FROM
THE TREE
TO THE
LABYRINTH

FROM THE TREE TO THE LABYRINTH

HISTORICAL STUDIES ON THE SIGN AND INTERPRETATION

UMBERTO ECO

Translated by Anthony Oldcorn

Harvard University Press

Cambridge, Massachusetts
London, England
2014

Originally published as *Dall'albero al labirinto: Studi storici sul segno e l'interpretazione,*
by Umberto Eco, copyright © 2007 RCS Libri S.p.A.

Chapters 11 and 12, "The Language of the Austral Land" and "The Linguistics of Joseph
de Maistre," were originally published in *Serendipities,* by Umberto Eco, translated by
William Weaver. Copyright © 1998 by Columbia University Press. Reprinted with
permission of the publisher.

Library of Congress Cataloging-in-Publication Data

Eco, Umberto.
   [Dall'albero al labirinto. English]
   From the tree to the labyrinth : historical studies on the sign and interpretation /
Umberto Eco ; translated by Anthony Oldcorn.
      pages   cm
   "Originally published as Dall'albero al labirinto: Studi storici sul segno e
l'interpretazione, by Umberto Eco, © 2007 RCS Libri S.p.A."
   Includes bibliographical references and index.
   ISBN 978-0-674-04918-5 (alk. paper)
   1. Semiotics—History.   2. Language and languages—Philosophy—History.
I. Oldcorn, Anthony, translator.   II. Title.

P99.E2613 2014
121'.68—dc23
2013015258

Contents

Introduction

At the second congress of the International Association for Semiotic Studies (Vienna, July 1979) I presented a number of "Proposals for a History of Semiotics." I recommended that we intensify historical studies on the various theories of the sign and of semiosis over the centuries, first of all because I considered it a necessary contribution to the history of philosophy as a whole, and secondly because I was convinced that to do semiotics today one needed to know how it was done yesterday, however much it might have been disguised as something else. And what better place to begin than from that "Coup d'oeil sur le développement de la sémiotique" with which Roman Jakobson had opened the first international congress of the association five years earlier?

I suggested three lines of research. The first had narrower ambitions, since it was confined to those authors who had spoken explicitly about the relation of signification, starting with the *Cratylus* and with Aristotle, down through Augustine and eventually to Peirce—but without neglecting the authors of treatises on rhetoric like Emanuele Tesauro or the theorists of universal and artificial languages like Wilkins or Beck.

My second line of research involved a close rereading of the whole history of philosophy with a view to finding implicit semiotic theories even where they had apparently not been explicitly developed, and the chief example I gave was that of Kant.

Finally, my third suggestion was intended to cover all those forms of literature in which symbolic and hermeneutical strategies of any kind were deployed or developed (among them, for instance, the works of the Pseudo-Areopagite). I cited as examples manuals of divination (texts like Guglielmo

Dorando's *Rationale divinorum officiorum*), the medieval bestiaries, the various discussions of poetics, down to the marginal notes of writers and artists who had reflected in one way or another on the processes of communication.

Anyone familiar with the bibliography of semiotics over the last thirty years knows that my appeal was anchored on the one hand in already developed or developing historiographical interests, while on the other it voiced an urgency that was already, so to speak, in the air: over the past thirty years, the contributions to an historical reconstruction of theories of the sign and semiosis have been many, so many that we are already in a position (provided someone could be found with the will and the energy to take on the task) to plan a definitive history of semiotic thought, by various authors and in several volumes.

For my own part, in the course of this thirty-year period, I have continued to elaborate the occasional personal offering, even returning from time to time to a topic previously explored—not to mention that chapter in semiotic history to which I devoted my *La ricerca della lingua perfetta* (1993), translated as *The Search for a Perfect Language* (1995). Such, then, is the origin and nature of the essays gathered in the present volume.

They were conceived under various circumstances, some for strictly academic occasions, others as discourses addressed to a broader general public. I decided not to attempt to rewrite them in a more uniform style, and I have kept the apparatus of notes and references in the case of the more specialized contributions and the conversational tone in the case of the more essayistic pieces.

I trust that even readers whose interests are not specifically semiotic (in the professional sense of the word) will be able to read these writings as contributions to a history of the various philosophies of language or languages.

|

From the Tree to the Labyrinth

1.1. Dictionary and Encyclopedia

For some time now the notions of dictionary and encyclopedia have been used in semiotics, linguistics, the philosophy of language and the cognitive sciences, to say nothing of computer science, to identify two models of *semantic representation,* models that in turn refer back to a general representation of knowledge and/or the world.

In defining a term (and its corresponding concept), the *dictionary* model is expected to take into account only those properties *necessary and sufficient* to distinguish that particular concept from others; in other words, it ought to contain only those properties defined by Kant as *analytical* (analytical being that a priori judgment in which the concept functioning as predicate can be deduced from the definition of the subject). Thus the analytical properties of dog would be ANIMAL, MAMMAL, and CANINE (on the basis of which a dog is distinguishable from a cat, and it is logically incorrect and semantically inaccurate to say of something that it is a dog but it is not an animal). This definition does not assign to the dog the properties of barking or being domesticated: these are not necessary properties (because there may be dogs incapable of barking and/or hostile to man) and are not part of our knowledge of a language but of our *knowledge of the world.* They are therefore matter for the *encyclopedia.*

In this sense semiotic dictionaries and encyclopedias are not directly comparable to dictionaries and encyclopedias "in the flesh," so to speak, to the published products, in other words, that go by the same name. In fact, dictionaries "in the flesh" are not usually composed according to the dictionary model: a normal dictionary, for instance, may define "cat" as a feline mammal, but usually adds details of an encyclopedic nature that concern the cat's fur, the shape of its eyes, its behavioral habits, and so on and so forth.

If we wish to identify a dictionary in its pure form—to which various contemporary theoreticians in the field of artificial intelligence still refer when they speak (see section 1.7 below) of "ontologies"—we must return to the model of the *Arbor Porphyriana* or Porphyrian tree, in other words to the commentary on Aristotle's *Categories* written in the third century A.D. by the Neo-Platonist Porphyry in his *Isagoge,* a text that throughout the Middle Ages (and beyond) will be a constant point of reference for any theory of definition.

1.2. The Dictionary

1.2.1. The First Idea of the Dictionary: The Arbor Porphyriana

Aristotle (*Posterior Analytics,* II, iii, 90b 30) says that what is defined is the essence or essential nature. Defining a substance means deciding, among its attributes, which of them appear to be essential, and in particular those that are the cause of the fact that the substance is what it is, in other words, its *substantial form.*

The problem is coming up with the right attributes that can be predicated as elements of the definition (*Posterior Analytics,* II, xiii, 96a–b). Aristotle gives the example of the number 3: an attribute such as being certainly applies to the number 3, but also to anything else that is not a number. On the other hand, the fact of being odd applies to the number 3 in such a way that, even if it has a wider application (it also applies, for instance, to the number 5), it nonetheless does not extend beyond the class of numbers. These are the attributes we must look for "up to the point where, although singly they have a wider extension of meaning than the subject, collectively they have not; for this must be the essence of the thing" (II, xiii, 96a 35). What Aristotle means is that, if we define man as MORTAL, ANIMAL and RATIONAL, each of these attributes, taken on its own, can also be applied to other beings (horses, for example, are animal and mortal, and the gods, in the Neo-Platonic sense of the word, are animal and rational), but, taken altogether, as a defining "group," MORTAL RATIONAL ANIMAL applies only to man, and in a way that is absolutely reciprocal.

A definition is not a demonstration: to reveal the essence of a thing is not the same as to prove a proposition about that thing; a definition says *what* something is, whereas a demonstration proves *that* something is (II, iii, 91a 1), and, consequently, in a definition we assume what a demonstration must on the contrary prove (II, 3, 91a 35). Those who define do not prove that something exists (II, iii, 92a 20). This means that for Aristotle a definition is concerned with *meaning* and has nothing to do with processes of *reference* to a state of the world (II, iii, 93b 30).

To find the right way to construct good definitions, Aristotle develops the theory of *predicables,* that is, of the ways in which categories can be predicated of a subject. In his *Topics* (I, iv, 101b 17–25) he identifies only four predicables (genus, proprium or unique property, definition, and accident), while Porphyry—as we shall see—will speak of five predicables (genus, species, difference, proprium, and accident).[1]

In a lengthy discussion in the *Posterior Analytics* (II, xiii), Aristotle outlines a series of rules to develop a proper division, proceeding from the most universal genera to the *infimae species,* identifying at each stage of the division the proper difference.

This is the method followed by Porphyry in the *Isagoge.* The fact that Porphyry develops a theory of division in a commentary on the *Categories* (where the problem of difference is hardly mentioned) is a serious matter for debate (see, for instance, Moody 1935), but it is not particularly relevant to our analysis.

In the same way, we may sidestep the *vexata quaestio* of the nature of universals, a question that Boethius bequeaths to the Middle Ages, taking the *Isagoge* itself as his point of departure. Porphyry declares his intention (we do not know how sincere he is) of setting aside the question of whether genera and species exist in and of themselves or if they are concepts of the mind. However that may be, he is the first to translate Aristotle in terms of a tree, and

---

1. Probably Aristotle does not include difference among the predicables because it appears when, registered along with genus (*Topics* I 101b 20), it constitutes the definition. In other words, definition (and therefore species) is the result of the conjunction of genus and difference: if we add definition to the list there is no need to include difference; if we include species there is no need to include definition; if we include genus and species there is no need to include difference. Furthermore, Aristotle does not list species among the predicables because species is not predicated of anything, being itself the ultimate subject of every predication. Porphyry will insert species in the list because species is what is expressed by definition.

it is certainly difficult to avoid the suspicion that, in so doing, he is indebted to the Neo-Platonic notion of the Great Chain of Being.[2] We may safely ignore, however, the metaphysics that underlies the *Arbor Porphyriana,* given that what interests us is the fact that this tree, whatever its metaphysical roots, is conceived of as a representation of logical relationships.

Porphyry delineates a *single* tree of substances, whereas Aristotle uses the method of division with a great deal of caution and, we might add, a great deal of skepticism. He seems to give it considerable weight in the *Posterior Analytics,* but to be more circumspect in *On the Parts of Animals* (642b et seq.), where he gives the impression of being prepared to construct different trees depending on which problem he is dealing with, even when it comes to defining the same species (see the whole discourse on animals with horns, apropos of which see Eco 1983a).

But Porphyry outlined a single tree of substances, and it is through this model, and not the more problematical discussion in the real Aristotle, that the idea of a dictionary structure of definition is transmitted, via Boethius, down to our own day, even though present-day proponents of a dictionary-based semantics may not know to whom they are indebted.

Porphyry, we were saying, lists five predicables: genus, species, difference, proprium, and accident. The five predicables establish the mode of definition for each of the ten categories. It is possible, then, to imagine ten Porphyrian trees: one for substances, which allows us, for example, to define man as MORTAL RATIONAL ANIMAL, and one for each of the other nine categories—a tree of qualities, for example, in which purple is defined as a species of the genus red.[3] Therefore there are ten possible trees, but there is no tree of trees because Being is not a *summum genus.*

There can be no doubt that the Porphyrian tree of substances aspires to be a hierarchical and finite whole of genera and species. The definition Porphyry gives of "genus" is purely formal: a genus is that to which a species is subordinate. Conversely, a species is what is subordinate to a genus. Genus and species are mutually definable and therefore complementary. Every genus placed on a high node of the tree includes the species that depend upon it;

---

2. On this topic Lovejoy (1936) remains fundamental.

3. Aristotle says that accidents too are susceptible of definition, though only with reference to a substance; see *Metaphysics* VII 1028a 10–1031a 10.

every species subordinate to a genus is a genus for the species subordinate to it, down to the base of the tree, where the *specie specialissime,* or "second substances," such as man, for instance, are collocated. At the highest fork is the *genus generalissimum* (represented by the name of the category), which cannot be a species of anything else. A genus can be a *predicate* of its own species, whereas the species *belong* to a genus.

The relationship of species to their superior genera is a relationship of hyponyms to hyperonyms. This phenomenon would guarantee the finite structure of the tree since, granted a given number of *specie specialissime,* and given that for two (or more) species there is only one genus, then, as we proceed upward, in the end the tree inevitably tapers off till it reaches the root node. In this sense the tree would fulfill all the functions required of a good dictionary.

But a Porphyrian tree cannot be made up only of genera and species. If this were the case, it would take the form illustrated in Figure 1.1.

In a tree of this kind man and horse (or man and cat) could not be distinguished from one another. A man is different from a horse because, though both may be animals, the first is rational and the second isn't. Rationality is the *difference* for man. Difference is the crucial element, because *accidents* are not required to produce a definition.[4]

Differences may be separable from the subject (such as being hot, being in motion, being sick), in which case they are simply "accidents" (things that may happen—from the Latin *accidere* [=happen]—to a subject or not happen). But they may also be inseparable: among these some are inseparable but still accidental (like having a snub nose), others belong to the subject in and of

---

4. As for the proprium, it belongs to a species, but is not part of its definition. There are different kinds of proprium—one that occurs in a single species but not in every one of its members (like the healing ability in humans); one that occurs in an entire species but not only in that species (like having two legs); one that occurs in the entire species and only there, but only at a given moment in time (like getting grey as you get older); and one that occurs in one and only one species and at all times (like the ability to laugh in humans). This last type is the one most frequently cited and has the relatively interesting characteristic of being reciprocable with the species (only humans laugh and those who laugh are all human). Nevertheless, the proprium is not essential to the definition because laughter is only an occasional behavior, and therefore an "accident," and does not characterize human beings in a constant and necessary manner.

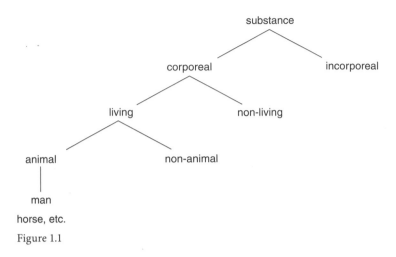

Figure 1.1

itself, or essentially, like being *rational* or *mortal*. These are the *specific* differences and are added to the genus to form the definition of the species.

Differences may be divisive or constitutive. For example, the genus LIVING BEING is potentially divisible into the differences *sensitive/insensitive,* but the *sensitive* difference may be compounded with the genus LIVING to constitute the species ANIMAL. In its turn ANIMAL becomes a genus divisible into *rational/irrational,* but the *rational* difference is constitutive, with the genus that it divides, of the species RATIONAL ANIMAL. Differences, then, divide a genus (and the genus contains them as potential opposites) and they are selected to constitute in practice a subordinate species, destined to become in its turn a genus divisible into new differences.

The *Isagoge* suggests the idea of the tree only verbally, but medieval tradition visualized the project as seen in Figure 1.2.

In the tree in Figure 1.2 the dotted lines mark the dividing differences, while the solid lines mark the constitutive differences. We remind the reader that the god appears both as an animal and as a body because, in the Platonic theology that constitutes Porphyry's frame of reference, the gods are intermediary natural forces and not to be identified with the One.[5]

---

5. Medieval tradition takes up this idea out of mere fidelity to the traditional example, just as all of modern logic assumes, without further verification, that the evening star and the morning star are both Venus.

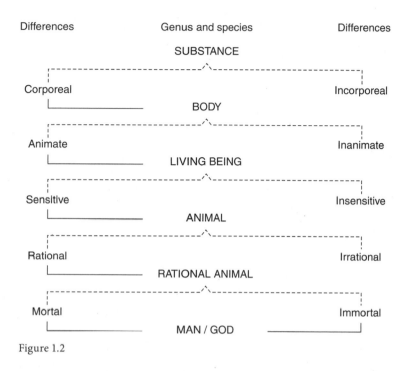

Figure 1.2

From the contemporary point of view of a distinction between dictionary and encyclopedia, the Porphyrian tree certainly introduces, with its differences, encyclopedic properties into a dictionary structure. In fact, being *Sensitive, Animate, Rational,* and *Mortal* are accidents identifiable in terms of knowledge of the world, and it is on the basis of its behavior that we decide whether a being is animate or rational, whether, in other words, it expresses ratiocinative capabilities by means of language. In any case, the end purposes of the tree are those of a dictionary, in which the differences are necessary and sufficient conditions to distinguish one being from another and to make the *definiens* or definer coextensive with the *definiendum* or definee, so that, if ANIMAL RATIONAL MORTAL, therefore of necessity *human,* and vice versa.

Once more, however, in its canonical version, this tree reveals its inadequacy, because it distinguishes, in a logically satisfactory fashion, God from man, but not, let's say, a man from a horse. If we had to define the horse, the tree would have to be enriched with further disjunctions: we would need, for

example, to divide ANIMALS into *mortal* and *immortal,* and the next species down—that of MORTAL ANIMALS—into *rational* (men) and *irrational*
(horses, for instance), even though, unfortunately, this subdivision, as is apparent in Figure 1.3, would not allow us to distinguish horses from donkeys,
cats, or dogs.

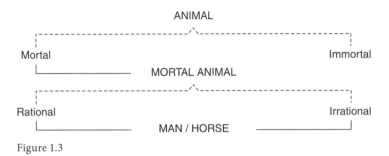

Figure 1.3

Even if we were willing to pay this price, however, we still could not rein-
troduce God into the tree. The only solution would be to insert the same
difference twice (at least) under two different genera (Figure 1.4).

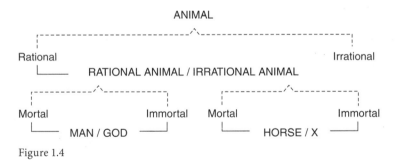

Figure 1.4

Porphyry would not have discouraged this decision, given that he himself
says (18.20) that the same difference "can often be observed in different species, such as having four legs in many animals that belong to different species."[6]

Aristotle too said that when two or more genera are subordinate to a superior genus (as occurs in the case of the man and the horse, insofar as they are

6. We are ignoring the fact that four-leggedness must be a proprium and not a difference, seeing that elsewhere two-leggedness is given as an example of a proprium.

both animals), there is nothing to prevent them having the same differences (*Categories* 1b 15 et seq.; *Topics* VI, 164b 10). In the *Posterior Analytics* (II, 90b et seq.), Aristotle demonstrates how one can arrive at an unambiguous definition of the number 3. Given that the number 1 was not a number for the Greeks (but the source and measure of all the other numbers), 3 could be defined as that odd number that is prime in both senses (that is, neither the sum nor the product of other numbers). This definition is fully reciprocable with the expression *three*. But it is interesting to reconstruct in Figure 1.5 the process of division by which Aristotle arrives at this definition.

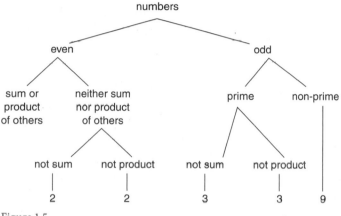

Figure 1.5

This type of division shows how properties like *not the sum* and *not the product* (which are differences) are not exclusive to any one disjuncture but can occur under several nodes. The same pair of dividing differences, then, can occur under several genera. Not only that, but the moment a certain difference has proved useful in defining a certain species unambiguously, it is no longer important to consider all the other subjects of which it is equally predicable (which amounts to saying that, once one or more differences have served to define the number 3, it is irrelevant that it may occur in the definition of other numbers).[7] Once we have said, then, that, given several subordinate genera, nothing prevents them having the

---

7. For a clear and unequivocal clarification of this point, see *Posterior Analytics* (II, 13, 97a 16–25).

same differences, it is difficult to say how many times the same pair of differences can occur.

In his *Topics* too (VI, 6, 144b), Aristotle admitted that the same difference may occur twice under two different genera (as long as they are not subordinate): "the earthbound animal and the flying animal are in fact genera not contained the one within the other, even though the notion of two-leggedness is the difference of both."[8]

If the same difference can recur a number of times, the finiteness and logical purity of the tree—which runs the risk of exploding into a dust cloud of differences, reproduced identically under different genera—are compromised. Indeed, if we reflect that species are a combination of genus and difference, and the genus higher up is in its turn a combination of another genus plus a difference (and therefore genera and species are abstractions, intellectual figments which serve to sum up various organizations of differences or accidents), *the most logical solution would be for the tree to be made up solely of differences,* properties that can be arranged into different trees according to the things to be defined, jettisoning the distinction between substances and accidents.

Many medieval commentators of the *Isagoge* appear to endorse this conclusion. Boethius in his *De divisione* (VI, 7) suggests that substances like pearl, ebony, milk, and some accidents like white or liquid may give rise to alternative trees. In one, for example, given a genus Liquids, with the differences *White/Black,* we would have the two species Milk and Ink; in the other, the genus White Things, with the differences *Liquid/Solid,* would generate the two species of Milk and Pearl (Figure 1.6).

True, in this passage Boethius is speaking only of accidents, but, in *De divisione* XII, 37, he applies the same principle to all divisions of genus ("generis unius fit multiplex divisio" ["a single genus is divisible in more than one way"]).[9]

Abelard says the same thing in his *Editio super Porphyrium* (150, 12), where he reminds us that "Pluraliter ideo dicit genera, quia animal dividitur per

8. It might be objected that *two-legged* or *not the sum* are indeed differences, but not specific; but we saw a moment ago in Figure 1.4 that specific differences such as *rational* may also occur twice (at least) under different genera.

9. See Boethius (1998: 33).

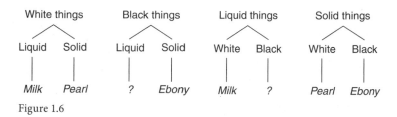

Figure 1.6

rationale animal et irrationale; et rationale per mortale et immortale dividitur; et mortale per rationale et irrationale dividitur" ("He [Porphyry] refers then to genera in more than one way, for animal is divisible into rational animal and irrational animal; and rational is divisible into mortal and immortal; and mortal is divisible into rational and irrational") (Figure 1.7).[10]

Figure 1.7

In a tree composed solely of differences, these can be continually reorganized following the description under which a given subject is considered, and the tree thus becomes a structure sensitive to contexts, not an absolute dictionary.

On the other hand, when Aristotle (who is interested in defining accidents as well as substances) asserts (*Posterior Analytics* I, 3, 83a, 15) that definitions must stick to a finite number of determinations, in either an ascending or a descending series, he does not in the least seem to be suggesting *that their number and function are already established by a previous categorical structure*. In fact in his various researches into natural phenomena, from the eclipse to the definition of ruminants, he shows a great deal

---

10. And in 157, 15, it is repeated again that a given difference can be predicated of more than one species: "Falsum est quod omnis differentia sequens ponit superiores, quia ubi sunt permixtae differentiae, fallit" ("It is false that every successive difference presupposes those that come before it, for that rule does not hold true in cases where the differences are mixed").

of flexibility in setting up subdivisions and suggesting trees in which genera, species, and differences exchange roles according to the problem one intends to resolve.

In *Posterior Analytics* II, 3, 90a, 15, he says that the eclipse is a deprivation of the sun's light by the earth's interposition. In order to define it this way we must suppose a division into genus and species like the one in Figure 1.8.

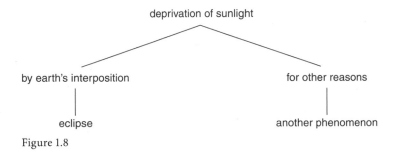

Figure 1.8

But what is the deprivation of the sun's light a species of? Are we talking about a tree that takes cognizance of the various kinds of deprivation (among which, let's say, are the deprivation of food and of life) or a tree that takes cognizance of various astronomical phenomena and opposes the radiation of the sun's light to its deprivation?

In II, 3, 93b, 5, the example of thunder is discussed. It is defined as extinction of fire in the clouds. Hence a tree as in Figure 1.9:

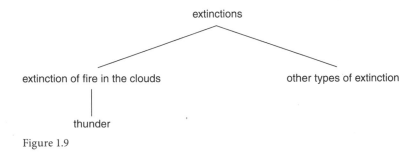

Figure 1.9

But what if the definition had been "noise produced by the extinction of fire in the clouds"? In that case, the tree would have to look like Figure 1.10.

As can be seen, in the first case thunder is a species of the genus extinction, in the second case of the genus noises.

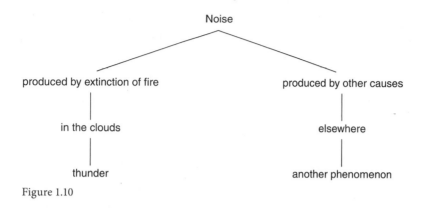

Figure 1.10

This flexibility is due to the fact that, when he is dealing with concrete phenomena, it is the philosopher's intention *to define them,* while a tree with a fixed hierarchy and a finite number of determinations serves only to *classify.* Merely classificatory, for example, is a device that embeds genera, species, and differences without explaining the nature of the *definiendum.* This model is that of the taxonomy of today's natural sciences, in which it is established, for instance, that a dog belongs to the genus CANIS, of the family of CANINES, of the suborder of FISSIPEDS, of the order of CARNIVORES, of the subclass of PLACENTALS, of the class of MAMMALS. This classification, however, does not tell us (and is not meant to tell us) either what the properties of a dog are or how to recognize a dog or refer to a dog. Every node of the classification is in fact a *pointer* that refers to another chapter of zoology in which the properties of Mammals, Placentalia, Carnivores, Fissipeds, and so on are specified.

A dictionary classification, then, does not serve to *define* a term but merely to allow us to use it in a logically correct fashion. Given, let's say, that the imaginary order of the Prixides is classified as belonging to the genus Prosides and the Prosides are a species of the genus Proceides, we do not need to know what the properties of a proceid or a prosid are to draw (true) inferences along the lines of: *if this is a prixid then it has to be a prosid,* and *it is impossible that something that is a prixid should not be a proceid.*

But these are not the bases which allow us to understand expressions in which terms like *prixid* and *proceid* appear: it is one thing to know that it is logically incorrect to say that a prixid is not a proceid; it is quite another to say what a proceid is, and, if it means anything to say that terms have a meaning, the classification does not supply that meaning.

Gil (1981: 1027) suggests that genera and species may be used as extensional parameters (classes), whereas only the differences decide the intensional regime. This is tantamount to saying that the meaning of a term depends on the differences and not on the genera or the species. Now, what makes it difficult to regiment the differences under a Porphyrian tree is that the differences are accidents, and accidents are infinite or at least indefinite in number.

The differences are qualities (and it is no accident that, while genera and species, which represent substances, are expressed by common nouns, the differences are expressed by adjectives). The differences come from a tree that is not the same as the substances, and their number is not known a priori (*Metaphysics* VIII, 1042a–1042b). Granted, Aristotle makes these remarks about nonessential differences, but at this point who can say which differences are essential and which not? Aristotle plays on a few examples (like *rational* and *mortal*), but when he speaks about species other than human, such as animals or artificial objects, he becomes much more vague and the differences multiply.

In theory we are entitled to put forward the hypothesis that Aristotle would not have been capable of constructing a finite Porphyrian tree, but in practice as well (on the basis, that is, of the philological evidence), when we read *On the Parts of Animals,* we see that he gives up *in practice* on constructing a single tree and readjusts complementary trees according to the properties whose cause and essential nature he wishes to explain (cf. Balme 1961 and Eco 1983a).

The notion of specific difference is, rhetorically speaking, an oxymoron. Saying *specific difference* is tantamount to saying *essential accident.* But this oxymoron conceals (or reveals) a far more serious ontological contradiction.

The thinker who understood the problem without prevarication (though he pointed it out with his customary prudence) was Thomas Aquinas. In his *De ente et essentia* he says that specific difference corresponds to substantial form (another ontological oxymoron, if we may put it that way, since the most substantial thing we can think of is identified with an accident). But Thomas's thought does not leave room for misunderstanding: what defines substantial form is difference as an accident.

In order to justify such a scandalous conclusion, Thomas excogitates—with one of his habitual strokes of genius—an extremely brilliant solution. There exist essential differences; but which and what they are we do not know;

what we know as specific differences are not the essential differences them-selves, but are, so to speak, signs of them, symptoms, clues, superficial man-ifestations of the being of something else that we cannot know. We infer the presence of essential differences through a semiotic process, with knowable accidents as our point of departure.[11]

That the effect is a sign of the cause is Thomas's customary idea (much of his theory of analogy depends on this assumption, which is, if we were to trace it back, Stoic in origin: effects are *indicative* signs). The idea reappears, for instance, in *Summa Theologiae* I, 29, 2 ad 3 and I, 77, 1 ad 7: a difference such as *rational* is not the real specific difference that constitutes the substantial form. *Ratio* (reason) as *potentia animae* (a power of the soul) appears outwardly *verbo et facto* (in word and deed), through exterior actions, psychological and physical behaviors (and those actions are accidents, not substances!). We say humans are rational because they demonstrate their rational powers by means of acts of cognition, or by an internal discourse (the activity of thought) or an external discourse, that is, by means of language (*Summa Theologiae* I, 78, 8 co.). In a decisive text in the *Contra Gentiles* (3, 46, n. 11), Thomas says that human beings do not know what they are *(quid est)*, but they know what they are like *(quod est)* insofar as they perceive themselves as actors in rational thought. We know what are our spiritual powers only "ex ipsorum actuum qualitate" ("from the nature of these same acts"). Thus *rational* is an accident, and so are all the differences into which the Porphyr-ian tree can be dissolved.

From this discovery, Thomas does not draw all the conclusions he should have regarding the possible nature of the tree of substances: he cannot bring himself (psychologically perhaps) to call the tree into question as a logical tool for obtaining definitions (something he could have done without go-ing out on a limb), because the entire Middle Ages is dominated by the conviction (however unconscious) that the tree mimics the structure of

---

11. "In rebus enim sensibilibus etiam ipsae differentiae essentiales ignotae sunt, unde significantur per differentias accidentales, quae ex essentialibus oriuntur, sicut causa significatur per suum effectum, sicut bipes ponitur differentia hominis" ("Even in the case of sensible things we do not know their essential differences; we indicate them through the accidental differences that flow from the essential dif-ferences, as we refer to a cause through its effect. In this way 'biped' is given as the difference of man"), Aquinas (1983, ch. V, paragraph 6, p. 63).

reality, and this Neo-Platonic conviction also affects the most rigorous of Aristotelians.

It is clear, however, if we follow its inner logic, that the tree of genera and species, however constructed, explodes into a swirl of accidents, into a nonhierarchizable network of *qualia*. The dictionary dissolves of necessity, as a result of internal tensions, into a potentially orderless and limitless galaxy of elements of knowledge of the world. It becomes, in other words, an encyclopedia, and it does so because it was already in fact an encyclopedia without knowing it, an artifice invented to camouflage the inevitability of the encyclopedia.

1.2.2. *The Utopia of the Dictionary in Modern Semantics*

We see a return to the dictionary model in the linguistics of the second half of twentieth century, when the first attempts appear to postulate or recognize—in order to define the contents expressed by the terms of a natural language—a finite system of *figures* possessing the same characteristics as a phonological system (based on a limited number of phonemes and their systematic oppositions). Thus, a *feature semantics* (features being primitive semantic atoms) was postulated, designed to establish the *conditions necessary and sufficient* for a definition of meaning, excluding knowledge of the world. In this way, in order to be recognized as a cat, something must have an ANIMAL feature, but it is not requested that it meows. These necessary and sufficient features are dictionary markers. Something along these lines was anticipated by Hjelmslev (1943[1961]) when he proposed to analyze the concepts corresponding to the twelve terms *ram, ewe, boy, girl, stallion, mare* through a combination of the *male/female* opposition and the assumed primitives SHEEP, HUMAN BEING, CHILD, HORSE.

Hjelmslev's was not the only modern proposal for a dictionary representation, though the many others proposed in the area of linguistics or of analytic philosophy, almost always in ignorance of Hjelmslev's proposal, did no more than repropose his model.[12]

---

12. See for instance the by now regrettably classic examples of Katz and Fodor (1963) or Katz (1972). For these problems, and for further references to the very extensive bibliography on the subject, see Eco (1984a: ch. 2) and Violi (1997 [English trans. Violi 2001]).

Reconsidering Hjelmslev's model, we see that a dictionary representation would allow us to solve the following problems (as Katz 1972 will suggest later): *synonymy* and *paraphrase* (a ewe is a female ovine); *similarity* and *difference* (the pairs ewe and mare and mare and stallion have some features in common, while we can establish on the basis of what other features they can be distinguished); *antonymy, complementarity,* and *contrariety* (*stallion* is the antonym of *mare*); *hyponymia* and *hyperonymia* (*equine* is the hyperonym of which *stallion* is the hyponym); *sensibleness* and *semantic anomaly* (*stallions are male* makes sense while *a female stallion* is semantically anomalous; *redundancy (male stallion); ambiguity* (the terms *bear* and *bull*, for example, have more than one meaning); analytical truth (*stallions are male* is analytically true, because the definition of the subject contains the predicate); *contradictoriness* (there are no male mares); *syntheticity* (that ewes produce wool does not depend on the dictionary but on our knowledge of the world); *inconsistency* (*this is a ewe* and *this is a ram* cannot be equally true if referred to the same individual); *semantic entailment* (if ram, then ovine).

Unfortunately this model does not permit us to represent what we must know about sheep and horses if we are to understand many discourses about them. It does not allow us, for instance, to reject expressions like *the stallion was bleating desperately like a ram* (justifiable only in a metaphorical context, and a very daring one at that), given that the mechanism of definition does not explain what sound horses naturally emit.

And this is not all. Even if a system of this kind could be implemented based on assumed *primitives,* and if SHEEP and HORSE were primitives, they would serve to define only a very limited share of the terms concerning part of the animal kingdom. How many primitive features would be needed to define all the terms in any given lexicon? And how do we define a "primitive" feature?

It has been said that primitives are innate ideas of a Platonic nature, but not even Plato succeeded in satisfactorily deciding how many or of what kind were the universally innate ideas (either there is an idea for every natural genus, like *equinity,* in which case the list is an open one, or there are a few far more abstract ideas, like the One, the Many, the Good, or mathematical concepts, which are insufficient to distinguish the meaning of lexical terms).

It has been said that primitives are elements of a whole that, by virtue of the systematic relationship between its terms, cannot be anything but finite:

but this would be a simplified Porphyrian tree or a tree of genera and species good only for the purposes of classification.

It is hard to define primitiveness by distinguishing between analytical and synthetic properties, a distinction severely criticized by Quine (1953a), in part because the notion of analyticalness is completely circular (if a property contained in the definition of a term is analytic it cannot be a criterion for establishing the appropriateness of a dictionary definition).

The possibility of positing a difference between *necessary* and *contingent* properties must also be excluded, because if it were necessary for a cat to be mammiferous and contingent for it to meow, then all "necessary" would mean is "analytic."

It has been proposed that *finiteness* is a requirement for a packet of primitives (primitives ought to be limited in number, considering that it would be anti-economical to have as many primitives as there are lemmata to define), but it is precisely the cataloguing of this finite number of semantic atoms that has turned out so far to be problematic.

It has been suggested that primitives are simple concepts, but it is difficult to define a simple concept (the concept of *mouse* seems more simple and immediate than that of *mammifer,* and it is easier to define concepts like *emphyteusis* than verbs like *to do*).

It has been suggested that they depend on our experience of the world, or that there are (as Russell 1905 suggested) "object-words" whose meaning we learn directly by ostension, and "dictionary-words" that can be defined by other dictionary-words—but Russell was the first to recognize that *pentagram* is a dictionary-word for most speakers, but would be an object-word for a child who grew up in a room in which the wallpaper was decorated with pentagrams.

The requirement of *adequacy* has been proposed (primitives should serve to define all words), but, if we consider as primitives sufficient to define the concept of "bachelor" features like HUMAN MALE ADULT UNMARRIED, why does it seem inadequate to call a Benedictine monk a bachelor? We would have to add other constrictions (for example, a bachelor is an adult human unmarried male *who has not taken a vow of chastity*), and with that we have introduced encyclopedic elements into our dictionary.

The requirements of *independence* (primitives should not depend for their definition on other primitives) and *absence of further interpretability* have been proposed, but not even HUMAN seems without further interpretability if we consider the whole debate over abortion and cloning that is taking place today precisely on the subject of what it means to be human. In reality, in any lexicon any term is potentially interpretable by means of other terms in the same lexicon, or other semantic devices, according to the criteria of *interpretance* and *unlimited semiosis* established by Peirce.

Lastly, if primitives are rooted in our way of thinking, the principle of *universality* suggests itself. It is assuredly possible that certain experiences related to our bodies are universal, such as *above/below, eat/sleep, be born/ die,* but in the first instance it is unthinkable that we can define all the objects and events in the universe in terms of these ideas, and, secondly, universal does not mean primitive, given that a universally understood concept such as *dying* needs to be further defined, as is demonstrated by the debates on end-of-life decisions and the harvesting of organs.

In the face of these criticisms, since the middle of the twentieth century, the conviction has made more and more headway, especially among the theorists of cognitivist semantics, that linguistic competence is always encyclopedic, and that in semantic representation no distinction can be made (except on a provisional basis and for the purpose of specific analyses) between linguistic knowledge and knowledge of the world.

But at this point we must abandon the vicissitudes of the dictionary to trace the historical evolution of the encyclopedia.

1.3. The Encyclopedias

The role of the encyclopedia has fluctuated over the centuries.[13] The word "encyclopedia" comes from *enkyklios paideia,* which signified a complete education in the Greek tradition.[14] The term "encyclopedia," however, makes

---

13. For a comprehensive historical survey, see Foucault (1966), Collison (1966), Binkley ed. (1977) (in particular the essay by Fowler), Beonio-Brocchieri Fumagalli (1981), Cherchi (1990), Schaer (1996), Salsano (1997), and Pombo et al. (2006) (and all Pombo's contributions on the Internet).

14. *Enkyklios* does not really mean, as it is usually translated today, "circular" education, in the sense of harmoniously complete, so much as "in the circle." Aristotle, in his *Nicomachean Ethics* and in the *De coelo* uses the adjective to mean "usual," "ordinary," in the meaning of "recurrent." But, according to some interpreters, the adjective refers to the form of the chorus: learning to sing certain hymns was an essential part of a boy's education, and therefore *enkyklios* would

its first appearance in the sixteenth century, first in a different form in Fleming Joachim Stergk's *Lucubrationes vel potius absolutissima kuklopaideia* (1529), and then in *The Boke Named The Governor* (1531) by Sir Thomas Elyot, who, in chapter XIII, on some reasons for the decline of education among English gentlemen, cites the encyclopedia as the sum total of knowledge, or the "world of science," or "the circle of doctrine." This same sum total of knowledge as a complete education is recommended by Gargantua to his son in book II, chapter 8 of Rabelais's *Gargantua and Pantagruel* (1532):

> That is why, my son, I urge you to employ your youth in making good progress in study [and virtue]. You are in Paris; Epistemon your tutor is with you; both can teach you: one directly and orally, the other by laudable examples.
>
> I intend and will that you acquire a perfect command of languages— first Greek (as Quintilian wishes), secondly Latin, and then Hebrew for the Holy Scriptures, as well as Chaldaean and Arabic likewise—and that, for your Greek, you mould your style by imitating Plato, and for your Latin, Cicero.
>
> Let there be no history which you do not hold ready in memory: to help you, you have the cosmographies of those who have written on the subject.
>
> When you were still very young—about five or six—I gave you a foretaste of geometry, arithmetic and music among the liberal arts. Follow that up with the other arts. Know all the canons of astronomy, but leave judicial astrology and the Art of Lullius alone as abuses and vanities.
>
> I want you to learn all of the beautiful texts of Civil Law by heart and compare them to moral philosophy.
>
> And as for the knowledge of natural phenomena, I want you to apply yourself to it with curiosity: let there be no sea, river or stream the fishes of which you do not know. Know all the birds of the air, all the trees, bushes and shrubs of the forests, all the herbs in the soil, all the metals

---

mean "the kind of education that a boy should have received." In fact this is the sense in which Vitruvius (*De architectura,* VI) interprets it, as "doctrinarum omnium disciplina," ("the disciple of all knowledge") and likewise Quintilian in *Institutio oratoria* (I, 10).

hidden deep in the womb of the Earth, the precious stones of all the Orient and the South: let none remain unknown to you.

Then frequent the books of the ancient medical writers, Greek, Arabic and Latin, without despising the Talmudists or the Cabbalists; and by frequent dissections acquire a perfect knowledge of that other world which is Man.

And for a few hours every day start to study the Sacred Writings: first the Gospels and Epistles of the Apostles in Greek, then the Old Testament in Hebrew. In short, let me see you an abyss of erudition.[15]

In book II, chapter 20, Thaumastes praises the young Pantagruel's culture, saying: "I swear he discovered, for my benefit, the true source, well and abyss of the encyclopedia of learning."

In 1536 we find the term in Juan Luis Vives's *De disciplinis,* in which he calls "encyclopedia" the various things that the educand must know, with explicit reference to Pliny and other classical encyclopedists.[16] As part of the title of a book the word appears in Paulus Scalichius de Lika's *Encyclopediae seu orbis disciplinarum tam sacrarum quam profanarum epistemon* (Basel, 1559).

1.3.1. Pliny and the Model of the Ancient Encyclopedia

No Greek encyclopedias, at least in the sense of compilations of previous knowledge, have survived. Of course, the works of Aristotle are an encyclopedia, ranging as they do from logic to astronomy and from the study of animals to human psychology. They are not presented, however, as a collection of shared knowledge, but as a fresh offering. Likewise, in a Latin context, rather than an encyclopedic collection of facts, Lucretius's *De rerum natura* aspires to be a systematic exposition of "scientific" truths.

The works that have been seen as examples of Greek encyclopedism are instead expressions, frequently incidental, of curiosity and wonder over fabulous lands and peoples: in this sense an encyclopedic component has been identified in the *Odyssey.* Encyclopedic interests are definitely present

---

15. English translation: Rabelais (2006: 48–49).

16. Cf. West (1997) for the idea suggested in Vives's *De disciplinis* of the encyclopedia as a constant expansion of information as a result of after-dinner conversation.

in Herodotus when he describes the marvels of Egypt and of other barbaric peoples. The Greek *Alexander Romance,* though its actual date is uncertain and its attribution to Callisthenes, a contemporary of Alexander, apocryphal, was probably composed at the beginning of the Hellenistic period and, while claiming to narrate the adventures of the famous Macedonian condottiere, presents itself in fact as a travel guide to marvelous places teeming with extraordinary creatures.

It was the mature Alexandrian period that produced many works of *paradoxography,* devoted to the presentation of remarkable things and events, such as the treatise devoted by Strato of Lampsacus to unusual animals, the *Mirabilia* of Callimachus, or that of Antigonus of Carystus, while the *De mirabilibus auscultationibus,* an assemblage or miscellany of little-known facts in the fields of botany, mineralogy, zoology, hydrography, and mythology, once attributed to Aristotle, can be assigned to Hellenistic circles of the third century B.C. Finally, we may speak of specialized encyclopedias in the case of later geographical compendia such as Pomponius Mela's *De situ orbis* (first century A.D.), Aelian's *De natura animalium* (second / third century) or the *Lives of the Philosophers* by Diogenes Laertius (second / third century).

But there is a line between the compendia of curious facts and erudite digressions (like the *Noctes Atticae,* composed by Aulus Gellius in the second century A.D., or specialized encyclopedias such as Pomponius Mela's) and an encyclopedia *in the global and organic sense of the word,* a work that aspires in other words to be an exhaustive catalogue of existing knowledge.

The Hellenistic world assigned the role that Roman and medieval scholars would eventually assign to the encyclopedia, not to a single volume that deals with everything, but to a collection of all existing volumes, the *library,* as well as to a collection of all *things* possible, the *museum.* The museum and library built in Alexandria by Ptolemy I (said to have held, depending on the period, between 500,000 and 700,000 volumes) formed the nucleus of a veritable university, a center for the collection, research, and transmission of knowledge.

The encyclopedic attitude took shape instead in Roman circles, in which the whole of Greek knowledge was gathered together, in a labor of appropriation of the patrimony of that *Graecia capta* which *ferum victorem cepit.*[17] An

---

17. "Captive Greece took captive her savage conqueror" (Horace, *Epistolae* 2, 1, 156).

early example is the *Rerum divinarum et humanarum antiquitates* of Terentius Varro (first century B.C.), of which only fragments have survived, which dealt with history, grammar, mathematics, philosophy, astronomy, geography, agriculture, law, rhetoric, the arts, literature, the biographies of famous Greeks and Romans, the history of the gods. We do possess, however, the 37 books of Pliny the Elder's *Historia Naturalis* (first century A.D., approximately 20,000 facts cited and 500 authors consulted), devoted to the heavens and the universe in general, the various countries of the world, prodigious births and burials, the earth's fauna, creatures of the deep, birds, insects, vegetables, medicines derived from vegetable and animal sources, metals, painting, precious stones and gems.

At first sight, Pliny's work appears to be a mere confused jumble of facts, with no structure, but, if we turn our attention to the immense index, we realize that the work begins in fact with the heavens, going on to deal with geography, demography, and ethnography, followed by anthropology and human physiology, zoology, botany, agriculture, gardening, natural pharmacology, medicine, and magic, before proceeding to mineralogy, architecture, and the plastic arts—setting up a sort of hierarchy proceeding from the original to the derivative, from the natural to the artificial—according to the arborescent structure illustrated in Figure 1.11.

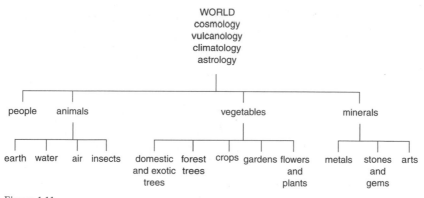

Figure 1.11

This aspect should also be borne in mind for what we will have to say about subsequent encyclopedias. An encyclopedia always relies for its organization on a tree—whose model is invariably, on a more or less conscious level, that of the binary subdivision of a Porphyrian tree. But the difference between the *Arbor Porphyriana* and the encyclopedic tree (which amounts, openly or in a dissimulated fashion, to a table of contents) is that the Porphyrian tree claims to use the terms of its disjunctions as primitives, not susceptible of further definition, and at the same time indispensable for defining something else, while in the encyclopedic index each node is referred to the notions that define it and will be presented in the course of the overall discussion. And in this sense classifications like those of the natural sciences also have or can assume the role of an index.

This difference is fundamental to an understanding of the history of encyclopedias and their indices. For a long time the encyclopedist used his index as a working tool that was basically *not* supposed to be of interest to the reader, whose need instead was for the information the encyclopedia contained—in other words, the encyclopedist was concerned with *where* he was going to put the crocodile, but he believed in principle that what the reader was interested in were the crocodile's empirical properties, not its place in the classification. Instead, this point of view gradually changed in the case of many modern encyclopedias, whose primary aim was precisely to provide a model of the organization of knowledge. It was some time, however, before the "plan" of an encyclopedia began to constitute an object of reflection or of meta-encyclopedic comment. For the reader, the encyclopedia appeared as a "map" of different territories whose edges were jagged and often imprecise, so that one had the impression of moving through it as if it were a labyrinth that allowed one to choose paths that were constantly new, without feeling obliged to stick to a route leading from the general to the particular.

The second aspect of how Pliny lays out a model for encyclopedias to come is that he does not speak of things he knows from experience but of things handed down to him by tradition, and he does not make the slightest effort to separate reliable empirical information from legend (he gives equal space to the crocodile and the basilisk). This point is extremely important in defining the encyclopedia as a theoretical model: *the encyclopedia does not claim to register what really exists but what people traditionally believe exists—and hence everything that an educated person should know, not simply to have knowledge of the world, but also to understand discourses about the world.*

This characteristic is already evident in the Hellenistic encyclopedias (a great many paragraphs in the pseudo-Aristotelian *De mirabilibus*, for example, employ a *verbum dicendi* such as "they say that" or "the story goes that" or "it is said that"), and it will remain a constant in medieval encyclopedias, as well as in those of the Renaissance and Baroque periods. Foucault reminds us that Buffon was astonished that in a sixteenth-century naturalist like Aldrovandi there was "an inextricable mixture of exact descriptions, quotations from other authors, fables relayed uncritically, observations which dealt indiscriminately with the anatomy, habitat, and mythological properties of an animal, and the uses that could be made of it in medicine or in magic." In fact, as Foucault goes on to comment:

> When one goes back to take a look at the *Historia serpentum et draconum,* one finds the chapter "On the serpent in general" arranged under the following headings: equivocation (which means the various meanings of the word serpent), synonyms and etymologies, differences, form and description, anatomy, nature and habits, temperament, coitus and generation, voice, movements, places, diet, physiognomy, antipathy, sympathy, modes of capture, death and wounds caused by the serpent, modes and signs of poisoning, remedies, epithets, denominations, prodigies and presages, monsters, mythology, gods to which it is dedicated, fables, allegories and mysteries, hieroglyphics, emblems and symbols, proverbs, coinage, miracles, riddles, devices, heraldic signs, historical facts, dreams, simulacra and statues, use in human diet, use in medicine, miscellaneous uses. Whereupon Buffon comments: "Let it be judged after that what proportion of natural history is to be found in such a hotch-potch of writing. There is no description here, only legend." And indeed, for Aldrovandi and his contemporaries, it was all legenda—things to be read. But the reason for this was not that they preferred the authority of men to the precision of an unprejudiced eye, but that nature, in itself, is an unbroken tissue of words and signs, of accounts and characters, of discourse and forms. When one is faced with the task of writing an animal's history, it is useless and impossible to choose between the profession of naturalist and that of compiler: one has to collect together into one and the same form of knowledge all that has been seen and heard, all that has been recounted, either by nature or by men, by the language of the world, by tradition, or by the poets. (Foucault 1970: 38–39)

Foucault sees this tendency as typical of the sixteenth-century *episteme*, whereas, as we have seen and as we will see, it is a characteristic of *every* idea of encyclopedia, from Pliny to the present day. In fact what distinguishes a contemporary encyclopedia like the *Britannica,* the French *Larousse* or the Italian *Treccani* from Pliny's encyclopedias or the medieval encyclopedias or Aldrovandi's encyclopedia and so on, is simply the critical attention devoted to separating legendary ideas from those that are scientifically proven (but only because today this difference too, ontological in nature, is considered part of what every educated person should know). Aside from this difference—which acquires relevance, let's say, between Francis Bacon (1561–1626) and Diderot and D'Alembert's mid-eighteenth-century *Encyclopédie*—a contemporary encyclopedia is also expected in principle to tell us everything that has been said, whether it be about sulfuric acid or Apollo or the sorcerer Merlin.

1.3.2. Medieval Encyclopedias

Compared with Pliny, medieval encyclopedias have a different origin and serve different purposes. If we are to understand their nature, we must begin with Augustine, whose concern was with the problem of the correct interpretation of Scripture and took into consideration, not only the signs produced by human beings in an effort to convey meaning, and the natural phenomena that may be interpreted as signs (*De doctrina christiana* II, 1, 1), but also, since Scripture speaks not only *in verbis* but also *in factis* (*De trinitate* XV, 9, 15), events and things of sacred history that have been supernaturally arranged so as to be read as signs.[18] Augustine taught how to resolve the question of whether a sign was to be understood in a literal or a figurative sense, and he said that we must suspect a figurative sense whenever Scripture appears to go against the truths of faith and moral behavior or gets lost in *superfluitates* or brings into play expressions not especially meaningful from the literal point of view (proper names, numbers and technical terms, elaborate descriptions of flowers, natural prodigies, precious stones, vestments and ceremonies, objects and events irrelevant from the spiritual point of view).

To interpret the figurative meaning of these facts we must appeal to our knowledge of the world. In *De doctrina christiana* (II, 57) Augustine insists at

---

18. These points will be further developed in Chapter 3 of the present volume.

length upon the fact that lacunae in our knowledge of things render figurative expressions obscure. If we are to understand why Scripture commands us to be as wise as serpents, we must know that, in the real world, the serpent offers its entire body to the aggressor in order to protect its head. And only if we know that the serpent, by forcing itself through the narrow entrance of its hole, sloughs off its old skin and is endowed with fresh strength, can we understand what the Apostle means when he explains how to put off the old man and put on the new man by passing through the "strait gate" (Matt. 7: 13).[19]

The same thing is true of precious stones and herbs. Knowing that the carbuncle shines in the dark illuminates many obscure passages of Scripture, while knowing that hyssop is effective in freeing the lungs from catarrh explains why it is said: "Purge me with hyssop and I shall be clean" (Psalm 51: 7). To understand why Moses, Elijah, and Jesus fasted for forty days we must bear in mind that the course of the day and that of the year are measured in terms of the number 4, the day according to divisions into four groups of hours that make up morning, midday, evening, and night, the year according to the four seasons. Similarly, we need to have a good knowledge of music: if we come across a mention of a psaltery with ten strings, we must be aware that the actual instrument does not call for that many strings if we are to deduce that what we have here is a reference to the Ten Commandments.

It is basically as a response to this need to interpret the Scriptures that medieval encyclopedias come into existence and circulate. They are different from Roman encyclopedias in that, although they too are concerned with explaining what the world is like, they are still more concerned to explain *how the sacred texts are to be understood*. To give a single example among the many possible, in the ninth century Rabanus Maurus insists that he speaks not only of the nature of things "sed etiam de mystica earumdem rerum significatione" ("but also of the mystical meaning of those things," *De rerum naturis,* PL 111, 12d).

The earliest encyclopedia of this type, however, antedates Augustine; we are referring to the first moralized bestiary, the *Physiologus,* a Greek work by an anonymous author composed in the early centuries A.D., though the Latin versions, each of which incidentally expands upon the original text, only appear toward the seventh century. This little work draws upon works

19. Biblical quotes, here and elsewhere, are from the King James Version.

by Pliny and other ancient authors (such as the *Polyhistor* of Solinus or the *Alexander Romance*) for information on the various animals, but to the description of each it adds an allegorical or moral interpretation. Here, for example, is the entry on "viper":

> John said to the Pharisees, "Ye generation of vipers" [Matt. 3:7 and Lk. 3:7]. Physiologus says of the viper that the male has the face of a man, while the female has the form of a woman down to her navel, but from her navel down to her tail she has the form of a crocodile. Indeed the woman has no secret place, that is, genitals for giving birth, but has only a pinhole. If the male lies with the female and spills his seed into her mouth, and if she drinks his seed, she will cut of the male's necessaries (that is, his male organs) and he will die. When, however, the young have grown within the womb of their mother who has no genitals for giving birth, they pierce through her side, killing her in their escape.
>
> Our Savior, therefore, likened the Pharisees to the viper; just as the viper's brood kills its father and mother, so this people which is without God kills its father, Jesus Christ, and its earthly mother, Jerusalem. "Yet how will they flee from the wrath to come?" [Lk. 3:7].[20]

As we see, the form and behavior of the viper are described so as to demonstrate why it is a figure for the Pharisees. Or, when he explains how the hedgehog climbs up the grapevine to get at the grapes, then throws the grapes down onto the ground and rolls on them so that the grapes are speared on his spines, whereupon he carries them back to his offspring, leaving the vine shoot bare, the intent is to represent the faithful who must remain attached to the spiritual Vine and not let the spirit of evil climb onto it and strip it of all its grapes.

Based on the model of the *Physiologus,* with few exceptions, are the medieval bestiaries, herbals, and lapidaries, and the various *imagines mundi,* from the *Etymologies* of Isidore of Seville in the seventh century, to the many bestiaries and encyclopedias of the twelfth century, down to Cecco d'Ascoli's thirteenth-century *L'Acerba.* All take Pliny as their point of departure and each incorporates the work of previous authors, offering therefore a fairly repetitive repertory of information.

----

20. English translation: Curley (1979: 15–16).

As is the case with Pliny, it appears that the classificatory criteria of the medieval encyclopedias are rather vague (why does Isidore classify the crocodile with the fishes? merely because it lives in the water?) and that they too therefore represent a mere accumulation of haphazard information. Nevertheless, the only example of a fortuitous assemblage is that provided by the *Physiologus,* given that the animals the author lists (the lion, the sun-lizard, the pelican, the owl, the eagle, the phoenix, the hoopoe, the viper, the ant, the sirens, the hedgehog, the fox, the panther, the whale, etc.) appear to be chosen at random. Evidently, this bestiary was only interested in animals to which tradition had assigned properties that lent themselves to an allegorical and moral interpretation. If, however, we examine the tables of contents of many medieval encyclopedias we observe that the way they are put together is only superficially casual (cf. Binkley 1997 and especially Meier 1997).

Isidore considers the seven liberal arts (grammar, rhetoric, dialectics, music, arithmetic, geometry, astronomy), followed by medicine, law, ecclesiastical books and offices, languages, peoples and armies, words, man, animals, the world, buildings, precious stones and metals, agriculture, wars, games, theater, ships, clothing, the home, and domestic chores—and one has to wonder what order lies behind a list of this kind, in which the entries dealing with animals are divided into Beasts, Small Animals, Serpents, Worms, Fish, Birds, and Small Winged Animals. But already in Isidore's day primary education was subdivided into the Trivium and the Quadrivium, and Isidore dedicates his first books in fact to these subjects, throwing in medicine for good measure. The chapters that follow, devoted to ecclesiastical laws and offices, are included because he was also writing for the learned, that is, for jurists and monks. Immediately afterward, another order becomes apparent: book VII takes as its point of departure God, the angels, and the saints and goes on to deal with mankind, then with the animals, and, from book XIII on, we proceed to consider the world and its parts, winds, waters, and mountains. Finally, with book XV, we arrive at inanimate but man-made objects, that is, at the various trades and métiers. Thus, though he syncretistically juxtaposes two criteria, Isidore does not throw things together randomly, and in the second part he follows an order of decreasing dignity of creatures, from God down to domestic implements.

The *De rerum naturis* of Rabanus Maurus also appears to be inspired by a casual order but in fact juxtaposes several traditional orders: it begins by following the criterion of decreasing dignity, and accordingly, starting with God, we move on to man, to the animals, to inanimate things, arriving finally at man-made things such as buildings, then the various trades are discussed, probably in the same order in which they were taught in the Carolingian Palatine school, and from the professions we proceed to philosophers, languages, precious stones, weights and measures, agriculture, military matters, games and theater, painting and colors, and the various tools used in cooking or in tilling the fields.[21]

In the thirteenth century, in his *De proprietatibus rerum,* Bartholomaeus Anglicus begins with a mixed order, following both dignity (from the angels to man) and the six days of Creation (the *hexameral* order). He then goes back and begins all over again with an order that may seem bizarre to us but apparently wasn't so for him, since he explains that, after speaking of the invisible world and of man, and dealing with the creation of the world and of time, he must now speak of the lesser things and of material creatures. And there follow the entries on air, birds, waters, mountains and regions, precious stones, herbs and animals, and finally various accidents like the senses, colors, sounds, scents, weights and measures, liquids. Bartholomaeus is respecting a philosophical order that is Aristotelian in origin, in that he speaks first of substances and then of accidents.

Furthermore, medieval readers must have perceived an order where we see only an accumulation of information, given that the organization of an encyclopedia also had a *mnemonic role* to play: a given order among things

---

21. If we find this order disconcerting, all we have to do is to consult, let's say, an Italian elementary school textbook from the 1930s containing scraps of ancient Roman history and the history of the nineteenth-century Risorgimento (skipping from Julius Caesar to Garibaldi), snippets of arts and literature (in the form of portraits of great men of the past), various lessons concerning life on the farm, notions of Fascism, a rudimentary introduction to racism. Anyone approaching such a text today with a scientific mentality would be unable to grasp the logic of its composition, but it contained all that the elementary school teacher was expected to impart as indispensable to the education of a child. Furthermore, if we were to compare the various morning schedules of a modern *liceo* or high school, we would be faced with incomprehensible leaps from organic chemistry to philosophy, from square roots to Petrarch. Or think again of the vagabond structure of many encyclopedias for children.

served to make them memorable, to remember the place they occupied in the image of the world (cf. Carruthers 1990 and Rivers 1997).

Little by little, the encyclopedias tend to make the order that governs them easier to follow: in the thirteenth century, Vincent de Beauvais's *Speculum majus,* with its 80 books divided into 9,885 chapters, already has the organization of a scholastic Summa. The *Speculum naturale* is inspired by a strictly hexameral criterion (the Creator, the sensible world, light, the firmament and the heavens, and so on, till we come to the animals, the formation of the human body and the story of mankind). The *Speculum doctrinale* treats of the human world and includes letters (philosophy, grammar, logic, rhetoric, poetics), morality, mechanics, and technical subjects, and, while the *Speculum morale* represents a sort of an ethical parenthesis (it is, incidentally, apocryphal), the *Speculum historiale* deals with human history or salvation history and has a chronological framework.

Order takes on a preponderant role, between the thirteenth and fourteenth centuries, with Raimon Llull's *Arbor scientiae (Tree of Science)*—a veritable portrayal of the Great Chain of Being through a representation of the great chain of knowledge—from which burgeon the *Arbor elementalis* (objects of the sublunar world made up of the four elements: fire, air, water, and earth, with precious stones, trees, animals), the *Arbor vegetalis,* the *Arbor sensualis,* the *Arbor imaginalis* (the mental images that are the similes of the things represented in the other trees), the *Arbor humanalis* (memory, understanding, will, and the various arts and sciences), and then the *Arbor moralis* (virtues and vices), the *Arbor imperialis* (government), the *Arbor apostolicalis* (the Church), the *Arbor caelestialis* (astrology and astronomy), the *Arbor angelicalis* (angelology), the *Arbor aeviternitalis* (the Otherworld kingdoms), the *Arbor maternalis* (Mariology), the *Arbor christianalis* (Christology), the *Arbor divinalis* (Divine attributes), the *Arbor exemplificalis* (the contents of knowledge), the *Arbor quaestionalis* (40,000 questions on the various professions).

1.3.3. From the Renaissance to the Seventeenth Century:
Toward the Labyrinth
Some of Llull's trees (the *Arbor elementalis,* for example) could still be interpreted as representations of the world and its parts, after the model of the *Arbor Porphyriana.* But, rather than a classification of reality, others suggest

a classification of knowledge about reality. This is the bent that the Llullism of the humanists and the Renaissance will appear to take, in which more or less tree-like structures are designed to organize universal knowledge into "chapters."[22] What we have here is not a classification of substances and accidents, but the *index* of a possible encyclopedia and an attempt to propose an organization of knowledge—an organization so important to the encyclopedist that at times the proposal is limited to the metalinguistic project of organizing this knowledge, putting off its actual investigation till a later date.

The *Margarita philosophica* of Gregor Reisch (1503) is still conceived in a postmedieval spirit. In it, the author, after devising an arboriform index that appears as a schematic frontispiece designed to facilitate consultation, proceeds to "fill it in" with 600 pages of actual encyclopedic information. But often the index is proposed without filling in the blanks, as we see, for instance, in the case of Politian, whose 1491 *Panepistemon* is a meticulously structured summary under the aegis of Philosophy personified as mother of the arts or *mater artium*.

Under the influence of Llull, the *Dialecticae institutiones* (1543) and the *Dialectique* (1555) of Pierre de la Ramée (also known as Petrus Ramus) both propose a rigorous method for listing in order, without repetitions or omissions, all the branches of knowledge—and the project will be taken up again in the *Encyclopaedia septem tomis distincta* of Johann Heinrich Alsted (1620). In the last case, starting with a series of *Praecognita disciplinarum,* we go on to the investigative tools (*lexica,* grammar, rhetoric, logic, oratory, and poetics) needed to confront the major questions addressed by so-called Theoretical Philosophy (metaphysics, pneumatics, physics, arithmetic, geometry, cosmography, uranometry, geography, optics, music), then on to Practical Philosophy (ethics, economics, politics, scholastics), arriving eventually at theology, jurisprudence, medicine, and the mechanical arts, as well as a hodgepodge of less well-organized disciplines (*farragines disciplinarum)* such as mnemonics, history, chronology, architectonics, down to issues like euthanasia, gymnastics, and tobaccology.

---

22. For the encyclopedic projects of the Renaissance and beyond, see the various contributions of Tega (1983, 1984, 1995, 2000, 2004), Vasoli (1978) and Pombo et al. (2006). For the Theaters of the World, cf. Rossi (1960) and Yates (1966).

Here the index is at the very heart of the encyclopedic project, the bones and nerves, as it were, of the discipline ("quasi ossa et nervos disciplinarum"), while the purpose of the project is the form that the universe of knowledge is supposed to assume. As Tega (1999: 113) remarks, "we should not expect to find in the encyclopedia the body, blood and spirit of each single discipline, but only a form devoid of any concrete and particular content." Alsted's is thus "the idea of an encyclopedia that not by accident takes as its model, not the work of the *polyhistor* or the philosopher or the scholar, but that of the architect whose job it is to produce a blueprint—or rather, in Alsted's case, a *table*—of a building that others will construct in stone and marble, while others still will decorate and fill it with objects."

This is because Alsted was working in a cultural climate in which a project of *Pansophia* was making headway, a form of universal wisdom that includes the entire encyclopedia of knowledge, foreshadowed in the so-called Theaters of the World, ideal architectural structures that attempt to encompass everything memorable, halfway between a mnemonics and an encyclopedia, whose most famous exemplar, never actually realized, remains that laid out in Giulio Camillo's 1550 *Idea del theatro*.[23] The index is intended to demonstrate that the reunification of knowledge is possible, and it does so because in such a climate the reorganization of knowledge is related to the utopian ideal of the reunification of the Christian world, but, like all utopias, it *announces* a reform without succeeding in bringing it about.

If the purpose of the *Arbor Porphyriana*, true to its Aristotelian inspiration, was to propose a methodology for "scientific" *demonstration* or better *definition*, the aim of the *pansophic index* was a *presentation* of the sciences (cf. Luisetti 2001: I, 1). In other words, pansophy is a *classification* of the

---

23. A scholar who, in the Baroque period, and precisely in the name of the pansophical ideal, will partially succeed in fleshing out his index is Jan Amos Komensky. With a general reform of society in mind and with an eye to implementing fresh pedagogical forms, in his *Didactica magna* (1628) and *Janua linguarum* (1631), to give the student an immediate visual apprehension of the things he was learning, Komensky attempted to classify the elementary notions according to a logic of ideas (the creation of the world, the four elements, the mineral, vegetable, and animals realms), while in his *Orbis sensualium pictus quadrilinguis* (1658) he devised a detailed illustrated nomenclature of all the world's fundamental objects as well as of human actions.

sciences, and we observed in section 2.1 how far removed classification is from definition.

The Renaissance and Baroque encyclopedia is therefore an ideal rather than a practical project that avoids "filling in" because, even if we were to exhaust the content of every discipline classified, the knowledge we would end up with would always be incomplete, just like the knowledge of any single individual. As far as the encyclopedia goes (as Alsted reminds us, in the "Admonitio" with which his *Encyclopaedia* begins), individuals "are like so many 'containers,' each of which is capable of holding a content in keeping with its receptive capacity, none of which, however, is able to contain in itself the whole of knowledge" (Tega 1999: 114).

But, precisely because knowledge is never complete, Ramus begins to conceive of an encyclopedia that can also take into consideration the constitution of disciplines as yet unknown or ill-defined. It is with Francis Bacon that the idea first appears of an encyclopedia based upon data derived from scientific experimentation and criticism of the erroneous opinions expressed in the past (the *idola*)—an *open* repertory, in other words, in a continuous process of development. Bacon's *Novum Organum* (1620) contains an appendix entitled "Parasceve ad historiam naturalem et experimentalem" ("Introduction to Natural and Experimental History") in which, after clarifying that we must steer clear of appealing to the authority of the ancients so as to avoid taking on apocryphal information, he draws up an ideal index which includes, in a reasonably logical order, celestial bodies, atmospheric phenomena, the earth, the four elements, natural species (mineral, vegetable, and animal), man, diseases and medicine, the arts, including the culinary arts, equitation, and games. Salomon's House, envisaged in his *New Atlantis* (1627), is an encyclopedic museum, and we can certainly speak of *farragines disciplinarum* apropos of his *Sylva Sylvarum* (1626), in which, taking into account only the first Century of the Table of Experiments, we find, jostling up against one another, considerations, for instance, concerning the nature of flame and the different techniques for coloring hair and feathers.

The metaphor of the *sylva* or forest is significant. A forest is not ordered according to clear binary disjunctions; instead it is a labyrinth. The labyrinth is explicitly mentioned in the preface to the *Instauratio Magna* (1620): "Aedificium autem hujus universi, structura sua, intellectui humano contemplanti, instar labyrinthi est; ubi tot ambigua viarum, tam fallaces rerum et signorum

similitudines, tam obliquae et implexae naturarum spirae et nodi, unde-
quaque se ostendunt" ("But the universe to the eye of the human understanding is framed like a labyrinth; presenting as it does on every side so
many ambiguities of way, so many deceitful resemblances of objects and
signs, natures so irregular in their lines, and so knotted and entangled").[24]
To the contemplating intellect, the edifice of the universe manifests itself as
a labyrinth, with a maze of ambiguous routes, of deceptive appearances of
things and signs, of winding and complicated nodes and spirals—and we
will see eventually, apropos of the rhizomic nature of an encyclopedia, how
truly prophetic this vision of "obliquae et implexae naturarum spirae et nodi"
would prove to be.

In this labyrinth, which no longer presents itself as a logical division but as
a rhetorical accumulation of notions and topics arranged under *loci,* the
Latin verb *invenire* (=to find or discover) no longer means to find something
one already knew existed, sitting in its proper place, ready to be used for the
purposes of argument, but truly to discover some new thing, or the relationship between two or more things, that one was previously unaware of. Such a
situation represents (as Rossi 1957, IV and V reminds us) the complete and
radical refusal of any preestablished hierarchy among beings. Pursuing an idea
that will be taken up again later by Leibniz, in the *Advancement of Learning*
Bacon points out that, if a secretary of state is obliged to accumulate a series
of records in his official place of business, he will classify them according to
the nature of the document (treaties, instructions, etc.), whereas in his private study he will keep all the papers that require his immediate attention
together, even though they may be of a heterogeneous nature. The Great
Chain of Being is a thing of the past, and from now on every subdivision will
invariably be made in context and directed toward a specific end.

1.3.4. The Cannocchiale aristotelico *of Emanuele Tesauro*
We have seen how with Bacon the idea of *inventio* (the noun derived from
the verb *invenire*) undergoes a sea change and, instead of referring to the
search for something already familiar, is transformed into the discovery of
something not yet known. But in this case hunting through the repertory of

---

24. Proemium, Epistle Dedicatory, Preface, and Plan of the *Instauratio Magna*
by Francis Bacon, in Eliot (1909, vol. 39, p. 126).

knowledge is like rummaging through an immense warehouse whose extent is not yet known, and rummaging not simply to put what one finds, whatever it may be, to use, but to construct, so to speak, a bricolage, discovering new syntheses, connections and dovetailings among things that at first sight did not appear to have any reciprocal relationship.

An encyclopedic model is paradoxically offered by Emanuele Tesauro's *Cannocchiale aristotelico* ("Aristotelian Telescope," 1665). I say "paradoxically" because, in the very century in which the model of Galileo's telescope comes into its own as the paradigmatic instrument for the development of the natural sciences, Tesauro proposes a telescope named after Aristotle as an instrument for renewal of what today we would call the human sciences, and the instrument he proposes is metaphor. In the *Cannocchiale*, however, we recognize the fundamental nucleus of Aristotelian rhetoric (of which more in section 1.8.1), and the model of metaphor is proposed as a means of discovering unfamiliar relations among the elements of knowledge, though Tesauro's interest, unlike Bacon's, is rhetorical rather than scientific.

To construct a repertory of known things, scrolling through which the metaphorical imagination may be led to discover unknown relationships, Tesauro develops the idea of a Categorical Index. He presents his index (with Baroque complaisance for the "marvelous" invention) as a "truly secret secret," an inexhaustible mine of infinite metaphors and ingenious conceits, given that genius is nothing more or less than the ability to "penetrate the objects deeply hidden beneath the various categories and compare them among themselves"—the ability, in other words, to unearth analogies and similarities that would have passed unnoticed had everything remained classified under its own particular category.

It is sufficient, then, to inscribe in a book Aristotle's ten categories, the Substance and the nine Accidents, and then list under each category its Members and under each Member the Things "subject to it."

All we can do for our present purposes is to give a few meager examples of the extensive catalogue Tesauro provides (susceptible in any case of constant expansion). Thus, under the category of Substance, are to be recorded as Members the Divine Persons, Ideas, the Fabulous Gods, Angels, Demons, and Sprites; then, under the Member Heaven, the Wandering Stars, the Zodiac, Vapors, Air, Meteors, Comets, Torches, Thunderbolts, and Winds; and then, under Earth, Fields, Solitudes, Mountains, Hills, and Promontories; under

Bodies, Stones, Gems, Metals, Herbs; under Mathematics, Orbs and Globes, Compasses, and Squares; and so on and so forth.

Likewise, for the category of Quantity, under the Quantity of Size are listed the Small, the Large, the Long, and the Short; under the Quantity of Weight, the Heavy and the Light. For the category of Quality, under Sight we find the Visible and the Invisible, the Apparent, the Handsome and the Misshapen, the Bright and the Dark, the White and the Black; under Scent, Sweet Odor and Stench—and so on through the categories of Relation, Action and Passion, Site, Time, Place, and State.

When we take a closer look at the Things subordinate to these Members, we find that, under the category of Quantity and the Member Size, among small things we find the angels (which fit within a point), the incorporeal forms, the pole as the unmoving point of the sphere, the zenith and the nadir; among Elementary Things the spark of fire, the droplet of water, the grain of sand, the scruple of stone, the gem, and the atom; among Human Things, the embryo, the *abortus,* the pigmy, and the dwarf; among Animals, the ant and the flea; among Plants, the mustard seed and the crumb of bread; among the Sciences, the mathematical point; in Architecture the tip of a pyramid; under *Lanaria,* the metal tip of a lace, and so on with a list that goes on for two pages.

We have no need to ask ourselves just how congruous this list is. Incongruity seems to be typical of all of the efforts made in the Baroque period to give an account of the global contents of a field of knowledge, just as it is equally characteristic of many seventeenth-century projects for artificial languages. Gaspar Schott, in his *Technica curiosa* (1664) and his *Joco-seriorum naturae et artis sive magiae naturalis centuriae tres* (ca. 1666) gave notice of a work published in 1653, whose author's name he claims to have forgotten. In fact the anonymous author seems to have been a certain Pedro Bermudo (1610–1648), a Spanish Jesuit who presented in Rome an *Artificium* or *Arithmeticus nomenclator, mundi omnes nationes ad linguarum et sermonis unitatem invitans. Authore linguae (quod mirere) Hispano quodam, vere, ut dicitur, muto.*[25] It is doubtful whether Schott's is a faithful description, but the issue is irrelevant, since, even if Schott had reworked the project after his

---

25. The last words of the title *(vere, ut dicitur, muto)* are probably a play on words, since, according to Schott, the author was dumb *(muto)*, and in Castilian *Bermudo* is pronounced almost the same as *Ver-mudo* (cf. Ceñal 1946).

own fashion, what interests us is the incongruity of the list. The *Artificium* provided for forty-four fundamental classes, which are worth listing here, giving only a few examples in parentheses:

1. Elements (fire, wind, smoke, ash, hell, purgatory, and the center of the earth). 2. Celestial entities (stars, thunderbolts, the rainbow). 3. Intellectual entities (God, Jesus, speech, opinion, suspicion, soul, stratagem, or ghost). 4. Secular states (emperor, barons, plebs). 5. Ecclesiastical states. 6. Artificers (painter and sailor). 7. Instruments. 8. Affections (love, justice, lust). 9. Religion. 10. Sacramental confession. 11. Tribunal. 12. Army. 13. Medicine (doctor, hunger, clyster). 14. Brute beasts. 15. Birds. 16. Reptiles and fish. 17. Parts of animals. 18. Furnishings. 19. Foodstuffs. 20. Beverages and liquids (wine, beer, water, butter, wax, resin). 21. Clothing. 22. Silk fabrics. 23. Wools. 24. Canvas and other woven cloths. 25. Navigation and spices (ship, cinnamon, anchor, chocolate). 26. Metals and coins. 27. Various artifacts. 28. Stones. 29. Jewels. 30. Trees and fruit. 31. Public places. 32. Weights and measures. 33. Numerals. 39. Time. 40. Adjectives. 41. Adverbs. 42. Prepositions. 43. Persons (pronouns, titles such as Your Eminence). 44. Travel (hay, road, highway robber).[26]

Around 1660 Athanasius Kircher had composed a *Novum hoc inventum quo omnia mundi idiomata ad unum reducuntur* ("New invention by which all the languages of the world can be reduced to one") still surviving only in manuscript form,[27] which proposed a fairly elementary grammar and a dictionary of 1620 "words," in which he endeavored to establish a list of fifty-four fundamental categories capable of being represented by means of iconograms. His iconograms recall those in use today in airports and stations—sometimes they represent an object, such as a small wineglass, sometimes they are purely geometrical (a rectangle, a triangle, a circle), while some of them are superficially inspired by Egyptian hieroglyphs. Without going into detail (see Marrone 1986 and Eco 1993: 9), we may simply note that the fifty-four categories of the *Novum Inventum* also constitute a notably

---

26. Leibniz will discuss the inappropriateness of this arrangement by classes in his early work, *Dissertatio de arte combinatoria* (1666).

27. Mss. Chigiani I, vi, 225, Biblioteca Apostolica Vaticana; see Marrone (1986).

incongruous list, including as they do divine, angelic, and celestial entities, elements, human beings, animals, vegetables, minerals, the dignities and other abstract concepts of Llull's *Ars Magna,* beverages, clothing, weights, numbers, hours, cities, foodstuffs, family, actions like seeing or giving, adjectives, adverbs, the months of the year. But let us get back to Tesauro.

Tesauro follows the bent of his time. But what seems to us a lack of the systematic spirit is on the contrary evidence of the effort made by the encyclopedist to avoid arid classification according to genera and species. It is the as yet unordered accumulation (or barely ordered, in Tesauro's case, under the rubrics of the ten categories and their members) that will later permit the *invention* (in the Baconian sense, not of recovery but of discovery) of unexpected and original relationships between the objects of knowledge. This impression of a "hodgepodge" is the price we have to pay, not to achieve completeness but to eschew the poverty of any classification in the form of a tree.

We have only to see what Tesauro makes of his warehouse of notions. If we were searching for a good metaphor for a dwarf (though for Tesauro discovering metaphors means, as it did for Aristotle, coming up with new definitions for things or discovering everything that can be said about a given object), from this repertory we could already derive the definitions of Myrmidon (the name is related to "ant") or the little mouse at whose birth the mountains were in labor. But to this index there is added another that, for every small thing, depending on which of the ten categories we consider, decides, under Quantity, what the small thing is commensurate with or what parts it has; under Quality, whether it is visible or what deformities it has; under Relation, to whom or with what it is related, whether it is material and what form it has; under Action and Passion, what it can and cannot do, and so on. And once we have asked ourselves what the small thing is commensurate with, the Index ought to refer us, for example, to "the Measure of the Geometric Finger."[28]

Proceeding in this way through each category, we could say of the dwarf that he is shorter than his own name, more an embryo than a man, a fragment of humanity, far smaller than a thumb, so insubstantial as to be without color, sure to be the loser in a fight with a fly, so tiny you can't tell whether he is sitting, standing or lying down, and so on.

The Index, precisely because of its labyrinthine nature, allows us to make connections between each object and every other object—so that it seems that

---

28. For the Geometric Finger, see Eco (1996a: 96).

all Tesauro's *metaforeta* or metaphor maker can do (and all he delights in doing) is deriving new knowledge from the deconstruction of a Porphyrian tree.

Although, out of devotion to Aristotle, Dante's "master of all those who know" (*Inferno* IV, 131), and his works, Tesauro opted to call his index "categorical," what he in fact provides is a procedure to pursue the infinite paths of a labyrinth, in which the subdivisions according to categories are nothing more than provisional and ultimately arbitrary constructions designed to contain somehow or other material that is in a constant state of ferment.

1.3.5. *Wilkins*

The point of greatest tension between tree and labyrinth is reached in seventeenth-century England, in the ambit of the Royal Society, where various projects for an a priori *philosophical language* (such as Lodwick's *A Common Writing*, Becks's *The Universal Character*, Dalgarno's *Ars signorum* or the *Essay towards a Real Character and a Philosophical Language* by Wilkins) are formulated, in which "characters" comprehensible to people who speak different languages are called upon to represent a global structure of the world.

What these systems discuss is the possibility of representing the meanings of each term through a punctiliously exhibited hierarchical arrangement of subdivisions from genera to species, while at the same time giving an account of the nonregimentable multiplicity of notions that common speakers have at their disposal. The problem these systems find themselves having to face is that, if one chooses a tree classification, according to the dictionary model, it is impossible to give an account either of the meaning of the terms or the nature of the things designated, and therefore the nodes of every tree-like classification must be filled in with encyclopedic specifications, with sums of properties, in other words, that can neither be defined   .
or classified.

Referring the reader to Eco (1993) for a more detailed analysis of these systems and the relevant bibliography, we will confine ourselves in this context to considering briefly Wilkins's *Essay towards a Real Character*, the most complete and fully worked-out project of them all. Wilkins conducted a kind of colossal review of all knowledge and produced a table of 40 major Genera, proceeding to subdivide them into 251 peculiar Differences, from which he derived 2,030 Species (presented in pairs). The table of 40 Genera (Figure 1.12) starts out with very general concepts like Creator and World

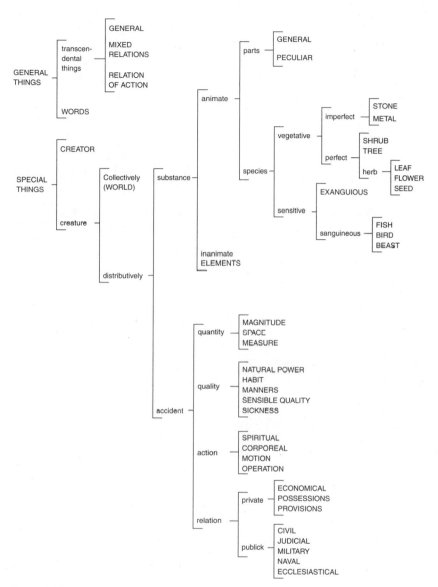

Figure 1.12

and, by means of a division into substances and accidents, animate and inanimate substances, vegetative and sensitive creatures, arrives at Stones, Metals, Trees, Birds, or accidents like Magnitude, Space, Sensible Qualities, Economical Relations.

More detailed still are the tables that allow us to arrive at individual species, in which Wilkins proposes to classify, for instance, even a beverage like beer, in order to represent the entire notional universe of a seventeenth-century Englishman. With regard to this system of ideas (which Wilkins, clearly erring on the side of ethnocentricity, presumes to be common to all mankind), the "real characters" that he proposes are signs (which assume both a written form, almost hieroglyphic in nature, and an oral form, transcribed in pronounceable alphabetic characters). Thus, if *De* signifies *Element,* and *Deb* the first difference *(Fire),* then *Deba* will denote the first species, which is *Flame.*

Here, however, we are not interested in Wilkins's writing proposals (essential though they may be to his project for a universal language), but in the criteria he uses to organize the notions. Once again, the mere classification does not permit us to recognize a Flame or to assert that it burns. Even when we get down to the single species we find divisions according to which, given the category Viviparous Clawed Beasts, subdivided into Rapacious and Non-Rapacious, under Rapacious we find *Cat-kind* and *Dog-kind,* the latter being divided into European and Exotic, the European further divided into Amphibious and Terrestrial, the Terrestrial into Bigger (Dog/Wolf) and Lesser (Fox/Badger), as we see in Figure 1.13.

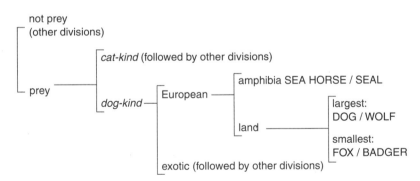

Figure 1.13

As usual, not only is it impossible to distinguish a dog from a wolf, but, in addition, the information that the "characters" of Wilkins's alphabet transmit is simply that the dog (*Zita* in the universal language) is "the first member of the specific pair of the fifth difference of the genus Beasts."

It is not until we consult the extremely crammed encyclopedic tables which Wilkins places after his classifications that we learn that viviparous animals have feet with toes, rapacious animals usually have six sharp incisors and two long fangs to hold their prey, the *Dog-kind* have round heads which distinguish them from the *Cat-kind* whose heads are more oblong in shape, while the largest of the canines are subdivided into "domesticated-tame" and "wild-hostile to sheep": this is the only way for us to grasp the difference between a dog and a wolf.

Wilkins's philosophical language *taxonomizes* but it does not define. In order to define, the system must have recourse to a miscellany of information expressed in a natural language that takes the form of an encyclopedia.

The defect that becomes evident in Wilkins's failure is the same defect that undermines any notion of a dictionary that sets itself the aim of being rigorous. In order for a dictionary to be totally independent of any additional knowledge of the world, its terms must be *primitives* not further definable—otherwise the tree would forfeit its nature as a device capable of guaranteeing the exactitude of the definitions it generates. But, in Wilkins's case, it is clear that the mass of encyclopedic information underlying the organization of the tables according to supposed primitives is in fundamental contradiction with the compositional character according to traits that appeared to be being realized in his "characteristic" language. The primitives are not primitives. Not only are Wilkins's species combinations of genera and differences (a weakness already typical of a Porphyrean Tree, given that the differences are accidents not subject to hierarchization), but furthermore they are *names* used as hooks on which to hang encyclopedic descriptions.

Nevertheless, precisely because it is impure, Wilkins's system is susceptible of another reading, no longer as a dictionary but as a *hypertext,* in our contemporary meaning of the term. If a hypertext links every node or element of its repertory, by means of a multiplicity of internal cross-references, to a multiplicity of other nodes, one could imagine a hypertext regarding animals that inserts *dog* into a general classification of mammals, in a tree of *taxa* that also includes cats, oxen, and wolves. But if in that tree one *points* to *dog* (precisely in the modern computer sense of clicking on it), one is directed to a repertory of information concerning the properties and habits of dogs. Selecting another type of connection, one can also access a list of the various roles played by dogs in different historical periods, or a list of images of dogs in art history. Perhaps this is where Wilkins was headed, when he thought of considering Defense both in terms of the duties of the citizen as well as in terms of military strategy.

1.3.6. Leibniz

Still, we cannot credit Wilkins with an idea he never formulated. The figure who did in some sense express it was Leibniz, perhaps because the opposition between dictionary and encyclopedia characterized his entire research. In fact, starting with his 1666 *Dissertatio de arte combinatoria*, explicitly inspired by Llull, he will pursue throughout his life the ideal of a *characteristica universalis,* a rational language, based on a limited number of primitives and logical rules, that would permit wise men to sit around a table and arrive at the truth by way of a *calculemus* ("let us calculate"). But he quickly becomes convinced that there is no assurance that the primitive terms one arrives at cannot be further broken down into components, and he admits that at best they may be *postulated* as such for the convenience of the calculus. In such a context, he is more concerned with the *form* of the propositions that the calculus is able to generate than he is with the meaning of the terms—and he compares in fact his *characteristica* to an algebra that can be applied, with quantitative rigor, to qualitative notions. And, like algebra, it is a form of *cogitatio caeca* (or "blind reasoning") that allows us to perform calculations, and to arrive at exact results, using symbols of whose significance we are not able to have a clear and distinct idea. In so doing Leibniz certainly launched the development of a formal logic in which the symbols do not refer back to a precise idea but stand *in its stead.*

But when on the other hand he thinks in terms of a review of universal knowledge, Leibniz assumes an entirely different stance, and in various writings he compares an encyclopedia to a library as a general inventory of all knowledge. In his 1679 *Consilium de Encyclopaedia nova conscribendi methodo inventoria,* he proposes an encyclopedia that would take in rational grammar, logic, the arts of memory, universal mathematics and its technical applications (geodetics, architecture, optics), mechanics, the science of the physical and chemical properties of bodies, mineralogy, botany and agronomy, animal biology and medicine, ethics, geopolitics, and natural theology. As was the case for Bacon, this encyclopedia must remain *open:* its order will be discovered little by little as science progresses, and it must also include the unwritten knowledge that is dispersed among people of different professions.

In his *Nouveaux essais sur l'entendement humain,* written in 1703–1705, he reminds us that the encyclopedia must have "many cross-references from one place to another, given the fact that most things can be seen from several different points of view, and a truth can be collocated in different places according to the different relationships it has: the people who organize a library often do not know where to classify certain books and remain undecided among two or three equally appropriate placements" (VI, 31). What Leibniz has in mind is what we would call a polydimensional encyclopedia, in which allowance has been made for multiple transversal connections (Gensini 1990: 19).

1.3.7. *The* Encyclopédie

In fact Leibniz anticipates the project later theorized by D'Alembert in the opening pages of the *Encyclopédie,* and it is on the basis of Leibniz's suggestions that, with the advent of the Enlightenment, the premises for a critique of any attempt to found an a priori system of ideas begin to take shape. The Enlightenment encyclopedia is determined to be critical and scientific: it refuses to censor any belief, even those considered erroneous, but it exposes them for what they are (see, for instance, the entry on the unicorn, which appears to describe the animal according to tradition, but at the same time underscores its legendary nature). Following the model of the ancient encyclopedia, it aspires to give an account of the entirety of human knowledge, even the "mechanical" knowledge associated with arts and crafts.

True, the model of the Enlightenment encyclopedia is based on a kind of tree-like pattern (Figure 1.14).

But D'Alembert, in his "Preliminary Discourse" to the *Encyclopédie,* while providing information concerning the criteria according to which the work was organized—not immediately obvious given its alphabetical rearrangement—develops on the one hand the metaphor of the tree while

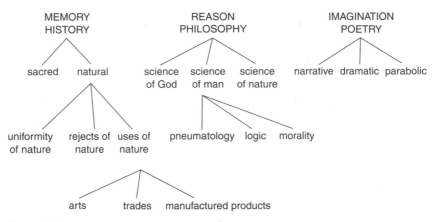

Figure 1.14

simultaneously calling it into question, speaking instead of a "terrestrial globe" and of a labyrinth:

> The general system of the sciences and the arts is a sort of labyrinth, a tortuous road which the intellect enters without quite knowing what direction to take. . . . However philosophic this disorder may be on the part of the soul, an encyclopedic tree which attempted to portray it would be disfigured, indeed utterly destroyed. . . .
>
> Finally, the system of our knowledge is composed of different branches, several of which have a common point of union. Since it is not possible, starting out from this point, to begin following all the routes simultaneously, it is the nature of the different minds that determines which route is chosen. . . .
>
> It is not the same with the encyclopedic arrangement of our knowledge. This consists of collecting knowledge into the smallest area possible and of placing the philosopher at a vantage point, so to speak, high above this vast labyrinth, whence he can perceive the principal sciences and the arts simultaneously. From there he can see at a glance the objects of their speculations and the operations which can be made on these objects; he can discern the general branches of human knowledge, the points that separate or unite them; and sometimes he can even glimpse the secrets that relate them to one another. It is a kind of

world map which is to show the principal countries, their position and their mutual dependence, the road that leads directly from one to the other. This road is often cut by a thousand obstacles, which are known in each country only to the inhabitants or to travelers, and which cannot be represented except in individual, highly detailed maps. These individual maps will be the different articles of the *Encyclopedia* and the Tree or Systematic Chart will be its world map.

But as, in the case of the general maps of the globe we inhabit, objects will be near or far and will have different appearances according to the vantage point at which the eye is placed by the geographer constructing the map, likewise the form of the encyclopedic tree will depend on the vantage point one assumes in viewing the universe of letters. Thus one can create as many different systems of human knowledge as there are world maps having different projections. . . .

. . . But often such an object, which because of one or several of its properties has been placed in one class, belongs to another class by virtue of other properties and might have been placed accordingly. Thus, the general division remains of necessity somewhat arbitrary.[29]

D'Alembert's discourse still suffers from an unresolved tension between the model of the tree and the model of the map. It becomes clear that the sum of our knowledge (present, but also, as it was for Leibniz, future) extends like a geographical map without borders, within which infinite itineraries are possible. But, given that the *Encyclopédie,* in its printed form, is in alphabetical order, one knows one will need to resort to a number of reductive strategies.

What we already have, however, is a first hint at the ideal model of an encyclopedia, that is, a hypothetical compendium of *all* of the knowledge available to a given culture.

1.4. The Maximal Encyclopedia as Regulatory Idea

The encyclopedia is potentially infinite because it is forever *in fieri,* and the discourses we construct on its basis constantly call it into question (in the same way in which the latest article by a nuclear scientist presupposes a series

---

29. English translation: D'Alembert (1963: 46–49).

of encyclopedic notions concerning the structure of the atom, but at the same time introduces new ones that render the old ones moot).

The Maximal Encyclopedia is not content with merely recording what "is true" (whatever meaning we may choose to give to this expression). It records instead everything that has been claimed in a social context, not only what has been accepted as true, but also what has been accepted as imaginary.

It exists as a *regulating principle:* yet this regulating idea, which cannot constitute the starting point for a publishable project because it has no organizable form, serves to identify portions of encyclopedias that can be activated, insofar as they serve to construct *provisional hierarchies* or *manageable networks,* with a view to interpreting and explaining the interpretability of certain segments of discourse.

This encyclopedia is not available for consultation in toto because it is the sum total of everything ever said by humankind, and yet it has a material existence, because what has been said has been deposited in the form of all the books ever written and all the images ever made and all the evidential items that act as reciprocal *interpretants* in the chain of semiosis.

Having become transformed over the centuries from an (attainable) utopia of *global* knowledge into an awareness of the impossibility of global knowledge, but with the certainty of the *local* availability of the elements of this knowledge, no longer the project for a book, but a method of investigation addressing the general and omnivorous library of culture in its entirety, the Maximal Encyclopedia was envisaged in poetic terms by Dante, when, in Canto 33 of his *Paradiso,* as he finally attains the vision of God, he is unable to describe what he saw except, precisely, in terms of an encyclopedia:

> In its profundity I saw—ingathered
> and bound by love into one single volume—
> what, in the universe, seems separate, scattered:
>   substances, accidents, and dispositions
> as if conjoined—in such a way that what
> I tell is only rudimentary.
>   I think I saw the universal shape
> which that knot takes; for, speaking this, I feel

a joy that is more ample. That one moment
  brings more forgetfulness to me than twenty-
five centuries have brought to the endeavor
that startled Neptune with the Argo's shadow![30]

The encyclopedia is the only means we have of giving an account, not only of the workings of any semiotic system, but also of the life of a given culture as a system of interlocking semiotic systems.

As I have shown elsewhere (see, for instance, Eco 1975), from the moment one takes the route of the encyclopedia, two theoretically crucial distinctions are lost: (i) in the first place, that between natural language and other semiotic systems, since properties expressed in nonverbal form can also constitute part of the encyclopedic representation of a given term or corresponding concept (in the sense that a potentially infinite number of images of dogs are part of the encyclopedic representation of the notion "dog"); and (ii) in the second place, the distinction between semiotic system as object and theoretical metalanguage. It is impossible in fact to create a metalanguage as a theoretical construct composed of a finite number of universal primitives: such a construct, as we have seen, explodes, and when it explodes it reveals that its own metalinguistic terms are nothing other than terms of the object language—though they may be used *provisionally* as not susceptible of further definition.

The encyclopedia is dominated by the Peircean principle of *interpretation* and consequently of *unlimited semiosis*. Every expression of the semiotic system is interpretable by other expressions, and these by still others, in a self-sustaining semiotic process, even if, from a Peircean point of view, this flight of interpretants generates habits and hence modalities of transformation of the natural world. Every result of this action on the world must, however, be interpreted in its turn, and in this way the circle of semiosis is on the one hand constantly opening up to what lies outside and on the other constantly reproducing itself within.

Furthermore, the encyclopedia generates ever new interpretations that depend on changing contexts and circumstances (and hence semantics incorporates within itself pragmatics). Therefore we can never give it a definitive and closed representation: an encyclopedic representation is never

---

30. English translation: Dante (1982: Paradiso XXXIII: 85–96).

global but invariably local, and it is activated as a function of determined contexts and circumstances. The expression "dog" occurring in a universe of discourse regarding fireplace furniture generates different interpretants from the same expression occurring in a universe of discourse regarding animals; while, within a discourse on animals, the same expression generates different ramifications of interpretants depending on whether the subject is zoology or hunting.

1.5. Labyrinths

D'Alembert spoke of a labyrinth, and he naturally attempted to express the concept through that of a map, without, however, being able to speak of the topological model of a polydimensional network. The Porphyrian tree represented an attempt to reduce the polydimensional labyrinth to a bidimensional schema. But we have observed how, even in this simple classificatory instrument, the tree regenerated the labyrinth (of differences) at every fresh step.

We must first reach a consensus on the concept of labyrinth, because labyrinths come in three varieties (cf. Santarcangeli 1967; Bord 1976; Kern 1981). The classic labyrinth of Cnossos is *unicursal:* there is only one path. Once one enters one cannot help reaching the center (and from the center one cannot help finding the way out). If the unicursal labyrinth were to be "unrolled," we would find we had a single thread in our hands—the thread of Ariadne which the legend presents as the means (alien to the labyrinth) of extricating oneself from the labyrinth, whereas in fact all it is is the labyrinth itself.[31] The unicursal labyrinth, then, does not represent a model for an encyclopedia (Figure 1.15)

The second type is the Mannerist labyrinth or *Irrweg.* The *Irrweg* proposes alternative choices, but all the paths lead to a dead point—all but one, that is, which leads to the way out (Figure 1.16). If it were "unrolled," the *Irrweg* would assume the form of a tree, of a structure of blind alleys (except for one).[32] One

---

31. In this labyrinth, by the way, there has to be a Minotaur, just to make the experience interesting, seeing that the pathway through it (setting aside the initial disorientation of Theseus, who doesn't know where it will lead) always leads where it has to lead and can't lead anywhere else.

32. In this case there is no need for a Minotaur; the Minotaur is the visitor himself, misled as to the nature of the tree.

Figure 1.15

Figure 1.16

can take the wrong path, in which case one is obliged to retrace one's steps (in a certain sense the *Irrweg* works like a *flowchart*).

The third kind of labyrinth is a *network,* in which every point may be connected with any other point (Figure 1.17).

A network cannot be "unrolled." One reason for this is because, whereas the first two kinds of labyrinth have an inside and an outside, from which one enters and toward which one exits, the third kind of labyrinth, infinitely extendible, has no inside and no outside.

Since every one of its points can be connected with any other, and since the process of connection is also a continual process of correction of the connections, its structure will always be different from what it was a moment ago, and it can be traversed by taking a different route each time. Those who travel in it, then, must also learn to correct constantly the image

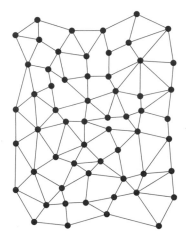

Figure 1.17

they have of it, whether this be a concrete (local) image of one of its sections, or the hypothetical regulatory image concerning its global structure (which cannot be known, for reasons both synchronic and diachronic).

A network is a tree plus an infinite number of corridors that connect its nodes. The tree may become (multidimensionally) a polygon, a system of interconnected polygons, an immense megahedron. But even this comparison is misleading: a polygon has outside limits, whereas the abstract model of the network has none.

In Eco (1984b: ch. 2), as a metaphor for the network model, I chose the *rhizome* (Deleuze and Guattari 1976). Every point of the rhizome can be connected to any other point; it is said that in the rhizome there are no points or positions, only lines; this characteristic, however, is doubtful, because every intersection of two lines makes it possible to identify a point; the rhizome can be broken and reconnected at any point; the rhizome is antigenealogical (it is not an hierarchized tree); if the rhizome had an outside, with that outside it could produce another rhizome, therefore it has neither an inside nor an outside; the rhizome can be taken to pieces and inverted; it is susceptible to modification; a multidimensional network of trees, open in all directions, creates rhizomes, which means that every local section of the rhizome can be represented as a tree, as long as we bear in mind that this is a fiction that we indulge in for the sake of our temporary convenience; a global description of the rhizome is not possible, either in time or in space; the rhizome justifies and encourages contradictions; if every one of its nodes can be connected with every other node, from every node we can reach all the other nodes, but *loops* can also occur; only local descriptions of the rhizome are possible; in a rhizomic structure without an outside, every perspective (every point of view on the rhizome) is always obtained from an internal point, and, as Rosenstiehl (1979) suggests, it is a short-sighted algorithm in the sense that every local description tends to be a mere hypothesis about the network as a whole. Within the rhizome, thinking means feeling one's way, in other words, *by conjecture.*

Naturally it is legitimate to inquire whether we are entitled to deduce this idea of an *open-ended* encyclopedia from a few allusions in Leibniz and an elegant metaphor in the *Encyclopédie,* or whether instead we are attributing to our ancestors ideas that were only developed considerably later. But the fact that, starting from the medieval dogmatics of the *Arbor Porphyriana* and by way of the last attempts at classification of the Renaissance, we slowly evolved toward an open-ended conception of knowledge, has its roots in the Copernican revolution. The model of the tree, in the sense of a supposedly closed catalogue, reflected the notion of an ordered and self-contained cosmos with a finite and unalterable number of concentric spheres. With the Copernican revolution the Earth was first moved to the periphery, encouraging changing perspectives on the universe, then the circular orbits of the planets became elliptical, putting yet another criterion of perfect symmetry in crisis, and finally—first at the dawn of the modern world, with Nicholas of Cusa's idea of a universe with its center everywhere and its circumference nowhere, and then with Giordano Bruno's vision of an infinity of worlds, the universe of knowledge too strives little by little to imitate the model of the planetary universe.

1.6. The New Encyclopedic Models

Whether or not this was the unconscious model for a new ideal of encyclopedic knowledge, it must be said that the first real efforts at creating semantic representations in encyclopedic form did not get underway until the second half of the twentieth century and only after a fierce debate regarding the shortcomings of any dictionary representation.[33]

---

33. The first proposals for switching to encyclopedic representations are to be found in Wilson (1967). There followed Eco (1975), Haiman (1980), Eco (1984a), Marconi (1992, 1999), and Violi (1997).

Clearly, although the idea of the encyclopedia as postulate and ideal model is infinite, all that could be attempted were limited and *local* representations, which however did not exclude the possibility of their progressive and potentially limitless enrichment.

The new encyclopedic models assumed a number of formats, among them:

(i) Matrices representing the presence or absence of traits chosen ad hoc to account for the differences among items belonging to the same semantic subset, such as *chair, armchair, sofa,* etc. (cf. Pottier 1965).

(ii) Contextual selection models (specifying the various meanings a given lexeme may take on in different contexts) (cf. Eco 1975, 1984a).

(iii) Models by Cases that include Agents, Objects, Instruments, Purposes (the verb "to accuse," for example, is defined as an action in which a human Agent communicates to a human Object by means of a verbal Instrument with the Purpose of revealing to him that the action of another human Object is evil; whereas "to criticize" is explained as the action of a human Agent who by means of a verbal Instrument speaks to a human Object with the Purpose of demonstrating that the action of another human Object is open to censure; or else the verb "to kill" is analyzed as the action of a human Agent which causes a change of state, from living to dead, of an animated X— further specifying, by the use of the English verb "to assassinate," that the X in question must be a political figure) (cf. Fillmore 1968, 1969, 1977).

(iv) Representations that take into account, in the case, for instance, of a term like "water," the properties that determine its extension or its referent (its being H_2O); labels of a quasi-dictionary variety, such as being Natural and Liquid; as well as stereotypical notions like Colorless, Transparent, Tasteless, Odorless, Thirst-Quenching (cf. Putnam 1975, 12).

(v) Representations that take into account all possible properties of a term and specify, for a chemical element for example, odor, color, natural state, atomic number, effects, history, etc. (cf. Neubauer and Petöfi 1981).

None of these proposals, however, had had recourse to network structures. It is in the field of artificial intelligence that frame-, script- or scenario-type representations appear, registering each stage of a sequence of typical events (for instance, what does "going out to a restaurant" mean: entering, sitting down at a table, ordering from the menu, eating, requesting the bill, etc.)—all models that have proved successful in the field of artificial intelligence, where, in order for a computer to understand a text and draw conclusions from it, it must first be provided with all of the competences with which (even without their being aware of it) the average human being is endowed (cf. Schank and Abelson 1977; Schank and Childers 1984).

But it is with Quillian (1968) that the notion of a *semantic network,* structured as a labyrinth of interconnected nodes, first appears. To simplify things, all we have to do is take another look at Figure 1.17. Any node can be taken as the point of departure or *type* of a series of other nodes *(tokens)* that define it (let's say the point of departure is *dog* and that this node is defined by its links with *animal, quadruped, able to bark, faithful,* etc.). Each of the defining terms may in its turn become the *type* of another series of *tokens.* For instance, *animal* could be exemplified by *dog,* but also by *cat,* and would include *quadruped* but also *biped;* or, if a node *cat* were to be identified, it would be defined by a number of nodes it shared with the definition of *dog,* such as *animal* and *quadruped,* but it would also refer to nodes like *feline,* which it shares with *tiger,* and so on.

A network model implies the definition of every concept (represented by a term) through its interconnection with the universe of all the concepts that interpret it, each of them ready to become the concept interpreted by all the others.

If we were to expand the network of linked nodes ad infinitum, from a concept assumed as *type* it would be possible to retrace, from the center to the outermost periphery, the entire universe of the other concepts, each of which may in its turn become the center, thereby generating infinite peripheries.

Such a model is also susceptible of a two-dimensional graphic configuration when we examine a local portion of it (and in a computer simulation, in which the number of *tokens* chosen is limited, it is possible to give it a describable structure). But it is not in fact possible to represent it in all its complexity. It would have to be shown as a kind of polydimensional network, endowed with topological properties, in which the paths become longer or shorter, and every term gains in proximity with the others, by way of shortcuts and immediate contacts, while remaining at the same time linked to all the others according to historically mutable relationships.

It has been said that, if we assume a maximal notion of competence about the world, the meaning of a term would then consist of all the true propositions in which it has appeared or could appear. In fact, this would presuppose the ideal model of the encyclopedia. But in scientific practice and the way in which, in our daily lives, we try to make sense of sentences, we do not make a global appeal to the encyclopedia for every sentence, and it is the content that selects the local zones of competence that must be activated. Two flexible criteria may be assumed: (i) information is potentially part of the *average* encyclopedic competence if it can be supposed to be sufficiently shared by a collectivity (which may also be a "regional" collectivity—in this sense the definition of *neutrino* would form part only of the regional competence of a community of nuclear physicists—see the concept of Specialized Encyclopedia discussed below in section 1.9); (ii) the format of the network to be activated is prescribed by the contexts and the circumstances of the proposition (accordingly, if someone uses the word *torus* in speaking of topology a network is constituted which is concerned with mathematical objects, and all concepts regarding the fields of architecture, anatomy, and botany are excluded).

While in an ideal encyclopedia there are no differences between necessary and contingent properties, it must be admitted that, within a specific culture, certain properties appear to be more *resistant to negation* than others, on account of the fact that they are more salient: it could feasibly be denied, for instance, in the light of a new system of classification, that a *sheep* is *ovine,* or again this particular trait might not be deemed necessary to the understanding of the term *sheep* in the sentence: "the sheep was bleating in the field." There can be no doubt, however, that it is hard to deny that a sheep is an animal—and the characteristic also remains implicit for the comprehension of the example we just cited. It has also been observed (Violi 1997: sect. 2.2.2.3) that some traits seem to be more *resistant* than others, and that these uncancelable traits are not only categorical labels such as ANIMAL or PHYSICAL OBJECT. In the life of semiosis we realize that we are also reluctant to cancel some "factual" properties that appear more salient and characteristic than others.

To explain why certain properties appear more resistant than others, Violi (1997: sect. 7.2) distinguishes between essential and typical properties: it is essential that a cat be an animal; it is typical that it meows. The second property can be canceled, but not the first. But if this were to be the case we would be back again to the same old difference between dictionary and encyclopedic properties. Violi (1997: sect. 7.3.1.3) instead considers properties that are functional and certainly encyclopedic in nature to be similarly uncancelable: hence it is difficult to say of something that it is a box and at the same time deny that it can contain objects (if it couldn't it would be a *fake* box).

Often, however, in order to construct and presuppose a local portion of encyclopedia needed for the comprehension of a determined context, we must resort to simplified local representations that set aside many properties that are otherwise (in other contexts) resistant.

In Eco (1984b: sect. 2.3.4) I gave the example of a dialogue between a wife and her husband at midnight in a suburban home. The wife looks out the window and says with a preoccupied air, "Honey, there's a man in the garden." The husband takes a look and says, "No, honey, that's not a man." The husband's reaction certainly violates a pragmatic rule because it provides less information than the situation calls for, since denying the presence of a man could on the one hand suggest that what is there is a child or a cat, while on the other hand it could also lead his wife to imagine something more dangerous (why not an invader from outer space?).

In this context, when she is afraid there may be a man there, the wife surely does not assign to the term the properties of rationality, bipedality, or the ability to laugh—all properties that in that context are *narcotized* (cf. Eco 1979a: ch. 5) and considered irrelevant, but instead those of a living being, capable of movement and aggression and therefore potentially—at night and in someone else's garden—dangerous. Because it is also part and parcel of the infinite encyclopedic properties of *man* to be prone to take up a life of crime (don't we all know that *homo homini lupus,* man is a wolf to men?) The husband ought then to adjust his iteration on the basis of a *local* encyclopedic representation, as in Figure 1.18, one that he conjecturally considers shared (given the circumstances) by his wife.

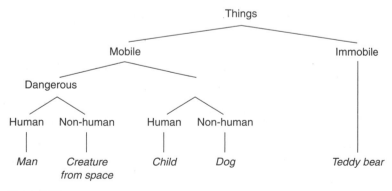

Figure 1.18

If the husband wishes to calm his wife down he must either exclude immediately the property of mobility (by saying, for example, that what she saw was
the shadow of a tree) or deny any suggestion of properties suggesting danger-
ousness (in which case he might say that it wasn't a man but a stray dog).

The ad hoc construction of a local portion of encyclopedia, that organizes
only the properties pertinent to the context, is the only strategy that will allow the husband to interact in a reasonable way with his concerned wife.

1.7. The "Ontologies"

In the most recent research on artificial intelligence and the cognitive sciences, the notion of semantic networks has given rise to a theory of *ontologies*. Despite the inappropriate use of a concept like "ontology," which has
quite a different meaning in philosophy, the term is used in this context to
refer to the *categorical organization* of a portion of universe that may take
the form of any kind of classificatory tree or semantic network. In this
sense, the husband in the example just considered could (without being
aware of it, like Molière's Monsieur Jourdain who spoke in prose without
being aware of it) have constructed an ontology.

According to one recent definition, an ontology is "a specification of a
representational vocabulary for a shared domain of discourse—definitions of
classes, relations, functions, and other objects" (Gruber 1993: 199). The definition is very broad and can be adapted both to a complex semantic network
and to a mere classification. In fact, in much of the literature on ontologies,
the starting point is the model of the *Arbor Porphyriana*, used to exemplify
the most common semantic relationship, that is, that of *subsumption* (see, for
instance, Sowa 1991, 2000). If this seems disappointing, it occurs because the
producers of ontologies are responding as a rule to practical needs (even supplying a business firm with a satisfactory organization of its data and products) and sometimes a tree structure can serve that purpose.

There are ontologies in the form "part-of," in which, for example, the
meaning of *car* is analyzed, representing its various components and functions (see, for instance, Barsalou 1992: 30). From the theoretical point of
view, they do not go much further than the representations already present
in various versions of encyclopedia semantics—except that a particular
representational structure is devised to give instructions to a computer.

Other times graphs are designed in which each node has not just one single superordinate but allowance is made for multiple heredities and a node may derive properties from each single superordinate node or from all of them.

There is some discussion as to whether the ontologies should be *adequatist,* that is, maximal, or *reductionalist,* that is, referred to a single universe of discourse. It is usually conceded that the domain of an ontology should not be complete but simply cover the area of interest that produces it. In the vast literature on the subject the ontologies are sometimes no more than ingenuous diagrams designed to illustrate perfectly intuitive links and differences, classifications in the most traditional sense of the word—like those used in the natural sciences since Linnaeus—or mere shorthand notes or mnemonic devices. Even apart from the nonchalance with which the word "ontology" is used to indicate (and to sell) representations so dissimilar in scope and purpose, the variety of the models suggests that, if they really reflect states and structures of the mind, this would mean that our brain articulates its competence through different data-organization models depending on the problem to be resolved or committed to memory.

The aspects that make ontologies interesting are highlighted by Smith (2003): (i) they do not pretend to be representations of the world but of our modes of conceptualization in given domains—sometimes representing also commonsense knowledge; (ii) therefore an ontology has nothing to do with questions of ontological realism and is a purely pragmatic undertaking; (iii) the entities present in an ontology possess only the properties represented in that structure (we would add that the others are narcotized because they are irrelevant to the specific universe of discourse). As Smith remarks, it is as if Hamlet, whose hair is not mentioned in Shakespeare's tragedy, was neither bald nor nonbald, but instead was *a man without properties* as far as his hair was concerned.

In this sense, an ontology, however clumsy and ingenuous it may be, is the local representation of a portion of encyclopedic knowledge relevant for the purposes of a given universe of discourse.

1.8. Ontologies and Semiosic Creativity

It appears that, if we are to understand a text or the meaning of a word, we need an underlying ontology, as is shown in the example illustrated in

Figure 1.18. In the same way, it seems obvious that if the encyclopedia, as Leibniz already opined, is a body subject to a constant process of renewal and expansion, many expressions produced in the context of a given culture can contribute toward changing the current encyclopedia. The contentions of Copernicus, for instance, and later those of Galileo and Kepler noticeably modified the encyclopedia of the modern world (which from that moment on did not stop citing the theories of Ptolemy but placed an asterisk in front of them to show they were mistaken).

But, alongside these cases of scientific innovation, or transformation of common sense, there are cases of artistic creativity in which a new text requires—if it is to be understood in all its innovative aspects—that our encyclopedia be modified.

1.8.1. Metaphor as a Tool for Producing New Ontologies
In this historical rereading of the adventures of the encyclopedia we must once again return to Aristotle, to consider an aspect of his thought that has apparently nothing to do with the history of definitions, either dictionary or encyclopedic. We are talking about his theory of metaphor.

What makes Aristotle's theory of metaphor interesting for us today is not simply the fact that it is the first rigorous discussion of this trope, but above all the fact that this first theorization of metaphor does not consider it as a mere ornament of discourse but assigns it a cognitive function.[34]

The key suggestion in the *Poetics* is to be found in 1459a 8, where the author declares that metaphor is the best of all the tropes because understanding metaphor means "knowing how to recognize similarity" or "the related concept." The verb he uses is *theorein,* which means to perceive, to investigate, to compare, to judge. It is then clearly a *verbum cognoscendi.* Aristotle gives examples of banal metaphors, such as those from genus to species *(there lies my ship)* or from species to genus *(Verily ten thousand noble deeds hath*

---

34. This was the topic of the seminar in which Chapters 2 and 3 in this volume had their origin. Its purpose was to attempt to establish how and to what extent Aristotle's proposal had been accepted throughout history. For a complete overview reaching down to the present day, see the miscellany edited by Lorusso (2005), in which, for the analysis of the Aristotelian texts, we refer the reader to the contributions of Manetti (2005), Calboli Montefusco (2005), and Calboli (2005).

Odysseus wrought), but he already lists metaphors that are more interesting poetically when he speaks of the metaphor from species to species *(with blade of bronze drew away the life).* As for the metaphor by analogy he appears to be listing expressions that are already quite solidly codified such as *the shield of Dionysus* (god of wine) for the cup and *the cup of Mars* (god of war) for the shield or the evening as the old age of the day. But he identifies an effective and original poetic expression in *sowing the god-created light,* said of the sun, perhaps by Pindar, and he likewise appreciates a quasi-riddle like *a man I saw who on another man had glued the bronze by aid of fire,* said of the suction cup or cupping glass. These are cases in which the poetic invention leads us to investigate the similarity, suggested, but not immediately evident.

The relevant passages in the third book of the *Rhetoric* are far more in number. What arouses wonder *(to thaumaston)* is pleasing; metaphor manifests itself *(phainesthai)* when we examine *(skopein)* a possible correspondence or analogy. The talent for metaphor is not something that can be learned from others, and therefore it is not a matter of mere imitation but of invention. The examples he gives of analogy are not in the least banal, as in the famous example (1405a) in which pirates refer to themselves as "purveyors." The rhetorical move is persuasive because it insinuates that the plunderer and the merchant share a characteristic in common, since both of them facilitate the transfer of goods from a source to the consumer. The identification of the characteristic they share (in addition to being brazen) is daring, because other discordant characteristics, such as the opposition between a peaceful means and a violent one, are narcotized, but it is undeniably ingenious and provokes surprise, encouraging us to reconsider the role of the pirate in the economy of the Mediterranean.

Aristotle declares that metaphors should be drawn from things that are not evident, just as in philosophy the sagacious mind recognizes, discovers, perceives *(theorein)* similarities between distant things (1412a 12). On the other hand, in 1405b he says that metaphors imply enigmas. When, apropos of the *asteia* (1410b 6 et seq.), he says that the poet calls old age *kalámen* or "a withered stalk," he specifies that such a metaphor is productive of a knowledge *(gnosis)* through their common genus, inasmuch as both belong to the genus of things that have lost their bloom. Elegant enthymemes are those which help us learn in a new and rapid way and, in this as in other cases, the *verbum cognoscendi* used is *manthanein,* to learn. Those enthymemes are efficacious that are understood little by little as they are spoken and were previously unknown, or those we understand only at the end. In such cases we say that *gnosis gínetai* ("knowledge comes to be"). Moreover, the obvious metaphor, which is not at all striking, is rejected. When the metaphor makes us see things the opposite from the way we thought they were, it becomes evident that we have learned something, and our mind seems to say: "That's the way it was, and I was mistaken about it."

Metaphors, then, "put the thing before our eyes" *(to poiein to pragma pro ommaton).* This notion of "putting something before our eyes" is repeated several other times in the text, and Aristotle appears to insist on it with conviction: a metaphor is not a mere transfer but a transfer that is immediate in its evidence—but clearly unfamiliar, unexpected, thanks to which things are seen in action (1410b 34), or better, signified in action.

As for the many examples provided by the text, especially those that concern similes (1406b 20 et seq.), it is certainly difficult to say whether they may have sounded bold to the ears of Aristotle's contemporaries, but all of them appear to be examples of original witticisms. The same can be said of the passage on the *asteia* (1411b 22). All the examples are provocative and so little used previously that they are attributed to a specific author. To call triremes *painted millstones* and taverns *the mess-rooms of Attica* is a fine way to show something in a new light.

But *what is it* that metaphor as a cognitive mechanism makes us see in a fresh light? Things themselves, or the way we were accustomed to seeing (and representing) things?

It appears that it is only in contemporary culture that we have realized that, in order to be understood, metaphors often require us to reorganize our categories. As Black (1979: 39–40) remarks, "some metaphors enable us to see aspects of reality that the metaphor production helps to constitute. But that is no longer surprising if one believes that the world is necessarily a world under a certain description—or a world seen from a certain perspective. Certain metaphors can create such a perspective."[35]

---

35. On the fact that metaphor constructs rather than discovering a similarity and is a source of fresh knowledge, not so much because it makes us know a given thing better but above all because it makes us discover a new way of organizing things, see, in addition to Black, Ricoeur (1975: 246) and Lakoff and Johnson (1980: 215).

Still, when Aristotle said that the invention of an effective metaphor "puts before our eyes" for the first time an unfamiliar relationship between two things, he meant that metaphor compels us to reorganize our knowledge and our opinions. Let us return to the *Rhetoric* (1405a) and the metaphor by which pirates are said to be *purveyors* or *suppliers.* Now, before the appearance of this metaphor there was nothing to associate an honest merchant who acquires, transports by ship, and resells his merchandise with a pirate who steals someone else's merchandise. The astuteness of the metaphor consists in compelling us to identify a hierarchical organization of property that, on a lower level, distinguishes a violent action from a pacific one, but, on the higher level, lumps together genera and species of those who transport merchandise upon the sea. In this way the metaphor unexpectedly suggests a socially useful role for the pirate, at the same time leading us to suspect that there may be something not altogether above board about the transactions of the merchant. In this way, the categorical field becomes reorganized no longer on the basis of moral or legal considerations but on the basis of economic activity.

We have already remarked how, in seeking various explanations for the eclipse, Aristotle tried out various "ontologies" (and we are not going too far in using the term in the quintessentially modern sense we just recognized). Similarly, when, in *On the Parts of Animals,* he must decide, on the basis of empirical observations, which of the various biological phenomena are causes and which effects, Aristotle finds himself faced with the fact that ruminants (animals, that is, with four stomachs) have horns and lack upper incisors—with the embarrassing exception of the camel, which is a ruminant lacking upper incisors, but without horns.

Aristotle first proposes a definition whereby horned animals are animals which, since they have four stomachs—which makes internal rumination possible—have redirected the hard matter of the teeth into the formation of horns. In order to make the camel fit into this categorical organization, Aristotle must suppose that it did not need to redirect the hard matter into horns (because, being large, it had no need for further protection), but instead it deflected it to the gums and palate (Figure 1.19).

But why are ruminants the way they are? The fact that they are ruminants explains why they have horns, but having horns does not explain why they are ruminants. Faced with the need to define the category of ruminants,

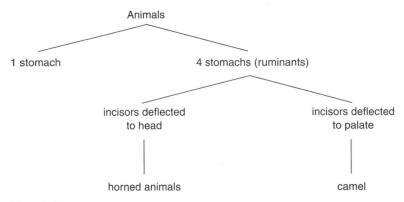

Figure 1.19

Aristotle puts forward the hypothesis that ruminants have deviated the hard matter from the mouth to the head for reasons of defense and have developed four stomachs as a consequence (Figure 1.20).

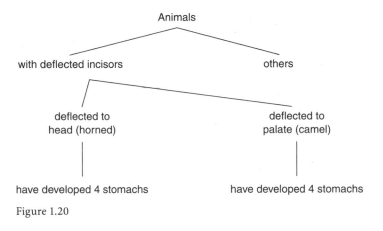

Figure 1.20

   As we can readily see, these two definitions presuppose two different categorical organizations, in the first of which it is the fact of being a ruminant that determines the deviation of the incisors and makes possible the development of horns, in the other it is the deviation of the incisors for the purposes of defense that produced the four stomachs. The truth is that Aristotle, in suggesting a number of hypotheses regarding causes and effects, in no way attempts to construct pseudo-Porphyrian trees. He merely shows extreme flexibility in selecting as a genus what was previously a species and vice versa. In other words, he never tells us that the definition is based on an underlying ontological structure, rather what he does is to propose a methodology of division that makes an adequate definition possible. It is not the underlying tree that makes the definition possible, it is the definition that imposes an underlying tree, frequently ad hoc. But in his theory of metaphor Aristotle goes still further: he suggests that a creative and original use of language obliges us *to invent a new ontology*—and therefore, we might add, to enrich to some degree our encyclopedia.

Naturally, the new ontology is only valid as far as the comprehension of the creative text that imposes it is concerned. But we are entitled to suppose that, once the creative text has imposed a new ontology, however *local*, somehow or other it leaves a trace in our encyclopedia.

1.8.2. Joycean Ontologies

In my essay "The Semantics of Metaphor" (in Eco 1984c), a kind of reduced ontology was constructed, made up of all the expressions that appear in a certain section of Joyce's *Finnegans Wake*, and an attempt was made to justify the various puns as passages among a series of phonetic, synecdochic, metonymic, or metaphoric associations.

The experiment was intended to demonstrate how, starting from whatever point of the textual universe one might chose as a sample, one could attain, by multiple and continuous pathways, as in a garden of forking paths, any other point.

In the schema presented in Figure 1.21,[36] we may observe how the term *Neanderthal* evokes by phonetic association three other terms: *meander, Tal* (German for "valley") and *tale* ("story," in English), which combine to form the punning coinage cited in the book, *meandertale*. In the associative trajectory, however, intermediate nodes are created, provided by terms all of which appear in the text of *Finnegans Wake* and only there. At this point the associations may be phonetic or semantic in nature.

These interconnections demonstrate, moreover, how each term may become in its turn the archetype of an associative series that would lead us to

---

36. It will be observed how this reconstruction of a fragment of encyclopedia within Joyce's text was reminiscent of the model in Quillian (1968), adopted in Eco (1975).

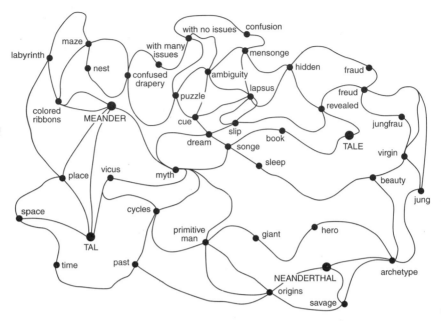

Figure 1.21

identify, sooner or later, other associative chains. The whole diagram has a purely orientative value, in the sense that it reduces the associations numerically and dimensionally, but if we proceed from this ontology to Joyce's text, we observe that all the associations registered by the network have been developed (in other words, we see how that ontology had its origin in the need to render explicit the associations that that text intended to provoke). Indeed, every association produces a pun that defines the book. The book is *a slipping beauty* (and hence a sleeping beauty who as she sleeps generates a series of *lapsus* through semantic slips, mindful of an error, etc.), a *jungfraud's messonge-book* (where, to the associations already cited, that of *message* is added), a labyrinth (or *meandertale*) in which we find *a word as cunningly hidden in its maze of confused drapery as a fieldmouse in a nest of coloured ribbons* (the expression that gave rise to the schema, which naturally would have been clearer had the various circuits been colored differently). As a final synthesis, in the pages of the book the neologism *meanderthalltale* becomes the metaphorical stand-in for all that can be said about the book itself and which is said by the associative chains identified in the network.

In the associative sequences, semantic rather than phonetic in nature, the terms are associated through identity or similarity of properties (not real, but culturally *imputed*). If we reread the associative sequences we see that each of them could be constructed by referring to a "notional field" accepted in a given culture or to one of those typical linguistic *carrefours* or crossroads theorized by Trier, Matoré, and others. A survey of the notional fields acquired by a given culture would explain not only why *Freud* and *Fraud* may be connected, by phonetic similarity, but also *Freud-dream* and *Freud-Jung.*

Let us consider, for example, the sequence generated by *Tal:* on the one hand it refers us to *space* and *place,* genera of which *Tal* is, so to speak, the species. But *space* in turn refers to *time* since the relationship between space and time is a typical relationship of complementarity. The relationship between time and the past and between time and the cycles *(corsi e ricorsi)* of Giambattista Vico arises from a more or less textbook contiguity.

This means that on the one hand all of the connections were certainly culturalized before Joyce justified them by pretending to institute them or discover them, while on the other they become evident to us (and allow us to reconstruct the ontology underlying the text) only because Joyce brought them to light (by making obvious the relationships among the terms of a *domain* that he himself brought into focus).

What makes the pun creative is not the series of connections (which potentially precedes it because they are already culturalized): it is the decision to oblige us to construct, by way of an unfamiliar ontology, *short circuits* that are possible but not yet evident. Between *message* and *dream* there is no phonetic similarity and only a weak semantic contiguity (whereby, but only in certain cultures, or as part of a psychoanalytic *koiné,* a dream is a message), and to bring them together the reader has been obliged to make the leap over unconnected points of the diagram so as to get from *songe* to *mensonge* or from *message* to *mensonge.* But from that moment—from the moment when the text has spoken—those points are no longer unconnected.

Language, carrying to creative outcomes the encyclopedic process of unlimited semiosis, has created a new polydimensional network of possible connections. This creative "gentle violence," once set in motion, does not leave unaffected the collective encyclopedia (and indirectly, not even the one shared by those who have not read Joyce). It has left behind a trace, a fruitful wound.

1.9. The Formats of the Encyclopedia

1.9.1. From the Individual to the Maximal

However intriguing this reconstruction of a "Joycean ontology" may have proved to be, it cannot be denied that the model of a reduced labyrinth illustrated in Figure 1.21 is infinitely more impoverished than *Finnegans Wake* taken as a whole. As useful as it has been in understanding a series of implicit and explicit connections at the basis of a number of puns, and as instructive as it perhaps is as a miniaturization of an encyclopedic network, nevertheless, just like the rest of the ontologies we have spoken of so far, it fatally reduces the riches of the Maximal Encyclopedia (of which the entire text of *Finnegans Wake* is in any case only a part) to which it certainly refers us, though by means of a work of domestication.

We remarked in section 1.4 that a Maximal Encyclopedia cannot be consulted in its entirety because it represents the sum total of everything that was ever thought or said, or at least of everything that could in theory be discovered, to the extent to which it has been expressed through a series of materially identifiable interpretants (graffiti, stelae, monuments, manuscripts, books, electronic recordings)—a sort of World Wide Web far richer that the one to which we have access through the Internet.

Pavel (1986) invited us to try a fascinating mental experiment. Let us suppose that an omniscient being is capable of writing or reading a *Magnum Opus* that contains all of the true assertions regarding both the real world and all possible worlds. Naturally, since we can speak of the universe using different languages, and since each language defines it in a different way, there exists a Maximal Collection (Pavel calls it the "Total Image") of *Magna Opera*. Let us now suppose that God charges a number of angels with writing Daily Books for each individual human being, in which they take note of all the propositions (concerning the possible worlds of that individual's desires and hopes and the real world of his acts) that correspond to a true statement in one of the books that make up the Maximal Collection of *Magna Opera*. The collection of Daily Books belonging to a given individual must be produced on the Day of Judgment, along with the collection of the Books that assess the lives of families, tribes, and nations.

But the benevolent genie who writes a Daily Book is not content to align true statements: he connects them, evaluates them, builds them into a system. And since on the Day of Judgment individuals and groups will each have a defending angel, the defenders will rewrite for each individual another astronomical series of Daily Books in which the same statements will be linked together in different ways, and differently compared to the affirmations of some of the *Magna Opera*.

Since infinite alternative worlds make up each of the infinite *Magna Opera,* the angels will write an infinite number of Daily Books in which affirmations that are true in one world and false in the other will be mingled together. If we further hypothesize that some of the genies may be clumsy and mix up affirmations registered as mutually contradictory by a single *Magnum Opus,* what we will end up with will be a series of compendiums, miscellanies, compendiums of fragments of miscellanies that amalgamate strata of books of different origins, and at that point it will be very difficult to say which books are truthful and which fictional, and with respect to what original. We will have an astronomical infinity of books each of which will straddle different worlds and we will no doubt consider as true stories that others have considered as fictional.[37]

This gives us a good idea of what the Maximal Encyclopedia might look like, if we substitute for the angels the human beings who took time to leave behind their traces (from the bison depicted in the Altamira caverns to the invention of writing and beyond). The legend Pavel narrates gives a reasonable representation of our situation when confronted by the universe of affirmations that we are accustomed to accept not as "true" but in any case enunciated.[38]

In the preceding sections we saw how, confronted with the virtual immensity of the Maximal Encyclopedia (a regulatory hypothesis, a stimulus to the understanding of sentences of every type), we usually attempt to reduce its format, to construct local representations with the purpose of understanding

37. Pavel (1986: 64–70).
38. On the *Metrôon* as a warehouse of memory, see Esposito (2001: 107–110).

a single context. Nevertheless, this entire dialectic between local and global is not so simple. In other words, recognizing it does not mean answering a question but formulating one. When in a given context we endeavor to reconstruct the portion of encyclopedia probably activated by some enunciator, to what format of the encyclopedia are we referring? Clearly, if a child tells us that the sun has moved, in our understanding of what the child means we do not refer the statement to complex cosmographical notions concerning a galactic revolution of the sun, but instead to the set of "ingenuous" habits of perception on the basis of which we say that the sun rises and sets. But what encyclopedic format do we refer to when we are talking to a scientist, to an educated person, to a farm laborer, to an inhabitant of a far-off country?

In *Kant and the Platypus* I discussed the difference between Nuclear Content (NC)—a set of interpretants on the basis of which both a lay person and a naturalist can agree on the properties evoked by the term *mouse,* both understanding in the same way the sentence *there is a mouse in the kitchen*—and Molar Content (MC), which represents the specialized knowledge that a naturalist may have of a mouse. We are justified, then, in thinking that on the one hand there is a Median Encyclopedia (shared in the present case by both the naturalist and the common native speaker) and on the other an unmanageable plethora of Specialized Encyclopedias, the complete collection of which would constitute the unattainable Maximal Encyclopedia. Accordingly, we could imagine the states (or strata) of what Putnam has called the social division of linguistic labor by hypothesizing a kind of solar system (the Maximal Encyclopedia) in which a great many Specialized Encyclopedias describe orbits of varying circumferences around a central nucleus (the Median Encyclopedia), but at the center of that nucleus we must also imagine a swarm of Individual Encyclopedias representing in sundry and unforeseeable ways the encyclopedic notions of each individual.

In section 1.3.3 we alluded to Alsted's notion according to which, with respect to the encyclopedia, individuals are like so many containers, each capable of holding a content commensurate with his or her receptive capacity, and none capable of containing in themselves the whole sum of knowledge. In any kind of communicative interaction, it is clearly necessary to presuppose and infer the format of the individual encyclopedia of the persons speaking to us, otherwise we would attribute to them intentions (and knowledge) that they do not have. This is basically why we so frequently bring into play the *principle of charity*. But as a rule (except when we are dealing with anomalous interlocutors such as a child, a foreigner from a remote and unknown culture, or a mentally challenged individual) out of considerations of economy we have recourse to what we consider to be a Median Encyclopedia. Though its extent is difficult to measure, a Median Encyclopedia is identified with the contents of a given culture.

So, just as knowledge of the works of Plato (except for the *Timaeus*) were not part of the Median Encyclopedia of medieval culture, in which notions about Plato came from Neo-Platonic sources, in the same way part of our current Western encyclopedia is the idea that the Ptolemaic system was believed to be true in the past whereas today it is considered erroneous (without its having been forgotten). To sum up, we might say that the Median Encyclopedia is represented by an encyclopedia in the publisher's sense of the word—and probably a mid-sized one-volume encyclopedia and not the thirty-two volumes of the 2010 *Britannica*.[39]

The fact that it is a Median Encyclopedia does not mean that all of its contents are shared by all members of a given culture, but rather that it is *shareable* (we will examine in more detail later, in section 1.9.5, the concept of "latency" of information). Even an educated person may have forgotten (or

---

39. It has been suggested that the concept of a semiotic encyclopedia corresponds to Lotman's idea of the semiosphere: "Imagine a room in a museum, where exhibits from different eras are laid out in different windows, with texts in known and unknown languages, and instructions for deciphering them, together with explanatory texts for the exhibitions created by guides who map the necessary routes and rules of behaviour for visitors. If we place into that room still more visitors, with their own semiotic worlds, then we will begin to obtain some thing resembling a picture of the semiosphere" (Lotman 2005: 213–214). In point of fact Lotman's semiosphere would appear on the one hand to be still vaster than a Maximal Encyclopedia because it also contains the private and idiosyncratic notions of the individual visitors; on the other hand, it is, so to speak, regulated by someone (the organizers) and therefore appears rather to be the territory of a culture that has set up rules to distinguish a Median Encyclopedia from the Specialized Encyclopedias.

never have known) the date of Napoleon's death, but that person knows that the information is accessible and usually knows where to find it. This is why it is said that a cultivated person is not someone who knows the dates of the beginning and the end of the Seven Years War, but someone who can come up with them in a couple of minutes.

The Median Encyclopedia cannot be identified with an extensive library containing thousands, even millions of volumes, because such a library, though it may not be commensurate with the Maximal Encyclopedia, nevertheless encompasses the Median Encyclopedias of exotic cultures, of past civilizations, and ideally all of the Specialized Encyclopedias, past and present. That library is instead merely an attempt to approximate the Maximal Encyclopedia, fatally incomplete because the Maximal Encyclopedia does not contain only those ideas that have been committed to the written word.

The fact that, not just the Maximal Encyclopedia, but even the "parody" of it represented by a normal library should provoke the vertigo of a knowledge so exaggeratedly extensive that nobody could ever capture or contain it in their own individual memories, leads us to the problem of memory and forgetfulness; the problem, in other words, of the Vertigo of the Labyrinth.

1.9.2. *The Vertigo of the Labyrinth and the* Ars Oblivionalis

Since classical antiquity, the problem of the need to forget appears contemporaneously with the development of mnemonic techniques by which to commit to memory the maximum possible amount of information (especially in the centuries in which information was not as readily obtainable and transportable as it has since become, with the invention first of printing and subsequently of electronic devices). In *De oratore* (II, 74), for example, Cicero cites the case of Themistocles, who was gifted with an extraordinary memory. When someone offered to teach him an *ars memorandi,* Themistocles replied that his interlocutor would be doing him a greater service if he taught him how to forget what he wished to forget than if he taught him how to remember ("gratius sibi illum esse facturum, si se oblivisci quae vellet quam si meminisse docuisset"), inasmuch as he would prefer to be able to forget something he did not wish to remember than to remember everything that he had once heard or seen ("cum quidem ei fuerit optabilius oblivisci posse potius quod meminisse nollet quam quod semel audisset vidissetve meminisse").

Themistocles's concern, incidentally, anticipates (and perhaps inspires) the anxiety of Borges's Funes the Memorious, who remembered each and every detail of his experiences and perceptions, to such an obsessive and unbearable degree, down to the mere rustling of a leaf heard decades earlier, that he was practically unable to think.

The problem of the excess of memory explains why one of the terrors of the practitioners of mnemonics was that of remembering so much as to confound their ideas and forget practically everything as a result. It seems, in fact, that at a certain point in his life Giulio Camillo had to excuse himself for his state of confusion and for the gaps in his memory, citing as an explanation his protracted and frantic application to his theaters of memory. On the other hand, in his polemic against mnemotechnics, Cornelius Agrippa *(De vanitate scientiarum)* claimed that the mind is rendered obtuse by the memorative art's resort to "monstrous" images and, being so overburdened, is led to madness. Hence, subterraneously parallel to the fortunes of the *ars memoriae,* the reappearance from time to time of the phantasm of an *ars oblivionalis* (see Eco 1987a and Weinrich 1997).

In the twentieth lesson ("Lettione XX") of the *Plutosofia* of Filippo Gesualdo (1592), the "methods for oblivion" are reviewed.[40] Gesualdo excludes mythical solutions such as drinking the waters of Lethe. He is aware that Johannes Spangerbergius in his *Libellus artificiosae memoriae* (1570)[41] had already reminded his readers that people forget from corruption, that is, from forgetfulness of past species, by diminution (old age and sickness), and from ablation of their cerebral organs. Likewise, it is obvious that we can forget by repression and suppression, drunkenness and drugs, but all these are cases of natural occurrences that must be studied and are studied elsewhere.[42]

---

40. [*Translator's note:* On Gesualdo, among others, see Barbara Keller-Dall'Asta, *Heilsplan und Gedächtnis: zur Mnemologie des 16. Jahrhunderts in Italien* (Heidelberg: Universitätsverlag Winter, 2001).]

41. The work of Johannes Spangenberg appeared under this title in 1570, but another version with the title *Libellus de comparatione artificiosae memoriae* had appeared in 1539. It would be subsequently published as *Artis memoriae seu potius reminiscentiae* in 1603, *Ars memoriae* in 1614, etc.

42. To these causes we might add the mystics' techniques for detachment from the world and from one's own memories. These are certainly techniques that aim at voluntary forgetfulness, but what is to be forgotten is so global as to coincide

Gesualdo, however, is intent upon developing an art of forgetting that employs the same techniques as an art of remembering,[43] and he advises:

First, having recited, and wishing to consign the images to oblivion; either in the daytime with closed eyes or in the dark and quiet of the night, you should go wandering with your mind through all the imagined places, evoking an obscure nocturnal gloom that hides all of them, and proceeding in this fashion, and going back a number of times with the mind and not seeing any images, every figure will soon disappear.

Second, go peering into all the places with the mind, back and forth, and contemplate them empty and bare, as they were formed for the first time without any images in them, and this operation should be performed several times.

Third, if the persons in the places are persistent, let them be seen by the mind from all angles many times, and let them be contemplated in the same way they were first set up, with bowed heads and dangling arms, without any additional images.

Fourth, just as the painter pastes over and whitewashes his paintings to cancel them, so we too can cancel the images with colors painted over them. And these colors are white, green or black; imagining over the places white curtains, green sheets or black cloths; and going over the places a number of times with these veils of colors. And one can also imagine the places stuffed with straw, hay, firewood, merchandise, etc.

Fifth, I consider it an excellent rule to put in place new figures; because just as one nail drives out another, so forming new images and putting them in the places already imagined, cancels the first images from our memory. It is true that it is necessary to imprint them with great care and mental effort and to repeat them frequently in the dark

---

with the annihilation of one's own self-awareness. This being the case, I would prefer to speak of spiritual ablation, not of a technique for canceling local portions of our memory.

43. [*Translator's note:* A fundamental strategy in the art of memory consisted in collocating mnemonic images or figures in a series of designated "places" along a familiar route that the orator would follow with his mind's eye observing the images to be remembered. The art of forgetting consists, then, in eliminating these "places" or reminders. See, for example, Yates (1966) and Eco and Migiel (1988).]

and quiet of the night, so that the intense and vivid idea of the second ones drives out the first Ideas.

Sixth, imagine a great storm of winds, hail, dust, ruined buildings and places and temples, a flood that leaves everything in a state of confusion. And when this noxious thought has continued for a while and been repeated several times, finally go walking among the places with your mind, imagining the weather bright and calm and peaceful, and seeing the places empty and bare as they were formed for the first time.

Seventh, after the longest period of time possible, imagine an Enemy, terrible and fearsome (the more cruel and bestial and belligerent the better) who, with a troop of armed companions, enters and passes impetuously among the places and with scourges, cudgels and other weapons drives out the likenesses, assaults the people, shatters the images, puts to flight through doors and windows all of the animals and animate persons who were in the places,

Until, after the tumult has passed and the ruin, seeing the places with a mind recovered from its terror, they will be seen bare and vacant as before. And if this destruction were to occur at the hands of hostile armies, such as the Turks and Pagans, it would be even more effective, because that terror confounds everything and sets everything upside down.[44]

We do not know whether anyone ever put the artifices Gesualdo recommended into practice, but we are entitled to suspect that all these stratagems made it easier to remember than to forget whatever it was the practitioner wanted to forget, and to remember it with even greater intensity—as occurs when lovers try to blot out the image of the person who has abandoned them.[45]

---

44. [*Translator's note:* My translation from Eco's text (AO)].

45. Note that we cannot make an exception either for the most blatant cases of political censure—such as the photographs of the Stalinist period in which the images of the former leaders declared to be heretics and shot have been removed—precisely because that act of violence kept the memory of those eliminated alive in the collective memory. Similarly, the various attempts at revisionism, such as the theory that Kennedy's death did not occur as the official records have it, because—as we will see later—in cases that involve the (presumed) correction of an error or a debate over two possible solutions to a problem, the tendency is to retain, not just the solution assumed to be correct, but both horns of the dilemma.

The physiological and psychological reasons why an *Ars oblivionalis* is impossible depend on the contiguity/similarity dialectic on which the classical mnemotechnical systems are founded. If object x has been imagined to be in contact with object y, or if object x is in some way homologous with object y, every time object x is evoked so is object y. But if this is how the *Artes memoriae* work, it is hard to see how one can imagine an object x that, when evoked, somehow acts on our cerebral cortex by canceling y. Jakobson (1956) described the structures of the different types of aphasia and how they manifest themselves, but he did not say how they can be produced artificially. It is no accident, however, if Jakobson, in order to explain the internal mechanics at least of a neurophysiological problem like aphasia, if not its causes, should appeal to the paradigmatic and syntagmatic axes, two categories from the linguistic and semiotic domain. This suggests that we could view the arts of memory (of forgetting as well as recalling) in semiotic terms.

1.9.3. Mnemotechnics as Semiotics

There can be no doubt that any mnemotechnical strategy belongs to the field of semiotics, if one accepts a definition of the sign as something that stands in the eyes of someone in place of something else in some respect or capacity. To associate in some way a y with an x means to use the one as the signifier and expression of the other. To make a knot in one's handkerchief is certainly a semiosic strategy, as was the trail of white pebbles or beans that the character in the fairytale dropped making it possible for the children to find their way back out of the wood. These are two different kinds of strategy, because the knot in the handkerchief is an arbitrary sign for whatever one decides to associate with it, whereas the trail of pebbles institutes a vectorial homology between the sequence of pebbles and the path to be followed and stands for that specific path and not for any other possible path—but all this tells us is that different mnemotechical strategies call into play different semiosic procedures.

The earliest Greco-Roman mnemotechnics present themselves as a sequence of empirical solutions based upon associations inspired by rhetorical criteria—relying, in other words, as Aristotle suggested, "on something similar or contrary or closely connected."[46] We have the hint of a system

---

46. When, in the *Rhetorica ad Herennium* (III, xx, 33), to remember the idea of witnesses *(testes)*, the orator is urged to imagine a goat's testicles *(testes)*, what we

when these same classical mnemotechnics propose the organized institution of places, such as a memory palace or a city, even though the organic structure of the loci is often used to accommodate random series of *res memorandae* or things to be remembered. But the more elaborate systems certainly present themselves as a semiotics in the Hjelmslevian sense of the term, in other words as a system that posits a plane of expression, form, and substance correlated with a plane of content, form, and substance. Now, speaking of the form of the content implies speaking of a systematic organization of the world. And this is not all: in principle there is nothing that is constitutionally expression or content, given that, if, in a function of signs based on a system A, x is the expression of y, in another system B, y can become the expression of x—or, to give another example, nothing prevents us conceiving of two semiotics, in one of which visual images stand for sequences of letters of the alphabet while in the other letters of the alphabet stand for visual images.

Mnemotechnics that exhibit some aspects of a semiotics are those systems in which: (i) on the level of expression there appears a system of loci designed to accommodate figures that belong to the same iconographic field and exercise the function of lexical units; (ii) at the level of content, the *res memorandae* are in their turn organized into a logical-conceptual system such that, if this system could be translated in terms of another visual representation, the mnemotechnic could function as the plane of expression of a second mnemotechnic whose contents would become the system of loci and images that made up the plane of expression of the first mnemotechnic.

For example, in the *Thesaurus artificiosae memoriae* of Cosma Rosselli (Venice, 1579), the theater of planetary structures, celestial hierarchies,

---

have is an etymological association. When, in the same work (III, xxi, 33), to recall the line of verse, "Iam domum itionem reges Atridae parant" ("And now the kings, sons of Atreus, prepare their return home"), a complex image is conjured up to evoke the families of the Domitii and the Reges (a purely phonetic association), as well as a still more complex image of actors preparing for the roles of Agamemnon and Menelaus, which plays on the one hand on genealogical memories and on the other on semantic analogies—we do not have the impression that any systematic criterion is involved, indeed we are even entitled to wonder whether what we are presented with is really a useful mnemotechnical device, seeing that in any case the author also advises his reader to learn the line by heart.

infernal circles, organized in detail, that he presents is at the same time a lexical system and an organization of the world. Rosselli's mnemotechnics is a semiotics because what institutes something as expression and as content is its sign function, not the nature of the thing. Anything at all can become functive expressive or content functive. A frequently recurrent expression in Rosselli is *e converso* and its equivalents: *x* may stand for *y* or *e converso*. Incidentally, entities previously placed among the loci may be used as figures and vice versa.[47]

The objection could be raised that many mnemotechnics are not semiotics in the Hjelmslevian sense because their planes are *conformal:* the correlation between unit of expression and unit of content is not between one term and another and is in any case not arbitrary. There exists an isomorphic relationship between the planes, and therefore for Hjelmslev these mnemotechnics, more than semiotics, would be *symbolic systems.* Take, for instance, the convention (found in a number of authors) by which the system of grammatical cases is associated with parts of the body—in which it is not arbitrary, at least in the author's intentions, to associate the nominative case with the head, the accusative with the breast that can be beaten, the genitive and the dative with the hands that hold and offer, and so on. Nevertheless, it should not be a matter of excessive concern whether a mnemotechnic is a symbolic system. In the first place, because we have reached a point where we consider as semiotic systems, albeit with their own particular characteristics, systems that Hjelmslev would have seen as symbolic, giving up on analyzing their possible articulations. And secondly, because the conformity of the mnemotechnical planes is either doubtful or weak and ambiguous; while the presumed iconic relations that they bring into play are fairly debatable. Rosselli, for example, claimed that the correlation must be based on similarity, but he failed to exhaust the many ways in which one thing may be similar to another ("quomodo multis modis, aliqua res alteri sit similis") (*Thesaurus,* p. 107). There was, for instance, a similarity of substance (the human being as the microcosmic image of the macrocosm) and of

---

47. "Ne mireris, quod quae pro locis supra posuimus, pro figuris nunc apta esse dicamus. Loca enim praedicta pro figuris (secundum diversos respectos) servire poterunt" ("You should not be surprised if we now say that what earlier we posited for the loci is also true for the figures. For the loci previously described could serve [according to various aspects] as figures," *Thesaurus,* p. 78).

quantity (the ten fingers for the ten commandments), correlation by meton-ymy and antonomasia (Atlas for the astronomers or for astronomy, the bear for irascibility, the lion for pride, Cicero for rhetoric),by homonymy (the four-legged dog for the constellation of the Dog Star), by irony and contrast (the fatuous individual for the wise one), by vestigial traces (the wolf's spoor for the wolf, the mirror in which Titus admired himself for Titus), by a word pro-nounced differently (*sanguine* for *sane*), by similarity of name (Arista for Ar-istotle), by genus and species (leopard for animal), by pagan symbol (the eagle for Jove), by peoples (Parthians for arrows, Scythians for horses, Phoenicians for the alphabet), by the signs of the zodiac (the sign for the constellation), by relation between an organ and its function, by a common accident or attribute (the crow for the Ethiopian), by hieroglyphic (the ant for foresight).

At this point the criteria become so vague that, as many mnemotechnical theorists recommend, it is advisable to commit to memory the relationship that connects a place or a figure to a *res memoranda*. Which is tantamount to saying that practically all mnemotechnics were based on relationships chosen almost arbitrarily and were therefore, more than symbolic systems, semiotics, however imperfect. But however imperfect they might be, they were, nonetheless, tentative semiotics. To say that in a functive of a symbolic nature the correlation is badly formulated does not exclude the possibility that the functive be proposed as such.

It is the semiotic nature of mnemotechnics that makes it impossible to construct an art of forgetfulness on the mnemotechnical model, because it is a property of every semiotic system to permit *the presentification of ab-sence*. It is a venerable topos to recognize that that all semiotic systems are characterized by their ability to actualize, if only in the possible world cir-cumscribed by our assertions, the nonexistent. This is why, as Abelard points out, the sentence *nulla rosa est* ("there is no rose") actualizes to some extent, at least in the mind's eye, the rose.[48]

---

48. This is why the logical discussions concerning existential presuppositions, or on the truth value to be assigned to the assertion *Yesterday Piero met his sister* if we could truthfully assert that Piero has no sisters, appear ingenuous and lack-ing in common sense. It is in fact unlikely that someone will respond to the first assertion with *Your assertion does not make sense because Piero has no sisters*. It is highly likely that the answers will be: (i) Whose sister? (presumption of error in the identification of the individual); (ii) You must have been dreaming (reference to existence in a possible world); (iii) Just what do you mean by sister? (presumption

Worth (1975) is the author of an essay entitled "Pictures Can't Say Ain't" in which he argues that no image in a mnemotechnic can act by canceling out what it refers to (illustrating just how provocative Magritte was when he painted a pipe with the caption "Ceci n'est pas une pipe" [This is not—or *ain't*—a pipe]). But the fact is that the words of a verbal language too— whether or not they can say "ain't," since existence can be predicated only in a proposition and not in an isolated term—cannot say "do not take into consideration—or forget—what I am naming."

It is not possible to use any expression to make one's content disappear, because a semiotics is by definition a mechanism for making things *present to the mind,* and is therefore a mechanism for producing intentional acts.[49] At most, mnemotechnics, like other semiotics, can lead to forgetfulness (albeit accidentally) thanks to two phenomena: interference among data and excess of data. Setting aside interference among data, which is a psychological rather than a cultural phenomenon, let us concentrate on the desire to forget in order to avoid an excess of information.[50]

---

of lexical error); I didn't know Piero had any sisters (correction of one's previous conviction). This occurs because every assertion, rather than presupposing, *posits,* makes present in the universe of discourse, by its semiotic power, the entities it names, albeit as entities in a possible world (cf. Eco and Violi 1987).

49. In Canetti's *Auto-da-fé* Professor Kien, endowed with a prodigious memory, records in a notebook all the idiocies he is trying to forget—an ironical narrative invention if ever there was one.

50. There exist casual mechanisms by which an idea or expression is not forgotten but confused instead with other ideas or expressions. In such cases confusion can occur both between expressions (confusion by pseudo-synonymity, such as mixing up the terms *paronomasia* and *antonomasia*), or between an expression and two different meanings, say, or notions or definitional contents (like not remembering whether *fragola* in Italian means "strawberry" or "raspberry"). Both of these phenomena never occur by subtraction (something is there that subsequently disappears), but by addition (two notions or terms become superimposed in your memory and you no longer know which one is correct). The phenomenon usually occurs the first time we make a mistake; someone gives us the correct information; and from then on we remember the error and the correction together, without recalling which is which. The dilemma left a more lasting impression than its solution, and it is the former and not the latter that stayed in our mind. The same thing often happens with the pronunciation of a word in a foreign language. There are no voluntary devices for forgetting, but they do exist for not re-

1.9.4. Ars Excerpendi

While we already encountered the problem in Themistocles-Cicero, the dread of excess certainly increases with the invention of printing, which not only makes available an enormous quantity of textual material, but also facilitates access to it for the man in the street and "leads to the transition, in not much more than a couple of centuries, from the primacy of remembrance to the primacy of forgetting" (Cevolini 2006: 6). Thus, we witness the development of an art not unknown in the centuries of manuscript culture but which acquires central importance in the culture of print, the *ars excerpendi,* the art, that is, of compiling abstracts or summaries so as to retain only such knowledge as is judged indispensable, and to let marginal information fall by the wayside.

In any case, what we may call the Themistocles complex returns over and over again in the course of cultural history, and one of its most dramatic manifestations is assuredly the second of Nietzsche's *Untimely Meditations,* on the advantages and disadvantages of historical studies for life. The text begins with a statement that could be another of the sources for Borges's Funes:

> In the case of the smallest or of the greatest happiness, however, it is always the same thing that makes happiness happiness: the ability to forget or, expressed in more scholarly fashion, the capacity to feel *unhistorically* during its duration. He who cannot sink down on the threshold of the moment and forget all the past, who cannot stand balanced like a goddess of victory without growing dizzy and afraid, will never know what happiness is—worse, he will never do anything to make others happy. Imagine the extremest possible example of a man who did not possess the power of forgetting at all and who was thus condemned to see everywhere a state of becoming: such a man would no longer believe in his

---

membering properly: you must multiply the semiosis. We may try to forget the medieval mnemonic rhyme invented to remember the moods of the first syllogistic figure (Barbara, Celarent, Darii, Ferio) by training ourselves to repeat over and over for several days a corrupted version "Birbiri, Celirant, Doria, Fario," until we are no longer able to recall which of the two formulas is the correct one. We do not forget by cancelation but by superposition, not by producing absence but by multiplying the presences.

own being, would no longer believe in himself, would see everything flowing asunder in moving points and would lose himself in this stream of becoming: like a true pupil of Heraclitus. He would in the end hardly dare to raise his finger. Forgetting is essential to action of any kind, just as not only light but darkness too is essential for the life of everything organic. A man who wanted to feel historically through and through would be like one forcibly deprived of sleep, or an animal that had to live only by rumination and ever repeated rumination. Thus: it is possible to live almost without memory, and to live happily moreover, as the animal demonstrates; but it is altogether impossible to *live* at all without forgetting. Or, to express my theme even more simply: *there is a degree of sleeplessness, of rumination, of the historical sense, which is harmful and ultimately fatal to the living thing, whether this living thing be a man or a people or a culture.* (Nietzsche, *Untimely Meditations*, p. 62)

This is the starting point for an analysis of the negative effects of the excess of historical studies which, now they have reached such an unbearable complexity and richness, oppress the memory of a culture to such an extent as to make it unsuited for life. And now, on the crest of this wave of vitalistic admonitions, comes the call for youth to develop an art of forgetfulness (Nietzsche 1874: 351, and see also Weinrich 2004: ch. VI).

One of the interesting things about this text is that, on the heels of these declarations that appear to address the individual's need for survival, the emphasis changes to the need for a systematic forgetting on the part of cultures in general. This switch is of capital importance because, once the impossibility of voluntarily forgetting what the individual memory has recorded has been demonstrated, then cultures present themselves as systems that function, not only to preserve and hand down information useful to their survival as cultures, but also to cancel the information judged to be in excess. The culture does not make individuals forget *what they know,* but it keeps from them finding out *what they do not know yet.* In other words, while it may be difficult for individuals to forget that they got burned on the stove a few minutes ago, a culture, using the manipulative techniques we will get to later, can impose silence and therefore *no longer inform* individuals that, let's say, in the year 1600 Giordano Bruno got burned (in a big way) in Rome's Campo dei Fiori. Or, to put it differently, a culture can remove from Lotman's semiosphere (discussed in Note 38) certain elements that will no longer be exposed to the visitor's view.[51]

A century and a half after Nietzsche's text, reflection on cultural forgetting has become commonplace and, despite Nietzsche's urgent cry of alarm, the process of cancelation continuously performed by a culture simply in order to stay alive has come to seem normal. Identifying memory and culture, today we study the acts of forgetting that a culture mobilizes through various kinds of cancelation, which can range from out and out censure (the erasure of manuscripts, bonfires of books, *damnatio memoriae,* forgery of documentary sources, negationism) to forgetfulness out of shame, inertia, remorse, down to those processes current in the exact sciences in which it is decided that not only those hypotheses proven to have been erroneous but even the efforts and procedures followed to arrive at those that turned out to be correct are expunged from the specialized encyclopedia of a particular science because they are no longer useful (see Paolo Rossi 1988, 1998), while certain disciplines go so far as to consider obsolete any contribution published more than five years ago.

If our Specialized Encyclopedias are subject to processes of forgetting, so much more so is the Median Encyclopedia of a given culture. It guarantees remembrance of the important historical facts or the principles of physics, but it omits an infinite amount of information that the collectivity has *repressed,* because it was judged no longer useful or pertinent. For instance, the Median Encyclopedia tells us all we need to know about the death of Julius Caesar but nothing about what his widow Calpurnia did after his assassination; it provides precious details about the progress of the Battle of Waterloo but does not give us the names of all the participants—and so on and so forth. These are extremely useful "forgettings," made so as not to overload the collective memory with more than it can bear—and without rendering the filtered or censored facts irretrievable, since there do exist specialized individuals (such as historians or archaeologists) capable of bringing them to light. In such cases, the collective memory sometimes picks up on the data, restoring them to the Median Encyclopedia, and sometimes decides instead to leave them in some specialized "reservation."

---

51. For these operations performed by a culture, see also Demaria (2006).

The forgetfulness filtering performed by the Median Encyclopedia does not depend on the will of an individual or on a conscious act of the collective will: it occurs out of a kind of inertia, sometimes even from natural causes, like the cancelation of everything that was ever known about Atlantis, if Atlantis ever existed.

The problem of filtering by the Median Encyclopedia was in any case not unknown to the medieval encyclopedists—even though they seem to us to be intent on handing on everything that tradition had handed on to them. In the *Libellum apologeticum* that serves as an introduction to his *Speculum Majus,* Vincent of Beauvais is already shocked by the proliferation of knowledge ("videbam praeterea, iuxta Danielis prophetiam . . . ubique multiplicatam esse scientiam" ("Furthermore, I saw, as in the prophecy of Daniel, that knowledge was everywhere increased") (*Libellum,* 1).[52] This is why he decides to make his encyclopedia a *florilegium,* in other words, *a selection of the best of his reading.* That the selection is not immune from the suspicion of censorship is confirmed by his citation of the so-called *Decretum Gelasianum, De libris recipiendis et non recipiendis,* a compendium of what was apocryphal and what was canonical in Holy Scripture anachronistically attributed to the fifth-century pope Gelasius I: "denique Decretum Gelasii papae, quo scripta quaedam reprobantur quaedam vere approbantur, hic in ipso operis principio ponere volui, ut lector inter autentica et apocripha discernere sciat, sicque rationis arbitrio quod voluit eligat, quod noluerit reliquat" ("therefore I decided to put at the very beginning of this work the decree of Pope Gelasius, according to which certain writings are disapproved and certain others rightly approved, so as to allow the reader to distinguish between the authentic and the apocryphal and choose with the guidance of reason what he wants and reject what he does not want"). Nevertheless, Paulmier-Foucart and Lusignan (1990) admit that "certain texts have survived only because they were included in the *Speculum Majus.*"

All a culture does, then, is to select the data for its own memory. It may not do what Stalin did when he erased from historical photographs the faces of the comrades he had sent to their deaths, or what Orwell's Big Brother did when he corrected the news in *The Times* every morning. But when we read that some English secondary schools have proposed abolishing the teaching

---

52. Cited in Brown (2012: 109).

of the Crusades so as not to offend the sensibilities of their Muslim students, it becomes apparent that culture is a continual process of rewriting and selecting information.

1.9.5. Cancelation, Cross-reference, Latency

Still, there is a difference between the Plinian and medieval encyclopedias and the structures of a modern Median Encyclopedia. The first premonitions of this change can already be seen in the encyclopedias of the sixteenth and seventeenth centuries. Let us recapitulate: an *Arbor Porphyriana* aspired to provide a definitive image of the Great Chain of Being; and that image (had it been exhaustive and had it included all of the beings in the universe—a hypothesis that was formally impossible, as we have seen) would have been definitive in the sense that all its nodes appeared to be primitives. When one knows that a man is Animate, one knows intuitively all one needs to know, and there is no need for any science to define what Animate is to distinguish it from what is Inanimate (even though medieval science often does so). Similarly, when Pliny's encyclopedia or those of Rabanus Maurus or Honorius of Autun explain to us the "nature of things" or the "image of the world," they assume that they have told us all we need to know, to such a degree that we need a well-trained art of memory to remember it.[53]

The form of the modern encyclopedia, on the other hand, is that of naturalistic classification in which, if we say that a horse is an Ungulate, this taxonomical node is understood as a *link* (exactly in the hypertextual sense of the term) that refers us to a repository of specialized knowledge—and it is there that the properties of the ungulates will be specified (see, in this connection, Eco 1997, 3 and 4).

In this sense it has been said that in speaking of the modern encyclopedia, more than of forgetting, it is appropriate to speak of the "latency" of knowledge (Cevolini 2006: 99). It is not as if the information *in excess* (the object of

---

53. "This was precisely what the medieval encyclopedia . . . aspired to, not only through the topical arrangement of knowledge, but also, more concretely, by means of diagrams, miniatures, illuminated initials, and so on. With a single image it was possible to embrace the whole of being, from God to the angels, from man to the stones, and retain it in the memory thanks to the power of the imagination" (Cevolini 2006: 96).

Specialized Encyclopedias—and even the information in excess vis-à-vis a Specialized Encyclopedia, such as, for example, the history of astronomical theories proven to have been erroneous) is actually forgotten. It is, so to speak, "frozen," and all the expert has to do is to take it out of the freezer and put it in the microwave to make it available once again, at least as much as is needed to understand a given context. This latency is represented by the model of the library or the archive (or even the museum)—containers always available even though no one may currently be using them, and even if they haven't been used for centuries (see Esposito 2001, ch. 4 especially paragraph 4.4).

If we now return to paragraphs 1.3.5 and 1.3.6 we will see how both Wilkins and Leibniz anticipated these techniques of latency that constitute the form that modern cultures came up with to get around the Vertigo of the Labyrinth.

1.9.6. The Maximal Encyclopedia and Virtuality

In this sense every encyclopedia refers back to ever vaster portions of knowledge, through a series of cross-references that has been defined as virtual. In the background is the truly virtual encyclopedia, the Maximal Encyclopedia. The Maximal Encyclopedia is virtual in nature, not only because we never know where it stops; the fact is that it contains potentially *even what it in fact (today) no longer contains.*

We remarked that the Median Encyclopedia does not record the names of all those who fought in the battle of Waterloo. But what would happen if a scholar wanted to reconstruct that list today? Let's say he has access to archives that have remained unexplored until now, or that he acquires a document similar to the catalogue of the Thousand, the volunteers who sailed from Quarto to Sicily with Garibaldi in 1860 (now readily available even on Wikipedia). That scholar would be exploiting forgotten and repressed portions of the Median Encyclopedia that are still part and parcel of the Maximal Encyclopedia.

We know that in his *Poetics* Aristotle cites tragedies of which no record survives. What encyclopedia do these works belong to? For the present only the fact that Aristotle cited the mere *title* of these works forms part of the Median Encyclopedia (or at least of a Specialized Encyclopedia). If one day (as was the case with the Gnostic texts of Nag Hammadi) some of these plays were to be discovered buried in a jar in the desert, they *would have al-*

ready been part of the Maximal Encyclopedia, even if no one up till then could have claimed so, while from that time on they would be part of one or more Specialized Encyclopedias. But what would happen if on the other hand they were never found and our knowledge of them continued to be limited to an acquaintance with their titles?

For the very fact that there are good reasons to believe they once existed, we would continue to think that they *might* form part of the Maximal Encyclopedia, even though for the moment they belong to it only in a virtual and optative fashion–or else that they are part of it but only in the possible world in which they have been discovered, or that they were part of the Median Encyclopedia of Aristotle's day.

The Maximal Encyclopedia, then, despite the fact that its name we have been giving it suggests that, to quote Anselm, it is something *quo nihil majus cogitari possit* ("than which something greater cannot be thought"), is in fact an accordion-like structure, and one day it could expand beyond anything we dream of today. Which offers no small encouragement to future research.

1.9.7. The Text as Producer of Forgetfulness

At this point, we understand how, every time we construct a local "ontology" in order to disambiguate a proposition in a given context (as we observed in paragraph 1.7), we are performing *ad hoc* the same operation that a culture performs in constructing its own Median Encyclopedia. We prune, we narcotize, we eliminate some notions, retaining only those we consider pertinent.

How do we go about identifying—in our efforts to pinpoint the appropriate context—the notions to prune? We consider the context as if it was a text, and we behave exactly as we behave when we are trying to understand a text. A text (in addition to being a tool for inventing and remembering) is also *a tool for forgetting*, or at least for rendering something latent.[54]

---

54. On textuality as one means of creating forgetfulness, see Lotman and Uspensky (1975), as well as Demaria (2006: 43): "Cultural memory is the result of different strategies of selection of what may become a memory—that is, of different enunciative praxes which form identities in different ways."

Classical mnemonics could not be used for forgetting because a mnemonic technique is a *mutilated semiotics*. A semiotics in the Hjelmslevian sense is a system that—in addition to a lexicon—also contains rules for syntactic combination, and allows us to develop discourses, or, in other words, texts. A mnemonic technique on the other hand was more like a simple dictionary or a repertory of significant units that cannot be combined among themselves. A mnemonic technique did not facilitate the articulation of mnemotechnical *discourses*.

But if a mnemonic technique, insofar as it is a semiotics, cannot be used to forget, a semiotics that is not a mnemonic technique can produce forgetfulness or cancellation at the level of the textual processes themselves.

If in a semiotics the correlation is not based on simple automatic equivalence ($a = b$), but on a principle of inferentiality, however elementary (if a, then b), the meaning of an expression is a potentially huge package of instructions for interpreting the expression in different contexts and drawing from it, as Peirce would have it, all the most remote inferential consequences, in other words, all its interpretants. On these bases we ought then to know in theory every possible interpretant of an expression, whereas in practice we know (or remember) only the portion that is activated by a given context. Interpreting the expression in context means magnifying certain interpretants and narcotizing others, and narcotizing them means removing them temporarily from our competence, if only for the duration of the current interpretation (cf. Eco 1979, 1984).

If the interpretation of a sign, as Peirce maintained, always makes us learn "something more," this something more (in a given context) is always learned by giving up something less, that is, by excluding all the other interpretations that could have been given of the same expression in another context.

If, as a matter of principle (and on the strength of the ideal global encyclopedia), knowing how many miles Paris is from Bombay is part of the meaning of the name *Paris*, when we are reading *Les Misérables* we learn many things about Paris, but we are expected to forget the distance (and to act as if we had forgotten it—if we already knew it) between Paris and Bombay.

There are many cases in which, in the course of the interaction between a reader and a text, instances of forgetfulness occur, encouraged in some way by the text itself. If, as I recalled in my *Role of the Reader* (1984), a text is a strategy that aims at stimulating a series of interpretations on the part of a Model Reader, there may be texts that presuppose, as part of their strategy, a presumption of forgetfulness on the reader's part and direct and encourage it. Often the text wants something to be read, so to speak, in a subliminal fashion, and then consciously disregarded as being of little relevance. The most explicit case of encouraged forgetfulness is provided by the mystery novel. To cite one of the most famous examples, *The Murder of Roger Ackroyd* by Agatha Christie, it is no secret that the novel intends to surprise the reader in its denouement with the revelation that the narrator is the murderer. To make the revelation still more telling, the author must convince readers that they fell into the trap not as a result of the author's manipulation but because of their own naiveté (in other words, the author wants readers to admire the cleverness with which the narrator not only makes them fall into the trap, but then insists that they assume the responsibility themselves for having done so). To this end, in the final chapter, entitled "Apologia," the novel's first-person narrator assures the reader that he had not in fact kept anything from him. *"I am rather pleased with myself as a writer. What could be neater, for instance, than the following?"* And at this point the narrator—and with him the author—lists a series of rapid allusions, all present in the text, that the reader can only have forgotten due to their strategical irrelevance, but which, had they been interpreted along the lines of a syndrome of suspicion, would have anticipated the revelation of the truth. Naturally the reader could not be expected to harbor suspicions vis-à-vis the narrator, and herein lies the relish of the game, but the entire novel appears to be the very epitome of textually encouraged forgetfulness. The Sicilian novelist Leonardo Sciascia rightly observes, in his afterword to Christie's novel in the Mondadori "Oscar del Giallo" series, that "Poirot arrives at the conclusion that Dr Sheppard is guilty by reading everything that the narrator has to tell us; in other words, by reading the same story we are reading." But Poirot is more than Christie's model reader, he is her accomplice and he does what she did not want her model reader to do.

A series of short stories by Jorge Luis Borges and Adolfo Bioy-Casares, *Six Problems for Don Isidro Parodi*, appears to be based on the same procedure, but taken to the nth degree, indeed, I am tempted to say, to the point of metaphysical parody. Listening to the stories and reports of a series of bizarre and unreliable characters, Don Isidro, who is serving a sentence of life imprisonment, never fails to solve the mystery, and he succeeds because he recognizes as pertinent a certain piece of information mentioned in the account. With the result that the reader cannot help wondering why he too was not a winner, since he was dealt the same narrative cards as Don Isidro. Borges's subtlety lies in the fact that the details accumulated in the story are so many, and all of them given the same degree of emphasis (or, if you will, the same zero degree of emphasis), that there was no apparent reason for the reader to recall detail A rather than detail B. Indeed, there is no apparent reason why detail A should be stressed as pertinent by Don Isidro. The fact is that Don Isidro is a monster, even more so than Borges's other character Funes the Memorious, because not only does he never forget anything, but within the flux of memories that obsesses him he is able to single out the one detail that counts for the purposes of the solution.

In point of fact, by presenting a character who remembers everything, Borges's text speaks to us meta-narratively of a reader who does not remember anything, and of a text that does everything in its power to induce him to forget.

All the texts we have cited induce forgetfulness through a cluttered over-abundance of details. No one can remember everything was in Leopold Bloom's drawer as described in the penultimate chapter of Joyce's *Ulysses*. Given that what we have is a microcosm containing everything, no one can say what was in there (unless they have read the chapter several dozen times—though in that case we would be dealing with mechanical memorization, as when someone learns a poem by heart).

It may be argued that the forgetfulness produced by a text is transitory, a collateral effect, ascribable to considerations of interpretive economy. True, one cannot forget an existential tragedy by immersing oneself in a good novel (at best one's distraction is of limited duration), but it is equally true that certain individuals claim to have dulled the ache of a painful memory by devoting themselves heart and soul to an engrossing task. Be that as it may, what a text does is not what Gesualdo had in mind when he laid out a series of impossible techniques for eliminating a particular item from our memory. Nevertheless, when we re-read the passage quoted in section 1.9.2, we realize that Gesualdo, without being aware of it, was describing metaphorically the way a text somehow makes us put into parentheses (in other words, forget, at least for as long as we continue reading) what it has no intention of speaking about.

A text in fact obscures that immense portion of the world it is not concerned with; it paints it over with a coat of whitewash; it substitutes for the images we have of the world those that belong exclusively to its own possible universe, so that, with Gesualdo's "great care and mental effort," it is the latter that are imprinted and remain dominant in our imagination. And still more so if we read the text (or look at it, if it is a visual text) as though we were isolating ourselves with it or in it "in the dark and quiet of the night," in such a way that "the intense and vivid idea" of the fresh images "drives out the first Ideas." A text, if it absorbs our attention, cancels the world that existed prior to the text, about which it is silent, to which it makes no reference, as if its discourse were "a great storm of winds, hail, dust, ruined buildings and places and temples, a flood that leaves everything in a state of confusion," as if, with respect to the external world, it were "an Enemy . . . who, with a troop of armed companions, enters and passes impetuously among the places and with scourges, cudgels and other weapons drives out the likenesses, assaults the people, shatters the images, puts to flight through doors and windows all of the animals and animate persons who were in the places," and finally presents us with another universe "clear, calm and quiet."

We might analyze the various cultures of the past by considering the texts that helped eliminate a series of notions from their Median Encyclopedia. It was the rigoristic polemic of so many Fathers of the Church that led to the suppression of so many pagan texts, texts that the Renaissance would subsequently rediscover—irony of the processes of cancelation!—in the same monastic libraries where they had nonetheless been preserved. It was the excess of texts of *histoire événementielle* that led to the neglect of the data for a history of material relations, data that only at considerable cost subsequent schools of historiography were able to recover in the byways of the Maximal Encyclopedia.

To conclude, if cultures survive, one reason is because they have succeeded in reducing the weight of their encyclopedic baggage by placing so many notions in abeyance, thus guaranteeing their members a sort of vaccination against the Vertigo of the Labyrinth and the Themistocles/Funes complex.

The real problem, however, is not the fact that cultures *pare down* their encyclopedias (which is, in any case, a physiological phenomenon), but rather that what has been placed in abeyance can always be recovered. For this reason the regulatory idea of a Maximal Encyclopedia is a powerful aid to the *Advancement of Learning*—and having to confront ever and anon the Vertigo of the Labyrinth is often the price we must pay for calling into question the laziest of our ontologies.

2

Metaphor as Knowledge

Aristotle's Medieval (Mis)Fortunes

In Chapter 1 we observed that Aristotle's major contribution to the theory of metaphor lay in the emphasis he placed on its cognitive value. Since we are accustomed to seeing the Middle Ages as the age of the rediscovery of Aristotle and indeed of his near-canonization, it should prove interesting to inquire whether the Middle Ages somehow picked up on and profited from this suggestion of his. Let us say from the outset that our investigation was sparked by the conviction that the answer is in the negative. What we must try to understand, then, is why there exists no medieval theory of metaphor as an instrument of knowledge, at least in the aforementioned Aristotelian sense. The answer, which we will attempt to document in what follows, is that not only did medieval authors gain access to the *Poetics* and the *Rhetoric* at a very late date, but they also became acquainted with these texts in translations that were, to say the least, somewhat misleading. We will see later (in Chapter 3) what the other sources of medieval reflection on metaphor were, and what other tools (such as, for example, the concept of *analogia entis* or "analogy of being") they did attribute a cognitive function to.

Paper delivered at the Scuola Superiore di Studi Umanistici of the University of Bologna in March 2001 as part of a series of lectures on the fortunes of Aristotle's theory of metaphor. Revised and expanded, especially as regards the contribution of Giles of Rome, and published as a collaborative effort by myself and Costantino Marmo with the title "La teoria aristotelica della metafora nel Medioevo," in Lorusso (2005). The present version is a reelaboration of my 2001 paper, but takes into account observations and clarifications made by Marmo.

2.1. The Latin Aristotle

It is no secret how protracted and tormented were the fortunes of the *Aristoteles Latinus*. In the sixth century Boethius had translated the entire *Organon*, but for centuries only one section of it, the so-called *Logica Vetus*—translations, in other words, of the *Categories* and the *De interpretatione*, accompanied by a version of the *Isagoge* by Porphyry and a number of treatises by Boethius on categorical and hypothetical syllogisms, on division and on topics—was in circulation, and that for the most part in a corrupt form.[1] Boethius had also translated the *Prior Analytics*, the *Topics*, and the *Sophistical Refutations*, but these works did not circulate at all until they were revised or retranslated, from Greek or Arabic,[2] along with the *Posterior Analytics*, in the twelfth century. True, this last-named work had also been translated by Boethius, but his version had been lost and remained practically unknown.[3] With the twelfth century the *Libri Naturales* also make their appearance: the *Physics*, the *De coelo et mundo*, the *De generatione et corruptione*, the *Meteorologica*, the *De anima*, the *Parva Naturalia* are translated, first from Arabic then from Greek. The *Metaphysics* too appeared, first in partial form in a *translatio vetustissima* by James of Venice, while another extended portion appeared—translated from the Greek—in the same century (the so-called *translatio media*). Thomas Aquinas will own a complete version only when William of Moerbeke, completing his rendering, will make Book K available to him. Partial versions of the Greek text of the *Libri Morales* also go back to

---

1. Boethius's contributions were the *Introductio in syllogismos categoricos*, *De categoricis syllogismis*, *De hypotheticis syllogismis*, *De divisione* and *De differentiis topicis* (PL 64). Only in the thirteenth century would William of Moerbeke bring forth new translations of the Aristotelian treatises, in addition to a translation of Ammonius Hermiae's Greek commentary on the *De interpretatione*.

2. Boethius's translation of the *Sophistical Refutations*, for example, was revised by James of Venice in the twelfth century and retranslated in the thirteenth century by William of Moerbeke. Its circulation, however, was modest.

3. It is only with the translation from the Greek by James of Venice (twelfth century), its revision by William of Moerbeke (thirteenth century), together with the translation from the Arabic by Gerard of Cremona (end of the twelfth century) and the commentary of Robert Grosseteste (ca. 1230), that this text will enter medieval culture, becoming fully integrated into the so-called *Logica Nova*.

the twelfth century. In the mid-thirteenth century Robert Grosseteste translated the *Nicomachean Ethics,* later revised by Moerbeke, and it will be the 1260s before the latter will provide a complete version of the *Politics.* It is likewise in the thirteenth century that Michael Scotus made versions of the books on animals from the Arabic, while at a slightly later date Moerbeke will also translate them from Greek. A rendering of *De motu animalium* by yet another translator was known to Albertus Magnus.

Coming to the two texts that most concern us, we note that Moerbeke did not translate the *Poetics* until 1278—in other words, after Thomas's death in 1274[4]—while Averroes's *Middle Commentary*—composed in 1175—appears, translated by Hermann the German (Hermannus Alemannus), around 1256.

In the same year Hermann translated the *Rhetoric* from the Arabic. This translation is accompanied by the anonymous *Translatio Vetus,* from the Greek. And finally, around 1269 or 1270, there appears a version from the Greek by Moerbeke.

Thus, the *Rhetoric* and *Poetics,* when they finally appear in Latin, do so at an advanced date (and at a moment when a *Logica Modernorum* is on the rise—more interested in the *Organon* than in the remainder of Aristotle's works). Thomas is the typical example of a thinker who was not influenced by any suggestion of Aristotle's on this subject, and his theory of metaphor that "non supergreditur modum litteralis sensus" ("does not exceed the literal sense") offers sufficient proof of this fact.[5]

2.2. The *Poetics:* Averroes's Commentary and Hermann's Translation

Averroes did not know Greek, he scarcely knew Syriac, and he was reading Aristotle in a tenth-century Arabic translation, derived in turn from a Syriac version.[6] Both he and his sources have trouble rendering the various

---

4. Furthermore, only two manuscripts are known from this period. It is not until Giorgio Valla's 1495 Latin translation from the Greek that the *Poetics* will enter the world of the Humanists. Valla was unaware of Moerbeke's translation.

5. The quote from Thomas is from Quodlibet VII, q. 6 a. 3 ad 2 (http://www .corpusthomisticum.org/q07.html#68283). We will have more to say on this topic in Chapter 3.

6. The Middle Commentary on the *Poetics* appeared in English in Butterworth (1986). The text of Hermann can be found under the title *Averrois expositio seu*

aspects of Greek poetry and dramaturgy to which Aristotle refers, and consequently try to adapt their examples to the Arabic literary tradition. Imagine what the Latin reader was able to make of Aristotle with the aid of Hermann the German's Latin translation of an Arabic text, based in turn on an attempt to fathom the Syriac version of an unknown Greek original!

Furthermore, Hermann decided to translate only Averroes's commentary, because, on account of the different metrical systems and the obscurity of the lexicon, he was not able to make complete sense of Aristotle's work from the Arabic version, as he remarks in his "Proem."[7]

Today we possess an English translation of Averroes's Arabic text (Butterworth 1986) and, when we compare the two, we must admit that Hermann did not go wrong on the fundamental points. But he certainly adds to the confusion when he attempts to translate the poetic examples from Arabic; and he occasionally decides to replace them with Latin examples taken from the rhetorical tradition. When, for instance, Averroes proposes as an example of metaphor a fine line of Arabic poetry "the horses of youth and its trappings have been removed" (Butterworth 1986: 61), meaning that, in old age, love and war, activities associated with youth, are no longer practicable, Hermann substitutes the tired old chestnuts, *pratum ridet* ("the meadow smiles") and *litus aratur* ("the strand is plowed").[8] In addition he gets badly tangled up in the rhetorical terminology. He translates what was intended as the term for metonymy as *translatio* and the

---

Poetria Ibn Rosdin in Minio-Paluello (1968). Citations from either work are to the pages of these modern editions.

7. "Postquam, cum non modico labore consummaveram translationem Rhetorice Aristotelis, volens mittere ad eius Poetriam, tantam inveni difficultatem propter disconvenientiam modi metrificandi in greco cum modo metrificandi in arabico, et propter vocabulorum obscuritatem, et plures alias causas, quod non sum confisus me posse sane et integre illius operis translationis studiis tradere latinorum" ("After having completed, with no small labor, my translation of Aristotle's *Rhetoric,* and wishing to dedicate myself to his *Poetria,* I found myself confronted with enormous difficulties, because of the difference between Greek and Arabic metrical scansion, the obscurity of the terminology, and for a number of other reasons, so that I am not sure I can really offer the translation of that work to the schools of the Latins without misrepresentation") (p. 41).

8. P. 42. On the circulation of these canonical examples, see Chapter 3.

term for metaphor as *transumptio,* but when Averroes cites both as species of the genus "substitution," he proceeds to use the term *concambium* (p. 42). When Averroes says that poetic discourse is *imitative,* Hermann translates with the adjective *imaginative,* with quite drastic results for the comprehensibility of the text (ibid.).

Things go from bad to worse when Averroes, for "peripeteia" and "anagnorisis," uses terms equivalent to "reversal" and "discovery"; the best Hermann can come up with is *circulatio* and *directio,* choices that are of little help in making the concepts clear (p. 53).

But the blame is not all Hermann's. Butterworth is convinced that the Middle Commentary has been unjustly condemned and is more useful than previously thought, and he may be right as far as the comprehension of Averroes goes, but he is overindulgent with Averroes when it comes to a proper understanding of Aristotle.

Many readers will recall Borges's 1947 short story entitled "Averroës' Search" (in Borges 1998) in which the Argentinian writer imagines Abū al-Walīd Muḥammad ibn-Aḥmad ibn-Muḥammad ibn-Rushd (aka Averroes) as he endeavors to write a commentary on Aristotle's *Poetics.* What bothers him is that he does not know the meaning of the words "tragedy" and "comedy," which he had already come across nine years earlier when reading the *Rhetoric.* The problem is an obvious one, since these artistic forms were unknown in the Arabic tradition. The irony of Borges's story stems from the fact that, while Averroes is struggling over the meaning of these obscure terms, beneath his windows a group of children is role-playing, impersonating a muezzin, a minaret, and a congregation, in other words, they are performing theater, but neither they nor Averroes are aware of the fact. Later on, somebody tells the philosopher about a strange ceremony he once witnessed in China, and from the description the reader is able to deduce that it was a theatrical performance—but the characters in the story are not so perceptive. At the end of this veritable comedy of errors, Averroes returns to his meditations on Aristotle and concludes: "Aristu [Aristotle] gives the name "tragedy" to panegyrics and the name "comedy" to satires and anathemas. There are many admirable tragedies and comedies in the Qur'àn and the mu'allaqat of the mosque" (Borges 1998: 241).

Readers tend to attribute this paradoxical situation to Borges' imagination, but what he describes was precisely the quandary that beset

Averroes.[9] In the Middle Commentary, everything Aristotle has to say about tragedy is referred by Averroes to poetry in general, and more particularly to the poetic forms known as *laudatio* (praise) and *vituperatio* (blame). This epideictic poetry makes use of representations, but—though Averroes reminds us how men take pleasure in imitating things, not only in words but also through images, song, and dance—he speaks of them as exclusively verbal representations. Such representations are intended *to instigate to virtuous actions,* and their intent, then, is moralizing. Aristotle's *pragma* thus becomes a virtuous and voluntary operation (Hermann: "operatio virtuosa, que habet potentiam universalem in rebus virtuosis, non potentiam particularem in unaquaque rerum virtuosarum" ["a virtuous deed that has a universal power with respect to virtuous matters, not a particular power with respect to one or another virtuous matter"] [p. 47]). Averroes understands that poetry tends toward the universal, and that its end is to arouse pity and fear in order to impress the minds of the audience. But for him these procedures too are calculated to render persuasive certain moral values, and this moralizing notion of poetry prevents Averroes from understanding Aristotle's notion of the fundamentally cathartic (and not didactic) function of the tragic action.

The situation becomes still more "Borgesian" when Averroes finds himself obliged to comment on *Poetica* 1450a 7–14, where Aristotle lists the six components of tragedy. For Aristotle, as we know, these are *mythos* (plot), *ethos* (character), *lexis* (diction), *dianoia* (thought), *opsis* (spectacle), and *melos* (song or melody). Averroes interprets the first term to mean "mythic statements" (Hermann translates "sermo fabularis"), the second as "character" (Hermann: "consuetudines"), the third as "meter" (Hermann: "metrum seu pondus"), the fourth as "belief," that is, as "the ability to represent what exists or does not exist in such and such a way" (Butterworth 1986: 78); for Hermann: "credulitas" or "potentia representandi rem sic esse aut sic non esse" ("the ability to represent the thing as it is or as it is not"). The sixth component is correctly interpreted as "melody" *(tonus),* but evidently Averroes is thinking of a poetic melody, not of the presence of musicians onstage.

---

9. Borges probably got his information from Marcelino Menendez y Pelayo's meticulous summary of the two commentaries in volume 1 of his *Historia de las ideas estéticas en España* (1883).

Things get more (or less) dramatic when we come to the fifth component, *opsis*. Averroes cannot envisage a spectacular representation of actions, and in translating *opsis* as *nazar* he has in mind something that leads to the "discovery of the correctness of a belief" (Butterworth 1986: 76),[10] in other words a type of argumentation that demonstrates the correctness of the beliefs represented (for moral purposes). And all Hermann can do is to go along, so he translates "consideratio, scilicet argumentatio seu probatio rectitudinis credulitatis aut operationis non per sermonum persuasivum (hoc enim non pertinet huic arti neque est conveniens ei) sed per sermonem representativum" ("an examination or argument or proof of the correctness of a belief or the correctness of a deed, not by means of a persuasive statement [for that is not applicable to this art nor appropriate for it] but by means of a representative statement").

Having failed in this way to grasp the meaning of spectacle, Averroes goes on to remark (Butterworth 1986: 79) that epideictic poetry "does not use the art of dissimulation and delivery the way rhetoric does," and Hermann translates "non utitur carmen laudativum arte gesticulationis neque vultuum acceptione sicut utitur hiis retorica" ("laudatory verse does not take advantage of the art of gesticulation nor of putting on facial expressions the way rhetoric does") (p. 49). On the other hand, Averroes had been led astray by 1450b 15 et seq., where Aristotle says that spectacle, however effective it may be, is not essential to the poetic art, since tragedy can also function without performance and without actors. In this way, Aristotle's concession (tragedy can also be read) is transformed into the elimination of the *opsis*. Consequently, at least in the form in which it reaches its medieval readers, Aristotle's text appears to exclude the only truly theatrical aspect of tragedy.

Finally, we have a total misunderstanding apropos of 1451b 1–14, where Aristotle opposes poetry to history, in the sense that poetry narrates possible actions, either probable or necessary, but always general, while the historian expounds real but particular events. Here Averroes radically misinterprets: he says that the poet speaks of existing and possible matters and that he often speaks about general things, while "the one who invents parables and stories" (in other words, those who for Aristotle were the historians)

---

10. For Averroes, see Butterworth (1986: 75–79); for Hermann, see Minio-Paluello (1968: 48–49).

feign false things, inventing individuals who do not exist and finding names
for them (Butterworth 1986: 83–84). Hermann translates "poete vere po-
nunt nomina rebus existentibus, et fortassis loquuntur in universalibus"
("the poets on the other hand use names for existing [*viz*. individual] things,
and sometimes they also speak in general terms") (p. 52) and, transforming
the historian into a *fictor* (in other words, a narrator of fables), he says that
he "fingit individua quae penitus non habent existentiam in re, et ponitur
eis nomina" ("he invents individuals who do not exist at all in reality, and
gives them names").

Averroes seems sensitive to the thematics of metaphor, as he brings it up
right away at the start of his commentary (Butterworth 1986: 60–61), whereas
Aristotle himself has nothing to say about it and confines himself to discussing imitation. For Averroes, poetic compositions are imitative when they
compare one thing to another, and he gives the example of cases in which
one thing is described "as if" it were another (speaking of these "particles of
comparison," Hermann will use the term "*sinkategoremata similitudinis*"
("the syncategorematic terms of the comparison") (p. 42);[11] but he also cites
cases of "substitution," a generic procedure of which metaphor and metonymy are subspecies. Apropos of metaphor Averroes speaks immediately of
analogy, that is, of a four-term relationship. In this same context he makes an
affirmation typical of Arabic philosophy, which will come to have a notable
influence on Latin thought, namely, that *poetics belongs to the art of logic*.[12]

In another context, not found in Aristotle, Averroes, discussing sense-
perceptible things represented by means of other equally sense-perceptible
things, seems to be alluding to metaphors, since he speaks of the knowledge
produced by the names of constellations like Cancer (in the sense of "crab").
He appears to be saying that these juxtapositions generate uncertainty (at
least they are introduced by expressions of uncertainty) and therefore some
kind of cognitive effort, while comparisons that do not generate uncertainty
are less interesting (p. 97). Hermann translates: "Quedem earum sunt ut fiat
representatio rerum sensibilium per res sensibiles quarum natura sit ut quasi

11. [*Translator's note:* The *Shorter Oxford English Dictionary* defines "syncategorematic" as follows: "Of a word: having no meaning by itself, but only in conjunction with one or more other words or concepts."]

12. For the fortunes of this thesis, see Marmo 1990.

in dubio ponant aspectorem, et estimare faciant eum presentes esse res ip-
sas" ("Among them is for the representation of sense-perceptible things to
be made by means of sense-perceptible things, such that anyone who looks
at them becomes uncertain and fancies that they are indeed those things")
(p. 59). Here we could be getting close to a cognitive notion of tropes. But a
little earlier Averroes has declared that these imitative pictures must con-
form to commonly used formulas in a clear fashion, so as not to create difficulties. The doubt is resolved when we realize that he is commenting on
1454b 19–21, where ways of making the recognition or agnition more interesting are analyzed, and therefore the uncertainty is due to the recogniz-
ability of characteristic signs or tokens (Aristotle is talking about scars,
necklaces, etc.). Perhaps it is because Averroes is not thinking of *coups de
théâtre* that he treats the matter with some hesitancy (otherwise he would
never have introduced the Cancer example), and Hermann follows him with
the same hesitant confusion.

Metaphor also seems to crop up apropos of 1455a 4–6. Aristotle is concerned with agnition through syllogism, as when, in Aeschylus's *Libation
Bearers (Choephoroi)*, Electra argues that someone identical to herself has arrived, but nobody is identical to her except Orestes. Averroes interprets this to
mean that what is being spoken of is an individual who is like another individual because of a similar constitution or temperament (p. 104). Hermann is
drawn by this discourse on similarity to speak of *metaphorica assimilatio*
("metaphorical comparison") (p. 60), which is quite evidently a misreading.

We do come to metaphor apropos of 1457b et seq. A noun, as Aristotle
says, can be "ordinary" or "rare" or "metaphorical" or "ornamental" (along
with other categories less interesting from our point of view). Averroes (Butterworth 1986: 121–122) accepts this distinction, as does Hermann (p. 67),
who defines metaphor as *primarium, intromissum aliunde, transumptum,*
or *facticium* ("original, introduced from elsewhere, taken over from an ex-
trinsic usage, or artificial"). Similarly observed is the Aristotelian distinction between metaphors from genus to species and vice versa, from species
to species, or by analogy, and even the example of old age as the evening of
life is preserved.

Averroes however (as well as his translator) follows the letter of Aristotle:
it is certainly useful to use unusual words if one wishes to strike the reader's
imagination, but one must not exaggerate, so as not to fall into riddles. As

for the passage in 1459a 8, in which Aristotle introduces the knowledge of the related concept (with the verb *theorein*), Averroes does not seem to grasp the suggestion and confines himself to saying that "when the similarity in the substitution is very strong, it makes both the imitation and the understanding more excellent" (Butterworth 1986: 134). Hermann translates "quando enim commutatio vehementis fuerit assimilationis, inducet bonitatem imaginationis et comprehensionem complectiorem rei representatae simul" ("when indeed the reciprocal opposition is that of a very strong similarity, it leads to both the good quality of the imagery and a more comprehensive understanding of the thing it represents") (p. 71). All this is certainly much weaker than it was in Aristotle's text.

Overall, it is difficult to say what effect Averroes's commentary might have had on the imagination of the Latins, since what they were confronted with were metaphors taken from Arabic poetry inadequately translated by Hermann. They certainly must have sounded odd to the ears of the Latin reader, and they might therefore have suggested an invitation to be daring. And what can we say of the effect that might have been produced by metaphors such as "Iam sol inclinatur et nondum perfecisti, et subdivisus in horizonte est quasi oculus strabi vel lusci" ("Now the sun is declining but has not completely set, it appears split on the horizon like the eye of a squinter or a person with one eye") or "Non est denigratus oculos antimonio pulvere, ut nigros habent oculos a natura" ("Someone who has blackened their eyes with kohl is not like someone who has black eyes by nature") (pp. 59–60)?

In fact we have only to consult the few medieval commentaries devoted to Averroes's treatise, prior at least to the use made of it by Giles of Rome (Egidius Romanus). These texts are reproduced by Dahan (1980: 193–239) and represent a series of glosses on the *Translatio Hermanni,* a *Quaestio in Poetriam* and the *Expositio super Poetriam* of Bartholomew of Bruges. They consist of fairly pedestrian summaries of Averroes's text, which add nothing useful either to the comprehension of Aristotle or that of Averroes. At most, in the first glosses, where Hermann speaks of *translatio* and *transumptio* as two species of *concambium,* two examples (taken perhaps from Boethius's *De consolatione)* are adduced, "sicut enim se habet liberalis ad pecuniam, sic mare ad aquas" ("just as a liberal person handles money, so does the sea its waters") and "sicut mare arenis siccis aquas ministrat, sic liberalis egentibus pecuniam" ("just as the sea pours its waters on the dry sands, so liberal persons hand out money to those in need"), which appear to be two instances of *transumptio.*

2.3. The *Poetics:* William of Moerbeke's Translation

Compared with the commentary of Averroes/Hermann, Moerbeke's translation strikes us as considerably more faithful to Aristotle, though at times it too falls victim to misleading Greek manuscripts.[13] When in 1457b 32 Aristotle says that a shield could be called a "a wineless wine bowl" *(aoinon),* Moerbeke reads *oinou* and translates "puta si scutum dicat 'fyalam' non Martis sed vini," "as if you were to call the shield, not the cup of Mars but a wine cup") (p. 27).

Faced with the riddle of the dry suction cup, and following the reading he found in his manuscript, he translates "virilem rubicundum ut est ignitum super virum adherentem" ("a manly red like something fiery sticking to a man") (p. 28). But he translates "seminans deo conditam flammam" ("sowing the god-created flame"), as well as other citations, correctly.

Tragodia and *komodia* are translated correctly (albeit with a simple calque). But let us not forget how obscure these terms could appear to a man of the Middle Ages: according to William of Saint-Thierry (*Commentarius in Canticum canticorum,* PL 180), a comedy is a story that, though it may contain elegiac passages that speak of the pains of love, ends happily; for Honorius of Autun (*De animae exilio et patria,* PL 172), tragedies are poems that deal with war, such as Lucan's *Pharsalia,* while comedies, like the works of Terence, sing of weddings. Dante too refers to his work as a *Commedia* not because it is a theatrical work but because it has a very happy ending. Hugh of Saint Victor (*Didascalicon* II, 27, PL 176) says that the art of performance gets the name of "theatrical" art from the word "theater," a place where the ancient peoples gathered for amusement, and in theaters dramatic events were recited aloud, with readings of poems or representations involving actors and masks. In the *Poetria* of John of Garland (Johannes de Garlandia), we find a classification of literary genres in which tragedy is defined as "carmen quod incipit a gaudio et terminat in luctu" ("a poem that begins in rejoicing

---

13. Moerbeke's translation of the *Poetics* also appears in Minio-Paluello (1968). The page references in parenthesis are to the pages of this edition.

and ends in lamentation"), while comedy is "carmen jocosum incipiens a tristitia et terminans in gaudium" ("a light-hearted poem beginning in sadness and ending in rejoicing") (cf. De Bruyne, Études II, iii, 3). One of the few texts in which an idea of classical tragedy can be identified (based, however, on hearsay) is the *Ars versificatoria* of Matthew of Vendôme (II, 5, in Faral 1924), where among the arts tragedy is cited "inter ceteras clamitans boatu" ("shouting various loud cries in the midst of the group"), which (citing Horace, *Ars Poet.* 97) "projicit ampullas et sexquipedalia verba" ("spews forth bombast and sesquipedalian words") and, continues Matthew, "pedibus innitens coturnatis, rigida superficie, minaci supercilio, assuetae ferocitatis multifarium intonat conjecturam" ("relying on buskin feet, an inflexible appearance, and a menacing brow, thunders forth a multitude of warnings, all with her customary ferocity"). Not much to go on as a clue to Aristotle's concept of tragedy, but enough to recognize what ancient theatrical actions were like, seeing that the theater the Middle Ages had in mind evoked the antics of minstrels and *histriones,* along with the sacred mystery play.

Accordingly, in Moerbeke's translation (pp. 9–10), mimesis is rendered as *imitatio,* pity and fear with *misericordia* and *timor, pathos* with *passio;* the six parts of tragedy become *fabula, mores, locutio, ratiocinatio, visus,* and *melodie;* it is understood that *opsis* has to do with the mimic action of the *hypocrita* or actor; *peripetie* and *anagnorisees (idest recognitiones)* are mentioned; and the distinction between the poet and the historian is clear. The oppositions between a clear and a pedestrian style are faithfully presented, though *glotta* is translated as *lingua,* making the nature of the barbarism somewhat less than transparent. Moerbeke translates 1457b 6 et seq., where metaphor is defined, in an acceptable manner.

In the crucial 1459a, 8, where Aristotle says that "to use metaphor well implies an ability to see the likenesses in things," and he uses in this context the verb *theorein,* Moerbeke translates "nam bene metaphorizare est simile considerare" ("for to coin good metaphors is to consider likeness") (p. 29). Perhaps the verb *considerare* has a weaker connotation than the Greek word, but it points in any case to the universe of knowledge.

To sum up, the Latin reader could have acquired a reasonable idea of Aristotle's text from Moerbeke, but with nothing that underscored with particular energy the cognitive aspect of metaphor's implications.

2.4. Aristotle's *Rhetoric:* Hermann the German's Translation

In section 2.1 we recalled that three translations of the *Rhetoric* had appeared: one from the Arabic by Hermann the German, an anonymous *Translatio Vetus,* and, between 1269 and 1270, the version of William of Moerbeke, from the Greek. For a long time the received wisdom concerning Hermann's *Rhetoric* was imprecise. The title, *Averroes in Rhetoricam,* led some scholars to conclude that it was a translation of Averroes's Middle Commentary. Then, because of the existence of other manuscripts that bore the title *Didascalia in Rhetoricam Aristotelis ex glosa Alpharabi* (whereas al-Farabi's commentary was incomplete from the start), it was believed that Hermann's text was based solely on Arabic sources. Only quite recently (Bogges 1971) was it determined that Hermann had translated the text of Aristotle from the Arabic, inserting passages from Averroes's commentary and from Avicenna's *Shifa* when the manuscripts at his disposal were lacunary (but invariably making the insertion explicit). In his translation of al-Farabi's glosses, Hermann explicitly claims to have translated Aristotle's *Rhetoric* from Arabic to Latin, and he repeats the claim in the prologue to his translation of the *Rhetoric.*

We shall consider later the problems that this extremely arduous translation, of whose insufficiencies the translator himself was fully aware, posed for the Latin reader. Furthermore, we know of only two complete manuscripts and one fragmentary one, which leads us us conclude that it had a very limited circulation.[14]

An example of the translator's embarrassment is provided by the notion of *ta asteia.* At the end of chapter 10 Hermann decides to skip portions of the text of Aristotle that he is unable to translate, and he goes on to comment: "Plura talia exempla ad idem facientia, quia greca sapiebant sententiam non multum usitatam latinis, dimissa sunt, et subsequitur quasi conclusio auctoris" ("Many like examples of the same import have been omitted for they smacked of the Greek idiom not much used by the Latins, and the author's conclusions as it were follow immediately after"). To say nothing of the fact that in one manuscript (Toledo, cf. Marmo 1992: 32 n. 8) in chapter 11 we find: "Ideoque pulchre dicit Astisius in suis transsumptionibus quasi

---

14. For all this information and the passages cited, see Bogges (1971).

ante oculos statuende ea que transumendo loquitur" ("And this is why Astisius expresses himself so well in his transumptions that almost place what he is talking about by transference before your very eyes"). Where the form *Astisius* suggests that the Arabic original had interpreted *asteia* as a proper name, and that Hermann had gone along with this interpretation.

2.5. The *Rhetoric: Translatio Vetus* (V) and William of Moerbeke's Translation (M)

With reference to the key points of Aristotle's text listed in section 2.1, let us now examine the solutions provided by V and M.[15]

1404b 3. That what is "foreign" is delectable and *thaumaston* (i.e., exciting wonder) is clear enough both in V ("mirabiles enim absentium, delectabile autem mirabile est" ["for those who are admirable are different, but what is admirable is delightful"]) and in M ("admiratores enim advenarum sunt, delectabile autem quod mirabile est" ["for those who admire are strangers, but what is admirable is delightful"]).

1405a 9. V says that "manifestum et delectabile et externum habet maxime metaphora, et assumere non est ipsam ad alio" ("metaphor has most especially evidence, delight and strangeness, and it cannot be received from someone else"). M translates "evidentiam et delectationem et extraneitatem habet maxime metaphora, et accipere ipsam non est ab alio" ("metaphor has most especially distinctness, delight and strangeness, and it cannot be taken from someone else"). Both let it be understood that good metaphors are not made by merely imitating those already codified.

1405a 9. Verbs like *phainesthai* and *skopein* are rendered in V with *videri* and *intueri* and by M with *apparire* and *intendere*. They are in other words *verba cognoscendi*.

1405a 10. V does not get the quip about pirates calling themselves purveyors and translates "et latrones se ipsos depredatores vocant" ("and pirates call themselves predators"). M on the other hand speaks appropriately of *acquisitores*.

---

15. Textual references and page numbers are to Schneider (1978). References to the original are to Aristotle (1926).

1405b 13. The idea that metaphor puts matters before our eyes is properly understood ("in faciendo rem coram oculis" in V and "in faciendo rem pre oculis" in M). Similarly, all subsequent translations of the same expression are correct.

1406b 4. The translators are embarrassed, and not without reason, by the distinction between *metaphora* and *eikon*. V first translates *eikon* as *conveniens,* producing the obscure expression "est autem et conveniens metaphora" ("moreover a metaphor is also befitting"), but right afterward he translates the same term with *ymagines.* M translates it as *assimilatio.* In both translations, however, the context makes it clear that what is involved is a simile (for both, Achilles "ut leone fremit" or "fremuit" ["roars like a lion"]).

1410b 10 et seq. We come now to the definitions of *ta asteia* ("witty and popular sayings"). V renders the term with *solatiosa* and M conserves *asteia.* Especially in the latter case, we can only suppose that the medieval reader had no idea what they were talking about (see, in Marmo 1992, the misunderstandings that ensue in Giles of Rome's commentary). One might have expected the concept to be clarified by the plentiful examples supplied by Aristotle, but unfortunately the translation of these pithy sayings is unsatisfactory. Many of Aristotle's examples are completely skipped. In V the triremes like "parti-colored mills" become "milonas curvas," and in M "molares varios." Sisyphus's stone that rolls ruthlessly down to the plain becomes in V "lapis . . . inverecundus ad eum qui est inverecundus" ("a stone . . . shameless to him who is shameless") and in M "lapis . . . qui inverecundus ad facile verecundabilem." ("a stone . . . that is shameless to someone who is easily contemptible"). The spear-point that speeds eagerly through the warrior's breast is not translated in V, while in M it appears as the inexplicable "gibbosa falerizantia." In V the metaphor of stubble for old age becomes the incomprehensible "quando enim dicit senectutem bonam, facit doctrinam et cognitionem propter genus" ("for when he says that old age is good, he teaches and imparts knowledge to us through the genus"), while M translates more appropriately "quando enim dixit senectutem calamum fecit disciplinam et notitiam per genus" ("when he called old age a stalk, he taught and delivered a notion through its genus"). In 1412a 5, Archytas's metaphor on the similarity between an arbitrator and an altar (both a refuge for someone who has suffered an injustice) in V becomes "sicut Archites dixit idem esse propter hanc et altare" ("just as Archytas said that there was no difference *because of this*"), perhaps because his manuscript, instead of "diaiteten" [=arbitrator], read "dia tauten"); M on the other hand is not guilty of the same error. We may well wonder how much intellectual stimulation a medieval reader might have felt in the face of such obscure pseudo-inventions that often come across as insipid or meaningless.

Curiously, in the same passage, both translators accurately render the conceptual aspect. In V good enthymemes "faciunt nobis doctrinam expeditam" ("they teach us expeditiously"), and in this connection mention is made of "cognitio" (which is Aristotle's *gnosis* or "knowing"). M says that good enthymemes "faciunt nos addiscere celeriter" ("make us learn quickly") and that "cum hoc quod dicuntur notitia fit" ("which are understood the moment they are stated"). Similarly, it is clear, though elliptically expressed, that metaphor must make us see the thing in action and that, like philosophy, it must make us "inspicere" (a good translation of *theorein*, "to contemplate or consider") a resemblance "a propriis et non manifestis" ("proper to the object, yet not obvious") (V), while M speaks less forcefully, but with clarity, of a witty saying that makes us "bene considerare similitudinem in multibus distantibus" ("consider carefully similarity in many disparate things"). When V finds himself faced (in 1412a 17) with the term "epiphaneia" he boldly transliterates it as "epyphania" (while M does not grasp the meaning of apparition and revelation and says "in superficie," ["on the surface"]).

Correctly rendered is the passage in 1412a, in which Aristotle says that, when confronted with a witty juxtaposition, the surprised reader recognizes that he had not seen things as they were and had been mistaken (even though, immediately following, V, after attempting to translate Stesichorus's apophthegm of the grasshoppers that will sing to themselves from the ground, skips a short passage on riddles and translates the notion of "novel expressions" with "inania"). M on the other hand translates the passage on riddles (which are able to say new things ["nova dicere"]) and gets across the idea of the unexpected word ("inopinatum") and the paradox it produces.

To sum up, the two versions might have given some inkling of Aristotle's position, but it is doubtful whether the meaning of the technical terms was immediately evident, and the translations of the examples were certainly of no help in understanding the definitions any better.

2.6. The Medieval Misfortunes of the *Poetics* and the *Rhetoric*

The scant attention the Middle Ages paid to these two translations can be explained in a number of ways. In the first place, up until the twelfth century, rhetoric had belonged to the *trivium*, but poetics was not included. Thus, observes Dahan (1980), poetics is ignored by Alan of Lille (in his *Anticlaudianus*), Honorius of Autun, Hugh of Saint Victor, Robert Grosseteste (in his *De artibus liberalibus*), John of Dacia (in his *De divisione scientiae*), and many others.

Around the twelfth century, another division of the sciences becomes prevalent, one Stoic in origin, according to which philosophy is subdivided into logic, ethics, and physics, and at this point both poetics and rhetoric were considered part of logic. The idea is already present in Augustine, but see Isidore of Seville's definition in *Etymologiae* II, 24, 3: "Philosophiae species tripartita est: una naturalis, quae graece physica appellatur...; altera moralis, quae graece ethica dicitur...; tertia rationalis, quae graece vocabulo logica appellatur" ("There are three kinds of philosophy: one natural [*naturalis*], which in Greek is 'physics' [*physica*]...; a second moral [*moralis*], which is called 'ethics' [*ethica*] in Greek...; a third rational [*rationalis*], which is named with the Greek term 'logic' [*logica*].")[16]

Later in the twelfth century, through the agency of Gundisalvo, the Arabic classification, in which poetics and rhetoric are seen as an integral part of Aristotle's *Organon* (see, for instance, Avicenna's *Shifa* and the *De scientiis* of al-Farabi), becomes established in the West. It was in fact an aid to students of logic that Hermann presented his translation: "suscipiant igitur, si placet, et huius editionis Poetriae translationem viri studiosi, et gaudeant se cum hac adeptos logici negotii Aristotilis complementum ("May then learned men, should it be deemed desirable, take up also the translation of this edition of the *Poetria* and rejoice to achieve with it a completion of the logical works of Aristotle").

Though he did not know Aristotle's *Rhetoric*, Albertus Magnus considers rhetoric a logical discipline (see, for instance, *Liber de praedicabilibus* I, 4); and in the *Liber Primis Posteriorum Analyticorum* he includes poetics

---

16. See Barney, Lewis, Beach, and Berghof (2006, p. 79).

under logic (cf. Dahan and Rosier-Catach 1998: 77, as well as Marmo 1990: 159–163).[17]

As parts of logic, poetics and rhetoric were understood to be persuasive discourses that could be used for political and moral ends, and it is in fact Gundisalvo who defines poetics as forming part of civil science, which is in its turn part of eloquence, whose purpose is to delight and instruct both in science and proper behavior.

The thinker who crystallizes the Arabic position (rhetoric and poetics as part of logic, and their moral and civic orientation) is Roger Bacon (cf. Rosier-Catach 1998). Bacon, inspired by Gerard of Cremona's translation of al-Farabi's *De scientiis,* is intent, in his *Moralis Philosophia* (the seventh part of his *Opus Majus*), on establishing a method for convincing the infidel of the superiority of Christianity, and he finds it in rhetorical and poetic discourse. He is seeking a "sermo potens ad inclinandum mentem" ("speech with the power to persuade the mind"); and language (he affirms in *Opus Majus* III) is more effective than any war. If dialectical and demonstrative arguments could move the speculative mind, poetics and rhetoric can move the practical intellect (*Opus Majus* III).

Poetic argument has nothing to do with truth or falsehood. Poetics is the study of ways of moving the listener emotionally by means of a magniloquent style, and the greatest example of poetic discourse is provided by the Holy Scriptures. In the *Moralis Philosophia* imitation *(similitudo)* is seen as the way of comparing, for instance, virtue to light and sin to things that are hideous.

It is Bacon again, in his *Communia Matematica,* who will state that poetic argument uses fine discourses so that the soul may be overcome by the love of virtue and learn to hate vice. To this end ornaments such as meter and rhythm can be useful, as is the case in the texts of Scripture.[18]

---

17. To find classifications that include poetics in an autonomous position, we must wait for Giles of Rome, though Dahan (1980: 178) already finds anticipations of this position in William of Conches and Richard of Saint Victor.

18. "Hoc argumentum utitur sermonibus pulchris et in fine decoris, ut rapiatur animus subito in amorem virtutis et felicitatis, et in odium vicii et pene perpetue que ei respondent. Et ideo sermones poetici qui sunt completi et pulchritudine et efficacia movendi animum debent esse ornati omni vetustate loquendi prosaice at astricti omni lege metri et ritmi, sicut Scriptura Sacra . . . ut

Independently of Bacon, the idea that poetics and rhetoric are part of logic and are concerned with moral and civil knowledge made more and more headway among those who approached the first translations of Aristotle. It is understandable, then, that the thinkers who debated such problems were not especially interested in the semiotics of *elocutio,* and hence in the technical study of metaphors, but focused their attention more on methods of argumentation.

Thomas demonstrates his familiarity with these translations (except, of course, Moerbeke's translation of the *Poetics*), but, in his commentary on *Posterior Analytics* I, he sees logic as judicative *(Prior and Posterior Analytics),* sophistic *(Sophistical Refutations)* and inventive *(Topics, Rhetoric, and Poetics).* Hence, "poetae est inducere ad aliquod virtuosum per aliquam decentem representationem" ("the poet's task is to lead us to something virtuous by some excellent description").

Buridan will allude to the fact that poetics, while it doesn't put things clearly like rhetoric does, still has the same educative intentions in mind, "scientiam delectabiler obscurare nititur, per verborum transumptionem," "it endeavors to obscure knowledge delightfully by metalepsis" (cf. Dahan 1998: 186).

But Bacon is the one who points to another reason for the scant currency of these translations and interpretations of Aristotle: they were badly translated and hard to fathom. Bacon says that he knew Hermann personally. In *Moralis philosophia* VI he claims that Hermann confided in him ("dixit mihi") that he was insufficiently versed in logic to translate the *Rhetoric* well, and for the same reasons had not dared to translate the *Poetics,* confining himself to translating Averroes's commentary. So, Bacon observed, we can never really know what Aristotle thought about poetics, we can only

---

decore et suavitate sermonis animus subito et fortiter moveatur" ("This is argument makes use of beautiful and decorous speech so that the soul will be immediately raised to the love of virtue and happiness and to the hatred of vice, and will scarcely ever be attracted to it. And so poetic speeches that are complete, beautiful and efficacious in moving the soul ought to be dressed out in all proper forms of prosaic speech, and abide by all the laws of meter and rhythm, just like Sacred Scripture . . . so that by the decor and sweetness of the language, the soul may be strongly and immediately moved"), (cf. Hackett 1997: 136, n. 6).

"get a whiff" of it, not savor it, as is the case with wine that has been poured too many times from one container to another.[19]

Bacon claims in *Opus Majus* I that the moderns neglect two books of logic, one of them translated with a commentary by al-Farabi, the other an exposition of Aristotle by Averroes, translated without reproducing the philosopher's original text.[20] In *Opus Majus* III he points out once again that there are few Latin translations of Aristotle's logic and Averroes's commentaries, and that the few versions extant are not read.[21] Again, in the *Moralis Philosophia* (V, 255), he cites Averroes's commentary on the *Poetics* as the only available source for Aristotle's text, but he recognizes that it too is known to only a few.[22] In *Opus Majus* III he complains about the translations of Aristotle's works, executed

---

19. *"Studiosi homines possunt a longe olfacere eius sentenciam, non gustare: vinum enim, quod de tercio vase transfusum est, virtutem non retinet in vigore"* ("Learned men can get a distant whiff of his meaning, but not taste it. For a wine that has been poured into three successive containers does not keep its virtue in all its strength") (*Moralis Philosophia* VI, 267, cited in Rosier-Catach (1998: 95), to whom we are also indebted for the references that follow).

20. "Moderni . . . duos libros logicae meliores negligunt, quorum unus translatus est cum Commentum Alpharabii super librum illum, et alterius expositio per Averroem facta sine textu Aristotelis est traslata" ("The Moderns neglect the two best books on logic, one of which has been translated with the commentary of al-Farabi, while the commentary on the other composed by Averroes has been translated without Aristotle's text").

21. "Quoniam autem libri Logica Aristotelis de his modis, et commentarii Avicennae, deficiuntur apud Latinos, et paucae quae translata sunt, in usu non habentur nec leguntur, ideo non est facile esprimere quod oporteat in hac parte" ("On the other hand, since the books of Aristotle's Logic regarding these methods, together with Avicenna's commentaries, are not available to the Latins, and the little that has been translated is not used or read, it is no easy matter to express what needs to be expressed in this part").

22. "Quoniam vero non habemus in latino librum Aristotelis de hoc argomento ideo vulgus ignorat modum conponendi ipsum; sed tamen illi, qui diligentes sunt, possunt multum de hoc argumento sentire per Commentarium Averrois et [forse in] librum Aristotilis, qui habetur in lingua latina, licet non sit in usu multitudinis" ("Since we do not have, in Latin, Aristotle's book on this subject [Bacon is alluding to the *Poetics*], most people therefore do not know the way it was composed; those, however, who are studious can learn much on this topic from Averroes's Commentary and the book by Aristotle that we do possess in the Latin language, though not many people make use of it").

"cum defectu translationis et squalore," ("crudely and with defective translation")—with the result that nothing can be understood–and he remarks what a loss this has been for the culture of his time.

From these texts we may deduce that Bacon was not yet acquainted with Moerbeke's translation of the *Rhetoric*, which would not appear in fact until later and which he might perhaps have treated with greater indulgence. But Bacon's strictures, which are extremely severe on almost all the translators without proposing new criteria for a correct translation (cf. Lemay 1997), indicate to us that, though they may have enjoyed some limited currency, Averroes's texts were familiar to few, and viewed with suspicion by those who knew them. It appears that the translations were not readily available in university circles, though in any case Bacon operated outside of those circles. Thomas cites a brief excerpt from Hermann's translation of the *Rhetoric* in the *Contra Gentiles;* and later, in *Summa Theologiae* I–II, 29, 6, he will quote it once more, but this time in Moerbeke's version. Moerbeke's translation will in fact enjoy greater popularity, it will circulate in numerous manuscripts, and it will form the basis for the commentary on the *Rhetoric* composed by Giles of Rome between 1272 and 1274.[23]

Precisely because he has available a less improbable translation than those that came earlier, Giles's theory of metaphor strikes us as unquestionably more mature. In both Marmo (1998) and chapter 7 of Eco and Marmo (2005) (written entirely by Marmo), we see how Giles worked out a strategy of critical collation among the different versions.

But at this point we are nearing the end of the thirteenth century. Giles's commentary will be followed by those of John of Jandun and Buridan,[24] too late, we might say, for Aristotle's theory of metaphor to have any decisive influence on scholastic thought. As will be seen in Chapter 3, medieval metaphorology will have other founding texts and other outcomes.

What we have attempted to demonstrate here is how the absence of a cognitive theory of metaphor in the golden age of scholasticism was largely due to the inadequacy of the existing translations.

---

23. Interest in the two Aristotelian texts apparently reawakens in the fourteenth century, when citations from Hermann's translation appear in several florilegia; see Bogges (1970).

24. Still unpublished; see Marmo (1992).

3

From Metaphor to *Analogia Entis*

3.1. Poetics and Rhetoric

In Chapter 2 we saw how the notion of the cognitive value of metaphor, as outlined in Aristotle, was without influence on the thought of the Latin Middle Ages. Our next step will be to see whether and how a notion of metaphor not directly related to Aristotle's definitions developed in medieval circles.

Ideas concerning the *figurae elocutionis* reach the Middle Ages from classical rhetoric, especially from the rhetorical works of Cicero, from the *Rhetorica ad Herennium* (formerly attributed to Cicero), and from Quintilian, as well as via Latin grammarians like Donatus and Priscian. To what extent Aristotle's notions become transformed as they are handed on by these authors is fairly evident from the divisions of metaphor proposed by Quintilian (*Institutio* VIII, 6). Whereas, for the Aristotle of the *Poetics* (1457b), metaphor meant the transferral of the name appropriate to one thing to another thing, Quintilian too (*Institutio oratoria* 8, 6, 1) speaks of "verbi vel sermonis a propria significatione in aliam cum virtute mutatio" ("a shift of a word or phrase from its proper meaning to another, in a way that has positive value"), in such a way that not only is the form of the words changed, "sed et sensuum et compositionis" ("but also the forms of sentences and of composition"). But Aristotle distinguished metaphors based on transferral from

This is a shorter, edited version of a paper delivered at a seminar at the Scuola Superiore di Studi Umanistici of the University of Bologna in March 2001 in the context of a series of talks on the fortunes of Aristotle's theory of metaphor. It appeared in Lorusso (2005).

genus to species, species to genus, species to species or by analogy, while Quintilian, though he speaks of comparison (as in *this man is a lion,* which is an abbreviated simile), considers comparisons or substitutions between animate genera (*steersman* for *charioteer*), between animate and inanimate *(he gave the fleet more rein),* inanimate and animate (*the wall of the Argives,* for the resistance they oppose), and the attribution of animation to something inanimate *(the river Araxes, who spurns bridges).* The four modes are further divided into subspecies that contemplate changes from rational to rational, irrational to rational, rational to irrational, irrational to irrational, from the whole to the parts and vice versa.

What remains Aristotelian in Quintilian is the notion that the metaphor, in addition to being an ornament (as it is when we speak of *lumen orationis* or of *generis claritas*), may also be an instrument of knowledge, when it finds a name, and therefore some semblance of a definition, for something that otherwise would not have one—when farmers, for instance, speak of the buds of the vine as gems or of crops as thirsty. But it cannot be said that Quintilian insists further on this function, which, more than cognitive, might be called "lexically substitutive," since it serves to make up for *penuria nominum* or the scarcity of names for things.

Another suggestion came from Donatus (fourth century), in whom Quintilian's scheme was taken up with a hint of semic analysis: in fact metaphor is spoken of as a *translatio* from animate to animate, inanimate to inanimate, animate to inanimate, inanimate to animate, with all the appropriate examples.[1]

---

1. "Tropus est dictio translata a propria significatione ad non propriam similitudinem ornatus necessitatisue causa.... Metaphora est rerum uerborumque translatio. Haec fit modis quattuor, ab animali ad animale, ab inanimali ad inanimale, ab animale ad inanimale, ab inanimali ad animale: ab animali ad animale, ut *Tiphyn aurigam celeris fecere carinae;* nam et auriga et gubernator animam habent: ab inanimali ad inanimale, ut *ut pelagus tenuere rates;* nam et naues et rates animam non habent: ab animali ad inanimale, ut *Atlantis cinctum assidue cui nubibus atris piniferum caput* et cetera: nam ut haec animalis sunt, ita mons animam non habet, cui membra hominis ascribuntur: ab inanimali ad animale, ut *si tantum pectore robur concipis;* nam ut robur animam non habet, sic utique Turnus, cui haec dicuntur, animam habet" (*Ars maior* III, 6, ed. Holtz, pp. 668–669). "A trope is an expression taken out of its proper meaning to a similar improper

There follows the definition of all of the other tropes, and it is interesting to point out that for allegory and enigma Donatus bases himself on an implicit criterion accepted throughout the Middle Ages and still valid for modern rhetoric. Taken at face value, a metaphor may appear to be absurd (semantically unacceptable), and we must therefore assume (today we would say *by implicature*) that we are dealing with a figurative usage. On the other hand, we have allegory when the letter of the text is meaningful but we must infer a secondary sense on the basis of certain contextual clues (as Augustine teaches, but we will get to that later). Donatus gives the example of Virgil's "et iam tempus equum fumantia soluere colla" ("and now it is time to unyoke the necks of our smoking steeds" [*Georgics* II, 542]), to say that it is time to end the poem, and, though this may strike us as a valid metaphor, Donatus is right to point out that it does not seem unreasonable for someone to want to remove the horses' harnesses (though odd in that particular context), and that therefore this is an example of allegory and not of metaphor. The same criterion holds true for enigma.[2]

---

one for the purpose of embellishment or necessity. . . . Metaphor is the transformation of things or words. This takes place in four ways, from the animate to the animate, from the inanimate to the inanimate, from the animate to the inanimate, from the inanimate to the animate—from the animate to the animate, as *Tiphyn aurigam celeris fecere carinae* [P. Terentius Varro Atacinus, *Argonautae*]; for both *auriga* 'driver' [or 'charioteer': Lewis and Short] and *gubernator* 'guider' [steersman,' 'pilot': Lewis and Short] have souls—from inanimate to inanimate, as *ut pelagus tenuere rates* (Aeneid 5.8) 'when the ships gained the deep'; for neither *naves* 'ships' nor *rates* 'rafts, ships' are alive—from animate to inanimate, as A*tlantis cinctum assidue cui nubibus atris piniferum caput*; (Aeneid 4.248) 'Atlas, whose pine-wreathed head is always encircled by black clouds,' for these are animate, *mons* 'mountain,' to which human members are attributed, is not alive—from the inanimate to the animate, as *si tantum pectore robur concipis* (Aeneid 11.368) 'if in your heart you nourish such strength,' since *robur* 'strength' is not alive; likewise also Turnus, to whom these things are said, is a living being" (Trans. Jim Marchand, online at http://www9.georgetown.edu/faculty/jod/texts/donatus.3.english.html).

2. "Allegoria est tropus, quo aliud significatur quam dicitur, ut *et iam tempus equum fumantia soluere colla*, hoc est 'carmen finire' . . . Aenigma est obscura sententia per occultam similitudinem rerum, ut *mater me genuit, eadem mox gignitur ex me*, cum significet aquam in glaciem concrescere et ex eadem rursus effluere" ("Allegory is a trope, in which one signifies something different from what one says, as in "and now it is time to unyoke the necks of our smoking steeds"

Nevertheless, in these definitions of Donatus it is not specified to what extent obscurity is a vehicle of knowledge. Finally, we find something in Donatus that recalls Aristotle's *eikon*, that is, the simile: "Icon est personarum inter se vel eorum quae personis accidunt comparatio, ut '*os humerosque deo similis*'" ("Icon [or simile] is the comparison between persons or between the properties that belong to them, such as 'godlike in face and shoulders'") (*Ars maior* III, 6, ed. Holtz, p. 673).[3]

Among early medieval definitions, the following is taken from the *Etymologiae* of Isidore of Seville (I, 37. 2): "metaphora est verbi alicujus usurpata translatio, sicut dicimus 'fluctuare segetes,' 'gemmare vites'" ("metaphor is an adopted transference of some word, as when we say 'cornfields ripple' or 'the vines put forth gems'), which is clearly derived from Cicero and Quintilian, from the second of whom Isidore borrows the distinction of the passage from animate to animate, animate to inanimate, and so on. There is no hint that these substitutions have a cognitive function, indeed "things are transferred very elegantly from one kind to another for the sake of beauty, so that the speech may be greatly adorned" (I, 37, 5).

Isidore is among those, and there are some among the moderns, who—while they are prepared to accept a metaphor like *fluctuare segetes*—consider its opposite, *segetare fluctus* inacceptable,[4] as if its unprecedented boldness were an offence to metaphorical common sense, while they find the interchange of a bird's wings and a ship's oars reciprocal, precisely because both *are said*: "alae navium et alarum remigium *dicuntur*" (ibid., my emphasis). A good metaphor, then, is something that "is [already] said." It appears, then, that there is little room left for uncodified daring, which evidently "non dicitur . . ."("is not said").

(Virgil, *Georgics*, II, 542), in other words, to finish the poem. An enigma (or riddle) is a proposition that is obscure because of a secret resemblance between things, such as 'my mother gave birth to me and she will soon be born out of me,' which means that water is changed into ice and then will flow once again from the ice") (*Ars maior* III, 6, ed. Holtz, pp. 671–672).

3. The Virgilian simile is from *Aeneid*, I, 589.

4. The idea probably comes from Demetrius Phalereus (*On Style,* 79): not all metaphors are interchangeable: the *auriga* may be called *gubernator* and vice versa, but, though we may call the lower slopes of the mountain *the foot of Mount Ida* we cannot call human feet *slopes.*

Donatus's definitions are found almost verbatim in the *De schematibus et tropis* of the Venerable Bede, and from there they are handed on with minimal variations to a number of later medieval texts. Compared to Donatus, what changes, if anything, are the citations and the comments on them.[5]

It is never made explicit whether the trope is witty because of its difficulty, though it is implied that it should be clarified by the reading of the text's interpreter. The tradition will tend to privilege readily comprehensible tropes over obscure and ingenious ones.

An invitation to moderation could already be found in the *Rhetorica ad Herennium* (IV, 45): Translationem pudentem dicunt esse oportere, ut cum ratione in consimilem rem transeat, ne sine dilectu temere et cupide videatur in dissimilem transcurrisse" ("They say that a metaphor ought to be restrained, so as to be a transition with good reason to a kindred thing, and not seem an indiscriminate, reckless and precipitate leap to an unlike thing").[6] Alcuin (*De rhet.*, in Halm 1863: 37) reminds us that we must learn the good things that past authors have done, and when one has become accustomed to their manner of speaking, one will inevitably speak in an ornate style.

Alcuin affirms that the function of good metaphors is to make clearer something that could not be said in any other words, though exaggerations are to be avoided. Literary education, at least as organized from the *Schola Palatina* on, is based on imitation of the ancients, and the metaphorical ar-

---

5. Ab inanimali ad inanimal, ut Zachariae undecimo: *Aperi, Libane, portas tuas.* Item psalmo VIII: *Qui perambulat semitas maris.* Translatio est enim a civitate ad montem, et a terra ad mare, quorum nullum animam habet. Ab animali ad inanimal, ut, Amos I: *Exsiccatus est vertex Carmeli.* Homines enim, non montes, verticem habent. 4, Ab inanimali ad animal, ut, Ezech. XI: *Auferam a vobis cor lapideum.* Non enim lapis, sed populus animam habet (PL 90, 179D–180B). "From inanimate to inanimate, as in Zechariah 11, 1: 'Open thy doors, O Lebanon.' And likewise in Psalms 8, 8: 'whatsoever passeth through the paths of the seas.' In fact the metaphor is from the city to the mountain and from the land to the sea, and neither of these things is animate. From animate to inanimate, as in Amos 1, 2: 'and the [head] of Carmel shall wither.' In fact, men have heads, not mountains. From inanimate to animate, as in Ezekiel 11, 19: 'I will take the stony heart out of [your] flesh.' In fact, the stone is not animate, but people have a soul". Examples follow of transferrals to birds, beasts, and so on.

6. The Latin quote is from Cicero 1954, p. 345.

senal too must stick to tried and true models. The examples given are the canonical ones *(gemmare vites, luxuriari messem, fluctuare segetes),* and the question of how far one may experiment with overbold metaphors is answered with an appeal to moderation, and a provocative metaphor such as the term of abuse *stercus curiae* ("the droppings of the curia or court") is consequently rejected.[7]

Centuries later, a refined proto-humanist like John of Salisbury in his *Metalogicon* will inform us that grammar provides the tropes, but "solis eruditissimis patet usus eorum: unde et lex eorum arctior est, qua non permittuntur longius evagari. Regulariter enim proditum est, quia figures extendere non licet" (I, 19) ("The employment of tropes, just as the use of schemata, is the exclusive privilege of the very learned. The rules governing tropes are also very strict, so that the latitude in which they may be used is definitely limited. For the rules teach that we may not extend figures") (I, 19).[8]

He will cite Quintilian reminding us that "virtus enim sermonis optima est perspicuitas et facilitas intelligendi" ("what is desirable first and foremost in language is lucid clarity and easy comprehensibility") and he will say that tropes are motivated by necessity or ornament.

Again, it is John (*Metalogicon* III, 8) who, while he praises metaphors which highlight what we would call the physical resemblance between two things, condemns expressions like "the law is the measure (or image) of things that are just by their very nature" because in the concept of law there is nothing that resembles either measure or image (in point of fact he takes the example from *Topics* VI, 2, 140, 7 et seq.).

---

7. "Undecumque licet ducere translationes? Nequaquam, sed tantum de honestis rebus. Nam summopere fugienda est omnis turpitudo earum rerum, ad quas eorum animos qui audiunt trahet similitudo, ut dictum est *morte Africani castratam rem publicam* et *stercus curiae*: in utroque deformis cogitatio similitudinis" ("Are we free to make metaphors out of anything we choose? Not at all, only from decent things. In fact we must avoid at all costs any vulgarity in the things to which the simile draws the attention of one's listeners, as when someone said 'The republic was castrated by the death of Scipio Africanus' or the expression 'the dung of the senate'; in both cases the conception of the comparison is dishonorable") (Halm 1863: 38).

8. See McGarry 1955, p. 56.

Does this perhaps mean that medieval poets were incapable of inventing unprecedented metaphors? Naturally, the whole history of medieval poetry is there to affirm the opposite, and we still find Dante's "aiuola che ci fa tanto feroci" ("the garden plot that makes us so aggressive," *Pd* 22, 151) or "Galeotto fu il libro e chi lo scrisse" ("Galahad was the book and whoever wrote it," *Inf* 5, 137) admirable in their boldness. And that is not all: much of medieval poetry and prose frequently succumbed to the fascination of enigmatic expression. We have only to think of the so-called *Hisperica Famina* (cf. De Bruyne 1946: 1:4, and Herren 1974), or of the *Epitomae* of that bizarre seventh-century rhetorician Virgil of Bigorre (cf. Polara 1979), not to mention the hermetic *trobar clus* of the Provençal poets.

Nevertheless, it seems that the very authors who show their appreciation for enigmas and obscurity by composing such texts or quoting them admiringly are far more circumspect when it comes to theory. Virgil of Bigorre, for instance, says that there are poetic compositions which aspire to wit and whimsy, which he calls *leporia* (calling to mind Aristotle's *asteia*), but he reminds us that in so doing poetry is distinct from rhetoric because it is cramped and obscure ("angusta atque oscura," *Epitomae* IV, 6). The word-polishers ("tornores logi," IV, 7), are therefore to be condemned; the *leporia* displays a certain *mordacitas* but does not always escape mendacity. Can we say "sol in occasu metitur maria," when no created thing, not even the setting sun, can plumb *(metiri)* the depths of the seas? Better to say "sol in occasu tinguit mare." Can we say "ventus e terra roborum radices evellit altas" (IV, 8), when we know that the wind only makes oaks quake and does not tear them up by their roots? We might say that for Virgil inventing neologisms, coming up with outlandish etymologies, and composing riddles in cipher was all in a day's work, but when it came to metaphors you had to watch where you were headed.

Among the Provençal poets (cf. De Bruyne 1946: 2:332), Allégret warns us that his verse will seem incomprehensible to fools, and Bernart de Venzac promises veridical words that will be a source of perturbation for the wise and scandal for the foolish, unless they accept a double reading. Guiraut de Borneill, however, while defending on the one hand the obscure style ("I will seek and lead by the reins fair words burdened with a meaning at once strange and natural that not everyone will discover"), on the other hand opts for the *trobar plan* or *leu chanso* over the *trobar clus,* and recognizes that it makes more sense to write intelligibly than to tangle up the words ("Qu'eu cut c'atretan grans sens / es, qui sap razo gardar, / com los motz entrebeschar" ["I think that it's just as much good sense / if one can keep to the point, / as to twist my words around each other"]).

It is true that, in the various discussions of the lofty style, the perplexity that must be aroused in the mind of the reader, in such a way that the diversity of the examples may dispel boredom, is often praised and "tamquam cibum aurium, invitet auditorem" ("like food for the ears, invite your listeners") (Geoffrey of Vinsauf, *Documentum de modo et arte dictandi et versificandi* Faral: 272);[9] usually, however, the examples do not concern difficult metaphors, but amplifications and descriptions that produce hypotyposis, as when, to say that travelers go on board ship and prepare for the voyage, the writer is advised to compose eight lines describing the action and making it vivid.

In other words, we seem to be witnessing a gap between poetic practice and rhetorical theorization. It appears, from the theoretical point of view, that straightforward, immediately comprehensible metaphors, preferably already codified, are to be preferred.

Geoffrey of Vinsauf (*Poetria nova,* 1705–1708) will affirm that there are three ways to develop one's style: through the art whose rules one follows, through custom to which one conforms, and through the imitation of models. John of Salisbury (*Metalogicon* I, 24) tells us how Bernard of Chartres conducted his classes: he pointed out what was simple and in conformity with the rules, he demonstrated the grammatical figures, the rhetorical colors and the subtleties of argumentation and, to teach the *splendor orationis* ("splendor of discourse"), he demonstrated the marvels of *translatio* (in other words, metaphor) "ubi sermo ex causa probabili ad alienum traducitur significationem" ("whereby speech is transferred to some alien meaning for a most likely cause"). The student who did not observe his strictures was educated "flagellis et poenis." ("with whipping and punishments"). But he did not punish plagiary, though he pointed it out—as if to say that theft was preferable to having an overbold metaphor betray the *causa probabilis,* or the affinities acceptable between metaphorizer and metaphorized.

---

9. For the citations from Matthew of Vendôme, Geoffrey of Vinsauf and John of Garland, see Faral (1924).

Be that as it may, in the classical rules for distinguishing the lofty style, the mediocre and temperate, the vicious or extenuated, the bucolic or pastoral and humble, the georgic and mediocre, and the epic or sublime or grand styles— from the *Rhetorica ad Herennium* to the *Schola Vindobonensia ad Horatii Artem poeticam* (probably dating from the eleventh century) to the *De ornamentis verborum* of Marbode of Rennes, down to the *artes poeticae* of the twelfth and thirteenth centuries (Matthew of Vendôme, Geoffrey of Vinsauf, and John of Garland)—the examples of the words to be preferred are always canonical: *lychnos* is preferable to *lucerna;* in referring to Karolus, it belongs to the lofty style to say that he is "Ecclesiae clypeus et pacis columna" ("the shield of the Church and a column of peace"), but vicious to say he is "clava pacis" ("the cudgel of peace"); it is temperate or mediocre to say he is "Ecclesiae custos" ("the guardian of the Church") and vicious that he is "militiae baculus" ("the staff of the military"); it is humble to say "In tergo clavem pastor portat, ferit inde—presbyterum, cum quo ludere sponsa solet" ("the shepherd carries a club on his shoulder, then he strikes the priest with it, who is wont to sport with his wife"), but it is vicious to say "Rusticus a tergo clavem trahit et ter tonse (or pertonso)—testiculos aufert, prandia laeta facit" ("the peasant takes the club from his back and tears off the priest's testicles, of which he makes a good meal"). And even the metaphorical terms defining the styles are themselves defined by the tradition, "fluctuans et dissolutum, turgidum et inflatum, aridum et exsangue" (Matthew of Vendôme, *Ars versificatoria* I, 30).

What is most appreciated in metaphors is the *color rhetoricus* they bring with them, and hence their ornamental value, since for the theoreticians of medieval poetics the proper end of poetry is invariably grace and elegance: for Matthew of Vendôme (*Ars* III, 18) "fiunt autem tropi ad eloquii suavitatem" ("the tropes are made for the pleasantness of the discourse").

A somewhat singular attempt to provide a logical-semantic rule for the generation of good metaphors is the one proposed by Geoffrey of Vinsauf, who in his *Documentum de arte dictandi et versificandi* (Faral: 285–289) endeavors to establish codified procedures, based on the identity of properties between metaphorizer and metaphorized.[10] Hence, it is established that

---

10. "Considerandum est verbum, quod debet transferri, de quibus dicatur proprie; et, si ad aliam rem debeat transferri, cavendum est ut in ea proprietate sit similitudo. Sic autem debet inveniri similitudo: perscrutandum est in illo verbo

the verb *nasci* (to be born) is properly used only of animals, but it has something in common with other actions, such as "to begin." In which case, we can say "nascuntur flores" (in the sense that the flowers begin to be "incipiunt esse"), or "nascitur istud opus," or "nata est malitia in diebus nostris" ("evil is born in our day"). And, by an analogous procedure, we can say "pubescit humus." For Geoffrey, this artifice "est planissima via ad inveniendum translationes" (Faral: 287).

Some historians (Dronke 1986: 14–16 and Bertini 2003: 35) have identified in Geoffrey a precise notion of the cognitive function of metaphor, in the sense in which it would be taken up by Dante in his Letter to Cangrande della Scala (*Epistole* XIII, 29), where he says of the things seen during his celestial journey that, since they cannot be expressed "sermone proprio" ("in everyday language"), they must be spoken of "per assumptionem metaphorismorum" ("by the employment of metaphors"). Nevertheless—setting aside Dante, to whom we will return—Geoffrey repeats that in constructing metaphors it would be wrong not to draw the properties from among those that are "expressissime et apparentissime similia" ("most expressly and apparently similar," II, 3, 17–18). Obviously, milk and snow are white, and honey is sweet, but Geoffrey does not seem to advise identifying properties that are nonself-evident in order to create unexpected likenesses. Indeed (in II, 3) he denounces as "turgidus et inflatus" ("turgid and inflated') that style "qui nimis duris et ampullosis utitur translationibus," ("which has recourse to crude and bombastic metaphors"), such as saying "ego transivi per montes belli" ("I have crossed over the mountains of war") instead of settling for "per difficultates belli" ("the hardships of war").

And in fact the same author, in his *Poetria nova* (765 et seq.), suggests the use of prefabricated metaphors, so to speak. Instead of "aurum fulvum, lac

---

quiddam commune, quod pluribus conveniat quam illud verbum; et quibuscumque aliis commune conveniat proprie, conveniet illud verbum traslative" ("You have to consider what the word to be used metaphorically can appropriately be used for; and if it is to be used metaphorically for something else, you must make sure that the comparison fits with its proper use. The comparison is to be found in the following way: one must seek carefully in that word something in common, something that fits other things in addition to that word; and whatever other thing what they have in common is suited to, that word will also be suited metaphorically") (Faral: 286).

nitidum, rosa praerubicunda, mel dulcifluum, flammae rutilae, corpus nivis album" ("tawny gold, limpid milk, a rose redder than red, smooth-flowing honey, ruddy flames, a body white as snow") it is better to say "dentes nivei, labra flammea, gustus mellitus, vultus roseus, frons lactea, crinis aureus" ("snow-white teeth, lips of flame, a taste like honey, rosy cheeks, a milk-white brow, golden hair). It is acceptable to say that spring *paints* the earth with flowers, that fair weather *soothes,* that the winds *are sleeping,* that deep valleys *lie,* because, by transferring human actions to nonhuman things, man sees himself in nature, as in a mirror. But this is still the canonical procedure of the anthropomorphization of the inanimate. Furthermore, though Geoffrey may venture a rule which we have dubbed logical-semantic, in point of fact he does not suggest any criterion for the proper identification of the relevant properties.

3.2. References and Examples in Philosophical Thought

We might expect greater commitment on the part of the philosophers, who deal with the correct meaning of terms and the difference between univocal and equivocal signs. In her essay *"Prata rident"*, Rosier-Catach (1997) examines a canonical topos in medieval doctrinal thought: the metaphor of the smiling meadow (already present in *Ad Herennium* 4). It is striking how this same example occurs over and over again in very different authors, from Abelard to Theodoric of Chartres and William of Conches, down to Thomas Aquinas, eventually spilling over into the discussions of analogy or *translatio in divinis,* in other words, the use of metaphors to speak of God.

Abelard's point of departure is an annotation in Boethius's commentary on the *Categories,* according to which, if one calls the "gubernator" (helmsman) of a ship its "auriga"(charioteer), and if one does so "ornatus causa," there is no ambiguity. Abelard says he agrees, because in that case the text assumes the transferred meaning only for a limited time, as occurs when one says "ridere" instead of "florere" of a meadow (*Glossae super Predicamenta,* in Geyer 1927: 121). The transferred meaning does not occur *per institutionem* but only in a specific context, "per abusionem translationis, ex accidentale usurpatione" ("for an abuse of metaphor, as a result of a casual inappropriate use." *Super Peri herm.,* in Geyer 1927: 364). What we have here is not an instance of *translatio aequivoca* based on *penuria nominum.* The case is instead somewhat similar to that of *oppositio in adiecto* ("opposition in the attribute"), as in *homo mortuus,* where *homo* signifies (here and here alone) "corpse."

William of Conches *(Glosae in Priscianum)* will speak of *locutio figurativa* more or less as Abelard does (Rosier-Catach 1997: 161–164). Robert Kilwardby says that in the case of the trope the expression is not understood as "intellectus primus" but as "intellectus secundus," not "simpliciter" but "secundum quid." The *Flores Rhetorici* (by the twelfth-century Master of Tours) speaks of words united in "decente matrimonio," and there appears to be a timid allusion to the inferences that can be drawn from a metaphor, so that from "prata rident" one may proceed to "prata luxuriant floribus or prata floribus lasciviunt." Here Rosier-Catach (1997) speaks of evidence of awareness of metaphorical productivity, but we personally find the allusion if anything quite tenuous. In the same vein the *Dialectica Monacensis* (II, 2, in De Rijk 1962–1967, II: 561) finds it extravagant and inappropriate to hazard the following syllogism: "Quicquid ridet habet os—pratum ridet—ergo habet os" ("Whatever smiles has a mouth—the meadow smiles—therefore it has a mouth").

From a logical point of view, the position could not be more reasonable. And yet, if we want to know how to go about making metaphor an instrument of new knowledge and invention, we have only to see what the Jesuit Emanuele Tesauro, in the baroque period, is able to make of a "fair flower of rhetoric" that by his day was beginning "to stink." We have only to read the lengthy analysis in the *Cannocchiale aristotelico* (ed. Zavatta, 1670: 116 et seq.) dedicated to the smile of the meadows, where he demonstrates how many new ideas and revelatory images can spring from a productive development of the initial trope. For upward of five pages of variations by inference on the original nucleus, in a virtuoso pyrotechnic display of baroque wit, Tesauro shows how the metaphor can give rise to infinite ways of seeing the fecundity of the meadows: *"Iucundissimus pratorum RISUS, RIDIBUNDA vidimus prata, RIDENTER prata florent, Pratorum RISIO oculos beat, RIDENTISSIME prata gliscunt . . ."* ("The most delightful smile of the meadows, we have seen the meadows smile, the meadows smile in flowering, the smiling of the meadows delights our eyes, the meadows rejoice most smilingly"). Whereupon he proceeds to invert the metaphor, *"Hac in solitudine MOESTISSIMA videres prata. Sub Canopo squalida ubique prata LUGENT"* ("In such solitude you would see the meadows most mournful. Under the bright star of Canopus the mournful meadows are weeping"), or, by the subtraction of human properties, we get, *"Prata RIDENT sine ore. RISUS est sine cachinno"* ("The meadows smile without a mouth. The smile is without laughter"), and, by the extension of the metaphor to component parts of the meadow or to the whole earth, we get *"Virides rident RIPAE. Laeta exultant GRAMINA, Fragrantissimi rident FLORES. Alma ridet TELLUS. Rident SEGETES"* ("The verdant banks smile. The grasses exult joyfully. The most sweet-smelling flowers smile. The life-giving earth smiles. The crops smile.") And Tesauro enthusiastically continues:

> Che se hora tu ligherai questa proprietà del rider de' prati, con le cose *Antecedenti, Concomitanti* & *Conseguenti:* tante *Propositioni,* & *Entimemi* arguti, ne farai germogliare; che tanti fiori apunto non partoriscono i prati al primo tempo. Chiamo antecedenti le Cagioni di questo metaforico Riso; cioè: il ritorno del Sole dal tropico hiberno al Segno dell'Ariete. Lo spirar di Zefiro fecondator della terra. I tiepidi venti Australi. Le piogge di Primavera. La fuga delle neui. Le sementi dell'Autunno. Onde scherzando dirai: *SOLI arridentia prata reditum GRATVLANTVR, Vis scire cur prata rideant?* ... *Suavissimis AUSTRI delibuta suauijs, subrident prata, Dubitas cur prata rideant? IMBRIBVS ebria sunt.* (Tesauro 1968, pp. 117–118)[11]

And so on and so forth. And if we may grant a human smile to the meadows, why not grant them also the features that accompany the smile? Hence,

---

11. "For if you now put this property of the smiling of the meadows together with its antecedents, concomitants and consequences, you will generate so many witty propositions and enthymemes that the fields themselves in springtime do not produce so many flowers. I call antecedents the causes of this metaphorical Smile: that is, the return of the sun from the hibernal tropic to the sign of Aries. The wafting of Zephyr fecundator of the earth. The warm Austral winds. The rains of Springtime. The retreat of the snows. The autumn seedtime. Thus you will say: Amico SOLI arridentia prata reditum gratulantur. Vis scire cur prata rideant? ... Suavissimis Austri delibuta suauys, subrident prata.Dubitas cur prata rideant? Imbribus ebria sunt" ("The laughing meadows salute their friend the sun on his return. Do you want to know why the meadows are smiling? ... Smothered with the cloying kisses of the Auster wind, the meadows smile. Do you not know why the meadows smile. They are drunk with the rains").

"*Pulcherrima pratorum FACIES*. Et se la faccia ha le sue membra: ancor dirai; *Tondentur falce virides pratorum COMAE, CRINITA frondibus prata virent. Micantes pratorum OCULI, flores*" ("'*The FACE most fair of the meadows*.' And if the face has all its attributes, then you will say: 'The green LOCKS of the meadows are mown by the sickle. The meadows are green with their COIFFURE of leaves. The flowers are the flashing EYES of the meadows'" (ibid., p. 118).

This appeal to Tesauro, however, merely serves to underscore, by way of contrast, the timidity of all medieval theories of metaphor.

3.3. Metaphor, Allegory, and Universal Symbolism

Why does the Middle Ages confine metaphor to a merely ornamental function and fail to recognize, at least on the theoretical level, its cognitive possibilities? The answer is twofold: (i) for the Middle Ages, our only teacher, who speaks through "real" metaphors *(in rebus)*, is God, and all man can do is to uncover the metaphorical language of creation, and (ii) if man would speak of God, then no metaphor is equal to the challenge, and no metaphor can account for his unfathomable nature any more than literal language can.

If we wish to study this aspect of medieval culture and its implicit semiotics, we must establish precise distinctions between metaphor, symbol, and allegory—which is what we did in Eco (1985), and to which we will return later.[12] For now, we may speak generically of *figural* language for all those cases where *aliud dicitur, aliud demonstratur,* in which there is some kind of *translatio* from one term or a string of terms (or better, from the contents they express) to another, which somehow constitutes its secondary meaning.[13] What

---

12. Pépin (1958, 1970) and Auerbach (1944) have demonstrated with a wealth of examples that the classical world, too, understood "symbol" and "allegory" as synonyms, just as their patristic and medieval exegetes did. The examples, in which the term "symbol" is also used for those didactic and conceptualizing representations that in another context will be called "allegories," range from Philo to grammarians like Demetrius, from Clement of Alexandria to Hippolytus of Rome, from Porphyry to the Pseudo-Dionysius the Areopagite, from Plotinus to Iamblichus.

13. We encounter various formulations of this maxim, as a definition of trope or allegory, in Cicero (*De oratore*, 3.41.166): *ut aliud dicatur, aliud intelligendum sit* ("so that one thing may be expressed and another understood"); Donato (*Ars*

interests us here is how the Middle Ages fixes its attention on phenomena of secondary or *figural* meaning, which are not those of literary metaphor.

Our starting point is Paul's First Epistle to the Corinthians 13:12: "Nunc videmus per speculum et in aenigmitate, tunc autem facie ad faciem" ("For now we see through a glass, darkly; but then face to face"). The most elegant solution poetically speaking is that supplied by the *Rhythmus alter,* formerly attributed to Alan of Lille (PL 210: 578C–579C):

> Omnis mundi creatura,
> Quasi liber, et pictura
> Nobis est, et speculum.
> Nostrae vitae, nostrae mortis,
> Nostri status, nostrae sortis
> Fidele signaculum.
> Nostrum statum pingit rosa,
> Nostri status decens glosa
> Nostrae vitae lectio.
> Quae dum primo mane floret,
> Defloratus flos effloret
> Vespertino senio.
> Ergo spirans flos exspirat,
> In pallorem dum delirat,
> Oriendo moriens.
> Simul vetus et novella,

---

maior III, 6), Ambrose (*De Abraham libri duo*, I, 4, 28): *Allegoria est cum aliud geritur et aliud figuratur* ("We have allegory when one thing is presented and we imagine another"); Augustine (*Sermo* 272): *Ista, fratres, ideo dicuntur sacramenta, quia in eis aliud uidetur, aliud intelligitur* ("These things, brethren, are therefore called sacraments, because in them one thing appears and something else is intended"); Cassiodorus (*Expositio Psalmorum*, VII. 1,80): *schema quod dicitur allegoria, id est inversio, aliud dicens, aliud significans* ("The figure called allegory, that is, inversion, says one thing and means another"); Bede (*De schematibus et tropis*, II.2.12): *Allegoria est tropus quo aliud significatur quam dicitur* ("Allegory is a figure that signifies something different from what it says"); and Isidore (*Etymologiae* I.37.22): *Allegoria est alieniloquium. Aliud enim sonat, et alius intelligitur* ("Allegory is other-speech, because it says something literally and something else is understood").

Simul senex et puella
Rosa marcet oriens.
   Sic aetatis ver humane
Iuventutis primo mane
Reflorescit paululum.[14]

The world is to be interrogated as if every item with which it is furnished had been put there by God to instruct us in some way. As Hugh of Saint Victor will remark, the sensible world "quasi quidam liber est scriptus digiti Dei" ("is like a book written by the finger of God") (*De tribus diebus* VII, 4), and, according to Richard of Saint Victor, "habent tamen corporea omnia ad invisibilia bona similitudinem aliquam" ("and yet all corporal things bear some resemblance to the goods we cannot see") (*Benjamin major* II, 13).

The fact that the world is a book written by the finger of God is seen not so much as a cosmological notion as an exegetical necessity. In other words, this universal symbolism starts out primarily as scriptural allegorism and goes on to become what has been defined as "universal symbolism."

Commentators spoke of allegorical interpretations well before the birth of the patristic scriptural tradition: the Greeks interrogated Homer allegorically; in Stoic circles there arose an allegorist tradition which saw the classical epic as a mythical cloaking of natural truths; there existed an allegorical exegesis of the Jewish Torah, and in the first century Philo of Alexandria attempted an allegorical reading of the Old Testament.

In an attempt to counterbalance the Gnostic overemphasis on the New Testament, to the total detriment of the Old, Clement of Alexandria proposes viewing the two testaments as distinct and complementary, while Origen perfects this position by insisting on the necessity of a parallel reading. The Old Testament is the figure of the New, it is the letter of which the

---

14. "Every created thing in the world is like a book or a painting or a mirror to us. A faithful image of our life, of our death, of our state, of our fate. The rose depicts our state, and on our state provides a fitting commentary, a teaching for our lives. Though it blossoms in the early morning, it fades a petalless flower in the old age of evening. Thus the flower expires respiring, while it withers pale and wilting, dying as it is born. At once a dotard and a damsel, at once a maiden and an ancient, the rose is rotting as it rises. So the springtime of mankind blossoms briefly in the early morning of our youth."

other is the spirit, or, in semiotic terms, it is the expression of which the New is the content (or one of the possible contents). In its turn, the New Testament has a figural meaning, inasmuch as it is a promise of future things. With Origen the "theological discourse" is born, which is no longer—or no longer simply—a discourse on God, but on His Scripture.[15]

Origen already speaks of a literal sense, a moral (psychic) sense, and a mystical (pneumatic) sense. Hence the triad—*literal, tropological,* and *allegorical*—that will later become the foursome expressed in the famous distich of Augustine of Dacia (thirteenth century): "littera gesta docet—quid credas allegoria—moralis quid agas—quo tendas anagogia" ("the letter tells us what went down—the allegory what faith is sound—the moral how to act well—the anagogy where our course is bound").

From the beginning, Origen's hermeneutics, and that of the Fathers of the Church in general, tends to favor a kind of reading that has been defined as "typological": the characters and events of the Old Testament are seen, because of their actions or their characteristics, as types, anticipations, foreshadowings of the characters of the New. Some authors (such as Auerbach 1944, for example) attempt to discern something different from allegory, when Dante, instead of allegorizing openly—as he does, for instance, in the first canto of the *Inferno* or in the procession in the Earthly Paradise—brings onstage characters like Saint Bernard who, without ceasing to be living and individual figures (in addition to being authentic historical personages), become "types" of superior truths on account of certain of their concrete characteristics. Some would go so far as to speak, apropos of these examples, of "symbols." But in this case too, what we are probably dealing with is allegory: the vicissitudes, interpretable literally, of one character, become a figure for another (at best what we have is an allegory complicated by Vossian antonomasia, inasmuch as the characters embody certain of their outstanding characteristics).

However we describe this typology, it requires that what is figured (whether a type, a symbol, or an allegory) be an allegory not *in verbis* but *in factis.* It is not the words of Moses or the Psalmist, qua words, that are to be read as endowed with an secondary meaning, even though they appear to be

---

15. Cf. De Lubac 1959–64, Compagnon 1979, Bori 1987, and, on the twelfth century, Valente 1995.

metaphorical expressions: it is the very events of the Old Testament that have been prearranged by God, as if history were a book written with his hand, to act as a figure of the new dispensation.

A useful distinction between facts and words may be found in Bede's *De Schematibus et tropis,* but Augustine had already addressed this problem, and he was in a position to do so because he had been the first, on the basis of a profoundly assimilated Stoic culture, to create a theory of the sign. Augustine distinguishes between signs that are words, and things that may function as signs, since a sign is anything that brings to mind something else, over and above the impression the thing makes on our senses (*De Doctrina Christiana* II, 1, 1).[16] Not all things are signs, but all signs are certainly things, and, alongside the signs produced by man intentionally to signify, there are also things, events, and characters that can be assumed as signs or (as in the case of sacred history) can be supernaturally arranged as signs so as to be read as signs.

In this way Augustine teaches us to distinguish obscure and ambiguous signs from clear ones, and to resolve the question of whether a sign is to be interpreted in a literal or in a figurative sense. Tropes like metaphor or metonymy can be easily recognized because if they were taken literally the text would appear meaningless or childishly mendacious, but what about those expressions (usually involving a whole sentence or a narration, and not a simple term or image) that have an acceptable literal meaning and to which the interpreter is instead led to assign a figurative meaning (as is the case, for example, with allegories)? A metaphor tells us that Achilles is a lion, and from the literal point of view this is a lie, but an allegory tells us that a leopard, a she-wolf, and a lion are encountered in a dark wood, and the statement could perfectly well be taken at face value.

To get back to the author of the *Rhythmus alter,* more than a metaphor, what we have here is an allegory, indeed, it represents a set of instructions for decoding allegories. He does not say *life is a rose* (an expression that would be absurd if taken literally). Instead, he lists all the qualities that pertain to the rose, qualities which (while still remaining literally comprehensible) become or may become (if the proper interpretive tools are

---

16. On Augustine's semiotics, see Manetti 1987, chap. 10, and Vecchio 1994.

provided) an allegory of human life. In fact, before listing the properties of the rose, he informs us that it is a depiction of our state ("nostrum statum pingit rosa"), and goes on to furnish the necessary elements to make the parallel clear.

How do we understand that something that has an acceptable literal meaning is to be understood as an allegory? Augustine, discussing the hermeneutical rules proposed by Tyconius (*De doctrina christiana* III, 30, 42—37, 56), tells us that we must suspect a figurative sense whenever Scripture, even if what it says makes literal sense, appears to go against the truth of faith or decent customs. Mary Magdalene washes the feet of Christ with perfumed ointments and dries them with her own hair. Is it thinkable that the Redeemer would submit to such a lascivious pagan ritual? Obviously not. So the narrative must be a representation of something else.

But we must also suspect a secondary meaning whenever Scripture gets lost in *superfluitates* or brings into play expressions poor in literal content. These two considerations are amazingly subtle and modern, even if Augustine found them already suggested by other authors.[17]

We have *superfluitas* when the text spends an inordinate amount of time describing something that might have a literal sense, but without the *textually economical* reasons for this descriptive insistence being clear. We have semantically poor expressions when proper names, numbers, or technical terms show up, or insistent descriptions of flowers, natural prodigies, stones, vestments, or ceremonies—objects or events that are irrelevant from the spiritual point of view. In such cases, we must presume—since it is inconceivable that the sacred text might be indulging a taste for ornament—that *aliud dicitur et aliud significatur,* one thing is said and another is intended.

Where are we to look for the keys to decoding, since the text must after all be interpreted "correctly," that is, according to an approved code? When he

---

17. See, for instance, Jerome (*In Matt.* XXI.5) *cum historia vel impossibilitatem habeat vel turpitudinem, ad altiora transmittimur* ("When the story speaks of impossible things or turpitudes, we are being directed toward higher things"); or Origen (*De Principiis*, 4.2.9, and 4.3.4), according to whom the Holy Spirit interpolates into the text superfluous little details as a clue to its prophetic nature.

speaks about words, Augustine knows where to look for the rules—in classical grammar and rhetoric. But if Scripture speaks not only *in verbis* but *in factis* (*De doctrina christiana* II, 10, 15)—if there is, in other words, *allegoria historiae* in addition to *allegoria sermonis* (cf. *De vera religione* 50, 99)—then one must resort to one's knowledge of the world.[18]

Hence the resort to the encyclopedia, which traces an *imago mundi,* giving us the spiritual meaning of every worldly thing or event mentioned in Scripture. The Middle Ages inherited fascinating descriptions of the universe as a collection of marvelous facts from pagan culture: from Pliny to the *Polyhistor* of Solinus or the *Alexander Romance.* All they had to do was to moralize the encyclopedia, attributing a spiritual meaning to every object in the world. And so, following the model of the *Physiologus,* the Middle Ages began to compile its own encyclopedias, from the *Etymologiae* of Isidore of Seville to the *De rerum naturis* of Rabanus Maurus, to Honorius of Autun's *De imagine mundi* or Alexander Neckham's *De naturis rerum,* to the *De proprietatibus rerum* of Bartholomaeus Anglicus and the *Specula* of Vincent of Beauvais. The task was to provide, backed by the authority of tradition, the rules of correlation that would make it possible to assign a figural significance to any element in the physical world. And since authority has a nose of wax, and since every encyclopedist is a dwarf on the shoulders of the encyclopedists who went before him, they had no problem, not only in multiplying meanings, but in inventing new creatures and properties, that (on account of their curiouser and curiouser characteristics) would make the world into one immense speech act.

At this point what is dubbed indifferently "medieval symbolism" or "allegory" takes separate paths. Separate at least in our eyes, which are looking for a handy typology, though these modes in fact interpenetrate continuously, especially when we consider that poets too will soon start writing allegorically like Scripture (see below what we have to say about Dante).

We may distinguish, then, under the generic heading of symbolism (or the *aliud dicitur aliud demonstratur*), a series of different attitudes (Figure 3.1).

---

18. See too *Epistola* 102.33: *sicut humana consuetudo verbis, ita divina potentia etiam factis loquitur* ("Just as it is the custom of human beings to express themselves in words, so the divine power expresses itself in actions").

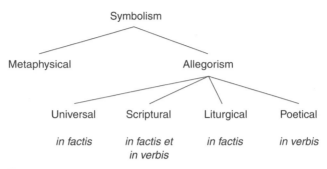

Figure 3.1

What we may call "metaphysical pansemiosis" does not interest us in the present context. This is the approach of Scotus Eriugena, for whom every element with which the world is furnished is a theophany that refers back to its first cause: "nihil enim visibilium rerum corporaliumque est, ut arbitror, quod non incorporale quid et intelligibile significet (De divisione naturae" ("there is nothing among visible and corporeal things that I can think of that does not signify something incorporeal and intelligent") (*De divisione naturae*, 5, 3). Like the Victorines, Eriugena does not speak simply of the allegorical or metaphorical resemblance between terrestrial bodies and celestial things, but in particular of their more "philosophical" significance, which has to do with the uninterrupted series of causes and effects known as the Great Chain of Being (cf. Lovejoy 1936).

Universal allegorism is that of the encyclopedias, bestiaries, and lapidaries: it represents a fabulous and hallucinatory way of looking at the universe, not for what it makes apparent but for what it might allude to: the difference, with regard to metaphysical pansemiosis, lies in the different philosophical awareness, in the metaphysical foundation, to be precise, of the ulterior meaning of sensible and corporeal things.[19]

We have already spoken of scriptural allegorism and will do so again shortly; and what liturgical allegorism might consist of is intuitive.

———

19. On the use of myths in twelfth-century philosophy (by William of Conches, Abelard, Hildegard of Bingen, and others), cf. Dronke 1974, who in his first chapter points to a series of keywords connected with symbolism (or allegorism), such as *aenigma, fabula, figura, imago, integumentum, involucrum, mysterium, similitudo, symbolum*, and *translatio*.

Poetic allegorism is that abundantly employed by secular poetry: Dante's dark wood, say, or the whole of the *Roman de la Rose*. It imitates the modes of scriptural allegorism, but the facts presented are fictitious. If anything, oriented as it is toward moral edification, it may at most aspire to a cognitive function. But it is precisely in the case of the allegory of poets that a nexus of interesting problems comes to the fore.

The Middle Ages abounds in allegorical readings of poetic texts (cf. De Bruyne 1946, I, 3, 8). Fables provide the first instance: naturally they speak of happenings that are patently false (talking animals and the like), though they do so with the intent of communicating a moral truth. If we read the various treatises that prescribe ways of correctly reading poetic texts (see, for instance, the *Dialogus super auctores* of Conrad of Hirsau), we will see that what they consist of are exercises in textual analysis. Faced with a poetic text, we must ask who is its author, what was the author's purpose and intention, the nature of the poem or the genre to which it belongs, and the order and number of the books before going on to examine the relationship between *littera, sensus,* and *sententia.* As Hugh of Saint Victor observes in his *Didascalicon,* the *littera* is the ordered disposition of the words, the *sensus* is the obvious and simple meaning of the phrase as it appears at first reading, and the *sententia* is a more profound form of understanding, which can only be arrived at through commentary and interpretation.[20]

All the authors insist on the primary need to examine the letter, expound the meaning of difficult words, justify the grammatical and syntactical forms, identify the figures and tropes. At this point one proceeds to interpret the

---

20. "Expositio tria continet, litteram, sensum, sententiam. Littera est congrua ordinatio dictionum, quod etiam constructionem vocamus. Sensus est facilis quaedam et aperta significatio, quam littera prima fronte praefert. Sententia est profundior intelligentia, quae nisi expositione vel interpretatione non invenitur. In his ordo est, ut primum littera, deinde sensus, deinde sententia inquiratur. Quo facto, perfecta est expositio" ("Exposition involves three things: the letter, the sense and the inner meaning. The letter is the congruous arrangement of words, which we also call construction. The sense is a certain plain and straightforward meaning that the letter presents on the surface. The inner meaning (*sententia*) is the deeper understanding that can be discovered only through interpretation and commentary. Among these the order is: first the letter, then the sense and lastly the inner meaning. And when this is done, the exposition is complete") (III, 8).

meaning intended by the author, as this is suggested by the letter of the text. Then, to the hidden meaning, according to the formula *aliud dicitur et aliud demonstratur*. Now, it would appear that opinions differ concerning the distinction between *sensus* and *sententia*. For some interpreters analyzing a fable by Aesop or Avianus, the *sententia* would be the moral truth contained in the fable, according to which, in the fable of the wolf and the lamb, wolves are evil and lambs are good. But is this meaning, which the author makes so explicit beneath the *integumentum* or covering of the parable, the *sensus* or the *sententia*? For some interpreters, fables have a *parabolic* meaning, offered immediately to the reader, while the *sententia* would be a more deeply hidden allegorical truth, similar to that of the Scriptures (cf. De Bruyne 1946: 2:326–327).

We have only to read Comparetti's *Vergil in the Middle Ages* (1885) to see what sources the invitation to the Middle Ages to read the Roman poet allegorically came from. Medieval scholars may have been familiar with a commentary on Homer by Donatus that has since disappeared; they certainly knew Servius's commentary and Macrobius's observations on Virgil. Virgil was considered not only the greatest of poets (Homer was merely a legend, and his actual texts were unknown) but also the wisest of men. Accordingly, Bernard of Chartres, John of Salisbury, or Bernardus Sylvestris, among others, read the first six books of the *Aeneid* as a representation of the six ages of life. But what difference is there between this search for the epic's allegorical *sententia* and the discovery of the parabolic meaning of a fable? The parabolic meaning seems to depend closely on the literal meaning, at a less subtle level than that of the allegorical *sententia*.

Ulrich of Strasbourg (*De summo bono* I, 2, 9; cf. De Bruyne 1946: 2:314) says that fables, though they evidently say false things, can be taken as true, since the thing meant is not that conveyed by the words but by the sense that those words express. Alexander of Hales suggested adding to the four senses of Scripture (historical, allegorical, moral, and anagogical) the parabolic sense, which he reduced to the historical, distinguishing, however, within the historical sense, the sense *secundum rem,* in other words, the literal sense of the facts narrated, and that *secundum similitudinem,* as occurs in parables.[21]

---

21. "De parabolico intellectu dicendum quod reducitur ad historicum. Sed historia dicitur dupliciter secundum rem et secundum rei similitudinem. Secundum rem, sicut in rebus gestis: secundum similitudinem sicut in parabolis. Parabola enim est

De Bruyne (1946: 2:312–313) attempts to systematize these differences between the various senses in the following way: the literal sense may be *proper* (or historical, in which an account is given of the actual events), *figurative* (typical, in the sense in which the individual represents the universal), *parabolic* and moral (in the secular sense, as in fables), or *allegorical* (or typical-figural, *in factis*); the spiritual sense, on the other hand, may be *tropical* (or moral) or *anagogical*.

At this point, we should underscore a difference between the metaphorical sense (in which the letter appears to be mendacious, unless we understand it to be figurative) and the moral sense of the fable, which could be ignored without the fable ceasing to signify things that are understandable, though considered false. But perhaps to the medieval mind it seemed equally false that a meadow could smile or that an animal could talk, only, in the first case, the falsity was *in adjecto* and, in the second, in the course of the events narrated. On the other hand, in these instructions for reading texts, the importance of identifying the metaphors is stated, but it does not seem that particular hermeneutical efforts are to be brought into play, whereas if one reads Aesop one must make an interpretive effort, however minimal, to understand the moral truth the author wished to express. The fact is we are faced with three different senses: (i) the sense of the metaphors, which, as we have seen, never poses a problem; (ii) the parabolic sense of the fables, in which we must indubitably attribute to the author a moralizing intent, if we are not to remain attached to the mendacious letter—and yet this moral sense is not obscure but evident; and (iii) the sense of the allegory, which allows us to know *per speculum et in aenigmate*.

To make things still more complicated, we find in doctrinal circles impatience with the allegorical interpretation of secular poetry, and John of Salisbury, for instance, will say that, since humane letters must not draw a

---

similitudo rerum, cum per rerum differentem similitudinem ad id, qod per ipsam intelligitur, pervenitur" ("As for the meaning of parables it must be said that it can be reduced to the historical narrative. But the narrative is defined in two ways, with respect to the thing itself and with respect to the likeness of the thing. With respect to the thing, as in what actually happened; with respect to the likeness of a thing, as in the parables. In fact the parable is a relation of likeness among things, when, through the different resemblances among things, we arrive at the knowledge of what it is intended to convey") (*Summa, Tractatus Introductorius* I, 4 ad 2).

veil over sacred mysteries, it is ridiculous, harmful, and useless to look for anything beyond the literal sense (*Polycraticus* VII, 12).[22]

This knot will be loosed, in exemplary but—to our way of thinking—astonishing fashion, by Thomas Aquinas.

3.4. Metaphor in Thomas Aquinas

Thomas (*Summa Theologiae* I, 1, 9) asks if the use of poetic metaphors in the Bible is permissible, and he seems to come to a negative conclusion, when he quotes the current opinion by which poetry is an *infima doctrina* or inferior teaching. And he seems to share this opinion when he says that "poetica non capiuntur a ratione humana propter defectus veritatis qui est in eis" ("human reason fails to grasp the import of poetical utterance on account of its deficiency in truth") (*Summa Theologiae* II–II, 101. 2 ad 2). However, this affirmation should not be taken as a putdown of poetry or as a definition of the poetic in eighteenth-century terms as *perceptio confusa*. Instead, it is about recognizing poetry's status as an *art* (and therefore of *recta ratio fact-*

---

22. "Divinae paginae libros, quorum singuli apices divinis pleni sunt sacramentis, tanta gravitate legendos forte concesserim, eo quod thesaurus Spiritus sancti, cujus digito scripti sunt, omnino nequeat exhauriri. Licet enim ad unum tantummodo sensum accommodata sit superficies litterae, multiplicitas mysteriorum intrinsecus latet. Et ab eadem re saepe allegoria fidem, tropologia mores variis modis aedificat. Anagoge quoque multipliciter sursum ducit, ut litteram non modo verbis, sed rebus ipsis instituat. At in liberalibus disciplinis, ubi non res, sed duntaxat verba significant, quisquis pro sensu litterae contentus non est, aberrare mihi videtur, aut ab intelligentia veritatis, quo diutius teneantur, se velle suos abducere auditores, Polycraticus VIII, 12. *Quod aliter legendi sunt libri divini, aliter gentilium libri*" ("I would perhaps concede that the Holy Scriptures, whose every tittle is filled with holy signs, should be read with such solemnity for the reason that the treasure of the Holy Ghost by whose hand they have been written cannot be entirely plumbed. For although on the face of it the written word lends itself to one meaning only, manifold mysteries lie hidden within, and from the same source allegory often edifies faith and character in various ways. Mystical interpretation leads upward in manifold ways, so that it provides the letter not only with words but with reality itself. But in liberal studies where not things but words merely have meaning, he who is not content with with the first meaning of the letter seems to me to lose himself, or to be desirous of leading his auditors away from an understanding of truth that they may be held by him for a longer period") (Pike 1938, p. 264).

ibilium or right judgment regarding things to be made), in which *making* is naturally inferior to the pure *knowing* of philosophy and theology.

Thomas had learned from Aristotle's *Metaphysics* that the efforts at story-telling of the earliest poet theologians represented a childlike form of ratio-nal knowledge of the world. In fact, like all Scholastics, he is uninterested in a doctrine of poetry (a subject for the authors of rhetorical treatises who taught in the Faculty of Arts and not in the Faculty of Theology). Thomas was a poet in his own right (and an excellent one at that), but in the pas-sages in which he compares poetic knowledge with theological knowledge, he conforms to a canonical opposition and refers to the world of poetry merely as an unexamined alternative. He is impervious to the idea that poets can express universal truths, because he has not read Aristotle on the subject, and he therefore sticks to the received wisdom that poets recount *fabulae fictae.* On the other hand, he admits that the divine mysteries, which go beyond our ability to understand, must be revealed in allegorical form: "conveniens est sacrae scripturae divina et spiritualia sub similitu-dine corporalium tradere" ("Holy Scripture fittingly delivers divine and spiritual realities under bodily guises") (*Summa Theologiae* I, q. 1, a. 9 co.). As for the reading of the sacred text, he specifies that it is based first and foremost on the literal and historical sense: when Scripture says that the Hebrews went out of the land of Egypt, it relates a fact; this fact is compre-hensible and constitutes the immediate denotation of the narrative dis-course. But the *res,* the things of which the sacred text supplies the record, were arranged by God as signs. The spiritual sense, then, is that meaning by means of which the things signified by the language refer to other things, and it is based accordingly on the literal sense. Thus, God disposes the same course of events, subject to his divine providence, to endow them with a spiritual meaning.[23]

---

23. "Illa vero significatio qua res significatae per voces, iterum res alias signifi-cant, dicitur sensus spiritualis, qui super litteralem fundatur, et eum supponit" ("The meaning, however, whereby the things signified by the words in their turn also signify other things is called the spiritual sense: it is based on and presup-poses the literal sense") (Gilby 2006: 37–39). "Deus adhibet ad significationem ali-quorum ipsum cursum rerum suae providentiae subjectarum" ("God uses the very course of the things subject to his providence to signify certain other things") (*Quodlibet* VII. q. 6 a.3 co).

What we have here is not a rhetorical procedure, as would be the case with tropes or allegories *in verbis;* instead what we have are pure allegories *in factis,* in which it is the things themselves that act as signifiers of higher truths.[24]

Up until this point Thomas would not have been saying anything new. But in his allusions to the literal sense he emphasizes a rather important notion, namely that the literal sense is *quem auctor intendit.* Thomas does not speak of a literal sense as the sense of the sentence (what the sentence says denotatively according to the linguistic code to which it refers), but rather as the sense attributed to the act of enunciation! Accordingly—we are interpreting Thomas's words—if the sentence says that teeth are *made of snow,* we are not to understand that, grammatically speaking, the sentence expresses a mendacious proposition. The speaker's intention, in using that metaphor, was to say that the teeth were white (*like* snow) and therefore the metaphorical construction is part of the literal sense, because it is part of the content that the speaker intended to say. In *Super epistulam ad Galatas* too, Thomas reminds us that both *homo ridet* and *pratum ridet* (figurative sense) are part of the literal sense (VII, 254). In *III Sent.* he says that in scriptural metaphors there is no falsehood (38, 1, ad 4).[25]

In short, Thomas is prepared to speak of a secondary or spiritual meaning only when senses can be identified in a text that the author *did not intend to communicate, and did not know were being communicated.* And this is the case for an author (like the author of the Bible) who narrates facts without knowing that they have been prearranged by God as signs of something else.

While we may speak, then, of a secondary sense of Scripture, things change when we move on to secular poetry or any other human discourse that does

---

24. "Sensus spiritualis . . . accipitur vel consistit in hoc quod quaedam res et figuram aliarum rerum exprimuntur" ("The spiritual sernse can be grasped or consists of this: that certain things are expressed in a figurative way through other things") (*Quodl.* VII. q. 6. A. 2 co.; see also *I Sent.* 3.3 ad 2).

25. "Quia in figurativis locutionibus non est sensus verborum quem primo aspecto faciunt, sed quem proferens sub tali modo loquendi favere intendit, sicut qui dicit quod partum ridet, sub quadem rei similitudine intendit significare prati floritionem" ("Because figurative locutions do not have the meaning they seem to have at first sight, but the meaning the person speaking in that way intends to give them: such as when someone says, The meadow smiles, intending to express the flowering of the meadow using a similitude") (Cf. Dahan 1992).

not concern sacred history. In fact at this point Thomas makes an important affirmation, which in a nutshell is this: allegory *in factis* is valid only for sacred history, not for profane history. God, so to speak, has limited his role as manipulator of events to sacred history alone, but we must not look for any mystic meaning after the Redemption—profane history is a history of facts not of signs: "unde in nulla scientia, humana industria inventa, proprie loquendo, potest inveniri nisi litteralis sensus" ("hence in no science discovered by human industry can we find, strictly speaking, anything beside a literal sense") (*Quaestiones quodlibetales* VII q. 6 a. 3 co.).

On the one hand this move—inspired by the new Aristotelian naturalism— calls into question universal allegorism, with its bestiaries, lapidaries, encyclopedias, the mystical symbolism of the *Rhythmus alter,* and the vision of a universe populated by entities at a high symbolic temperature. And naturally it sounds like an out-and-out repudiation of allegorical readings of the pagan poets. On the other hand, it tells us that when, in secular poetry, a rhetorical figure occurs (including metaphor) there is no spiritual sense, only a *sensus parabolicus,* which *is part of the literal sense.*[26]

When, then, in the Scriptures Christ is designated through the figure of a goat (a scapegoat) what we have is not *allegoria in factis,* but a simple poetic procedure: *allegoria in verbis.* The poetic expression is not a symbol or an allegory of divine or future things, it simply signifies—parabolically and therefore *literally*—Christ (*Quaestiones quodlibetales* VII, 6, 15).[27]

There is no spiritual meaning in poetic discourse or even in Scripture when they use rhetorical figures, because that is the meaning the author intended, and the reader easily identifies it as literal on the basis of rhetorical rules. But this does not mean that the literal level (as the parabolic and therefore rhetorical sense) cannot have more than one meaning. Which means in other words, though Thomas does not say as much *apertis verbis* (because

---

26. "Fictiones poeticae non sunt ad aliud ordinatae nisi ad significandum" ("Poetic fictions have no other objective but to signify") and their meaning "non supergreditur modum litteralis sensus" ("Does not go beyond the mode of the literal sense") (*Quodl.* VII.6.16, ob. 1 and ad 1).

27. "Nam per voces significatur aliquid proprie et aliquid figurative, nec est letteralis sensus ipsa figura, sed id quod est figuratum" ("For words can signify something properly and something figuratively; in the latter case the literal sense is not the figure of speech itself, but the object it figures") (*S. Th.* Ia q.1. a. 10 ad 3).

the problem does not interest him), that there may be more than one level of meaning in secular poetry. Except that those different levels of meaning, couched in the parabolic mode, belong to the literal sense of the sentence as understood by its enunciator. To the extent that, since the author of the Scriptures is God, and God can understand and intend many things at the same time, it is possible that in the Scriptures there are *plures sensus* or several meanings, even according to the merely literal sense.

Likewise, we may speak of a simple literal meaning for liturgical allegory too, which employs not merely words but also gestures, colors, and images, since in that case the administrator of the rite intends to say something precise by means of a parable and we must not look, in the words that he formulates or prescribes, for a secret unintended meaning. Though the ceremonial precept, as it appeared in the old law, may have had a spiritual sense, when it was introduced into Christian liturgy it assumed a significance that was purely and simply parabolic.

Thomas reorganizes a series of scattered notions and implicit convictions that explain why the Middle Ages paid so little attention to the analysis of metaphor. If what the author intended to say literally must be clearly understood through the trope, any attempt to create bold and unexpected metaphors would compromise their natural literalness. Medieval theory would not have been able to accept as a good metaphor or simile Montale's bold comparison between life (and its travails and frustrations) and walking along a wall that has fragments of broken glass cemented on top of it, because the similarity had not been codified.[28]

3.5. Dante

Dante does not appear to pay the slightest attention to Thomas's strictures (cf. Eco 1985). In *Epistola XIII*, explaining to Cangrande della Scala the keys

---

28. [*Translator's note:* The allusion is to the poem *Meriggiare pallido e assorto*, from twentieth-century poet Eugenio Montale's first collection of verse *Ossi di seppia* (1927), which concludes: "E andando nel sole che abbaglia / sentire con triste meraviglia / com'è tutta la vita e il suo travaglio / in questo seguitare una muraglia / che ha in cima cocci aguzzi di bottiglia" ("And walking in the blinding sun / to feel with sad surprise / how the whole of life and its labor / is in this following a high wall / topped with sharp shards of bottle glass").]

for reading his poem, he says that the work is *polysemos,* that it has several senses, and he lists the four canonical levels—literal, allegorical, moral, and anagogical.[29]

To clarify what he means he gives a biblical example, citing Psalm 114: "In exitu Israel de Egipto, domus Jacob de populo barbaro, facta est Judea sanctificatio eius, Israel potestas eius" ("When Israel went out of Egypt, the house of Jacob from a people of strange language; Judah was his sanctuary and Israel his dominion").

Dante reminds us that according to the letter the meaning is that the children of Israel went out of the land of Egypt at the time of Moses; according to the allegory the meaning is that we are redeemed by Christ; according to the moral sense that the soul goes from the darkness and sorrow of sin to a state of grace; and according to the anagogical sense the Psalmist says that the blessed soul emerges from the slavery of earthly corruption into the freedom of eternal glory.

The controversy surrounding this *Epistola* is well known, whether, that is, it is the work of Dante or not, but as far as our problem is concerned, the discussion is irrelevant: even if the *Epistola* had not been written by Dante it would nonetheless reflect a medieval idea that deserves our attention.

On the other hand, in the *Convivio* Dante positions himself no differently. It is true that the second treatise, which concerns allegory, recognizes that "the theologians take this sense differently from the poets," but immediately afterward the author affirms that it is his intention to interpret the allegorical mode in the sense of the poets. And the sense of the poets is that

---

29. "Ad evidentiam itaque dicendorum sciendum est quod istius operis non est simplex sensus, ymo dici potest polisemos, hoc est plurium sensuum; nam primus sensus est qui habetur per litteram, alius est qui habetur per significata per litteram. Et primus dicitur litteralis, secundus vero allegoricus sive moralis sive anagogicus" ("For the elucidation, therefore, of what we have to say, it must be understood that the meaning of this work is not of one kind only: rather the work may be descibed as 'polysemous,' that is, having several meanings; for the first meaning is that which is conveyed by the letter, and the next is that which is conveyed by what the letter signifies; the former of which is called literal, while the latter is called allegorical or moral or anagogical") (*Epistole,* XIII, 7). Dante Alighieri, *Epistole,* a cura di Arsenio Frugoni e Giorgio Brugnoli, in *Opere minori,* tomo II, Milano-Napoli, Riccardo Ricciardi Editore, 1979, p. 611).

by which allegory transmits, under the "cloak" of fable, "a truth hidden under a beautiful fiction. Thus Ovid says that Orpheus with his lyre made beasts tame, and trees and stones move towards himself; that is to say that the wise man by the instrument of his voice makes cruel hearts grow mild and humble, and those who have not the life of science and art move to his will" (Dante 1909: 73).

This would appear to be another expression of deference to the parabolic sense, such as we found in the case of the fables. But now let us see what Dante does, for instance, with the poem "Voi che 'ntendendo il terzo ciel movete") ("You who with your understanding move the third heaven"). He devotes chapters II–IX to explaining how it speaks *literally* of the angels and the heavens, with ample astronomical clarifications, and he devotes the following chapters to the allegorical explanation: "I say that by heaven I mean science and by heavens the sciences, because of three similarities the heavens have chiefly with the sciences. . . . For each moving heaven moves around its center, which, as to its movement, does not move, and so each science moves around its subject," and so on, taking care in addition to remind us how the Gentle Lady of the *Vita nuova* represented Philosophy. And this is the allegorical sense, fairly well hidden, like that of Scripture.

In the *Convivio,* however, both the literal sense and the allegorical sense are presented as *intended* by the author, and we are basically still talking about an allegory *in verbis.* In *Epistola XIII,* on the other hand, something further is suggested.

Prima facie, as an example of an allegorical reading the author interprets facts narrated by the Bible. It could be objected (see Pépin 1970: 81) that here Dante is citing not the *fact* of the Exodus but the *words* of the Psalmist who speaks of the Exodus—a difference Augustine was already conscious of (*Enarrationes in psalmos* CXIII). But a few lines before citing the psalm, Dante speaks of his own poem, and he uses an expression that some translations, more or less unconsciously, attenuate. For example, the Italian translation of the Latin *Epistola* by Frugoni and Brugnoli, in the Ricciardi edition of Dante's minor works, makes Dante say "the first meaning is the one we have from the letter of the text, the other is the one we have from what was meant to be signified by the letter of the text" ("il primo significato è quello che si ha dalla lettera del testo, l'altro è quello che si ha da quel che si volle significare con la lettera del testo") (*Epistole XIII,* 7, 20). If this were the case, Dante would still be talking about a parabolic meaning, intended by the author. But the Latin text says: "primus sensus est qui habetur per litteram, alius est qui habetur per significata per litteram," and here it seems that Dante means to speak of the things "that are signified by the letter" and therefore of an allegory *in factis*, and there is nothing in the Latin to justify that "was meant to be signified" ("che si volle significare") which appears in the Italian version. If he had wished to speak of the intended sense, Dante would not have used the neuter plural *significata* but some other expression such as *sententiam.*

How can we talk about an allegory *in factis* apropos of events narrated in the context of a secular poem, whose mode, Dante tells us in the course of the letter, is "poeticus" and "fictivus"?

There are two possible answers. If we assume that Dante was an orthodox Thomist, then we can only conclude that the *Epistola,* which clearly runs counter to Thomist principles, must not be authentic. In that case, however, it would be odd that all of Dante's early commentators (Boccaccio, Benvenuto da Imola, Francesco da Buti, and so on) have followed the path indicated by the epistle. But the most economical hypothesis is that Dante, at least as far as his definition of poetry went, did not follow Thomas's opinion.

Dante believes that poetry has philosophical dignity, not only his own poetry but that of all the great poets, and he does not accept the dismissal of the poet-theologians decreed by Aristotle in his *Metaphysics* (and commented upon approvingly by Saint Thomas). Sixth among so much wisdom (along with Homer, Virgil, Horace, Ovid, and Lucan—as he remarks in *Inferno,* IV, 48), he never ceased to read *both* the facts of mythology *and* the other works of the classical poets as if they were allegories *in factis,* a practice that, despite Thomas's *caveat,* was cultivated in Bologna in the period during which Dante resided there (cf. Renucci 1958). These are the terms in which he speaks of poets in the *De vulgari eloquentia* (I, 2, 7), in the *Convivio,* and in many other places, and in the *Divine Comedy* he has Statius openly affirm that Virgil taught those who came after him "like someone who goes at night and carries his lamp behind him and does not help himself" (*Purgatorio* XXII, 67–69): the poetry of the pagan poet conveys additional meanings of which the author is unaware. And in his *Epistola VII* Dante offers an allegorical interpretation of a passage from Ovid's *Metamorphoses,* seen as a prefigurement of the destiny of Florence.

For Dante, then, the poet continues Holy Scripture after his own fashion, just as in the past he had confirmed or even anticipated it. He believes in the reality of the myth he has produced as he tends to believe in the allegorical truth of the classical myths that he cites, along with historical personages assumed as *figurae* of the future, even mythological personages like Orpheus. And Cato of Utica himself will be judged worthy of signifying, along with Moses, Christ's sacrifice (*Purgatorio* I, 70–75), even God himself (*Convivio* IV, 18, 15).

If this is the poet's task, to figure by means of a poetic lie facts and events that function as signs, in imitation of the signs of the Bible, then we can understand why Dante would propound to Cangrande della Scala what has been defined by Curtius as his "self-exegesis" and by Pépin as his "self-allegoresis." It is plausible that Dante thought of the secondary meaning of his poem as being close to the secondary meaning of the Bible, in the sense that at times the poet himself, when inspired, is not aware of all he is saying. For this reason he invokes divine inspiration (addressing Apollo) in the first canto of *Paradiso*. And if the poet is someone who "when Love inspires him notes, and in the same way as Love dictates within goes signifying" (*Purgatorio* XXII, 52–54), in order to interpret what he is not always aware that he has said, we may then use the same procedures reserved by Thomas for sacred history. If a poetic text were entirely literal-parabolic, it is not easy to see why the poet would clutter up various passages with enunciatory instances in which he invites the reader to decipher what is hidden "beneath the veil of the strange verses" (see, for example, *Inferno* IX, 61–63).

That said, we are bound to admit that, as far as his manner of interpreting metaphors goes, Dante does not break with the ideas of his time and in particular with those of Thomas. Let us take the *Vita nuova,* and confine ourselves to examining how Dante explains the sonnet "Tanto gentile e tanto onesta pare." The poem contains a number of metaphorical expressions, such as "benignamente d'umiltà vestuta," "dolcezza al core," not to mention the invitation, addressed to the soul, to sigh *(sospirare)*. Well, Dante makes it immediately clear that "this sonnet is so easy to understand . . . that it has no need of any division." And the same is true for the other compositions he comments on: he clarifies the general philosophical meaning, but it does not occur to him to explain the metaphors. If we turn to the *Convivio,* we find something very similar. Indeed, it is curious that, in explaining "Amor che ne la mente mi ragiona" (and I would argue that the verb "ragiona" ["reasons, speaks"] is already a first metaphorical expression, to say nothing of the fourth verse, in which the intellect "disvia" ["goes off track"]), not only does Dante fail to explain his metaphors, but, in order to explain the profound meaning of his poem, he employs liberal quantities of additional metaphors as if they were readily comprehensible: "Lo quale amore poi, trovando la mia disposta vita al suo ardore, a guisa di fuoco, di picciolo in grande fiamma s'accese; sì che non solamente vegghiando, ma dormendo, lume di costei nella mia testa era guidato" ("Finding my life disposed toward ardor, this love later blazed up like a fire, from a small to a great flame, so that not only while I was awake but also during my sleep the light of her penetrated my mind"), going on to speak of the "abitaculo del mio amore" ("the dwelling of my love"), its "multiplicato incendio" ("spreading fire"), and so on. Similarly, apropos of "Voi che 'ntendendo," whereas the *canzone* itself, philosophical in its content, does not contain many metaphors, in his commentary the author piles on metaphors intended to explain the text but which he makes no effort to explain, such as "trapassamento," "vedovata vita," "disposarsi a quella immagine," "molta battaglia intra lo pensiero," "rocca della mia mente," and so on. For Dante too, then, metaphors are *completely* part of the literal (intended) meaning and do not require any effort of interpretation.

We have only to observe what happens when in *Epistola XIII* to Cangrande della Scala he explains how the poet has attempted to render the ineffability of the divine vision. Dante obviously cites Pseudo-Dionysius, and, even if he had not done so, we would have known perfectly well where the theme of the unutterability of God came from. He further warns us that "multa namque per intellectum videmus quibus signa vocalia desunt: quod satis Plato insinuat in suis libris per assumptionem metaphorismorum" ("in fact with the aid of our intellect we see many things for which we lack verbal expressions: which is sufficiently demonstrated by Plato in his works when he makes use of metaphors") (*Epistola XIII*, 29). And, even using a very conservative definition of whether an expression is used metaphorically, in *Paradiso* 33, 55–145, we can identify seventy-seven metaphors and similes— some of which are among the most striking in the poem. But throughout the *Epistola*, it does not even occur to Dante, who seems determined to explain everything, and brings in philosophy and theology to elucidate what it was he wanted to say, to comment upon these metaphors. When he cites the opening lines of the *Paradiso,* "The glory of him who moves all things / penetrates and shines throughout the universe," he confines himself to saying that what he says is "bene dictum," explaining that the glory of God "penetrat, quantum ad essentiam; resplendet, quantum ad esse" ("it penetrates as to its essence, it shines as to its being") *Epistola XIII,* 23). He says, in other words, what philosophical purposes these two metaphors are used for, but he feels no need to say in what way glory (in any case already a metaphorical expression) can be said to *penetrate* and *shine.*

3.6. The Symbolic Theology of Pseudo-Dionysius

At this point it remains to be seen whether metaphor, having forfeited its cognitive function in poetry and in the text of Scripture, could still assume a revelatory function in a theory of divine names—where the challenge is to name someone whom no literal expression can give a proper account of.

In the wake of Neo-Platonism, in the sixth century the idea of the One as unfathomable and contradictory enters the Christian world, through the agency of Pseudo-Dionysius the Areopagite (hereinafter "Dionysius"). In his works the Divinity is named negatively as something that is

> the Cause of all [and] is above all and is not inexistent, lifeless, speechless, mindless. It is not a material body, and hence has neither shape nor form, quality, quantity, or weight. It is not in any place and can neither be seen nor be touched. It is neither perceived nor is it perceptible. It suffers neither disorder nor disturbance and is overwhelmed by no earthly passion. It is not powerless and subject to the disturbances caused by sense perception. It passes through no change, decay, division, loss, no ebb and flow, nothing of which the senses may be aware. None of all this can be either identified with it nor attributed to it. . . .
>
> . . . It is not soul, or mind, nor does it possess imagination, conviction, speech, or understanding. Nor is it speech per se, understanding per se. It cannot be spoken of and it cannot be grasped by understanding. It is not number or order, greatness or smallness, equality or inequality, similarity or dissimilarity. It is not immovable, moving or at rest. It has no power, it is not power, nor is it light. It does not live, nor is it life. It is not a substance, nor is it eternity or time. It cannot be

grasped by the understanding since it is neither knowledge nor truth. It is not kingship. It is not wisdom. It is neither one nor oneness, divinity nor goodness. Nor is it a spirit, in the sense in which we understand that term. (*The Mystical Theology*, trans. Luibheid, pp. 140–141)[30]

And so on in this vein for page after page of dazzling mystical aphasia.

How then can we speak of divine names? How can we do this if the Transcendent surpasses all discourse and all knowledge, if it abides beyond the reach of mind and of being, if it encompasses and circumscribes, embraces and anticipates all things, while itself eluding their grasp and escaping from any perception, imagination, opinion, name, discourse, apprehension, or understanding? (*The Divine Names,* trans. Luibheid, p. 53).

Not knowing what else to name it, Dionysius calls the divinity "the brilliant darkness of a hidden silence" and "the ray of the divine shadow which is above everything that is" (p. 135). At first blush, these appear to be oxymorons, expressing a contradiction, and therefore the impossibility of an unambiguous definition; they are nonetheless oxymorons based upon metaphors.

Dionysius, however, continues to insist that no metaphor or symbol can express the divine nature. But in so doing he swings back and forth between a kind of mystagogic attitude (under the influence of various non-Christian sources) and a symbolic theology, designed to help even the simple-minded comprehend the nature of God.

From the mystagogic point of view God is ineffable, and the only way to speak adequately of him is to be silent: as we ascend from lower to higher things "we shall find ourselves not simply running short of words but actually speechless and unknowing," (*The Mystical Theology*, trans. Luibheid, p. 139). When someone speaks, it is to hide the divine mysteries from those who cannot penetrate them: "it is most fitting to the mysterious passages of scripture

---

30. This and subsequent quotations from the works of Pseudo-Dionysius are from Pseudo-Dionysius 1987. On this sixth-century Greek author, sometimes referred to as Denys or Dennis, and erroneously believed to have been the magistrate of the Athenian Areopagus converted by Saint Paul (Acts, 17, 34), see Rorem 1993.

that the sacred and hidden truth about the celestial intelligences be concealed through the inexpressible and the sacred and be inaccessible to the *hoi polloi*. Not everyone is sacred, and, as scripture says, knowledge is not for everyone" (*The Celestial Hierarchy*, trans. Luibheid, p. 149). Symbolic discourses regarding God are "the protective garb of the understanding of what is ineffable and invisible to the common multitude" (*Letter Nine*, trans. Luibheid, p. 283).

This mystagogic attitude is continually contradicted by the opposite attitude, the theophanic conviction (and it is this mode that will fascinate Eriugena) that, since God is the cause of all things, he is rightly nameless and yet all names are fitting, in the sense that every effect points back to its Cause (*The Divine Names*, trans. Luibheid, p. 56). In this way the form and figure of a man are attributed to God, or that of fire or amber, his ears are praised and his eyes and his hair, his countenance, his hands, his shoulders, his wings, his arms, his back, and his feet "They have placed around it such things as crowns, chairs, cups, mixing bowls and similar mysterious items" (*The Divine Names*, trans. Luibheid, pp. 56–57).

The symbolic theology that attempts to make the nature of God comprehensible through similes or "aistheta symbola" ("perceptible symbols") (*Letter Nine*, trans. Luibheid, p. 281) swings between these two extremes. Still, it must be clear that these symbolic references are always inadequate. Hence the need for these representations to display their feebly hyperbolic nature (if I too may be permitted an oxymoron):

Furthermore, I doubt that anyone would refuse to acknowledge that incongruities are more suitable for lifting our minds up into the domain of the spiritual than similarities are. High-flown shapes could well mislead someone into thinking that the heavenly beings are golden or gleaming men, glamorous, wearing lustrous clothing, giving off flames which cause no harm, or that they have other similar beauties with which the word of God has fashioned the heavenly minds. It was to avoid this kind of misunderstanding among those incapable of rising above visible beauty that the pious theologians so wisely and upliftingly stooped to incongruous dissimilarities, for by doing this they took account of our inherent tendency toward the material and our willingness to be lazily satisfied by base images. At the same time they enabled that part of the soul which longs for the things above actually to rise up. Indeed the sheer crassness of the signs is a goad so that even the materially inclined cannot accept that it could be permitted or true that the celestial and divine sights could be conveyed by such shameful things. (*The Celestial Hierarchy*, trans. Luibheid, p. 150)

At the very end of this citation Dionysius continues with an apparent contradiction: he observes that "there is nothing which lacks its own share of beauty" (ibid., p. 150), given that Scripture states that God saw everything He had made, "and behold, it was very good" (Gen. 1:31). But what we have here is a bow in the direction of that pancalistic sensibility that will pervade the entire Middle Ages. The problem is rather that at this point Dionysius introduces the idea, which will return with some frequency throughout his corpus, of naming through *dissimilar similarity* or *inappropriate dissimilarity* (see, for example, chapter 2 of *The Celestial Hierarchy*, trans. Luibheid, p. 138), whereby the divinity is sometimes given a lowly name: "Sometimes the images are of the lowliest kind, such as sweet-smelling ointment and corner stone, Sometimes the imagery is even derived from animals so that God is described as a lion or a panther, a leopard or a charging bear. Add to this what seems the lowliest and most incongruous of all, for the experts in things divine gave him the form of a worm" (*The Celestial Hierarchy*, trans. Luibheid, p. 152).[31]

Concerning this point, it has frequently been understood that for Dionysius the name that best expresses the inexpressibility of the divine nature is based on an inverse analogy, according to which what is emphasized are not the similar but the opposed properties. Some occultist interpretations of these passages speak of an image of God reflected as it were on the surface of the terrestrial sea in inverted symmetry (and this would be the sense in the famous passage from Paul's First Epistle to the Corinthians 13:12, where he says that we see now "through a glass darkly"). If this were indeed the case we might expect a theory of inverse analogy, which would go a long way toward confirming the idea of a symbolic naming that obscures in order to spur the intelligence to seek further—and we would therefore be quite close to the idea of metaphor as cognitive process. And this could be tied in with

---

31. To be precise it is the psalmist who says he is a worm in Psalm 22, 6, though it is possible that an allegorical interpretation might see the psalmist as a prefiguration of Christ.

a strong suggestion from Aristotle (see *Rhetoric* 1405a): "since opposites are in the same class, you do what I have suggested if you say that a man who begs 'prays,' and a man who prays 'begs'; for praying and begging are both varieties of asking." And it would be quite a challenge to require a semiotics of metaphor to account for a process by which two things are substituted for each other based, not on the properties they have in common, but on the maximum tension between opposite properties (like calling the sea solid, God malevolent, the gaze of the Medusa benevolent, and so on). To tell the truth, none of the examples given by Dionysius constitutes a case of dissimilar similarity (in the above sense), but at most of audacious similarity, linking the divine and the human on the basis of "unseemly" resemblances, but resemblances nonetheless.

The most extreme case of dissimilarity is cited in *Letter Nine,* which examines a passage from Psalm 78 in which God appears to get drunk. Since the image of a divinity shamelessly intoxicated is unacceptable, Dionysius engages in a prodigious example of exegetic subtlety only to conclude as follows:

> In our terminology, inebriation has the pejorative meaning of an immoderate fullness, being out of one's mind and wits. It has a better meaning when applied to God, and this inebriation must be understood as nothing other than the measureless superabundance of good things which are in him as Cause. As for being out of one's mind and wits, which follows drunkenness, in God's case it must be taken to mean that incomprehensible superabundance of God by virtue of which his capacity to understand transcends any understanding or any state of being understood. He is beyond being itself. Quite simply, as "drunk," God stands outside of all good things, being the superfullness of all these things. He surpasses all that is measureless and his abode is above and beyond all that exists (*Letter Nine,* trans. Luibheid, p. 287).

A memorable example of an author clutching at allegorical straws, whereas all the Psalmist is doing is describing the wrath of God: "Then the Lord awaked as one out of sleep, and like a mighty man that shouteth by reason of wine" (Ps. 78:65). Describing God as wrathful is in keeping with the Bible's normal process of anthropomorphization; and what we have here is actually a simile: God awakens so full of wrath as to appear to be drunk. A powerful image, that truly *puts before our eyes,* as Aristotle has it, the wrath of God, but which Dionysius, with his lack of interest in the mechanism of metaphor, does not see, his attention being concentrated on the subtler exercises of allegory. So that, as Augustine points out, seeing that the literal sense appears repugnant, we look *in factis* for a spiritual sense.

The real problem is that Dionysius does not make a clear distinction between metaphor and allegory and tends to lump both together in the category of the symbolic. The difference between metaphor and allegory has already been made abundantly clear. What constitutes a symbol, compared with these two rhetorical techniques, is still an open question at this point in time and will remain so for centuries (see Eco 1984a: ch. 4): an image in the form of a luminous glowing mandala may be thought of as a symbol in a number of cultures, without its being either an allegory or a metaphor. After all, maybe the best way to grasp Dionysius's hallucinated semiotics is to reconsider Goethe's famous distinction:

> There is a great difference, whether the poet seeks the particular for the sake of the general or sees the general in the particular. From the former procedure there ensues allegory, in which the particular serves only as illustration, as example of the general. The latter procedure, however, is genuinely the nature of poetry; it expresses something particular, without thinking of the general or pointing to it. Allegory transforms the phenomenon into a concept, the concept into an image, but in such a way that the concept always remains bounded in the image, and is entirely to be kept and held in it, and to be expressed by it.
>
> Symbolism . . . transforms the phenomenon into idea, the idea into an image, and in such a way that the idea remains always infinitely active and unapproachable in the image, and even if expressed in all languages, still would remain inexpressible. (Goethe, Maxims and Reflections, Nos. 279, 1112, 1113)

Now, we might expect Dionysius to consider allegories as didactic procedures (or procedures calculated to conceal the truth from the eyes of the profane) and symbols as epiphanies that make secret knowledge evident. The truth is that all the examples of symbolic theology provided by Dionysius have nothing whatsoever to do with a modern theory of symbols, nor do they propose an alternative. Let us consider a few examples.

In chapter 2 of *The Celestial Hierarchy* (trans. Luibheid, p. 148), Dionysius affirms that the Scriptures use poetic forms to represent formless celestial intelligences. It is unclear whether by poetic forms he means allegories *(in verbis)* or metaphors. And in the passage previously cited in which he speaks of God being named through the lowliest creatures, such as the bear and the lion, the example Dionysius has in mind is clearly Hosea 5:12–14, where God, still angry with Israel, says that he will be unto Ephraim as a moth, and to the house of Judah as rottenness, and unto Ephraim as a lion, and as a young lion to the house of Judah. The moth and the young lion are not "symbols" of the divinity. The Bible does not say that God is a moth or a lion, but that in a certain circumstance He will behave as His children are used to seeing the moth and the lion behave. These are perfectly comprehensible similes or metaphors (*in verbis* naturally) to which the prophets have accustomed us. Thomas Aquinas would have said that what the biblical author *intended to say literally* was that God, at the height of his wrath, was not about to give his erring children any respite.

Similarly, when in *Letter Nine* (trans. Luibheid, pp. 286–287) Dionysius speaks of those "occult and audacious enigmas" in which the Scriptures compare divine things to dew or honey, he is still thinking of Hosea 14:5, where the Psalmist says, "I will be as the dew unto Israel," or Psalm 19:9–10, where he affirms that "the judgments of the Lord are . . . sweeter also than honey and the honeycomb." This time God is not angry but most loving, and the metaphor makes this clear. In no sense, however, is honey a symbol of God.

It should be obvious that these metaphors are comprehensible, because the traditional attributes of honey are its pleasant taste and sweetness, of the moth its annoying persistence, of dew its beneficial fertilizing qualities. When Dionysius is afraid that his audience may not be familiar with all the properties of the metaphorical vehicle, he lists them, as any self-respecting encyclopedist of the early centuries A.D. would have done. In *The Celestial Hierarchy*, for example, speaking of the symbolic presentation of fire, he points out that the Scriptures give us examples of flaming chariot wheels, fiery animals, men radiating fire, braziers of red-hot coals, rivers of flame, and he observes: "And indeed it seems to me that this imagery of fire best expresses the way in which the intelligent beings of heaven are like the De-ity" (p. 183), and he proceeds to list a series of properties traditionally associated with fire. Fire passes through all things without mixing with them, it cannot be grasped but it seizes everything, it lies hidden until it finds the proper kindling, it transforms things, it vivifies them with its heat, it shuns adulteration, it tends upward, it penetrates, it moves by itself and makes other things move, it embraces everything but nothing can contain it, it is efficient, powerful, and when ignored it appears to be dead, but it springs unexpectedly to life when stirred, it flings itself upward and cannot be checked, and so on. With such an encyclopedia it is easy to produce not just metaphors but whole allegories based upon fire. Fire is not an obscure symbol that names without naming, that alludes without revealing: when intimately known in its very nature, as Dionysius shows that he knows it, it puts before our eyes the supernatural realities of which it is a metaphor or an allegory, and it does so effortlessly.

The same can be said of light, and of the sun as the source of light, to which Dionysius devotes a number of fine pages in the *Divine Names* (trans. Luibheid, p. 74), pages that will inspire many medieval theorists of the aesthetics of light (see Eco 1956, 1987).

The pages of the *Divine Names* in which Dionysius says that God can be called Good, Beauty, or Being belong to a different register. In this case he is not talking about earthly entities, animals, objects, natural phenomena capable of becoming images, or metaphors of divine things. Here he is talking about what the Scholastics will call the transcendental properties of Being. The problem is that we, knowing the moth from experience, can compare it to God, but we are able to say that something is good or beautiful only insofar as we are able to see that certain things in our experience participate in a reflected fashion in the properties of the divinity. "For we recognize the difference in intelligible beings between qualities that are shared and the objects which share them. We call 'beautiful' that which has a share in beauty, and we give the name of 'beauty' to that ingredient which is the cause of beauty in everything. But the 'beautiful' which is beyond individual being is called 'beauty' because of that beauty bestowed by it on all things, each in accordance with what it is" (*The Divine Names*, trans. Luibheid, p. 76).[32]

---

32. Thomas will comment: "Ostendit quomodo Deo [pulchrum] attribuitur. . . . Dicit ergo primo quod in Causa prima, scilicet Deo, non sunt dividenda pulchrum

Likewise, what is suprasubstantially Good and Beauty is "that which truly is and which gives being to everything else" (*The Divine Names,* trans. Luibheid, p. 98). "Every being and all the ages derive their existence from the Preexistent. All eternity and time are from Him. The Preexistent is the source and is the cause of all eternity, of time and of every kind of being" (*The Divine Names,* V, 5, trans. Luibheid, pp. 98–99).

What we have here is a leap. Here the trajectory is no longer *upward* (from the moth to God) but *downward,* from God to whatever is good and beautiful. The divine names belong strictly speaking to the divinity, and only at a subordinate level to things. This subordination, however, is not of a metaphorical order, but of a metaphysical one. If the properties of the moth are similar to those of God, it is because of a defect of our imagination. This is the only way can imagine the implacability of God's wrath (which is obviously something quite different). The simile is couched *in verbis,* and the *verba* are clearly inadequate to express an object so sublime. Therefore the metaphor from low to high appears capable of making us know, by putting the thing before our eyes; but it makes us know in an extremely pallid fashion what is by definition unknowable. The properties of beautiful things on the other hand are what they are because they participate in the beauty of the divinity. The similitude is not *in verbis* but *in re.* The sharing of transcendental properties by creatures is always a pallid sharing, but it is not a pallor of the imagination (or of language); instead the pallor is ontological.

---

et pulchritudo. . . . Deinde . . . ostendit qualiter attribuuntur creaturis; et dicit quod in existentibus, pulchrum et pulchritudo distinguuntur secundum participans et participatum, ita quod pulchrum dicitur hoc quod participat pulchritudinem; pulchritudo autem participatio primae Causae quae omnia pulchra facit: pulchritudo enim creaturae nihil est aliud quam similitudo divinae pulchritudinis in rebus participata" (In librum beati Dionysii De divinis nominibus expositio IV, 5: 335 and 337). "He demonstrates how beauty can be attributed to God. . . . He says first of all that in the First Cause, i.e., in God, the beautiful and beauty are not to be separated. . . . He then proceeds to demonstrate how they are attributed to creaures; and he says that in existing things the beautiful and beauty are distinguished with respect to participation and participants. Thus, we call something 'beautiful' because it is a participant in beauty. Beauty, however, is a participation in the First Cause, which makes all things beautiful. So that the beauty of creatures is simply a likeness of the divine beauty in which things participate" (Eco 1988, p. 27).

This is tantamount to saying that in the symbolic theology of Dionysius
there is no room for a coherent theory of metaphor, and so be it. But this position implies a fine cognitive dilemma. In fact we have it on faith that God is
Goodness and Beauty, but in what precise way He suprasubstantially possesses these properties we do not know. Or rather, either we know it by illumination or arcane knowledge, or we must imagine it in a pallid fashion taking
the properties of things as our point of departure. A problem of which Thomas
Aquinas (who is not a cultivator of any hidden or mysteriosophic science of
the divinity) is fully aware when, from these very same pages of Dionysius, he
derives the idea of knowledge *by analogy*: somehow or other, "prout possumus," to the best of our abilities, we must elevate ourselves from earthly things
to knowledge of the First Cause (*Expositio Sancti Thomae* V, 3, n. 668). Are we
justified in saying, then, that such knowledge is merely metaphorical?

3.7. The *Analogia Entis*

Rosier-Catach (1997: 167–173) cites a number of cases in which the canonical example of *prata rident* serves to highlight the difference between metaphor and *translatio in divinis*. Boethius (*De Trinitate* IV, 1, 5, 21) had already
remarked that when predications had to do with God, the things predicated
are thereby modified. Gilbert of Poitiers *(Dialogus Everardi et Ratii)* will say,
apropos of the ten categories of Aristotle *(praedicamenta),* that "si quis ad
divinam verterit praedicationem, cuncta [praedicamenta] mutantur" ("if one
proceeds to the predication of divine things, all the [categories] change").
Theodoric of Chartres follows the dictum of Dionysius, according to which
a substantial predicate does not mean that God is a substance, but that he is
beyond all substance.

So, in the case of predication *in divinis,* it is not the thing that is predicated, only the name. At the same time, the idea makes headway that, despite
this difference, the predicate "quodam modo innuit nobis substantiam" ("in
a certain way suggests the substance to us"). As a result, what we have is not
an unbridgeable divarication, and predication by pure negation, but instead
some form of *connotation.*

To what extent the difference between univocal predication and predication *in divinis* posed an insurmountable problem is confirmed by the *Regu-
lae theologicae* of Alain of Lille, in which a distinction is made (somewhat

obscurely) between: (i) the transfer of the name and the thing, as in "linea est longa," where length, which is the property of the body, is said of the line that distinguishes it and makes it possible to call it "long"; (ii) the transfer of the thing, as in "seges est laeta," where the thing (in this case *laetitia* or gladness) is attributed to the subject, the cornfield; (iii) the transfer of the name alone, as in "monachus est albus"—in which the white monk is not himself white (we are talking about a white-robed Cistercian). But this is precisely the way we say "Deus est iustus."

Later in the text, however, Alain admits that God is called just "a causa quia efficit iustum" ("rightly, since he brings about justice"). Here we are close to the position taken by Dionysius, for whom Goodness and Beauty really are divine properties and may be applied to earthly things only insofar as, through participation, they cause something very similar in them. In that case it is not simply a question of transferring the name: indeed it would not even be a metaphor (judging by the above-cited classification).

Since this is not the place to venture into the boundless territory of the discussions on the *analogia entis* (pointing out the frequently subtle differences between one author and another, right down to the Second Scholasticism of the Counter-Reformation, from Cajetanus to Suarez, we will simply attempt to see what were the basic models for univocal and equivocal discourse that inspired the whole of Scholastic debate. And the fundamental model is always the one derived from Aristotle (see Owens 1951) and from Boethius's commentary.

The discourse on equivocity is already present in the *Metaphysics*, where Aristotle discusses how being can be "said in many ways." After saying that there is a science that considers being in and of itself, when we might have expected his first tentative definition of the object of this science, he repeats as the only possible definition what had appeared in his first book (992b 18) only as a parenthetical observation: "being is said in many ways" ("to de on leghetai men pollachos")—according to multiple meanings (1003a 33).

In fact, Aristotle reduces these many ways to four. Being is said: (i) as accidental being (this is the being predicated by the copula, whereby we say that a man is white or standing); (ii) as true—it may be true or false that the man is white, or that man is an animal; (iii) as potentiality and act, whereby, while it may not be true that this healthy man is ill right now, he could become ill, and (as we might say today) we can think of a possible world in which it is true that this man is ill; and finally (iv) as *ens per se* or as *substance.* However we speak of being, we say it "with reference to a single principle" (1003b 5–6), that is, to the substances: "The first meaning of being is the essence that signifies the substance (semainei ten ousian)" (1028a 14–15).

Is this saying in a number of ways an equivocal way of saying? Aristotle is unclear on this point. In the *Categories* (1, 1a) he says that we have *homonymy* or *equivocity* when entities that require a different definition have a single name in common. The classical example is *zoon,* used both for an animal and a painting, a homonymy that exists in Greek. It should be said that medieval thinkers, who did not know Greek, failed to grasp this homonymy, thinking that the word animal was used both for the animal and the image of the animal, and that Aristotle gave a broader meaning to equivocity than they did. See, for example, Thomas Aquinas: "Philosophus largo modo accipit aequivoca, secundum quod includant in se analoga" ("The philosopher takes equivocal terms in a broad sense, so they include analogous terms") (*Summa Theologiae* I, 13, 10 ad 4).

As Aristotle sees it, we find ourselves faced with an example of accidental *equivocation* (in the Middle Ages they would have said it was due to *penuria nominum*). We have *synonymity* or *univocality* when the term corresponds to a single definition (when, that is, *zoon* is said of a man or an ox). And finally, we have *paronymity* when things are designated by the same term but with a different grammatical ending ("the grammarian" [*grammatico*] when it stands for "grammar" [*grammatica*]). Owen (1951) makes it clear that Aristotle considers equivocity or univocality to be properties, not of the term itself, but of the things for which a single term is used.[33] Thus, we have univocality when a single term is used for what is expressed by a single definition, and equivocity when we have a single term for two things that correspond to two different definitions.

Different uses of a term are broadly discussed in the *Topics* (I, 15, 106a 1–8), where Aristotle takes on for the first time the question of a twofold way of employing terms: it is one thing to say that justice and courage are called

---

33. See, however, the observations of Lo Piparo (2000: 60–61) who criticizes current translations of the beginning of the *Categories* which define synonymy and homonymy as properties of things and not of names. Owens (1951) would reflect a post-Aristotelian theory of synonymy.

"good" univocally (because goodness is part of the definition of both) and it is another to say in various ways that what is conducive to health is good. The allusion here is to the original Aristotelian example, widely discussed in the Middle Ages, according to which both people in good health and the medicine conducive to good health, not to mention urine as a sign of good health, are dubbed "healthy."

In the *Nicomachean Ethics* (I, 6, 1096b 23–29) the question of why honor, wisdom, and pleasure are called "goods" comes up again. The three things are different, and yet the use of the term is not an example of casual equivocation. Are they called "good" because they depend upon a single cause ("aph'enos") or because they are directed toward the same end or good ("pros hen")? Or is it by analogy, following the example of sight that is good for the body just as the intellect is for the soul? Here Aristotle clearly distinguishes the first case from true analogy, which sets up a proportion among four terms.[34]

In Boethius's Latin translation of Porphyry's *Isagoge,* "aph'enos" and "pros hen" are rendered respectively as "ab uno" (the term "medical" used both for the doctor himself and for the doctor's potions and instruments) and "ad unum" (the classical example of "healthy" said of the body, the medicine, and the urine). Clearly, however, the first example is a relatively weak one, since it could be reduced to a case of paronymy. In fact the concept that remains central in Aristotle is that of *pros hen.* Briefly put, to be named for the cause one proceeds from or for the end toward which one tends is to all intents and purposes the same thing (we could say that the relationship is based on a common cause, whether it be efficient or final). What we have, then, are two forms of equivocity, *pros hen,* which the scholastic tradition will dub *analogy of proportion* (and, in the case of Cajetanus, of *attribution*), and that by analogy, which the scholastic tradition will dub *analogy of proportionality.* For convenience sake, from now on we will use the two terms *attribution,* which for Aristotle was not a form of analogy, and *proportionality,* which for Aristotle was the only form of analogy.

Aristotle explains the attribution in the *Metaphysics* (K. 3, 1060b 36–1061a 7) where he takes as examples of speaking "in several ways" the adjectives *medical* and *healthy*: they are used in reference to *(pros)* the same thing: a medical dis-

---

34. A convincing treatment of analogy in Aristotle can still be read in Lyttkens 1952.

course and an instrument are both called "medical" because the medical discourse proceeds from medical science and the instrument is useful to that science; in like manner, things that are signs or causes of health are termed "healthy." Now, health is something that is only found in a body and is not present in the color of the urine or that of the medicine (we ought to speak, then, of a patently equivocal situation in which a single term is referred to things that have different definitions). Both the urine and the medicine, however, refer to health. Just as the term *being* is used in various senses but with reference to one central idea *(pros hen),* and is therefore not equivocal, the same goes for the term "healthy." Both express a common notion *(legonthai kath'en).*

Attribution is a relationship involving two terms: medicine is healthy because it causes health, and we cannot say that medicine is to the sick body as health is to the healthy body. The case of analogy is different. Here four terms are required, as we are also reminded in the *Poetics* and the *Rhetoric.* The stone is shameless because it is to Sisyphus as the shameless man is to his victim (*Rhetoric,* III, 11, 1412a 5, in Bollingen ed., p. 2253). Now, whereas the examples of attribution are always given as instances of the stereotyped use of language (healthy medicine, healthy urine), for Aristotle the analogy is an instrument of knowledge, and he makes use of it, when it serves him, in his books on nature too. "The underlying nature can be known by analogy" (*Physics* I, 7, 191a, in Bollingen ed., p. 326).

At this point let us reconsider the very nature of metaphor. As proposed in Eco (1984a: sect. 3.8.3), let us suppose that metaphor and metonymy can be explained on the basis of a componential analysis in the form of an encyclopedia which in the definition of a given term includes its form (or morphological aspect), cause, matter, and end (or function).

	Property 1, form
Sememe A	Property 2, cause
	Property 3, matter
	Property 4, end or function

The idea was already present among the Scholastics: see, for instance, how Thomas (*De principiis naturae,* 6) admits that sometimes the like properties are predicated with respect to the cause, and at others with respect to the end.

To formulate the metonymy *drink a glass* (container for content), it is not necessary to compare two terms: one identifies in the encyclopedic definition of the glass the fact that it contains wine; the substitution is therefore one of semic interdependence within the same sememe. To call the glass *the shield of Dionysus* on the other hand I must compare the properties of Dionysus and the god of war Ares, recognize that in both the same morphological property appears (a typical instrument or emblem), identify a property that the two instruments have in common (both being round and concave in form), and activate the exchange. In both cases the substitution first occurs on account of the semic identity among sememes, then two sememes are crossed with two semes.

Now, it appears that metaphor imposes a comparison between two entities that were previously separate, thereby increasing our knowledge, whereas metonymy presumes prior knowledge of the thing played upon. Hence the greater cognitive power of metaphor.

Attribution seems to be akin to metonymy: we call medicine "healthy" because we already know that the property of medicine is to procure health. But if this is the case, then many of the metaphors cited by Aristotle, from genre to species and vice versa, are in fact forms of metonymy or synecdoche, given the fact that genre ought to be a property of the species. Just as being an animal is a property of mankind, and makes it possible for Francesca da Rimini to address Dante with the vocative "O aminal grazioso e benigno," similarly standing still is a property of being at anchor. We have only to look at Emanuele Tesauro's *Cannocchiale aristotelico* ([1670]1968: 284). He has no qualms about calling metaphors from genre to species and vice versa "analogiae attributionis."

On the other hand, when Aristotle calls the stone shameless, he is attributing to it a property (certainly justified by the context) that had not previously been recognized. Let us take another look at the example calling pirates commercial purveyors. First of all, a four-term analogy is set up: the pirates are to the transportation of stolen property as merchants are to that of the goods they acquire. The impression of identifying a genre X, of which pirates and purveyors are both species, is a consequence of the analogical operation. In fact it takes two independent sememes and identifies in them a common property (that of being *transporters* of goods). Only when we have understood the metaphor can we say that pirates and purveyors belong (unexpectedly) to the same genre, or the same whole. The property they share, surprisingly brought to the fore, becomes a common genre.

$$\begin{matrix} & \text{purveyors} \\ \text{transporters} & \\ & \text{pirates} \end{matrix}$$

The entire Scholastic discussion of the *analogia entis* (despite the great variety of its outcomes) is fundamentally based on a choice between analogy of attribution and analogy of proportionality, and the examples are similar to those given by Aristotle when it comes to finding attributions or proportions between medicine and health and meadows and smiles.

The real problem, already looming in Dionysius, arises when the divine names come into play. When we say that medicine is healthy is that the same kind of attribution as saying that God is Good? We recognize the properties of health and we are familiar with the properties of both medicine and urine (one causes health, the other reveals it). Combining together known properties, we perform the attribution. What happens, however, in the case of the divine names?

There are only two possible solutions.[35]

(i) We know the goodness of things *per prius* and we infer *per posterius* that the cause of this goodness must exist in God. But what we have at this point is an inference from something known to something that must exist, but whose nature is unknown to us. And it is not enough to suppose that the cause must somehow resemble the effect. All the more since, in the course of his discussion of analogy, Thomas (in *Summa Theologiae* I, 45, 7, for example, following the lead of Augustine) distinguishes two types of likeness between cause and effect. The effect may represent "quantum ad similitudinem formae" ("by reason of the similarity of its form") and this is the case with the "repraesentatio imaginis" ("the representation of an image"), in other words, of the statue of Mercury that resembles Mercury. But it can also represent by "causalitas causae" ("the causality of the cause"), in which case there

---

35. For an examination of Thomas's theories on analogy from the point of view of their evolution, see Marmo 1994: 305–320 (with more exhaustive references to the literature on the subject).

is no morphological likeness but rather "repraesentatio per vestigium" ("representation by way of a visible trace"), as occurs both in the relationship between smoke and fire and that between a man and the footprints he leaves behind him. (Thomas—following Albertus Magnus—grants that the footprints may resemble the form of the foot, but he points out that the imprint of the foot is not similar to the man who left it and therefore cannot tell us who that man was.[36] In *Scriptum super libros Sententiarum* I, 8, 1, 2 he gives the example of the sun, which produces heat but is not hot in itself.) If then we go back from the goodness of things to their divine cause, we do so out of *causalitas causae,* but we have no idea of what this goodness is like. We call Goodness the cause of goodness merely to make up for the *penuria nominum,* and hence a case of equivocation. It is as if, seeing smoke and not knowing anything about the fire that caused it is, we were to name this unknown quantity Hypersubstantial Smoke, thinking that what we were faced with was an example of *repraesentatio imaginis* and not *repraesentio per vestigium.* Let us consider the disturbing consequences of such a solution: if the mechanism of attribution were still valid, given that, among our actions and among the events of the world, some things are bad (a crime, rotten food, an illness), why do we not attribute the cause of these things to God, thereby making him responsible for Evil? Because we know a priori that there is no Evil in God (whereas there is Goodness). But if we already knew that, there was no need to look for an analogy. All that remains, then, is the second conclusion.

(ii) We know (by faith or revelation) the attributes of the Divinity, and it is therefore *per prius,* on the basis of these attributes, that we predicate *per posterius* the goodness of terrestrial things. We know, in other words, that God is ontologically Good *per prius* and that things are good *per posterius,* insofar as they share in the goodness of the Divinity. The attribute "good" characteristic of a certain thing is the equivalent of the attribute "animal" that characterizes a cat. We understand that a cat is an animal because we already know what an animal is. Thus we have a predication of a metonymi-

---

36. Which is after all the situation faced by Robinson Crusoe: he sees the footprints in the sand and knows they must have been made by a human being, but he as yet has no inkling that they were left by a particular "savage" whom he will call Friday.

cal type from one known thing to another known thing: the attribution
does not lead us to discover anything we did not already know.

Alternatively, predication *in divinis* implies an analogy of proportionality. But, in the case of the Aristotelian analogy, we discover an identity of
properties between two things both of whose properties are known (the
discovery involves the unsuspected relationship established between two
known things). In an analogy extended *in divinis,* on the other hand, the
trick would be to identify (and this would be truly unsuspected) an identity
of properties between something about which we know everything and
something about which we know nothing. In other words, the proportion
established is not (as was the case with the shield of Ares and of the cup of
Dionysus) $A:B=C:D$, but $A:B=x:y$, where x and y are unknown properties.
This would in fact be the proportionality according to which we could say
that human knowledge bears the same relation to the human mind as divine
knowledge does to the divine mind. The most one could hazard is that between divine knowledge and the divine mind (both unknown) a relationship is established *in some way* similar to the one established between human knowledge and the human soul. But similar how? By *repraesentatio
imaginis* or by *causalitas causae?* The comparison established between Achilles
and the lion works as long as we already know what the wrath of Achilles is
like, as well as the fierceness of the lion, and only then does the wrath of
Achilles appear more convincing. But saying that divine Knowledge is to
the divine Mind what human knowledge is to the human mind teaches us
less than the comparison does about Achilles. In the second case, the wrath
of the warrior, of which we already have some inkling, is reinforced through
the comparison with the lion with the attributes of fierceness and courage.
We learn something new. In the case of predication *in divinis,* we learn that
something, we don't know what, bears a pale resemblance to human intelligence. Accordingly, if predication *in divinis* were analogy of proportionality
it would teach us less than a good metaphor teaches us.

Unless we already know what God is and what his qualities are, in which
case the analogy would tell us something interesting about whatever is compared to God, not about God, about Whom we already know all there is
to know.

It could be argued that the cases in which God is truly spoken of metaphorically are exempt from this criticism. The poetic metaphors of the Bible

that speak of a God raging like a lion or as persistent as a woodworm tell us something about his wrath or his obstinacy. Granted. But these metaphors are not designed to reveal to us God's nature, which is unknown, but the effects of his operations, which we already know. They do not posit an unknowable God but a God already anthropomorphized, like the pagan gods. Proceeding from the known to the known, these metaphors place something before our eyes, but in the mode of a simile. We are on this side of, or in any event outside of, an analogical discourse *in divinis*.

This is the fundamental weakness with any discussion of the *analogia entis,* and in fact all it permits the philosopher to discover is what the philosopher already knew on faith. It is no accident that discussions of the *analogia entis* engender prodigies of subtlety, but end up dissipating with the Scholasticism of the Post-Reformation. In fact, whenever we have to speak of the divine attributes, if we assume a Platonic-Augustinian position, then we already know everything about God for innate reasons, and only because we have this knowledge of the divine can we say that something shares (pallidly) in His Goodness or another of the transcendental properties of being. These appear to be the terms in which authors like Alexander of Hales, who speaks of the soul as "imago Dei," or Bonaventure, for whom the soul possesses "principia per se nota," handle analogy. And analogy is not so much a pathway to knowledge as a proportion known by illumination (see Lyttkens 1952: 123–153).

Otherwise we must take experience as our starting point, in which case the *analogia entis* is reduced to the rational demonstration of God's existence, or to the formula that basically reiterates Thomas's five ways: given a chain of cause and effect in the world, ergo there must exist a causeless first cause. Apart from the fatal weakness of the argument (the ergo that leads up to the final conclusion is exactly what was supposed to be proved—that is, just as the things of the world suppose a chain of causes and effects, so the chain of causes and effects of the world supposes an otherworldly cause—an argument that fails to withstand Kant's criticism), we should note that what the five ways tell us at the most is that God must exist, not what God is like.

In point of fact, any discussion of analogy only serves to remind us that all we can predicate of God is Goodness, Truth, Fullness of Being, Unity, Beauty, but nothing further. And it can only come up in a culture that already assumes that God is Goodness, Unity, Truth, and Beauty.

Precisely on account of this dramatic impasse, which will lead to its col-
lapse, the *analogia entis* has less cognitive value than a good metaphor.

3.8. Conclusion

The poetry and prose of the Middle Ages abound in metaphors, while contemporary theory, be it philosophical or poetic and rhetorical, is inadequate
to account for this richness. This should not surprise us, as it is a commonplace that the culture of the time frequently shows a dichotomy between
theory and practice. The typical example is music, a field in which the doctrinal discussion is extremely abstract, based on Pythagorean models, *re-
licto aurium iudicio* ("setting aside the judgment of the ears"), as Boethius
remarked, and as a result deaf to the evolution of musical practice (see Eco
1987 and Dahan 1980: 172). But at least in the case of music there is an explanation, which is, as we mentioned, the weight of the Pythagorean tradition as transmitted by Boethius. Can we find a similar reason in the case of
the theory of metaphor?

We can, and it lies in the weight that the commentary on Aristotle's *Categories* had throughout medieval doctrinal culture thanks to the mediation
of Porphyry.

Let us take another look at what we said in Chapter 1 (section 1.2.1) apropos of the *Arbor Porphyriana:* that it makes it possible, in other words, to
classify, but not to define. In order to define, the tree would have to introduce many more differences than it actually does, or it would have to resolve
itself into a network of differences. Every time Aristotle is faced with explaining a metaphor he has recourse to local "ontologies" that are far more
flexible than a tree of genera and species.

Now, the doctrinal thought of the Middle Ages is unable to wean itself
away from the model provided by the *Arbor,* and as a consequence, while it
can easily understand and justify substitutions from genus to species and vice
versa, it finds itself in difficulties when it comes to talking about the multiplicity of properties that enter into play in metaphorical substitutions. It is
worth noting that Geoffrey of Vinsauf, who was not a philosopher, was not
the only one to point out the need to take into consideration *all* of the possible properties of an object: philosophers and theologians too, when it came
to analyzing a metaphor, were perfectly well aware of what, often peripheral,

characteristics formed the basis of the amalgam of the two sememes. But when it came to constructing a theory of metaphorical invention (considering the subtleties they were capable of when discussing problems of logic), they found themselves without a sufficiently flexible semantic model, and they were loath to call into question the canonical model of the Porphyrian tree that had been such an integral part of their intellectual formation.

Why this instinctive reluctance to challenge the world order established by the *Arbor Porphyriana?* If what we said at the conclusion of Chapter 1 is true, resorting to flexible, even unexplored, "ontologies" to explain metaphorical expressions meant admitting that ontologies, like the Porphyrian tree itself, were practical, provisional tools, and not definitive images of the structure of the world and the Great Chain of Being. And not even the most faithful devotees of Aristotle in those centuries could escape the influence of Neo-Platonism (Thomas Aquinas himself commented not only on Aristotle but also on Dionysius).

To construct or suggest the possibility of an unexpectedly adequate ontology, we do not have to start with the supposition that the universe must always be seen according to a single organizational model according to preordained genera and species. But it was precisely this idea of an "ontological revolution" that could not even cross the mind of a medieval thinker, because their very image of the world was conceived along the model of a stable *Arbor Porphyriana.*

This helps us understand, I believe, why a historical period so rich in extraordinary metaphors (audaciously proposed by its poets) found itself unable to elaborate a theory of metaphor as an instrument of fresh knowledge.

4

The Dog That Barked (and Other Zoosemiotic Archaeologies)

By no means soft on Scholasticism, in his *De dignitate et augmentis scientiarum* (I, 24), Francis Bacon, after reminding us that Scylla had the face and bosom of a young and beautiful woman, points out that she subsequently revealed herself (according to Virgil's *Eclogue VI*, 75) "candida succinctam latrantibus inguina monstris" ("with howling monsters girt about her white

---

The second part of this essay chapter incorporates a research project that first appeared under my name, together with those of Roberto Lambertini, Costantino Marmo, and Andrea Tabarroni. The project took shape in a seminar on the history of semiotics at the University of Bologna (during the academic year 1982–1983). After being presented at the Settimane di Studio del Centro Italiano di Studi sull'Alto Medioevo (see Spoleto 1985), it was published in English in Eco and Marmo, *On the Medieval Theory of Signs* (1989). For the present book, I have rewritten it, taking into account contributions that have appeared more recently, unburdening it of a number of quotations and erudite notes, and changing the order of the sections. Our original research project identified the classifications in order of complexity, regardless of whether they had appeared before or after one another, whereas in this version I have followed the chronological order, at least within the two traditions—Stoic-Augustinian and Aristotelian-Boethian—because what most concerned me was to underscore the conflict, continually latent, between the correlational and inferential notions of the sign. Hence, while I refer the reader to the original version (cited passim throughout these following notes as *Latratus canis* 1989) for a more detailed discussion, the other three authors are not to be considered responsible for the present draft. It should be understood, however, that, without their collaboration, my own ideas on the *latratus canis* would have remained as inarticulate as the *gemitus infirmorum*. [*Translator's note:* The essay "On Animal Language in the Medieval Classification of Signs," co-authored by Umberto Eco,

waist").[1] Whereupon Bacon goes on to comment that in the writings of the Scholastics one finds concepts appealing at first sight, but which, when you delve more deeply into their distinctions and divisions, rather than proving fertile and capable of generating benefits for human life, "in portentosas et latrantes quaestiones desinunt" ("end in monstrous altercations and barking questions").[2]

Roberto Lambertini, Costantino Marmo, and Andrea Tabarroni, first appeared in English in *Versus* a special number (38–39 [1984]: 3–38) of the periodical *Versus. Quaderni di Studi Semiotici* dedicated to Medieval Semiotics, and subsequently in the symposium edited by Eco and Marmo, *On the Medieval Theory of Signs* (1989: pp. 3–41); the English version appears to have been a collective effort by the authors, revised by Shona Kelly. For a partial summary of their conclusions, see also the chapter "Interpreting Animals," in Eco's *The Limits of Interpretation* (1990b, pp. 111–122)—a reprint, with negligible editorial corrections, of the article "*Latratus canis*" that appeared in English, attributed to Eco alone, in the periodical *Tijdschrift voor Filosofie* 47 (1985): 3–14. Between these two publications, another similarly abbreviated version, close but not identical to the last two mentioned, and once again recognized as the fruit of a collaboration, was included in a symposium on semiotics, namely, Umberto Eco, Roberto Lambertini, Costantino Marmo, Andrea, and Tabarroni (1986), "*Latratus canis*' or: the Dog's Barking," in John Deely, Brooke Williams, and Felicia E. Kruse (eds.), *Frontiers in Semiotics* (1986, pp. 63–73). What follows is a new English translation of Eco's Italian text, itself revised for inclusion in the present volume. It is somewhat misleading that Eco chooses to refer in the notes that follow to the original collaborative article, "On Animal Language in the Medieval Classification of Signs," as *Latratus canis*.]

1. The translation is from Virgil (1999: 66–67).

2. [*Translator's note:* The corresponding passage in the *Advancement of Learning* (1604) runs as follows: "so that the fable and fiction of Scylla seemeth to be a lively image of this kind of philosophy or knowledge; which was transformed into a comely virgin for the upper parts; but then *candida succinctam latrantibus inguina monstris* ("with howling monsters girt about her white waist," Virgil, *Eclogue VI,* 75), so the generalities of the schoolmen are for a while good and proportionable; but then when you descend into their distinctions and decisions, instead of a fruitful womb for the use and benefit of man's life, *they end in monstrous altercations and barking questions*." The dichotomous image may coincidentally remind us of Shakespeare's Lear (without the barking): "Down from the waist they are Centaurs,/Though women all above:/But to the girdle do the gods inherit,/Beneath is all the fiends.'"]

The Scholastics could never have suspected that at the beginning of the seventeenth century their exquisite *quaestiones* would be rudely defined as "barking" *(latrantes)*, particularly since, in a number of those *quaestiones*, they had devoted their respectful and benevolent attention to nothing less than the barking of the dog. What did they have to say on the subject? Did they have anything new to say or did they simply repeat traditional notions handed down from the ancient world?

4.1. Animals from Antiquity to the Middle Ages

4.1.1. The Soul, Rights, and Language of Beasts in Antiquity
In myths and fables animals never quit talking, and these anthropomorphic fantasies reveal how we human beings have always been fascinated by our inscrutable fellow travelers, always at the ready with promises of troubling and illuminating revelations.

As for the philosophers and encyclopedists, a comprehensive survey would take up too much space, and the relevant bibliography is extremely vast. We will therefore confine ourselves to a particular consideration of those arguments that, among the various animals, are concerned with the dog. The comparison between the philosopher and the dog recorded (albeit tongue in cheek) by Plato (*Republic* II, 375a–376b) is well known. Well-bred dogs are gentle toward their familiars and aggressive toward strangers, and this demonstrates a happy trait in their nature: "your dog is a true philosopher, I venture to say." The dog can tell a friendly figure from a hostile one purely on the grounds that he is familiar with the one and not the other: How can we deny a certain learning ability to a creature who is able to distinguish friends and strangers simply on the basis of knowledge or ignorance?

The Latin Aristotle makes a distinction between mere *sound (sonus)* and *voice (vox)* or utterance, and in *De anima* (II, 429b) he says that a sound can be defined as a "voice" when it is emitted by an animated being and is significant *(semantikos)*. In any case, animal sounds are not emitted according to convention (they are not symbols, but *manifestations* of something at a symptomatic level) and they are *agrammatoi*, that is, not articulate (see, for instance, *De interpretatione* [*On Interpretation*] 16a and *Poetics* 1456b).

We will return to these distinctions later, because they will become central in the medieval debate. Aristotle asserts in his *Politics* that man is the only animal to possess the faculty of language, but this tells us nothing yet about the animals, because, as we will see, ever since antiquity there have been three recurring problems that crop up in this regard: (i) whether animals have a soul, or at least some form of intelligence; (ii) whether they communicate in some way among themselves and with us; and (iii) whether we should respect their dignity by abstaining from killing them and eating their flesh.

The Aristotelian texts that discuss point (i) are the subject of widespread debate, because, though Aristotle, in defining the soul as "the first actuality of a natural body possessed of organs" (*De anima* [*On the Soul*] II, i, 412b), could not deny a soul to animals, it is often unclear what kind of intelligence he means to attribute to them, given that not only was he clear about the distinction between the sensitive and the rational souls, but he drew distinctions among the intellective qualities of different animal species, without reaching any definitive conclusions (*De anima* II, 413b–414a).

What is certain is that the *Historia animalium* (*History of Animals*) (VIII and IX), for example, claims that many animals exhibit traces of psychic qualities (though these may be merely *analogous* to those of humans), inasmuch as certain beasts display kindness and courage, timidity, fear, and cunning, and quite often something approaching sagacity—so that at times these virtues appear to differ from those possessed by human beings only in degree. Aristotle even seems to suggest an evolutionary progress (from plant to animal and from animal to man), in which it is not easy to draw lines of demarcation. Some animals do not confine themselves to procreating in a specific season, and, while many devote themselves to providing food for their offspring only to abandon them later, others are endowed with memory and live longer in the company of their young, establishing forms of social collaboration. Still others are capable of giving or receiving instructions, both in their intraspecies relationships as well as with humans, whose commands they appear to understand. The *Metaphysics* (A, 1) states that animals are naturally endowed with sensation, but the more intelligent ones are those in which sensation gives rise to memory, and it is they who are more apt to learn than those without the ability to remember (and this is where the dog comes in). All animals unable to hear sounds (the bee, for instance) may be intelligent, but they lack the ability to learn, while those that possess, in addition to memory, the sense of hearing (see also the *Posterior Analytics* II, 19) are able to learn. Finally, in the *Nicomachean Ethics* (VI, 7, 1141a), Aristotle declares that, since it can remember the past, the superior animal is capable of foreseeing its future needs.

In the *Dictionary of the History of Ideas* entry on "Theriophily" by George Boas (1973–1974), the citations range from Anaxagoras to Diogenes, from Democritus to Xenophon, from Philemon to Menander and Aristophanes, not to mention Theophrastus. But it is the notion of love or admiration for the animal world that is too sweeping.

Among Stoics, Academicians, and Epicureans, a debate had arisen about the possibility of an animal *logos,* for which the Stoic fragments offer plenty of evidence, though it is often contradictory (for a synthesis, see Pohlenz 1948–1955: I and II). The Stoics distinguish between a *logos endiathetos,* internally configured, that is, and a *logos prophorikos,* capable of manifesting itself externally. Now, whereas for Epicurus the difference between an animal voice (*vox*) and a human voice was simply one of degree, for the Stoics names are imposed by an explicit decision on the part of a rational mind, and therefore the various abilities attributable to animals are merely the consequence of an innate instinct of self-preservation. Along the same lines, Seneca (*Ad Lucilium epistulae morales,* III, cxxi) will remind us that animals are conscious of their own makeup, which explains their various abilities, and they have innate knowledge, but they are not endowed with reason.[3] The adherents of the New Academy on the other hand professed more indulgent opinions with regard to the intellectual capacities of animals.

But it is precisely in the context of the Stoic debate that an argument comes to the fore, unanimously attributed to Chrysippus, and destined for great popularity. We will cite two versions of it.[4] The one that is more famous

---

3. Seneca, *Ad Lucilium Epistulae Morales,* with an English translation by Richard M. Gummere, Harvard University Press, Cambridge, Massachusetts, 1917, vol. III, pp. 397–411 ["On Instinct in Animals"].

4. On the history of these two versions, see Giuseppe Girgenti, in his commentary on the Italian translation of Porphyry's *De abstinentia* (*Astinenza dagli animali,* Milano, Bompiani, 2005, n. 22 to Book III).

today and more frequently quoted is that in Sextus Empiricus's *Outlines of Pyrrhonism* (I, 69):

> And according to Chrysippus, who shows special interest in irrational animals, the dog even shares in the far-famed "Dialectic." This person, at any rate, declares that the dog makes use of the fifth complex indemonstrable syllogism when, on arriving at a spot where three ways meet, after smelling at the two roads by which the quarry did not pass, he rushes off at once by the third without stopping to smell. For, says the old writer, the dog implicitly reasons thus: "The creature went either by this road, or by that, or by the other: but it did not go by this road or by that: therefore it went by the other."[5]

Sextus assumes, with respect to Chrysippus's argument, a position closer to that of the Academicians (as will Porphyry in his *De Abstinentia* [*On Abstinence from Killing Animals*], in open polemic with the Stoics). Sextus reminds us in fact (again in his *Outlines of Pyrrhonism,* I, 65–77) that, through its behavior, the dog displays further aptitude for reflection and comprehension: it is able to choose between foods that are good for it and foods that are harmful; it is able to procure its food by hunting; it recognizes people's merits by wagging its tail when it sees those with whom it is familiar and darting at strangers (it can therefore distinguish between right and wrong); it often shows prudence; and, finally, since it is capable of understanding its own passions and of mitigating them, it is able to remove its own splinters and clean its wounds, it knows it must keep the wounded limb immobile, and it can identify the herbs that will alleviate its pain. Thus, it shows that it possesses a *logos*. It is true that we do not understand the words of the animals, but then, we don't understand the words of the barbarians either, who can assuredly speak; and therefore it is not absurd to believe that animals speak. And dogs certainly make different sounds in different circumstances.

But the information provided by Sextus does not appear till the second and third century A.D., while the discussion goes back somewhat earlier. It appears, for example, in the first century A.D. in the dialogue *De animalibus*

---

5. Sextus Empricus, *Outlines of Pyrrhonism,* I, 69, trans. R. G. Bury, Cambridge, Massachusetts, Harvard University Press, 1955, pp. 41–43.

(On Animals) of Philo of Alexandria. Philo's brother Alexander speaks in favor of animal intelligence, citing in fact the classical example:

> A hound was in pursuit of a beast. When it came to a deep [ditch] which had two trails beside it—one to the right and the other to the left, *and* having but a short distance yet to go, it deliberated which way would be worth taking. Going to the right and finding no trace, it returned and took the other. Since there was no clearly perceptible mark *there* either, with no further scenting it jumped into the [ditch] to track down hastily. This was not achieved by chance but rather by deliberation of the mind. The logicians call this thoughtful reckoning "the fifth complex indemonstrable syllogism": for the beast might have escaped either to the right or to the left or else may have leaped. (*De animalibus* 45)[6]

In point of fact, for Chrysippus all the argument proved was that the instinctive behavior of animals *prefigured* a logical behavior, and in the dialogue Philo follows the Stoic line, polemically responding to Alexander:

> Even the assertion of those who think that hounds track by making use of the fifth mode of syllogism is to be dismissed. The same could be said of those who gather clams or any other thing which moves. That they seem to follow a definite pattern is *only* logical speculation on the part of those who have no sense of philosophy, not even in dreams. Then one has to say that all who are in search of something are making use of the fifth mode of syllogism! These and other similar *assertions* are delusive fantasies of those more accustomed to the plausibility and sophistry of matters than to the discipline of examining the truth.
>
> We agree that there are some decent and good qualities which are applicable to animals and many other functions which help preserve and maintain their courage; these are observed by sight. There is certainty

---

6. As Sextus himself explains in *Outlines of Pyrrhonism* II, 158 (p. 253), the fifth nondemonstrable argument "deduces from a disjunctive premiss and the opposite of one of its clauses the other clause," as for example "Either it is day or it is night; but it is not night; therefore it is day." Naturally, in the version with the crossroads (as opposed to the one with the ditch) what we have is a "multiple syllogism."

in everything perceived *or* discerned in all the various species. But surely *animals* have no share of reasoning ability, for reasoning ability extends itself to a multiplicity of abstract concepts in the mind's *perception* of God, the universe, laws, provincial practices, the state, state affairs, and numerous other things, none of which animals understand. (*De animalibus,* 84–85)[7]

One of the fundamental texts in the polemic has got to be Plutarch's *De sollertia animalium (On the Intelligence of Animals),* which appeared at an unspecified date between 70 and 90 A.D. Plutarch's position is decidedly anti-Stoical and—like Porphyry's *De abstinentia*—is concerned not just with animal intelligence but with the respect we owe animals. Though the original Greek title translates as "Whether Land or Sea Animals Are Cleverer," and the Latin *sollertia* is weaker than the Greek *phronesis* (and tends to suggest a practical intelligence guided by experience), there can be no doubt that Plutarch is endorsing the thesis of animal rationality and polemizing against the doctrines of those who would deny it. Of course animal rationality is imperfect compared with that of humans but—the argument is common throughout the polemic—similar differences also exist among humans. All living beings share sensitivity and imagination and are capable of perception. But we cannot perceive without the participation of reason, because the data perceived may escape our attention unless an intelligent behavior intervenes to highlight and interpret it (what we experience with our eyes and ears does not result in sensations without the involvement of our rational faculties). (This argument is still extremely current in contemporary cognitivism.) If this were not the case, Plutarch argues, it would be impossible to explain why

---

7. [*Translator's note:* Philo's Greek original survives only in a sixth-century Armenian translation. This and the previous quote are from Abraham Terian, *Philonis Alexandrini De Animalibus: The Armenian Text with an Introduction, Translation, and Commentary,* Chico, California, Scholars Press, 1981, pp. 87 and 103–4. The English translator criticizes the "syntactical awkwardness" of the Armenian text, and his own translation is in fact quite unidiomatic. In our transcription of the first citation, Terian's term "shaft," which would seem to indicate a vertical cavity, has been replaced by "ditch," indicating a horizontal barrier, more in keeping with the context.]

animals not only perceive but also recall their perceptions and deduce from them notions they commit to memory by which to plan actions useful to their survival.[8]

This is the opening ploy in a polemic aimed ultimately at Aristotle and in general at all those who hold, as do the Stoics, that the behavior of animals is *as if* it were rational behavior. That would be like saying, argues Plutarch, that it is *as if* the swallow were to build its nest, *as if* the lion felt anger, *as if* deer were timorous—or, worse still, *as if* animals could see, *as if* they emitted sounds, *as if* they were alive.

Different capacities certainly exist, and they exist among animals just as they exist among humans, admits Plutarch, but to say that some beings have weaker rational faculties than others does not mean that they don't have them at all: "Let us rather say that they possess an infirm and murky intellect, like an eye afflicted with feeble and blurred vision." He is no doubt referring to the Academicians when he affirms that animals have a share in reason because their behavior proves that they have intentions, preparation, memory, emotions, care for their offspring, gratitude for benefits received, resentment toward those who have caused them suffering, courage, sociability, temperance, and magnanimity.

There follows a plethora of examples drawn from the observation of animal behavior and finally (969 B) Chrysippus's argument appears. Indeed, it is preceded by the example of the fox, used by some peoples to test the solidity of the ice: the fox edges slowly forward with its ear cocked listening for the flow of the current beneath the surface of the ice and, if it hears it, concludes that it has reached a layer of thin ice and stops. Chrysippus's dog behaves in the same way.

True, at this point Plutarch tries to attenuate the force of the proof: it is perception itself, through the scent left by its quarry, that guides the dog, not a syllogism. But the undermining of Chrysippus's argument does not impugn his final conclusion: we must oppose those who would deny reason and intelligence to animals.

---

8. See *Plutarch's Moralia*, XII, Trans. by Harold Cherniss and William Helmbold, Cambridge, Massachusetts, Harvard University Press, 1957, pp. 309–479. The same volume (pp. 487–533) contains the dialogue *Bruta animalia ratione uti* mentioned below.

In another dialogue, *Bruta animalia ratione uti* ("Beasts are Rational"), to those who object that it is an exaggeration to attribute reason to beings without an innate notion of the divinity, Plutarch replies by recalling the atheism of Sisyphus. Hence his rejection of a carnivorous diet, and his concession—though through gritted teeth—that we may put down noxious animals.

In his *De natura animalium (On the Nature of Animals)* Claudius Aelian (third century A.D.), setting aside the examples of dogs who have fallen in love with human beings (I, 6), speaks in VI, 9, of how dogs are capable of taking care of domestic tasks, so that it is enough for a poor man to have a dog who can take the place of a servant; in VI, 26, we have a series of anecdotes probably taken from Pliny—examples of dogs who laid down and died next to the bodies of their masters, of King Lysimachus's dog who insisted on sharing the fate of death along with his master even though he could have escaped, a theme that returns in VII, 10, where we hear of dogs who identified with their barking the assassins of their masters, while in VIII, 2, the virtues and feats of hunting dogs are remembered. Aelian picks up on Chrysippus's argument:

> If even animals know how to reason deductively, understand dialectic, and how to choose one thing in preference to another, we shall be justified in asserting that in all subjects Nature is an instructress without a rival. For example, this was told me by one who had some experience in dialectic and was to some degree a devotee of the chase. There was a Hound, he said, trained to hunt; and so it was on the track of a hare. And the hare was not yet to be seen, but the Hound pursuing came upon a ditch and was puzzled as to whether it had better follow to the left or to the right. And when it seemed to have weighed the matter sufficiently, it leapt straight across. So the man who professed himself both dialectician and huntsman essayed to offer the proof of his statements in the following manner: The Hound paused and reflected and said to itself: "The hare turned either in this direction or in that or went ahead. It turned neither in this direction nor in that; therefore it went ahead." And in my opinion he was not being sophistical, for as no tracks were visible on the near side of the ditch, it remained that the hare must have jumped over the ditch. So the Hound was quite right also to jump

over after it, for certainty that this particular Hound was good at tracking and keen-scented.[9]

The facts that Aelian's source is clearly Philo (seeing that he speaks of a ditch
instead of a crossroads), and that he is well known for upholding the Stoical
position, prevent him from drawing a positive conclusion from the example in
favor of the canine *logos,* and lead him to prudently attribute the wisdom of the
dog's choice not to a chain of reasoning but to a natural instinct.

It seems to me that posterity took up the argument more in Sextus's sense
that in Philo's. The third book of the *De abstinentia* of Porphyry (third–
fourth century A.D.) is attuned to the anti-Stoical polemic. The arguments
offered in favor of animal intelligence serve to back up a "vegetarian" thesis
against their slaughter. Animals express their interior states, and the fact
that we do not understand them is no more embarrassing than that we do
not understand the language or thought of the Indians or the Scythians
(and there are individuals and peoples who claim to comprehend the language of animals, as is proven by Philostratus, in his *Life of Apollonius of
Tyana,* for whom the Arabs understand the language of the birds). As a consequence, we cannot define animals as being without reason simply because
we do not understand them. Nor is it a convincing argument to say that only
certain animals like ravens and magpies can imitate human language, because not only can humans not imitate the languages of the animals, they
cannot even understand all five *(sic)* human languages.

There follow the usual references to the various animal abilities and to
how the dog interacts intelligently and communicates with his master; we
then proceed to the citation of Chrysippus's argument (III, 6, 1), recalling
that, according to Empedocles, Pythagoras, Plato, and Aristotle, the dog participates in discourse (III, 6, 6) and that the difference between internal
discourse and external discourse for Aristotle is merely a difference between
more and less. This is not all: animals are able to teach their young, the male
shares sympathetically the birth pangs of the female, they display an acute
sense of justice and sociability, they have sharper senses than ours, and if at

---

9. Aelian, *On the Characteristics of Animals,* With an English Translation by
A. F. Schofield, Cambridge, Massachusetts, Harvard University Press, 1958–9,
vol. II, Book VI, para. 59 (pp. 81–83).

times their reasonableness seems inferior to ours this does not mean that it is to be denied:

> Let it be agreed, then, that the difference is a matter of more and less, not of complete deprivation, nor or a have and a have-not. But just as in the same species one has a healthier body and another a less healthy, and there is also as great difference with regard to illness and in good or bad constitutions, so it is for souls: one is good, another bad. Among bad souls, some are more so, others less so. Nor is there sameness among good souls: Socrates is not good in the same way as Aristotle or Plato, and in people of similar reputation there is not sameness. So, even if we think more than they do, animals are not to be deprived of thinking, any more than partridges are to be deprived of flying because falcons fly more.[10]

We might see in this passage from Porphyry, just as we saw in Plutarch, to say nothing of certain passages in Aristotle's *Historia animalium,* the nucleus of those proto-evolutionist solutions which, in the late seventeenth and early eighteenth centuries, will be proposed, in polemic against the mechanism of Descartes, by two authors who, through their references and citations, show themselves to be familiar with these classical discussions. We have in mind the Jesuit Ignace Gaston Pardies (*Discours de la connoissance des bestes,* Paris, 1672)—who cites Aristotle's *Historia animalium, De anima,* and *De memoria,* Herodotus, the dispute between Stoics and Academics, and the Saint Basil of the *Hexaemeron*—and the Protestant David Renaud Boullier (*Essai philosophique sur l'âme des bêtes,* published anonymously in 1728) who cites both Aristotle and Aelian. In Bouillier, more explicitly than in Pardies, the idea of a gradual development of species is set forth. Even among human beings there are various stages of development— the soul of a child is less developed than that of an adult—but this gradual development takes place not only in the span of a single lifetime but also from the lowest to the highest of living species. He concludes (and perhaps we may allow a man of his day a certain measure of "political incorrect-

---

10. Porphyry, *On Abstinence from Killing Animals,* trans. by Gillian Clark, Ithaca, NY: Cornell University Press, 2000, p. 85.

ness") there are fewer differences between a monkey and a native of Africa than between a native of Africa and a European bel esprit. The souls of animals cannot conceive of God, but acknowledging that their souls belong to a less advanced stage of development than ours is not the same as demonstrating that they do not have one.

We will reencounter this proto-evolutionary position in the much better-known discussion between Buffon and Condillac. Buffon, in his *Histoire naturelle* II and III (1749), and later in his "Discours sur la nature des animaux" (*Histoire* IV, 1753), while denying thought to animals, admits that "nature descends by degrees and imperceptible nuances" and a freshwater polyp could be seen as the last of the animals and the first of the plants—and in *Histoire* IV there also appears the idea of the ass as a degenerate horse, which allows us a glimpse, though Buffon distances himself from the idea, of the perspective of a transformation of species. Condillac on the other hand (*Traité des animaux*, 1755) polemically defends the thesis of animal intelligence, and, since for him all higher abilities evolve out of sensation, he concludes that recognizing that animals are capable of developing their sensations means placing them at an evolutionary stage immediately below humans. Animals do not speak like humans, but the difference lies in a different level of complexity, "du plus au moins"—an expression that sounds almost like a quote from Porphyry.

Porphyry meanwhile (to get back to him) maintains that even the vices of animals (such as jealousy) are signs of intelligence. Be that as it may, there is one vice that animals do not have, unlike humans, and that is treachery toward those who love them. They have no cities, but neither do the Scythians, who live in caravans. They do not have written laws, but laws did not exist among humans so long so they lived in a state of natural felicity. Maybe they do not hold counsel (though that cannot be demonstrated), but not all human groups do. For these and other reasons it is demonstrated that animals possess reason—even though it may be defective in many cases—and hence the need to respect them.

Apart from the argument of Chrysippus, the text that exerted most influence on posterity from the first century A.D., and in particular on the medieval encyclopedists, is Pliny's *Naturalis historia* (*Natural History*). In it he deals with the language of fish (book IX) and birds (book X, including birds that can speak), but what he has to say about canine intelligence in VIII, 61, is worth quoting, considering that all those who will write about the subject subsequently appear basically to be echoing his text (or referring back to the same sources):

> Many also of the domestic animals are worth studying, and before all the one most faithful to man, the dog, and the horse. We are told of a dog that fought against brigands in defence of his master and although covered with wounds would not leave his corpse, driving away birds and beasts of prey; and of another dog in Epirus which recognized his master's murderer in a gathering and by snapping and barking made him confess the crime. The King of the Garamantes was escorted back from exile by 200 dogs who did battle with those that offered resistance. The people of Colophon and also those of Castabulum had troops of dogs for their wars; these fought fiercely in the front rank, never refusing battle, and were their most loyal supporters, never requiring pay. When some Cimbrians were killed their hounds defended their houses placed on waggons. When Jason of Lycia had been murdered his dog refused to take food and starved to death. But a dog the name of which Duris gives as Hyrcanus when King Lysimachus's pyre was set alight threw itself into the flame, and similarly at the funeral of King Hiero. Philistus also records the tyrant Gelo's dog Pyrrhus; also the dog of Nicomedes King of Bithynia is recorded to have bitten the King's wife Consingis because she played a rather loose joke with her husband. Among ourselves the famous Vulcatius, Cascellius's tutor in civil law, when returning on his cob from his place near Rome after nightfall was defended by his dog from a highwayman; and so was the senator Caelius, an invalid, when set upon by armed men at Piacenza, and he did not receive a wound until the dog had been dispatched. But above all cases, in our own generation it is attested by the National Records that in the consulship of Appius Julius and Publius Silus when as a result of the case of Germanicus's son Nero punishment was visited on Titius Sabinus and his slaves, a dog belonging to one of them could not be driven away from him in prison and when he had been flung on the Steps of Lamentation would not leave his body, uttering sorrowful howls to the vast concourse of the Roman public around, and when one of them threw it food it carried it to the mouth of its dead master; also when his corpse had been thrown into the Tiber it

swam to it and tried to keep it afloat, a great crowd streaming out to view the animal's loyalty.

Dogs alone know their master, and also recognize a sudden arrival as a stranger; they alone recognize their own names, and the voice of a member of the household; they remember the way to places however distant, and no creature save man has a longer memory.[11]

4.1.2. The Transmigration of the Problem in the Middle Ages

Did the Middle Ages know of these texts? The Platonic texts no, but Aristotle's *Analytics* will become known at least in the twelfth and thirteenth centuries, and in the same period the *Metaphysics* and the *Nicomachean Ethics* will also begin to circulate. Knowledge of the *Politics* and the *Historia animalium* will come a bit later.

But, in any case, the Middle Ages was familiar with Pliny and, through him, with a whole vast repertory of sources dealing with the animal world.[12] It is to Pliny that the entire encyclopedist tradition in general refers: we need only cite Isidore of Seville, who reminds us that there is no creature more intelligent than the dog:

The Latin word "dog" *(canis)* seems to have a Greek etymology, for the animal is called *kuon* in Greek. Still, some people think it is named for the sound *(canor)* of barking because it is loud, whence also the word "sing" *(canere)*. No animal is smarter than the dog, for they have more sense than the others. They alone recognize their own names; they love

---

11. Pliny, *Natural History,* vol. III (Books VIII–XI), translated by H. Rackham, Cambridge, MA: Harvard University Press, 1940, pp. 101–103.

12. See, for example, Columella: "Now, as I promised in the earlier part of my treatise, I will speak of the dumb guardians of the flocks, though it is wrong to speak of the dog as a dumb guardian; for what human being so clearly or so vociferously gives warning of the presence of a wild beast or of a thief as does the dog by its barking? What servant is more attached to his master than is a dog? What companion more faithful? What more wakeful night-watchman can be found? Lastly, what more steadfast avenger or defender?" (*De re rustica,* books V–IX, trans. E. S. Forster and Edward Heffner, Cambridge, MA, Harvard University Press, 1954, pp. 305–307). C. Julius Solinus, too, addresses the barking of the dog in his *Collectanea rerum mirabilium* VI.

their masters; they defend their master's home; they lay down their life for their master; they willingly run after game with their master; they do not leave the body of their master even when he has died. Finally, it is part of their nature not to be able to live apart from humans. There are two qualities found in dogs: strength and speed.[13]

What the sources are for the Middle Ages' familiarity with Chrysippus's dog is uncertain, but we have already seen that the argument of the dog as syllogist appears early on in patristic culture: for Saint Basil (*Hexaemeron*, Homily IX) this is the example used to demonstrate that the dog has a faculty similar to reason. After this Chrysippus's dog makes its appearance in the bestiaries; for example in the twelfth-century *De Bestiis* sometimes attributed to Hugh of Fouilloy (and previously attributed to Hugh of Saint Victor, but more likely anonymous).[14] Later it will be mentioned by Gregory of Rimini as evidence of the fact that animals too possess the "notitia complexa de sensibilibus" (*Lectura super primum et secundum Sententiarum* I, 3, 1, 1).

The Middle Ages did not enjoy direct access to Porphyry's *De abstinentia*, first translated into Latin in the fifteenth century by Marsilio Ficino, but information regarding his arguments had been transmitted by Saint Jerome (*Adversus Jovinianum*) and, apropos of abstaining from animal meats, by Augustine (*Civitas Dei* I, 20, and *Confessions* III, 18, where the problem of abstinence is dismissed as a pagan prejudice).

---

13. Stephen A. Barney, W. J. Lewis, J. A. Beach, Oliver Berghof with the collaboration of Muriel Hall, *The Etymologies of Isidore of Seville*, Cambridge: Cambridge University Press, 2006, p. 253. Likewise, see also Rabanus Maurus, *De rerum naturis*, VIII *De bestiis.*

14. "Canis vero ubi vestigium leporis cervive reperit, et ad diverticulum semitae venerit, et quoddam viarum compitum, quod partes in plurimas scinditur, ambians singularum semitarum exordium, tacitus secum ipse pertractat, velut syllogisticam vocem sagicitate colligendi ordoris demittens. Aut certe, inquit, in hanc partem deflexit, aut in illam. Aut certe in humc se anfractum contulit, sed nec in stam, nec in illam ingressus est, superest igitur ut in istam partem se contulit, et sic falsitate repudiata in veritatem prolabitur" (*De bestiis*, III, 11, PL 177 86d). A similar text from the same period is found in the Cambridge Bestiary, except that the dog is pursuing, not a hare, but a deer.

In Scholastic circles too the question of the souls of animals was not explored to any significant extent because, although in the wake of the Aristotelian tradition the notion that animals had a soul had never been called into question, they were merely granted, in addition to the vegetative soul, a *sensitive* soul. A sensitive soul may have instincts but it clearly lacks rationality or the ability to exercise free choice, as Thomas Aquinas concludes, precisely apropos of Chrysippus's argument, in *Summa Theologiae*, I–II, 13, 2.[15]

---

15. "It would seem that irrational animals are able to choose. For choice 'is the desire of certain things on account of an end,' as stated in *Ethics* iii, 2, 3. But irrational animals desire something on account of an end: since they act for an end, and from desire. Therefore choice is in irrational animals. Further, the very word *electio* (choice) seems to signify the taking of something in preference to others. But irrational animals take something in preference to others: thus we can easily see for ourselves that a sheep will eat one grass and refuse another. Therefore choice is in irrational animals. Further, according to *Ethics* vi, 12, '*it is from prudence that a man makes a good choice of means.*' But prudence is found in irrational animals: hence it is said in the beginning of *Metaph.* i, 1 that 'those animals which, like bees, cannot hear sounds, are prudent by instinct.' We see this plainly, in wonderful cases of sagacity manifested in the works of various animals, such as bees, spiders, and dogs. For a hound in following a stag, on coming to a crossroad, tries by scent whether the stag has passed by the first or the second road: and if he find that the stag has not passed there, being thus assured, takes to the third road without trying the scent; as though he were reasoning by way of exclusion, arguing that the stag must have passed by this way, since he did not pass by the others, and there is no other road. Therefore it seems that irrational animals are able to choose. On the contrary, Gregory of Nyssa [*Nemesius, *De Nat. Hom.* xxxiii.] says that '*children and irrational animals act willingly but not from choice.*' Therefore choice is not in irrational animals. "I answer that, Since choice is the taking of one thing in preference to another it must of necessity be in respect of several things that can be chosen. Consequently in those things which are altogether determinate to one there is no place for choice. Now the difference between the sensitive appetite and the will is that, as stated above (Q[1], A[2], ad 3), the sensitive appetite is determinate to one particular thing, according to the order of nature; whereas the will, although determinate to one thing in general, viz. the good, according to the order of nature, is nevertheless indeterminate in respect of particular goods. Consequently choice belongs properly to the will, and not to the sensitive appetite which is all that irrational animals have. Wherefore irrational animals are not competent to choose. Not every desire of one thing on account of an end is called

Furthermore, a sensitive soul, unlike a rational soul, could not be immortal. Indeed Thomas, who holds that the rational (and immortal) soul is introduced by God into the fetus only when the brain is fully formed several months after conception (*Summa Theologiae* I, 90), came to the conclusion that even human embryos, which possess only a sensitive soul, could not participate in the resurrection of the flesh (*Supplementum* 80, 4).

This allowed Thomas to justify the slaughtering of animals for alimentary purposes: the inferior forms of life are ordered toward the survival of the superior forms, and therefore vegetables serve as food for animals and animals for man.[16]

---

choice: there must be a certain discrimination of one thing from another. And this cannot be except when the appetite can be moved to several things. "An irrational animal takes one thing in preference to another, because its appetite is naturally determinate to that thing. Wherefore as soon as an animal, whether by its sense or by its imagination, is offered something to which its appetite is naturally inclined, it is moved to that alone, without making any choice. Just as fire is moved upward and not downward, without its making any choice. "As stated in *Phys.* iii, 3 *'movement is the act of the movable, caused by a mover.'* Wherefore the power of the mover appears in the movement of that which it moves. Accordingly, in all things moved by reason, the order of reason which moves them is evident, although the things themselves are without reason: for an arrow through the motion of the archer goes straight towards the target, as though it were endowed with reason to direct its course. The same may be seen in the movements of clocks and all engines put together by the art of man. Now as artificial things are in comparison to human art, so are all natural things in comparison to the Divine art. And accordingly order is to be seen in things moved by nature, just as in things moved by reason, as is stated in Phys. ii. And thus it is that in the works of irrational animals we notice certain marks of sagacity, in so far as they have a natural inclination to set about their actions in a most orderly manner through being ordained by the Supreme art. For which reason, too, certain animals are called prudent or sagacious; and not because they reason or exercise any choice about things. This is clear from the fact that all that share in one nature, invariably act in the same way" (*Summa Theologiae*, I–II, 13, 2).

16. "Nullus peccat ex hoc quod utitur re aliqua ad hoc ad quod est. In rerum autem ordine imperfectiora sunt propter perfectiora, sicut etiam in generationis via natura ab imperfectis ad perfecta procedit. Et inde est quod sicut in generatione hominis prius est vivum, deinde animal, ultimo autem homo; ita etiam ea quae tantum vivunt, ut plantae, sunt communiter propter omnia animalia, et animalia sunt propter hominem. Et ideo si homo utatur plantis ad utilitatem animalium, et animalibus ad utilitatem hominis, non est illicitum, ut etiam per philos-

The themes of Porphyry's *De abstinentia* were alien to the medieval mentality, and the problem of the suffering of animals did not occasion much distress, given that human beings were sufficiently prone to suffering themselves.[17]

The fact that Saint Francis of Assisi could not only profess brotherly love toward animals but was also able (at least according to the powers attributed to him in Franciscan circles) to convince a wolf by reasoning with him, was evidence of a mystically provocative attitude at odds with the opinions officially shared by the philosophical and theological culture of the time.

So the thinkers of the Middle Ages do not appear to have been tempted by what we have termed "proto-evolutionist" tendencies. Even if we read onto-

---

ophum patet, in I Polit. Inter alios autem usus maxime necessarius esse videtur ut animalia plantis utantur in cibum, et homines animalibus, quod sine mortificatione eorum fieri non potest. Et ideo licitum est et plantas mortificare in usum animalium, et animalia in usum hominum, ex ipsa ordinatione divina, dicitur enim Gen. I, ecce, dedi vobis omnem herbam et universa ligna, ut sint vobis in escam et cunctis animantibus. Et Gen. IX dicitur, omne quod movetur et vivit, erit vobis in cibum" (*Summa Theologiae* II–II, 64, 1).

17. Though it may not be the first, the most famous gesture of renewed respect for animals is the celebrated passage in Montaigne ("Apology for Raymond Sebond," *Essays* II, 12), in which, in addition to defending the existence of a linguistic faculty in animals (since he does not see how their ability to complain, rejoice, call upon each other for help and utter amorous invitations can be defined otherwise), he observes how the constructive behavior of birds and spiders evinces a capacity for choice and thought: "Take the swallows, when spring returns; we can see them ferreting through all the corners of our houses; from a thousand places they select one, finding it the most suitable place to make their nests: is that done without judgment or discernment? And then when they are making their nests (so beautifully and so wondrously woven together) can birds use a square rather than a circle, an obtuse angle rather than a right angle, without knowing their properties or their effects? Do they bring water and then clay without realizing that hardness can be softened by dampening? They cover the floors of their palaces with moss or down; do they do so without foreseeing that the tender limbs of their little ones will lie more softly there and be more comfortable? Do they protect themselves from the stormy winds and plant their dwellings to the eastward, without recognizing the varying qualities of those winds and considering that one is more healthy for them than another? Why does the spider make her web denser in one place and slacker in another, using this knot here and that knot there, if she cannot reflect, think or reach conclusions?" (*The Complete Essays*. Translated and edited with an introduction and notes by M. A. Screech, Penguin Books, 1991, pp. 508–509).

genesis in terms of philogenesis, the development from the vegetative soul to
the sensitive soul and eventually to the rational soul was not seen as a *continuum,* and (given the Thomistic notions cited above) the transition in the
fetus from the vegetative soul to the rational soul was, so to speak, a "catastrophe" attributable to direct divine intervention. Still, Rosier-Catach (2006)
points out, in a passage from Dante's *Convivio* (III, 7, 6), the idea of a more
or less continuous gradation from the souls of the angels to the souls of humans to the souls of the animals, a gradation that strikes her as definitely
"contrary to the teachings of the Church":

> And since in the intellectual order of the universe the ascent and de-
> scent are almost by continuous gradations from the lowest form to the
> highest and from the highest to the lowest, as we see in the order of
> beings capable of sensation; and since between the angelic nature, which
> is intellectual being, and the human nature there is no gradation but
> rather the one is, as it were, continuous with the other by the order of
> gradation; and since between the human soul and the most perfect
> soul of the brute animals there is also no intermediary gradation, so it
> is that we see many men so vile and in such a state of baseness that
> they seem to be almost nothing but beasts. Consequently it must be
> stated and firmly believed that there are some so noble and so lofty in
> nature that they are almost nothing but angels, for otherwise the hu-
> man species would not be continuous in both directions, which is
> impossible.[18]

These observations did not prevent Dante from affirming in the *De vulgari eloquentiae* (I, 2, 5) that animals are incapable of speech and have no
need of it (just as angels are endowed with an ineffable intellectual capacity,
so that each one understands the thoughts of each of the others, or rather all
of them read the thoughts of all of the others in the mind of God). Because
they do not have individual but only specific passions, knowing their own
they also know those of their congeners, and they have no interest in knowing those of animals of a different species. Likewise demons have no need of

18. Dante Alighieri, *Il Convivio* (= The Banquet), translated by Richard Lan-
sing, New York: Garland, 1990.

discourse because they all know reciprocally the degree of their own perfidiousness. (And we cannot even attempt to transform Dante into an evolutionist *ante litteram* simply because he permitted himself the rhetorical hyperbole of addressing his lady as an angel!)

The Middle Ages was not insensitive to the presence of animals. Indeed it was almost obsessively concerned with them in its bestiaries. But, rather than speaking (as occurs in the tradition of the fable), those animals are themselves the *signs* of a divine language. They "say" many things, but without being aware of it. This is because what they are or what they do become figures of something else. The lion signifies the Redemption by canceling its tracks, the elephant by attempting to lift its fallen companion, the serpent by sloughing off its old skin. Characters in a book written *digito Dei* ("with the finger of God"), the animals do not produce language, instead they themselves are words in a symbolic language. They are not observed in their actual behaviors, but in those attributed to them. They do not do what they do but what the bestiaries would have them do, so that they can express through their behavior something of which they are totally incognizant.

This is not all. As mere signs they are completely polyvocal; they serve to communicate different things according to the circumstances and properties highlighted. To confine ourselves to the dog, Rabanus Maurus (IX century) explains why and by virtue of what contradictory properties the dog may represent either the devil, the Jews, or the Gentiles,[19] while in the anonymous

---

19. "Canis autem diversas significationes habet, nam ut diabolum uel Iudeum siue gentilem populum significant. Vnde propheta dominum precatur dicens in Psalmo: Erue a framea anima meam, et de manu canis unicam meam. Nam in meliore parte canis ponitur, ut in Ecclesiaste ubi scriptum est: Melior est canis uius leone mortuo. Hic leonem diabolum, canem uero gentilem vel hominem peccatorem accipiendum puto, qui deo melior dicitur: Quod ad fidem et pententiam posit venire, hinc de Iudeis scrptum est: Conuertantur ad uesperum et famem patientur, ut canes circuibunt ciuitatem. Canes intelleguntur muti sacerdotes uel inprobi ut in ecclesia: Canes muti non ualentes lactare. Canes Iudei in Psalmo: Quoniam circumdederunt me canes multi. Canes populus gentium ut in euangelio: Non est bonum sumere panem filiorum et mittere canibus ad manducandum. Canes heretici ut in Deuteronomio: Non inferes precium canis in domum dei tui. Et in apostolo: Videte canes uidete malos operarios uidete concisiones. Canis uero uoracissimum animal, atque inportunum, consueuit illas domus latratibus defendere, in quibus edacitatem suam nouit, accepto pane saciate, his

eleventh-century *Libro della natura degli animali* or in the *De Bestiis* attributed to Hugh of Fouilloy the fact that it swallows its own vomit allows the dog to be chosen as a symbol of the repentant sinner, and in the *Bestiario moralizzato di Gubbio* (thirteenth–fourteenth century) the dog that dies defending its master becomes a symbol of Christ who died for our salvation.

Things are not so very different in the case of the Renaissance emblem books, which are far more dependent on the medieval bestiaries than is commonly thought. Some historians have seen this as a development of the theme of canine intelligence (see, for example, Höltgen 1998), given that, in the best-known source for the emblem books, Horapollon's fifth-century *Hieroglyphica* (I, 39), the dog is singled out to represent a sacred scribe or a prophet or an embalmer or the spleen or the sense of smell or laughter or a sneeze (or a magistrate or a judge). But from this abundance of references it is evident that the dog (or any other animal for that matter) lends itself to many interpretations. In the texts that develop the theme in the Renaissance and Baroque periods, such as, for example, Picinelli's *Mondo simbolico* (1653) or the various versions of Valeriano's *Hieroglyphica* (between 1556 and 1626), the dog is represented as a symbol of magnanimity, generosity, courage, obedience, love of sacred literature, remembrance of things past, and memory of

---

merito conparantur Iudei qui Christianae fidali munere salo contigit, ut qui ante fuit persecutor Christiani nominis, postea diuino munere iungeretur apostolis. Canes homini rixosi uel detractors alter utro se lacerantes, ut in apostolo: Quod si inuicem mordetis et comedetis uidete ne ab inuicem consumamini. Catuli abusiue dicuntur, quarumlibet bestiarum filii, nam propriae catuli canum sunt, per diminutionem dicti. Lynciscile dicuntur ut ait Plinius canes nati ex lupis et canibus. Cum inter se forte miscuntur, solent et Inde feminas canes noctu in si alligatas admitti, ad tigres bestias a quibus in siliri et nasci, ex eodem faetu canes adeo acerrimos et fortes, ut in complexu leones prosternant. Catuli ergo significant gentiles, unde est in evangelio, quod Sirofaenissa mulier, cui dominus ait: Non est bonum sumere panem filiorum et mittere canibus, respodit ei dicens: Etiam domine. Nam et Catelli edunt de micis quae cadunt de mensa dominorum suorum. Mensa quippe est scriptura sancta quae nobis panem uitae ministrat. Mice puerorum interna sunt misteria scripturarum, quibus humilium solent corda refici. Non ergo crustas, sed micas de pane puerorum edunt. Catelli quia conversi ad fidem, qui erant despecti in gentibus non littere superficiem in scripturis sed spiritalium sensuum, quia in bonis attibus proficere ualeant inquirunt" (Rabanus Maurus, *De naturis rerum* VIII).

benefits received, while, at the same time, it is an emblem of sacrilege, stupidity, adulation, buffoonery, and impudence. In Alciati's one hundred and sixty-fifth emblem "Inanis impetus" ("Antagonism that achieves nothing"), a dog gazes up at the moon as if in a mirror convinced there is another dog up there, and he bays, but the moon continues on its course, and the dog's bay is carried away vainly on the wind. And in emblem 175 "Alius peccat, alius plectitur" ("One sins and another is punished"), the dog who bites the stone that has been thrown at him is incapable of harming his aggressor. Finally, in an allegory of Logic that appears in the various editions of Gregor Reisch's *Margarita philosophica* we find two hunting dogs symbolizing the pursuit of knowledge, but one represents truth and the other falsehood—which does not offer much of a guarantee of canine sagacity.

Still, there is an area of discourse, for the most part indifferent to the universe of symbols, in which we encounter references to animal behavior based on nonfanciful observations, and this occurs in the discussions of language on the part of grammarians, to say nothing of philosophers and theologians, where we encounter canonical references, not merely to articulated language, but also to various forms of interjection or vocal emission, such as the moaning of the sick, the lowing of oxen, the chirping of chickens, the pseudo-language of magpies and parrots, and especially and most frequently the barking of the dog.

Encountering these references so frequently, we get the obvious impression that each author is borrowing from predecessors a well-worn topos, and is therefore simply repeating concepts handed down by tradition. The dog's bark is a victim of the inertia of the *auctoritates*, while the examples migrate automatically from text to text.[20]

---

20. To complicate things further, another element comes into play. Medieval thought is to put it mildly obsessed with two objects of investigation, God and man. Observe what happens in the theory of definition from Porphyry's *Isagoge* down to Ockham. Porphyry's tree ought to be seen as a logical artifice that permits us to define every element of our cosmic furniture, but in fact it is invariably exemplified in abbreviated form, in such a way as to distinguish unequivocally man from the divinity. As we observed in Chapter 1, none of the available examples of the *Arbor Porphiriana* serves to define unambiguously the horse or the dog, to say nothing of plants and minerals. Irrational animals find a place there only to furnish a pole of comparison with the rational animals. Whereupon the

And yet it pays to proceed cautiously in the case of medieval writers, who realized (if we may be allowed to cite another famous topos) that the nose of their *auctoritas* was made of wax and could be reshaped *ad libitum*. The first thing a student of the Middle Ages must do when coming across the same term and—to all intents and purposes—the same concept, is to suspect that this terminological identity masks or conceals an idea that is almost always novel and in each case different.

If, out of a taste (also medieval) for summing up systems of definitions in trees of the Porphyrian kind, one begins to construct (for every author who mentions the barking of the dog or similar utterances) taxonomies of the various species of utterances and sounds, one becomes aware that, depending on the author, the moaning of the sick and the barking of the dog occupy different positions. Which leads us to suspect that, when different authors spoke of the *latratus canis,* they had in mind a different zoosemiotic phenomenon, and that this difference in classification implied a difference in underlying semiotics.

Sometimes, to discover the soul of a philosophical system we must latch on to symptoms at its periphery. Which amounts to saying that sometimes we can better understand the Thomistic system through the implications it produces in a *quaestio quodlibetalis* than by starting with the *Summae Theologiae* (to which, however, we must obviously return). This may not be true in every case, but one thing that is sure is that an inquiry into the barking of the dog demonstrates that not only is there a medieval semiotics, but there are in fact many.

4.2. *Latratus Canis*

4.2.1. *Names and Signs*
To account for the embarrassing position of the *latratus canis* in medieval linguistic theories we must bear in mind the fact that Greek semiotics, from the *Corpus Hippocraticum* to the Stoics, draws a clear distinction between a

---

medieval theory of definition leaves them to their fate and fails to provide pointers for distinguishing a dog from a horse, let alone a dog from a wolf. In order to have adequate taxonomical instruments at our disposal, we must await the naturalists and theorists of artificial languages of seventeenth-century England (see Slaughter 1982 and Eco 1993).

theory of names (in other words, of verbal language) and a theory of signs. The signs *(semeia)* are natural phenomena, which today we call symptoms or indices, whose relationship to what they signify is based on the mechanism of inference: if such and such a symptom, then such and such a malady; if this woman produces milk, then she has given birth; where there's smoke, there's fire. Words, on the other hand, bear a different relationship to the things they name or the concept they signify, and this relationship is the one sanctioned by the Aristotelian theory of definition. It is a relationship of equivalency or mutual substitutability.

Now, these two semiotic lines begin to merge in the Stoics, and this fusion will be explicitly recognized by Augustine (in the *De magistro*, in the *De doctrina christiana*, and in the *De dialectica*).[21] In Augustine a science of the *signum* as the supreme genus takes shape, of which both symptoms and words, the mimetic gestures of actors and the blare of the military trumpet, are species. Still, not even in Augustine is the dichotomy definitively resolved between the relationship of inference, which binds a natural sign to the thing it is a sign of, and the relationship of equivalence, which binds a linguistic term to the concept it signifies or the thing it designates.

By now medieval semiotics is aware of both lines of thought, but is not yet fully capable of perfecting their unification. This is why, as we shall see, the *latratus canis* will occupy a different position in different classifications, depending on whether they are classifications of signs in general or of *voces*. Because the classification of *signa* is Stoic in origin, while the classification of *voces* is Aristotelian.

4.2.2. The Stoic Influence: Augustine

In his *De doctrina christiana* (II, 1–4), Augustine proposes his famous definition of the sign. A sign is something which, over and above its sensible aspect, brings to mind something different from itself, like the spoor left by an animal, the smoke from which one infers the presence of fire, the moan that indicates pain, the bugle that communicates orders to a troop of soldiers. Signs are therefore either *natural* or *given*. *Signa naturalia* are those that

---

21. I refer the reader to the chapter on "Signs" in Eco (1984b: 14–45), which was based on my entry "Segno" in volume 12 (1981) of the *Enciclopedia Einaudi*. See also Todorov (1982).

make something manifest independently of any intention, like the smoke that indicates fire or the tracks left by the animal or even the anger that shows in a face without the angry person wishing to show it. The *signa data* on the other hand are those emitted in order to communicate the movements of the mind or the contents of one's thought. We only *signify* in order to produce in the mind of someone else what we already have in our own. But, on the one hand, what is in the mind of the person emitting the sign is not necessarily a concept; it can also be a psychological state or a sensation; on the other hand, the sign produces *something* in the mind of the addressee, not necessarily a concept. This is why Augustine places among the *signa data* both the words of Scripture (in addition of course to human words) and the signs produced by animals, and, in a humane touch, he evokes for us not only the utilitarian relationship between the rooster and the hen in search of food but also the cooing of the turtle dove calling for her mate.[22]

---

22. "For a sign is a thing which, over and above the impression it makes on the senses, causes something else to come into the mind as a consequence of itself: as when we see a footprint, we conclude that an animal whose footprint this is has passed by; and when we see smoke, we know that there is fire beneath; and when we hear the voice of a living man, we think of the feeling in his mind; and when the trumpet sounds, soldiers know that they are to advance or retreat, or do whatever else the state of the battle requires. Now some signs are natural, others conventional. Natural signs are those which, apart from any intention or desire of using them as signs, do yet lead to the knowledge of something else, as, for example, smoke when it indicates fire. For it is not from any intention of making it a sign that it is so, but through attention to experience we come to know that fire is beneath, even when nothing but smoke can be seen. And the footprint of an animal passing by belongs to this class of signs. And the countenance of an angry or sorrowful man indicates the feeling in his mind, independently of his will: and in the same way every other emotion of the mind is betrayed by the tell-tale countenance, even though we do nothing with the intention of making it known. This class of signs, however, it is no part of my design to discuss at present. But as it comes under this division of the subject, I could not altogether pass it over. It will be enough to have noticed it thus far. Conventional signs, on the other hand, are those which living beings mutually exchange for the purpose of showing, as well as they can, the feelings of their minds, or their perceptions, or their thoughts. Nor is there any reason for giving a sign except the desire of drawing forth and conveying into another's mind what the giver of the sign has in his own mind. We wish, then, to consider and discuss this class of signs so far as

He leaves us no choice, then, but to attribute to him the classification shown in Figure 4.1.

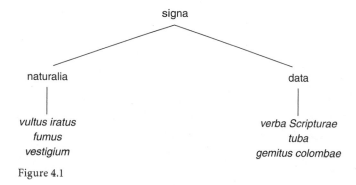

Figure 4.1

Except that at this point Augustine realizes that he has gone too far, and in his final paragraph he corrects himself, leaving in suspense the question as to whether the call of the dove or the groans of the sick are truly to be considered phenomena of signification. If it were not for this correction, the "language" of the dove would have been firmly situated alongside the words of Holy Scripture. And since it is the latter that he is concerned with, he chooses to shelve the other issue for the time being.

---

men are concerned with it, because even the signs which have been given us of God, and which are contained in the Holy Scriptures, were made known to us through men—those, namely, who wrote the Scriptures. The beasts, too, have certain signs among themselves by which they make known the desires in their mind. For when the poultry-cock has discovered food, he signals with his voice for the hen to run to him, and the dove by cooing calls his mate, or is called by her in turn; and many signs of the same kind are matters of common observation. Now whether these signs, like the expression or the cry of a man in grief, follow the movement of the mind instinctively and apart from any purpose, or whether they are really used with the purpose of signification, is another question, and does not pertain to the matter in hand. And this part of the subject I exclude from the scope of this work as not necessary to my present object" (Augustine, *On Christian Doctrine*, II, 1–3, online trans. by J. F. Shaw, from *Select Nicene and Post-Nicene Fathers*, at http://www.ccel.org/ccel/augustine/doctrine .iv.iii.ii.html). On the doctrine of the sign in Augustine, see Manetti (1987), Vecchio (1994), and Sirridge (1997).

4.2.3. *The Stoic Influence: Abelard*

One solution to the riddle of the dove will make its appearance (albeit some-what problematically) with Abelard. In his *Dialectica* (I, iii, 1), the classifica-tion he espouses (which in any case does not depart from the Augustinian distinction) can be reduced to the Aristotelian-Boethian model (to be dis-cussed later): meaningful *voces* may be divided into those than are mean-ingful *naturaliter* and those whose meaning proceeds *ex impositione* or *ad placitum* ("by convention"); and among the natural utterances he cites the barking of the dog (as an expression of anger).[23]

But in his *Ingredientibus,* another opposition is associated with that be-tween *naturaliter* and *ex impositione,* namely, that between *significativa* and *significantia.*[24]

---

23. "Liquet autem ex suprapositis significativarum vocum alias naturaliter, alias ad placitum significare. Quecumque enim habiles sunt ad significandum vel ex natura vel ex impositione significative dicuntur. Naturales quidem voces, quas non humana inventio imposuit sed sola natura [contulit], naturaliter [et non] ex impositione significativas dicimus, ut ea quam latrando canis emittit, ex qua ip-sius iram concepimus. Omnium enim hominum discretio ex latratu canis eius iram intelligit, quem ex commotione ire certum est procedere in his omnibus que latrant. Sed huiusmodi voces que nec locutiones componunt, quippe nec ab homini-bus proferuntur, ab omni logica sunt aliene" (Petrus Abaelardus, *Dialectica,* First complete edition of the Parisian manuscript, With an introduction by L. M. De Rijk, Ph.D., Second, revised edition, Assen: Van Gorcum 1970, p. 114).

24. "Significare Aristotelis accipit per se intellectum constituere, significati-vum autem dicitur, quidquid habile est per se ad significandum ex institutione aliqua sive ab homine facta sive a natura. Nam latratus natura artifex, id est Deus, ea intentione cani contulit, ut iram eius repraesentaret; et voluntas hominum no-mina et verba ad significandum instituit nec non etiam res quasdam, ut circulum vini vel signa quibus monachi utuntur. Non enim significare vocum tantum est, verum etiam rerum. Unde scriptum est: nutu signisque loquentur (Ovid, *II Trist.* 453). Per 'significativum' separat a nomine voces non significativas, quae scilicet neque ab homine neque a natura institutae sunt ad significandum. Nam licet un-aquaeque vox certificare possit suum prolatorem animal esse, sicut latratus canis ipse esse iratum, non tamen omnes ad hoc institutae sunt ostendendum, sicut la-tratus est ad significationem irae institutus. Similiter unaquaeque vox, cum se per auditum praesentans se subgerat intellectui, non ideo significativa dicenda est, quia per nullam institutionem hoc habet, sicut nec aliquis homo se praesentans nobis dum per hoc quod sensui subjacet, de se dat intellectum, sui significativus

In order for a word to be *significativa* it must be an *institutio*. This *institutio* is not a convention (like the *impositio*); instead it is a decision that lies behind both the *impositio* and the natural *significativeness,* and could come very close to intentionality. Words signify in fact by means of the institution of human will, which orders them *ad intellectum constituere,* that is, to produce concepts. Seeing that by his day the barking of the dog must have become a canonical citation, Abelard declares that it is significant of anger and pain, just like a human expression designed to communicate something, because it is instituted by nature, in other words by God, to express this meaning. Thus, the bark can be distinguished from those phenomena that are merely *significantia,* that is, symptomatic, such as, for example, that same bark that, heard from a distance, allows us merely to conclude that there is a dog somewhere over yonder.

If a man, then, hears a bark and infers that there is a dog present, this is a symptom being used, by inference, to draw a signification, but the fact that it becomes significant does not imply that it has been instituted as significative. On the other hand, when the dog barks, it does so to express a specific concept (anger or pain or rejoicing), in other words, in order to *constituere intellectum* (produce concepts) in our minds. Abelard does not say that the dog does so of its own free will: the dog is acted upon by another will, belonging to the natural order (a sort, we might say, of *agent will*).[25] But it is still

---

dicitur, quia licet ita sit a natura creatus, ut hoc facere possit, non est ideo creatus, ut hoc faciat. 'Significativum vero magis ad causam quam ad actum significandi pertinet, ut sicut non omnia significativa actualiter significant, ita non omnia actu significantia sint significativa, sed ea sola quae ad significandum sunt instituta" (*Logica "Ingredientibus,"* Glosses on the Peri Hermeneias. In Bernhard Geyer, *Peter Abaelards Philosophische Schriften,* Münster, Aschendorff, 1927, pp. 335–336).

25. An explanation of why in the case of animals nature acts as a sort of agent will (comparable to "agent intellect") is provided by Albertus Magnus, *De anima* II [*De voce qualiter fiat*], iii, 22: "Et cum duo sint in anima, affectus scilicet doloris vel gaudii et conceptus cordis de rebus, non est vox significans affectum, sed potius conceptum. Cetera autem animalia affectus habentia sonos suos affectus indicantes emittunt et ideo non vocant; et quaecumque illorum plurium sunt affectuum sunt etiam plurium sonorum, et quae levioris sunt complexionis, et ideo aves plurium sunt garrituum quam gressibilia. Et illae quae inter aves sunt latioris linguae, et melioris memoriae, magis imitantur locutionem et ceteros sonos, quos audiunt. Licet enim bruta habeant imaginationem, sicut superius ostendimus, tamen non moveretur ab ipsis imaginatis secundum rationem imaginatorum, sed a

an intentional agent. Abelard is quite clear: a thing is significative because of the act of will that produces it as such, not because of the fact that it produces meanings.

Accordingly, Abelard's taxonomy should be translated as in Figure 4.2.

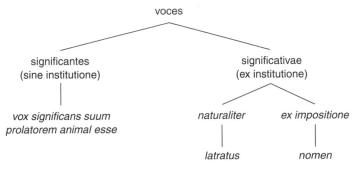

Figure 4.2

Apropos of which, it could be said that where there is *institutio,* there is some form of code, a correspondence (natural or conventional) between *signans* and *signatum,* which cannot be simply a matter of conjecture. But the *voces significantes* remain a matter for conjecture and therefore inference, and in this sense Abelard sticks to the Stoic distinction that distinguishes between speech act and index or cue.

4.2.4. Boethius's Reading of De interpretatione *16a*

This distinction, however, is not so evident in the semiotics clearly derived from Aristotle. Now, if we are to appreciate most of the discussions that follow, we must take as our point of departure, as the Middle Ages did, *De interpretatione* 16a, where, with the purpose of defining nouns and verbs, Aristotle makes a number of statements about signs in general. Let me attempt a *translatio media,* which, while taking into account our current versions,

---

natura et ideo omnia similiter operantur; una enim hirundo facit nidum sicut alia, et haec imitatio est naturae potius quam artis.Ideo anima imaginativa in eis non regit naturam, neque agit eam ad opera, secundum diversa imaginata, sicut facit homo, sed potius regitur a natura et agitur ad opera ab ipsa, ei ideo fit quod licet habeant apus se imaginata, tamen ad exprimendum illa non formant voces. Affectus autem laetitiarum et tristiarum magis profundatur in natura quam in anima, et ideo illos exprimunt sonis et garritibus."

endeavors above all to give an account of those aspects that particularly struck the translators and interpreters of the Middle Ages:

> The sounds of the voice *(ta en te phone)* are symbols *(symbola)* of the affections *(pathematon)* of the soul, just as the letters of the alphabet *(grammata)* are symbols of the things that are in the voice *(en te phone)*. And as the letters of the alphabet are not the same for all men, in the same way neither are the sounds. Nevertheless, sounds and letters are basically signs *(semeia)* of the affections of the soul, which are the same for everyone, and likewise things *(pragmata)*, of which the affections of the soul are similar images *(omoiomata)*, are the same for everyone. (16a, 1–10)
>
> A name is a sound endowed with meaning *(phone semantīke)* by convention *(kata syntheken)*. (16a, 20–21)

Lo Piparo (2003) has proposed a radically different interpretation of this passage,[26] but in the present instance we are concerned, not with the

---

26. According to this reading the affections of the soul are not mental images of things, but modes of being of thought, cognitive modalities (like thinking, being afraid, or experiencing joy). The *pragmata* are not real things or facts in general (otherwise how could we explain why Aristotle says elsewhere in his works that we can think of nonexistent or false hybrids like the *hircocervus* or phenomena whose existence we are unable to prove (such as squaring the circle or the *commensurability* of the diagonal). Likewise, "those things that are in the voice" could be transformations, differentiations, or articulations that are proper to the human voice. Finally, an expression like *kata syntheken* does not mean that linguistic *voces* are related to the affections of the soul by means of convention, but that they are articulate, the effect of a syntactic composition (and for this very reason the *voces* emitted by animals, which are inarticulate, cannot express thoughts). At the same time the interpretation of the *omoiomata* is also called into question. It would refer to the fact that there exists a relationship of structural similarity between logical-cognitive operations and events in the world. In conclusion, the passage from Aristotle should be reinterpreted as follows: "The articulations of the human voice and the logical-cognitive operations of the human soul are different from each other and complementary, just as written articulations and articulations of the voice are. And just as the minimal units with which and in which writing is articulated are not the same for all mankind, neither are the minimal units in which the linguistic voice is articulated. On the other hand, the logical-cognitive operations of which the vocal and graphic units are the natural physiognomic signs are the same for all mankind, and likewise the same for all

philological exegesis of Aristotle, but with seeing how the Middle Ages read this text; and the current interpretation was that what we have on the one hand are things, which impress their images upon the soul (which constitutes their *species*), while on the other we have the linguistic symbols (sonorous and graphemic) that refer to the affections of the soul, or mental images, *ad placitum*. But, if this is how the text is to be understood, we ought to draw another conclusion from it: that sounds and letters (independently of their meaning) are also indices *(semeia)* of the affections of the soul. An idea that may appear banal in itself (like saying that if someone speaks it is because they have something in their heads that they want to say), but which becomes less banal when we see the advantage that Thomas derives from it indirectly, when he lets it be understood that we do not recognize that man is a rational animal through direct knowledge of his essence, but because he manifests his rationality though language.

Boethius's Latin translation, upon which medieval thinkers will base themselves, runs as follows (my emphasis):

> Sunt ergo ea quae sunt in voce, earum quae sunt in anima passionum *notae;* et ea quae scribuntur, eorum quae sunt in voce. Et quemadmodum nec litterae omnibus eaedem, sic nec eaedem voces; quorum autem hae primorum *notae* sunt, eaedem omnibus passiones animae sunt; et quorum hae similitudines, res etiam eaedem. . . .
>
> Nomen ergo est vox significativa secundum placitum sine tempore, cuius pars est significativa separata . . . Secundum placitum vero, quoniam naturaliter nominum nihil est, sed quando fit *nota;* nam designant et inlitterati soni, ut ferarum, quorum nihil est nomen.[27]

---

mankind are the facts with which the logical-cognitive operations of the human soul are in a relation of similarity" (Lo Piparo 2003: 187).

27. *De Interpretatione,* in *Aristoteles Latinus* II, 1–2, ed. L. Minio-Paluello, Bruges-Paris, Desclée de Brouwer, 1965, pp. 5, 4–11 and pp. 6, 4, 11–13. The following is a translation of Aristotle's original Greek text: "Now spoken sounds are symbols of affections in the soul, and written marks symbols of spoken sounds. And just as written marks are not the same for all men, neither are spoken sounds. But what these are in the first place signs of—affections of the soul—are the same for all; and what these affections are likenesses of—actual things—are also the same . . . A name is a spoken sound significant by convention, without

Boethius, then, translates with the same word, *nota,* both of the Aristotelian terms, *symbolon* and *semeion.* What Aristotle meant to say was that the twofold relationship word/concept and letters of the alphabet/words is symbolic, or, as the Middle Ages will interpret it, is based on convention (and for this reason varies from one language to another), whereas the relationship between concept and thing is iconic.

But if we translate *semeion* with *nota,* and understand it to mean "sign" in the contemporary meaning of the word (the sense in which we also speak of a linguistic sign), what Aristotle appears to be saying is that words are symbols *and* signs of concepts, and that consequently the two terms are synonyms. In addition to leaving in abeyance the idea, previously referred to, that Aristotle was saying that the fact that words are spoken is an *index, proof,* or *symptom* of the fact that concepts exist in the mind of the speaker, it also leaves in abeyance the whole universe of indiciary signs, and in this sense it poses a number of serious problems that we will come to grips with in due time.

For the moment let us consider a telling example. When Aristotle says, in *De interpretatione* (16a 19–20, 26–29)—this at least was the way he was read in the Middle Ages—that a name is a *vox significativa* by convention, and that no sound is a name for natural reasons but is such only when it *becomes,* by convention, a symbol, he adds that inarticulate sounds, like those made by the beasts, *manifest (delousi)* something, though none of them is a name.

Aristotle does not say that the sounds made by the beasts signify or designate something, he says they manifest it, as a symptom makes manifest its cause. But the Middle Ages, as we shall see, has no trouble translating the Greek *delousi* with the Latin *significant.* Boethius's translation, by rendering symbol and index with the same term *nota,* obliterated the distinction and favored their identification.[28] But the Middle Ages will have no problem in-

---

time, none of whose parts is significant in separation . . . I say 'by convention' because no name is a name naturally but only when it has become a symbol. Even inarticulate noises (of beasts, for instance) do indeed reveal something, yet none of them is a name." *Aristotle's Categories and De Interpretatione,* Translated with Notes and Glossary by J. L. Ackrill, Oxford: Clarendon Press, 1963, pp. 43–44.

28. Boethius translates *semeion* as *nota* on his own initiative, whereas he finds the identification of *symbolon* with *nota* already sanctioned by Cicero (*Topica* VIII, 35), on whom he comments as follows: "Nota vero est quae rem quamque designat. Quo fit ut omne nomen nota sit, idcirco quod notam facit rem de qua

terpreting the sounds made by animals as *voces significativae,* even though not the same as *nomina* (and various commentators explain that in such cases Aristotle is not talking about *voces* but about *soni,* because not all animals, on account of the structure of their phonatory organs, can utter *voces,* and many simply produce sounds).[29]

The barking of the dog, which means that the dog is angry, appears in Boethius as an example of a *vox significativa,* though not *ad placitum,* but *naturaliter:* "canum latratus iram significat canum"—and, by the same token, *voces naturaliter significativae* are also the moans of the sick.[30]

---

praedicatur, id Aristoteles symbolon nominavit" (*In Topicis Ciceronis Commentaria* IV, PL. 64, col. 1111 B). And here Boethius establishes the equivalency, as characteristic properties of *nota,* between *rem designare* and *rem notam facere,* in other words, between the significative function proper to Aristotle's *symbolon* and the inferential or symptomatic function of *semeion.*

29. See *Latratus canis* ("On Animal Language"), p. 29, n. 20, and *De Resp.* 476 a 1–b 12; *Hist. An.* 535 b 14–24; *De an.* 420 b 9–14. And along the same lines Boethius, *In Librum Aristotelis De Interpretatione Commentaria majora,* PL 64, col. 423 D, where he explains that fish and cicadas do not have a voice but produce sounds with their gills or with their chests. Similar observations are found in Thomas (*In l. De Int.,* 1, IV, 46) as well as in Pseudo Aegidius Romanus (*In Libros Peri hermeneias Expositio,* Venetiis 1507, fol. 49rb). The example of the *latratus canis* is already present in Ammonius, whose work, however, was only translated into Latin in 1268 by William of Moerbeke (*Commentaire sur le Peri Hermenneias,* ed. G. Verbeke, *Corpus Latinum Commentariorum in Aristotelem Graecorum* I. Louvain-Paris: Nauwelaerts 1961, p. 47: "Hoc autem 'secundum confictionem' separat ipsum a natura significantibus vocibus. Tales autem sunt quae irrationalium animalium voces. Extraneo enim aliquo superveniente, canis latrans significat extranei praesentiam. Sed non secundum aliquam confictionem et condictionem ad invicem emittunt talem vocem canes" ("'By convention' distinguishes [the name] from the vocal sounds significant by nature. Such are the vocal sounds of the irrational animals. For, when a stranger suddenly appears, a dog by his bark signifies the presence of the stranger; but dogs do not produce this sort of vocal sound according to any convention or agreements among themselves"). Ammonius, *On Aristotle's* On Interpretation 1–8, Translated by David Blank, Ithaca, N.Y.: Cornell University Press, 1996, p. 39.

30. "Neque solum nomen vox significativa est, sed sunt quaedam voces quae significant quidem, sed nomina non sunt, ut ea quae a nobis in aliquibus affectibus proferuntur, ut cum quis gemitum edit, vel cum dolore concitus emittit clamorem. Illud enim doloris animi, illud corporis signum est, et cum sint voces et significent quamdam vel animi vbel corporis passionem, nullus tamen gemitum clamoremque

And so, under the genus *voces significativae* we find a species that according to Aristotle should have belonged among the *semeia*. In this category, Boethius and those who follow him lump together, along with the barking of the dog, the *gemitus infirmorum,* the whinny of the horse and the sounds made by those animals that have no *vox* but have "tantum sonitu quodam concrepant."[31]

Boethius assuredly understands that these *voces* signify *naturaliter,* because they evidently reveal their cause according to the (symptomatic) model of inference, but, having obfuscated the distinction between the doctrine of indices and the doctrine of names, he neglects an important fact: that natural sounds do not have an emitter, unless, as sometimes occurs in certain processes of divination, they are interpreted *as if* they had been emitted intentionally by a supernatural agent. The moaning of the sick and the barking of the dog, however, have an emitter, though we are not in a position to affirm that the emission was deliberate. But Boethius also singles out the whinny of the horse: "hinnitus quoque equorum sepe alterius equi consuetudinem quaerit,"[32] when the horse whinnies to call another horse, and hence whinnies with a definite intention. In fact, in the same passage, Boethius says that "ferarum quoque mutorum animalium voces interdum aliqua significatione praeditas esse perspicimus." We are dealing, then, with *voces* endowed with some meaning. But endowed by whom (before the advent of Abelard's idea of an "active will")? By the beast emitting them or by the human hearing them?

---

dixerit nomen. Mutorumque quoque animalium sunt quaedam voces quae significant: ut canum latratus iras significant canum, alia vox autem mollior quodam blandimenta XXXX decsignat, quare adjecta differentia separandum erat nomen ab his omnibus quae voces quidem essent et significarent sed nominis vocabulum non tenerentur" (*In De Int. Comm. Maj.,* PL 64, col. 420 C–D).

31. See *In l. De Int. Comm. Maj.,* PL 64, col. 423 A–B: "Nec vero dicitur quod nulla vox naturaliter aliquod designet, sed quod nomina non naturaliter, sed positione significent. Alioqui habent hoc ferarum, mutorumque animalium soni, quorum vox quidem significat aliquid, ut hinnitus equi consueti equi inquisitionem, latratus canum latrantium iracundiam monstrat, et alia huiusmodi. Sed cum voces mutorum animalium propria natura significant, nullis tamen elementorum formulis conscribunt. Nomen vero quamquam subjacet elementis."

32. Cf. Saint Thomas Aquinas and Tommaso de Vio Cajetan, *Aristotle On Interpretation*: Commentary by St. Thomas and Cajetan (Peri hermeneias), trans. from the Latin with an introd. by Jean T. Oesterle, Milwaukee, Wis.: Marquette University Press, 1962.

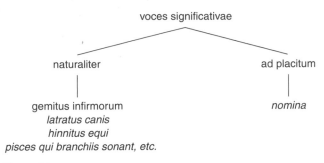

Figure 4.3

We can immediately see that the *latratus canis* (and all the other sounds animals make) may enjoy a double status: on the one hand the dog speaks to other dogs and on the other the dog speaks to humans. But in the second case, the alternative is still twofold: either humans understand the dog's bark because they have acquired a habit that makes them apt at interpreting symptoms (like the sailor who has learned how to interpret the signs in the sky), or else humans have acquired a habit that makes them apt at interpreting the language the dog uses to talk to them. These are two distinct zoosemiotic problems (while yet another problem remains on the back burner: if and in what way the dog understands the language the human uses to address him).

We must conclude, then, that with Boethius a classification of *voces* is inaugurated which has two characteristics: it melds together the Stoic classification of signs (as *voces significativae naturaliter*) and the Aristotelian classification of *voces* (as *nomina ad placitum*), and it leaves in abeyance the problem of the intentionality of the utterance of the *vox*.

Consequently, this classification—consolidating a series of basically analogous positions taken by a number of authors, from Boethius to Peter of Spain, Lambert of Auxerre, Garland the Compotist, and others—would appear as in Figure 4.3.[33]

---

33. See pp. 27–28, n. 15, in *Latratus canis* ("On Animal Language"), the references to Garlandus Compotista, *Dialectica* III (ed. De Rijk. Assen: Van Gorcum, 1959, pp. 64, 24–28); in L. M. De Rijk, *Logica Modernorum* (Assen: Van Gorcum, 1967, II, pt 2, p. 78, 7–16), the *Abbreviatio Montana*, p. 149, 15–24; the *Ars Emmerana*, p. 179, 12–19, the *Ars Burana*, p. 358, 1–7, the *Introductiones Parisienses*, p. 380, 11–18, the *Logica 'Ut dicit'*, p. 418, 5–9, the *Logica 'Cum sit nostra'*, p. 463, 7–17, the *Dialectica Monanensis*. For the thirteenth century, Peter of Spain, *Tractatus, called afterwards*

4.2.5. *The Thomist Reading of* De interpretatione *16a*

Thomas Aquinas will not depart from this classification, though his taxonomy is more complex. Taking into account the remarks appearing passim in his commentary on the *De interpretatione,* whereas, at IV, 38 et seq., he seems to concern himself with a classification of the *voces,* reserving the appellation *signum* only for the *voces significativae,* in IV, 46, on the other hand, where he attempts to explain why Aristotle, in speaking of animal sounds, used the term *soni* and not *voces* (it was necessary, Thomas explains, to take into consideration the sounds of animals which, not being furnished with lungs, are not capable of uttering vocal sounds), he suggests the possibility of a more detailed classification, which considers the *sonus* as a genus.

The Aristotelian translation available to Thomas was not yet that of William of Moerbeke (who was shrewd enough to translate *symbolon* and *semeion* correctly as two distinct notions), but basically that of Boethius, whose Latin term for both semiotic phenomena is *nota* (which the commentary then proceeds to read as the equivalent of *signum*).

Bearing in mind the probable sources he was relying on,[34] his classification could be summed up as in Figure 4.4.

This classification betrays a number of influences. In the first instance, along the lines of Saint Augustine, Thomas calls every meaningful *vox* a *signum*. But, in II, 19, he speaks of a *signum* also apropos of the military trumpet *(tuba),* which is evidently not a case of *sonus vocalis.* It would appear, then, that a *signum* for him was any case of meaningful utterance, vocal or nonvocal. But, having translated the two Aristotelian terms with *signum=nota,* he takes no account of the inferential nature of the Stoic *semeia,* ignores every type of index except *sonus,* and places evident indices like the moaning of the sick and the sounds made by animals among the meaningful *voces.*

4.2.6. *Transcribability and Articulation*

In the second place there appears in Thomas a distinction between *voces litteratae* and *articulatae* and *voces illitteratae* and *non articulatae.* The

---

'*Summulae Logicales*' (ed. De Rijk. Assen: Van Gorcum, 1972, pp. 1, 23, 2, 9) and Lambert of Auxerre, *Logica* (ed F. Alessio. Florence, La Nuova Italia, 1971, p. 7).

34. All prior manuals of logic began their treatment with a definition of *sonus* as a genus of *vox.* In his commentary on *De interpretatione* (IV, 38), Thomas will likewise affirm that "vox est sonus ab ore animali prolatus, cum imaginatione quadam."

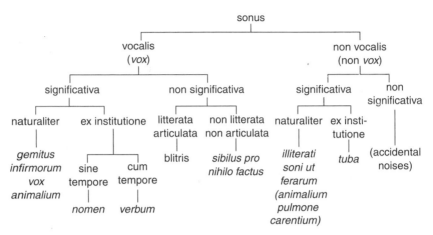

Figure 4.4

opposition *litteratae/illitteratae* appears to go back directly to the text of
Aristotle, where he speaks of utterances that are *agrammatoi* (like those of
the animals), that is, which cannot be transcribed with letters of the alphabet. Which would explain why *blitris* (a typical example used by the Stoics
and subsequently in the Middle Ages, along with *buba* and *bufbaf,* of vocal
utterances that, though transcribable, signify nothing) appears among the
voces litteratae, though it is not meaningful. The problem is rather that of
defining what is meant by *articulata* (with its opposite *non articulata*).

It is unclear whether articulation concerns the sounds only or their graphemic transcription as well, and Aristotle's texts are not explicit on this issue.[35]
In his commentary on the *De interpretatione,* Boethius (col. 395 D) appears
determined to unite the two types of articulation. Some ideas become clearer
if we go on to read Priscian:[36] we recognize, in fact, a line of thought that is
found in the grammatical tradition, and also in authors like Vincent of Beauvais.[37] A *vox articulata* for Priscian is one that is "copulata cum aliquo sensu

---

35. But see Lo Piparo (2003, IV, 9).

36. *Institutiones Grammaticae,* I, cap, de 'voce" (ed. M. Herz, in *Grammatici
Latini* II, Leipzig, 1855, reprint Hildesheim 1961, pp. 5–6).

37. See *Latratus canis* ("On Animal Language"), p. 29, n. 20. The influence of
Priscian's classification is discernible from the beginning of the eleventhth century onward, when, thanks especially to the influence of the Irish grammarians
operating on the continent, in particular in the context of the Carolingian cul-

mentis eius qui loquitur," and utterances are no longer classified according to a binary taxonomy, but following the matrix represented in Figure 4.5.

	articulata	inarticulata
litterata	quae possunt scribi et intellegi ut 'homo' et 'arma virumque cano'	coax (ranarum vox)
illitterata	sibilus hominis, gemitus	cra (vox corvina) mugitus, crepitus

Figure 4.5

This matrix presents two distinct problems. The lesser problem concerns its
internal coherence, given that the croaking of the frog appears to be transcribable in letters of the alphabet—see Aristophanes's *brekekex koax koax*—while
the lowing of the ox is not. But the classification probably represents current
linguistic usage (simply put, that it was more customary to spell out the croaking of the frog than the lowing of the ox), and Priscian was likely referring to a
panoply of examples handed down to him by the Greek tradition. The second
problem concerns Thomas's solution. If Thomas is following Priscian, it is hard
to understand why the difference between articulation and nonarticulation appears to distinguish nonmeaningful utterances *(non significativa)*, while it is
absent from the branch devoted to meaningful utterances *(significativa)*—in
which the names are articulate and lettered, but not the animal sounds.

The fact is that behind this complex of questions there lurk a number of
semiotic problems that are by no means negligible. Thomas's classification is
anticipated by Ammonius.[38]

---

tural renaissance, his authority begins to supplant that of Donatus in the principal Episcopal schools (see Holz 1981). Analogous positions are to be found in Alcuin's *Grammatica,* in the *Excerptio de arte grammatica Prisciani* of Rabanus
Maurus, in Sedulius Scottus's *In Donati artem maiorem,* etc. Later the same classification will be borrowed, for example, by Petrus Helias in his *Summa super
Priscianum maiorem,* by Vincent of Beauvais in his *Speculum Doctrinale,* and
eventually by Simon of Dacia in his *Domus Gramatice.*
38. "Dupliciter enim ea quae simpliciter voce divisa, videlicet in significativam
et non significativam, litteratam et illitteratam, quarum hanc quidem articulatam,

After he has made it clear that for him being *litterata* (in other words, transcribable in letters) is the same thing, in the case of a *vox,* as being *articulata,* Ammonius seems to place the difference *articulata / non articulata* twice under two different genera, so that his classification can only be transcribed in the form of a matrix, as was the case for Priscian's (Figure 4.6).

Thomas (*In 1. De Int. Exp.* IV, 38) appears to take up only the first part of Ammonius's suggestion, and he writes: "Additur autem prima differentia, scilicet significativa, ad differentiam quarumcumque vocum non significantium, sive sit vox litterata et articulata, sicut "blitris," sive non litterata et non

---

hanc autem inarticulatum vocant" ("Let vocal sound *simpliciter* be divided twice into two, i.e., into significant and meaningless, and into lettered and unlettered, the former of which is called 'articulate' and the latter 'inarticulate'"). Ammonius, then, appears to put articulation only among the differences characterizing the *voces illitteratae.* "Accidet enim hanc quidam esse vocem significativam et litteratam ut homo, hanc autem significativam et illitteratam ut canis latratus, hanc autem non significativam et litteratam ut blituri, hanc autem non significativam et illitteratam ut sibilus quae fit frustra et non gratia significandi aliquid aut vocis alicuius irrationalium animalium repraesentatio, quae fit non gratia repraesentationis (haec enim iam significativa), sed quae fit inordinate et sine intentione finis" ("For there will be vocal sound which is significant and lettered, like 'human being,' vocal sound which is significant and unlettered, like the bark of a dog, vocal sound which is meaningless and lettered, like '*blituri*,' and vocal sound which is meaningless and unlettered, like whistling which is done for no reason and not to signify anything or the imitation [by a man] of some vocal sound made by irrational animals when it happens not in order to mimic (for that would already be significant), but in a random and purposeless manner"). Ammonius, *On Aristotle's* On Interpretation 1–8, Translated by David Blank, Ithaca: Cornell University Press, 1996, p. 40. *(Commentaire sur le Peri Herm., op. cit., pp. 59, 3–60).* Thomas was doubtless familiar with Ammonius in William of Moerbeke's translation. In his commentary on the *De Interpretatione* (IV, 39) he echoes one of its typical lines of argument: "Sed cum vox sit quedam res naturalis, nomen autem non est aliquid naturale sed ab hominibus institutum, videtur quod non debuit genus nominis ponere vocem, quae est ex natura, sed magis signum, quod est ex institutione, ut diceretur: nomen est signum vocale; sicut enim convenientius definiretur scutella, si quis diceret quod est vas ligneum, quam si quis diceret qupod est lignum formatum in vas." In his commentary the example Ammonius gave was that of the throne (pp. 76). What is more worthy of note is that, shortly afterward (IV, 40), Thomas appears not to accept Ammonius's proposal to define *nomen* by taking *signum* as its genus. This is why in Figure 4 we preferred to insert *sonus* as our genus. See in this connection *Latratus canis* ("On Animal Language").

	significativa	non significativa
articulata	"homo"	blitris
non articulata	latratus	sibilus

Figure 4.6

articulata, sicut sibilus per nihilo factus." Why does Thomas seem to be embarrassed by a classification that would suggest a matrix rather than a tree?

The problem seems to lie with the very nature of a tree (of Porphyrian inspiration), which proceeds by genera, species, and specific differences. In other words, the problem arises when, starting from a series of definitions given in discursive form, one attempts to regiment them in the form of a Porphyrian tree (something Thomas did not do, though it was precisely because he did not do so that the problem facing him did not become evident). As we demonstrated in Chapter 1 apropos of the Porphyrian tree, in order to give an account of any organization of the universe (even, as in the present case, a classification of signs and *voces*), the same pair of differences ought to be reproduced over and over again under different genera. If Thomas had followed this procedure, the difference *litterata/illitterata*, like that between *articulata* and *inarticulata*, should have appeared under two distinct genera (Figure 4.7).

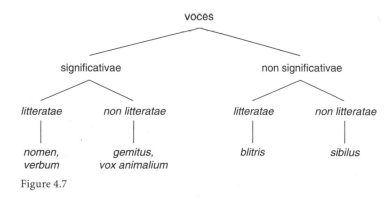

Figure 4.7

But, once he had accepted the principle that the same difference may be placed under two different genera, he ought to have reproduced it also under the signs that are meaningful *ex institutione*, where *tuba* or trumpet appears, seeing that—according to Aristotle, *De anima* 420b, 5–8—we have articulability among musical sounds too (to say nothing of their transcribability in musical notation).

In that case, the tree-like structure would have given way to a system of interconnected nodes, which, as Chapter 1 suggested, Thomas may have caught a glimpse of but could not admit. Independently, however, of these considerations, what is clear is that the contradictions of Thomas's solution stem from the fact that he is playing a double (and irreconcilable) game. One is grammatical, and it required that the *voces* (lettered or not) be distinguished according to their articulatory possibilities—and this is what Priscian, as a good grammarian, did. The other was semantic, and it required that the difference be posited between meaningful and nonmeaningful *voces*. The two taxonomies could not coexist. Thomas appears convincing when he speaks of one issue rather than the other, but he reveals all his uncertainty when he attempts (albeit motivated simply by a desire for taxonomical clarity) to put the two discourses together into a single system.

At this point, we could leave Thomas to his fate, gratified by the fact that once again our pursuit of the barking dog has succeeded in revealing the weaknesses or contradictions of a system. At most, we could point out that Thomas does not use *articulata* in the same sense as Priscian (that is, "endowed with meaning"), but in the same sense as Ammonius, and that consequently *blitris* is an example of a *vox non significativa* that nonetheless has a phonetic articulation and at the same time can be transcribed alphabetically. But it is precisely this observation that leads us to wonder why Priscian (and the grammarians who follow him) attributed to *articulata* a connection with meaning. Nota bene, it is not that they try to meld a taxonomy of articulations with one of signification, but that they take practically for granted that there is a connection, which they do not however explore, between articulation and meaning. In the first instance we could argue that they assumed that one articulates only to express something—and this was the hypothesis that was made in *Latratus canis* 1989.

In fact, when we go back to Ammonius's commentary, we see that he makes explicit and implicit reference to Plato's *Cratylus*, suggesting that there is a close link between *articulatio* and *significatio*. In Plato's dialogue, Socrates expounds the notion according to which whoever invented the first names created them in imitation of things, endeavoring to reproduce, through the coordination of letters and syllables, their nature. In other words, there would be a relationship of an iconic type between the phonological structure of the *signans* and the ontological structure of the *signatum*. A theory very close to this is found among the Stoics.[39] So it becomes comprehensible why Priscian, heir to a grammatical tradition with its roots in Stoicism, goes so far as to identify the *articulatio* of the *vox* with its *significatio,* followed in this by all medieval grammarians,[40] while, in the logical-philosophical tradition (untouched by the grammatical tradition), the *articulatio* has nothing to do with the meaning, but concerns the *litteratio,* and hence the possibility of the written translation of the sound.[41]

However that may be, it is obvious that among the grammarians the barking of the dog was on track for an unhappy ending. All the grammarian is interested in are the sounds articulated by humans, observant, precisely, of a *grammar,* in order to express meanings. The sounds made by animals are of no interest. Accordingly, in the texts of the grammarians the barking of the dog is destined to occupy an increasingly marginal position. For, if the first hypothesis (the influence of the *Cratylus*) were to be valid, then, given that the meaningfulness of the name is the consequence of an original relationship of iconicity, hence the *articulatio,* the *voces* of the animals, by common consent neither articulate or articulable, would not represent a

---

39. See Max Pohlenz, *Die Stoa. Die Geschichte einer geistigen Bewegung,* Göttingen, Vandenhoeck und Ruprecht, 1948–1955 and Pinborg (1962: 155–156).

40. See *Latratus canis* ("On Animal Language"), p. 31, n. 25. This identification is particularly explicit in John of Dacia's *Summa grammatica,* and it appears in the second half of the fourteenth century in a manual of logic like the *Summulae Logicales* of Richard of Lavenham (see Spade 1980: 380–381), where the pseudo-language of parrots is discussed, citing Isadore and an epigram of Martial's.

41. The position of the grammarians on the relationship between meaning and articulation would appear less original if we were to accept the reading of *De Interpretatione* proposed by Lo Piparo (2003) mentioned in Note 27 above. If *kata syntheken* is not to be interpreted as *ad placitum* but "by virtue of articulation, by syntactic composition of sounds otherwise deprived of meaning," we might be entitled to suspect that the grammatical tradition had somehow been influenced by an original reading of Aristotle. And in that case the grammarians would not have considered it implicit that one articulates in order to express something, but rather that a linguistic articulation was necessary if one was to express oneself conceptually. If this was the case it would be more comprehensible why for them articulation was so closely tied to the meaning to be expressed.

subject of great interest. Animals are not aware that *nomina sunt consequentia rerum,* and they are not capable of imitating the nature of things.[42]

4.2.7. Back to Thomas

Clearly, at this point, we may skip the tradition of the grammarians. What interests us instead is the tradition of the philosophers, who continue to

---

42. For a more detailed discussion see *Latratus canis* ("On Animal Language"), p. 13, n. 16, and p. 17, nn. 29 and 36, where the somewhat anomalous solution of a contemporary of Thomas, the Pseudo-Kilwardby, is also considered. Influenced by Priscian, he is inclined to exclude animal voices from the field of conventional signification, and yet, unlike the other grammarians and Modistae who will come later, he attempts a classification of all *signa.* In his system, then, animal sounds are indeed excluded from the *voces significativae,* only to reappear, albeit with some ambiguity, among the *signa naturalia.* "Ad hoc dicendum quod diversae sunt scientiae de signis. Signorum enim quaedam significant aliquid ex institutione et quaedam significant naturaliter ut effectus generaliter sive sit convertibilis sive non convertibilis cum sua causa est signum suae causae. Quod patet tam in genere naturae quam in genere moris. In genere naturae fumus est signum ignis non convertibile et defectus luminis sive eclipsis a corpore luminoso est signum interpositionis tenebrosis corporis. Similiter in genere moris delectatio, quae est in operationibus, est signum habitus voluntarii, sicut dicit Philosophus in secundo Ethicorum ubi dicit quod opportet signa facere habituum delectationem vel tristitiam in operationibus. Et sic patet quod effectus generaliter est signum suae causae. Unde Philosophus primo Posteriorum demonstrationes factas per effectum vocat syllogismos per signa in illa parte: 'Quoniam autem ex necessitate sunt circa unumquodque.' Secundum quorundam expositionem signorum vero quae significant ex institutione quaedam sunt instituta ad significandum tantum, quaedam sunt instituta ad significandum et sanctificandum. Signa ultimo modo sunt signa legis divinae de quibus nihil ad praesans. Quae autem sunt instituta ad significandum tantum quaedam sunt voces, de quibus dicit Philosophus quod sunt notae passionum. . . . Et de talibus signis est scientia rationalis quia rationis est componere partes vocis et ordinare et ad significandum instituere, non naturae vel moris, ut postea patebit. Quaedam autem sunt res ut signa metaphysica (?) sicut sunt gestus et nutus corporei, circuli et imaginationes de quibus nihil ad praesens." (See "Roberti Kilwardby quod fertur Commenti super Priscianum maiorem Extracta," ed. K. M. Fredborg et al., *Cahiers de l'Inst. du Moyen-Age grec et latin* 15, 1975, pp. 3–4). [*Translator's note:* In n. 29 to the collaborative essay alluded to at beginning of these notes, "On Animal Language in the Medieval Classification of Signs," Eco suggests, after citing the same Latin passage by Kilwardby, that, instead of "imaginationes" in the last sentence, the text ought to read "imagines."]

grant the dog and his bark a position of honor in the classification of signs. This is also because the philosophers, in addition to the classifications they elaborate, following the lead of the *De interpretatione,* are constantly induced to make supplementary observations. Take Thomas, who, in *Sententia libri Politicorum* (I, I/b), comes back once more to the difference between human and animal *voces.* Since, he affirms, nature never does anything gratuitously but always has a definite purpose, it is obvious that, although various animals possess a "voice," only humans possess a *locutio* and, though there may be animals capable of repeating human words, we cannot say that they talk, because they do not understand what they are saying, but utter the words they have learned out of mere habit. Animal "voices" serve to express sadness or delight and other passions (and once again the barking of the dog is cited and the roar of the lion: "et haec sibi invicem significant per aliquas naturales voces, sicut leo per rugitum et canis per latratum"), while humans, instead of these *voces,* use interjections. But only human *locutio* is able to signify things useful and harmful, just and unjust, good and evil.[43]

Here Thomas takes a step forward. He recognizes that, just as humans have ways of signifying to each other, alternately and intentionally, sadness and delight, the same is true of animals, and he thus touches on a problem that will be treated at greater length by Roger Bacon, who will distinguish between the moan that the sick man utters inadvertently and the interjection that he utters intentionally, following a certain linguistic convention, to signify the same pain, in however conceptually imperfect a manner.[44]

---

43. See *Latratus canis* ("On Animal Language"), n. 30. This theme is developed in the *De anima* of Avicenna, where the opposition between human language and the *voces* of the animals is placed in relation with the diversity of ends toward which communication is ordered: among humans these are infinite since they are determined by our social existence, while among animals they are few and dictated by natural instinct (*Liber de Anima seu Sextus de Naturalibus* V, ed. S. van Riet, Louvain, Leiden, 1968, p. 72, 42–48).

44. "Interiectiones omnes sunt mediae inter istas voces nunc dictas scilicet: significativae naturaliter et inter voces plene significantes ad placitum . . . Interiectiones enim imperfecte significant ad placitum et parum significant per modum conceptus propter quod vicinantur vocibus illis quae solum per modum affectus subiect isignificant cuiusmodi sunt gemitus et cetera quae facts sunt. Gemitus enim et suspiria et huiusmodi naturaliter et per modum solius affectus excitantis animam intellectivam significant, quae per interiectiones gemendi et dolendi et suspirandi et admirandi et huiusmodi significantur per modum conceptus, licet

But, in this way, within the same Thomist system, the *latratus canis* changes position, as if, halfway between the *voces significativae naturaliter* (among which we find the *gemitus*) and the *voces ad placitum* (where we find spoken language), we were to locate an intermediate zone, in which humans produce (paralinguistically, we would say today) interjections, while dogs bark. In fact, in this revised classification, the real difference between human and canine language lies not in the opposition intentional/unintentional (vaguely touched upon, but basically eluded), and not only in that between natural and *ad placitum,* but in the opposition between the interjection and the ability of human language to express abstractions by means of which humans set up *domum et civitatem* ("ergo homo est naturale animal domesticum et civile")—an affirmation that Thomas takes up from Aristotle's *Politics* 1253 at 9–30, where Aristotle opposes human language, capable of producing concepts and abstractions, to the inarticulate sounds of animals, expressive merely of pleasure or pain.

4.2.8. Roger Bacon

Not unmindful of Augustine's provocation, enter at this point Roger Bacon. The classification of signs outlined in Bacon's *De signis* strikes us in many ways as syncretistic and as yet unresolved. The eccentricities of this classification find their explanation in a project whose results will be seen in later semiotics, especially in Ockham. Briefly, up until Bacon, thanks to the Aristotelian vulgate, words signify the passions of the soul (concepts, universal species), species bear an iconic relationship to things, and words, through the mediation of species, serve to name things *(nominantur singularia, sed universalia significantur, "they name individual things while they signify universals").* With the *De signis,* on the other hand, words begin to signify directly individual things, of which the *species intelligibiles* are the mental counterpart. But the link between words and species becomes secondary and is reduced to a purely symptomatic relationship. Bacon has grasped the

---

imperfecti" (*De signis,* I, 9 in Karin M. Fredborg, Lauge Nielsen and Jan Pinborg, eds., "An Unedited Part of Roger Bacon's *Opus Maius:* "De Signis," *Traditio* 34 [1978], p. 75–136). In general on the problems raised by the classification of interjections in the medieval grammatical tradition, see Pinborg (1961). And see also *Latratus canis* ("On Animal Language").

difference between *symbola* and *semeia* in *De interpretatione* 16a but, on the basis of a philologically correct reading, he elaborates a philosophically unfaithful reading. In other words, he erases the fact that for Aristotle words *may* be symptoms of the passions of the mind, but *in the first instance* they *signify* them directly, and he concludes that words are symptoms of the species that are formed in the mind.[45] We have endeavored to reconstruct Bacon's classification in Figure 4.8.

In commenting on this figure, let us say at once that that the "natural signs" ought to correspond to those of Augustine, which are produced without any intention, but it is unclear on what grounds Bacon distinguishes between those of the first and those of the third type. It would appear that, whereas in the third type we have a clear relationship of cause and effect, in those of the first type we have simply a relationship of concomitance among events (in the case of those classified as necessary the concomitance is certain, while for the probable ones it is uncertain). But it remains obscure why the ground being wet as a probable sign of a previous rain shower is not classified among the *vestigia*. Still more embarrassing is the curious collocation

---

45. "Si vero obiciatur in contrarium quod Aristoteles in librum Perihermeneias dicit voces significare passiones in anima, ut Boethius exponat de speciebus et in libro illo loquitur de partibus enuntiationis vel enuntiatione, quae significant ad placitum et tunc partes orationis sive voces impositae rebus significabunt ut videtur species ad placitum, dicendum est quod Aristotele a principio capituli de nomine intendit loqui de vocibus, ut sunt signa ad placitum, sed ante illud capitulum loquitur in universali de signis sive ad placitum sive naturaliter, quamvis ascendat in particulari ad illa signa, quae intendit, scilicet ad nomen et verbum prout significant res ad placitum. Et quod loquitur in universali de signis, manifestum est per hoc, quod dicit quod intellectus sunt signa rerum et voces signa intellectuum ety scriptura est signum vocis, certe intellectus non est signum rei ad placitum, sed naturale, ut dicit Boethius in Commento, quoniam eundem intellectum habet Graecus de re, quam habet Latinus, et tamen diversas voces proferunt ad rem intellectam designandam. Voces autem et scriptura possunt ad placitum significare aliqua, et alia ut signa naturalia. Unde vox imposita rei extra animam, si comparetur ad ipsam rem, est vox significativa ad placitum, quia ei imposita est. Si vero ad speciem propriam ipsius vocis, tunc est signum naturale in triplici modo signi naturalis, ut habitum est prius. Si vero ad speciem rei nec antequam cognoscetur res per eam, quia opportet quod actu intelligatur res per speciem et habitum nominata et vocata et repraesentata per vocem, antequam vox sit signum speciei ipsius rei" (*De signis* V, 166, op. cit., p. 134.).

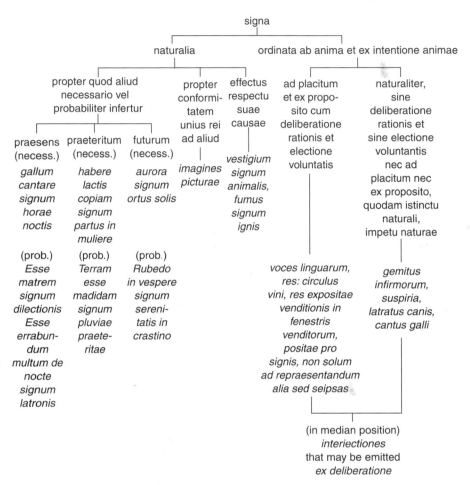

Figure 4.8

of the *imagines* (intentionally produced by man) among the natural signs. Bacon explains this with the fact that what is made intentionally is the object (the statue), while the resemblance between the statue and the real person is due to a certain homology between the form of the *signans* and that of the *signatum*.[46] What interests us more is the classification of the signs produced by an intention of the soul, where Bacon perceives an intention even

---

46. Augustine was far more subtle in his *De doctrina Christiana* II, xxv, 38–39, where he recognized the largely conventional nature of images and mimic representations.

in the case of sounds emitted instinctively, without any intervention on the part of reason or even will, as an immediate movement of the sensitive soul (such as the moaning of the sick and animal noises).

Now, the signs ordered by the soul, but without rational deliberation or election of the will, are said to function *naturaliter*. They have, however, nothing to do with the natural signs. The latter were called natural with reference to nature as substance; the former are called natural because they are set in motion by a movement of nature. Be that as it may, the distinction is clear: the *signa naturalia* do not appear as the consequence of an intention, on the part of either humans or animals, while the moaning of the sick and the barking of the dog have their origin in a movement of the sensitive soul that tends to express what the animal (human or no) is feeling. And so in this classification the barking of the dog, without being placed alongside Holy Scripture and separated from the mourning of the dove, as it was in Augustine, is not a mere symptom either.

Furthermore, it is worth pointing out that the crow of the rooster appears twice in this classification. There is a cockcrow that is a sign of what time of day it is and a cockcrow that is instead a *linguistic act,* even if we do not happen to understand its purport.

When Bacon compares these two cases he uses a different terminology. When the cockcrow appears among the signs *ordinata ab anima,* it is referred to as "cantus galli," while when it appears as a symptom it is referred to as "gallum cantare": "cantus galli nichil proprie nobis significat tamquam vox significativa, sed gallum cantare significant nobis horas." The natural sign is not the cockcrow itself, but the fact that the cock crows (the Stoics would have called it an incorporeal). Now, in the *De signis,* whom the cock is crowing to (whether to other cocks or to humans) is not specified, but the same theme is picked up again in the *Sumulae Dialectices.*[47]

---

47. "Vocem alia significativa, alia non, significativa. Non significativa est per quam nichil auditui representatur, ut 'bubo' etc.; vox significativa est per quam omne animal interpretatur aliquid omni vel alicui sue speciei—omne vero animal potest hoc facere, quia natura non dedit ei vocem ociosam. Et hoc possumus videre manifeste, quai gallina aliter garrit cum pullis suis quando invitat eos ad escam et quando docet eos cavere a milvo. Bruta autem animalia interpretantur omni individuo sue speciei, ut asinus omni asino, leo omni leoni, sed homo non interpretatur omni homini, set SED alicui, quia Gallicus Gallico, Graecus Graeco, Latinus Latino et hec solum. Nullum eciam animal interpretatur alicui individuo

Here Bacon is quite clear: a significant *vox* is the one by which any animal can communicate with another animal of the same species, in other words there are *voces significativae naturaliter* that all members of a species understand, and others (the ones that are *ad placitum*) that are understood only by subgroups of the same human species, as is the case with articulate languages. That animals understand each other can be seen from their behavior, as when, for example, the mother hen warns her chicks of the threat of the hawk. So the rooster speaks with different words according to the circumstances and is understood by the other members of his species, just as the ass is understood by the ass and the lion by the lion. All humans need is a little training, and they too will be able to understand the language of the beasts. As will be further clarified by Pseudo-Marsilius of Inghen:[48] the dog certainly barks in order to signify something, and it is irrelevant whether

---

alterius speciei nisi inproprie adminus per suam vocem propriam nichil interpretatur nisi eis qui sunt de sua specie, tamen si ex industria et assuetudine posit aliquod animal uti voce alteriius, ut pica voce hominis, potest aliquo modo inproprie et non naturaliter significare alii quam sue speciei ut homini; et forte quamvis homo posit aliquid comprehendere per vocem pice, non tamen est illa vox proprie significativa, cum non fit a pica sub intentione significandi, et quamvis homo possit aliquid apprehendere per talem vocem , pica tamen pice nihil significat per illam. Similiter cantus galli nichil proprie nobis significat tamen vox significativa, set SED gallum cantare significat nobis horas, sicut rubor in mane significant nobis pluviam. Vocum significativarum alia significativa ad placitum, alia naturaliter. Vox significativa naturaliter est que ordinatur ad significandum, ut gemitus infirmorum et omnis vox ferarum vel sonus. Vox significativa ad placitum est que ex institucione humana aliquid significant" (*Opera hactenus inedita Rogeri Baconi*, fasc. XV, ed. R. Steele. Oxonii, Clarendon Press, 1940, p. 233, 20 234, 13).

48. "Est tamen sciendum quod ad cuiuslibet vocis prolationem prencipalitur duo instrumenta naturalia sunt necessaria, scilicet pulmo et vocalis arteria. Ex isto patet quod latratus canum etiam est sonus vox et quando arguitur 'tamen non fit cum intentione aliquid significandi' respondetur negando assumptum. Neque oportet quod omnes intelligent illum latratum, sed sufficit quod illi intelligant qui sciunt proprietatem et habitudinem canum. Nam latratus canum uni significat gaudium, alteri autem iram." (*Commentum emendatum et correctum in primum et quartum tractatus Petri Hyspani Et super tractatibus Marsilij de Suppositionibus, ampliationibus, appellationibus et consequentiis* (Hangenau, 1495, s. p.; reprint Frankfurt, Minerva, 1967 with title *Commentum in primum et quartum tractatum Petri Hispani.*) See *Latratus canis* ("On Animal Language").

everyone understands what he means, it is enough that those who understand the characteristics and habits of dogs understand.

This said, the table of zoosemiotic situations has been fully explored: the
dog who speaks to the dog, the dog whose bark man interprets because he
knows the dog's habits and therefore his language, and even the animal who
speaks human words, like the magpie or the parrot (but this is a case of
learned behavior and mechanical execution on the animal's part, and the
problem has nothing to do with a theory of signs).[49]

With Bacon's espousal of the zoosemiotic revaluation of an Augustine
who is closer to Greek culture, the barking dog definitively joins the ranks
of those who, in one way or another, express themselves, because the behavior of animals who twitter, howl, squeak, and roar as they go about their associative lives will henceforth be regarded with a greater sensitivity to the
facts of nature.[50]

---

49. We might add to the list a number of marginal phenomena (mentioned in
Latratus canis, "On Animal Language"). Take, for example, Thomas's observations
on the miraculous or magical instances of talking animals reported by Scripture
(*Quaestiones disputatae de potentia Dei*, VI, 5): "Ad tertium dicendum, quod locutio
canum, et alia huiusmodi quae Simon Magus faciebat, potuerunt fieri per illu-
sionem, et non per effectus veritatem. Si tamen per effectus veritatem hoc fierent,
nullum sequitur inconveniens, quia non dabat ani daemon virtutem loquendi,
sicut datur mutis per miraculum, sed ipsemet per aliquem motum localem sonum
formabat, litteratae et articulatae vocis similitudinem et modum habentem; per
hunc autem modum etiam asina Balaam intelligitur fuisse locuta (Numbers XXII,
28), Angelo tamen bono operante, ("*Reply to the Third Objection*. Speaking dogs
and like works of Simon the magician were quite possibly done by trickery and not
in very truth. If, however, they were genuine, it matters not: since the demon did
not give a dog the power of speech miraculously as when it is given to the dumb;
but by some kind of local movement he made sounds to be heard like words composed of letters and syllables. It is thus that we may understand Balaam's ass to
have spoken [*Numbers*, XXII, 28], although in this case it was by the action of a
good angel"). *On the power of God* (*Quæstiones disputatæ de potentia Dei*) by Saint
Thomas Aquinas. Literally translated by the English Dominican fathers. Three
books in one. Westminster, Md.: Newman Press, 1952, p. 186. Dante too deals with
talking animals in the *Convivio* (III, vii, 8–10), where he cites the magpie and the
parrot, and in the *De vulgari eloquentia* (I, ii, 6–8), where he cites the examples *de
serpente loquente ad priumum mulierem, de asina Balaam, de piscis loquentibus*.

50. It is a slow process. If, as late as 1603, Fabrici d'Acquapendente can compose a
treatise *De brutorum loqui* in which he takes up once again the classical arguments

It is no accident that we are now entering a period in which the figurative arts too have progressed, in their representation of nature, from the stylizations of the Romanesque to the realism of the Gothic.

Exit the allegorical animal of the bestiary. From now on, whimpers, barks, whinnies, and roars ring out in the symbolic forest inhabited by the beasts, who now say whatever they feel like saying and not what the *Physiologus* would have them say, thereby refusing to become *quasi liber et pictura* and just being themselves.[51]

---

concerning communication among animals and their passions, in 1650, Athanasius Kircher, in his *Musurgia Universalis* (I, 14–15), is interested in the sounds uttered by the various animals and makes an accurate study of the syntax, if not the semantics, of the monkeys of the Americas, of cicadas, grasshoppers, frogs, and various types of birds, with accurate pentagrammatical transcriptions that take into account different structures, including the *pigolismus,* the *glazismus,* and the *teretismus,* distinguishing the sounds made by the mother hen when laying and those with which she calls her chicks—and revealing himself to have been an expert pioneer bird watcher. His was no longer a philosophical reflection on the possibility of animal language, such as occurred in the Middle Ages: Kircher devoted a vast portion of his treatise to the examination of the various phonatory organs of the animals in order to explain the possibility or impossibility of their "languages."

51. The phrase *quasi liber et pictura* is a line from the Latin poem quoted in Chapter 3 (section 3.3). At this point we may even find ourselves annoyed by the barking of a dog which has abandoned the pages of the theologians and invaded the nights of lovers and robbers. Two centuries after Bacon (1544), Michelangelo Biondo will reveal a trick to stop a dog barking, which he apparently learned from the thieves themselves, interrupted in the course of their night's work, as well as from lovers, disturbed as they attempted to scale their mistress's balcony. All you have to do is to swallow or drink a dog's heart, duly baked and reduced to a powder: "Accepimus a quibusdam, quod cum quis latratum canis vult cohibere ne illi sit impedimento in quibusdam peragendis (quod maxime amantibus ad amantes accedentibus nocere solet et furibus nocturnis) itaque cor canis edat, quamvis dicunt quidam quod potatum praestantius est; ideo ustum redigatur in pulverem et deglutiatur, quoniam latratum canis comprimet; quod furibus et amantibus dimittimus credendum." Which is a bit like catching a bird by sprinkling salt on its tail. See *De canibus et venatione libellus,* "Ad latratum," Rome 1544. Partial ed. in *Arte della caccia,* ed. G. Innamorati, vol. 1, Milano, Panfilo, 1965.

5

Fakes and Forgeries in the Middle Ages

The modern reader, nurtured on philology, is aware that many forgeries were perpetrated in the course of the Middle Ages. But were the people of the Middle Ages similarly aware? Did they recognize the notion of forgery? And if they recognized the notion, was it the same as our own?

In formulating these questions, we find ourselves compelled to analyze a series of terms—like falsification, fake, forgery, false attribution, diplomatic forgery, alteration, counterfeit, facsimile, and so on—that we nowadays take for granted. If we are to decide whether similar concepts existed in the Middle Ages, we are inevitably obliged to take a closer look at our own contemporary concepts.

It is no accident that dictionaries and encyclopedias, in defining falsification, place the emphasis on malicious intent, introducing—without defining them—concepts such as counterfeit, spurious, apocryphal, pseudo, and so on. *Webster's Unabridged Dictionary*, for instance, defines *forgery* as "the act of forging, fabricating or producing falsely; especially the crime of fraudulently making, counterfeiting, or altering any writing, record, instrument,

A revised version of "Tipologia della falsificazione" ["A Typology of Forgery"], in Setz (1988), originally given at the Internationaler Kongress der MGH, Munich, September 16–19, 1986. My theoretical (rather than historical) essay, "Falsi e contraffazioni," was developed on the basis of this publication (see Eco 1990a). [*Translator's note*: Relevant also is Eco's entry (published in English) "Fakes in Arts and Crafts" in Eco 2004c (4:3571–3580).

register, note and the like to deceive, mislead or defraud; as the forgery of a document or of a signature."[1]

The dictionaries are also vague on the distinction between spurious, apocryphal, and pseudo. Spurious is used for nonauthentic or falsified works and documents, but also for an illegitimate child born from an adulterous relationship. In the natural sciences, it refers to organs that resemble other organs without having their function. For example, the spurious ribs are two lower ribs on either side of the skeleton that do not reach as far as the sternum; in zoology, the spurious or bastard wing (or alula) is a tuft of accessory flight feathers growing on the first digit of the bird's wing, behind the wing's angle, in some cases substituted by a nail or spur; in botany, it indicates an apparatus or organ that resembles another organ with a different structure or function.

---

1. Equally unsatisfactory are the German definitions in the *Brockhaus Enziklopädie* (1968) ("Zweck vorgenommene Nachbildung, Veränderung oder historisch irrefhrende Gestaltung eines Gegenstandes (hierzu Tafeln), eines Kunstwerkes, eines literar. Denckmals, einer Unterschrift usf.") or the *Meyers Grosses Universal Lexikon* ("der Herstellen eines unechten Gegenstandes oder das Verändern eines echten Gegenstandes zur Tauschung im Rechtverkehr—dadegen Imitation"). The following definitions are from the standard Italian dictionary of Nicola Zingarelli *(Vocabolario della lingua italiana)*. "Falso ... A agg.: ... 2 Che è stato contraffatto, alterato con intenzione dolosa ... SIN. Truccato. CONTR. Autentico. ... 4 Che non è ciò di cui ha l'apparenza ... SIN. Illusorio. ... B s. m. ... 3 Falsificazione, falsità ... 4 Opera d'arte, francobollo, documento e sim. contraffatto." "Falsificare ... Contraffare, deformare, alterare con l'intenzione e la consapevolezza di commettere un reato." "Falsificazione ... 1 Atto, effetto del falsificare ... SIN. Alterazione, contraffazione. 2 Documento o atto artificiosamente prodotto per sostutuire un originale perduto o guasto o per creare testimonianza dolosa." "Contraffare ... 2 Alterare la voce, l'aspetto e sim., spec. per trarre in inganno ... 3 Falsificare." "Facsimile ... 1 Riproduzione esatta, nella forma della scrittura e in ogni particolare, di scritto, stampa, incisione, firma. 2 fig. Persona o cosa assai simile a un'altra." "Pseudo- ... primo elemento ... che, in parole composte della terminologia dotta e scientifica, significa genericamente 'falso' ... In vari casi indica analogia esteriore, qualità apparente, semplice somiglianza puramente estrinseca, o qualche affinità con quanto designato dal secondo componente." "Spurio ... 1 Illegitimo ... 2 Privo di genuinità, di autenticità." "Apocrifo ... 2 Detto di testo, spec. letterario, falsamente attribuito a un'epoca o a un autore. SIN. Spurio."

In German the same phenomenon is rendered with the prefix *pseudo*. Webster gives *apocryphal* as a synonym of *spurious* ("Apocryphal: various writings falsely attributed... of doubtful authorship or authenticity... spurious"). In fact, *apokryphos* originally meant occult and secret; apocryphal gospels and other biblical writings got the name because people weren't allowed to read them—and as such they were excluded from among the canonical books. Hence, "apocryphal" came to signify "excluded from the canon." Subsequently, late Jewish authors attribute their writings to the ancient prophets, and these books are termed *pseudonymous* or *pseudoepigraphical*. It should be observed, however, that Catholics describe the non-canonical books as apocryphal, while the books accepted in the Greek version of the Septuagint are said to be *deuterocanonical*. For Protestants on the other hand it is the deuterocanonical books that are apocryphal while the ones Catholics call apocryphal are pseudoepigraphical.[2]

5.1. The Semiotics of Forgery

Given the complexity of the notion of forgery, if we are to understand what might have been considered a forgery in the Middle Ages, we must proceed to clarify the various related concepts.[3]

5.1.1. Doubles

The first thing we must consider is the semiosic concept known as *replicability*. The most complete instance of replicability is the *double*, a physical *token* that has all the characteristics of another physical token, at least from a* practical point of view, insofar as both possess all the pertinent traits prescribed by an abstract *type*. In this sense, two chairs of the same model or two sheets of office paper are both doubles of one another, and the perfect homology between the two tokens is established with reference to their type. Doubles do not lend themselves to the deceit of falsification in that every token has the same practical value as every other, and each one can substitute for the other. A double is not identical with another double (in the

---

2. See also Haywood (1987: 10–18).

3. For the terminology of this section see the chapter "Theory of Sign Production" in Eco (1979b).

Leibnizian sense of indiscernibility), in other words, two tokens of the same type are—and are recognized as—two different physical objects. Nevertheless, they are considered interchangeable.

Theoretically speaking, we have two reciprocal doubles when, given two objects, Oa and Ob, their matter displays the same physical characteristics, in the sense of their molecular composition, and their form is similar, in the mathematical sense of congruence (the features to be compared for similarity are determined by the type). But who is to determine the criteria for similarity? The problem of doubles is ontological in theory, but pragmatic in practice. It is the user who decides under which description—that is, from what practical standpoint—the two matters and the two forms are, ceteris paribus, "objectively" similar, and therefore, from the practical point of view, interchangeable. Under a microscopic analysis, or in the light of other chemical tests, it could be proven that two sheets of office paper of different brands display fairly relevant differences, but a normal user habitually sees them as doubles (and hence interchangeable) in every respect.

5.1.2. Pseudo-Doubles

We have a case of pseudo-doubles when only one token of the type (the privileged token) takes on a special value in the eye of one or more users, for one or all of the following reasons: (i) on account of *temporal priority,* such as occurs for instance when the first product off the assembly line of particular model of automobile (if it can be identified as the first) is displayed in a museum as a unique specimen;[4] (ii) because that particular token contains evidence of previous possession, as occurs in the case of a copy of a book

---

4. Often a minimal material or formal variant serves to characterize the object as a *unicum:* two dollar bills of the same value are doubles as far as their use goes, but not from the bank's point of view, since their serial numbers are different. Even in a case of perfect reproduction, the token that received the number first is considered theoretically "original." Hence the interesting question whether we are to consider authentic a fake bill printed (with fraudulent intent) on authentic watermarked and security-threaded stock, with the plates of the Mint, by the director of the Mint in person, who assigns it the same number as another bill legally printed a few moments earlier. If it were ever possible to determine the priority of its printing, only the first bill would be authentic. Otherwise one would have to decide to arbitrarily destroy one of the two bills and consider the other the original.

with an inscription by the author or the signature of an illustrious former owner; (iii) because that token has been used in a special context (this would be the case with the Holy Grail, the chalice used by Jesus Christ at the Last Supper, if it could ever be discovered and authenticated); (iv) because the particular token is of such material and formal complexity that no attempt to imitate it can reproduce all the characteristics recognized as relevant (a typical case would be an oil painting on canvas painted in a particular style with special paints, so that the chromatic shadings, the microscopic grain of the canvas, the flow of the brushstrokes—all features judged indispensable to the total fruition of the object—can never be completely imitated.[5] In all of the above cases, for various reasons, these "unique" objects become the type of themselves, and any reproduction of these objects, when not honestly presented as a facsimile or imperfect copy produced for a didactic or documentary purpose, is made with a *false identification* in mind.[6]

---

5. The modern concept of the work of art as an unrepeatable *unicum* privileges its originality and its formal and material complexity, which, taken together, constitute the concept of *authorial authenticity*. Naturally in the practice of critics and collectors the notion of originality often prevails over the presence of relevant structural features. As a result, even a perfect copy of a statue, which reproduces, using the exact same materials, every aesthetically relevant feature of the original, is downgraded only because it is denied recognition of the privilege of originality. Problems of this sort crop up for the plastic and figurative arts but not for written texts, since any reproduction, be it printed or manuscript, of the same poetic text is assumed, for critical purposes, to be a perfect double of the original type (see the distinction between autographic versus allographic arts in Goodman 1968). They do, however, occur among bibliophiles, where in fact value is placed on the particular material consistency which renders one token (a copy of a rare book) something unique compared with other copies of the same book (evidence of possession, state of preservation, width of the margins, etc.).

6. A recent phenomenon is that of commercial facsimiles of precious illuminated manuscripts, in which the colors, the tactile feel of the gold leaf, the wormholes, and the transparency of the parchment are all reproduced with absolute fidelity, though the manuscript is not reproduced on real parchment but on paper (though it contrives to imitate the consistency of the original parchment). Even the reproduction of real parchment would display, when submitted to chemical tests, characteristics different from the antique original. And even if the reproduction were to be printed on recovered ancient parchment the same tests would demonstrate that the characters printed on it were made by mechanical means. And in any

5.1.3. False Identification

We have false identification when, given a hypothetical object Oa, produced by author A in historical circumstances t_1, and, given another object Ob, produced by author B in historical circumstances t_2, somebody (an individual or a group) decides that Ob is identical with Oa, to the point of being indiscernible. In the concept of falsification the malicious intentions of the falsifier are generally implicit. The problem of malice on the part of B, the author of Ob, seems to us irrelevant: he is fully aware that Ob is not identical to Oa, but he may have produced it with no intention to deceive, as an exercise, as a joke, or by mere chance. The *Constitutum Constantini (Donation of Constantine)* was probably first produced as a rhetorical exercise, and it was only in later centuries that (in good or bad faith) it came to be considered authentic (see De Leo 1974). What interests us more is the intention of the person performing the false identification (the Identifier) who asserts that Oa and Ob are identical (of course, in a case of malice aforethought, the Identifier and author B of Ob may be one and the same person).

Historical forgery does not belong in this category. It concerns a document Ob, produced by B, who is entitled to produce it as his own, but whose purpose in producing it is to assert (in a mendacious fashion) something inexact or invented. This is the case, for instance, when someone writes a letter bearing false witness, a report that misrepresents the results of a scientific experiment, a dispatch or communiqué issued by a government that lies about the results of an election (electoral fraud), and so on. A historical forgery is an instance of a deliberate lie and in this sense it is to be distinguished from a diplomatic forgery, which we will come to later.[7]

---

case the ancient parchment used for the reproduction would not be the original parchment of the manuscript.

7. In the same way we do not have false identification in *texts written under a pseudonym* when A (usually a famous person or someone otherwise known) produces O but would have it believed that it was produced by an unknown B (the identity of two objects is not an issue in such a case); in cases of *plagiarism,* in which B produces an object Ob which he presents as his own work, but using wholly or in part an object Oa produced by someone else (where B however does all he can to ensure that Ob will not be identified with Oa); or in cases of *aberrant decoding,* in which a text O, written according to a code C1, is interpreted as if it were written according to a code C2. Examples of this last practice are the oracular

5.2. Difficulties of Authentication Procedures

In order for a process of false identification to occur a culture must have criteria, considered somehow objective, by which to establish indiscernibility or equivalence between objects, and therefore criteria for establishing the authenticity of an object Ob. These criteria can be valid (i) for objects that were not produced for communicative purposes, such as paleontological finds, objects in use in archaic or primitive cultures (which can be interpreted as signs, symptoms, traces, or clues to events distant in space and time); or (ii) for objects produced for explicitly communicative purposes (documents, visual works of art, hieroglyphic inscriptions, epigraphs, etc.). Both kinds of objects are generally understood to be "documents," though objects belonging to type (ii) are considered both for their expression and their content, while objects belonging to type (i) are evaluated only for their expression, seeing that the content (or meaning) attributed to them by the addressee did not exist for the sender (the archaic producer of an iron knife blade undoubtedly intended to signify the practical function of the object he was constructing, but only the modern archeologist reads that knife as a sign of the fact that, when it was produced, people knew how to work iron).

The contemporary disciplines of identification (which we will refer to generically as philological disciplines) recognize four methods of authentication. We will see, case by case, that the criteria available to medieval culture were far more vague.

5.2.1. Authentication at the Level of the Material Support of the Text
We have physicochemical methods for determining the period of fabrication and the quality of the material support (parchment, paper, canvas, wood, etc.). Nowadays these methods are considered sufficiently scientific, and therefore intersubjectively verifiable, but the medieval scholar almost never had the opportunity to encounter original documents in their original language

---

reading of Virgil as a Christian author in the Middle Ages, in the Baroque period the false interpretation of Egyptian hieroglyphics on the part of Athanasius Kircher, in modern times the reading of Dante as if he were writing in the secret code of the so-called sect of the Fedeli d'Amore (see Pozzato 1989). But in this kind of exercise there is no question of identification between two physical objects.

(even the translators were working from manuscripts at a considerable remove from their archetypes), and all they knew of past civilizations were
seriously contaminated ruins. Christianity discovers history (the sequence
creation-original sin-redemption-parousia), but not historiography. It knows
the past solely through the information handed down by tradition. The legal
opinions handed down in the High Middle Ages ascertaining the counterfeit nature of the documents produced by one of the litigating parties confine themselves at best to a discussion of the authenticity of the seal. Remi of
Trèves asks Gerbert d'Aurillac (the future pope Sylvester II) to send him one
of his leather armillary spheres, and Gerbert (an enthusiast of the classical
authors) asks for a copy of Statius's *Achilleid* in exchange. Remi sends it to
him; but the *Achilleid* was left unfinished by its author. Gerbert is unaware
of this and accuses Remi of sending him a defective manuscript and, to
punish him, sends him an inferior painted wooden sphere. Gerbert had no
accredited sources for knowing the physical conditions of the original manuscript (see Havet 1889: 983–997 and Gilson 1952: 228–229).

The cautionary tale of the reception and translations of the *Corpus Dionysianum* is an episode worthy of reflection. When Byzantine emperor Michael II the Stammerer sent it as a gift to Frankish king Louis the Pious in
827 as the work of a disciple of Saint Paul who was the first bishop of Paris,
no one thought to question its authenticity. The testimony of the donor, the
prestige of the alleged author, the interest of the text—all were sufficient
guarantees. Scotus Eriugena had doubts about the identity of Paul's disciple
and the first bishop of Paris, but not about the venerable age of the text.

5.2.2. Authentication at the Level of Textual Manifestation
The form of the document must be in keeping with the rules of formation of
the period to which it is attributed. The first example of philological analysis
based on the form of the expression was provided in the fifteenth century by
Lorenzo Valla (*De falso credita et ementita Constantini donatione declama-
tio*, XIII), when he demonstrated that the use of certain linguistic expressions in Latin was completely implausible at the beginning of the fourth
century A.D. Isaac Casaubon (*De rebus sacris et ecclesiasticis exercitationes*,
XIV) proved that the *Corpus Hermeticum* was not a Greek translation of an
ancient Egyptian text, because it did not contain a single trace of Egyptian
idiomatic expressions. Modern philologists have shown that the Hermetic

Asclepius was not translated, as was once believed, by Marius Victorinus, because in all his writings Victorinus always put the conjunction *etenim* at the beginning of the sentence, whereas in the *Asclepius* the word occurs in the second position twenty-one times out of twenty-five.

According to the semiosic system, recourse is made to paleographic, epigraphic, lexicographic, grammatical, iconographic, and stylistic and other criteria. These methods are today judged sufficiently scientific, even when based on conjecture. The Middle Ages had no paleographic criteria, and its lexicographic, grammatical, and stylistic criteria were fairly vague. Men like Augustine and Abelard, and eventually scholars like Thomas Aquinas, recognized the problem of establishing the reliability of a text on the basis of its linguistic features. But, apropos of the text of the Bible, Augustine, who had small Greek and less Hebrew, in the pages where he discusses the technique of *emendatio,* advises at most to compare the various Latin translations with each other, in order to make a conjecture, taking account of the differences, about the "correct" reading of the text. He is looking for a "good" text, not the original text, and he rejects the idea of checking the Hebrew version because he believes it has been manipulated by the Jews: hence, not only does he not go back to the presumed original, he mistrusts it. Better a translation inspired by God that an original corrupted by a malicious intent (*De doctrina christiana* 2, 11–14).

As Marrou (1958) remarks, none of his commentaries presupposes a preliminary effort to establish a critical text. There is no analysis of the manuscript tradition. Saint Augustine is content to compare the largest possible number of manuscripts and to take into consideration the largest possible number of variants.

When Saint Jerome's translation *ex hebraeo* conflicts with that of the Septuagint, Augustine tends to suspect Jerome's translation, because he considers the Septuagint divinely inspired. He never chooses the Vulgate over the Septuagint. In the *De civitate Dei* (15, 10–11), in calculating the age of Methuselah, the text of the Septuagint (but not the Vulgate) is contradictory, since it has Methuselah die after the Flood, but Augustine refrains from committing himself, suggesting the hypothesis of a correction introduced by the perfidious Jews to undermine the confidence of Christians vis-à-vis the Septuagint version. It is curious that Augustine should think that the Hebrew original might be corrupt (a useful suspicion on the part of a philologist), while he is not overly concerned over the corruptness of the translations, convinced that he can resolve the issues with a bland comparative approach, in which the last word will be uttered not by philology but by a righteous will to interpret and fidelity to traditional knowledge (see Marrou 1958: 432–434).

Bede and other authors analyze the rhetorical figures of Holy Scripture, but they are ignorant of the Hebrew original, and the language they are analyzing is that of a translation. It is not until the thirteenth century that an effort will be made to return to the Hebrew original with the help of converted Jews (see Chenu 1950: 117–125 and 206).

In any case, etymological practice has much to teach us about the weakness of medieval philology, whether the etymologies in question be those of Isidore of Seville or Virgil of Toulouse. Medieval etymology has nothing to do with the history of the lexicon. It is philosophical, theological, moral, or poetic. Every medieval etymology is, from the etymological point of view, a fake.

As for their insensitivity to language, the case of the thirteenth-century Modistae (see Chapter 7) is exemplary: all of their speculative grammar is an example of philological highhandedness. They attempt to elaborate a general theory of language on the basis of a single language, Latin. They do not believe that other languages displaying other grammatical (and therefore mental) structures exist. They identify *modus essendi* and *modus significandi*. Their ethnocentric impermeability is equal only to that of those twentieth-century Anglo-Saxon linguists who construct theories of linguistic universals on the basic of a single language, English.

True, the Abelard of *Sic et non* invites us to beware of words used in an unusual sense, of the corrupt state of a text as a sign of a work's inauthenticity, but the practice will remain imprecise, at least down to Petrarch and the proto-humanists.[8]

5.2.3. Authentication at the Level of Content

In this case we must decide whether the categories, the taxonomies, the styles of argument, the iconographic configurations, and similar phenomena can be traced back to the cultural universe to which the document is

---

8. This continuing ascendency of logic over grammar in the thirteenth century was accurately described by Gilson (1952) in the chapter of his *Philosophie au Moyen Age* entitled "L'exil des belles-lettres."

attributed. Even for the modern period such criteria are highly conjectural in nature, though they appeal to relatively accepted notions with regard to the "worldview" typical of a given historical period.

Medieval intellectuals had some idea of content screening; at least during the Scholastic period, they attempted to verify whether a text attributed to a certain author displayed modes of thought in keeping with the cultural universe to which the author belonged. Abelard advises his readers to beware of passages in which the author cites only other people's opinions, often contradictory, in which the words have a different meaning depending on the author cited. Like Augustine in the *De doctrina christiana,* Abelard recommends checking the context. But this contextual principle is invalidated by his next recommendation: to give greater weight, in doubtful cases, to the most qualified authority.

Thomas Aquinas takes up the criterion of textual and historical contextuality, giving precedence to usage over the lexicographical meaning; and implicit in this criterion is that the usage be that of the period referred to (*Summa Theologiae* I, 29, 2 ad 1). Thomas concentrates on the *modus loquendi,* that is, on the philosophical style, and he is able to establish that at certain points Dionysius the Areopagite or Augustine speak in a certain way because they are following the usage of the Platonists. He goes in search of the *intentio auctoris,* but his examination is not historical but theoretical. He does not always ask himself whether, at the time of the supposed production of the text, people thought in that way, but rather whether that way of thinking was "correct," and therefore to be attributed to the supposed doctrinal authority. "In quantum sacra doctrina utitur philosophicis documentis, non recipit ea propter auctoritatem dicentium sed propter rationem dictorum" ("Inasmuch as sacred doctrine makes use of the teachings of philosophy for their own sake, it does not accept them on account of the authority of those who taught them, but on account of the reasonableness of the doctrine") (*In Boet. De Trinitate* 2, 3 ad 8).[9]

Credit is denied to the name of the presumed author (a previous false identification is called into question), but this is done by demonstrating that the alleged author could not have thought what the text says, or think it in the way the text says it.

---

9. http://www.logicmuseum.com/authors/aquinas/superboethiumq2.htm.

Let us see how Thomas proceeds in reattributing the *De causis,* an operation that, when we take the period into account, may be defined as philological—but only in a metaphorical sense. Thomas's argument goes as follows: until yesterday this book was thought to be by Aristotle, but now we have William of Moerbeke's translation of the *Elementatio theologica* of Proclus. Given the similarity of the two texts, we believe that the second is derived from the first, of which it is an Arabic variant, since it comes to us from the Arabic, and its content is not Aristotelian but Platonic. There can be no doubt that we are dealing with an attitude that is already mature, but in this connection it must be observed that these so-called procedures of authentication are based on a concept of authenticity different from our modern criteria.

Thomas repeatedly uses the term *authenticus,* but for him (and for the Middle Ages in general) the term signifies, not "original," but "true." *Authenticus* expresses its value, its authority, its credibility—not the genuineness of a text's provenance. Apropos of the *De causis* he says: "ideo in hac materia non est authenticus" *(II Sent.* 18, 2, 2, ad 2*),* but he means that the text is not authentic because it is not in the spirit of Aristotle. In *De ver.* 1, 1 ad 1, rejecting the attribution of the *Liber de spiritu et anima* to Augustine, he declares "non est authenticus nec creditur esse Augustini," but the reasons he gives are purely theoretical (see Chenu 1950: 111).

As Thurot (1869: 103–104) remarks, when explaining texts, the glossators do not attempt to grasp the thought of their author, but to teach the same science that is supposed to be explained therein: "An authentic author, as he was called at the time, cannot be deceived or contradict himself, and neither can he follow a defective plan or be in disagreement with another authentic author."

5.2.4. Authentication with Reference to Known Fact
In such cases our modern philological disciplines establish whether what the document refers to was indeed the case (or could be known) at the time it was supposedly produced. For example, analyses of the alleged correspondence between Churchill and Mussolini demonstrate the patent falsity of certain letters dated 1945—in spite of the fact that the paper (the material support) is authentic—on the basis of obvious contradictions of known fact. One letter is alleged to have been written from an address where Churchill

had not been living for years, another is dated May 7, though in it Churchill refers to events that did not occur until May 10 of that year.

This criterion seems not only "scientific," but also intuitively obvious. In reality, however, it is very modern. In fact, not only does it presume historical knowledge and the ability to establish on the basis of incontrovertible documentation whether something happened or not in that particular way; it also presupposes that we do not lend credence to the prophetic gifts of the ancient authors.

There is no need to go looking for violations of this principle in the Middle Ages—for the simple reason that we can find a mind-boggling example in the Renaissance. At the height of Humanism, the writings of the supposed Hermes Trismegistus show up at the court of Cosimo de' Medici, and everyone from Pico della Mirandola to Ficino and beyond is inclined to consider them a product of the ancient world and divinely inspired. The reasoning of these authors, who nevertheless knew both Greek and Hebrew, is not fundamentally different from that of their medieval predecessors: the hermetic texts are divinely inspired because, although they were written before Jesus Christ, they contain the same teachings! They are considered authentically ancient only because they anticipate "prophetically" events (or ideas) that happened later. As we have seen, it will be a good century before Casaubon will turn this criterion on its head: in addition to analyzing expressive forms and forms of content, and demonstrating that the texts of the *Corpus Dionysianum* contain stylistic traits typical of the Hellenistic period, he will recognize that, if these texts contain echoes of Christian concepts, they must have been composed in the early centuries of the Christian era.

5.3. Three Categories of False Identification

At this point we are in a position to identify three chief forms of false identification.

5.3.1. Strong False Identification
It is asserted (in good or bad faith) that an object Ob is identical (or coincides with) an object Oa, already well-known and famous, where B is an anonymous author, whereas A is an author who is well-known and famous.

Oa is instead physically different from Ob and between the two objects there
exists merely a relationship of apparent formal homology.

FIRST CASE. A person knows full well that Ob cannot be identified with Oa,
because it was produced subsequently by imitation, but still considers the
two objects to be equivalent as far as their value and function is concerned
and, since he does not possess the notion of authorial originality, he presents the one as identical to the other. This is the case with ingenuous nonfe-
tishistic collecting, as occurred with the Roman patricians who considered
themselves aesthetically satisfied with a copy of a Greek statue and were not
above labeling it or having it signed "Phidias" or "Praxiteles." It is the case
with the tourists in Florence who admire the David of Michelangelo outside
the Palazzo Vecchio, unconcerned that it is a copy of the original preserved
elsewhere. A paradoxical variant of this possibility is the authorial fake: the
same author A, after producing Oa, produces, following the same specifications, a perfect double Ob, morphologically indistinguishable from Oa. From
the ontological point of view, the two objects are physically and historically
distinct, but from the point of view of their aesthetic value they are both
equally valuable. Cases of this kind (see the controversy over the fake De
Chiricos that some critics believe were painted by De Chirico himself) offer
embarrassing food for thought for a critique of the fetishistic concept of the
work of art as *unicum*.

SECOND CASE. A person is aware that Ob is simply an imitation of Oa and
cannot be identified with it and does not believe the two objects to be equivalent. But, in bad faith, he pretends (and declares) that Ob is identical to Oa.
This is a case of falsification in the strict sense, of a copy identified with the
original, or of counterfeiting of currency. The practice has been widespread
since classical antiquity, and during the Renaissance collectors commis-
sioned fake coins and statues, often simply for the pleasure of completing
their collection.

THIRD CASE. We have a variant of the two previous cases when B transforms Oa into Ob. For example, during the last century the bibliophile Guglielmo Libri manipulated original manuscripts stolen from libraries public
and private, dismembering them, altering the notes of provenance and pos-

session, adding false signatures. In a similar way people performed unfaithful restorations on paintings and statues that denatured the work, or they eliminated or covered over parts of the body subject to censure, or broke up the panels of a polyptych. All these operations may have been done in good or bad faith (believing or not believing that Ob was still identical to Oa), or believing or not believing that the work was manipulated in a spirit faithful to the *intentio auctoris*. In reality, the objects we consider ancient, original, and authentic works of art have instead been transformed by the action of time and by man—and they have undergone amputations, restorations, alterations, loss of color. To this category belongs the neoclassical dream of Greek art as "white," whereas the original temples and statues were polychrome. In this way, a typology of falsification may lead us to reflect critically on our own ideology of authenticity.

FOURTH CASE. A person is unaware that the two objects are not identical, or believes that Oa and Ob are the same object. Obviously he is not concerned with the problem of their interchangeability and presents Ob as authentic. This was a common state of affairs in the Middle Ages, but it can also occur today in the case of an erroneous authentication made in good faith.

5.3.2. Weak False Identification or Presumption of Interchangeability
Oa and Ob are known to be physically different, but it is agreed that, when described in a certain way and for certain practical purposes, the one is equivalent to the other, and they are presented as completely interchangeable.

This was the case in general in the Middle Ages for all translations. The translation was the only text that supplied information about the original, and it was considered a substitute for the original, even though it was known to be a version from another language (usually unknown). This was also the case for transcription from one codex to another. From the point of view of modern philology these translations and transcriptions were all unfaithful, in addition to which translator and transcriber would consciously alter the text, amputating it or censuring it. To this category we may also assign the various kinds of hidden censure that translations and copies were subject to, and even certain cases of aberrant decoding produced by an annotation that led the copyist to interpret one expression as if it was the same as another.

The Middle Ages was very flexible in its attitude toward translations. In paragraph IV, v, 7, 134, of the *De divinis nominibus* of Pseudo-Dionysius, Hilduin's first version translated *kalon* as *bonum* and *kallos* as *bonitas*. Eriugena translates the first term as *bonum* but the second as *pulchrum;* and lastly John the Saracen renders both with *pulchritudo* and *pulchrum*. These are substantial differences that reveal, as De Bruyne (1946: 1:5, 2) points out, a profound cultural transformation. But the Saracen himself, in a letter to John of Salisbury (PL 193, 2599), will claim that he translated according to the meaning, not according to the letter. The Saracen was lexically correct, but probably for the wrong reasons, at least in terms of the official lexicography of his day, since, in the following century, Albertus Magnus will continue to debate the two terms and to assert that *kalos* with one "l" means goodness, not beauty.[10]

5.3.3. Pseudo-Identification

This is the case of apocryphal or pseudoepigraphical objects. It is asserted that an object Ob is identical to (or coincides with) an object Oa, except for the fact that Oa no longer exists, or never existed, and in any case has never been seen by anyone. Oa is qualified as exceptional, either because of the name of its author or because in reality the tradition has handed down inaccurate information about its supposed existence. To lend credence to a pseudo-identification we have to be somehow familiar with a set of objects *a* (Oa1, Oa2, Oa3, etc.), all produced by a well-known and famous author A. From set *a* an abstract type is extracted which does not take into consideration the features of objects *a* but instead the supposed specifications according to which they were formed, or the way in which A apparently produced them (style, type of materials used, etc.). Ob was produced according to these specifications, and it therefore is asserted that Ob is a previously unknown product by A.

FIRST CASE. Someone is aware that Oa does not exist and is familiar only with Ob. He therefore knows that they cannot be identified with each other.

---

10. In the *De pulchro et bono,* another case of false attribution—to Thomas Aquinas—and this time not just on the part of the Middle Ages but all the way down to our own century (see Chapter 8 in this volume). For a discussion of *kalon,* see the introduction by Pietro Caramello to the Marietti edition of the *De divinis nominibus.*

But he believes in good faith that Ob may serve all the purposes that Oa would have served, and as such he presents it in place of Oa, whereas Ob is merely an ersatz of Oa. This is the typical case of the *diplomatic forgery (reine formale Falschung)*. While the historical forgery *(reine Falschung)* concerns a formally genuine document that contains inexact or invented information (such as the authentic confirmation of false privileges), the diplomatic forgery is a document expressly created to assert privileges that may in fact have really been conceded but whose original documentation has been lost. Examples are the false documents produced by monks to backdate or extend the possessions of their abbeys, where we may suppose that the monks, on the basis of tradition, were convinced that they had truly obtained the privileges in question and were simply attempting to affirm them in a public manner.

SECOND CASE. Someone knows that Oa does not exist, and does not believe that Ob is equivalent and interchangeable with Oa. Nevertheless, in bad faith, he insists on declaring the two objects (one real, the other virtual) to be identical, or on the authenticity of Ob, with intent to deceive. This is the case of the modern diplomatic forgery, of fake genealogical trees produced to confirm otherwise unattested pedigrees, of apocryphal documents produced with malicious intent. This is probably the case of the poem *De vetula,* produced in the thirteenth century, but immediately attributed to Ovid. We may suppose that the person or persons who placed the *Corpus Dionysianum* into circulation in the eighth century, attributing it to a disciple of Saint Paul, were instead aware that the work had been fabricated much later, but they nonetheless decided to attribute it to an uncontestable *auctoritas*. To this category there also belong the cases of attribution to an author by no means well-known and famous, but who becomes so when he is presented as ancient and when characteristics are attributed to him that make him an authority. This is the case with a number of nonexistent chroniclers to whom the Abbot Trithemius attributed spurious works.[11]

In all of these cases, in addition to the documentary forgery, a historical falsification is also committed, in other words, lies are circulated regarding

---

11. This of course is also the case with artistic fakes, like the fake Dutch masters painted fifty years ago by the extraordinarily talented contemporary artist Han van Meegeren.

events of the past. The pseudo-identification is invoked to subrogate the historical lie.

THIRD CASE. Someone is unaware that Oa does not exist and does not know that it is not identifiable with Ob. Therefore that someone has no problem considering them identical. Independently of whether or not he believes in the interchangeability of the two objects, he claims in any case that they are identical, thereby affirming the authenticity of Ob. This appears to have been the case with those who thought the *Corpus Dionysianum* was the work of a disciple of Saint Paul, unaware that it had been produced at a later date, and those who considered the *De causis* to be a work by Aristotle and not by an Arabic follower of Proclus. It is certainly the case with all those who believed and continue to believe in the authenticity of the book of Enoch, and to the men of the Renaissance who attributed the *Corpus Hermeticum* not to Hellenistic authors but to a mythical Hermes Trismegistus who supposedly lived before Plato at the time of the Egyptians and could probably be identified with Moses. In the modern period, we have the case of Heidegger (1915) who writes a commentary on a *Grammatica Speculativa* believing it to be the work of Duns Scotus, while a few years later it will be proven to be the work of Thomas of Erfurt. It goes without saying that a false attribution of this kind also leads to aberrant decoding.

A variant of this case of pseudo-identification is attribution to a pseudo-author: we have only one text Ob, whose author is unknown, and it is decided to attribute it to an author A, information about whom is uncertain. This seems to have been the case with the attribution of the treatise *On the Sublime* to a certain Pseudo-Longinus.

5.4. What Do We Mean by "Knowing That"?

In sketching this semiotics of falsification we have implicitly made use of an epistemic operator like "knows that" which poses a number of problems. What does it mean to say that someone *knows* that Oa and Ob are not identical? The only case of false attribution in which we can know that Oa and Ob are not identical is the one in which someone presents us, for example, with a perfect reproduction Ob of the *Mona Lisa,* when we are standing in front of the original Oa exhibited in the Louvre, and affirms that the two objects are indiscernibly the same object. This is of course an improbable event, but even if was to occur the doubt would remain whether Ob was the authentic *Mona Lisa* and Oa a fake maliciously (or erroneously) hung on the gallery wall. And what does it mean to *know* that Oa never existed? Except for the case in which there are irrefutable proofs that Oa once existed and has been destroyed (as is probably true of the Hanging Gardens of Babylon or the temple of Diana at Ephesus), usually the assertion "Oa does not exist" is understood simply to mean "there are no proofs of its existence."

Modern philology has developed techniques of identification to establish whether an Ob is identical to an Oa, but these procedures presuppose that we know the properties Oa has or should have. Now, the techniques by which we establish the characteristics of Oa are the same as those by which we identify Ob. In other words, in order to say that a reproduction of the *Mona Lisa* is not authentic, somebody has to have analyzed and authenticated the original *Mona Lisa* using the same techniques used to decide that the reproduction of it is different. For modern philology the traditional evidence that the *Mona Lisa* in the Louvre was put there, let's say, by Leonardo right after painting it is not enough. This fact must be proven by means of documents, but for these documents too the question of their authentication must be posed. And if there is any doubt about the documents, the presumed original of the *Mona Lisa* is analyzed to decide whether its material and morphological attributes lead us to conclude that it was painted by Leonardo.

Our modern culture, therefore, must assume that (i) a document authenticates traditional information and not vice versa; (ii) authenticity means historical primitivity and authorial originality (this is the only way to establish the priority of Oa over Ob); and (iii) primitivity and originality are established by considering the object as a sign of its origin, and the techniques of authentication described in section 5.2 are applied to this end.

These checks call for scientific and historical knowledge of which the Middle Ages had only a vague and ambiguous grasp, for reasons intimately connected with its concept of historical truth.

5.5. Historical Truth, Tradition, and *Auctoritas*

The Middle Ages could not conceive of a document that would authenticate traditional data because the only reliable form of documentation it possessed was traditional data.

The Middle Ages could only argue based on the testimony of the past, and the past had chronological abscissas that were quite vague. The medieval procedure of recourse to authority has the form of a synecdoche: an author or a single text stands for the globality of tradition and always functions outside of any context. Le Goff (1964: 397–402) has remarked that the medieval form of wisdom is folkloristic, and is symbolized by the proverb. Feudal law and practice are sanctioned by custom.

The same Le Goff cites a 1252 lawsuit between the servants of the chapter of Notre Dame de Paris in Orly and the canons: the canons say the servants must pay tithes because tradition requires it. The oldest inhabitant of the region is consulted and he says that it has been that way "a tempore a quo non extat memoria" ("from time immemorial"). Another witness, the archdeacon Jean, affirms that he has seen certain ancient documents in the chapter which attest to the existence of the custom, and the chapter has put its faith in these documents out of respect for the antiquity of the writing. No one of course thought to check the existence, let alone the nature, of the documents: it was sufficient to hear they existed, for centuries.

For the Middle Ages, the problem of tradition, in historiography and hermeneutics, is that it does not have to be reconstructed: it is already given from the beginning; it must simply be recognized and interpreted in the proper way.

Apart from the data of tradition, only one document is recognized, and it is the text (translated) of the Holy Scriptures. Other documents are not distinguished as original and nonoriginal: they have either been handed down or they don't exist. If they have been handed down, they are true only insofar as they agree or can be made to agree with the truth of Scripture: "Certus enim sum, si quid dico quod Sacrae Scripturae absque dubio contradicat, quia falsum est" ("For I am certain that, if I say anything which clearly opposes Holy Scripture, it is false") (Anselm, *Cur Deus homo*, 1, 18, PL 153, 38).

Still, the problem is not so simple, because, in order to establish the truth of Scripture, it must be correctly interpreted. After Origen proposed the principle of the complementarity of the two testaments and their parallel reading, the problem arose of how to legitimate their interpretations. On the one hand a correct interpretation must legitimize the Church, but on the other what decides whether and how an interpretation is correct is the interpretive tradition, legitimized by the Church as the guardian of truth: an embarrassing situation, and the origin of every theory of the hermeneutical circle (see Compagnon 1979).

This is why the Middle Ages must amass a treasury of authoritative opinions, or *auctoritates*. In the course of the philosophical and theological debate, authority materializes in the form of quotes that become "authentic" opinions and therefore authoritative in themselves. They are clarified, when they are obscure, by their glosses, but these too must come from an "authentic" author.

As Grabmann remarks (1906–1911), when it came to the explanation of Scripture, historical grammatical interpretations or independent research on the concepts and connections of the biblical text carried no weight; what counted were above all collections of passages extrapolated from the Fathers of the Church. Pre-Scholastic theological literature "is placed under the sign of reproduction," and appeals to *florilegia* and *catenae*. But little by little the original manuscripts of the Fathers are neglected or lost, and their opinions survive only in the *florilegia*. When we consider that this process occurs through free transcriptions and translations, we can see how the modern idea of authenticity could find itself in considerable difficulty.

Furthermore, the *florilegia* are arranged for the most part in alphabetical order, which excludes the kind of systematic classification that might have made for comparison and discussion of contradictory passages. With the twelfth century, the *florilegia* and traditional opinions are supplemented by *sententiae modernorum magistrorum*, even though these so-called modern masters are such only by academic convention (as authors of *glossae magistrales*), and Thomas often dares to contradict them ("haec glossa magistralis est et parum valet," ["this is a master's annotation and has little value"] *In I Timeum* 5, 2).[12]

To the anarchy of the authorities, the Middle Ages proved incapable of opposing a practice of verification of historical originality. Scrutiny (and the dialectical discussion intended to resolve contradictions) was not philological but philosophical. Hence the decision, asserted without hypocrisy in the twelfth century, to treat authorities with a pinch of salt. "Authority has a nose

---

12. See Grabmann (1906–1911, esp. Part IV of the first volume, devoted to the transmission of traditional knowledge), and Chenu (1950: 128–129). On how anthologies may give rise to a series of misunderstandings concerning originals that no one reads any more, see Ghellinck (1939: 95 and 105).

of wax, in other words, it can be bent in different directions" ["Auctoritas cereum habet nasum, id est in diversum potest flexi sensum," Alain de Lille, *De fide catholica* 1, 30]). Authorities must be accepted, but, given their insufficiencies and contradictions, they must be interpreted reverently, *exponere reverenter*, and, as Chenu notes (1950: 122), we should make no mistake over the meaning of this expression: what we are dealing with are small but efficacious adjustments, fine-tuning, rectifications to the meaning of the text.

5.6. On the Shoulders of Giants

Bernard of Chartres, as we know, supplied the moral and historical justification for these interpretive liberties, with his famous aphorism that compared contemporary thinkers to dwarves standing on the shoulders of giants.[13] But the same idea (if not the metaphor of the dwarves) appears six centuries earlier in Priscian, and this brings us to the question of whether the aphorism is modest or presumptuous in its intent. In fact it can be interpreted in the sense that what we know today, though we may know it somewhat better, is what the ancients have taught us, or, alternatively, that, however much we owe to the ancients, we know far more than they did. A similar aphorism, that appears in Saint Bernard of Clairvaux (Bernardus Carnotensis) and speaks of gleaners following in the footsteps of the reapers, leaves no room for doubt, because the gleaners gather only the gleanings left behind by the reapers. Where Priscian stood remains ambiguous: for him it seems that the moderns are more *perspicacious* than the ancients, though not necessarily more *learned*.[14]

---

13. "Dicebat Bernardus Carnotensis nos esse quasi nanos gigantium humeris insidentes, ut possimus plura eis et in remotiora videre, non utique proprii visus acumine aut eminentia corporis sed quia quia in altum subvehimur et extollimur magnitudine gigantes" ("Bernard of Chartres used to say that we were like dwarfs seated on the shoulders of giants. If we see more and further than they, it is not due to our own clear eyes or tall bodies, but because we are raised on high and upborne by their gigantic bigness"), *Metalogicon* (1159) bk. 3, ch. 4. Translation from Henry Osborn Taylor *The Mediaeval Mind* ([1911]1919) vol. 2, p. 159. See Jeauneau (1967: 79–99) and Merton (1965).

14. An interesting link between Priscian and Bernard could be William of Conches, who mentions dwarves and giants in his glosses on Priscian's *Institutio-*

But perhaps we should be debating not the meaning of the aphorism but how it has been interpreted in various historical periods. What does William of Conches mean when, commenting on the aphorism, he declares that the moderns are "perspicaciores" ("more perspicacious") than the ancients? It is no accident that, taking Newton as his point of departure, Merton (1965) sees the aphorism as decisive in the modern debates over influence, collaboration, borrowing, and plagiarism. But the notion of plagiarism, and the idea of staking one's life on being or not being the first to see something, can exist only in a period in which what is prized in every field of discourse is originality, or in the spirit of that modernity characterized by Maritain with the telling formula to the effect that, after Descartes, every thinker becomes a "debutant in the absolute." In the Middle Ages that was not how it was at all.

In the Middle Ages what was true was true because it had been upheld by a previous authority, to the point that, if one suspected that the authority had not espoused the new idea, one proceeded to manipulate the evidence, because authority has a nose of wax. It comes naturally to the Middle Ages to employ the aphorism, because the mode of discussion typical of the period is the commentary or the gloss. One must always take a giant as one's point of departure. But it is up for grabs whether a medieval thinker using the aphorism is vindicating the superiority of the moderns or arguing for the continuity of knowledge.

To read the aphorism in a Hegelian sense we do not have to wait for Hegel, but neither must we assume that Bernard thought like Newton. Newton knew

---

nes grammaticae. William's text precedes that of John of Salisbury and was written in the years when William was chancellor at Chartres. But, while the first version of William's glosses dates back to before 1123 (John's *Metalogicon* is dated 1159), before Neckam, Peter of Blois, and Alain de Lille, all three cited by Merton, we find the aphorism in 1160 in a text from the school of Laon and later, around 1185, in the Danish historian Sven Aggesen. In the thirteenth century, the aphorism also appears in Gérard of Cambrai, Raoul of Longchamp, Gilles de Corbeil, Gérard of Auvergne, and, in the fourteenth century, in Alexandre Ricat, physician to the kings of Aragon, or other doctors like Guy de Chauliac and Ambroise Paré, as well as in Daniel Sennert. Gregory (1961) identifies it in Gassendi. Ortega y Gasset, in "Entorno a Galileo" (*Obras completas* V, Madrid 1947: 45), speaking of the succession of generations, says that men stand "one on the shoulders of another, and the one who is on top enjoys the impression of dominating the others, but he ought to realize that at the same time he is their prisoner."

full well that, since Copernicus, a revolution in the universe was under way; Bernard didn't even know that revolutions in knowledge were possible.

Indeed, since one of the recurrent themes of medieval culture is the progressive senescence of the world, Bernard's aphorism could be interpreted to mean that, given that *mundus senescit* (the world is getting older and older), and inexorably at that, the best we can do is to play up some of the advantages of this tragedy.[15]

On the other hand, Bernard, following Priscian, uses the aphorism in the context of a debate on grammar, in which what is at stake are the concepts of knowledge and imitation of the style of the ancients. Nothing to do then with notions like the cumulative nature and progress of theological and scientific knowledge. Still, Bernard (our witness is still John of Salisbury) scolded those among his pupils who slavishly imitated the ancients, saying that the problem was not writing like them, but learning from them to write as well as they did, so that, in the future, "someone will be inspired by us as we are inspired by them."[16] Therefore, though not in the same terms as we read it today, an appeal to independence and courage was nonetheless present in his aphorism. And it is not without significance that John of Salisbury takes up the aphorism no longer in the context of grammar but in a chapter in which he is discussing Aristotle's *De interpretatione*.

A few years earlier Adelard of Bath had inveighed against a generation that considered acceptable only the discoveries made by the ancients, and in the coming century Siger of Brabant will declare that *auctoritas* by itself is not enough, because we are all men exactly like those we are inspired by, and therefore "why should we not devote ourselves to rational research like them?" (Beonio-Brocchieri Fumagalli 1987: 232). We are clearly on the threshold of modernity. But we have a long way to go as far as the concept of originality and the neurosis of plagiarism are concerned.

5.7. *Tamquam ab iniustis possessoribus*

The Middle Ages copied without acknowledgment because that was the way it was done and ought to be done. What's more, a notion akin to that con-

---

15. See, for example, the chapter on the spatial and temporal structures of the Middle Ages in Le Goff (1964).

16. See McGarry (1955: 167).

tained in the aphorism was anticipated by Augustine and developed by Roger Bacon, when he said that if we find good ideas in pagan texts we are entitled to appropriate them as ours "tamquam ab iniustis possessoribus," ("as it were from unjust possessors") because, if the ideas are true, then Christian culture has every right to them. This explains why medieval notions of forgery and what is fake are very different from our own.

True, the falsification of *auctoritates* is an act of critical freedom that reaffirms the principle of discovery against every kind of dogmatic constraint. But this liberation is obtained at the expense of what we would define today as "philological correctness." If the dwarf is to see further than the giant he can and must adjust the giant's thought to show that innovation does not contradict tradition. *Non nova sed nove* ("Not new things, but in a new way"). This is why medieval culture could not avoid a casual approach to philology.

Let us close with a significant example. Thomas's choice of translations seems never to be inspired by philological considerations. His commentary on the *De interpretatione* follows the translation by Boethius, despite the fact that he already had William of Moerbeke's new version available to him, and without realizing that Boethius was guilty of a misreading of considerable interpretive importance. In *De interpretatione* 16a Aristotle says that words are *symbola* of the passions of the soul, but shortly thereafter he adds that they can also be taken as *semeia* of the same passions, and hence as symptoms. The passage can be explained as meaning that words are conventional symbols, but they may also be interpreted as symptoms of the fact that the speaker has something on his or her mind. As we already saw in Chapter 4 on the barking of the dog, Boethius translates both Greek terms with *nota* (a fairly vague multipurpose expression), which leads Thomas to interpret both cases with the word *signum*—a choice that seriously compromises a correct reading of the text.

But note what happens with Roger Bacon, who was so convinced that, in order to snatch the truth from the infidel, "tamquam ab iniustis possessoribus," we have to know languages, to be able to check the translations—an ideal shared by Robert Grosseteste and in general by the Oxford Franciscans ("Cum ignorat linguas non est possibile quod aliquid sciat magnificum, propter rationes quam scribo, de linguarum cognitione," *Opus Minus*, p. 327). Bacon knows Greek and perhaps he realizes Boethius's error. But even after realizing it, for reasons that have to do with his own theory of signs, he continues to see the relationship between words and things as purely symptomatic, as if Aristotle had used the term *semeion* in both instances (*De signis,* V, 166).

Bacon is aware that a translation Ob is not the equivalent of the original Oa, but he has no qualms in transforming Oa into a third text that simply turns Ob upside down. He certainly acted without any clear intention to deceive, and felt authorized to do what he did because he was convinced that in so doing he was better serving the interests of truth. But the truth was *his* truth, not the truth of the original text.

It is episodes like this that lead us to conclude that, though there were forgeries in the Middle Ages, what was missing was the awareness of forgery. Medieval notions of true and false attribution and manipulation of a text were not the same as ours.

5.8. Conclusions

We could say, as tradition has it, that the new philological awareness begins with Petrarch, and subsequently with Lorenzo Valla. But the fact that this awareness surfaced does not mean that European culture changed its attitude toward its sources overnight. The proof, furnished by Casaubon, of the Hellenistic origins of the *Corpus Hermeticum* appeared at the beginning of the seventeenth century, but even afterward, and for a considerable length of time, most of European culture continued to believe in the text's antiquity.

We would be better advised to reflect on the regeneration of the processes of falsification in the contemporary world. Setting aside the fabricators who continue to repeat the time-honored counterfeiting techniques (false attributions, fake genealogical tables, copies of paintings), we find ourselves faced, in the political universe and in the mass media, with a new form of falsification. Not only do we have false information, but also apocryphal documents, placed in circulation by a secret service or a government or an industrial group, and leaked to the media, in order to create social turmoil, confusion in public opinion. We speak of "false information," without appealing to epistemological considerations, because the news is bound to be discovered as false sooner or later. Indeed we might say that it is disseminated as true precisely in order for it to be revealed as false a little time later.

Its purpose in fact is not to create a false belief but to undermine established beliefs and convictions. It serves to destabilize, to throw suspicion upon powers and counterpowers alike, to make us distrust our sources, to sow confusion.

We conclude then that the people of the Middle Ages falsified in order to confirm their faith in something (an author, an institution, a current of thought, a theological truth) and to uphold an order, whereas our contemporaries falsify in order to create distrust and disorder. Our philological age can no longer permit itself falsifications that present themselves as truths because it knows they will be unveiled in no time; and it operates instead by spreading falsifications that have no fear of philological examination, because they are destined to be unmasked immediately. We are not dealing with an isolated fake that masks, hides, and confuses, and to that end endeavors to seem "true." It is the quantity of falsifications recognizable as such that functions as a mask, because it tends to undermine the reliability of all truth.

We do not know how the people of the Middle Ages, with their ingenuous concept of authenticity, would have judged this brash and cynical concept we have of noningenuous falsification. One thing is for sure: no historical period has the right to moralize about any other.

6

Jottings on Beatus of Liébana

Read today in a secular spirit, the Apocalypse or Revelation of Saint John the Divine can be savored as an exercise in Surrealism, without the reader feeling the urge to reduce its absurd or oneiric elements to a decipherable letter. Or it could be interpreted as an exercise in mystical symbolism, lending itself to every possible interpretation, a stimulus for the most unbridled flights of the imagination, and consequently anyone proposing to assign a precise meaning to the text would be accused of betraying its rich poetic suggestion. The Middle Ages on the other hand, true to the Pauline admonition, knew that, before seeing truth face to face, "videmus per speculum et in aegnigmate" ("we see through a glass darkly"), and enigmas or riddles, ever since the time of the Sphinx, are there to be solved. The Middle Ages, then, was within its rights to interpret the Apocalyse as an allegory; and the keys for interpreting any allegory correctly have to be absolutely precise.

The text certainly employs similes—and metaphors as well—that present no problems of interpretation ("His head and his hairs were white like wool, as white as snow. . . . and his voice as the sound of many waters."). Nevertheless, taken as a whole, it is an allegory, a rhetorical figure in which the text may be taken literally (what is to prevent seven stars and seven lamps of fire from manifesting themselves?), though it seems more profitable from the

---

A reworking of my essay "Palinsesto su Beato" (Eco 1973), a commentary that first appeared in the sumptuously illustrated Franco Maria Ricci edition of *Beato di Liébana* (1973), and "Jerusalem and the Temple as Signs in Medieval Culture," in Manetti (1996: 329–344). [*Translator's note:* English citations from the Apocalypse are from the King James Version (KJV)].

hermeneutical point of view to interpret every character, figure, or event with reference to a key (hence, for example, the seven stars are the angels of the seven Churches and the seven lamps are the seven Churches themselves).[1]

Once we are in possession of the necessary keys, reading allegory is like solving a puzzle—and etymological wordplay was never so legitimate as it is in this case, if we interpret this riddling as the enigmatic language of a form of mysticism.

Interpreting the Apocalypse allegorically, however, is not all that easy, because the keys are not always supplied by the text. The Seer tells us what the seven stars are, but he does not spell out clearly who the beast rising up out of the sea is. He tells us the dragon is Satan, but he does not tell us immediately who the beast rising up out of the earth is—he will define him later as a false prophet, but he will confound his identity in a Kabbalistic conjuring of numbers and dynastic hocus-pocus. He speaks of a battlefield, Armageddon, recognizable in Hebrew tradition, and then he alludes to two witnesses who according to modern interpreters are Saints Peter and Paul, but whom Saint Bonaventure identifies instead as Enoch and Elijah (*Hexaem* I, 3, iii).

The vision, then, is in the allegorical mode, but it seems to go only halfway toward out-and-out allegory. When, in describing the procession in the Earthly Paradise toward the end of *Purgatory*, Dante says: "Beneath the handsome sky I have described, / twenty-four elders moved on, two by two, / and they had wreaths of lilies on their heads" (*Pg.*, XXIX, 82–84), his modern commentators inform us that these are the twenty-four elders of the Apocalypse. But in more than one modern commentary on the Apocalypse we are told that the four and twenty elders represent the twenty-four priestly classes (Rossano 1963), while equally frequent is the interpretation that would prefer to identify them with the twelve patriarchs and the twelve apostles. Saint Jerome, on the other hand, saw them as the twenty-four books of the Old Testament. Such an identification obliges us to interpret in turn the four beasts (the lion, the calf, the flying eagle, and the beast with the face as a man) as the four Gospels of the New Testament—something the traditional iconography usually does in fact do, on the evidence supplied once more by Saint Jerome. In another, modern commentary on the Apocalypse, however,

---

1. For the differences between metaphor and allegory, see Chapter 3 in the present volume.

Angelini (1969) suggests that the four beasts are beings of a superangelic nature. Can we assert that, for its author John, there existed a terminus a quo for this backward flight, from signifier to signified, a point at which they meant something precise?

If we attempt to consider the Apocalypse of Saint John as a text that can be anchored to *things,* we discover that it too, like the episode in Dante's *Purgatory,* is allegory in the second degree, an allegory that cites, as its own meaning, another allegory, namely Ezekiel 1:10; and who is to say that Ezekiel in his turn was not citing figures from Assyrian mythology? And so on and so forth. One signified functions only in the context of other signifieds linked to the same isotopy (books of the Old Testament-books of the New, or Heavenly Senate-cherubic intelligences, etc.), and the text as a whole, organized as it is as an open allegory, defies a univocal reading.

Such is the text that Beatus (730–785)—abbot of Liébana, chaplain to Queen Osinda, wife of Silo, king of Oviedo in northern Spain—finds himself confronted with in his *Apocalipsin libri duodecim.* Though the Apocalypse itself occupies no more than a few dozen pages, in the Sanders edition (1930) Beatus's commentary occupies 650, and in the edition published by Italy's Poligrafico dello Stato more than 1,000, while one of its average manuscripts runs to 300 leaves, written recto and verso and including the illustrations.[2]

To speak of Beatus is in fact to speak also and above all of the Mozarabic miniatures that illustrate all the so-called *Beati* produced between the tenth and eleventh centuries, in an amazing spate of fabulously beautiful books, such as the *Beatus* of Magius (970), the *Beatus* of San Millan de la Cogolla (920–930), the *Beatus* of Valcavado (970), the *Beatus* of Facundo (1047), the *Beatus* of San Miguel (tenth century), the *Beatus* of Gerona (975), the *Beatus* of the Catedral de Urgell, the *Beatus* of the monastery of the Escorial, and the *Beatus* of San Pedro de Cardeña (all three between the tenth and eleventh centuries), and the *Beatus* of Saint-Sever (1028–1072).

---

2. References for the citations from Beatus's *Commentarius* that follow are to the critical edition by Sanders (1930) (S followed by the page number) as well as to that of the 1985 Poligrafico dello Stato edition (B followed by the page number). For a monumental five-volume illustrated catalogue of the illustrations, see Williams 1994–2005.

In theory, the study of the written commentary and the study of the miniatures constitute two distinct problems (the history of biblical exegesis and the iconography of Christian art),[3] which would eventually require us to consider the connection between the boom of the *Beati* (two or three centuries after the composition of the commentary itself) and the history of millenarianism (see Eco 1973). But, though it is our intention to deal only with Beatus's commentary, we must constantly bear in mind the miniatures it inspired, since, while not always faithful to the commentary, they are heavily indebted to the fascination it exerted.

6.1. *Apertissime*

Beatus is not what we would call a "great" writer, and not simply because he lived in one of the most unsettled centuries of the Early Middle Ages, if we consider that the Venerable Bede—who died when Beatus was still a child—displays far greater intellectual vigor. Naturally Bede lived at the dawn of the English renaissance, while Beatus writes in a Christian Spain entrenched in its isolation at the edges of a hostile world of infidels. But this is not the point, and we must concede that Beatus was a farrago-prone epigone whose Latin syntax would make anyone's hair stand on end, even somebody accustomed to the piquant corruptions of medieval Latin. It is a miracle that it

---

3. The illuminations in the Beatus manuscripts have a preeminent place in the development of the figurative arts of the Middle Ages. Their influence spread along the "ways of Saint James," along the four roads, that is, which criss-crossed Europe and were taken by pilgrims on their pilgrimage to Santiago de Compostela. Along these roads the great abbey churches of the Romanesque period rose. The churches fulfilled several functions: organizational, hospitable, liturgical, and especially didactic. The church itself was, so to speak, a book made out of stone. The figures on its portals and capitals told the believers stopping there all they needed to know for the salvation of their souls: the mysteries of the faith, the precepts of virtuous behavior, the phenomena of nature, the elements of a more or less fabulous geography, tall tales of exotic peoples and monstrous creatures. For a long time, the West, having emerged from the Middle Ages, lost the knack of deciphering the meanings of many of these representations, so obvious to the medieval spectator or reader. It will be art historian Emile Mâle (1922, vol. I, ch. 2) who will identify the references to the Apocalypse that have their source in the illuminated *Beati*. See also Focillon (1938).

was not included among the voluptuous readings of Huymans's Des Esse-
intes, who might well have savored its "stammering grace, the often exquisite clumsiness of the monks stirring the poetical left-overs of Antiquity into
a pious stew. . . . the workshop turning out verbs of refined sweetness, sub-
stantives smelling of incense, and strange adjectives, crudely fashioned out
of gold in the delightfully barbaric style of Gothic jewellery."[4]

If what distinguishes this "Gothic jewelry" is a taste for accumulation and
obsessive verbal *entrelacs,* Beatus is a past master of the art, combining as he
does his lack of originality with an excess of earnestness. He acknowledges
his role as compiler—bringing together all of the commentaries that authors
more famous than he have previously composed; he lines them up without
citing his sources at all or citing them incorrectly, unendingly repeating his
own long-winded explanations, getting lost in rambling analyses of one passage while dismissing another with no more than a passing allusion; he borrows or steals wholesale from Augustine or Tyconius, seemingly without
stopping to ask himself whether what he filches makes sense (such as when,
for example, he speaks of the persecutions of the Christians in Africa as if
they were taking place in his own day, whereas in fact the Christians involved were those contemporary with Tyconius, several centuries earlier).
And yet, just when you are getting used to the idea that all he is doing is repeating what other people have said, you unexpectedly discover that he has
changed a word, eliminated a clause, altered an inflection—and all of a sudden the entire meaning of the commentary has been altered. Without letting it show, Beatus has renewed the tradition.

At the beginning of his commentary, Beatus transcribes an entire passage
which he attributes to Saint Jerome, but eleven centuries later we discover it
is by Priscillian of Avila (Sanders 1930: XX). He inserts texts several pages
long by other writers without any acknowledgment, and then confesses
debts of little or no account. He is not agreeable reading, he resists interpretation, he blatantly contradicts himself time and time again, he uses the
same Latin citation in two different crucial places, once with the ablative,
the other with the accusative ("mille annis" . . . "mille annos"). His contemporaries could not help noticing his interminable repetitiveness, and yet the
success he enjoyed was unprecedented. He influenced generation after gen-

---

4. Huysmans 2003, p. 39.

eration of readers and spawned a plethora of illuminated manuscripts such as not even the Four Evangelists inspired. His own time probably admired him for his excess of mediocrity—if you utter one banality you sound foolish, if you utter two you're a bore, but utter 10,000 and in no time you're Flaubert, the author of that catalogue of clichés, *Bouvard et Pécuchet*. Or maybe the secret of Beatus's popularity lies in his ability to transport his reader into a cultural discourse of the past, constructing a world of his own unrelated to the world of reality—something that appealed in general to the people of the Middle Ages, and which must have been even more attractive in a period in which reality was not always easy to take.

Beatus—confronted with a biblical text that defies any rational interpretation—is determined to explain everything, and he insists that everything be made clear and transparent. If the text is ambiguous—and heaven only knows it is—Beatus is dead set on eliminating every last ambiguity.

Camón Aznar (1960) has attempted to present Beatus's project as a manifestation of Hispanic national culture: as the East, in the guise of the Muslim occupation, was busy invading Visigothic Spain, Beatus, a representative of Spanish Visigothic culture, takes on an Oriental text seething with prophetic imagery, cutting it down to Western size, explaining everything, leaving no image vague or ambiguous. Within the very dichotomies of the text, everything that is confused, undifferentiated, and incomprehensible is attributed to the realm of evil. The people, the beasts, the desert, everything elemental, all are identified with the Devil.

In this way, what we have is the paradox of a text written in the spirit of Western clarity that will act as the inspiration for a series of exercises in Mozarabic art, typical instead of an imagination profoundly permeated with Oriental suggestions. The text can come to grips with the spirit of Oriental prophecy only by establishing every image as a precise cipher that can be translated and adapted to exhortatory ends, while the illustrations themselves are vibrant with expressionistic tensions, straining and contorting themselves to communicate something else, something more (Camón Aznar 1960: 24).

It could be objected that the other commentaries do the same thing, but the point is that Beatus churns out twelve whole books and hundreds and hundreds of pages, while Bede's commentary, for instance, occupies only seventy-seven columns in the *Patrologia Latina,* in other words, about 120 normal pages. But Bede, it is immediately obvious, is repeating a number of classical interpretations and moving swiftly on, whereas Beatus leaves no interpretive stone unturned, skips not a single detail, dedicates as many as ten pages to a single verse, in an attempt to find a "rational" (to his mind) solution for every exegetical problem.

Perhaps the appeal to a typically Hispanic culture is not strictly speaking indispensable. Beatus explains everything because the spirit of the Middle Ages inclined writers to want to translate all the hidden senses of a written text. It is just that in Beatus this obsession with exegetical exhaustiveness is more consuming than it is in others.

In his commentary on Apocalypse 4:1–6, having referred to the elders, he continues without batting an eye: "ecce apertissime manifestavi patriarcharum et apostolorum chorum" ("behold I have shown unquestionably the chorus of the patriarchs and the apostles") (*Commentarius* III, S 270). This adverb *apertissime* is a minor masterpiece of the medieval mentality, because the last thing that would occur to us is that the twenty-four elders refer *unquestionably* to the patriarchs and the apostles. And it is even more curious, if one is reading the text convinced, as Beatus was, that it was written by John the Apostle, that the Seer of Patmos, who is therefore still alive and well, should see *himself* as one of the twenty-four figures who surround the throne of the Lord. But at this point Beatus is speaking on the basis of an exegetical tradition represented by the Fathers of the Church, and he behaves exactly like the army of interpreters of the Apocalyse that his own text will inspire. He speaks as if there were reading codes for every allegory.

Prior to Beatus, Hippolytus of Rome, Tyconius, Tertullian, Irenaeus, Lactantius, Saint Jerome, Augustine, and many others had laid the groundwork for an authorized reading of Scripture. And hence it makes perfect sense that the elders should represent the patriarchs and the apostles *unquestionably*.

Nevertheless, the medieval tradition is not strictly unanimous in its interpretations. Bede—in his *Explanatio Apocalypsis* (PL, 93)—agrees with Beatus about the elders, but apropos of the beasts, after stating that "haec animalia multifarie interpretantur" ("these animals are interpreted in various ways"), he associates the lion with Matthew and the beast with the face as a man with Mark, a rather singular solution, since the exegetical tradition has accustomed us to the opposite attribution. Furthermore, for Bede the reasons why each of the animals are associated with a given evangelist are quite different from those advanced by Beatus. Finally, Bede alludes to the fact that at times the beasts, instead of signifying the Evangelists, signify the entire Church. And subsequently, when he comes to interpret the figure of the Lamb, which would appear to be so solidly connected with the image of Christ, Bede reminds us that in the Lamb Tyconius saw the Church. Bede is more subtle than Beatus, as can be seen in the critical clarity with which he points out that there can be more than one interpretation: "Dominus qui agnus est innocenter moriendo, leo quoque factus est mortem fortiter evincendo" ("The Lord, who, dying innocently, is a lamb, in boldly conquering death also became a lion").

Bede is aware, in other words, of what students of medieval Christian iconography know today, that is, that the same animal or the same flower may signify realities as opposed as God and the Devil, since in the domain of the symbolic we are perpetually encountering interconnected homonymies and synonymies. He knows that interpretation is an exercise in high rhetoric, and he cites at the beginning of his commentary the seven rules for the reading of the sacred texts enunciated by Tyconius, several of which are nothing more or less than rules for the interpretation of rhetorical figures.[5]

---

5. The rules, set forth in the *Liber regularum* (and discussed at length by Augustine in his *De doctrina christiana* III, 30–37) are: 1. "Of the Lord and his Body": Christ is sometimes presented as the head of the Church and sometimes as the Church itself, his Mystical Body. 2. "On the Double Body of Christ": a somewhat obscure rule, partly because Augustine, in his commentary, taken up, for example, by the Venerable Bede, outmaneuvers Donatist Tyconius, seizing the occasion to interpret him in an anti-Donatist key: it is not true that only the just belong to the Church and are worthy of administering the sacraments, instead the Church is a *Corpus Permixtum*, made up, that is, of good and bad members, whom God will separate on the Day of Judgment; for now, the Church is "bipartite." 3. "On Promises and the Law" deals with the discussion of grace versus good works. 4. "Of Species and Genus": Holy Scripture sometimes speaks of a specific entity designating by metonymy the vaster genus: it says "Jerusalem" or "Solomon" and means the Church and all its members. 5. "Of the Times": based explicitly on the principle of synecdoche or the part for the whole—the Apocalypse speaks of 144,000 elect to indicate the assembly of all the Saints, who are somewhat more, and it speaks of times in the same way. 6. "Of Recapitulation": sometimes the author of Scripture lists a temporal sequence of events, then he adds one that seems to be the continuation of the series but is in fact their recapitulation or the repetition of something

Bede knows that hermeneutics is an interpretive choice—a principle that Beatus, so convinced of the correctness of his own decodifications, seems to be less aware of. This may be why it is his text, and not that of Bede, that was destined to become so popular and influential, because it is untroubled by exegetical doubts and appears to read the Apocalypse like an open book.

The truth is, however, that Beatus is well aware that the sacred text is open to multiple interpretations. Augustine had said so in no uncertain terms, providing extremely telling examples, in books 11 and 12 of his *Confessions* where he explains that Scripture may be understood on several levels. If we take an expression like "In the beginning God made," one interpreter sees the beginning as referring to Divine Wisdom, while another sees it as referring to the beginning of things. And if one sees heaven and earth as prime matter, another sees heaven and earth as already formed and distinct, while yet another believes that the word "heaven" designates spiritual nature in its perfected form and the word "earth" corporeal matter in all its formlessness.

The fact is, says Augustine, that it is God Himself who inspires the prophets and patriarchs in such a way that they conceive *ab initio* all of the meanings that may be attributed to their words. When there is disagreement over which of two meanings should be attributed to an expression used by Moses, Augustine wonders whether both senses may not be true at the same time, with space left over for a third or fourth meaning that remains to be discovered, "quam ut unam veram sententiam ad hoc apertius ponerem, ut excluderem ceteras, quarum falsitas me non posset offendere" ("rather than set down my own meaning so clearly as to exclude the rest, which, not being false, could not offend me"). What's to prevent us believing that all meanings were foreseen by this great servant of the Lord?

Thus, on the one hand, the medieval interpreter operates with a sort of theoretical empiricism, passing unconcernedly from one meaning to another, citing an authority as irrefutable at one moment and putting words into his mouth at another, appealing to an illustrious Father of the Church when it

---

already said (this is a rule that helps overcome the sense of flashback that the Apocalypse communicates to the reader when certain events appear to occur twice). 7. "Of the Devil and his Body": repeats the rule, once more metonymical, according to which we speak of Christ as both head and body of the community of the Elect.

suits him and ignoring him when he encounters another interpretation that seems to be more convincing (excluding, naturally, those "quarum falsitas me non posset offendere"—itself a little masterpiece of medieval hermeneutics). On the other hand, he remains firmly convinced that his reading is illuminated by divine grace, taking his interpretation to be the only one possible and buttressing it with proofs—proofs completely alien to our concept of scientific rigor.

Inspired by this laissez-faire dogmatism (if I may be permitted an oxymoron), the interpreter behaves as if there was only one code, whereas everyone knows that there are many, but nobody seems to mind. In this way, if we must speak of a medieval symbolic code, we must bear in mind that it is a code full of semantic bifurcations, an honest-to-goodness dictionary of synonyms and homonyms, in which one image may suggest many realities and a real object many different images—all of them true because what God has to say is vast and complex, every language inadequate, and we must try to grasp it as best we can, a little at a time.

Nonetheless, as we remarked, Beatus belongs to the school of those who would have the text say what it has to say in the most unambiguous way possible. So, to explain why the twenty-four elders are *unquestionably* the patriarchs and the apostles, he plunges into a numerological demonstration that is just as conclusive for him as dropping a weight off the Tower of Pisa was for Galileo. He has no misgivings about the fact that the Church is duodecimally constituted on the model of the twelve tribes of Israel and, since twelve is the number of hours in the day and twelve the number of hours in the night, therefore twelve is the number of the apostles and twelve the number of the patriarchs and of the prophets who, as representatives of the Law, were the only sources of light during the long night that preceded the advent of Christ (*Commentarius* III, S 271, B 450).

It follows that in the New Testament Christ is incarnate, and his appearance is called light and day, and he is called, in the words of the prophet, a sun, the sun of justice ("ecce vobis, qui timete Dominum, orietur sol justitiae," ["But unto you that fear my name shall the Sun of righteousness arise,"] [Mal. 4:2]), because he elected the twelve apostles as the hours of the day, and he said of them "vos estis lux mundi" ("you are the light of the world") (Matt. 5:14). And he supplemented the number of the twelve apostles with the body of bishops (ibid.).

So went the hermeneutic delirium of Beatus's ruminations; and the result was that, not merely his contemporaries, but posterity too (as evidenced by the number of illuminated manuscripts his commentary generated), fell completely under his spell.

Beatus goes still further. He interprets as "self-evident" signs, not only the images of the major figurations (the elders, the beasts), but also the minimal characteristics described in the text. Thus, the four beasts are endowed with six wings and are full of eyes for reasons that are once again *unquestionable:* because, being the Four Evangelists, they understand and perceive all of the divine mysteries, past and to come. And they are lion, calf, man, and eagle because Mark was the first to speak of John the Baptist who loved the desert ("in hoc autem forma leonis est" ["in this then is the form of the lion"]), and Luke began with a reference to the spirit of the priesthood citing Zachariah ("bene ergo Lucam similem vitulo dicit, vitulus enim in persona ponitur sacerdotum sicut dixit Esaya" ["therefore he is right to say that Luke is like a calf, in fact the calf is represented in the person of the priests, as Isaiah says"]), Matthew was the one who insisted on the earthly and human generation of Christ, hence the image of the man, and finally John was the theorist of the Word that comes down from heaven and to heaven returns, so he is aptly symbolized by the eagle (S 278 et seq., B 462 et seq.).

6.2. Seeing Scripture

Beatus personifies a typical medieval tendency according to which the imagination—even the theological imagination—is eminently visual. It is no accident that Beatus's text produced so many illuminated illustrations. The illuminators illustrated his text a posteriori, but Beatus was already writing a text to be illustrated, because the sacred text he had in front of him seemed to have been imagined as a series of vivid pictures.

Modern biblical exegesis appears to view this pictorial tendency with suspicion, as an historical residue from which John's text must be freed if we are to interpret it correctly:

The modern Western reader must also beware of the tendency to translate the figures and scenes presented by the author into pictures. The author is in fact making use of conventional symbolic materials, without concern for the figurative effects thereby produced. A reader attempting to picture or imagine a Lamb with seven horns and seven eyes, or a dragon with seven heads and ten horns, wondering, for example, how the ten horns were distributed on the seven heads, would be off on the wrong track. Instead we must translate the symbols intellectually, without stopping to consider their effect on the imagination. Therefore, since the number seven is the symbol of fullness, the seven horns and the seven eyes signify that the Lamb possesses the fullness of power (the horns) and the fullness of knowledge (the eyes). (Rossano 1963: 342)[6]

The fact is that the medieval interpreter could not and would not read the text in this way, and did precisely the opposite, first of all because he was ignorant of those Oriental traditions of which the modern philologist has such a clear historical and ethnographical awareness. Therefore, if the text said seven heads and ten horns, it had to be taken literally. Second because, already in Beatus's day, and even more after it, thinking in pictures was the preferred way—and for the vast masses of the illiterate, however rich and powerful they might be, who laid their eyes on an illuminated manuscript or any other pictorial representation, it was the privileged way, the only way even, in which they could understand and commit to memory the contents of the sacred text. It was therefore essential—especially for those with pedagogical intent—to picture events and characters visually down to the tiniest detail. And the more monstrous and marvelous the detail, the more the imagination was awakened and the interpretive passion inflamed. A visual symbol crammed with details is bound to be richer in meanings, as we know from the evidence of dreams. And, as occurred in the Latin mnemonic tradition (as well as the Greek), which the Middle Ages knew in part from the surviving texts and in part at second hand, for an item of knowledge to be stored in our memories it had to be associated with a scene, the more astonishing and terrible the better (see Carruthers 1990).

We will not go so far as to say—overestimating the influence of mnemonic techniques—that the entire apocalyptic tradition is nothing more than an

---

6. [*Translator's note*: Unless otherwise attributed, translations of Italian secondary sources, here and elsewhere, are my own, from Eco's text.]

attempt to embody in memorable images a few moral and eschatological principles. But we feel confident in asserting that the medieval passion for apocalyptic *imagerie* is partly the result of the influence of the ancient arts of memory.

Beatus's attitude toward the text, then, was the opposite of that of the modern interpreter: the scenes must be transposed into visual images, the interpreter must be concerned with the resulting pictorial effect, because the cryptography, the mystical enigma, depend on that effect. And if there are ten horns and seven heads, we must ask ourselves how these numbers, incongruous in themselves, can be represented congruously. The problem for the illuminator, who must solve the problem pictorially, is the same as that for the commentator, who must solve it symbolically. And the commentators often find themselves stymied because they are endeavoring to translate the text with an illustrator's mentality. Beatus's *Commentarius* is a glaring example of this predicament.

Let us see how this impulse to translate the text into clear visual images leads our scrutinist to misrepresent the text. We will start from the beginning, from John's vision of the one seated on a throne and the four beasts (chapter 4) and from its most likely source: Ezekiel's vision in the book that bears his name (Ezek. 1:4–26).

Ezekiel speaks of a whirlwind coming out of the north: and a great cloud, and a fire infolding it, and brightness about it: and out of the midst thereof, that is, out of the midst of the fire, "as it were the resemblance of amber." And in the midst thereof the likeness of four living creatures and this was their appearance: there was the likeness of a man in them. Every one had four faces and four wings, straight feet and the soles of their feet were like the sole of a calf's foot, and they sparkled like the color of burnished brass. And they had the hands of a man under their wings on their four sides. And these four living creatures turned not when they went but went straight forward.

So far so good. Up to now the vision looks like something that can be pictured. But at this point the prophet declares that, in addition to the face of a man, the creatures had the face of a lion on the right side and the face of an ox on the left side, and they also had the face of an eagle. Their wings were stretched upward, two wings of every one were joined one to another, and two covered their bodies. Their appearance was like burning coals of fire, and like the appearance of lamps.

Another confusing fact: although Ezekiel had said (twice) that they turned not when they went and all four went straight forward, he now informs us that the living creatures ran and returned as the appearance of a flash of lightning, and behold one wheel on the earth by the living creatures, with his four faces, And the appearance of the wheels and their work was like unto the color of a beryl, and they four had one likeness: and their appearance and their work was as it were a wheel in the middle of a wheel. And they went in four directions, and they turned not when they went, and their rings were full of eyes round about them four. And when the living creatures went, the wheels went by them; and when the living creatures were lifted up from the earth, the wheels were lifted up, and "whithersoever the spirit was to go, they went, thither was their spirit to go; and the wheels were lifted up over against them: for the spirit of the living creature was in the wheels" (Ezek. 1:20).

As we will have occasion to observe in a moment, it is clear that Ezekiel is not, so to speak, indulging in ekphrasis, but recounting a series of oneiric events. But let us proceed with our reading of his text: now above the firmament that was over the living creatures' heads was the likeness of a throne, as the appearance of a sapphire stone: and upon the likeness of the throne was the likeness as the appearance of a man above upon it. "And I saw as the colour of amber, as the appearance of fire round about within it, from the appearance of his loins even upward, and from the appearance of his loins even downward, I saw as it were the appearance of fire, and it had brightness round about. As the appearance of the bow that is in the cloud in the day of rain." "This," declares Ezekiel, "was the appearance of the likeness of the glory of the Lord. And when I saw it, I fell upon my face, and I heard a voice of one that spake" (Ezek. 1:27–28).

This is the same vision that appears, in an abridged form, in Apocalypse 4:2–8, with the difference that John seems to start where Ezekiel left off. The throne in the firmament appears right away, and on the throne someone is seated, similar in appearance to a jasper and a sardine stone. A rainbow like an emerald surrounds the throne. Around the throne are twenty-four seats and upon the seats are seated twenty-four elders clothed in white raiment, with crowns of gold on their heads. From the throne (before which burn seven lamps of fire, which are the seven Spirits of God) proceed lightnings and thunderings and voices. Before the throne is a sea of glass like crystal. "*In the midst of the throne and round about the throne* were four beasts full of eyes before and behind. And the first beast was like a lion, the second beast like a calf, and the third beast had a face as a man, and the fourth was like a flying eagle. And the four beasts had each of them six wings about him; and they were full of eyes within . . ." (Apoc. 4:6–8).[7]

At first blush John's text appears to be a copy of Ezekiel's, except for the fact that in Ezekiel each of the living creatures had the face of all four animals. John makes the same vision easier to picture: each of the beasts has the face of a different animal. In Ezekiel the creatures have four wings, in John six,[8] and naturally Beatus, after expressing his amazement that the wings are not part of the normal endowments of the four animals (including the

---

7. The Latin version of the Apocalypse quoted by Beatus (*Commentarius* III, S266, B442, S267, B459) is slightly different from the Vulgate but the basic sense is the same, as is the case with the KJV. We reproduce here Beatus's Latin source text along with the corresponding text from the KJV (which we already followed closely in the body of the chapter): "Et ecce thronus positus erat in caelo, et supra thronum sedens, et qui sedebat similis erat aspectui lapidi iaspidis et sardino; et iris in circuito sedis, similis aspectui zmaragdino; et in circuitu throni vidi sedes viginti quattuor, et supra sedes viginti quattuor seniores sedentes in veste alba, et in capitibus eorum coronas aureas. Et de sede procedunt fulgura et voces et tonitrua. Et septem lampades ignis ardentis, qui sunt septem spiritus Dei. Et in conspectu throni sicut mare vitreum simile cristallo. Et vidi *in medio throni et in circuito throni* quattuor animalia plena oculia ante et retro. Animal primum simile leonis, et secundum animal simile vituli, et tertium animal habens faciem hominis, et quartum animal simile ad aquilae volantis. Haec quattuor animalia singula eorum habebant alas senas: et in circuitu et intus plena sunt oculis" ("And, behold, a throne was set in heaven, and one sat on the throne. And he that sat was to look upon like a jasper and a sardine stone: and there was a rainbow round about the throne, in sight like unto an emerald. And round about the throne were four and twenty seats: and upon the seats I saw four and twenty elders sitting, clothed in white raiment; and they had on their heads crowns of gold. And out of the throne proceeded lightnings and thunderings and voices: and there were seven lamps of fire burning before the throne, which are the seven Spirits of God. And before the throne there was a sea of glass like unto crystal: and in the midst of the throne, and round about the throne, were four beast full of eyes before and behind. And the first beast was like a lion, and the second beast like a calf, and the third beast had a face as a man, and the fourth beast was like a flying eagle. And the four beasts had each of them six wings about him; and they were full of eyes within") King James 4:2–8.

8. John combines together several different visions, and in this case his inspiration is Isaiah 6:2. See the commentary on the Apocalypse by Lupieri (1999).

eagle, which is only supposed to have two), indulges in the usual allegorical interpretations. Furthermore, the eyes are not on the wheels, or on the wings of the four beasts, but on the beasts themselves (and the Greek text of the Apocalypse in any case confirms this reading).

Nevertheless, John does not entirely succeed in escaping the influence of the text of Ezekiel. Before the throne is a transparent sea like crystal, and "in the midst of the throne and round about the throne" are the elders. The same expression is found in the Latin text used by Beatus ("in medio throni et in circuitu throni"). The expression seems to be obscure, because on the throne is the One Seated, and it is difficult to see how the elders can be in the midst of the throne at the same time. To resolve this embarrassing contradiction, a modern commentator, Angelini (1969), eliminates the second mention of the throne and translates in such a way that the elders seem to be, not in the midst of the throne, but in the midst of the sea of crystal that stretches before the throne: "Facing the throne stretched a billowing sea of transparent crystal, and in the midst and around were four beasts full of eyes in front and behind." A violence done to the text to make it more reasonable. But why should a vision be reasonable?

Not surprisingly, at this point a perplexed Beatus remarks that "quaestio oritur" ("a question arises"), and he gets out of it by revealing that what the text sometimes refers to as a throne and sometimes as a seat is none other than the Church, upon which obviously is seated Christ our Lord, but in which dwell, thanks to his largesse, also the gospels, the Evangelists, and the elders, who cannot be said to dwell outside the Church.

An elegant solution perhaps, but at odds with the rest of his exegetical method, which is that of "visualizing" or projecting the facts of the story in space. For proof of our contention, we have only to look at the illuminators, who are not sure how to get around it and represent this topological problem variously in different images.

For instance, in the *Beatus* of Ferdinand and Sancha of Madrid—and this is also the case in the majority of the other *Beati*—the limited space available leads the illustrator to reduce the number of the elders from twelve to eight, and there is only one wheel placed in the center. As in many *Beati*, the Seated One is depicted as a lamb (because Beatus identifies him as Christ), but it is not clear whether or not the eyes are represented, whether, that is, the eyes are to be interpreted as the ones around the throne of the lamb or those that appear on the wings of the four *animalia*. What is more important, however, is that the illuminator fails to render the sense of movement that the words of the text suggest, that the four beasts, that is, are evidently on the move, and appear now in the midst of and now around the throne (Figure 6.1).

Figure 6.1

A more interesting case is that of the *Beatus* of San Millán, in which, with a fine torsion of the figures that has an expressionist feel to it, the illuminator at least tries to convey the movement of the beasts: he does not have them mount *onto* the throne, but he does manage to suggest their whirling motion around the throne of the Lamb (Figure 6.2).

Figure 6.2

In the *Beatus* of San Severo (Figure 6.3), the artist endeavors to convey somehow the movement of at least one of the four beasts, showing the lion about to invade the circular area around the throne.

Figure 6.3

Medieval culture has no trouble translating biblical texts into images, because its roots are in Greek culture, which is eminently visual. Every epiphany of the sacred in classical Greece occurs in the form of an image and—for obvious reasons—of a fixed image. It is no accident if the literary genre of ekphrasis—the minutely detailed description of statues and pictures, so as to render them, through the skilled use of verbal language, practically visible—has its origin and development in Greek culture. Hebrew culture, on the other hand, was eminently oral. In Plato's *Timaeus* the Demiurge creates the universe using geometrical figures, whereas in the Bible it is by means of a verbal act that God creates the world. The Greeks *saw* their gods; Moses only *hears* God's voice.

Now a voice can certainly evoke images, but those images will not be necessarily immobile. On the other hand, while both Ezekiel and John claim to have had a vision, they do not say that what they saw was a gallery of fixed images. And it is significant that they do not speak in the present tense, as someone does when they are describing a picture that they still have before their eyes, but in the past or the imperfect, as we might do if we were narrating a dream in which the events came one after the other. Every visionary experience is of necessity oneiric, and what the Seer sees has the same sense of *flou* and lack of preciseness as what we see in a dream. Today we would say that the vision takes the form of a *cinematographic* event, in which the images occur one after the other. This is why it is possible to see the Seated One on a throne, upon whose image, through a series of fade-outs, the living creatures are then superimposed, and, in the following sequence, in which everything has changed position, the Seated One again on the throne, the living creatures around it, and the Lamb between them. All of the Apocalypse has this dreamlike rhythm: events occur more than once—the beast is given up for dead and once again we see it in combat, Babylon is said to have collapsed and it is still there awaiting its castigation, and so on.

If we reread the vision as the description of a sequence in motion (bearing in mind that Ezekiel said that "the living creatures ran and returned as the appearance of a flash of lightning"), all the contradictions disappear. What we have is a succession of movements and metamorphoses. The image of the dream would have been a help to Beatus in solving his quandaries, but Beatus thought in terms of synchronic images motionless in space with no passage of time to alter them.

6.3. Other Impossible Visualizations

Naturally, it is not just Beatus who attempts to translate biblical visions into representable images. Take what happens with the description of the Temple. The Temple does not appear in the Apocalypse, and Beatus does not mention it, but it certainly provides the inspiration for John's vision of the Heavenly Jerusalem. Now, all of the medieval attempts to visualize the various biblical descriptions of the Temple suffer from the same failing as Beatus: their insistence on seeing as fixed images what were in fact oneiric and metamorphic visions.

The Old Testament offers two meticulous descriptions of the Temple of Jerusalem: one in 1 Kings and the other in Ezekiel. The description in 1 Kings is more precise, today we might say "user-friendly":

And the house which king Solomon built for the LORD, the length thereof was threescore cubits, and the breadth thereof twenty cubits, and the height thereof thirty cubits. And the porch before the temple of the house, twenty cubits was the length thereof, according to the breadth of the house; and ten cubits was the breadth thereof before the house. And for the house he made windows of narrow lights. And against the wall of the house he built chambers round about, against the walls of the house round about, both of the temple and of the oracle: and he made chambers round about: The nethermost chamber was five cubits broad, and the middle was six cubits broad, and the third was seven cubits broad: for without in the wall of the house he made narrowed rests round about, that the beams should not be fastened in the walls of the house. And the house, when it was in building, was built of stone made ready before it was brought thither: so that there was neither hammer nor axe nor any tool of iron heard in the house, while it was in building. The door for the middle chamber was in the right side of the house: and they went up with winding stairs into the middle chamber, and out of the middle into the third. So he built the house, and finished it; and covered the house with beams and boards of cedar. And then he built chambers against all the house, five cubits high: and they rested on the house with timber of cedar. (1 Kings 6:2–10)

Not so exact is the lengthy description in Ezekiel (40:5–49, 41:1–26, and 42:1–20), which, precisely because of its apparent incoherence, seems apt to challenge its exegetes to the most reckless feats of interpretation:

And behold a wall on the outside of the house round about, and in the man's hand a measuring reed of six cubits long by the cubit and an hand breadth: so he measured the breadth of the building, one reed; and the height, one reed. Then came he unto the gate which looketh toward the east, and went up the stairs thereof, and measured the threshold of the gate, which was one reed broad; and the other threshold of the gate, which was one reed broad. And every little chamber was one reed long, and one reed broad; and between the little chambers were five cubits; and the threshold of the gate by the porch of the gate within was one reed. He measured also the porch of the gate within, one reed. Then measured he the porch of the gate, eight cubits; and the posts thereof, two cubits; and the porch of the gate was inward. And the little chambers of the gate eastward were three on this side, and three on that side; they three were of one measure: and the posts had one measure on this side and on that side. And he measured the breadth of the entry of the gate, ten cubits; and the length of the gate, thirteen cubits. The space also before the little chambers was one cubit on this side, and the space was one cubit on that side: and the little chambers were six cubits on this side, and six cubits on that side. He measured then the gate from the roof of one little chamber to the roof of another: the breadth was five and twenty cubits, door against door. He made also posts of threescore cubits, even unto the post of the court round about the gate. And from the face of the gate of the entrance unto the face of the porch of the inner gate were fifty cubits. And there were narrow windows to the little chambers, and to their posts within the gate round about, and likewise to the arches: and windows were round about inward: and upon each post were palm trees. (Ezek. 40:5–16)

And so on in the same vein. Imagine trying to reconstruct a model of the Temple based on this description with the aid of a measuring tape and a conversion table. In addition to which, medieval interpreters did not even have a conversion table for the measurements, to say nothing of the corruption of the data that would have occurred thanks to the manifold translations, and manuscript transcriptions of translations, that they had at their disposal. But, come to that, even a twenty-first-century architect would find it a challenge to translate these verbal instructions into a project drawing.

It is interesting to observe the pains the medieval allegorists go to in their determination to *see* the Temple as Ezekiel describes it (and in their efforts to picture it they attempt to provide instructions for its ideal reconstruction; see De Lubac 1959–1964, II, 7, 2). The Hebrew tradition itself admitted the impossibility of a coherent architectural reading: in the twelfth century Rabbi Solomon Ben Isaac agreed that no one could ever figure out the arrangement of the northern chambers, where they began to the east and how far they extended to the west, and where they began on the one side and how far they extended on the other (see Rosenau 1979). Furthermore, Ezekiel himself does not claim to have seen a real construction but a "*quasi* aedificium" ("*as* [*it were*] the frame of a city," Ezek. 40:2, my emphasis), while the Fathers of the Church, just as they granted that the vision of the four living creatures defied literal explanation, also declared that the measurements of the building were inconceivable in physical terms, given, for example, that the gates would have to have been wider than the walls.

Thus, interpreters like Hugh of Fouilloy, in his *De claustro animae* (XII century), though he based himself on 1 Kings 6 (less confused and confusing than Ezekiel's vision), confined himself to analyzing the mystical significance of the Temple. The Temple in fact stands for the body of Christ and that of every Christian ("nostrum spirituale templum" ["our spiritual temple"]), the cedars of Lebanon stand for the most glorious men of all times, and Hiram's builders who hewed the stones are the good monks who know how to smooth the irregularities and imperfections of the rough stone (in other words, the souls of their brethren), making them even and harmoniously disposed. And the splendor of the precious metals and stones was the splendor of charity. Cutting the stones signified cutting away human vices. Solomon employed 30,000 workmen, and this number is a multiple of 3 and 10 and, setting aside the mystical meanings of the number 10, 3 is the number of the Trinity, of the three eminent good works (prayer, fasting, and alms deeds), the three virtues of reading, meditation, and preaching, and so on.

Confronted with the measurements of the Temple, rather than trying to interpret them literally, Hugh comments upon the spiritual significance of its dimensions (the length of the building means patience, its breadth means charity, its height means hope, etc.) (chapter XVII, PL 176, 1118).

Other commentators struggled instead to reconstruct the Temple because, if we buy into the idea (Augustinian in origin) that, when faced in Scripture with expressions that seem to convey an excess of basically superfluous information, such as numbers and measurements, we should be on the lookout for an allegorical meaning, bearing in mind that biblical allegory was *in factis* not *in verbis*. Therefore, that a reed was six cubits long was not a mere verbal affirmation or *flatus vocis,* but a fact that had actually occurred, and that God had so predisposed so that we could interpret it allegorically. Hence, a realistic reconstruction of the Temple *had* to be possible, otherwise it would mean Scripture had lied.

And so, in his *In visionem Ezechielis,* we find Richard of Saint Victor—in a polemical stance vis-à-vis the Fathers of the Church, who had advised interpreters to stick to a spiritual reading—laboring over his calculations and producing plans, elevations and cross sections, deciding, when two measurements are impossible to reconcile, that one of them must refer to the whole edifice and the other to one of its parts—in a desperate attempt (doomed, alas, to failure) to reduce the *quasi aedificium* to something a medieval master builder could really have constructed (see De Lubac 1959–1964: II, 5, 3).

6.4. The Jerusalem of Beatus

As for the Heavenly Jerusalem, Christian thought had transformed the biblical Jerusalem into a theological image, idealizing and, so to speak, disincarnating the real historical city. The first transformation of Jerusalem occurs at the end of the Apocalypse, where it is said of the city that

> her light was like unto that of a stone most precious, even like a jasper stone, clear as crystal; and [she] had a great wall and high, and had twelve gates, and at the gates twelve angels . . . on the east three gates; on the north three gates; on the south three gates; and on the west three gates. And the wall of the city had twelve foundations, and in them the names of the twelve apostles of the Lamb . . . And the city lieth foursquare, and the length is as large as the breadth: and he measured the city with the reed, twelve thousand furlongs. . . . And he measured the wall thereof, a hundred and forty and four cubits. . . . And the building of the wall of it was of jasper; and the city was pure gold, like unto clear glass. And the foundations of the wall of the city were garnished with all manner of precious stones. The first foundation was jasper; the second, sapphire; the third, a chalcedony; the fourth, an emerald; the fifth, sardonyx; the sixth, sardius; the seventh, chrysolite; the eighth, beryl; the ninth, a topaz; the tenth, a chrysoprasus; the eleventh, a jacinth; the twelfth, an amethyst. And the twelve gates were twelve pearls; every several gate was of one pearl: and the street of the city was pure gold, as it were transparent glass. . . . And the city had no need of the sun, neither of the moon, to shine in it, for the glory of God did lighten it, and the Lamb is the light thereof. (Apoc. 21:11–23)

Thus, Jerusalem ceases to be a geographical place in order to become the image of the Heavenly Jerusalem. Rather than urbanistic, John's description is architectural, with special insistence on the aesthetic aspects. Moreover, his description is clearly inspired by that of Ezekiel, in which the construction is not rectangular, as it is in other biblical texts, by based upon squares.

The vision of the Heavenly Jerusalem could not fail to fascinate Beatus of Liébana and, centuries later, his illustrators. But more than anything else, he appears to be fascinated by three aspects: Jerusalem's foursquare perfection, its measurements, and the splendor of its precious stones and its golden decorations. Beatus in fact is a forerunner of the aesthetics of the threefold criterion of beauty: integrity, proportion, and light, but he lacked the philosophical categories that would have allowed him to focus in on the reasons for his admiration. He therefore proceeds by confused interjections and inexact calculations.

The chief aspect of Jerusalem that strikes him seems to be the fact that the city shines like a gem without the need for an external light source. Jerusalem has no need of stellar illumination to shine; she radiates light from within herself like a soul internally illuminated by grace. The twelve gates are figures of the twelve apostles, the twelve prophets, and the twelve tribes of Israel. Twelve gates, twelve angels at the gates (a number John plucks out of nowhere, without any previous scriptural support), and twelve foundations, produce the number thirty-six, the number of hours Christ spent in the Sepulcher. The city is square as a reminder of the Four Evangelists, given that its breadth is the same as its length. Following the Vulgate that speaks of twelve thousand by twelve thousand cubits, Beatus decides to multiply twelve by ten to produce 120, which is (according to the Acts of the Apostles) the number of souls who have received the Holy Spirit. Then he adds to the 120 the 24 elders of the Apocalypse and comes up with 144, which is the measurement of the wall of Jerusalem in cubits. And we could go on and on, showing how every number, every detail of the city's layout, permits Beatus to unearth ever newer and more prodigious allegorical allusions.[9]

---

9. The only way the people of the Middle Ages could appreciate any treasure or architectural harmony was by experiencing it in the same terms in which the Apostle had described the Heavenly Jerusalem. Suffice it to quote the example of Suger, abbot of Saint Denis (twelfth century), who in his *Liber de rebus in administratione sua gestis* and in his *Libellus alter de consecratione ecclesiae Sancti Dionisii* (PL 186), speaking of how he feels when he contemplates the treasures he has accumulated for his church, explicitly cites Jerusalem, and its Temple, proudly regarding himself as a second Solomon and referring to his church as a second temple.

In order to obtain a "readable" result, Beatus has no qualms in having recourse to citations that he presents as faithful, but which are in fact altered ever so slightly, changing a word here, eliminating an aside there, or modifying an inflection.

6.5. *Mille Annos*

What makes the Apocalypse fascinating for the Middle Ages is the substantial ambiguity of chapter 20, verses 1–15, which it will be useful to cite in full here. Here we can read it in the King James Version but we are obliged to put in a footnote the text as it was quoted by Beatus, which was lacunary at certain points with respect to the Vulgate:

And I saw an angel come down from heaven, having the key of the bottomless pit and a great chain in his hand.

And he laid hold on the dragon, that old serpent, which is the Devil, and Satan, and bound him a thousand years.

And cast him into the bottomless pit, and shut him up, and set a seal upon him, that he should deceive the nations no more, till the thousand years should be fulfilled: and after that he must be loosed a little season.

And I saw thrones, and they sat upon them, and judgment was given unto them: and I *saw* the souls of them that were beheaded for the witness of Jesus, and for the word of God, and which had not worshipped the beast, neither his image, neither had received *his* mark upon their foreheads, or in their hands; and they lived and reigned with Christ a thousand years.

But the rest of the dead lived not again until the thousand years were finished. This is the first resurrection.

Blessed and holy *is* he that hath part in the first resurrection: on such the second death hath no power, but they shall be priests of God and of Christ, and shall reign with him a thousand years.

And when the thousand years are expired, Satan shall be loosed out of his prison. And shall go out to deceive the nations which are in the four quarters of the earth, Gog and Magog, to gather them together to battle: the number of whom *is* as the sand of the sea.

And they went up on the breadth of the earth, and compassed the camp of the saints about, and the beloved city: and the fire came down from God out of heaven, and devoured them.

And the devil that deceived them was cast into the lake of fire and brimstone, where the beast and the false prophet *are,* and shall be tormented day and night for ever and ever.

And I saw a great white throne, and him that sat on it, from whose face the earth and the heaven fled away; and there was found no place for them.

And I saw the dead, small and great, stand before God: and the books were opened: and another book was opened, which is the book of life: and the dead were judged out of those things which were written in the books, according to their works.

And the sea gave up the dead which were in it; and death and hell delivered up the dead which were in them: and they were judged every man according to their works.

And death and hell were cast into the lake of fire. This is the second death.

And whosoever was not found written in the book of life was cast into the lake of fire.

Taken literally, this chapter could mean that, at a certain point in human history, Satan will be cast into prison and, during the entire time of his imprisonment, the kingdom of the Messiah will be realized on earth, and all of the elect will participate in it, rewarded with a "first resurrection." This period will last for the 1,000 years of the Devil's captivity. Then the Devil will be freed for a certain period of time, then once more defeated. At this point the enthroned Christ will begin the Last Judgment, human history will be fulfilled, and (we are now at the beginning of chapter 21) there will be a new heaven and a new earth, the advent, that is, of the Heavenly Jerusalem.

The problem for the Christians of the early centuries is whether the 1,000 years of the Messiah's reign were still to come or whether they were the years that they themselves were living. If the first interpretation was correct they had to wait for a Second Coming of the Messiah and a kind of golden age (which had also been promised by a number of ancient religions), followed by a return of the Devil and his false prophet the Antichrist (as the tradition will gradually come to call him, although the Apocalypse itself speaks only in fact of a false prophet). And finally, the Last Judgment and the end of time. This is the dominant reading, with some fluctuation, down to Augustine.

In the fourth century the Donatist heresy gained a footing. True, it targeted the unworthy ministers of the cult, insisting that the sacraments that they administered were invalid; but to deny validity to the liturgical actions of a considerable portion of the official Church, and to set against it the purity of a rigoristically virtuous community illuminated by the Holy Spirit, was tantamount in the last analysis to setting against a Heavenly Jerusalem (yet to come) the new Babylon represented by the current Church.

Augustine's response (*De Civitate Dei* XX) is that neither the City of God nor the millennium are historical events that will be realized in this world; they are mystical events. The millennium John speaks of represents the period that stretches from the Incarnation to the end of history, therefore it is the period *we are already living*, the period in progress, completely realized in the living Church. It does not occur to Augustine to separate in day-to-day history the perfect members of the perfect city from the reprobates; he is well aware that human history is riddled with sin and error, even the history of the just who seek salvation in the body of the Church. Earthly history, then, will not be the site of a battle for the supremacy of the heavenly city— Armageddon is not of this world.[10]

With this solution, however, Augustine leaves the way open for two magnificent suggestions. The first concerns the earthly possibility of that City of God that he had already demonstrated was not of this world. What happened in Augustine's case was what happens with many polemists who, thinking to refute an argument, write a book that turns out to be such a

---

10. A curious failure to align one's spiritual discourse with earthly contingencies, when we recall that the *De civitate Dei* was written at precisely the same time as Alaric's Goths were putting Rome to the sack. But Augustine is too much of a philosopher to indulge in short-term prophecies. In any case, great long-term eschatological convictions arise precisely when, in the short term, there is little or nothing to hope for. Indeed, to the Christians who fear for the fall of Rome as the fall of their very civilization, Augustine says not to fear, because the City of God is something completely different, its destiny is not of this world, and in this world the just are bound to the reprobate in their alternate vicissitudes.

success that the argument in question is, if not bolstered, at least brought into the public eye. Accordingly, we will see how, in the course of subsequent history, the idea of the two cities will fascinate reformers and revolutionaries alike, all of them convinced that the City of God must be realized forthwith by the elect; what is needed, then, is a great battle, an Armageddon on earth, a revolution.

The second suggestion concerns the immediate advent of the Day of Judgment, and hence the expectation of the year 1000. If the millennium is not a promise for the future, but is going on here and now, if we are to interpret the Apocalypse correctly, the first thing that must come to pass is the end of the world. The fact that the interpreters were divided over doing the math—whether 1,000 years was to be taken as an approximate or precise figure, whether it was to be calculated from the year of Christ's birth, from his Passion, from the beginning or end of the persecutions: whether in other words the years were 1,000, 1,400 or 1,033—did not affect the fact that the end of the world must come sooner or later.

The history of the Apocalypse in the Middle Ages oscillates between these two possible interpretations, accompanied by alternate euphoria and dysphoria, as well as a perennial sense of expectation and tension. Because, either Christ must still be coming to reign for 1,000 years on earth or he has already come, in which case it won't be long before the Devil returns and with him the end of the world.

This is the context in which Beatus writes his commentary. History informs us that he wrote it for precise theological reasons. Elipandus, archbishop of Toledo, and Felix, bishop of Urgel, had resuscitated an old heresy, adoptionism, which denied the divinity of the Word, relegated to the role of adopted son of the Father. Spanish adoptionism was a "mitigated" form of the heresy and, while they accepted the fact that the Word was the natural son of the Father, they saw Christ in his human nature as merely an adopted son.

Beatus finds in the Apocalypse a text apt to display a Christ in his full consubstantial divinity and sonship, and he employs his commentary as a weapon. And he proves to be a winner, since later Charlemagne will convene two whole councils and a synod, in Germany and Italy, in the course of which the adoptionists will be condemned—and this may explain why the commentary created such a furor at the time.

Beatus lingers with lyric ardor, in a dazzling display of high medieval rhetoric, over the phrase "ab eo qui est, et qui erat, et qui venturus est" ("from Him who is, and who was, and who is to come") from which, with something of a non sequitur, he draws the proof of the divinity of Christ. But what fascinates him most is that Christ is coming as judge (venturus ad iudicandum)—and when he arrives at chapter 20 of the Apocalypse, in other words at the ambiguous prophecy of the millennium, he goes so far as to open with an invocation imploring God not to let him fall into error. He is aware that he is dealing with a fundamental issue.

The text of John tells him first of all that the angel casts the Devil into the abyss "till the thousand years should be fulfilled" (Apoc. 20:3). Then it says that "the souls of them that were beheaded for the witness of Jesus and for the word of God, and which had not worshipped the beast . . . lived and reigned with Christ a thousand years" (20:4). John goes on to specify that this reign is the "first resurrection," which is baptism, and concludes: "but they shall be priests of God and of Christ, and shall reign with him a thousand years" (20:6). Beatus admits that these 1,000 years are to be calculated from the passion of Our Lord and are therefore those of the earthly reign of the Church, which had been the opinion of Augustine. He repeats several times that the millennium spoken of, both for the Devil and the blessed, is the one in which he and his readers are living: "they will reign with the Lord now and in the future . . . when speaking of 1,000 years he meant of this world. . . ." And so on and so forth.

In order that there should be no misunderstanding, he conducts a subtle analysis of the verb tenses, since John says at a certain point that the blessed "have reigned" for 1,000 years, and elsewhere that they "will reign for a thousand years." Beatus, however, knows how to handle Holy Scripture and reminds us that the prophets, speaking of what will happen to Christ, often use the past perfect tense ("et diviserunt vestimenta mea" ["they parted my garments among them"]) when they are obviously talking about something that is destined to happen in the future. Secondly, he states more than once that the use of 1,000 years is certainly an example of synecdoche in the manner of Tyconius, and probably means a longer period of time, at the same time he makes it quite clear that, though it may be a perfect number that indicates a longer period, 1,000 is still a number that implies closure and does not allude to the "perpetuum saeculum" or eternity.

Therefore, Beatus insists, John is speaking of the current millennium and the end of this world. Psychologically speaking, Beatus was, as Camón Aznar describes him, an author obsessed with the millennium and at the same time a rationalist, in the sense that he wanted at all costs to reduce the visionary suggestions of his favorite text to a series of comprehensible messages. And someone obsessed with the millennium is not so much interested in the fact that we are living it as that it is approaching its end.

Augustine, seemingly irritated by the literalist myopia with which the fanatics of the coming millennium read chapter 20 (he declares that many have reduced this passage to a kind of ridiculous fable [De Civitate Dei XX, 7]), found an elegant solution to the problem: what we are dealing with is a figurative expression that indicates the period in which the Church Militant will live in this world (he avoided prophesies as to how long this might be). Beatus, instead, feels obliged to compel John's text to express this concept literally in every word, every verb ending, every adverb. It is not that he wants to be right at all costs, he just wants the text to be *manifestissime* (most manifestly) transparent.

Thus, readers of Beatus's text found themselves faced with the end of the millennium as an incontrovertible historical event, which helps explain why his text had such a wide circulation, and why the better part of the illuminations that accompany it were made between the beginning and the end of the tenth century, in other words, when the first millennium was drawing to a close.[11]

---

11. The literature on the terrors of the year 1000 is extremely vast and contradictory. Focillon (1952) refuted the legend (dear to Romantic historians like Michelet) according to which, on the fatal night of December 31, 999, the Christian world kept vigil in its churches awaiting the end of the world. The texts of the period do not contain any hint of these terrors, and expressions such as *appropinquante fine mundi* ("since the end of the world is approaching") were standard rhetorical formulas. Finally, dating the year from the birth of Christ and not from the supposed creation of the world, though it had been in fashion for three centuries, was still not a universal practice. Robert II the Pious was given a penance of seven years in 998, a sign that nobody was expecting the world to end tomorrow. In 998 Abbo of Fleury, in his *Liber apologeticus,* mentions these apocalyptic beliefs, but he condemns them, dismissing them as fables. Nevertheless, another hypothesis has been proposed (see esp. Landes 1988): that the terrors really did exist among the populace, endemic but underground, stirred up by heretical preachers, and that the official literature does not mention them for reasons of censorship. Gouguenheim (2000), however, has pointed out that, not only is it difficult to come up with a text of the period that speaks explicitly of the

Just how profound was Beatus's visionary immersion in his play of verbal echoes (biblical citations, patristic influences, captious disputations) can be seen from the energetic fashion in which he inveighs against the dangerous heretics who held that the millennium was to be dated from the Incarnation onward, whereas for him there was no doubt that it had to be calculated starting from the Passion. But it is even clearer in the pages he devotes to the Antichrist.

Beatus is obsessed with the idea of the Antichrist, as is apparent from the very start (*Commentarius* I, S 44, B 73): "Incipit tractatus de Apocalypsin Iohannis in explanatione sua a multis doctoribus et probatissimis viris illustribus, diverso quidem stilo, sed non diversa fide interpretata, ubi de Cristo et ecclesia et de antichristo et eius signis primissime recognoscas" ("Here begins the treatise on the Apocalypse of John, which in the commentaries of many doctors and highly esteemed famous men has been interpreted in different ways, but not with different faith, in which what concerns Christ and his church and what concerns the Antichrist and his signs can be examined at the highest level"). The Apocalypse is a treatise on the Antichrist and how to recognize him.

On this subject Beatus did not only have the suggestions of the Apocalypse to go on. Quite apart from the readings in this sense of certain Old Testament prophets, the Gospels too spoke of the Antichrist, as did the First Epistle of Saint John.[12] Patristic literature also frequently referred to

---

terrors, but that the first authors to mention them are John Trithemius, in his *Annales Hirsaugiensis*, written at the beginning of the sixteenth century (and the allusion could well be an insertion by subsequent seventeenth-century editors), and Cesare Baronio, in his *Annales Ecclesiastici* in 1590. In which case, all of the literature on the terrors would be derived from these two extremely late sources. But, even if we were to admit that the terrors existed and any mention of them suppressed, a proof from silence is a very fragile proof. The Church had no reason to remain silent about the terrors, merely in order to stifle presumed heretical ideas. There was nothing in the least heretical about the notion that the world was about to end in the year 1000, since it could be buttressed by a reading of none other than Saint Augustine.

12. "For there shall arise false Christs, and false prophets, and shall shew great signs and wonders; insomuch that, if it were possible, they shall deceive the very elect" (Matt. 24:24). "And then if any man shall say to you, Lo, here is Christ; or lo, he is there; believe him not: For false Christs and false prophets shall rise, and

the Antichrist (we have only to think of the *De Antechristo* of Hippolytus in the third century), to say nothing of other more or less spurious texts.[13] But Beatus was not content with what he found already available. He plunges

---

shall shew signs and wonders to seduce, if it were possible, even the elect" (Mark 13:21–22). "Little children, it is the last time: and as ye have heard that antichrist shall come, even now are there many antichrists; whereby we know that it is the last time" (1 John 2:18); "Who is a liar but he that denieth that Jesus is the Christ? He is antichrist, that denieth the Father and the Son" (1 John 2:22); "And every spirit that confesseth not that Jesus Christ is come in the flesh is not of God: and this is that spirit of antichrist, whereof ye have heard that it should come; and even now already is it in the world" (1 John 4:3).

13. "And these are the signs of him: his head [is] as a fiery flame, his right eye shot with blood, his left [eye] blue-black, and he hath two pupils. His eyelashes are white, his lower lip is large; but his right thigh slender; his feet broad, his great toe is bruised and flat. This is the sickle of desolation" (*The Testament of Our Lord,* translated into English from the Syriac with Introduction and Notes by James Cooper, D.D. and Arthur John Maclean, M.A., F.R.G.S., Edinburgh, T. & T. Clark, 1902, 1, 11. Available online from the Cornell University library: http://www.archive.org/stream/cu31924029296170/cu31924029296170_djvu.txt.

"He is small, with thin legs, tall, a tuft of grey hair on his bald forehead, his eyebrows reach to his ears, he has a mark of leprosy on the back of his hand. He will change his shape in front of those who see him: at one time he will be a young man, at another an old man" (Apocalypse of Elijah 3:15–17 [third century]). "His face has a dark look, his hair is like the heads of arrows, his forehead is scowling, his right eye is like the morning star and his left like that of a lion. His mouth is a cubit broad, his teeth a span in length and his fingers are like sickles. His footprints are two cubits long and on his forehead is written: Antichrist" (Apocalypse of Saint John the Theologian [fifth century]).

It is uncertain whether Beatus was familiar with a tenth-century fragment in a manuscript from the monastery of Mont Saint-Michel: "His disciples said to Jesus: "Lord, tell us how to recognize him." And Jesus said to them: "He will be nine cubits tall. He will have black hair gathered like an iron chain. He will have in his forehead an eye that shines like the dawn. His lower lip will be thick and he will have no upper lip. The little finger of his hand will be the longest, his left foot broader. His posture similar."

He certainly knew Irenaeus of Lyon: "But when this Antichrist shall have devastated all things in this world, he will reign for three years and six months, and sit in the temple at Jerusalem; and then the Lord will come from heaven in the clouds, in the glory of the Father, sending this man and those who follow him into the lake of fire; but bringing in for the righteous the times of the kingdom, that is,

first of all into an incredible Kabbalistic speculation, teasing out the numerical hints of John's text to provide a mathematical matrix by means of which to identify the name of the coming Antichrist. Secondly, once he has declared that the Antichrist is bound to come, that he will destroy the community of the faithful, that the saints will need all of their spirit of martyrdom and perseverance to resist him, he launches into a prolonged diatribe to demonstrate that the Antichrist will seek to restore the Judaic law and will definitely be a Jew, taking up a theme common to most previous authors of apocalyptic treatises, but blithely forgetting that in his day his own country has fallen prey to a flesh-and-blood Antichrist in the person of the Muslim invader. It is not clear whether he was even aware of it (because after all the kingdom of Asturias where Beatus was active fell within the Frankish orbit) or whether he is resorting to some kind of code, since his Antichrist will not only impose circumcision but will have the added characteristic of not drinking wine, which would seem to allude to the Muslims, were it not for the fact that he will have the further distinction of not appreciating female embraces (something about which the Muslims might have begged to differ). What is more, the Antichrist—and this trait would not fit either the Muslims or the Jews—though himself *impurissimus,* will seduce the people by preaching, sobriety, and chastity. Here Beatus may be alluding to some rigoristic heresy, maybe one no longer even active in his own day, but combated in one of his sources.

Beatus's readers, however, did not stop to worry about the coherence of his narrative. They wanted to hear about the Antichrist. The fact is that the fortune of a text may be explained by something outside the text. After the year 1000 the medieval reader will develop a taste for tales of war, love, and magic, but in Beatus's day the Song of Songs couldn't hold a candle to the Apocalypse.

This is why the treatise of Adso of Montier-en-Der, *De ortu et tempore Antichristi* (PL 101, 1289–1293), came out in the tenth century, probably under Beatus's influence. Adso claims that the Antichrist will be born of the Jewish people and, born from the union of a father and a mother like the rest of mankind, and not, as some would have it, from a virgin, he will be entirely conceived in sin. From his first conception, the Devil will enter his mother's

the rest, the hallowed seventh day" (*Against Heresies,* V, 30, 4. Available online at http://www.newadvent.org/fathers/0103530.htm.

womb, he will be nourished in the womb by virtue of the Devil, and the power of the Devil will be always with him. And, as the Holy Spirit descended into the womb of the mother of Jesus Christ and filled it with his virtue, so the Devil will enter into the mother of the Antichrist and will fill her, surround her, and make her his own, possessing her within and without, so that, thanks to the cooperation of the Devil, she will conceive him in congress with a man, and he who will be born shall be wholly evil, iniquitous, and damned. And for this reason he shall be called the son of perdition. He will have wizards, witch doctors, diviners, and enchanters who will educate him in every iniquity, falsehood, and malefic art.

In the twelfth century Hildegard of Bingen will write that the son of perdition will come with all the wiles of the first seduction, and monstrous turpitudes, and black iniquities, with eyes of fire, ass's ears, the muzzle and mouth of a lion; and, inducing humankind to renounce God, he will smother their senses with the most horrendous stench, snarling with an enormous grimace and displaying his fearsome iron fangs (*Liber Scivias* III, 1, 14).

The popularity of the figure of the Antichrist is no doubt partly to be ascribed to the millennialist anxieties we have outlined. If we hope, however, to fully account for these anxieties, and with them for the success of Beatus, we must take into consideration, in addition to these theological considerations and a taste for symbolic storytelling, the *material* circumstances that went along with the state of crisis that was the life of the High Middle Ages. Beatus was not regaling his readers with happenings that might occur a few years or 1,000 years into the future, but with happenings that people in those still dark ages were accustomed to experiencing on a daily basis. We have only to read Benedictine Rodulfus Glaber's account in his *Historiarum libri* of events that occurred, not in Beatus's time, but after the millennium was already thirty years into the past, at the start of the year 1033. Rodulfus describes a famine brought on by weather so inclement that, as a result of the flooding, it was impossible to find a favorable moment either to sow or to reap. Hunger had made the entire populace, rich and poor alike, completely emaciated and, when there were no more live animals to eat, they were compelled to eat corpses "and other things it is too repugnant even to mention," to such a point that some people were reduced to devouring human flesh. Travelers were waylaid, murdered, cut into pieces, and roasted, and people who had left their homes in the hope of escaping the penury had their throats slit during the night by those who had offered them shelter. People even lured in children, offering them a piece of fruit or an egg, only to slaughter them and eat them.

In many localities corpses were dug up and eaten. Someone was discovered to have brought roasted human flesh to the market in Tournus and was burned at the stake; someone else suffered an identical fate because he went out at night in search of the place where the same meat had been buried. In a word, "that insane fury spread so far that abandoned cattle were safer from being carried off than were human beings" (*Historiarum liber* IV, 9–10).

Perhaps Rodolfus was still under the influence of his reading of Beatus. Otherwise it is difficult to understand how such horrible things could come to pass in the year 1033, since Rodulfus had earlier exulted (in book III, iv, 13) that in 1003 the rebirth of Europe had begun "shaking off, as it were, and ridding itself of its former senility, it had put on a pure white mantle of churches." But that was how Rodolfus was: in book V he will also narrate how the Devil once appeared to him. A sure sign that, after the year 1000 had gone by, people were laughing on one side of their faces to have come through unscathed and weeping on the other for fear their calculations were off and something even worse was still about to happen. But when he is not seeing the Devil but simply looking around him, Rodulfus seems to be a reliable chronicler. So his tales of hard times have an aura of truth.

What is to prevent, then, in times dominated by such a sense of *insecuritas,* the scholar reading Beatus, or the unlettered masses listening to someone else read Beatus, or seeing the same horrors depicted on the frescoed walls of their churches, thinking, along with Horace, "de te fabula narratur" ("this could be your story")? Even in our own day, on the silver screen, stories involving cataclysms and disasters that hold out no hope for the future but fuel (or hypnotically sublimate) our night sweats and nightmares continue to garner success.

7

Dante between Modistae and Kabbalah

7.1. The *De vulgari eloquentia*

In his *De vulgari eloquentia* (hereinafter *DVE*), to explain the existence of a plurality of languages, Dante sticks to the letter of the biblical account in Genesis, which he knew in the Latin text of the Vulgate. So we must stick to the Vulgate too, setting aside any philological concerns regarding its fidelity to the original Hebrew. In any case, as we shall see, Dante occasionally strays, with the highhandedness we have come to expect of him, even from the text of the Vulgate.

If the *DVE* is a treatise on language and speech acts, Genesis offered Dante many examples of primal "speech acts." The first thing we must agree on, however, is what "speaking" means. Certainly, every sign—as Augustine had already remarked—is something perceptible to the senses that serves to bring to mind something different from itself, but this definition (which could also refer to the knot I tie in my handkerchief to remind me of a task I must do) does not yet imply a communicative relationship articulated between two subjects. Rosier-Catach (2006) sees this communicative aspect underscored instead by definitions like the one in Calcidius's Latin translation of the *Timaeus*, later echoed by Thomas Aquinas ("ut Plato dicit, sermo ad hoc datus est nobis ut cognoscamus voluntatis indicia" ["As Plato says,

A reworking of "*Forma locutionis*" published in Vattimo (1992), which also appeared in English, with the title "The Perfect Language of Dante," in Eco (1995) and, in a somewhat different form, as "Languages in Paradise," in Eco 1998b.

speech was given to us so we could know signs of others' wills"], *De veritate* 9, 4, 7).[1] If Dante understood a speech act in this way, then we ought not to say that God "speaks" when he pronounces the *fiat lux,* as a result of which "there was light" (Gen. 1:3–4);[2] and the same could be said for other similar expressions used in the course of creation. Here God seems instead to know "how to do things with words," bringing into play a magic, operative, performative quality of the word—thus setting a dangerous precedent for all future followers of the occult sciences, convinced they can change the course of events simply by uttering a few para-Hebraic sounds. In the same way it is not clear what God was up to when, for example, He called ("appellavit") light "day" and darkness "night," seeing that He had no need to communicate those names to anyone, least of all Himself.

Dante is nonetheless aware of the fact that the Bible often speaks in a figurative way, and he does not make these divine "words" the object of his reflection, considering that, as far as he is concerned, it is evident that the gift of speech has been conferred on man alone ("patet soli homini datum fuisse loqui," *DVE* I, ii, 8). As he will repeat on a number of occasions, the ability to speak belongs only to mankind: the angels don't have it (they are gifted with an "ineffable intellectual ability," which allows each of them to understand the thought of all the others, or, alternatively, all of them read the thoughts of all the others in the mind of God) and the demons (who are already reciprocally aware of the depths of their own perfidy) don't have it either. And—we may add—if the angels have no use for speech, the same is even truer of God when He was creating the universe.

It is the intention of the *DVE,* therefore, to deal solely with human speech, inasmuch as man is guided by his reason, which in single individuals assumes different forms of judgment and discernment, and requires a faculty that will permit the speaker to transmit an intellectual content through signs perceptible to the senses, in a relationship between sound and sense

---

1. Or again: "Nihil est enim aliud loqui ad alterum, quam conceptum mentis alteri manifestare" ("For to talk to someone else means precisely to make known one's thoughts to them") (*Summa Theologiae* I, 107, 1.). This idea of a relationship with another person or persons reappears in various other authors.

2. Biblical quotes, here and elsewhere, are from the King James Version.

that he can recognize (in accordance with tradition) *ad placitum,* in other words, as conventionally agreed upon.[3]

Nevertheless, Dante still has to explain the episode recounted in Genesis 2:16–17, when the Lord speaks to man for the first time, placing at Adam's disposal all the resources of the Earthly Paradise, and commanding him not to eat of the fruit of the Tree of Good and Evil. Clearly, what we have here is an initial act of communication, which would contradict the idea that man was the first to use language. Dante gets out of this by affirming that the fact that God communicated something to Adam does not mean that He did so verbally, but (and this traditional idea comes from Psalm 148: "fire and hail, snow and frost, stormy wind fulfilling his command" ["ignis grando nix glacies spiritus procellarum quae faciunt verbum eius"—the verb "faciunt" in the Vulgate is ambiguous and could mean "that do his word" or "that make up his word"]) He could have expressed himself through atmospheric phenomena, such as thunderclaps and lightning.

Having clarified these issues, Dante might at this point have discussed how Adam spoke when the Lord (Gen. 2:19) formed out of the ground every

---

3. "Oportuit ergo genus humanum ad comunicandum inter se conceptiones suas aliquod rationale signum et sensuale habere; quia, cum de ratione accipere habeat et in rationem portare, rationale esse oportuit; cumque de una ratione in aliam nichil deferri possit nisi per medium sensuale, sensuale esse oportuit; quare, si tantum rationale esset, pertransire non posset; si tantum sensuale, nec a ratione accipere, nec in rationem deponere potuisset. Hoc equidem signum est ipsum subiectum nobile de quo loquimur: nam sensuale quid est, in quantum sonus est; rationale vero, in quantum aliquid significare videtur ad placitum" (*DVE* I, iii, 2–3). "So it was necessary that the human race, in order for its members to communicate their conceptions among themselves should have some signal based on reason and perception. Since this signal needed to receive its contents from reason and convey it back there, it had to be rational; but, since nothing can be conveyed from one reasoning mind to another except by means perceptible to the senses, it had also to be based on perception. For, if it were purely rational, it could not make its journey; if purely perceptible, it could neither derive anything from reason nor deliver anything to it. This signal, then, is the noble foundation that I am discussing, for it is perceptible, in that it is a sound, and yet also rational, in that this sound, according to convention, *(ad placitum)* is taken to mean something" (Dante 1996: I, iii, 2, p. 7. Subsequent citations in English are from Steven Botterill's translation (Dante 1996). Botterill's facing Latin text is based on the critical text established by Mengaldo (1979).

beast of the field and every bird of the air and brought them to the man to see what he would call them, and whatever the man called each living creature, that was its name ("omne enim, quod vocavit Adam animae viventis, ipsum est nomen eius"). Curiously enough, this role of Adam as nomothete (with the tremendous problem, touched on in Plato's *Cratylus,* and which will obsess the coming centuries, that is, on what basis did Adam name the animals—with the names *due* to them because of their natures or with those that he himself arbitrarily chose to assign, *ad placitum*) is ignored by Dante. Nor is that all. Disregarding the fact that, in order to name the animals, Adam must have spoken in some way, Dante confesses to being perplexed by the fact that "according to what it says at the beginning of Genesis" the first to speak was the "most presumptuous" Eve ("mulierem invenitur ante omnes fuisse locutam" ["we find that a woman spoke before anyone else"] *DVE* I, iv, 3), when she engaged in dialogue with the serpent, and he finds it unbecoming that such a noble act of the human race should have emerged, not from the lips of a man but from those of a woman ("inconvenienter putatur tam egregium humani generis actum non prius a viro quam a femina profluxisse" ["it may be thought unseemly that so distinguished an action of the human race should first have been performed by a woman rather than a man"] *DVE* I, iv, 3, p. 9).

In fact, this observation (apart from the puzzling display of antifeminism on the part of a poet who sang the praises of a *donna angelicata* or a mortal woman glorified as an angel)—if we exclude the doubtful "words" attributed to God, Adam is the first to speak—first of all when he names the animals, and then when he expresses his satisfaction with the appearance of Eve. Indeed, in the latter case, an entire utterance of his is cited for the first time: "dixitque Adam hoc nunc os ex ossibus meis et caro de carne mea haec vocabitur virago quoniam de viro sumpta est" ("And Adam said, This is now bone of my bones, and flesh of my flesh: she shall be called Woman, because she was taken out of Man"). Mengaldo (1979: 42) suggests that, since for Dante people speak to externalize the thoughts in their minds, and speech is therefore a dialogical phenomenon, what Dante meant to say was that what we have between Eve and the serpent is the first *dialogue,* and hence the first *linguistic act* expressed through the physical production of meaningful sounds. Which would lead us to believe that when Adam is pleased with the appearance of Eve and "says" what he says, maybe he says it to himself, and that (but perhaps we are overmodernizing Dante) the naming of the animals ought not to be considered a linguistic act but a mere metalinguistic foundation.

However we may wish to interpret this liberty that Dante takes as a reader of the Bible, Mengaldo's suggestion nonetheless prompts us to clarify what a *linguistic act,* as distinct from a language, meant for Dante, in other words to ask ourselves whether or not there is in Dante a critical awareness of the difference (to use the Saussurean terminology) between *langue* and *parole.*

Tendentious though he may be in the episode involving Eve, Dante is keen to defend his conviction that Adam ought to have been the first one to speak. And, despite the fact that the first sound uttered by human beings is usually a cry of pain, Adam's first utterance could only be a cry of joy and at the same time an act of homage to his creator. Therefore, Adam's first utterance must have been the name of God, *El* (*DVE* I, iv, 4, p. 9).

Confronted with this first linguistic act in human history, Dante must now come to grips with the issue he had proposed to deal with at the very beginning of the *DVE,* precisely because the plurality of languages confirmed by his experience finds its foundation and explanation in Genesis 11:1 and following. The story is a familiar one: after the Flood "the whole earth was of one language, and of one speech," but pride led mankind to vie with God and to construct a tower whose top might reach unto heaven, and the Lord, to punish their pride and prevent the construction of the tower, decides to confuse their languages.

It is true that in Genesis 10, speaking of the spreading abroad of the sons of Noah after the Flood, it is said: "By these [the sons of Japhet] were the isles of the Gentiles divided in their lands; every one after his tongue, after their families, in their nations" (10:5), and in almost the same words the concept was repeated for the sons of Ham (10:20) and the sons of Shem (10:31). This hint of a plurality of languages existing before Babel will prove a sticking point, not only for many interpreters of the Bible but also for the Utopians of the Perfect Language (see Eco 1993, English trans. 1995b). But Dante does not consider these passages.

He is clearly convinced that before the building of the Tower of Babel there existed a perfect language, which Adam had used when talking to God, and with which he had spoken to his descendants, and that the plurality of languages had come about only after the *confusio linguarum* or confusion of tongues. Demonstrating a knowledge of comparative linguistics exceptional in his day, Dante shows how the various languages that sprang from the confusion multiplied in a ternary fashion, first according to a division among the various parts of the world, then, within the area that today we would define as Romance, they split up into *langue d'oc, langue d'oil,* and *lingua del sì.* The last-named, the language spoken in Italy, has become further fragmented into a plurality of dialects that sometimes, in Bologna for example, vary from one quarter of the city to another. This is because man is a mutable animal in customs, habits, and languages, over the course of both time and space.

Dante's project for devising a more decorous and illustrious language (what he calls the *volgare illustre*) for the whole of Italy is to proceed to a critique of the various regional vernaculars, given that poets have always tended to keep a certain distance from the local dialect. His aim is to identify a vernacular that is *illustrious* (a bearer of light), *cardinal* (that functions as a cornerstone [*cardine*] for all the others), *aulic* or *regal* (worthy of its place in the palace of a national kingdom), and *curial* (the language of government, of the law courts, of instruction). This vernacular represents a kind of ideal rule that the best poets have come more or less close to, and by whose standards the existing vernaculars are to be judged.

The second, incomplete, portion of the *DVE* outlines the rules of composition for the one and only truly illustrious vernacular, the poetic language of which Dante considers himself to be the founder. But it is the first part of the treatise that interests us here.

The *DVE* defines the vernacular as the language children learn to use when they begin to articulate sounds, which they acquire by imitating their wet nurse, and he opposes it to a *locutio secundaria,* called grammar (*grammatica*) by the Romans. Grammar meant a language governed by rules that require extended study and of which one must acquire the *habitus.* This *locutio secundaria* is the scholastic Latin whose rules were taught in the schools of the day, an *artificial* idiom, "perpetual and incorruptible," the international language of the Church and the university, frozen in time into a system of rules and regulations by the grammarians who had laid down the law when Latin had ceased to be the living language of Rome.

Faced with this distinction, Dante states unequivocally that the vernacular is the nobler language because it was the first one used by the human race; because the whole world uses it "though with different pronunciations and using different words" (*DVE* I, i, 4); and lastly because it is natural whereas the other is artificial.

On the one hand, then, he affirms that the nobler language must fulfill the requirements of naturalness, while the recognized diversity of the vernaculars confirms their conventionality (and Dante admits that the relationship between signifier and signified, a consequence of the faculty of speech, is the product of convention, in other words, *ad placitum*). On the other hand, he speaks of the vernacular as a language everyone shares, even though vocabulary and pronunciation may vary. Since the whole of the *DVE* insists on the variety of languages, how are we to reconcile the idea that languages are many with the fact that the vernacular (natural language) is common to the whole human race? The answer is that it is "natural" and common to all to learn first of all a natural language without being aware of its rules, but that this occurs because all mankind has in common a natural predisposition for language, a natural linguistic faculty, which is embodied, in Scholastic terms, in different linguistic substances and forms (see also Marigo 1938: ch. 9, n. 23; Dragonetti 1961: 32).

Dante affirms in fact (*DVE* I, i, 2) that the ability to acquire one's mother tongue is natural, and this ability is common to all peoples despite the differences in vocabulary and pronunciation. He is not speaking then of a specific language, but of a general ability shared by all members of the species.

It is clear to him, then, that, while the language faculty is permanent and unchanging for all members of the species, natural languages on the other hand are capable of developing and becoming enriched over time, either independently of the wills of individual speakers or, on the contrary, as a result of their creativity—and the illustrious vernacular he is proposing to forge is meant to be a product of individual creativity. But it seems that between linguistic faculty and natural language he wishes to distinguish an intermediate moment.

In the opening chapter of the first part of the *DVE*, Dante, referring to his notion of the vernacular, uses terms such as *vulgaris eloquentia, locutio vulgarium gentium,* and *vulgaris locutio,* while he uses *locutio secundaria* for grammar. We could translate *eloquentia* in the generic sense either as "eloquence" or as "speech" or "manner of speaking." But the text contains a distinction among various lexical choices that is probably not casual. In certain cases Dante speaks of *locutio,* in others of *ydioma,* of *lingua,* or of *loquela.* He uses *ydioma,* for example, whenever he is referring to the Hebrew language (*DVE* I, iv, 1; vi, 1; and vi, 7), as well as in reference to the branching off of the world's languages, and the Romance languages in particular.

In I, vi, 6–7, in speaking of the *confusio linguarum* of Babel, Dante uses the term *loquela.* In the same context, however, he also uses *ydioma,* both for the languages of the confusion and the Hebrew language that remained intact. Similarly, he speaks of the *loquela* of the Genoese and of the Tuscans, but he also uses *lingua* for Hebrew and the dialects of the Italian vernacular. Writing again about the confusion of Babel. when he wants to say that, after its destruction, the builders of the Tower began to speak imperfect languages, he says that "tanto rudius nunc barbariusque locuntur," ("the more rudimentary and barbaric the language they now spoke") (*DVE* I, vii, 7, p. 14), while, a few lines down, referring to the original Hebrew language, the term used is "antiquissima locutione" ("the most ancient language") (*DVE* I, vii, 8, p. 14).

It might be thought that he uses all these terms as synonyms, if it were not for the fact that *ydioma, lingua,* and *loquela* are used only when what he is talking about is a Saussurean *langue,* while it seems that *locutio* is used in a more generic sense and shows up whenever the context appears to be suggesting the activity of *parole.* Apropos of certain animal cries, for instance, he says that such an act cannot be called a *locutio* because it is not a true linguistic activity (*DVE* I, ii, 6–7). What's more, Dante uses *locutio* every time Adam addresses God.

It would appear, then, that *ydioma, lingua,* and *loquela* are to be understood in the modern sense of "language," while *locutio* seems instead to stand for discursive acts.

In *DVE* I, iv, 1, Dante wonders who was the first human being to be given the faculty of speech *(locutio)* and what was the first thing said ("quod primitus locutus fuerit") and where, when, and to whom, and in what language ("sub quo ydiomate") was the first linguistic act ("primiloquium") emitted. I believe, incidentally, that we are entitled to translate "primiloquium" in this way, by analogy with "tristiloquium" and "turpiloquium" (*DVE* I, xi, 2; xiii, 4), used to describe the ugly manner of speaking of the Romans and the Florentines of his day.

Perhaps Dante wanted to stress the fact that Adam speaks to God before giving things their names, and that *God had therefore given him the faculty of speech before he constructed a language.*

But what language did Adam speak? Dante criticizes those who, like the Florentines, believe their own native language superior, whereas there exist many languages, and many of them are superior to the Italian vernacular. Next (*DVE* I, vi, 4), he concludes that, along with the first soul, God created at the same time a "certam formam locutionis" ("a certain form of language"). If we translate this expression as "a well-defined form of language" (as Mengaldo [1979: 55] does, how do we explain the fact that in *DVE* I, vi, 7 Dante states: "Fuit ergo hebraicum ydioma illud quod primi loquentis labia fabricarunt" ["So the Hebrew language was that which the lips of the first speaker moulded"]?

Dante explains that he speaks of *forma* "with reference both to the words used for things, and to the construction of words, and to the arrangement of the construction ("et quantum ad rerum vocabula et quantum ad vocabularum constructionem et quantum ad constructionis prolationem" [*DVE*, I, vi, 4]), allowing the inference that, by "forma locutionis" he is referring to a lexicon and a morphology, and hence to a language. But if we translate *forma* as "language," the following passage would be hard to fathom:

And this form (*forma*) of language would have continued to be used by all speakers, had it not been shattered through the fault of human presumption, as will be shown below.

In this form of language (*forma locutionis*) Adam spoke; in this form of language spoke all his descendants until the building of the Tower of Babel (which is interpreted as "tower of confusion"); this is the form of language inherited by the sons of Heber, who are called Hebrews because of it. To these alone it remained after the confusion, so that our redeemer, who was to descend from them (in so far as He was human), should not speak the language of confusion but that of grace.

So the Hebrew language was that which the lips of the first speaker moulded. (*DVE* I, vi, 4–7)[4]

---

4. "Qua quidem forma omnis lingua loquentium uteretur, nisi culpa presumptionis humane dissipata fuisset, ut inferius ostendetur. Hac forma locutionis locutus est Adam; hac forma locutionis locuti sunt omnes posteri eius usque ad edifi-

If we were to interpret "forma locutionis" as meaning a fully formed language, why then, in saying that Jesus Christ spoke Hebrew, does Dante use at one time *lingua* and at another *ydioma* (while, right afterward, in *DVE* I, vii, 7, recounting the episode of the confusion of tongues, *loquela* is the term chosen), whereas the expression "forma locutionis" is used only for the original divine gift? Furthermore, if we were to grant that "forma locutionis" signified only the faculty of speech, it is not clear why the sinners of Babel would have lost it (while the Hebrews kept it), seeing that the whole of the *DVE* recognizes the existence of a plurality of languages produced (on the basis of some natural faculty) after Babel.

Let us, then, attempt an alternative translation:

And it is precisely this form that all speakers would use in their language, if it had not been dismembered through the fault of human presumption, as we shall demonstrate below. *This is the linguistic form* in which Adam spoke: all of his descendants spoke *thanks to this form* until the building of the Tower of Babel—which is interpreted as the tower of confusion: this was *the linguistic form* that the sons of Eber, who were called Hebrews after their father, inherited. To them alone it remained after the confusion, so that our Redeemer, who was to be born of them through the human side of his nature, should enjoy, not a tongue of confusion, but a tongue of grace. It was, then, the Hebrew language *that the lips of the first speaker framed.*

What, however, is this linguistic form that is not the Hebrew language nor the general faculty of language and which was given to Adam as a divine gift but lost after Babel—and which Dante, as we shall see, is endeavoring to rediscover with his theory of the illustrious vernacular?

Corti (1981: 46 et seq.) has suggested a solution to the problem, based on the principle that Dante cannot be understood if he is seen simply as an

cationem turris Babel, que 'turris confusionis' interpretatur; hanc formam locutionis hereditati sunt filii Heber, qui ab eo dicti sunt Hebrei. Hiis solis post confusionem remansit, ut Redemptor noster, qui ex illis oriturus erat secundum humanitatem, non lingua confusionis, sed gratie, frueretur. Fuit ergo hebraicum ydioma illud quod primi loquentis labia fabricarunt" (*DVE* I, vi, 4–7).

orthodox follower of the thought of Thomas Aquinas. Dante appeals, depending on the circumstances, to various philosophical and theological sources, and there can be no doubt that he was influenced by various strands of that so-called radical Aristotelianism whose major representative was Siger of Brabant (whom Dante places in the Heaven of the Sun). But Boethius of Dacia too, one of the major representatives of the Modistae grammarians (and also in the Heaven of the Sun), was associated with the circles of radical Aristotelianism (and like Siger incurred the condemnation of the bishop of Paris in 1277). Dante is alleged to have been influenced by his *De modis significandi.* Corti sees the Bologna of his time as the seedbed from which these influences were passed on to Dante, either as a result of a personal stay there or through contacts between Bolognese and Florentine intellectual circles.

If such were the case, it would become clearer what Dante meant by "forma locutionis." It was the Modistae who argued for the existence of linguistic universals, that is, for a set of rules underlying the formation of any natural language. In the *De modis,* Boethius observes that it is possible to extract, from all existing languages, the rules of a universal grammar, distinct from either Latin or Greek grammar (*Quaestio* VI).

What God gave to Adam, then, was not the mere faculty for language, and not even a natural language, but the principles of a universal grammar, the formal cause, "the general structuring principle of language both as regards lexicon and as regards the morphological and syntactic characters of language, which Adam will frame little by little, as he goes on living and giving names to things" (Corti 1981: 47).[5] The *forma locutionis* given

---

5. Maria Corti's thesis has been challenged, especially by Pagani (1982) and by Maierù (1983): (i) there is no convincing proof that Dante knew Boethius of Dacia's work, (ii) in a number of instances Corti draws untenable analogies between the two texts, and (iii) the linguistic notions we find in Dante were already circulating among other philosophers and grammarians even before the thirteenth century. Even if we grant the first two points, however, there still remains the third, that the idea, that is, of a universal grammar enjoyed wide circulation in medieval culture and, as none of Corti's critics has placed in doubt, Dante was familiar with these discussions. To say, as Maierù says, that there was no need to be acquainted with Boethius's writings to know that "grammar is one and the same in all languages, even though there may be surface variations," because the same affirmation is already to be found in Roger Bacon, is if anything proof that Dante could indeed have been thinking of a universal grammar.

to him by God could be understood as a sort of innate mechanism reminiscent of the same universal principles studied in Chomsky's generative grammar.

It seems likely, then, that Dante believed that, with Babel, what had disappeared was the perfect *forma locutionis*—the only form that would permit the creation of languages capable of reflecting the very essence of things (the identity between *modi essendi* and *modi significandi*), of which the Hebrew spoken by Adam was the incomparable and perfect result—and that the surviving *formae locutionis* were incoherent and imperfect—just like the Italian vernaculars whose inability to express lofty and profound thought is pilloried by the poet.

If this is how the *DVE* is to be read, we can finally understand the nature of that illustrious vernacular that Dante claims to be tracking down like a perfumed panther, "whose scent is left everywhere but which is nowhere to be seen" (*DVE* I, xvi, 1).[6] It shows up here and there in the texts of the poets whom Dante considers major, but it still appears to be unformed, unregulated, unarticulated in its grammatical principles. Confronted with the existing vernaculars, natural but not universal, and with a universal but artificial grammar, Dante pursues the dream of a restoration of the Edenic *forma locutionis*, which is both natural and universal. Unlike many men of the Renaissance, however, who will go in search of a Hebrew language restored to its revelatory and magical powers, Dante's goal is to recreate the original conditions with an act of modern invention. The illustrious vernacular is to be a poetic language, his language, and it will be the means by which a modern poet is able to heal the post-Babelic wound. The whole of the second book of the *DVE* is not to be read as a mere treatise on style, but as an effort to create the conditions, the rules, the *forma locutionis* of the only conceivable perfect language, the Italian of Dante's poetry (Corti 1981: 70). This illustrious vernacular will possess the *necessity* (as opposed to the conventionality) of the original perfect language, because, just as the *forma locutionis* allowed Adam to speak with God, the illustrious vernacular will allow the

---

6. It was thought in the Middle Ages that the panther had a richly perfumed breath and left a trace of its passage wherever it had been. But, for the hunters who attempted to entrap it, it was practically impossible to locate. So they would smell its perfume but never succeed in catching it. This explains how the panther became a metaphor for poetry itself.

poet to make his words equal to the task of expressing what they have to express, which would otherwise be inexpressible.

This is why, instead of condemning the multiplicity of languages, Dante stresses their ability to renew themselves over time. It is on the basis of this faith in the creativity of language that he can aspire to invent a modern perfect language, without going hunting for lost models. If Dante had really thought that the Hebrew invented by Adam was the only perfect language, he would have done all he could to write his poem in Hebrew. The only reason he did not do so is because he thought that the vernacular he was called upon to invent would correspond to the God-given principles of universal form better than Adam's Hebrew had. Dante, with characteristic chutzpah, steps up to the plate as the new Adam.

7.2. *Paradiso* XXVI

If we turn now from the *DVE* to Canto XXVI of *Paradiso* (several years have gone by between the two), it looks as if Dante changed his mind. In the *DVE* it was unambiguously affirmed that Hebrew sprang as a perfect language from the God-given *forma locutionis,* and that was the language in which Adam addressed God, calling him *El.* In *Paradiso* XXVI, 124–138, however, Adam says:

> La lingua ch'io parlai fu tutta spenta
> innanzi che a l'ovra inconsummabile
> fosse la gente di Nembròt attenta:
>   ché nullo effetto mai razïonabile,
> per lo piacere uman che rinovella
> seguendo il cielo, sempre fu durabile.
>   Opera naturale è ch'uom favella;
> ma così o così, natura lascia
> poi fare a voi secondo che v'abbella.[7]
>   Pria ch'i' scendessi a l'infernale ambascia,

---

7. See in Marmo (1994: 124, n. 39) the interesting reference to Simon of Faversham, who claimed that there exists in language a difference between *natural* signification and *positive* (or conventional) signification.

I s'appellava in terra il sommo **bene**
onde vien la letizia che mi **fascia**;
   e EL si chiamò poi: e ciò **convene**,
ché l'uso d'i mortali è come fronda
in ramo, che sen va e altra vene.[8]

Adam affirms, not only that, born out of a natural disposition for speech, languages subsequently become distinguished from each other and grow and change thanks to human initiative, but also that the Hebrew spoken before the building of the Tower of Babel was no longer the same language that he had spoken in the Earthly Paradise. In Eden Adam had called God *I*, whereas later he was called *El*.

Saying that, by the time of the tower, Adam's Hebrew was a lost language might simply be a way to justify Genesis 10. But what is most striking is the odd notion that God might once have been called *I*, a choice that none of Dante's commentators has ever succeeded in explaining satisfactorily.

It has been suggested that *I* stands for the Roman numeral corresponding to the Arab numeral 1, and that it symbolizes therefore the perfect unity of God, but elsewhere in *Paradiso* (XIX, 128), the Roman numeral I stands for the smallest of quantities and is opposed to M, which stands instead for 1,000; it does not seem likely, then, that the poet would decide to designate the divinity with a numeral that indicates a minimal value.

A second interpretation appears to be inspired by a curious case of linguistic ethnocentrism—the conviction, that is, that there exists only one language and it is the most perfect one. The last thirteen cantos of Dorothy Sayers's English translation of the *Comedy* were completed after her death by Barbara Reynolds. Lines 133–136 of Canto XXVI in Reynolds's version read as follows:

---

8. "The tongue I spoke was all extinct before Nimrod's race gave their mind to the unaccomplishable task; for no product whatever of reason—since human choice is renewed with the course of heaven—can last forever. It is a work of nature that man should speak, but whether in this way or that nature then leaves you to follow your own pleasure. Before I descended to the anguish of Hell the Supreme Good from whom comes the joy that swathes me was named *I* on earth, and later He was called *El;* and that is fitting, for the usage of mortals is like a leaf on a branch, which goes and another comes" (Dante 1961: 379).

Ere I descended to the pains of Hell
Jah was the name men called the highest Good
Which swathes me in this joy. Thereafter *El*
His title was on earth. . . .

Clearly, if Dante's *I* had been preserved in the English, it might have been mistaken for the first person singular pronoun. It is understandable, then, that the translator should have changed it to *Jah*. We might be tempted to believe that *Jah* is simply the first syllable of Jahveh, if it were not for Reynolds's footnote, which suggests that Dante must have been thinking of Psalm 68:4, which she naturally cites in the King James Version: "Sing unto God, sing praises to his name; extol him that rideth upon the heavens by his name Jah, and rejoice before him."[9]

What makes this explanation "suspect"? The twin facts that unfortunately Dante did not know Hebrew and that neither was he especially conversant with the King James Version of the Bible.[10] The Bible Dante knew was the Vulgate, in which the verse in question is translated as follows: "Cantate Deo psalmum, dicite nomen ejus, iter facite ei qui ascendit super occasum Deus est nomen illi. Exultate in conspectus ejus." So the name of God Dante knew was *Deus* (for what it's worth, Luther's German translation also has, not *Jah*, but *Herr*).

For the same reasons we must exclude the hypothesis that Dante was influenced by Exodus 3:15, because in that case the Vulgate speaks of "Dominus Deus." As for the theory that Dante may have taken his *I* from the frequently used abbreviated Florentine form *i'* of the pronoun *io*—it is true that in Exodus 3:14 God says to Moses "Ego sum qui sum," but what he is saying is that his name is "Qui sum," in Hebrew *Ehyieh*.

There is yet another hypothesis. In the seventh book of his *Etymologies*, Isidore of Seville lists the traditional names of God in the Hebrew tradition

---

9. Even a contemporary Hebrew scholar like André Chouraqui translates: "Poétisez pour Elohim, chantez son nom; frayez passages au chevalier des nues: Yah est son nom! Exultez en face di lui!"

10. I am reminded of that nineteenth-century congressman from Texas who opposed the introduction of foreign language teaching in the schools declaring: "If English was good enough for the Lord Jesus Christ, it's good enough for me!"

and, along with El, Eloi, Eloe, Sabaoth, Elion, Eie, Adonai, Tetragrammaton, and Saddai, he also mentions *Ia* ("which is only applied to God, and which sounds as the last syllable of 'alleluia,' " *Etymologies*, p. 153). But if Dante had followed Isidore, whom he certainly knew, why did he use *I* and not *Ia*? Certainly not for metrical reasons (the only consideration that could justify the abbreviation), since his hendecasyllabic line would have scanned correctly in either case.

The mysterious appearance of this *I* can only be explained by concluding that Dante had changed his mind about Adam's original Hebrew, and that he had done so on the basis of information directly or indirectly acquired, just as we hypothesized that he had taken his idea of the *forma locutionis* from Modistae sources. We must therefore take one step, if not backward, at least to one side, and see what was happening at more or less the same time in Hebrew circles.

Let us take a look, then, at the principles of the Kabbalah of names, or ecstatic Kabbalah, theorized and practiced in the thirteenth century by Abraham Abulafia.[11]

The Kabbalah of names is practiced by reciting the names of God hidden in the Torah, playing on the various combinations of the letters of the Hebrew alphabet. The so-called theosophical Kabbalah, while making occasional recourse to practices of numerological reading through acrostics or anagrams, remained basically respectful of the sacred text. The Kabbalah of names, on the other hand, alters, rearranges, dismantles, and recombines the surface of the text and its syntagmatic structures, all the way down to the linguistic atoms constituted by the individual letters, in a process of continuous linguistic re-creation. If, in the theosophical Kabbalah, the text still stands between God and the interpreter, in the ecstatic Kabbalah, the interpreter stands between the text and God.

The practice of reading by permutation tends to provoke ecstatic effects. As Abulafia himself says:

And begin by combining this name, namely, *YHWH*, at the beginning alone, and examine all its combinations and move it and turn it about

---

11. All my information about Abulafia and the quotations that below come from Idel (1988a–c, 1989).

like a wheel returning around, front and back, like a scroll, and do not
let it rest, but when you see its matter strengthened because of the great
motion, because of the fear of confusion of your imagination, and the
rolling about of your thoughts, and when you let it rest, return to it and
ask [it] until there shall come to your hand a word of wisdom from it,
do not abandon it. Afterwards go on to the second one from it, *Adonay*,
and ask of it its foundation [*yesodo*] and it will reveal to you its secret
[*sodo*]. And then you will apprehend its matter in the truth of its language. Then join and combine the two of them [*YHWH* and *Adonay*],
and study them and ask them, and they will reveal to you the secrets of
wisdom. . . . Afterwards combine *Elohim,* and it will also grant you
wisdom. (*Hayyê ha-Nefes,* as cited in Idel 1988b: 21)

If in addition to this we consider the breathing techniques that are meant
to accompany the recitation of the names, we can see how the adept may
progress from syllabification to ecstasy and thence to the acquisition of magical powers, because the letters the mystic combines are the same sounds
with which God created the world. This aspect will become still more evident
in the fifteenth century. Apropos of Yohanan Alemanno, the friend and inspirer of Pico della Mirandola, Idel (1988a: 205) remarks: "the symbolic cargo
of language was transformed into a kind of quasi-mathematical command.
Kabbalistic symbolism thus turned into—or perhaps returned to—a magical
language of incantation."

All of this was possible because for Abulafia the atomic elements of the
text, its letters, had meaning in and of themselves, quite apart from the syn-
tagmata in which they occur. Every letter is already a divine name: "since for
the letters of the Name each letter is a Name in and of itself, be aware that
the Yodh is a name and YH is a name" (*Perush Havdalah de-Rabbi 'Akiva*).

The notion that the name of God can be expressed by a single letter of the
Tetragrammaton is also confirmed by the way in which the divine name is
written in many manuscripts. I am referring to Perani and Sgradini (2004:
131–143), where we see that it was the custom in medieval Hebrew texts to
represent the divine name with a calligraphic arrangement of a series of three
or four yodhs. The fact that these manuscripts were produced in an Italian
context encourages us to entertain the hypothesis that Dante was aware of
this tradition.

If we transliterate the yodh to an I, as Dante may have done, we have a possible source for the poet's volte-face. But this notion of the divine name is not the only idea that Dante seems to share with Abulafia.

According to the ecstatic Kabbalah, language is a universe unto itself, and the structure of language reflects the structure of reality. Already Philo of Alexandria had attempted in his writings to compare the intimate essence of the Torah with the Logos, the World of Ideas, while at the same time Platonic concepts had filtered into the Haggadic-Midrashic tradition, in which the Torah was perceived as the schema according to which God had created the world. The eternal Torah was therefore identified with Wisdom and in a number of passages with a world of forms, a universe of archetypes. In the thirteenth century, adopting an unmistakably Averroistic approach, Abulafia will postulate an equation between the Torah and the Active Intellect, "the form of all the forms of the separate intellects" *(Sefer Mafteah ha-Tokhahot).*

Nevertheless, for Abulafia, this matrix of all languages (which is one and the same as the eternal Torah, but not necessarily the written Torah) does not yet coincide with Hebrew. It appears that Abulafia makes a distinction between the twenty-two letters (and the eternal Torah) as matrix and Hebrew as the mother tongue of humankind. The twenty-two letters of the Hebrew alphabet represent the ideal sounds that must preside over the creation of each of the seventy other languages in existence. The fact that other languages have a larger number of vowels is a result of variations in the pronunciation of the twenty-two basic letters (the other foreign sounds would be called, in modern linguistic terms, allophones of the basic phonemes).[12]

---

12. Other Kabbalists point out that Christians are lacking the letter *heth* and the Arabs do not have the *pe;* and in the Renaissance Yohanan Alemanno will be of the opinion that the variations in pronunciation with regard to the twenty-two Hebrew letters are comparable to the sounds made by the different animals (some are like the grunt of a pig, others like the croak of a frog, others still like the honking of a crane). So that the very fact that they produce different sounds reveals that the other languages belong to peoples who have abandoned the proper conduct of life. In this sense, the multiplication of letters is considered to be one of the results of the confusion of Babel. Alemanno is aware of the fact that other peoples have recognized their own languages as the best in the world, and he cites Galen, for whom the Greek tongue is the most pleasing and the most respondent to the

For Abulafia the twenty-two letters represent all of the sounds naturally produced by the organs of phonation. It is the way the letters are combined that makes the creation of the different languages possible. The word *zeruf* (combination) and the word *lashon* (tongue) have the same numerical value (386): to know the laws of the combinatorial system is to possess the key to the formation of every language. Abulafia admits that the choice of representing these sounds by certain graphic signs is a matter of convention, but he speaks of a convention established between God and the prophets. He is perfectly familiar with the current theories of language according to which the sounds for certain things or concepts are conventional (because he found this Aristotelian and Stoic idea in authors like Maimonides), but he seems to overcome his embarrassment with a rather modern solution, implicitly distinguishing between conventionality and arbitrariness.

Hebrew had its origin in convention like all languages (Abulafia rejects the idea, endorsed by other scholars, some of them in the Christian camp, that a child left to itself from birth would automatically speak Hebrew), but Hebrew is still the Holy Mother Tongue because the names given by Adam were *in accord with nature* and not chosen arbitrarily. In this way, Hebrew was the *protolanguage,* and as such it was necessary if all the other languages were to be created, for "if such a language did not precede it there couldn't have been mutual agreement to call a given object by a different name from what it was previously cald, for how would the second person understand the second name if he doesn't known the original name, in order to be able to agree to the changes?" (*Sefer 'Or ha-Sekhel,* in Idel 1989: 13–14).

Abulafia bemoans the fact that, during the course of their exile, his people have forgotten their own original language, and his project is naturally for the Kabbalist to work toward the recovery of the true matrix of all seventy languages. It is the Messiah who will finally reveal the secrets of the Kabbalah, and the differences between languages will cease at the end of time, when all the existing languages will be reabsorbed into the Sacred Language.

Once again, we find that the positions of Abulafia and Dante have something in common. For Abulafia there existed an equation between the Torah and the Active Intellect, and the schema according to which God had cre-

---

laws of reason, but, not daring to contradict him, he admits that this is because there are affinities between Greek, Hebrew, Arabic, and Assyrian.

ated the world coincided with the linguistic gift he had given to Adam, a kind of generative matrix of all languages that did not yet coincide with Hebrew. We find, then, on the one hand, Averroistic influences in Abulafia, which lead him to believe in a single Active Intellect common to all mankind, and, on the other, undeniable and proven Averroistic sympathies in Dante—the conception, for instance, that Nardi (1985: ch. V) sees as having its origins in Avicenna and Augustine, of a divine Wisdom that offers its forms to the Possible Intellect. The Modistae too (especially the group based in Bologna) and other defenders of a universal grammar were no strangers to the Averroistic tradition. So here we have a shared philosophical position that (without insisting on a direct influence) might incline both thinkers to consider the gift of tongues as the handing-down of a *forma locutionis,* a generative matrix comparable to the Active Intellect.

This is not all. Historically speaking, Hebrew, for Abulafia, had been the *protolanguage,* but the Chosen People, in the course of the Diaspora, had forgotten that original language. Therefore, as Dante will say in the *Paradiso,* at the time of the confusion of Babel the tongue of Adam was "all extinct." Idel (1989) quotes an unpublished manuscript by a disciple of Abulafia which says:

> Anyone who believes in the creation of the world, if he believes that languages are conventional, he must also believe that they are of two types: the first is Divine, i.e., agreement between God and Adam, and the second is natural, i.e., based on agreement between Adam, Eve and their children. The second is derived from the first, and the first was only known to Adam and was not passed on to any of his offspring except for Seth, whom he bore in his likeness and his form. And so, the tradition reached Noah. And the confusion of the tongues during the generation of the dispersion [at the tower of Babel] occurred only to the second type of language, i.e., to the natural language. (Idel 1989: 17)

If we bear in mind that the term "tradition" refers to the Kabbalah, then the passage quoted is once more alluding to a linguistic knowledge, to a *forma locutionis* as a collection of rules for the construction of different languages.

If the original form is not a language, but the universal matrix of all languages, this confirms the historical mutability of Hebrew itself, but also the hope that that original form can be rediscovered and made to bear fruit once again (in different ways, obviously, for Dante and Abulafia).

All these remarks would make more sense if it could be demonstrated that Dante was familiar with Hebrew Kabbalistic thought and with Abulafia in particular.

Abulafia had come to Rome in 1260 and had stayed on in Italy until 1271, when he returned to Rome with the idea of converting the pope. Then he continued on to Sicily, where we lose track of him toward the end of the 1290s. His ideas, then, undoubtedly influenced Italian Jewish circles. In fact in 1290 we witness a debate between Hillel of Verona (who probably met Abulafia twenty years earlier) and Zerakhya of Barcelona, who arrived in Italy at the beginning of the 1270s (cf. Genot-Bismuth 1988: ch. II). Hillel, who had been frequenting intellectual circles in Bologna, writes to Zera-khya with a question first broached by Herodotus, that is, what language would a child brought up deprived of linguistic stimuli express itself in? For Hillel (who appears not to be aware, or chooses to ignore, that Abulafia had been of a different opinion), the child would express itself in the same Hebrew that had originally been given to man as part of his very nature. In his reply Zerakhya accuses him of having surrendered to the sirens of the "un-circumscised" of Bologna. The sounds produced by a child who had not been exposed to a linguistic education, he objects, would be similar to the barking of a dog, and it cannot be argued that the sacred language was given to man by his very nature, because the aptitude man possesses for language is merely potential, and the only way he learns to speak is through the education of his phonatory organs.[13]

This exchange is sufficient to demonstrate that Abulafia's themes were debated on the Italian peninsula, to be precise in the same Bolognese circles that influenced Dante (and where, according to Corti (1981), he might have picked up a number of ideas concerning the *forma locutionis*). But the research of Genot-Bismuth supplies additional details about the period, in which

---

13. Zerakhya uses a proof that we shall encounter after the Renaissance in other, Christian authors—cf. Brian Walton, *In Biblia polyglotta prolegomena* (1657) or Francisco Vallesio, *De sacra philosophia* (1652)—if the divine gift of an original sacred language had ever been made, every human being, no matter what their mother tongue, would have to have an innate knowledge of the sacred language as well.

we encounter a certain Yehudi Romano, who lectured to his coreligionists on Dante's *Comedy*, or Lionello di Ser Daniele who will do likewise, using a copy of the *Comedy* transliterated into Hebrew, to say nothing of a figure like Immanuel of Rome who, in his own poetic compositions, seems almost to parody Dante's themes, as if he were nursing the ambition of writing an anti-*Comedy* in Hebrew.[14]

We are not talking simply about the influence of Dante on Italian Jewish circles. Genot-Bismuth proves that the influences went both ways, going so far as to posit a Jewish origin for the theory of the four senses of Scripture mentioned in Dante's *Epistle XIII*—a bold thesis, when we think of the abundance of Christian sources Dante had at his disposal on that subject. Far less extravagant, and in many ways more convincing, is her thesis that Dante may have caught echoes of the Hillel-Zerakhya polemic in Bologna in the years following.

We might conclude that in the *DVE* Dante comes close to the position espoused by Hillel (or by Hillel's Christian inspirers, as Zerakhya suggested in his rebuttal), while in *Paradiso* XXVI he has become converted to Zerakhya's thesis, which was also that of Abulafia—though it is also true that, by the time he came to write the *DVE*, Dante could already have been familiar with both opinions.

Though Genot-Bismuth is able to document in detail a number of Jewish contributions to historiography that would appear as echoes and suggestions in the *De regimine principum* of Giles of Rome, it is enough for our purposes to recognize the existence of an intellectual climate in which ideas circulated as part of a constant polemic, made up of written and oral debates, between Church and Synagogue (cf. Calimani 1987: ch. VIII). Assuredly if, before the Renaissance, a Christian thinker had come close to embracing Hebrew doctrine, he would never have admitted it publicly. Like the Christian heretics, the Jewish community belonged—as Le Goff (1988) cogently puts it—to a category of outcasts that the official Middle Ages seemed to detest and admire simultaneously, with a mixture of fascination and fear, keeping them at a distance, but making sure the distance was close enough for the outcasts to be within reach. "What it called its charity towards them was like the attitude of a cat playing with a mouse" (Le Goff 1988: 316).

---

14. See Romano (2000). Cf. Battistoni (1995, 1999).

Before its rehabilitation by the Humanists, Christian notions of the Kaballah were hazy, and it tended to be lumped together with the black arts. On the other hand, it has been suggested (Gorni 1990: ch. VII) that Dante refers a little too insistently to various divinatory and magical arts (astrology, chiromancy, physiognomy, geomancy, pyromancy, hydromancy and, of course, necromancy). He appears to have been somehow familiar with an underground and marginalized culture of which the Kabbalah was confusedly a part, at least in popular opinion.

Thus, the interpretation of the *forma locutionis* as a universal matrix of language, even without referring it directly back to the Modistae, becomes still more persuasive.

The only drawback is that, in the absence of concrete proof of these contacts, this is all merely conjecture—as Busi (2004) pointed out in his review of Debenedetti Stow's (2004) book on Dante and Jewish mysticism, for whom the hypotheses we have just set forth are the object of passionate conviction, a conviction that results in her treating a number of hypotheses as if they were proofs.

Still, when all we have to work with are the texts, certain textual analogies, while they cannot be taken as irrefutable proofs, deserve nevertheless to be stressed, if for no other reason than to encourage further research.

We may close by imagining that, on his journey to Paradise—the one he took post mortem, not his literary journey—Dante actually met Abulafia. They may even be conversing amiably together at this very moment, smiling indulgently perhaps at the efforts we have been making to discover whether they had anything in common. And if at a certain point Adam too were to join in the conversation, it would be fascinating to discover what language the three of them were using to make themselves understood. But since the present author is somewhat skeptical concerning the existence of a Perfect Original Language, he prefers to think that the Angels will no doubt provide state-of-the-art simultaneous translation.

8

The Use and Interpretation of Medieval Texts

8.1. The Modernity of a Paleo-Thomist

In 1920 Jacques Maritain published *Art et scolastique (Art and Scholasticism)*[1] a slim volume containing 115 pages of text and 73 pages of notes (the most important of which are given titles of their own in the book's table of contents). In it the author assumed (i) that a medieval school of aesthetic thought, attributable in particular to Thomas Aquinas, had existed, and (ii) that this same school of thought was still sufficiently relevant to account for various aspects of contemporary modern art. Let us recall the climate of the

---

This chapter is a revisiting of two previous texts: "Storiografia medievale ed estetica teorica" (Eco 1961) and "L'esthétique médiévale d'Edgar de Bruyne" (Eco 2004a). The latter was also published in *Recherches de théologie et philosophie médiévales* 71 (2004): 219–232. On the difference between the *use* and the *interpretation* of texts, see Eco (1979, 1990). [*Translator's note:* I am grateful to Hugh Bredin and to his translation of Eco (1988) for his example and for helpful suggestions.]

1. *Art et scolastique,* first written between 1918 and 1919 and published in the periodical *Les lettres* in 1919, was issued in book form by the Librairie de l'Art Catholique in 1920. A copy of this edition, held in the University of Toronto library, can be read online at http://archive.org/stream/artetscolastique00mariuoft #page/n0/mode/1up. A second, revised edition appeared in 1927 (Paris: Rouart), with additional notes, as well as several new *annexes* (appendices or excursuses). The pages on poetry were extrapolated and reprinted, along with essays and poems by other authors, in the miscellany *Frontières de la poésie* [*The Frontiers of Poetry*] (Maritain 1935). The standard English version, *Art and Scholasticism and The Frontiers of Poetry* (Maritain 1962) was translated by Joseph W. Evans from the third and final revised French edition (1935).

time: avant-garde movements had been coming one after the other for forty
years; French philosophy was washing down the last scraps of positivism
with a strong draft of Bergsonism; Neo-Scholasticism, after its nineteenth-
century revival, was still flourishing in the episcopal seminaries, in perpetual polemic against contemporary thought, which for its part paid it not the
slightest bit of attention.

If, on the other hand, we can speak today of a medieval aesthetic school
of thought, and if no one believes any longer that the allusions to the beautiful contained in the *Summae* and *Commentaria* were simply scattered
and shapeless flotsam left over from the repertory of ancient philosophy, it
was not so pacifically accepted, in the opening decades of the twentieth
century, that the Middle Ages had had an aesthetic vision of its own (with
differences and nuances from one thinker to another and from one historical moment to another). People persisted in believing that the object of
investigation known today as the medieval school of aesthetic thought did
not exist. Furthermore, its texts did not exist either, since the texts that are
today recognized as such were understood at the time to be discussions of
metaphysics or physics or of the banal rules and regulations of technical
rhetoric.

There had of course been plenty of orthodox Neo-Thomistic thinkers,
who had reconstructed, shrewdly at times, at other times more ingenuously,
the aesthetic themes present in Thomas's work, presenting their reconstruc-
tions as theoretically valid for the modern world (driven by a Neo-Thomistic
faith in the *philosophia perennis*). But, on the one hand (and unlike Maritain), they had not attempted comparisons between medieval texts and the
artistic problems of later centuries, and, on the other (providing Maritain
with a series of negative examples), they had usually oscillated between historiographical reconstruction and their own theoretical projects, so that it
was not always easy to tell when it was Thomas speaking and when it was
them.[2] In any case, we had to wait until 1946 for the fundamental and histo-

---

2. We may cite Luigi Taparelli d'Azeglio ("Ragioni del bello secondo i principi di
San Tommaso," *Civiltà cattolica*, 1859–1860), Vincenzo Fortunato Marchese (*Delle
benemerenze di San Tommaso verso le belle arti*, Genoa, 1974), Pierre Vallet (*Idée
du beau dans la philosophie de Saint Thomas d'Aquin*, Louvain, 1887), J. Biolez
(*Saint Thomas et les Beaux Arts*, Louvain, 1896), Domenico M. Valensise (*Dell'estetica*

riographically correct texts of De Bruyne and Pouillon to appear. We will come to them in due course.

Art et scolastique, however, came out at the beginning of the 1920s. It was certainly not the work of a nineteenth-century Neo-Thomist, but clearly that of a modern who, though he would later acquiesce in the definition of "Paleo-Thomist" (1947: 9–10), also believed in Cocteau (still the irrepressible and acrobatic inventor of poetic fashions and fashionings) and enthused over the music of Satie, Milhaud, and Poulenc, and the paintings of Severini and Rouault. This man of the Middle Ages attempting to live in the contemporary world (he would eventually accentuate his social and political commit-

---

secondo i principii dell'Angelico Dottore, Rome, 1903), Paolo Lingueglia ("Le basi e le leggi dell'estetica secondo San Tommaso," in *Pagine di d'arte e di letteratura,* Turin, 1915), Octavio Nicolas Derisi (*Lo eterno y lo temporal en el arte,* Buenos Aires, 1942), as well as—but after Maritain—Leonard Callahan (*Theory of Aesthetics: According to the Principles of Saint Thomas,* Washington, DC, 1928), Adolf Dyroff ("Über die Entwicklung und der Wert der Ästhetik des Thomas von Aquin," *Archiv für systematische Philosophie una Soziologie,* 1929), Carlo Mazzantini ("Linee fondamentali di una estetica tomista," *Studium,* 1929), Thomas Gilby (*Poetic Experience: An Introduction to Thomistic Aesthetic,* New York, 1934), Josef Koch ("Zur Ästhetik des Thomas von Aquin," *Zeitschrift für Ästhetik,* 1931), Francesco Olgiati ("San Tommaso e l'arte," *Rivista di filosofia neoscolastica,* 1934), down to Mortimer Adler who, in his *Art and Prudence* (1937), attempted to apply Aristotelian aesthetics, seen through a Thomistic lens, to the cinema. Among these commentators perhaps the most original was Maurice de Wulf with his *Études historiques sur l'esthétique de Saint Thomas d'Aquin* (Louvain, 1896), which underscored the psychological elements in Thomistic aesthetics. Less historiographically reliable was his *Art et beauté* (1920), mixing as it does, and as did many similar works, philosophical historiography and militant metaphysics.

[*Translator's note:* It may be useful to point out that in what follows Eco will be using the term "aesthetic," not only with reference to the artistic experience, but in its broader sense of the appreciation of beauty. This is made clear in his 1956 dissertation on Aquinas, now translated into English by Hugh Bredin as *The Aesthetics of Thomas Aquinas:* "The concept of the aesthetic refers to the problem of the possible objective character, and the subjective conditions, of what we call the experience of beauty. It thus refers also to problems connected with the aesthetic object and aesthetic pleasure. The experience of beauty does not necessarily have art as its object; for we ascribe beauty not just to poems and paintings but also to horses, sunsets, and women—or even, at its limits, to a crime or a gourmet meal" (Eco 1988: 3).]

ment with the publication of *Humanisme intégrale*), who had arrived at Saint Thomas without completely forgetting Bergson,[3] now turned to interpret the problem of art and the beautiful according to the categories of Scholasticism. He did not address the problem of what was dead and what was still living in medieval thought: everything was evidently alive if he, well into the twentieth century, thought like a medieval. It was irrelevant that many of the Scholastic definitions he employed were filtered through a Bergsonian prism: indeed, this simply showed that the Middle Ages was not an island in history, but a dimension of the mind. It followed, according to what Maritain deemed to be "true," that Bergson was himself part of the *philosophia perennis*.

It is in this psychological dimension, which also involved a methodological dimension, that *Art et scolastique* was intended to be read. Only thus could one appreciate its freshness, its unexpected connections, the sudden leaps from ancient to modern, its "militant" vehemence. The culture of the 1920s was thus induced to reflect on the existence of a medieval aesthetic, presented, for better or for worse, as an instrument capable also of defining the artistic polemics of the present day.

On the one hand, the innate Cartesianism of French culture, cross-fertilized by the neoclassicism of the time (this was the same period in which Cocteau was championing Satie and Stravinsky in *Le coq et l'arlequin*), proved especially receptive to certain proposals that Maritain borrowed from the Scholastic tradition but which modern culture hailed as new, buried as they had been for centuries in ecclesiastical libraries. The revelation of a view of art as *recta ratio factibilium* ("right judgment regarding things to be made"), as a technical and practical *making*, an arrangement of materials conforming to an order dictated not just by the sensibility but chiefly by the intellect—and the beauty synthesized in the three touchstones of *integrity, proportion,* and *clarity*—could not fail to play a liberating role with regard to the manifold Romantic and Decadent liens and encumbrances that still weighed so heavily on aesthetic speculation. The same considerations explain the fortune, somewhat later, of Maritain in the United States, where this aesthetic, so close in its way to the Aristotelian tradition that the Anglo-Saxon world had

---

3. Let us not forget that in 1944 he published a collection of essays entitled *De Bergson à Thomas d'Aquin, essais de métaphysique et de morale* (New York: Éditions de la Maison Française).

never in fact abandoned,[4] would go so far as to garner the honors of wide-spread diffusion even in the pages of *Time* magazine.

Art et scolastique may deserve all the criticism we are about to level at it, but at the same time we are compelled to admit that it also encouraged many scholars to take up the study of medieval aesthetics. The price to be paid (and Maritain pays it down to the last cent) was that of not behaving in a historiographically responsible fashion and making free *use* of Thomas's texts instead of *interpreting* them. But, for an adept of the *philosophia perennis,* the difference between use and interpretation was not that important: if Saint Thomas was still contemporary (because, as they said in Neo-Scholastic circles, there is no progress in metaphysics), he could be read through the sensibility of a contemporary.

8.2. A Tendentious Reading

Maritain had no qualms about inventing nonexistent Thomistic citations. Take the case of that "pulchra enim dicuntur quae visa placent" ("things that please when they are seen are called beautiful") which in Maritain becomes "pulchrum est id quod visum placet" ("the beautiful is that which pleases being seen"). The difference appears to be negligible; but what in Thomas was practically a sociological observation ("people think that beautiful things are those that are pleasing to sight [or at the moment they are seen]"), is transformed into an *essentialist* definition, so much so that on the basis of that definition Maritain will proceed, as we will see, to identify this *visio* with an act of intuition of a very contemporary nature.[5]

What was the object discerned by the Thomistic *visio?* Thomas's words were unequivocal: it was the *claritas* possessed by the substantial form actualized in an ordered substance. What was the only way in which, within the

---

4. See my "The *Poetics* and Us" ["La Poetica e noi"] in Eco (2004b).

5. It is a known fact that nowhere in the Sherlock Holmes stories does Arthur Conan Doyle have his hero utter the famous phrase "Elementary, my dear Watson," and yet the remark is as frequently cited as "To be or not to be." The same thing has occurred with this formula of Maritain's, which has continued to be repeated as authentically Thomistic by a multiplicity of authors. Even De Munnynk (1923), writing as a critic of Maritain's method, continues to quote "pulchrum, est id quod visum placet" without batting an eyelid.

limits of Thomistic epistemology, this *visio* of the splendor of the substance was to be understood? As a complex act of judgment, permeated with intellect, that followed upon the primary abstraction of the *simplex apprehensio* ("direct apprehension"), and therefore as a mediated and complex act. This is the conclusion which, supported by the work of other scholars, we believe we have ascertained elsewhere (see Eco 1956).

For Maritain, on the other hand, the *visio* became the split-second and unique act of an "intellected sense" ("sens intelligencié"), grasping in a single instant, without the slightest effort at abstraction, the form at the very core of the matter. The beautiful for Maritain becomes:

> *id quod visum placet,* what pleases when it is seen; the object, in other words, of an intuition. . . . . Contemplating the object in the intuition that the senses have of it, the intellect rejoices in a presence, it rejoices in the luminous presence of something intelligible. . . . . If it turns away from the senses to abstraction and reasoning, it turns away from its own joy, and loses contact with this luminosity. To understand this, let us represent to ourselves that it is intellect and sense becoming one, or, if we may put it this way, an *intellected sense,* which gives place in the heart to aesthetic joy." (Maritain 1920: 174–175)[6]

What we have here is a typically modern kind of idea, which a medieval philosopher, rather than rejecting, would quite simply not have understood (see also, in this connection, Campanelli 1996: 93 et seq.). But even a contemporary historian would have to confess to a certain puzzlement reading that something that is *seen,* and therefore in some fashion perceived, must by the same token be *intuited.* We will return to this point. For the moment

---

6. *"id quod visum placet,* ce qui plaît étant vu, c'est-à-dire *étant l'objet d'une intuition.* . . . Contemplant l'objet dans l'intuition que le sens en a, l'intellect jouit d'une présence, elle jouit de la présence rayonnante d'un intelligible qui ne se révèle pas lui-même à ses yeux tel qu'il est. Se détourne-t-elle du sens pour abstraire et raisonner, elle se détourne de sa joie, et perd contact avec ce rayonnement. Pour entendre cela, représentons-nous que c'est l'intelligence et le sens ne faisant qu'un, ou, si l'on peut ainsi parler, le *sens intelligencié,* qui donne lieu dans le coeur à la joie esthétique" (1927: 252–254, n. 55).

all that is needed is to record the fact that from this point on Maritain proposes an idea of poetic knowledge as knowledge *through connaturality,* an idea he will explore more deeply in his later works.

We encounter the same distortion in his recovery of the definition of art as *habitus operativus* (explicated, we must admit, in exemplary fashion, with a wealth of philological data). This definition could not remain anchored to its medieval interpretation: later on De Bruyne and others would point out that it is only in a Franciscan context imbued with Platonism—and timidly at that—and thereafter, and more decisively, only with the dissolution of Scholasticism, in a climate of protohumanism and with the dawn of the Mannerist doctrines of *ingenium,* that a conception of the productive act will emerge in modern thought that recognizes the nucleus of the creative process in the presence of an original inner idea. In Thomas the doctrine of art is still classical. The *habitus operativus* ("a disposition to produce certain operations or acts") behaves according to fixed canons and, if the idea of art escapes being identified with mere imitation, it is only by having recourse to the recombining of memories of previous experiences, like that described by Horace in the first five lines of his *Ars Poetica.*

The limits of this doctrine prove too restrictive for Maritain. All he had to do was admit that he was speaking *after* Saint Thomas, but in that case he would not have been able to declare himself a "Paleo-Thomist." Accordingly, he blithely grafts onto his supposedly Thomistic picture the lesson of Bergson, and already in *Art et scolastique*—admittedly among the notes—he speaks of the work in progress not simply as a complex of traditional rules, but also as "raison séminale," intuition, and finally "schéma dynamique":

> "It is a simple vision, though virtually extremely rich in multiplicity, of the work to be made, grasped in its individual soul, seen as a spiritual seed or a *seminal reason* of the work, which has something to do with what Bergson calls the *dynamic schema,* which appeals not merely to the intellect but also the imagination and the sensibility of the artist" (Maritain 1920: 146–147, n. 93, my emphasis).[7]

---

7. "C'est une vue simple, bien que virtuellement très riche en multiplicité, de l'oeuvre à faire saisie dans son âme individuelle, vue qui est comme un germe spirituel ou une *raison séminale* de l'oeuvre, et qui tient de ce que M. Bergson

Even as Maritain writes, surrealism is on the doorstep, and symbolism is yielding its final fruits; Satie's neoclassicism cannot make him forget that the Late Romantic culture of symbolism has by this time identified art as a language appealing principally to feeling, the guardian of a mystery that ordinary words cannot *reveal*. Thus, in explicating the concept of *claritas*, he adheres to a definition he finds in *De Pulchro et Bono*, a little book that the most rigorous scholarship no longer attributed to Thomas but to Albertus Magnus (in point of fact even Maritain admits his uncertainty, deciding however to accept it as a reliable witness to Thomas's ideas).[8] The definition in question is of *claritas* as "resplendentia formae supra partes materiae proportionatas" ("a resplendence of form in the duly ordered parts of material objects"). But in Albertus Magnus there remains a Platonic emphasis, a dialectic between *esse* and *essentia,* in which form, shining through the matter it organizes, nevertheless is not fully identified with it, maintaining its ideal preeminence, whereas in Thomas, in the midst of a dialectic between *essence* and *concrete act of existing,* form becomes such only by individualizing itself in a concretely existing substance (see Eco 1956: ch. IV).

But this is not all. At this point Maritain, in a footnote, goes so far as to distance himself from Albertus Magnus, for whom the radiance of that form—be it Platonic or Aristotelian—was nonetheless comprehensible by whomsoever understood what type of object they were contemplating (a dog, a vase, a human body). For Maritain, on the other hand, the *claritas,* being clarity of form, is metaphysical clarity, clarity in itself, but not clarity for us. The principle of intelligibility of the thing, it is at the same time the principle of its mystery. Thus the beautiful is the splendor of a mystery. Moreover, it cannot be denied that Thomas himself, having reached the extreme limits of explanation of the essential reality of things, would have been brought up short before the mystery of participation by which they cling to being, thanks to the continuous creative intervention of the divinity. The

---

appelle *intuition* et *schéma dynamique,* qui intéresse non seulement l'intelligence, mais aussi l'imagination et la sensibilité de l'artiste" (1927: 277–278, n. 93).

8. Discovered in 1869 and at first attributed to Thomas, by the time Maritain was writing, the consensus inclined toward attributing it to Albertus Magnus (so much so that in 1927 Mandonnet would classify it among Thomas's *Opuscula spuria*). Maritain had therefore a number of indications that ought to have encouraged him to a greater prudence.

only way he could have explained this reality is by appealing to the analogical force of the language of theology. But the *analogia entis* is not the analogy of the symbolist and, however inadequate it may be, it is an instrument of clarification of the metaphysical mystery, in a cultural climate in which the intellectual possibility of knowledge of being is taken as implicit and what is stressed is our perception of the clarity of being and not its mystery. Maritain, on the other hand, stresses the mystery, elbowing Saint Thomas over toward Saint John of the Cross (as he will do systematically in 1932's *Les degrés du savoir* [*The Degrees of Knowledge*]) and medieval aesthetics toward the aesthetics of symbolism.

And let it not be thought that our suspicions are exaggerated: a few pages further on, as he prepares to explain the transcendental nature of the beautiful (that canonical given, by virtue of which, in medieval thought, the beautiful becomes concrete and solid and avoids the trap of subjective impression, becoming an objective attribute of truth and moral value, an inseparable property of being), Maritain has recourse to the words of Baudelaire, reminding us how, in its experience of beauty, the human mind has the sense of something that lies beyond it, of the tangible call of the beyond, and, in the melancholy of the ensuing moment, recognizes the evidence of a nature exiled in imperfection, aspiring toward the infinite that has just been revealed. Thus, little by little, the transcendental beauty of the Middle Ages is transformed into something akin to the Burkean and Kantian sublime, filtered through a Decadent sensibility.[9]

This, then, is the situation of *Art et scolastique*—a militant work that was to influence the writing of philosophical history, eliciting a number of studies (and saddling them with a series of interpretations as fascinating as they were incautious); a speculative work disguised as commentary, and hence fraught with contradictions.

8.3. After *Art et scolastique,* "Poetry" Takes Center Stage

In the essays gathered under the title of *Les frontières de la poésie* (1935), the author appeared to have rid himself of his false pose as historiographer to assume the physiognomy of the autonomous theorist; but it was only the

---

9. See Maritain (1920: 42–44, 48–49, and 185–186, n. 73).

diminished philosophical commitment of those essays that made him appear freer and more open-minded.

In *Frontières* the premises of *Art et scolastique* find ample development: if the medieval artist was the anonymous executor of the objective rules of his art, the artist that Maritain now portrays expresses "himself and his own essence," "provided that things resonate within him." The artist receives external reality "in the recesses of his feelings and his passion" ("dans les replis de son sentiment et de sa passion"), not as something other than himself but as something so completely identified with and absorbed in him as no longer to posit any difference between his own soul and the innermost aspects of the things he has made his own. Therefore poetic knowledge will be knowledge according to "resonance in subjectivity" ("résonance dans la subjectivité") (Maritain 1935: 194–197).

If the Scholastic theory of art was a theory of production, Maritain's theory becomes a theory of knowledge and, to get to this point, Maritain has evidently been compelled to enrich the Scholastic concept of *ars*. Hesitating to distort the category—so clear and well-defined—that Scholasticism had handed down to him (and that he himself in fact had expounded in *Art et scolastique*), he consequently sets alongside the concept of *art* that of *poetry*.

In the Scholastic tradition "poetry" is not an aesthetic category (as it is, let's say, for Croce (1902), who also applies it to literature in prose), nor, as *ars*, is it a form of knowledge: it is quite simply an operative *habitus* or a practical ability. Maritain's notion of poetry, then, is alien to medieval thought.

The nature of poetic practice is already sketched out in *Art et scolastique* and is also found, not only in *Frontières*, but also in subsequent works, as we will see in what follows. In short, while art is a practical operation governed by the laws of the intellect, poetry becomes an intentional emotion, the original inner spring that animates the rules of art from within. Art, therefore, begins later, with "the intellect and the will to choose" ("l'intellect et la volonté de choix").[10] Dangerously close to the idealistic formulation of a duality between lyrical intuition as inner expression and technical externalization as a mechanical addition, Maritain's duality nonetheless allows him to rediscover a deep level of knowledge belonging to the poetic moment, something that the medieval notion of art did not allow.

------

10. See Maritain (1920: 207, n. 130, and 217, n. 138), and Maritain (1935: 33, n. 1).

The poetic moment is an intuitive moment which calls into play not merely intellect but also emotion and sensibility. At that moment, the work appears as already virtually complete; it is "an intuitive and intentional emotion that carries within it far more than itself" ("émotion intuitive et intentionnelle qui porte en soi beaucoup plus qu'elle-même"), eager to lend existence to its phantasm, "an intuitive flash in which the entire work is virtually contained and which will unfold itself in the work" ("éclair intuitif . . . où toute l'oeuvre est contenue virtuellement et qui s'expliquera dans l'oeuvre"), and finally "it is above all as a precise emotion that it appears to the consciousness" ("c'est surtout . . . comme une émotion décisive qu'elle apparaît à la conscience") (Maritain 1935: 182–195). This is because it is the effect of a profound relationship with reality (the ultimate identification of the mystery of things with the mind of the artist): and therefore it can be understood as a moment of prelogical knowledge of reality, an instrument of metaphysical revelation.

All of this was not made explicit in *Art et scolastique*, nor does it appear in clear theoretical terms in *Frontières*. We find it, however, in a couple of later essays (which look forward to Maritain's *Creative Intuition in Art and Poetry* of 1953). These essays are "De la connaissance poétique" (1938a) and "Signe et symbole" (1938b). The date is significant: contemporary culture has returned, as a result of the injection of Surrealism, to a Romantic conception of art as an instrument of philosophy. The absolute to which it provides access is no longer that of the Romantics; nevertheless, Maritain's systematic framework allows him precisely to reinterpret the Surrealist lesson in terms of a metaphysic that is not that of the absurd but that of something significant and rich in positive determinations. In other words, poetry as an instrument, restored by Surrealism to its cognitive dignity, is now realigned according to the modalities of a Romantic aesthetic, but for the purposes of unveiling the universe of Saint Thomas, as seen by a Paleo-Thomist steeped in the modern aesthetic sensibility.

8.4. Poetic Discourse: Maritain vs. Thomas

There are a number of passages in Thomas in which he gives a definition of poetic discourse that is frankly discouraging (*Summa Theologiae* I, I, 9; II, 101, 2 ad 2). He speaks of poetry as an "infima doctrina" ("inferior learning") and opines that "poetica non capiuntur propter defectum veritatis qui est in eis" ("poetic matters cannot be grasped because they are deficient in truth"). This definition of the *modus poeticus* as inferior is fully justified in the context in which Thomas proposes it: that is, in a comparison between vernacular poetry and Holy Scripture and subsequently between poetry and theology; and, within the hierarchical system in which the sciences derive their dignity from the dignity of the object to which they apply, poetry is fated to be the loser. Its *defectus veritatis* or deficiency of truth derives from the fact that it narrates nonexistent things; it uses metaphors for the purposes of representation and to provide delight; it evades the strict control of reason and claims to be an instrument, not of knowledge, but instead of pleasure.[11]

It is true, as Curtius (1948: chs. XI and XII) clearly demonstrates, that it was on the basis of this same distinction between the poet and the theologian, and of certain affirmations made by Aristotle concerning the first poet-theologians, that protohumanists like Albertino Mussato began to adumbrate a notion of the revelatory role of poetry; but by then we will have abandoned the confines of Scholasticism and its inflexible epistemology. In the eyes of which, given its *defectus veritatis,* to interpret the *modus poeticus* as a *perceptio confusa* of the Baumgartian type would be, to say the least, a stretch.

Maritain (1938a–b), in contrast, goes back to Thomas's own writings in order to identify the *modus poeticus,* precisely because of its imprecise and representative nature, as knowledge by "affective connaturality with reality" ("connaturalité affective à la réalité"), a knowledge that is nonconceptualizable, inasmuch as it awakens within itself the creative profundities of the subject. Poetic knowledge is "inseparable from the productivity of the spirit" ("inséparable de la productivité de l'esprit") (1938a: 95–96).

What can the expressive and communicative instrument of this knowledge "by affective connaturality" be? It is the poetic symbol, which is a sign-image, something sensible that signifies its object by way of an analogy between sign and object, and therefore a sign, which, over and above its semantic effectiveness, obtains a practical result (by communicating an order, an appeal) by means of suggestion—an operation that Maritain does not hesitate to define as "magical" (1938a: 299 et seq.).

Nevertheless, no doubt because he did not believe that Thomas's own texts would support this interpretation, Maritain seeks confirmation in a

---

11. See, for a fuller treatment, Chapter 3 in the present volume.

Scholastic of the Counter-Reformation, to be specific, in John of Saint Thomas (1589–1644; aka John Poinsot, hereinafter "John").

Now, John's linguistic theory is a theory of philosophical language and he does not have the slightest interest in the possibilities of poetic language. The linguistic expression or term is what the proposition can be reduced to, as occurs in the case of the subject and the predicate; the term is both *vox* and *signum*, both mental and written, and it is *ex quo simplex conficitur propositio* ("that out of which a simple proposition is made"); it is a *vox significativa* (and therefore is not meaningless, unlike, for instance, the sound *blitiri*); and it is such *ad placitum,* that is, by stipulation or convention. Meaningful words *(voces significativae)* that have not been agreed upon, such as moans and groans, are excluded.[12]

Maritain, for his part, endeavors to find allusions to the "symbolic" value of images in certain citations from John (such as "ratio imaginis consistit in hoc quod procedat ab alio ut a principio et in similitudinem ejus, ut docet S. Thomas" ("the rationale of an image, therefore, consists in this, that it proceeds from another as from a principle and in a similitude or likeness of that other, as Saint Thomas teaches") (Deely 1985: 219). While it is true that Thomas states (in *Summa Theologiae* I, 35) that "species, prout ponitur ab Hilario in definitione imaginis, importat formam deductam in aliquo ab alio" ("the term *species*, as Hillary claims in his definition of the image, implies a form in one thing derived from another"), what he is talking about is the more traditional definition of the image as bound to the object by a relationship of likeness, not by convention, and this reading does not lend itself to a "symbolist" interpretation. Maritain, on the other hand, makes it the basis for a definition of the poetic symbol as a sign-image endowed with an analogical and ambiguous (or polysemic) relationship with the *signatum.*

---

12. See John of St. Thomas (1930). The *terminus* or term is "id, ex quo simplex conficitur propositio" ("that out of which a simple proposition is made") or "vox significativa ad placitum ex qua simplex conficitur propositio vel oratio" ("a vocal expression significative by stipulation, from which a simple proposition or sentence is constructed") (Deely 1985: 24); while the sign or *signum* is "id, quod potentiae cognoscitivae aliquid aliud a se repraesentat ("that which represents something other than itself to a cognitive power") (Deely 1985: 25). "Essentialiter enim consistit in ordine ad signatum" ("For the being of a sign essentially consists in an order to a signified") (Deely 1985: 218). See also Deely (1988) and Murphy (1991).

Thomas was not unaware of the existence of such sign-images capable of standing in a vaguely ambiguous position vis-à-vis the *signatum;* but he saw them as being the kind of visions that appear to prophets, announcing the fact, for instance, that there will be seven years of plenty by showing seven full ears of corn. This would be a purely poetic proceeding, and here again Thomas implies that it is inferior; so much so that he considers more valid and reliable those prophecies in which, instead of images, we have words, far less equivocal signs, and more desirable in a circumstance as delicate as that of the reception of the divine message.[13]

Saying, however, that in prophecy we encounter "poetic" procedures *does not mean that prophecy and poetic procedures are one and the same thing.*

Let us grant then, in order to get this false issue out of the way, that there does exist, in the authors to whom Maritain refers, a sign-image based on a relationship of analogy—and the fact that it is somewhat played down is surely not all that important, seeing that, here and elsewhere, what is at stake, as we have seen, is more a question of theology than one of aesthetics. Furthermore, the most reliable communicative vehicles are to be preferred, those that are, in other words, less "poetically" ambiguous. However, once the existence of sign-images had been recognized (as the entire allegorical tradition is there to attest), medieval thinkers invariably made every attempt to conventionalize them as much as they could, through their repertories of symbols, attributing a single meaning to every image (or at most a choice amongst four). If there are more—if, for example, in certain bestiaries, the lion may signify both Christ and the Devil—this is because of the overlapping of traditional associations. But the task of medieval hermeneutics,

---

13. "Secundum autem diversificantur gradus prophetiae quantum ad expressionem signorum imaginabilium quibus veritas intelligibilis exprimitur. Et quia signa maxime expressa intelligibilis veritatis sunt verba, ideo altior gradus prophetiae videtur quando propheta audit verba exprimentia intelligibilem veritatem. . . . In quibus etiam signis tanto videtur prophetia esse altior, quanto signa sunt magis expressa" ("Secondly the degrees of this prophecy are differentiated according to the expressiveness of the imaginary signs whereby the intelligible truth is conveyed. And since words are the most expressive signs of intelligible truth, it would seem to be a higher degree of prophecy when the prophet . . . hears words expressive of an intelligible truth. . . . In such like signs prophecy would seem to be the more excellent, according as the signs are more expressive") *Summa Theologiae* trans. by the Fathers of the English Dominican Province, II–II, 174, 3.

however much Maritain, as a reader of Baudelaire, would have preferred it, is not to cultivate a fruitful ambiguity, fraught with manifold suggestions, but on the contrary to identify as expeditiously as possible a definite meaning valid for the context at hand (which is usually scriptural).

The only way Maritain could have defended his position was by placing himself clearly outside the medieval tradition and declaring that modern man had turned the situation on its head. Incapable of choosing between the role of modern symbolist and that of ancient allegorist, on the one hand he throws a veil of ambiguity over his medieval sources, while on the other he undermines the comprehension of his personal proposals by making them sound like superannuated ruminations on Thomistic positions, whereas, if the truth were known, they are in reality assertions typical of contemporary aesthetics. It is not easy to keep one foot in Montparnasse and the other in the Street of Straw (Vicus Straminis=Ruelle au Fouarre). But this untenable ubiquity is the very essence of Maritain's aesthetic. It explains its fascination, however outmoded today, as well as the reason why it was so short-lived.

8.5. Creative Intuition vs. Agent Intellect

And so we come at last to a book like *Creative Intuition in Art and Poetry* (1953), meditated and composed in an English-speaking context by a more mature Maritain, enriched by his intense experience as a reader of contemporary poetic texts and partially weaned from his strict deference to the texts of the Middle Ages.[14]

Here Maritain no longer presents himself as an interpreter of Saint Thomas but as an autonomous thinker, developing the concept of poetry as revelation already outlined in his previous essays.

> By Poetry I mean . . . that intercommunication between the inner being of things and the inner being of the human Self which is a kind of divination. (3)

---

14. *Creative Intuition in Art and Poetry* began life as a cycle of six A. W. Mellon lectures in the fine arts given at the National Gallery of Art in Washington, DC, in the spring of 1952, and was published in 1953 for the Bollingen Foundation by Pantheon Books. Our quotations are taken from this edition.

In other words, poetry obliges us to consider the intellect both in its secret well-springs inside the human soul and as functioning in a non-rational (I do not say antirational) or nonlogical way. (4)

The integral conclusion must, therefore, it seems to me, be set forth as follows: On the one hand, as we have seen apropos of Oriental art, when art only intent on Things succeeds in revealing Things and their hidden meanings, it does also reveal obscurely, despite itself, the creative subjectivity of the artist. . . . On the other hand, when art primarily intent on the artist's Self succeeds in revealing creative subjectivity, it does also reveal obscurely Things and their hidden aspects and meanings—and with greater power of penetration indeed, I mean into the depths of this Corporeal Being itself and this Nature that our hands touch. . . . Our descriptive and inductive inquiry suggests that at the root of the creative act there must be a quite particular intellectual process, without parallel in logical reason, through which Things and the Self are grasped together by means of a kind of experience or knowledge which has no conceptual expression and is expressed only in the artist's work. (33–34)[15]

Nevertheless, in spite of the fact that this theory of poetic knowledge is patently in conflict with the medieval conception of art as *recta ratio factibilium* ("right judgment regarding things to be made"), as an intellectual creation, that is, which adheres to certain rules, Maritain, revealing an unsuspected acrobatic talent, endeavors to demonstrate that his position is not in conflict with Thomistic theory. Although, for the Middle Ages, art was a virtue of the practical intellect, for Maritain the set of rules by which the intellect operates are not rules ossified into a canon that antedates the creation of the work. This is where the notion of "creative intuition" comes in, super-

---

15. It is worth remarking that, in the second chapter of the book, Maritain appeals once more to the Scholastic theory of art, expounding it faithfully. But he continues to imply that primary intuition, a notion foreign to Scholastic theory, must preside over the organization of the operative rules. For Maritain creative intuition is the fundamental rule on which the artist's fidelity depends, and by whose standard it should be judged. For the medieval mind, on the other hand, the rules precede the productive act and its mental conception.

imposing itself on the canonical rules of making and breathing new life into them by virtue of an act that proceeds from the depths of the spirit.

There is no need to stress the fact that it is precisely this concept of an intuitive moment permeating the action and superimposing itself on the rules that is nowhere to be found in Thomas's aesthetics. Maritain seems to be affirming that the idea of creative intuition is peculiar to contemporary and modern poetics; and yet he reintroduces the intuitive moment in the context of classical philosophy when he states that all reasoning, deductive and syllogistic, is based in reality on an intuitive principle, on the existence, that is, of first principles that are not deduced but *seen*. The classical intuition of first principles, however, was still a modality of reason, the very law of its functioning; whereas the poetic intuition of the Moderns is an insight of the imagination: not a logical operation (which discovers) but the final effect of an imaginative operation (which creates).

Maritain does not appear sensitive to this difference. Indeed he maintains that there is no substantial difference between poetry and intellect, both are ascribable to the "same blood." The madness of the Surrealists and Plato's poetic mania, along with the profound intuition of principles (to say nothing of the mystical consciousness that ultimately constitutes the final step in any explicative process of being, as Maritain never tired of insisting), all have their common root in the spiritual makeup of mankind:

> My contention, then, is that everything depends, in the issue we are discussing, on the recognition of the existence of a spiritual unconscious, or rather, preconscious, of which Plato and the ancient wise men were well aware, and the disregard of which in favor of the Freudian unconscious alone is a sign of the dullness of our times. There are two kinds of unconscious, two great domains of psychological activity screened from the grasp of consciousness: the preconscious of the spirit in its living springs, and the unconscious of blood and flesh, instincts, tendencies, complexes, repressed images and desires, traumatic memories, as constituting a closed or autonomous dynamic whole. I would like to designate the first kind of unconscious by the name of *spiritual* or, for the sake of Plato, *musical* unconscious or preconscious; and the second by the name of *automatic* unconscious or *deaf* unconscious— deaf to the intellect, and structured into a world of its own apart from

the intellect; we might also say, in quite a general sense, leaving aside
any particular theory, *Freudian unconscious*. These two kinds of unconscious life are at work at the same time; in concrete existence their
respective impacts on conscious activity ordinarily interfere or inter-
mingle in a greater or less degree. . . . But they are essentially distinct
and thoroughly different in nature. (91–92)

It is enough to think of the ordinary and everyday functioning of
intellect, in so far as intellect is really in activity, and of the way in
which ideas arise in our minds, and every genuine intellectual grasping, or every new discovery, is brought about; it is enough to think of
the way in which our free decisions, when they are really free, are
made, especially those decisions which commit our entire life—to realize that there exists a deep nonconscious world of activity, for the intellect and the will, from which the acts and fruits of human consciousness and the clear perceptions of the mind emerge, and that the
universe of concepts, logical connections, rational discursus and rational deliberation, in which the activity of the intellect takes definite
form and shape, is preceded by the hidden workings of an immense
and primal preconscious life. Such a life develops in night, but in a
night which is translucid and fertile, and resembles that primeval diffused light which was created first, before God made, as Genesis puts it,
"lights in the firmament of heaven to divide the day from the night" so
as to be "for signs, and for seasons, and for days and years." (93–94)

If we are willing to forget the desperate syncretism of Maritain's ploy and
prepared to understand this "creative intuition" in terms of modern and
contemporary aesthetics, his argument appears, if not acceptable, at least
consistent.

What he is saying is that the foundation of a spiritual preconscious different from the unconscious of psychology is the foundation of a *primum* that is
both psychological and ontological, a sort of archetypal Realm of the Moth-
ers from which objective reality and personal spiritual activity itself both
draw their nourishment. In this way we can understand poetic knowledge to
be an affective connaturality that puts us into contact with the secret life of
being itself, and whose principal organ is none other than intuition, prelogical imaginative activity, the only activity capable of grasping a deep reality
that precedes logical distinctions and the duality of thought and being.

This is not an unheard-of philosophical position, and we cannot deny Maritain the right to espouse it. But Maritain insists on making Thomas's doctrine of the intellect the foundation of this conception.

Over and above the conscious rational arguments by means of which reason makes itself manifest, he tells us, there exist the very springs of creativity and love "hidden in the primordial translucid night of the intimate vitality of the soul" (94). Now, he continues: "the Schoolmen were not interested in working out any theory about the unconscious life of the soul" (and we are grateful to him for this admission) "yet their doctrines implied its existence" (96).

To declare that in a given philosophical system a certain problematic issue is not openly mooted, but that its constituent elements, and to some extent its solution, emerge from the system's very framework, is a legitimate position. A system is there to be interpreted, not only by contemporaries but also by posterity, and, since it claims to state truths about the world, it must be ready for any further developments in our knowledge of the world that might follow in its wake. But were *the premises of this doctrine* contained in Scholastic thought?

Maritain takes into consideration the Aristotelian notion of the agent intellect as inherited and elaborated upon by Thomas. The *agent intellect* engages in a process of intellectual abstraction performed on the contents of a *possible intellect,* which in and of itself would not be capable of a similar process of abstraction (given that it receives passively only what is presented to it by the senses). Maritain clearly embraces Thomas's solution, which is opposed to Arabic attempts to locate the agent intellect somewhere outside of the individual soul.

But, in the Thomistic doctrine of the agent intellect, there is no suggestion of any sort of unconscious activity. We could at best speak of a lightning-fast operation, instinctive perhaps, but of which we are fully conscious at the moment we avail ourselves of it, at the moment, that is, when we recognize the universal form in the individual experience.

In fact, in the following comment the problem of the unconscious does not seem to arise (we might also say that Maritain is honest enough, in paraphrasing Thomas's position, not to falsify its terms):

Thus, at a first step, the intelligible content present in the images, and which, in the images, was only intelligible in potency (or capable of *being*

made capable of becoming an object of intellectual vision), is made intelligible in act in a spiritual form (*specie impressa,* impressed pattern),
let us say, in an intelligible germ, which is received from the images by
the intellect, under the activation of the Illuminating Intellect. But this
is not yet enough for the attaining of knowledge. It is necessary that the
intelligible content drawn from the images should be not only intelligible in act, or capable of becoming an object of intellectual vision, but
intellected in act, or actually become an object of intellectual vision.
Then it is the intellect itself, which, having been impregnated by the
impressed pattern or intelligible germ, vitally produces—always under
the activation of the Illuminating Intellect—an inner fruit, a final and
more fully determined spiritual form (*species expressa),* the concept, in
which the content drawn from the images is brought to the very same
state of spirituality-in-act in which the intellect-in-act is, and in which
this now perfectly spiritualized content is seen, is actually an object of
intellectual vision. (97–98)

Here, Maritain's seductive language is already beginning to color, with a
kind of "imaginative efficacy," what is, in Thomas's version, one of the sim-
plest procedures of the human intellect.

From all of the various texts in which Thomas expounds his doctrine of
the intellect,[16] we may derive the following cognitive moments:

(i) when our eyes rest upon a concrete object, our external senses receive
by *immutatio,* or an act of receptivity on the part of the sentient bodily organ,
the various *qualitates sensibiles* inherent in the object, classified as *audibilia,
visibilia, odorabilia, gustabilia* and *tangibilia*—and they (our senses) receive
them in the same way in which wax receives the imprint of the seal, as a *species sensibilis,* still a material phenomenon but already separate from the
thing itself, and, so to speak, with a different makeup, "ut forma coloris in
pupilla, quae non fit per hoc colorata" ("like the form of a color in the pupil of
the eyes, which is not on that account colored") (*Summa Theologiae* I, 78, 3);

(ii) the external senses transmit this *species sensibilis* to the internal senses
(*sensus communis, phantasia, memoria, vis aestimativa,* or *cogitativa*);

(iii) common sense composes and reunites the various data received from
the external senses and elaborates the kind of iconic image of the object

---

16. For a reconstruction of the process in semiotic terms, see Pellerey (1984).

known as the *phantasma,* which is received in the repository of forms or *thesaurus formarum* of the *phantasia;*

(iv) it is at this point that the agent intellect comes into the picture, abstracting from the *phantasma* (which displays all of the qualities of the object, including those that are accidental or individual) the *species intelligibilis,* which is no longer individual but universal (Stone, Tree, Human Being) and offering it to the Possible Intellect as *locus specierum,* which recognizes the *quidditas* of the object, elaborates its universal concept, and performs other operations of elaboration of what was offered to it;[17]

(v) there is of course nothing secret about these essential characteristics, but they are inscribed in the simple and immediate figure—considered as this topological *terminatio*—of the object, since they are at one and the same time its principle of existence and its principle of definability. Point v is fundamental if we are to grasp the full extent of the license taken by Maritain;

(vi) the intellect has only one way to reconsider the characteristics of the concrete object with which the cognitive process began, and it does so through the *reflexio ad phantasmata;* in this reconsideration it certainly knows all of the individual characteristics of the object (in the sense that it "sees" them, so to speak, in the *phantasma*), though it cannot be said that it enters into contact with the individual object, because *cognitum est in cognoscente per modum cognoscentis* ("the known is in the knower in ways peculiar to the knower"), and the *phantasma* is not a material entity like the object. When the external senses received an impression of heat, they "felt" heat by *immutatio* or immutation. When the intellect performs the *reflexio ad phantasmata* or abstraction from phantasms, it "knows" that the object was hot, but it does not "feel" it.[18]

---

17. "Intellectus possibilis intelligit hominem non secundum quod est HIC homo sed in quantum est HOMO simpliciter, secundum rationem speciei" ("The possible intellect understands man, not as THIS man, but simply as MAN, according to man's specific nature") (*Contra gentiles* II, 73).

18. "Singulare in rebus materialibus intellectus noster directe et primo cognoscere non potest. Cuius ratio est, quia principium singularitatis in rebus materialibus est material individualis, intellectus autem noster, sicut supra dictum est, intelligit abstrahendo speciem intelligibilem ab huiusmodi material. Quod autem a materia individuali abstrahitur, est universale. Unde intellectus noster directe non est cognoscitivus nisu universalium. Indirecte autem, et quasi per quandam reflexionem, potest cognoscere singulare, quia, sicut supra dictum est, etiam postquam species

There is no direct connection between the image in the pupil and the concrete stone. Therefore, in the context of Thomas's epistemology a sort of transparent diaphragm is created situated between the intellect, the organ of abstraction, and the individual object, with all the properties that accrue to it from being made concrete in a *materia signata quantitate* ("quantatively determined matter").

To bridge this gap that occurs in every act of perception, the intellect has but one recourse: on the basis of what it "sees" in the *phantasma,* it is able to proceed to judgments ("this stone has such and such dimensions, it lies in such and such a place, it is illuminated by the sun, etc."). Therefore, in order to speak of the concrete stone, no act of *intuition* is involved (in Thomistic epistemology intuition *does not exist*), but an act of *judgment,* laborious, slow, agonizing, and painstaking.[19] Nevertheless, even if we resolve the ques-

---

intelligibiles abstraxit, non potest secundum eas actu intelligere nisi convertendo se ad phantasmata, in quibus species intelligibiles intelligit, ut dicitur in III de anima. Sic igitur ipsum universale per speciem intelligibilem directe intelligit; indirecte autem singularia, quorum sunt phantasmata. Et hoc modo format hanc propositionem, Socrates est homo" ("Directly and immediately our intellect cannot know the singular in material realities. The reason is that the principle of singularity in material things is individual matter, and our intellect—as said before—understands by abstracting species from this sort of matter. But what is abstracted from individual matter is universal. Therefore our intellect has direct knowledge only of universals. Indirectly and by a quasi-reflection, on the other hand, the intellect can know the singular, because, as mentioned before, even after it has abstracted species it cannot actually understand by means of them except by a return to sense images in which it understands the species, as Aristotle says [in *De anima* III]. Therefore, in this sense, it is the universal that the intellect understands directly by means of the species, and singulars (represented in sense images) only indirectly. And it is in this way that it formulates the proposition, 'Socrates is a man'") (*Summa Theologiae* I, 86, 1 co.). "Species igitur rei, secundum quod est in phantasmatibus, non est intelligibilis actu. . . . Sicut nec species coloris est sensata in actu secundum quod est in lapide, sed solum secundum quod est in pupilla" ("Wherefore the species of a thing according as it is in the phantasms is not actually intelligible . . . even so neither is the species of color actually perceived according as it is in the stone, but only according as it is in the pupil) (*Contra gentiles* II, 59).

19. On this resolution of the contemplation of the concrete in the discursive act of judgment, which characterizes Thomistic epistemology and is important if we

tion in these terms, we cannot deny that Thomas does not provide a satisfactory theory of knowledge of the individual—and consequently thinkers like Duns Scotus and Ockham will be led to seek other solutions.[20]

Hence, *it is not possible* that for Thomas the illuminating power of the intellect should instantaneously penetrate the individual recesses of the stone, seizing its eternal form in the quick of the matter with which it is imbued, in a unity that precedes the distinctions of reason, in an original and profound contact with the real, individualized in a form and made sensible in a matter dense with echoes and reverberations. *Pace* Maritain, Thomas's intellect cannot be identified with the profligacy of an intuition (in the modern sense of the term, and provided this idea of intuition remains viable and that we do not embrace Peirce's anti-intuitionist polemic) that seizes the veining of a piece of fruit, the nuances of a sunset, the texture of a layer of paint, and discovers in them the presence of that profound unity by means of which everything hangs together and is permeated by the same indivisible spiritual presence.[21]

---

are to understand the type of aesthetic that derives from it, we dealt at length in chapter 7 of Eco (1956) (English translation Eco [1988]). In what follows we will have occasion to mention the article by Roland-Gosselin, "Peut-on parler d'intuition intellectuelle dans la philosophie thomiste?" In open polemic with Maritain's positions, he concluded: "Sensation is an intuition of the sensible as such. Reflection, or psychological awareness, is an intuition of our acts, but determined primarily by their object. The other 'views,' more or less direct and immediate, that we have at our disposal do not attain the single reality. To reach concrete existence, that of things or the substantial existence of the ego, a detour or a discourse is called for." ["La sensation est une intuition du sensible comme tel. La réflexion, ou conscience psychologique, est une intuition de nos actes, mais déterminée premièrement par leur objet. Les autres 'vues' plus ou moins directes et immédiates, dont nous disposons, n'atteignent pas la réalité singulière. Pour rejoindre l'existence concrète, celle des choses ou l'existence substantielle du moi, un détour, ou un discours s'impose à elles"] (Roland-Gosselin 1930: 730).

20. Only the external senses know individual things, but it is probably a metaphor to say that they know, because in fact they register and do not know themselves (*Contra gentiles* II, 66). On the limits of Thomistic epistemology, see also Mahoney (1982).

21. In Eco (1956) we stated that this reconsideration of the concrete object occurs for Thomas only in the act of judgment. We could hardly compel him to say more, but the fact remains that in this way too the enjoyment of the concrete always

We might be tempted to think that Maritain—who had few qualms, despite the four centuries that separate the two, about turning with a certain insouciance from Thomas to John—is attributing to the former what he finds in his Counter-Reformation disciple. But when we go back and read the pages (*Cursus* III, 10, 4, pp. 322 et seq.) that John devotes to this very question of how the intellect is able to know singular material things, we observe that the disciple does not in fact break with the teachings of his master, but on the contrary, with the example of the Scotist "heresy" before his eyes, he ups the ante: "Non potest intellectus dirette ferri ad haec objecta prout modificata illis materialibus conditionibus, quae singularizant, se prout ad illis abstractis." It is only through the senses that an object is apprehended in its material particularities. When it is grasped "per modum quidditatis" ("in the mode of a definable character") by the intellect, then it is grasped "sine materialibus conditionibus loci et temporis etc" ("without the material conditions of place and time") (p. 325). To know means to abstract and to tend toward the individuation of the *quidditas*, setting aside those material particularities that make the object something singular. It is not so much that

---

takes place at rarefied intellectual heights, where the thing is considered only through the *reflexio* on what is already a phantasm. Could Thomas have failed to recognize that the thing, even after having been known (and reduced it to a phantasm), could be reconsidered through an activity that brought the senses into play once more? Not that he could not rule out the possibility that, after perceiving a thing a first time, we might perceive it again other times. He probably considered this event as a second act of perception, no different from the first, and his theory of knowledge obviously had to define the act of perception in its basic dynamic, without worrying about how often a human being may accidentally happen to perceive something. Which would perhaps explain why he was not interested in the type of experience that modern aesthetic theories have chosen to call intuitive because it seemed too complex to consider it as part of a process beginning over and over again, made up of hypotheses, inferences, trial and error. To conceive of such an idea, he would have had to speak not only of the possibility of a *reflexio ad phantasmata* but also of a subsequent *reflexio ad qualitates sensibiles*. In other words, he would have had to understand the comprehension of an object, not as a simple act, a *simplex apprehensio*, but as a never-ending process. Concerned, however, with guaranteeing the truth of our every perceptive contact with reality, he does not go so far; indeed he could not go so far. If we were to go back and come to terms with sensible experience after having grasped the *quidditas*, as if we might have made a mistake, then the entire doctrine of the intellect would be in trouble.

the intellect cannot grasp the singular; it cannot grasp the material that singularizes the object. John is citing Thomas (*Summa Theologiae* I, 86, 1 ad 3), where he says that "singulare non repugnat intelligibilitati inquantum est singulare, sed inquantum est materiale, quia nihil intelligitur nisi immaterialiter" ("the singular is incompatible with intelligibility not insofar as it is singular, but insofar as it is material, for nothing can be understood except immaterially").

In Maritain's account of the function of the agent intellect, when confronted with a concrete object such as a stone it confines itself to understanding "stone" and nothing else. For, if we insist on translating its function into modern terms, it has nothing to do with a preconscious activity of the soul, *but constitutes at most the transcendental possibility of conferring a form on the data of the senses.* Naturally, since Thomas is not Kant, the agent intellect does not "confer" anything of its own accord, it simply "recognizes" what was already there in the object but which, without its abstraction, would remain unknowable.

Now Maritain, in spite of being aware of all of the limitations of the Thomistic concept of the agent intellect, tends nevertheless to define this "fundamental source of light" as "hidden in the unconscious of the spirit." And in so doing, what he means by *unconscious* is what is instead *formal* (or, in Kantian terms, transcendental). That the effect of the operation of the agent intellect (that is, the concepts of all the things that I see and recognize according to universal species) may be repressed and stored in the psychological unconscious is a phenomenon that concerns psychology, not the theory of knowledge—and in any case it concerns modern psychology, not the psychology of Thomas. Failure to insist on this distinction means taking the agent intellect for something that it is not.

To say that "we know what we are thinking, but not how we are thinking" may be *ad mentem Divi Thomae;* but this does not make it legitimate to affirm that our knowledge is therefore the beginning of an intuition, at least insofar as we attribute this conclusion to Thomas. If intuition is a nondecomposable act, a swift vision of the spirit, intuition has nothing to do with knowledge *ad mentem Divi Thomae,* precisely because the act of knowledge in Thomas is *decomposable*—swift, instantaneous, if you will, but decomposable. Whereas *we,* in other words people who perceive and think every day, "know what we are thinking, but not how we are thinking," Thomas's

philosophy knows perfectly well (or presumes to know) how we are thinking and demonstrates how, breaking it down (or *decomposing it*) into each of
its successive phases.

And if an act is decomposable, where does intuition come in, the category
that philosophy has come up with to designate those acts that are not
decomposable—rationalizable through a series of successive moments that
render them by that very token a form of *discourse?*

Thomas, as Maritain realizes, speaks of knowledge by connaturality apropos of mystical knowledge.[22] But, in extending the concept to the aesthetic
experience (in saying, in other words, that aesthetic experience is a form of
mystical experience or vice versa), the Paleo-Thomist runs a twofold risk. The
first is for the aesthetic experience to seem closer to the *noche oscura* of the
mystics than to the ordered Scholastic vision—and, if he were not determined to be seen as a Paleo-Thomist at all costs, Maritain might even admit
it, since this after all is the position he arrives at. The second is for a position
typical of the modern mind—and of the modern mind with which Maritain
ought to find himself least in agreement—to be taken as implicit: namely,
that for contemporary man there is only one type of mystical relationship—
the aesthetic relationship—left (because God is probably dead). And this
would be fin-de-siècle aestheticism. Stephen Dedalus's confession at the end
of Joyce's *Portrait* points to no other conclusion. How does Maritain the
Paleo-Thomist get there? He gets there in an ambiguous way, especially as far
as his Thomism is concerned.

---

22. See *Summa Theologiae* II–II, 45, 2. There are certain acts of virtue that we
can judge and evaluate in the light of intellectual knowledge. But at the moment of
acting, if the *habitus* is deeply rooted in us, the rule acts via a certain connaturality
by which it is realized without our having a clear intellectual awareness. Knowledge by connaturality, if you like, but of a fixed rule, not the intuition of a hitherto
unknown possibility of being. *Sapientia* is a gift of the Spirit, the connate ability to
apply the right rule at the right moment. But *sapentia* presupposes the existence of
fixed rules, plastically adaptable to contingent situations, but always in accord with
a possibility that the intellect will subsequently be able to clarify. This is not the
kind of knowledge that implies a reconstruction of the world along lines forever
foreign to the intellect, understood by many of the Romantic and contemporary
poets whom Maritain cites in support of his claims (from Novalis to Rimbaud and
on to Char, Eluard, and John Crowe Ransom, etc.; see Maritain 1953: ch. 4).

The same mystical emphasis reappears when Maritain revisits another typically Thomistic (but not exclusively Thomistic) notion—that of beauty as a transcendental property of being (which implies the realizability of value at all levels of existence, albeit in analogical form). Maritain distinguishes between poetry—defined as the primary intuition with its correlative expressive impulse—and beauty. And the latter appears to him as a kind of ever-receding goal which poetry is constantly trying to catch up with, without ever completely succeeding. The poetic impulse brings into play the artistic capability, but this process always retains an element of the inchoate; it is never resolved in a final conquest but remains instead in a permanent state of tension—which is mystical or Platonic in nature. This tension could also be inferred from Thomas's doctrine of the transcendental nature of the beautiful, but only if Thomistic philosophy were to nurture such an anxiety in the face of the infinite that the presence of the *analogia entis* proved to be no longer satisfactory, and man were to seek, diabolically, by the roundabout routes of poetry, to violate a threshold that negative theology never crosses. A medieval notion if you will, though late medieval, typical of the Flemish and German mystics.

For Thomas, the beautiful is that "in cuius aspectu seu cognitione quietatur appetitus" ("in whose sight or cognition the appetite is quieted"), whereas the appetite for the infinite is never quieted in a mystic like Meister Eckhart: "nihil tam distans a quolibet quam ejus oppositum. Deus autem et creatura opponuntur ut unum et innumeratum opponuntur numero et numerato et numerabili" (*In Sapientiam,* VII, 14).[23]

Maritain's frequent citations from Poe and Baudelaire, as well as from other twentieth-century poets, are evidence of just how "modern" his anxieties are; but they fail to support his claim to be recovering Thomism. In point of fact, there is no need to go all the way back to medieval philosophy to clarify Maritain's position; we must look instead to the core of Romantic

---

23. It has been pointed out that the whole of Eckhart's implied aesthetics consists in the depiction of a tension toward a goal that is never realized, an aspiration that never finds rest. It finds its typical expression in the disproportionate verticalities of the Rhine cathedrals, whereas Thomistic aesthetics reminds us of the more composed Italian Gothic in which beauty is measured on a more human scale, capable of being perceived and enjoyed without requiring a violent laceration of the imagination and the sensibility (cf. Assunto 1961).

aesthetics. We need only reread what Schelling, an author cited by Maritain, had to say about art (*Werke* I, III). All of philosophy, according to Schelling, has its origin in an absolute principle that cannot be grasped or communicated through descriptions and concepts, but can only be intuited. This intuition is the "organ of philosophy." But since it is an intellectual intuition not a sensible one, it is a purely interior intuition, which can become objective only as a consequence of a second intuition—aesthetic intuition. Furthermore, if aesthetic intuition is intellectual intuition made objective, then art is the only true organ, and at the same time document, of philosophy, bearing constant and continual witness to what philosophy cannot represent externally, that is, the unconscious as it operates and produces. This is the root of the theoretical position spelled out in *Creative Intuition*.

In a form that has had such a telling influence on contemporary sensibility, especially in the Anglo-Saxon cultural circles that influenced the later Maritain, this same doctrine is to be found in Coleridge, as was usefully pointed out by Mayoux (1960).[24] It is not merely a question of similarities. Maritain is drawing on an entire tradition that nourished the poetry of the

---

24. For Coleridge, poetry is an act of analogical knowledge based on love. As he states in *On Poesy or Art*: "The artist must imitate that which is within the thing, that which is active through form and figure and discourses to us by symbols, as we unconsciously imitate those whom we love" (http://www.bartleby.com/27/17 .html). There exists, beyond the language of artificially stimulated hallucination, the possibility of a more authentic language of nature, through which the invisible communicates its existence to finite being. Nature is an alphabet, says Coleridge, and, obsessed by the mystery of the hieroglyph, he declares that what we call nature is a poem that lies hidden in a secret and mysterious script. In the years during which he composed what was to become his *Biographia Literaria*, Coleridge breaks with Kant and turns to Schelling, because he cannot tolerate Kant's critical inflexibility or confine himself to phenomena. In chapter 13 "On the imagination," he makes a demiurgic claim: "The primary IMAGINATION I hold to be the living Power and prime Agent of all human Perception, and as a repetition in the finite mind of the eternal act of creation in the infinite I AM" (Coleridge 1983, I, 304). See also the following quotation from *Anima Poetae*: "In looking at the objects of Nature while I am thinking, as at yonder moon dim-glimmering through the dewy window-pane, I seem rather to be seeking, as it were asking, a symbolic language for something within me that already and forever exists, than observing anything new."

last two centuries (it is no accident in fact that he frequently cites Coleridge), and, though he may invoke Saint Thomas, he is in fact getting closer and closer to the spirit of Romantic idealism: a paradoxical conclusion that he would no doubt be reluctant to accept, but that a conscientious exegesis cannot set aside *pro bono pacis.*

A reader of *Creative Intuition* unaware of its medieval allusions would certainly be fascinated by the whole conception of poetry as a magical act and would have to concede that it is defended with considerable rhetorical ability. But what is disturbing is the specious use of a thinker from the past to support the author's own theoretical position.

Still, what we have here, rather than a case of intellectual dishonesty, is a rather primitive conception of historiography. When someone operates with the metaphysical, historiographical, and methodological conviction that there exists only one philosophy and that that philosophy is a *philosophia perennis,* then the historiographical dimension, as understood by the modern philosopher, heir to historicism, ceases to exist. Nor is the initial act by which the attribute of perenniality is bestowed on a given historically determined philosophy an historiographical act: because its purpose is not to circumscribe the character of an historical phenomenon but to enunciate a truth regarding the nature of human thought.

Maritain's method of reading his medieval sources has a lot in common with that of the medieval philosopher who declared his respect for the *auctoritas* of the Fathers while claiming to be a dwarf on a giant's shoulders. When a medieval thinker was convinced of the truth of an assertion, he bolstered its legitimacy by claiming that it was to be found in his *auctores.* The most creative medieval philosophers, however, never recognized anything as true simply because it had been handed down from the Fathers. If anything, they did the opposite—when they found something they believed was true, they attributed it to the Fathers. They believed implicitly, then, not that everything that was part of tradition was true, but that everything that was true was part of tradition. Maritain does the same: attuned to all the subtleties of the modern sensibility, he welcomes its suggestions, attributing them, however, without further ado, to the sensibility of the Middle Ages. This behavior hides in fact an unconscious historicist conviction, which holds that the timeless treasure of truth *grows* and that the true Saint Thomas is not the Saint Thomas of the thirteenth century, for whom creative intuition does not exist, but the Saint Thomas of the twentieth century, who is now speaking through the lips of his faithful disciple. *Philosophia* is then *perennis*, not because, once formulated, it no longer changes, but precisely because it is constantly changing, and its definitive formulation always belongs to tomorrow. Which is an acceptable conclusion too, as long as it is made unequivocally clear (and even if, by making it clear, the appeal to the notion of a *philosophia perennnis* no longer has any meaning).

8.6. The Historiographical Lesson of De Bruyne

The extent of Maritain's historiographical highhandedness becomes clear when we compare it with the work of another author who, though likewise a Catholic and a Thomist by formation, was nonetheless able, in his work *as a historian,* to keep a distance between his own thought and that of the authors he studied. That author was Edgar De Bruyne.

De Bruyne published his *Études d'esthétique médiévale* in 1946. In 1940 he had brought out his *Philosophie van de Kunst* and in 1942 *Het Aestetisch beleven* and *De Philosophie van Martin Heidegger*. It is impossible to believe that a work of the amplitude of the *Études* (around 1,200 pages in the 1998 Albin Michel edition) could have been composed in the space of the three intervening years—years that were in any case among the most terrible and turbulent in Belgian history. What we had was instead the fruit of over a decade of research. The problems of medieval aesthetics had already been the subject, as we will see, of an essay De Bruyne wrote in 1930. But even making allowance for decades of work we can only marvel at how such a vast quantity of material, often unearthed in out-of-the-way pages of hundreds of works from Boethius to Duns Scotus, could have been assembled by a single man in such a brief span of time. Furthermore, let us not forget that at that time electronic searches and scanning technology did not exist, and all the material had to be laboriously hunted down in the thousands of pages of the *Patrologia Latina,* not to mention the other sources, and diligently catalogued (by hand, one imagines, working in goodness knows what monastic libraries). So we can't help smiling at the reaction, when the work appeared, of a number of critics who reproached De Bruyne for stopping at Duns Scotus and not considering Byzantine culture, for not citing Focillon and even for producing an anthology of quotations without arriving at a theoretical synthesis—thank heaven is all we can say, considering where the desire for a theoretical synthesis had led Maritain.[25]

To assess the impact of the work on the historiography of medieval aesthetics we have only to conduct a brief bibliographical survey. Croce consecrated 398 pages of his *Aesthetics* (1902[1950]) to the history of the problem: of these pages only *four* were devoted to the Middle Ages, and only to conclude that "almost all the tendencies of ancient aesthetics were continued through tradition and reappeared by spontaneous generation in the medieval centuries," but "it could be affirmed that the literary and artistic doctrines and opinions of the Middle Ages, with a few minor exceptions, are more valuable for the history of culture than for the general history of the science of aesthetics" (1902[1950]: 129).

Bosanquet in his *History of Aesthetic* (1904) allots a mere 30 out of a total of 500 pages to the Middle Ages, with the reductive heading "Some traces of the continuity of aesthetic consciousness throughout the Middle Ages." But he begins with the reevaluation of the medieval centuries by the pre-Raphaelites and Walter Pater, treating medieval thought, then, as the object of Decadent nostalgia and reminding the reader that modern aesthetics begins only when the problem of art criticism and that of the reconciliation of reason and sensibility are formulated—problems that the Middle Ages had ignored until the fourteenth century.

Saintsbury, in his *History of Criticism and Literary Taste in Europe* (1900–1904), speaks not of philosophers or theologians but of artists. He dedicates two chapters of the book to the Middle Ages ("Medieval criticism" and "The

---

25. For a review of these critiques, see Michel Lemoine's afterword to the 1998 Albin Michel edition. If we insist on looking for absences in De Bruyne's three volumes, the first great absence (somewhat surprisingly, since he belongs to the same Netherlandic culture) is Huizinga's *Waning of the Middle Ages*, published in 1919, which contains a number of acute observations on the medieval aesthetic sensibility (and not merely in the later centuries upon whose threshold De Bruyne chose to stop). On the other hand, talking about absences, Curtius, who had read everything, published his *European Literature and the Latin Middle Ages* [*Europäische Literatur und Lateinisches Mittelalter*] in 1948, and in it he fails to mention De Bruyne—perhaps because the Bruges edition, published two years earlier, seems to have had a practically clandestine circulation.

contribution of the medieval period to literary criticism"), discussing, however, only rhetorical theories, allegory, grammar, and so on.

Again, in 1935, Magnino's *Die Kunstliteratur* devoted only twenty-four pages to the medieval theory of art, while in 1937 *Die Literarästhetik des europäischen Mittelalters* by Glunz was more concerned with the evolution of literary taste than with aesthetic theory, though in the case of a few authors he did take into account the philosophical influence of Neo-Platonism.[26] The decisive year was 1946. By an amazing coincidence (or maybe not, if you subscribe to the notion of the Zeitgeist), there appeared in the same year the three volumes of De Bruyne's *Études d'ésthétique médiévale*, Pouillon's essay, "La beauté, propriété transcendantale chez les Scolastiques (1220–1270),"[27] which gathered together for the first time the various texts concerning the inclusion of beauty in the list of the transcendental properties of being, and Panofsky's book on Abbot Suger, in which the translation of Suger's text and Panofsky's commentary on it gave a lively and fascinating picture of the taste and aesthetic culture of a man of the twelfth century.[28]

With these contributions two phenomena of capital importance occurred: in the first place they demonstrated that the aesthetic problem had been present throughout the medieval centuries, not in a repetitive fashion but through a series of changes in perspective and genuine theoretical innovations (though almost always camouflaged by the use of a uniform philosophical lexicon); and, secondly, the various thinkers were treated correctly from a historiographical point of view, attempting that is to demonstrate what they had said with reference to the historical and theoretical framework of the philosophy of their time, without endeavoring to modernize them at all costs.

By 1954, within fifteen years of the appearance of the *Études*, Montano, in volume 5 of the *Grande Antologia Filosofica*, could devote 160 pages to an anthology illustrating aesthetics in Christian thought with commentaries clearly inspired by the *Études*. In the same year the forty-three pages on the Middle

---

26. But Edgar De Bruyne, reviewing Glunz in 1938 in the *Revue néo-scolastique de philosophie*, criticized him for not mentioning the great theoretical currents like the aesthetics of proportion and light, or the psychology of the Victorines.
27. See Pouillon (1946).
28. See Panofsky (1946).

Ages in the *History of Aesthetics* of Gilbert and Kuhn (revised edition), while they do not acknowledge De Bruyne, certainly take advantage of his work, presumably via secondary sources. There follow Eco (1956, 1959, 1987a), Simson (1956), Panofsky (1957), Holt (1957), Assunto (1961), and Kovach (1961). In 1962 the *History of Aesthetics* by Tatarkiewicz devotes an entire volume to the Middle Ages and, although the author advances a number of critical reservations with regard to the *Études,* he is clearly indebted to them. And we are entitled to wonder whether, without the *Études,* the four volumes of De Lubac's *Exégèse médiévale* (1959–1964), with their countless references to De Bruyne's pioneering work, would ever have seen the light of day.[29]

And this is only to cite the more important monographs, without counting the shorter contributions. From the 4 pages in Croce to Assunto's 500 and the 362 of Tatarkiewicz we can measure the extent of the change in perspective of which De Bruyne was the pioneer.

A development of these proportions can be explained, not only by the enormous mass of materials that De Bruyne made available to scholars, but also by the soundness of his historical method. Apart from Pouillon, who confined himself in any case to rediscovering and publishing texts, De Bruyne was the first to forget his own Thomism and to outline a genuine history of medieval aesthetic ideas as they had been formulated at the time, without any attempt to modernize them whatever it took. A commendable achievement, since only through this gesture of honest erudition was he able to render his idea of Middle Ages "up-to-date" (in the sense of interesting for the contemporary reader).

First and foremost, De Bruyne liberates the notion of a medieval aesthetic from its identification with the Thomistic aesthetic. He begins his *Études* by affirming that "studying the work of Saint Thomas Aquinas we frequently asked ourselves what was the historical and cultural background into which his reflections on art and beauty were to be placed."[30]

To respond to this initial query, he *de-Thomisticizes* medieval aesthetics, reminding us not only that the Middle Ages had reflected on art and the

---

29. In the index of names, however, the reader should remember to look for Bruyne and not *De* Bruyne.

30. The first study devoted by our author to Thomas is S. *Thomas d'Aquin. Le milieu.—L'homme.—La vision du monde* (Paris-Brussels: Gabriel Beauchesne, 1928).

beautiful well before Thomas, but also that there had not been a single school of aesthetics but many, each of them different in some respect from the others.

On the one hand, he demonstrated how Thomas came at the end of a tradition that could be traced back to Augustine and Boethius, and before that to Neo-Platonism and Pythagoreanism. And merely by doing this, he made it possible for those who followed him in restudying Thomas's aesthetics to see what sources had provided Thomas with some of his ideas; when he had followed in the wake of tradition without making any original contribution of his own; and when instead he had said something new. On the other hand, he pointed out that, side by side with a Thomistic aesthetics (to which previous scholarship had reduced the rich variety of medieval speculation),[31] there existed the aesthetics of the school of Chartres, of the Victorines, of Grosseteste, of Albertus Magnus, of Bonaventure, of Duns Scotus (and our list must end here, otherwise it would amount to reproducing the index of the *Études*).[32]

———————

31. Not by everyone of course. It is worth recalling the *Scriptorum de musica medii aevi nova series* by Edmond de Coussemaker (Paris, 1864–1876), Clemens Baeumker's *Witelo* (Münster, 1908), E. Lutz, "Die Ästhetik Bonaventuras," in *Festgabe zum 60: Geburstag Clem, Baeumker* (Münster, 1913), Johan Huizinga, *Herbst des Mittelalters* [The Waning of the Middle Ages] (Haarlem, 1919), Walter Müller, *Das Problem der Seelenschönheit im Mittelalter* (Berlin, 1926), Clare Riedl, *Grosseteste On Light* (Milwaukee, 1942), Karl Svoboda, *L'esthétique de Saint Augustin et ses sources* (Paris-Brno 1927), not to mention Menendez y Pelayo (1883), Edmond Faral (1924), J. Schlosser Magnino (1924), H. H. Glunz (1937), and Henri Pouillon (1939).

32. The goal of an historiographically correct reconstruction is not merely *not* to attempt to modernize one's authors. Presenting them as they actually were sometimes renews their relevance, in the sense that it allows us to understand better the relationships between ourselves and certain cultural phenomena that had hitherto been difficult to fathom. We may take as an example one of the most intriguing chapters of the *Études,* that on Hisperic–Latin (or Hiberno-Latin) aesthetics (the fourth chapter of the first volume). Today we possess reliable critical editions of the *Hisperica Famina* (Herren, 1974) and of the *Epitomae* and *Epistolae* of Virgil of Toulouse (Polara, 1979), but De Bruyne was compelled to work with nineteenth-century sources or directly with the *Patrologia*. The literary sensibility with which he revisits the phenomenon of the Asiatic style is completely modern (and at times betrays a penchant for the stammering Latin of the dark centuries almost worthy of Huysmans), even if some of his critics have blamed him for appealing too casually to categories such as "Baroque." True, he too was a man of his own day and had

De Bruyne's *Études* begin with Boethius and end with Duns Scotus. What changes occurred during this period? In this connection De Bruyne played a rather curious game—and it is unclear whether he was aware of the ambiguity of his position. On the one hand he endeavored to demonstrate that medieval aesthetics comprises a series of themes and ideas that span, often without modification, eight centuries of reflection on the beauty of God, nature, and art. Thus, in 1938, in a review of Glunz (1937), whereas Glunz had underscored, in our opinion correctly, an evolution in medieval taste, De Bruyne objected that it was problematic to speak, apropos of the Middle Ages, of evolution, because the various tendencies were always present, and he defined medieval artistic culture as "polyphonic." But, at the same time (and we have only to read the general index to the *Études*), it is apparent that, even though over the centuries the various authors constantly come back to the same themes, the material is arranged according to a historical and not a thematic sequence, beginning with Boethius and arriving eventually at Duns Scotus, while in his introduction he writes that he would have liked to dedicate a fourth volume to the period 1300–1450, thereby anticipating the possible objection that he had ended the story too abruptly.

De Bruyne also published, between 1952 and 1955, a history of aesthetics *(Geschiedenis van de aesthetica)* which begins with Greco-Roman thought, picks up on his work on the Middle Ages, and arrives via Dante at Humanism and the Renaissance, touching (though rather summarily) on the thought of later medieval authors like Buridan and Ockham and ending up with Denis the Carthusian (it is in these last pages that he finally cites Huizinga!). In this history of aesthetics it is more readily apparent that De Bruyne

---

a number of reservations regarding that "barbaric" taste, whereas you and I might be tempted to see those barbarians as precursors of James Joyce. Lemoine (1998), however, reminds us that, at the same time and apropos of the same texts, Henri Leclerc in the *Dictionnaire de l'Archéologie chrétienne et de liturgie* (1920), which he compiled with Fernand Cabrol, insisted that the Irish monks who composed and read the *Hisperica Famina* "were madmen who nowadays would find themselves relegated to an asylum for the mentally infirm." De Bruyne on the other hand was able to identify the links between these "demential" exercises and the miniatures of the Book of Kells and other masterpieces of Irish art, with the result that the pages he devotes to the Hisperic aesthetic are among the finest ever dedicated to this mysterious chapter of medieval culture.

had in mind an evolution over time of aesthetic thought—even if at this point he found himself having to come to grips with the phenomenon of the Renaissance, leaving behind the Middle Ages and its "polyphony."

In the case of the eight centuries he is concerned with, and however much he may stress a certain thematic coherence, he continually draws our attention to the presence of lines of development and therefore of a certain "progress." It would be going too far to attribute to him an Hegelian view of history, but he is certainly not unaware of transformations—we might go so far as to call them paradigm shifts—that do not allow us to speak of a Middle Ages that is constantly marking time. It would have been hard in fact for De Bruyne to deny that progress, when we consider how certain themes such as that of light assumed different valencies when they were transposed from the Neo-Platonic context of John Scotus Eriugena to that of the Aristotelian hylomorphism of the thirteenth century.

In 1947, fearful perhaps lest his *Études* not receive the circulation they deserved, De Bruyne published *L'esthétique du Moyen Age,* a more manageable volume of less than 300 pages, in a more compact format, in which he provided a kind of synthesis of his major work (this essay is reprinted as an appendix to the *Études* in the most recent Albin Michel edition of 1998). Unfortunately, out of concern perhaps that it would have made the book too cumbersome, De Bruyne fails to document any of his citations, referring his reader to the *Études* for his sources. As a consequence, the work, while too erudite for the nonspecialist reader, is of no use to the scholar. In any case, it is no longer arranged according to an historical sequence but thematically (the index refers to the sources, the sense of the beautiful, of art, and so on). The author is certainly at pains, in the context of one of these themes, to call attention to fresh developments,[33] but the polyphonic complexity previously mentioned becomes more evident, especially in a chapter devoted to the constants, in which the persistence throughout the period of the themes of musical proportion, light, symbolism, and allegory are underscored. We

---

33. See, for example, on p. 508, apropos of the sentiment of the beautiful: "It is not until the 13th century that the problem of distinguishing between the higher and the lower senses is posited in an explicit fashion" ["Ce n'est qu'au XIIIe siècle que le problème de la distinction des sens supérieurs et inférieurs se pose de manière explicite"].

may say, then, that De Bruyne was probably aware that his study was continuously open to two readings or to a single reading capable of exploiting the ongoing opposition between constants and innovations.

Be that as it may, De Bruyne's Middle Ages manages to deliver honest-to-goodness coups de théâtre (never of course announced with excessive stridency, in keeping with the custom of the day) perpetrated by authors who claimed to be nothing more than prudent and faithful annotators of the traditional texts whereas in reality, generation after generation, they were ensuring the evolution of both the aesthetic sensibility and the theories of art and the beautiful.

If one of the virtues of modernity is the intellectual courage whereby (according to a brilliant formulation by none other than Maritain) after Descartes every thinker is a debutant in the absolute, De Bruyne was not lacking in that virtue, as could be demonstrated by examining the texts in which he does not practice historiography but instead enunciates his own philosophy. If the Middle Ages made a virtue out of prudence, De Bruyne exercised that virtue as a historian. Reviewing in 1933, thirteen years before the publication of the *Études*, for the *Revue néoscolastique* a work by Wencelius, *La philosophie de l'art chez les néo-scolastiques de langue française* (1932), he contended that Thomas, contrary to what many Neo-Scholastic thinkers asserted, did not offer a complete aesthetic system: "we cannot see how the Angelic Doctor was able to reconcile in a truly organic whole what came to him from Neo-Platonism via Pseudo-Dionysius and what he borrowed from the Aristotelian theory of pleasures" (De Bruyne 1933: 416). Perhaps he had partially revised his judgment thirteen years later. What is striking, however, is his decision to consider his author in the light of philology and not apologetics.

8.7. The Problem of an Intellectual Intuition

In De Bruyne's review of Wencelius, we may discern, occasionally, between the lines, a polemical stance with regard to the use to which Maritain had put the texts of Saint Thomas. He criticizes Wencelius's exaggerated insistence on the objective and transcendental nature of the beautiful and insists instead on the relationship between beauty and the perceiving subject. As we have seen, this is the issue on which Maritain had overstepped the mark. De Bruyne makes it clear that to speak of the relationship with the subject is not the same as being "subjective" (an accusation that, especially given the historical moment, a philosopher inspired by Thomas could not countenance, given that subjectivity—what the nineteenth century had referred to as the "Kantian poison"—was the bête noire of the Neo-Thomists). He wrote that, if one wishes to speak about the transcendental nature of beauty, and at the same time about the relation of beauty to the knowing subject, all we need do is apply the Thomistic definition of God as Supreme Beauty to the pleasure of contemplating His beauty.

Maritain had attempted to identify both aesthetic pleasure and the creative act of the poetic imagination with an intuition that gave the impression of being overly subjective. As we see from his reading of the medieval authors, De Bruyne had realized that Maritain's intuition did not have much to do with a "Kantian" subject, but had instead a great deal to do with a mystical intuition in which the subject identifies with (immerses himself in) the ontological splendor that fascinates and inspires him, in a union in which the two aspirations appear to become intermingled.

For De Bruyne on the other hand it was a question of establishing a distinction between the knowing subject and the object known, and at the same time between the function of the intellect and that of the sensibility. This is why he never speaks, as does Maritain, of creative intuition. He does, however, speak of *intellectual intuition.*

And here, De Bruyne is guilty of the same sin as Maritain, when he insists on finding in Thomas at all costs something it is difficult to attribute to him.

Already, in 1930, De Bruyne had written "Du rôle de l'intellect dans l'activité esthétique" (in Rintelen 1930), and he would take up a number of the same themes in his *Esquisse d'une philosophie de l'art* (1930b). He refused to speak of aesthetic intuition as an irrational act, but thought of it as a sort of instinctive synthesis in which the intellect played a constitutive role. What he had in mind was not an abstract synthesis but a process in which feeling played an essential role. In this essay the intellect in the intuition figured as the formal principle of the intuition of the concrete.

We have already observed how difficult it is to identify in Thomas a principle of intuition of the concrete, but De Bruyne attempted to balance the books as best he could. What De Bruyne actually theorizes is a variant of the Kantian idea of the aesthetic experience as disinterested pleasure, purposiveness without a purpose, universality without a concept, and regularity without law. What Kant meant was that not only may one feel pleasure in a beautiful object without wishing to possess it or to avail oneself of it physically in some way (and thus far Thomas would have been in agreement), but that we perceive it as organized toward a particular end, whereas its purpose is its own self-subsistence—this is why we view it as if it were the perfect incarnation of a rule, whereas it is simply a rule unto itself. Thus, a flower is a typical example of a beautiful thing, and in this sense we can understand why what is constitutive of the judgment of beauty is universality without a concept. The aesthetic judgment is not the affirmation that all flowers are beautiful, but the judgment that limits itself to saying that this flower is beautiful. The necessity that leads us to say that this flower is beautiful does not depend on an abstract chain of reasoning but on our sensation of that individual flower. This is why in this experience what we have is a free play of the imagination and the intellect.

I believe we can affirm that De Bruyne's intellectual intuition is precisely this. Is it possible to find anything similar in the thought of Thomas? Can we speak of an intellectual intuition capable of bringing us to perceive an idea in the realm of the sensible without this idea being somehow already divorced from the sensible from which it has been abstracted?

In the same collection in which De Bruyne published his essay on the role of the intellect in aesthetic activity (Rintelen 1930), there appeared an article by Roland-Gosselin, "Peut-on parler d'intuition intellectuelle dans la philosophie Thomiste?", in which this possibility is denied on convincing grounds citing a good number of persuasive textual references. Roland-Gosselin emphasizes the fact that—if we take the term "intuition" as it is defined in Lalande's *Vocabulaire technique et critique de la philosophie,* as, in other words, "a direct and immediate view of an object of thought currently present to the mind and grasped in its individual reality"—we cannot find such an intuition of the individual in Thomistic epistemology. She added that an intuition of this kind could be found if anywhere in John of Saint Thomas (*Cursus* I; *Logica* II, 23, 1),[34] and it appears in any case in texts of the Franciscan school. In Thomas's corpus direct knowledge of the object

---

34. See Deely (1985: 29), where, however, it seems fairly clear that for John (Poinsot) the *notitia intuitiva* is that of things present to the senses and therefore is to be identified with sensation.

is possible only for creatures of pure spirit. As far as human knowledge is concerned, not even existence, place, or moment are the proper object of the senses, but are predicated by a more complex discursive act. In that first cognitive operation that is the *simplex apprehensio* ("direct apprehension"), all we have is the abstract apprehension of the essence. Human intellect is discursive and abstract—as a consequence (and this is my own personal comment on Roland-Gosselin), aesthetic pleasure too is perfected in the act of judgment that takes into account the individual elements recovered in the *reflexio ad phantasmata*.

Can we affirm that De Bruyne had occasion to reflect on the essay by Roland-Gosselin? Apparently not, since, even sixteen years later, in his *Études*, he is still seeking to identify in Thomas a theory of aesthetic intuition (in the second paragraph of the chapter dedicated to him).

In reconstructing Thomistic aesthetic thought De Bruyne insists particularly on what he considers the "discovery" of the *Summa Theologiae*, a discovery that for Thomas would mark a definite step forward with respect to his earlier writings.[35] De Bruyne points out how Thomas borrows from Alexander of Hales a principle that the other medieval authors had neglected: if for predecessors such as Albertus Magnus the beautiful was still definable in terms of objective qualities, Thomas defines it in relation to the knowing subject. The notion of *visa placent* accentuates the subjective act of enjoyment which becomes constitutive of the aesthetic experience.

De Bruyne obviously makes it clear that there can be no question of establishing a predominance of subjective activity over the objective qualities of the object, and he cites an unequivocal passage from Thomas's commentary *In de divinis nominibus* (398–399): "non enim ideo aliquod est pulchrum, quia nos illud amamus, sed quia est pulchrum et bonum, ideo amatur a nobis" ("in fact a thing is not beautiful because we love it, but, because it is beautiful and good, it is loved by us").[36] Still, it does not seem to him

---

35. Which goes to show once again that De Bruyne had a keen awareness of a diachronic development in medieval aesthetic themes. And it was in an implied polemic vis-à-vis his professed conclusions, *but using the same texts that he had made available,* that I originally entitled my 1959 survey *Sviluppo dell'estetica medievale* ("The *Development* of Medieval Aesthetics"). The English translation, by Hugh Bredin, is entitled *Art and Beauty in the Middle Ages* (Eco 1986).

36. The idea was already formulated in Augustine, *De vera religione* 32, 19.

without importance that the good and the beautiful, although they are the same thing, are differentiated *ratione:* if the good is what everyone desires ("respicit appetitum"), the beautiful *"respicit vim cognoscitivam"* ("relates to the knowing power"), and therefore *pulchra enim dicuntur quae visa placent* ("those things are called beautiful which please when seen") (*Summa Theologiae* I, 5 4 ad 1, my emphasis).

It is undeniable that for Thomas the beautiful, compared with the good, involves a relationship to the contemplative consciousness. Here, however, De Bruyne finds himself embarrassed by the fact that in the aesthetic experience there appear both a cognitive moment *(apprehensio, visio)* and what seems to him to be an emotive—today we would call it "passionate"—moment *(placet, delectat).* And he realizes the danger one might incur by following the route indicated by Maritain.

Can we concur with Maritain that aesthetic pleasure "is the quieting of our power of desire, which rests in the good that belongs to the cognitive power perfectly and harmoniously put into action" ("l'apaisement de notre puissance du désir, qui repose dans le bien propre de la puissance cognitive parfaitement et harmonieusement mise en acte"), to the point that "a being who, per absurdum, possessed only intellect, would have the perception of the beautiful in its roots and in its objective conditions, but not in the delight by means of which alone this perception is brought to completion" ("un être qui, par l'absurde, n'aurait que l'intellect, aurait la perception du beau dans ses racines et dans ses conditions objectives, mais non dans le plaisir par lequel seule cette perception est portée à son achèvement")? Or will we admit the thesis that Maritain is combating, namely, that the act of knowledge alone can produce the experience of the beautiful?[37]

In an attempt to disentangle this knot, De Bruyne reminds us that every natural operation in Thomas, including that of intelligence, occurs with a specific end in mind and presupposes an inclination, a tendency, a love. The "passionate" moment, then, of the aesthetic experience should come into play at the stage of the initial act of the knowing intellect. But there is no pleasure in or love for an object without a "practical" consciousness and (De Bruyne does not use this expression, though his discourse implies the concept) its

---

37. The quotations from Maritain refer to the 1927 edition of *Art et scolastique,* pp. 257, 259, n. 1.

concrete and individual perception. Which is tantamount to saying that one always loves, not childhood or the feminine gender, but *this* individual child or *this* woman). And so, once more, we are faced with the disquieting problem of the intuition of the concrete.

It is at this point, in the space of a single page, without insisting unnecessarily, that De Bruyne ventures as follows: "there is no aesthetic sentiment except insofar as intuitive knowledge itself satisfies us, thanks to its qualities of pure intuition: 'id cujus *ipsa apprehensio placet*, [the very apprehension of which pleases]'" (De Bruyne [1946]1998: 286).

Unfortunately, on this point the same objection already raised against Maritain is also valid for De Bruyne: do we have any reason to state that (in Thomas) the apprehension of something, if it is to produce pleasure, must be intuitive? It does not appear so, especially when we recall that the term *apprehensio* is used as a rule precisely for abstractive intellectual knowledge. And yet De Bruyne concludes that, when the *apprehensio*

has to do with the vision of corporeal beauty, it is neither purely sensible nor purely abstractive but essentially intuitive, in the sense that it presents itself psychologically as a synthetic unity. "Non enim proprie loquendum sensus aut intellectus cognoscunt, sed homo per utrumque." Intuition is an act of the whole man, in whatever way the connection between sensibility and mind is conceived. But in this intuition of the individual form, of which sensation is the first condition, it is the intellect that grasps, not just the meaning of the thing perceived, but also the value proper to pure perception [se rapporte à la vision du beau corporel, elle n'est ni purement sensible ni purement abstractive mais essentiellement intuitive, au sens où elle se présente psychologiquement comme une unité synthétique. "Non enim proprie loquendum sensus aut intellectus cognoscunt, sed homo per utrumque." L'intuition est l'acte de l'homme tout entier, de quelque forme que l'on conçoive le lien entre sensibilité et esprit. Mais dans cette intuition de la forme individuelle, dont la sensation est la première condition, c'est l'intellect qui saisit non seulement le sens de la chose perçue mais aussi la valeur propre de la perception pure.]

Is it enough to say that "non enim proprie loquendum sensus aut intellectus cognoscunt, sed homo per utrumque" (*De veritate* II, 6 ad 3—which, when you think about it, is practically a truism) to posit the concept of an intuitive synthesis? Not only does one statement not imply the other, Thomas always said the exact opposite: that sense and intellect, that is, do not know through a lightning synthesis, but in two separate phases. The senses appear first, and then, once the phantasm has been formed, the senses retire into the wings and the intellect steps onstage. But De Bruyne was in need of a principle of knowledge of the individual for which Thomas's aesthetics, sadly, made no allowance.

Thomas affirms that "the mind knows singulars through a certain kind of reflection, as when the mind, in knowing its object, which is some universal nature, returns to knowledge of its own act, then to the species which is the principle of its act, and, finally, to the phantasm from which it has abstracted the species. In this way, it attains to some knowledge (*aliqua cognitio*) concerning singulars."[38]

But this *aliqua cognitio* is insufficient to explain the delight one feels in observing how the form shines from the proportionate parts of the matter it organizes, nor to evaluate all the varieties of proportion it exhibits, nor to judge the integrity of the object appreciated. For all of this we must proceed to acts of judgment, to an activity of division and composition, in which we seize "proprietates et accidentia et habitudines" ("properties, accidents and relationships") (*Summa Theologiae* Ia, 85, 5 co.).

In this complex activity, which remains intellectual throughout, the aesthetic joy, even as it grasps the characteristics proper to the organized matter, remains an intellectual enjoyment, in which corporeality has a fairly reduced function. For Thomas the aesthetic *visio* is not something that differs from intellectual knowledge, but represents, if anything, one of its most complex levels. This is the limit of the Thomistic aesthetic (or for some readers, its strength, since aesthetic pleasure would no longer be an accident of the passions but a further exercise of the intellect).

---

38. "mens singulare cognoscit per quandam reflexionem, prout, scilicet, mens cognoscendo objectum suum, quod est aliqua natura universalis, redit in cognitionem sui actus, et ulterius in specimen quae est actus sui principium, et ulterius in phantasma a quo species est abstracta; et sic aliquam cognitionem de singulari accipit" (*Quaestiones disputatae de veritate* X, 5 co., trans. James V. McGlynn, S.J. http://dhspriory.org/thomas/QDdeVer10.htm.

This is Thomas's position, which stems from his inability to explain the knowledge of the concrete. It is too late to have him change his mind.

De Bruyne was playing a tricky game. On the one hand, he took into account his Belgian predecessors, like De Wulf, who had insisted on the fact that for Thomas the subject has a fundamental role in aesthetic perception—and De Wulf was certainly correct. On the other, he found himself faced with Thomas's unsatisfactory epistemology. He attempted therefore, relaxing his own historiographical rigor, to infer what Thomas *ought to have* said in order to make his position coherent and to lay the foundations for an aesthetic that would be satisfactory even to modern eyes.

He clearly shows his satisfaction when he is convinced that he recognizes an intellectual intuition in the Victorines or in Duns Scotus—and he is probably right; so this, we suspect, was why he considered his historical survey complete when he reached Duns Scotus. But if the Victorines and Duns Scotus agreed, so to speak, with De Bruyne, this does not mean that Thomas agreed with Scotus and the Victorines. In a word, the chapter on Thomas is really quite tormented and represents the "Maritainian fault" in De Bruyne's otherwise impeccable work. Which goes to show how difficult it is for a militant Thomist to admit that Thomas cannot always satisfy the legitimate theoretical desires of someone who is attempting to come to terms not only with Thomas but also with modern thought.

And yet, perhaps in a fit of prudence, in the chapter of the *Études* dedicated to Thomas, De Bruyne avoids using the expression "intellectual intuition." Maybe he really had been giving Roland-Gosselin's reaction some thought.

If writing the history of thought means letting the authors of the past say what they actually said and not what we would have them say, we must be consistent and accuse De Bruyne of this historiographical inaccuracy. While recognizing, however, that he must have been somehow aware that he was treading on thin ice, since he confined his reflections on intuition in Thomas to a mere two pages, almost en passant. So that, forgiving him this single moment of weakness, or of excessive love for his author, we may continue to insist on the great distance that separates Maritain's reading from his: the former consisting in a free *use* of the sources, the latter in an effort at *interpretation*.

9

Toward a History of Denotation

Denotation (along with its counterpart, *connotation*) is considered, depending on the context, as either a characteristic or a function (i) of individual terms (what does the word "dog" denote?); (ii) of declarative propositions (the sentence "the dog barks" may denote a state of the world, that there is a dog barking—but, if "the dog" is taken as denoting a species—all dogs, that is—then it could denote a characteristic common to the entire canine race); (iii) of nominal phrases and definite descriptions (the phrase "the President of the Republic" may denote, depending on the context and the circumstances of its utterance, either the actual president currently in power or the role provided for in a constitution). In each of these cases we must decide whether the denotation has to do with the meaning, the referent, or the act of reference. To sum up, by *denotation* do we mean what *is signified* by the term, *the thing named*, or, in the case of propositions, *what is the case* or *what is believed to be the case*, inasmuch as it forms the content of a proposition?

For structural linguists, "denotation" is concerned with meaning. For Hjelmslev (1943) the difference between a denotative semiotic and a connotative semiotic lies in the fact that the former is a semiotic whose expression plane is not a semiotic, whereas the latter is a semiotic whose expression plane

---

The original version of this essay was published in English with the title "Denotation" in Eco and Marmo (1989), and subsequently in Italian as an appendix to Eco (1997a). [*Translator's note:* This appendix was not included in the English translation of Eco (1997).] I would like to thank Mariateresa Beonio Brocchieri Fumagalli, Andrea Tabarroni, Roberto Lambertini, and Costantino Marmo for discussing the content with me and for their valuable suggestions.

is a semiotic. Barthes (1964) too formulates his position basing himself on Hjelmslev and develops a fully intensional idea of denotation, according to which, between a signifier and a first (or zero) degree signified, there is always a denotative relationship.

In componential analysis, the term has been used to indicate the sense-relationship expressed by a lexical term—such as the term "uncle," which expresses the relationship "father's brother" (see, for instance, Leech 1974: 238). In other words, in structuralist circles, denotation, referring back to Frege's (1892) distinction, is closer to *Sinn* than to *Bedeutung,* closer to meaning than to reference, and in Carnap's (1955) terms has more to do with intension than with extension.

It is, however, Frege's term *Bedeutung* that is ambiguous, and it should be replaced with *Bezeichnung* (which we may translate as "designation"), given that, in the vocabulary of philosophy, *Bedeutung* usually stands for "meaning," whereas *Bezeichnung* stands for "reference, designation" and for denotation in the extensional sense. Husserl (1970), for instance, says that a sign signifies or means *(bedeutet)* a signified and designates *(bezeichnet)* a thing. This is why, in the most recent tradition of Anglo-Saxon semantics inspired by Frege, *Bedeutung* is often rendered with "reference" or "denotation" (see, for example, Dummett 1973). And so the usage of the structuralists is completely turned on its head.

In the field of analytic philosophy, the whole picture underwent a radical change with Russell's essay "On Denoting" (1905), in which denotation is presented as different from meaning; and this is the direction followed by the entire Anglo-Saxon philosophical tradition. See, for instance, Ogden and Richards (1923) and Morris (1946), where it is said that when, for example, in Pavlov's experiment, a dog reacts to the bell, food is the *denotatum* of the bell, while the condition of being edible is its *significatum*.

In this sense, an expression denotes either the individuals or the class of individuals of which it is the name, whereas it connotes the characteristics on the basis of which such individuals are recognized as members of the class in question. If we go on to substitute (see Carnap 1955) the pairing *extension/intension* for the pairing *denotation/connotation*, then denotation becomes a function of connotation.

But even if we establish that denotation stands for extension, it may refer (i) to a class of individuals, (ii) to an actually existing individual (as in the case of the rigid designation of proper names), (iii) to each member of a class of individuals, (iv) to the truth value contained in an assertive proposition (with the consequence that, in each of these fields, the *denotatum* of a proposition is what is the case, or the fact that *p* is the case).

Very reasonably, Lyons (1977: 2:208) proposed using the term *designation* in place of *denotation,* and using *denotation* in a neutral fashion, between extension and intension: in this sense "dog" would denote the class of dogs (or perhaps some typical member, or exemplar, of the class), while "canine" would denote the characteristic whereby we recognize that it is correct to apply the expression. His proposal did not meet with much favor, however, at least in the analytical *koinè,* and therefore the polysemous nature of the term persists.

9.1. From Mill to Peirce

The term *denotation* was used in an explicitly extensional sense by John Stuart Mill in his *System of Logic* (1843, I, 2, 5): "the word white, denotes all white things, as snow, paper, the foam of the sea, etc., and implies, or in the language of the schoolmen, *connotes,* the attribute *whiteness*" (emphasis in original).

Peirce was probably the first to realize that there was something that did not jibe in this solution, despite the fact that he himself always used denotation in this extensional sense. Let us see how he uses the term on various occasions:

the direct reference of a symbol to its objects, or its denotation (CP 1.559)[1]

a Rhematic Indexical Sinsign [is] really affected by the real camel it denotes (CP 2.261)

a symbol . . . must denote an individual and must signify a character (CP 2.293)

every assertion contains such a denotative or pointing-out function (CP 5.429)

---

1. Here and elsewhere references to the standard edition of the *Collected Papers* (Peirce 1931–1958) appear under the abbreviation CP.

signs are designative or denotative or indicative, in so far as they, like a demonstrative pronoun, or a pointing finger, "brutally direct the mental eyeballs of the interpreter to the object in question" (8.350)

Peirce was well aware that, as far as connotation went, Mill was not in fact following, as he claimed to be, traditional Scholastic usage. The Schoolmen (at least up until the fourteenth century) distinguished between *significare* (meaning) and *appellare* (naming), and did not use *connotation* in opposition to *denotation*, but as an added form of signification:

> It has been, indeed, the opinion of all the students of the logic of the fourteenth, fifteenth and sixteenth centuries, that connotation was in those ages used exclusively for the reference to a second significate, that is (nearly), for a reference to a relative sense (such as father, brighter, etc.) to the correlate of the object it primarily denotes. . . . Mr. Mill has, however, considered himself entitled to deny this upon his simple authority, without the citation of a single passage from any writer of that time. (CP 2.393)

Peirce develops the same argument in *CP* 2.431, and he later points out that in the Middle Ages the most common opposition was between *significare* (to mean) and *nominare* (to refer to). He further observes how Mill uses—in place of the term *significare—connotare*, implicitly reserving *denotare* for designating, naming, or referring. Furthermore, he recalls a passage from John of Salisbury (*Metalogicus* II, 20), according to whom "nominantur singularia sed universalia significantur," concluding that unfortunately "the precise meaning recognized as proper to the word 'signify' at the time of John of Salisbury . . . was never strictly observed, either before and since; and on the contrary the meaning tended to slip towards that of 'denote'" (*CP* 2.434).

However, although Peirce lucidly realizes that at a certain point *significare* partially shifted from an intensional paradigm to an extensional one, he nevertheless fails to recognize that in ensuing centuries the term retains for the most part its intensional meaning. Thus, he accepts the fact that denotation is an extensional category (and took issue with Mill's work only with respect to connotation), whereas it is precisely the term *denotare* that, initially used halfway between extension and intension, finally (and the terminus ad quem is in fact Mill) took over as an extensional category. Peirce does not indicate when this happened for the first time, and he fails to do so because the question was far from lending itself to a simple solution.

9.2. From Aristotle to the Middle Ages

Plato had already made it clear that by pronouncing a single term (say, "dog") we can certainly signify a given idea, but only when we enunciate a proposition (such as "that dog barks") can we say that something *is the case,* and hence *say something is true or false.*

As for Aristotle, in the famous passage in *De interpretatione* (16a et seq.), he outlines a semiotic triangle in which words are on the one hand linked to concepts (or to the passions of the soul) and on the other to things. Aristotle says that words are "symbols" of the passions, and by "symbol" he means a conventional and arbitrary expedient. It is also true, however, as we will see in what follows, that he claims that words may be considered as symptoms *(semeia)* of the passions, but he says so in the same sense that any and every verbal utterance may first of all be a symptom of the fact that its speakers have something on their minds. The passions of the soul, on the other hand, are likenesses or icons of things. But, according to Aristotelian theory, things are known through the passions of the soul, without there being a direct connection between symbols and things. We name things and we mean their icons, that is, the corresponding ideas that the things arouse in our minds.[2] To indicate this symbolic relationship, Aristotle does not employ the word

---

2. Recently, Lo Piparo (2003) has proposed a different interpretation of the passage in question, according to which the passions of the soul are not mental images of things, but ways of being of thought, cognitive modalities (like reflecting, being afraid, feeling joy). In the same way, the *pragmata* cannot be things that already exist or facts in general, otherwise how are we to explain why, in other parts of his opus, Aristotle claims that we can think of nonexistent or false things like the chimera, or events that might exist but whose existence it is impossible to demonstrate. See the earlier references to Lo Piparo's theory in Chapter 4 of this volume, section 4.2.5. Nevertheless, even if we were to accept his reading, I do not think it would alter the nature of the problem under discussion.

semainein (which could almost be translated as "to signify"), though in many other circumstances he uses this verb to indicate the relationship between words and concepts (see Figure 9.1).

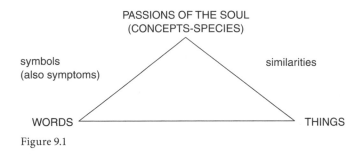

Figure 9.1

For Aristotle too, as for Plato, single terms taken in isolation do not make any statement about what is the case. They merely "mean" a thought. Sentences or complex expressions on the other hand also mean a thought; but only a particular kind of sentence (a statement or a proposition) asserts a state of affairs that is true or false. Aristotle does not say that statements "signify" what is true or false, only that they "say" (the Greek verb is *legein*) that something given A "belongs" (the verb is *uparkein*) to something given B.

Thus, from Aristotle on, we find ourselves faced with three questions that will be amply debated throughout the entire Middle Ages: (i) Do signs mean primarily concepts (and can refer to things only through the mediation of concepts), or do they can signify directly, designate, or denote things? (ii) What is the difference between referring to a class of individuals and referring to a concrete individual? (iii) Wherein lies the difference between the correlation *signs-concepts-individual things* and the correlation *sentences-propositional content-extralinguistic state of affairs?*

Not that medieval thinkers had all of these different issues clearly in mind from the word go. The most we can say is that question (i) became the object of debate, in terms of the opposition between *significare, nominare,* and *appellare,* very early on (at least from the time of Anselm of Canterbury). Question (ii) was probably framed for the first time by Peter of Spain with his distinction between *suppositio naturalis* and *suppositio accidentalis.* Question (iii) was variously addressed from Boethius onward—though while, among the commentators of Aristotle, the debate over the relationship of signification was conducted independently from that over true and false assertions, for a number of grammarians and theoreticians of the *suppositio,* the two issues were often superimposed, until such time as, with Roger Bacon and William of Ockham, they became completely interchangeable.

The fate of terms like *denotatio* and *designatio* is bound up with the history of the opposition *significatio–nominatio.* It would appear that, for a long time (at least until the fourteenth century), these terms were used sometimes in an intensional and sometimes in an extensional sense. The terms were already present in the traditional Latin lexicon and signified, among their many other meanings, "to stand as a sign for something"—regardless of whether that something was a concept or a thing. In the case of *designatio* the etymology speaks for itself, in the case of *denotatio,* however, we must bear in mind that the term *nota* indicated a sign, a token, a symbol, something that referred back to something else (see also Lyons 1968: ch. 9). According to Maierù (1972: 394), Aristotle's term *symbolon* was in fact generally translated as *nota:* "nota vero est quae rem quamquam designat. Quo fit ut omne nomen nota sit" ("a sign is that which designates any thing. Hence every name is a sign")(Boethius 1988: p. 108).[3]

It is important, then, to establish (i) what happened to the term *significatio;* and (ii) when *denotatio* (along with *designatio*) occurs in connection with *significatio,* and when, on the contrary, it occurs in opposition to it.

As far as *denotatio* goes, it is important to record its occurrence in each of the following three usages: (i) in a *strong* intensional sense (denotation is related to meaning); (ii) in a *strong* extensional sense (denotation is related to things or states of things); (iii) in a *weak* sense (denotation is undecided between intension and extension, but with good reason to lean toward intension). We will see that the weak sense is the predominant one at least up until the fourteenth century.

9.3. Boethius

From Augustine to the thirteenth century, the possibility of referring to things is always mediated by meaning. For Augustine, "signum est enim res

---

3. On Boethius's use of the term "nota" see our Chapter 4.2.4. For an English translation of this work by Boethius, see Boethius 1988.

praeter speciem, quam ingerit sensibus, aliud aliquid ex se faciens in cogitationem venire" ("a sign is something which, offering itself to the senses,
conveys something other to the intellect") (*De doctrina christiana* II, 1, 1)
and signification is the action a sign performs on the mind. Only through
this mediation can one refer to things (see Figure 9.2).

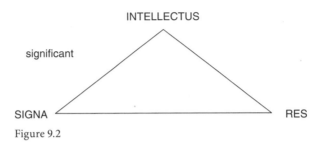

Figure 9.2

Boethius had already introduced the term *propositio* to indicate the complex expressions that assert that something is either true or false. It is difficult to decide whether by "proposition" he meant the expression itself or the
corresponding concept, but it is clear that truth or falsehood were connected with propositions and not with isolated terms. Boethius affirms that
the isolated terms signify the corresponding concept or the universal idea,
and he takes *significare*—as he does, though more rarely, *designare*—in the
intensional sense. Words are conventional tools that serve to make manifest
thoughts, *sensa* or *sententias* (*De interpretatione* I). Words do not designate
res subiectae but *passiones animae*. The most we can say of the thing designated is that it is "implied by its concept" (*significationi supposita* or *suppositum*, see De Rijk 1962–1967: 180–181).

In his first commentary on Aristotle's *Peri hermeneias*, II, in a discussion as to whether words refer directly to concepts or to things, in both
cases Boethius uses the expression *designare*. He says "vox vero conceptiones animi intellectusque significant" and "voces vero quae intellectus designant," and, speaking of *litterae, voces, intellectus, res,* he states that "litterae
verba nominaque significant" and that "haec vero (nomina) principaliter
quidem intellectus secundo vero loco res quoque designant. Intellectus
vero ipsi nihil aliud nisi rerum significativi sunt." In *Categories*, col. 159
B4–C8, he says that "prima igitur illa fuit nominum positio per quam
vel intellectui subiecta vel sensibus designaret." It seems to me that in

these examples *designare* and *significare* are considered as more or less interchangeable.

Therefore, for Boethius too, words signify concepts and it is only as a consequence of this that they may refer to things (see Figure 9.3).

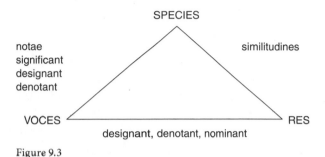

Figure 9.3

9.4. Anselm's *Appellatio*

It is thanks to the theory of *appellatio,* proposed in his *De Grammatico* by Anselm of Canterbury, that a more clear-cut distinction is posited between signifying and referring.

Building on Aristotle's theory of paronyms, Anselm says that, when we call a given individual a *grammaticus* or grammarian, we are using the term paronymically. The word still signifies the quality of being a grammarian, but it is used to refer to a specific person. To indicate reference, then, Anselm uses the term *appellatio,* while, to indicate meaning, he uses *significatio* (*De Grammatico,* 4, 30 et seq.). A distinction of this kind between meaning and appellation (or naming) is also observed by Abelard.

9.5. Abelard

In the case of Abelard it is not possible to identify a logical terminology established once and for all, since he frequently uses the same terms in more than one sense. Nevertheless, he is the first author in whom the distinction between the intensional and extensional aspects is clearly made (if not always consistently from the terminological point of view). While he speaks indifferently of *significatio de rebus* and *significatio de intellectibus,* he nevertheless considers the principal meaning of *significatio* to be (we would say) intensional, in conformity with the anti-Aristotelian tradition, for which *significare* means to *constituere* (or "to generate") a mental concept.

In his *Ingredientibus* (Geyer 1927: 307), Abelard states unambiguously that the intellectual plane is the necessary intermediary between things and concepts. "Not only is the *significatio intellectuum* a privileged *significatio*, it is also the only legitimate semantic function of a noun, the only one a dialectician must bear in mind when examining a discourse" (Beonio-Brocchieri Fumagalli 1969: 37).

But if we consider the various contexts in which terms such as *significare, designare, denotare, nominare, appellare* are compared and contrasted with one another, we are entitled to conclude that Abelard uses *significare* to refer to the *intellectus* generated in the mind of the listener, *nominare* instead for the referential function, and—at least in certain passages in the *Dialectica*, but in a way that leaves no room for doubt—*designare* and *denotare* for the relationship between a word and its definition or *sententia* (the *sententia* being what we would call the "encyclopedic" meaning of the term, whose definition represents a particular "dictionary" selection for the purposes of disambiguating the meaning of the term itself).[4]

We have already stressed, not only the frequently contradictory nature of Abelard's terminology, but also how the terms *designare* and *denotare* had

---

4. In the *Dialectica* (V, II, *De definitionibus;* De Rijk 1956: 594), it is clear that a *nomen* is *determinativum* of all the possible differences of something, and it is by hearing a name pronounced that we are able to understand *(intelligere)* them all. The *sententia* includes within itself all these differences, while the *definitio* posits only certain of them, those, that is, needed to determine the meaning of a name in the context of a proposition, eliminating all ambiguities: "Sic enim plures aliae sint ipsius differentiae constitutivae quae omnes in nomine *corporis* intelligi dicantur, non totam corporis sententiam haec definitio tenet, sicut enim nec hominis definitio *animal rationale et mortale* vel *animal gressibile bipes*. Sicut enim *hominis* nomen omnium differentiarum suarum determinativum sit, omnes in ipso opportet intelligi; non tamen omnes in definitione ipsius poni convenit propter vitium superfluae locutionis. . . . Cum autem et *bipes* et *gressibilis* et *perceptibilis disciplinae* ac multae quoque formae fortasse aliae hominis sint differentiae, quae omnes in nomine *hominis* determinari dicantur . . . apparet hominis sententiam in definitionem ipsius totam non claudi sed secundum quamdam partem constitutionis suae ipsius definiri. Sufficiunt itaque ad definiendum quae non sufficiunt ad constituendum."

continued to enjoy a remarkably vague definitional status down to his time. There are passages in which we encounter *designare* with a strong extensional sense, such as *Dialectica* (I, III, 2, 1, p. 119), where Abelard argues against those who maintain that syncategorematic words do not produce concepts, but merely indicate a number of *res subiectae*. In this passage Abelard goes on to speak of the possibility of designating things, and he seems to use *designare* to indicate the first imposition of names upon things (seen as a kind of baptism in which there is a strict designatory link between the namer and the thing named). See, for instance, *Dialectica* (I, III, 3, p. 114): "ad res designandas imposite."

It is also true, however, that in certain passages (see, for instance, I, III, 3, 1, p. 123), *designare* and *denotare* do not seem to have the same meaning, while in others (such as I, II, 3, 9, p. 97, and I, III, 3, 1, p. 121) the use of *designare* suggests an intensional interpretation.

Furthermore, there are two contexts (I, III, 1, 1, pp. 112–113) in which what is designated is the relationship between a name and its corresponding definition, and the denotation is explicitly linked to the meaning (or *sententia*) of an expression.

Taking issue with those who maintained that the things upon which the *vox* or name has been imposed are directly signified by the *vox* itself, Abelard stresses the fact that names signify "ea sola quae in voce denotantur atque in sententia ipsius tenentur." He then adds that words do not signify everything they can name, but what they designate by a definition. For example, Latin *animal* signifies a sensitive animal substance, and this is precisely what is *denoted* by (or in) the word (see Figure 9.4).

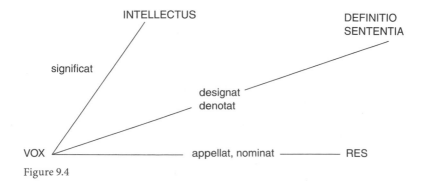

Figure 9.4

It is clear then that both designation and denotation continue to maintain a decidedly strong intensional sense and to refer to the relationship between an expression and its corresponding definitional content.

As for signification, it has nothing to do with the naming of things, since it continues to exist "nominatis rebus destructis" ("if the things named are destroyed"), making it possible to understand the meaning of *nulla rosa est* (*Ingredientibus,* Geyer ed., p. 309).

Abelard makes a further distinction between two specific meanings of *signification* that continue to be a source of perplexity even today. Spade (1982) has stressed the fact that for the Scholastics *significatio* is not the same as our "meaning": a term *significat* what it succeeds in bringing to someone's mind (and this is undoubtedly the sense intended by Augustine). In this way signification, unlike meaning, is a kind of causal relationship. Meaning (be it mental correlate, semantic content, intension, or any form of noematic, ideal, or cultural entity) is not represented in the Middle Ages—and throughout the entire Aristotelian tradition—by the term *significatio* but by *sententia* or *definitio.*

True, in the medieval tradition we find both *significare* in the sense of *constituere intellectus,* as well as the expression *significare speciem* (which seems more tied to a noncausal notion of signification), but this distinction seems to become clear only with Abelard: a word *significat* something to the mind causally, while the same word is correlated by way of designation and/or denotation with a meaning, that is, with a *sententia* or a definition.

Accordingly, we can say that what Abelard's theory envisaged was not a semiotic triangle, but a sort of square according to which a *vox:* (i) *significat intellectus,* (ii) *designat vel denotat sententiam vel definitionem,* and (iii) *nominat vel appellat res.*

9.6. Thomas Aquinas

In his commentary on the *De interpretatione,* Thomas Aquinas, who remains faithful to Aristotle's positions, after distinguishing the first operation of the intellect (perception) from the second ("scilicet de enunciatione affirmativa et negativa"), defines *interpretatio* as "vox significativa quae per se aliud significat, sive complexa sive incomplexa" ("significant vocal sound—whether complex or incomplex—which signifies something by itself") (*Proemium* 2). But immediately afterward he makes it clear that nouns and verbs are merely "principles" of interpretation, which is to be identified exclusively with the *oratio,* that is, with all those propositions "in qua verum et falsum inveniuntur."

At this point he uses *significare* for the nouns and verbs (I, ii, 14), as well as for those *voces* that signify naturally, such as the moaning of the sick and the noises made by animals; but, as far as human voices are concerned, they do not immediately signify the things themselves but the general concepts, and only "eis mediantibus" (through them) do they refer to *singularia* (I, 2, 15).

He later states that the name signifies its definition (I, ii, 20). True, when Thomas speaks of composition and division, that is, of affirmation and negation, he says the former "significat . . . coniunctionem," while the latter "significat . . . rerum separationem" (I, iii, 26), but it is clear that even here (where language refers to what is or is not the case) what is signified is an operation of the intellect. It is only the intellect, whose operations are signified, that may be defined as true or false with respect to the actual state of things: "intellectus dicitur verum secundum quod conformatur rei" (I, iii, 28). An expression can be neither true nor false, it is merely the sign that *significat* a true or false operation of the intellect.[5]

The verb *denotare,* in all of its various forms, occurs 105 times in the Thomistic lexicon (to which we may add two occurrences of the noun *denotatio*), but it appears that Thomas never used it in the strong extensional sense, in other words, he never used it to say that a given proposition denotes a state of affairs, or that a given term denotes a given thing.[6]

It is occasionally used with the sense of "to signify metaphorically or symbolically that . . ." See, for instance, the commentary *In Job* 10, where it is stated that the roaring of the lion stands for Job ("in denotatione Job rugitus leonis"). There is an ambiguous passage in *III Sent.* 7, 3, 2, which says: "Similiter est falsa: 'Filius Dei est praedestinatus,' cum non ponatur aliquid

---

5. "Unde haec vox, *homo est asinus,* est vere vox et vere signum; sed quia est signum falsi, ideo dicitur falsa" (I, iii, 31). "Nomina significant aliquid, scilicet quosdam conceptus simplices, licet rerum compositarum . . ." (I, iii, 34).

6. The preposition *per* "denotes the instrumental cause" (IV *Sent.* 1, 1, 4). Elsewhere he affirms that "praedicatio per causam potest . . . exponi per propositionem denotantem habitudinem causae" (I *Sent.* 30, 1, 1). Or "dicitur Christus sine additione, ad denotandum quod oleo invisibili unctus est . . ." (*Super Ev. Matthaei* 1, 4). In all these and in similar cases the term *denotatio* is always used in the weaker sense.

respectu cujus possit antecessio denotari." But it could be argued that what Thomas is talking about in this case is the mental operation that leads to the understanding of a temporal sequence.

9.7. *Suppositio*

Authors like Boethius, Abelard, or Thomas Aquinas, more concerned with the problem of signification than with that of denomination, were primarily interested in the psychological (today we would say "cognitive") aspects of language. Certain of our contemporary scholars, however, committed to the rediscovery of the first medieval manifestations of a modern truth-conditional semantics, find the whole question of signification to be a very embarrassing problem, upsetting as it does the purity of the extensional approach, firmly established apparently by the theory of *suppositio*.[7]

In its most mature formulation, supposition is the role a term, once inserted into a proposition, assumes so as to refer to the extralinguistic context. The road, however, that leads from the first vague notions of *suppositum* to the more elaborate theories like that of Ockham is long and winding. De Rijk (1962–1967, 1982, n. 16) has traced the path by which, in discussing the relationship between a term and the thing to which it refers, the notion of signification (understood as the relationship between words and concepts, or species, or universals, or definitions) becomes ever less important.

----

7. De Rijk (1962–1967: 206), for example, affirms that in Abelard "a point of view appears to prevail that is not based on logic" and that the term *impositio* "stands in most cases for *prima inventio*" and that "rarely is it encountered with the sense of denoting some actual imposition in this or that proposition emitted by some actual speaker. When even the *voces* are separated from the *res*, their connection with the intellect leads the author into the realm of psychology, or confines him to that of ontology, since the *intellectus* in its turn is referred to reality. The theory of predication too appears to be extremely influenced by the prevalence of perspectives that do not belong to logic." Hence, the medieval logicians "would have obtained better results if they had completely abandoned the very notion of signification" (De Rijk 1982: 173). But we cannot expect the medievals to think in terms of modern truth-functional semantics.

We may observe how, for instance (De Rijk 1982: 161 et seq.), the disciples of Priscian spoke of names as signifying a substance at the same time as a quality (a formula in which the latter no doubt represented the universal nature of the thing and the former the individual thing), so that as early as the twelfth century we find the verb *supponere* as the equivalent of *significare substantiam,* in other words, signifying the individual thing. It is true, however, that authors like William of Conches insist that names do not signify either substance or quality or a thing's actual existence, but only its universal nature, and that during the twelfth century the distinction is maintained between signification (of concepts and species) and denomination (the denotation of concrete individual things—see, for example, the *Ars Meliduna*).

It is, however, clear how, little by little, in the fields of logic and grammar, the cognitive is superseded by the extensional approach, and how "in successive phases, the real meaning of a term became the focus of general interest, with the consequence that reference and denotation became far more important than the over-abstract notion of signification. What a term signifies first and foremost is the concrete object to which it can correctly be applied" (De Rijk 1982: 167).

Notwithstanding this development, this novel point of view is not usually expressed using terms such as *denotatio,* whose semantic domain remains ill-defined.[8] Peter of Spain, for example, uses *denotari* in at least one passage (*Tractatus* VII, 68), in which he states that, in the expression *sedentem possibile est ambulare* ("to someone seated ambulating is possible"), what is denoted is not the concomitance between being seated and ambulating, but that between being seated and having the possibility *(potentia)* to ambulate. Once again, it is difficult to say whether *denotare* has an intensional or extensional function. Furthermore, Peter considers *significare* in an extremely broad sense, given that "significatio termini, prout hic sumitur, est rei per vocem secundum placitum representatio" (*Tractatus* VI, 2), and it is impossible to decide whether this *res* is to be considered as an individual or a universal (De Rijk 1982: 169).

---

8. In the Vienna commentary on Priscian (see De Rijk [1962–1967]: 245), a name "significat proprie vel appellative vel denotando de qua manerie rerum sit aliquid." Thus, *denotare* still appears to be connected with the significance of universal nature.

On the other hand, Peter does introduce an honest-to-goodness extensional theory simply by developing a notion of *suppositio* distinct from that
of signification (see also Ponzio 1983, who has an interesting reference to
Peirce, CP 5.320): what Peter says in fact is that *suppositio* and *significatio*
are different in that the latter is concerned with the imposition of a *vox* to
signify something, while the former is the meaning of the same term (which
already in and of itself and *in the first instance* signifies that given thing)
inasmuch as it stands for something particular.[9]

In Peter's theory, however, there is a difference between standing extensionally for a class and standing extensionally for an individual. What we have in
the first case is a natural supposition *(suppositio naturalis),* and in the second
an accidental supposition (ibid., 4). Along the same lines, Peter distinguishes
between *suppositio* and *appellatio:* "differt autem appellatio a suppositione et a
significatione, quia appellatio est tantum de re existente, sed significatio et
suppositio tam de re existente quam non existente" (*Tractatus* X, 1).

De Rijk (1982: 169) affirms that "Peter's natural supposition is the exact
denotative counterpart of signification." To be sure, we may insist that *homo*
signifies a certain universal nature and supposes all (possible) existing human beings or the class of humans. What Peter does not say, however, is that
homo signifies all existing human beings or that it denotes them, though the
entire question does not substantially change.

Up to this point, the terminological landscape that lies before us is still
somewhat confused, considering that each of the technical terms considered so far covers at least two different domains (except for "denotation" and
"designation," which are still more indeterminate). This is illustrated by the
diagram in Figure 9.5.

A significant change occurs with William of Sherwood, who "unlike Peter and the majority of 13th-century logicians . . . identifies the significative
character of a term with its referring exclusively to actually existing things"
(De Rijk 1982: 170–171).

---

9. "Suppositio vero est acceptio termini substantivi pro aliquo. Differunt autem
suppositio et significatio, quia significatio est per impositionem vocis ad rem sig-
nificandam, suppositio vero est acceptio ipsius termini iam significantis rem pro
aliquo. . . . Quare significatio prior est suppositione" (*Tractatus* VI, 3).

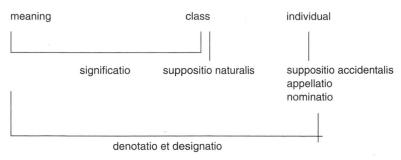

Figure 9.5

This will be the position of Roger Bacon, for whom signification becomes denotative in the modern extensional use of the term—despite the fact that he never employs a term such as *denotatio*.

9.8. Bacon

In his *De signis* (Fredborg et al. 1978, hereinafter *DS*), Bacon sets up a relatively complex classification of signs (fundamentally confirmed in other works by the same author, such as the *Compendium studii theologiae*), which presents a number of elements of interest to the semiotician. This classification has already been discussed,[10] and we saw that Bacon employs the terms *significare, significatio,* and *significatum* in a sense radically different from the traditional one.

In *DS* II, 2, he states that "signum autem est illud quod oblatum sensui vel intellectui aliquid designat ipsi intellectui." A definition of this kind might appear similar to that of Augustine—but only if we understand Bacon's "designat" as the equivalent of Augustine's "faciens in cogitationem venire." We must, however, point out two considerations that differentiate Bacon from Augustine. First of all, "oblatum sensui vel intellectui" implies that Bacon assumes a less radical stance than Augustine via-à-vis the sensible qualities of signs, given that he repeatedly admits that there may also be intellectual signs, in the sense that concepts too may be considered to be signs of things perceived. In the second place, for Augustine the sign produces something *in* the mind, while for Bacon a sign shows something (that exists outside of the mind) *to* the mind.

---

10. See Chapter 4 in the present volume.

Therefore, for Bacon signs do not refer to their referent through the mediation of a mental species, but are directly indicated, or posited, to refer immediately to an object. It makes no difference whether this object is an individual (something concrete), a species, a sentiment or a passion of the soul. What matters is that between a sign and the object that it is supposed to name *there is no preliminary mental mediation.* The mind steps in, so to speak, after the fact, to register the designation that has already taken place. As a result, Bacon uses *significare* in an exclusively extensional sense.

It should be borne in mind, however, that Bacon distinguishes natural signs (physical symptoms and icons) from signs "ordinata ab anima et ex intentione animae," in other words, signs produced by a human being with some purpose in mind.

Among the signs *ordinata ab anima* are words and other visible signs of a conventional nature, such as the *circulus vini* or barrel hoop that taverns displayed to identify themselves, and even the goods displayed outside shops, inasmuch as they signify that other members of the same class to which they belong are on sale within. In all of these cases Bacon speaks of *impositio,* that is, of a conventional act by means of which a given entity finds itself having to stand for something else. Clearly, for Bacon convention is not the same as arbitrariness: the merchandise on display is chosen conventionally but not arbitrarily (the objects act as a kind of metonymy, the member of the class for the class as a whole). The *circulus vini* too is designated as a sign in a conventional and nonarbitrary manner, inasmuch as it points to the hoops that hold the barrels together, and acts simultaneously as both synecdoche and metonymy, representing a part of the container that holds the wine ready to be sold.

But in *DS* most of the examples are taken from verbal language and hence, if we wish to follow Bacon's line of thought, it would be better not to stray too far from what is probably the paramount example of a system of conventional and arbitrary signs.

Bacon, however, is not so naïve as to say that words signify exclusively individual and concrete things. He contends that they name objects, but these objects may also exist in a mental space. Signs in fact can also name nonentities, such as infinity, a vacuum, the chimera, and nonbeing itself (*DS* II, 2, 19; see also II, 3, 27, and V, 162).

This implies that, even when words signify species, this occurs because they point extensionally to a class of mental objects. The relationship is always extensional, and the correctness of the reference is guaranteed only by the actual presence of the object signified. A word is truly significant if, and only if, the object it signifies *is the case*—if nothing else if it is the case that it is thought.

Admittedly, Bacon says (*DS* I, 1) "non enim sequitur: 'signum in actu est, ergo res significata est,' quia non entia possunt significari per voces sicut et entia," but this position cannot be equated to Abelard's insistence that even an expression like *nulla rosa est* signifies something. In the case of Abelard *rosa* was significant insofar as *significare* was considered from an intensional point of view, and, within this framework, the name signified the concept of the thing, even if the thing did not exist or had ceased to exist. Bacon's position is different: when one says "there is a rose" (and when there being a rose is the case), the meaning of the word is given by the actual concrete rose, but when one makes the same affirmation and no such rose exists, then the word *rose* does not refer to an actual rose, but to the image of the supposed rose that the speaker has in mind. There are two different referents, and in fact the sound *rose* itself is a token of two different lexical types.

Let us weigh carefully the following passage. Bacon states that "vox significativa ad placitum potest imponi . . . omnibus rebus extra animam et in anima," and he admits that we may name conventionally both mental entities and nonentities, but he insists on the fact that it is impossible to signify with the same *vox* both the individual object and the species. If, to name a species (or any other mental passion), one intends to use the same word already used to name the corresponding object, we must set in motion a *secunda impositio* (*DS* V, 162).

What Bacon intends to clarify is that, when we say "homo currit" ("the man is running") we do not use the word *homo* in the same sense as in the sentence "homo est animal" ("man is an animal"). In the first case the referent of the word is an individual, in the second a species. There are then two equivocal ways of using the same expression. When a potential customer sees the barrel hoop advertising wine in a wine shop, if there is wine, then the hoop signifies the actual wine. If there is no wine, and the customer is misled by a sign that refers to something that is not the case, then the referent of the sign is the idea or image of wine that has taken shape (erroneously) in the customer's mind.

For the people who know there is no wine, the hoop has lost its ability to signify, in the same way in which, when we use the same words to refer to things in the past or the future, we do not use them in the same sense as we do when we refer to actual things that are present. When we speak of Socrates, referring, that is, to someone who is dead, and express our opinions about him, in reality we are using the expression *Socrates* with a new meaning. The word "recipit aliam significationem per transsumptionem," it is used in an ambiguous way compared with the meaning it had when Socrates was alive. "Corrupta re cui facta est impositio, non remanebit vox significativa (*DS* IV, 2, 147). The linguistic term remains, but (as Bacon remarks at the beginning of *DS* I, 1) it remains only as a substance deprived of its *ratio* and of the semantic correlation that made its material occurrence a word.

In the same way, when a child dies, what is left of the father is the *substantia,* not the *relatio paternitatis* (*DS* I, 1, 38).

When we speak of individual things, "certum est inquirenti quod facta impositione soli rei extra animam, impossibile est (quod) vox significet speciem rei tamquam signum datum ab anima et significativum ad placitum, quia vox significativa ad placitum non significat nisi per impositionem et institutione," while the relationship between the mental species and the thing (as the Aristotelian tradition was also aware) is psychological and not directly semiotic. Bacon does not deny that species can be the signs of things, but they are so in an iconic sense: they are natural signs, and not signs *ordinata ab anima*. The *vox* thus signifies only the individual thing and not the species (*DS* V, 163). As has already been demonstrated, when we decide to use the same term to name the species, what we have is a second imposition.

Bacon subverts, then, once and for all the semiotic triangle implicitly formulated since Plato, according to which the relationship between words and referents is mediated by the idea, the concept, or the definition. At this juncture, the left-hand side of the triangle (the relationship, that is, between words and concepts) is reduced to a merely symptomatic phenomenon (see Figure 9.6).

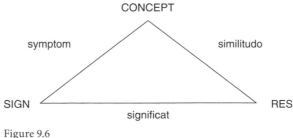

Figure 9.6

In Chapter 4, on the barking of the dog, we raised the question of whether Bacon had relied on Boethius's translation of *De interpretatione* 16a, in which both *symbolon* and *semeion* were translated into Latin with the same word, *nota,* or whether he might not have gone back to the original, concluding from it that words are first and foremost in an exclusively symptomatic relationship with the passions of the soul. Accordingly, he interprets (*DS* V, 166) the passage in Aristotle from his own point of view: words are essentially in a symptomatic relation with species, and at most they can signify them only vicariously *(secunda impositio),* while the only real relation of signification is that between words and referents. He disregards the fact that, for Aristotle, words were, so to speak, symptoms of the species with reference to a temporal sequence, but that in any case they *signified* the species, to the point that we can only understand things named through the mediation of species already known.

For Aristotle, and in general for the medieval tradition prior to Bacon, extension was a function of intension, and in order to ascertain whether something was in fact the case, one had first to understand the meaning of the statement. For Bacon, on the other hand, the meaning of the statement is the fact of which the referent is the case.

What is of most interest to Bacon is the extensional aspect of the entire question, and this is why the relationship of words to what is the case looms so large in his treatise, while the relationship of words and their meaning becomes at best a subspecies of the referential relationship.

We can thus understand why, in the context of his terminology, *significatio* undergoes a radical transformation from the meaning it had had until now. Before Bacon, *nominantur singularia sed universalia significantur,* but with Bacon and after him *significantur singularia,* or at least *significantur res* (though a *res* may be a class, a sentiment, an idea, or a species).

9.9. Duns Scotus and the Modistae

Duns Scotus and the Modistae represent a sort of highly ambiguous fringe between the extensional and intensional positions. In the Modistae we encounter a tortured dialectic between *modi significandi* and *modi essendi.* Lambertini (1984) has demonstrated how this point continues for the most part to remain ambiguous, not only in the original texts, but also in the context of modern and contemporary interpretations (see also Marmo 1994).

In the works of Duns Scotus too, we come across contradictory statements. In support of the extensionalist point of view, we find: "verbum autem exterius est signum rei et non intellectionis" (*Ordinatio* I, 27), while on the other hand, in support of the intensionalist position, we find "significare est alicuius intellectum constituere" (*Quaestiones in Perihermeneias* II, 541a). There are, however, passages that seem to espouse a compromise solution, opposed to be sure to that of Bacon, according to which, though the thing may be subject to transmutation, this is no reason for the *vox* that signifies it to change, because the thing is not signified insofar as it exists, but insofar as it is understood to be an intelligible species (*Quaestiones in Perihermeneias* III, 545 et seq.).

Thus there are scholars who would place Scotus among the extensionalists. Nuchelmans (1973: 196), for instance, referring to the commentary on the sentences (*Opus Oxoniense* I, 27, 3, 19), declares: "Duns Scotus already affirmed that what is signified by the vocal utterance is a thing rather than a concept." For others, such as Heidegger (1915),[11] Scotus is very close to a phenomenological view of meaning as a mental object. And finally, there are still others, like Boehner (1958: 219), who have no qualms about confessing their ongoing perplexity.[12]

9.10. Ockham

There has been considerable discussion as to whether Ockham's extensionalist theory is really as straightforward and explicit as might appear at first sight. If we consider in fact the four meanings of *significare* proposed by Ockham (*Summa logicae* I, 33), only the first has an unmistakable extensional sense. Only in this first meaning in fact do the terms lose their ability to signify when the object they stand for does not exist.

That said, even though we cannot be completely certain that Ockham used *significari* and *denotari* (invariably in the passive form) exclusively in

---

11. We have in mind the first and more reliable part of the text, dedicated to the true Scotus and not to Thomas of Erfurt.

12. Concerning this issue, see Pini (1999).

the extensional sense,[13] nevertheless in many passages he did use the two terms with this meaning.

What happens with Ockham—and had already happened with Bacon—is that the semiotic triangle is turned completely on its head once and for all. Words are not connected first and foremost with concepts and then, thanks to our intellectual mediation, to things: they are imposed directly on things and on states of affairs; and, in the same way, concepts too refer directly to things.

At this point, the semiotic triangle would look like Figure 9.7: there is a direct relation between concepts and things, given that concepts are the natural signs that *signify* things, and there is a direct relation between words and the things on which they impose a name, while he relation between words and concepts is completely neglected (see Boehner 1958: 221 and Tabarroni 1984).

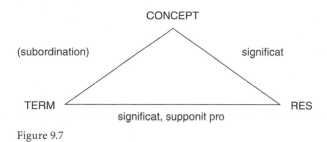

Figure 9.7

Ockham is familiar with the Boethius's dictum according to which "voces significant conceptus," but in his opinion it is to be understood in the sense that "voces sunt signa secundario significantia illa quae per passiones animae primario importantur," where it is clear that *illa* refers to the things, not the concepts. Words signify the same things signified by concepts, but they do not signify concepts (*Summa logicae* I, 1). In addition, there exists a rather disconcerting text in which Ockham, taking issue with the notion of an intelligible species, equates it with an image that cannot be more than a sign permitting us to remember something that we have already encountered as an individual entity: what is represented must be in some way already known, otherwise the representing image could never help us recognize the represented object. For instance a statue of Hercules would not help

---

13. For *significare,* see Boehner (1958) and for *denotari,* Marmo (1984).

me recognize the real Hercules if I had never seen Hercules before; and I could not tell whether the statue looked like Hercules or not.[14]

This text assumes (as an issue on which there exists general agreement) the fact that we are not able to imagine, on the basis of an icon, something previously unknown to us. This would seem to be at odds with our actual experience (take, for example, the case of the identikit photo), given the fact that people use paintings or drawings to represent the characteristics of persons, animals, or things they have never seen. Ockham's position could be interpreted in terms of cultural history as an example of aesthetic relativism: although he lived in the fourteenth century, Ockham was familiar for the most part with Romanesque and Early Gothic iconography, in which statues did not represent individuals in a realistic way, but universal types. When we view the portal of the Moissac cathedral or of Chartres, we have no trouble recognizing the Saint, the Prophet or the Human Being, but certainly not a unique individual. Ockham was unacquainted with the realism of Roman sculpture or the portrait tradition of later centuries.

There is nonetheless an epistemological explanation to account for such an embarrassing affirmation. If the concept is the only sign of individual things, and if its material expression (word or image) is merely a symptom of the inner image, then, without a prior *notitia intuitiva* of an object, the material expression cannot signify anything at all. Words and images cannot create or implant something in the mind of the addressee (as could occur in Augustine's semiotics), unless there already exists in that mind the only possible sign of experienced reality, namely, its mental sign. In the absence of that sign, the external expression ends up being the symptom of an *empty thought*. The subversion of the semiotic triangle, which for Bacon was the end point of a protracted debate, for Ockham is an inescapable point of departure.

There are convincing demonstrations of the fact that Ockham also used *significare* in the intensional sense—we refer the reader to Boehner (1958)

---

14. "Item repraesentatum debet esse prius cognitum; aliter repraesentans nunquam duceret in cognitionem repraesentati tamquam in simile. Exemplum: statua Herculis nunquam duceret me in cognitionem Herculis nisi prius vidissem Herculem; nec aliter possem scire utrum statua sit sibi similis aut non. Sed secundum ponentes speciem, species est aliquid praevium omni actui intelligendi objectum, igitur non potest poni propter repraesentationem objecti" (*Quaest. In II Sent. Reportatio*, 12–13). See also Tabarroni (1984).

and Marmo (1984) for all of those cases in which propositions maintain their meaning regardless of whether they are true or false. We are not concerned here, however, with Ockham's semiotics, but with his semiotic terminology. He clearly uses *supponere* in the extensional sense, inasmuch as *suppositio* exists "quando terminus stat in propositione pro aliquo" (*Summa logicae* I, 62). It is, however, equally evident that on more than one occasion Ockham uses *significare* (in the first meaning of the term) and *supponere* interchangeably: "aliquid significare, vel supponere vel stare pro aliquo" (*Summa logicae* I, 4; see also Pinborg 1972: 5).

It is, however, in the context of his discussion of propositions and suppositions that Ockham uses the term *denotari*. Consider, for example: "terminus supponit pro illo, de quo vel de pronomine demonstrare ipsum, per propositionem denotatur praedicatum praedicari, su supponens sit subiectum" (*Summa logicae* I, 62). If the term is the subject of a proposition, then the thing the term stands for *(supponit)* is the one of which the proposition denotes that the predicate is predicated.

In the phrase *homo est albus*, both terms *suppose* the same thing, and *it is denoted* by the whole proposition that it is the case that the same thing is both a man and white: "denotatur in tali propositione, quod illud, pro quo subiectum supponit, sit illud, pro quo praedicatum supponi" (*Exp. in Porph.* I, 72).

Likewise, *denotari* is used to indicate what is demonstrated to be the case by the conclusion of a syllogism: "propter quam ita est a parte rei sicut denotatur esse per conclusionem demonstrationis" (*Summa logicae* III, 2, 23; see also Moody 1935: sect. 6.3).[15]

---

15. "Sicut per istam 'Homo est animal' denotatur quod Sortes vere est animal. Per istam autem 'Homo est nomen' denotatur quod haec vox 'homo' est nomen . . . Similiter per istam "Album est animal," denotatur quod illa res, quae est alba, sit animal, ita quod haec sit vera: 'Hoc est animal,' demonstrandum illam rem, quae est alba et propter hoc pro illa re subjectum supponit. . . . Nam per istam: 'Sortes est albus' denotatur, quod Sortes est illa res, quae habet albedinem, et ideo praedicatum supponit pro ista re, quae habet albedinem. . . . Et ideo si in ista 'Hic est angelus,' subjectum et praedicatum supponunt pro eodem, propositio est vera. Et ideo non denotatur, quod hic habeat angelitatem . . . sed denotatur, quod hic sit vere angelus. . . . Similiter etiam per tales propositiones: 'Sortes est homo,' 'Sortes est animal' . . . denotatur quod Sortes vere est homo et vere est animal. . . . Denotatur quod est aliqua res, pro qua stat vel supponit hoc

The repeated use of the passive form suggests that a proposition *does not denote* a state of affairs: rather, *by means of a proposition a state of affairs is denoted*. It is, then, open to discussion whether *denotatio* is a relationship between a proposition and what is the case, or between a proposition and what is understood to be the case (see Marmo 1984). Through a proposition something is denoted, even if that something *supposes* nothing (*Summa logicae* I, 72).

Be that as it may, considering that (i) the *suppositio* is a extensional category, and the word "denotation" occurs so frequently in conjunction with the mention of the supposition' and that (ii) in all probability the proposition does not necessarily denote its truth value, but at least denotes to someone that something is or is not the case,[16] we are led to suppose that Ockham's example may have inspired some later thinkers to use the term *denotatio* in extensional contexts.

Thanks to the radical shift in meaning of the verb *significare* between Bacon and Ockham, at this point the term *denotare* is ready to be considered in an extensional perspective.

It is curious to observe how, if we consider Bacon and Ockham, this terminological revolution first affected the term *significatio* (involving *denotatio* almost exclusively as a side effect). But, from the time of Boethius on, the term *significatio* had found itself so tied in with the concept of "meaning" that it had been able to hold out, so to speak, more courageously against the incursions of the extensionalist point of view. Moreover, in centuries to come, we will continue to encounter *significatio,* once more used in an intensional sense (see, for example, Locke). Truth-conditional semantics on the other

---

praedicatum 'homo' et hoc praedicatum 'animal'" (*Summa,* II, 2). There is at least one example, taken from the *Elementarium logicae* and cited by Maierù, of *denotare* in the active voice, in which Ockham distinguishes between the two meanings of *appellare*. The first meaning is Anselm's, while, apropos of the second, Ockham writes: "aliter accipitur appellare pro termine exigere vel denotare seipsum debere suam propriam formam." It would seem that here *denotare* stands for "govern" (or "require") or postulate a coreference within the framework of the linguistic context.

16. For a similar use of *denotari,* see Ockham's *Quaestiones in libros Physicorum* III, partial edition by Corvino (1955).

hand was more successful in appropriating the more semantically ambiguous term *denotatio*.

The cognitivist tradition on the other hand did not follow the lead of using the term "denotation" in relation with meaning.[17] Be that as it may, after Mill we find the term "denotation" used more and more in reference to extension.

9.11. After Ockham

Do we have any reason to believe that Mill borrowed the idea of using *denotatio* as a technical term from Ockham?

There are in fact several reasons to suspect that Mill elaborated his *System of Logic* with reference to the Ockhamist tradition.

(i) Though he paid considerable attention to the intensional aspects of language, Mill formulated a theory of the denotation of terms in which he makes an affirmation similar to that expressed in Ockham's theory of supposition: "a name can only be said to stand for, or to be a name of, the things of which it can be predicated" (Mill [1898]1843: II, v).

(ii) Mill borrows from the Schoolmen (and he is the first to admit it—in II, v) the term "connotation" and, in distinguishing between connotative and nonconnotative terms, he states that the latter are defined as "absolute" terms. Gargani (1971: 95) traces back this terminology back to Ockham's distinction between connotative and absolute terms.

(iii) Mill uses *signify* in line with the Ockhamist tradition, at least as far as the first meaning assigned to it by the medieval philosopher goes. "A non-connotative term is one which signifies a subject only or an attribute only. A connotative term is one which denotes a subject, and implies an attribute" (II, v). Since the denotative function (in Mill's scheme of

---

17. Maierù (1972) cites Peter of Mantua: "Verba significantia actum mentis ut 'scio,' 'cognosco,' 'intelligo,' etc. denotant cognitionem rerum significatarum a terminis sequentibus ipsa verba per conceptum." Right after this sentence, Peter gives an example: "Unde ista propositio 'tu cognoscis Socratem' significat quod tu cognoscis Socratem per hunc conceptum 'Socratem' in recto vel oblique" (*Logica*, 19vb–20ra). It is evident that *denotare* and *significare* mean more or less the same thing, and that both terms are used to speak of propositional aptitudes—an intensional theme if ever there was one.

things) is performed in the first place by nonconnotative terms, it is clear that for Mill "to signify" and "to denote" are one and he same. See also: "the name . . . is said to signify the subjects *directly,* the attributes *indirectly;* it *denotes* the subjects and implies, or involves, or as we shall say henceforth, *connotes* the attributes . . . The only names of objects which connote nothing are proper names, and these have, strictly speaking, no signification" (II, v).

(iv) Mill probably opts for "denote" as a more technical and less prejudicial term than "signify," on account of its etymological opposition to "connote."

Nevertheless, we have seen that Ockham did not encourage the extensional use of *denotare* but at most influenced it. Where, in the history of the natural evolution of the term, are we to find the missing link?

The place to look is probably Hobbes's *De corpore* I, better known as *Computatio sive logica.*

It is a matter of general agreement that Hobbes was fundamentally influenced by Ockham, as Mill was by Hobbes. Mill in fact begins his discussion of proper names with an in-depth review of Hobbes's opinions.

We must, however, note that Hobbes does indeed follow Ockham as far as the theory of universals and propositions is concerned, but at the same time he develops a different theory of signification. For Hobbes in fact there is a clear-cut distinction between signifying (expressing the speaker's opinions, that is, during an act of communication) and naming (in the classic sense of *appellare* or *supponere,* on which see Hungerland and Vick 1981).

Mill ([1898]1843: II, 1) recognizes that for Hobbes names are above all the names of the ideas we have about things, but at the same time he finds in Hobbes proof supportive of the decision that "names, therefore, shall always be spoken of in this work as the names of things themselves," and the contention that "all names are names of something, real or imaginary . . . A general name is familiarly defined, a name which is capable of being truly affirmed, in the same sense, of each of an indefinite number of things." In these passages Mill is close to Hobbes, with the marginal difference that he dubs "general" the names that Hobbes on the other hand dubs "universal."

However, as we have noted, Mill uses "signify," not in the Hobbesian sense, but in that of Ockham, and, in place of the notion of "signifying" used by Hobbes, he prefers to employ "connote." Being deeply interested in connotation, and not realizing that his idea of "connotation" is not all that far away from Hobbes's "signification," Mill is convinced that Hobbes privileges nomination (Mill's "denotation") over signification (Mill's "connotation"). In his opinion, Hobbes, like the Nominalists in general, "bestowed little or no attention upon the connotation of words; and sought for their meaning exclusively in what they denote" (II, v).

This decidedly odd reading of Hobbes (as if he were Bertrand Russell) can be explained by the fact that Mill interprets Hobbes as if he were an orthodox follower of Ockham. But, if Mill considers Hobbes an Ockhamist, why does he attribute to him the idea that names denote? Mill claims that Hobbes uses *nominare* in the place of *denotare* (II, v), but he had probably observed that, in the *De corpore,* Hobbes used *denotare* in four cases at least—five in the English translation of Hobbes's Latin that Mill probably read, since he cites Hobbes's work as *Computation or Logic.*

As for the difference between abstract and concrete names, Hobbes says that "abstractum est quod in re supposita existentem nominis concreti causam denotat, ut 'esse corpus,' 'esse mobile' . . . et similia . . . Nomina autem abstracta causam nominis concreti denotant, non ipsam rem" (*De corpore* I, iii, 3). It should be underscored that for Hobbes abstract names do in fact denote a cause, but this cause is not an entity: it is the criterion that supports the use of an expression (see Gargani 1971: 86 and Hungerland and Vick 1981: 21). Mill reformulates Hobbes's text as follows: a concrete name is a name that stands for a thing; an abstract name is a name that stands for an attribute of a thing (1843, II, v)—in which "stand for" is Ockham's "stare pro aliquo." He adds, furthermore, that his use of words like "concrete" and "abstract" is to be understood as being in keeping with the usage of the Scholastics.

Mill probably extrapolates from this passage in Hobbes the idea that, if abstract names do not denote things, this is instead the case for concrete nouns. For Hobbes in fact "concretum est quod rei alicujus quae existere supponitur nomen est, ideoque quandoque suppositum, quandoque subjectum, graece ypoleimenon appellatur," and, two lines above, he writes that, in the proposition *corpus est mobile,* "quandoque rem ipsam cogitamus utroque nomine designatam" (*De corpore* I, 111,3). Thus, *designare* makes its appearance in a context in which it is linked on the one hand to the concept of supposition and on the other to that of denotation.

Since concrete names can be proper either to single things or to sets of individuals, we may say that, if there exists a concept of denotation developed by Hobbes, it is still halfway between between Peter of Spain's *suppositio naturalis* and his *suppositio accidentalis.* This is why Hungerland and Vick (1981: 51 et seq.) stress the fact that *denotare* could not have had for Hobbes the same meaning it has acquired in our contemporary philosophy of language, because it applies, not only to logical proper names, but also to the names of classes and even to nonexistent entities. But Mill does buy into such a perspective, and therefore could have interpreted Hobbes's *denotare* in an extensionalist mode.

In *De corpore* I, ii, 7, Hobbes states that "homo quemlibet e multis hominibus, phliosophus quemlibet et multis philosophis denotat propter omnium similitudinem." Denotation then once more concerns any and every individual who is part of a multitude of single individuals, insofar as *homo* and *philosophus* are concrete names of a class. In *De corpore* I, ii, 7, he adds that words are useful for syllogistic proofs, because, thanks to them, "unumquodque universale singularium rerum conceptus denotat infinitarum." Words denote concepts, but only of singular things. Mill translates this attitude along clearly extensional lines: "a general name . . . is capable of being truly affirmed of each of an indefinite number of things" (II, iii).

Finally, in *De corpore* II, ii, 2, Hobbes writes that the Latin name *parabola* may *denote* an allegory (parable) or a geometrical figure (parabola). It is not clear whether *denotat* here means *significat* or *nominat.*

To sum up:

(i) Hobbes uses *denotat* at least three times in such a way as to encourage an extensional interpretation, in contexts that recall Ockham's use of *significare* and *supponere.*

(ii) Although Hobbes does not use *denotare* as a technical term, he nonetheless uses it with some regularity and in such a way as to preclude its being interpreted as a synonym of *significare,* as Hungerland and Vick (1981: 153) have persuasively stressed.

(iii) Hobbes probably moved in this direction under the influence of the ambiguous alternative offered by the passive *denotari* that he encountered in Ockham, as well as in some logicians belonging to the Nominalist tradition.

(iv) Mill disregards Hobbes's theory of signification and reads *Computation or Logic* as if it belonged to a wholly Ockhamistic line of thought.

(v) Mill no doubt decided to oppose "denotation" (instead of nomination) to "connotation" under the influence of Hobbes's own use of *denotare.*

The above are of course merely hypotheses. The whole story of the give and take between Ockham and Hobbes and Hobbes and Mill has still to be written.

9.12. Conclusions

In the history of these philosophical terms, issues are clearly at stake which continue to be of considerable relevance from the semiotic and philosophical points of view. Mahoney (1983: 145) remarked on a curious contradiction, or at least a hiatus, between Bacon's epistemology and his semantics. From a gnoseological point of view, we can know a thing through its species, and we cannot name a thing if we do not know it. When we utter a *vox significativa,* then, it is because we have something in mind. From a semiotic standpoint, however, the opposite is what happens, or at least something substantially different: we apply the word directly to the thing, without any mediation of the mental image or the concept or the species.

Such is the paradox of any extensional semantics concerned with the relationship between a sentence and its truth conditions. Every extensional semantics, from Bacon to Tarsky, rather than considering the relation between words and meaning, concentrated on the relation between words and something that is the case. An extensional semantics so conceived does not address the problem of *how* we can know that p is the case. If instead we were to focus on this problem, we would need to be able to identify the mental processes or the semantic structures that make it possible to know or to believe that p is the case. We would need to identify the difference between knowing or believing that p is the case, and the fact that p is the case. But a strict extensional semantics is not concerned with these kinds of epistemological questions, seeing that its exclusive object of study is the formal relation between propositions and what is assumed to be the case. "Snow is white" is true only if snow is white. For an extensional semantics, the marginal and accidental fact that it is hard for us to know on what basis we may assume that snow *really* is white is not a problem

An intensional semantics on the other hand is invariably concerned with the description of our cognitive structures. It may not be capable of determining whether snow is or is not really white, but it seeks to imagine and

reflect upon the mental organization and encyclopedic structures that permit us to assume that snow is white.

Thus, in the last analysis, the history of the alternate fortunes of denotation
(and the fact that its status remains moot) turns out to be a symptom of the
unending dialectic between a cognitive and a truth-conditional approach.

10

On Llull, Pico, and Llullism

We have only to leaf through a few studies on Christian Kabbalism (for instance, Secret 1964; French 1972; Evans 1973) to meet up with the cliché of Ramon Llull the Kabbalist, served up with minimal variations. Llull as magus and alchemist appears in the context of magic in the Prague of Rudolf II, as well as in the library of John Dee, who "was deeply immersed in Llullism and apparently accepted the traditional attitude toward the Llullist-cabalist synthesis" (French 1972: 113). Llull is present in the works of professed Kabbalists (such as Burgonovus, Paulus Scalichius, and the superficial and credulous Belot)[1] as well as in those of the enemies of Kabbalism, like Martino Del Rio,[2] to the point that, when Gabriel Naudé came to write his *Apologie pour tous les grands hommes qui ont été accusés de magie* (Paris, 1625) he felt obliged to defend the poor Catalan mystic energetically against any suspicion of necromancy. To add to the confusion, "in a later Renaissance transforma-

---

A fusion of the following articles: "La lingua universale di Ramón Llull" (Eco 1991); "Pourquoi Llulle n'était pas un kabbaliste" (Eco 1992c); and "I rapporti tra *Revolutio Alphabetaria* e Lullismo" (Eco 1997a). These same themes are taken up in Eco (1993) [English trans. (1995)].

1. Burgonovus, *Cabalisticarum selectiora, obscvrioraque dogmata* (Venice: Apud Franciscum Francisium Senensem, 1569); Paulus Scalichius, *Encyclopedia seu orbis disciplinarum tam sacrarum quam prophanarum Epistemon* (Basel, 1559); Jean Belot, *Les Oeuvres de M. Jean Belot cure de Milmonts, professeur aux Sciences divines et célestes. Contenant la chiromence, physionomie, l'Art de Mémoire de Raymond Llulle, traité des divinations, augures et songes, les sciences stéganographiques etc.* (Rouen: Jean Berthelin, 1669).

2. *Disquisitionum magicarum libri sex* (Mainz: König, 1593).

tion, the letters B through K used in the Llullian *Ars* became associated with the Hebrew letters that the cabalists contemplated and that supposedly signified angel names and the attributes of God. These Hebrew letters, which were thought to have a summoning power over the angels, were the same ones used by practical cabalists like John Dee" (French 1972: 49).

Numerology, magic geometry, astrology, and Llullism are inextricably confused, in part because of the series of pseudo-Llullian alchemistic works that invaded the sixteenth-century scene. Furthermore, the names of the Kabbalah could also be carved on seals, and a whole magical and alchemical tradition made seals with a circular structure popular (Llull practiced his art on a circular wheel). And, for his part Athanasius Kircher, in his 1665 *Arithmologia,* also illustrated a number of magic seals in the form of numerical tables.[3]

However, what influence the Kabbalistic tradition had on Llull is not something we need to discuss in the present context. Llull was born in Majorca—a crossroads on the margins of Europe where encounters took place among Christian, Arabic, and Hebrew cultures, and it is certainly not impossible that someone living where three great monotheistic religions met could have been subject to the influence, visual at least, of Kabbalistic speculation. Llull's *Ars* combines letters on three concentric wheels and, from the very beginnings of the Kabbalistic tradition, in the *Sefer Yetzirah* ("Book of Creation," written at an uncertain date between the second and sixth centuries), the combining of the letters is associated with their inscription on a wheel. What is certain, however, is that nothing is further from Kabbalistic practices than Llull's *Ars,* at least as formulated by its founder.

10.1. What Exactly is Llull's *Ars*?

If we are to understand the internal mechanics of the *Ars,* we must first review a few principles of Llull's system of mathematical combinations.

We have *permutation* when, given *n* different elements, every possible change in their order has been realized. The typical case is the anagram.[4]

---

3. *Arithmologia, Sive De abditis Numerorum Mysterijs* (Rome: Ex Typographia Varesij, 1665).

4. The number of possible permutations is given by the factorial of *n* (*n!*) which is calculated: $1*2*3* \ldots *n$. For example, three elements ABC can be combined in

We have *disposition* when *n* elements are arranged *t* by *t*, but in such a way that the order also has differential value (AB and BA, for instance, represent two different dispositions).[5] We have *combination* when, if we have to arrange *n* elements *t* by *t*, inversions of order are not relevant (AB and BA, for instance, represent the same combination).[6]

The calculus of the permutations, dispositions, and combinations may be used to solve a number of technical problems, but it could also be used for the purposes of discovery—to delineate, in other words, possible future "scenarios." In semiotic terms, what we have is a system of expression (made up of symbols and syntactic rules) such that, by associating the symbols with a content, various "states of things" (or of ideas) can be imagined. In order for the combinatory system to be most effective, however, it must be assumed that there are no restrictions on thinking all possible universes. Once we begin to designate certain universes as not possible, either because they are improbable in the light of the evidence of our past experience or because they do not correspond to what we consider to be the laws of reason, then external criteria come into play that induce us, not merely to discriminate among the results of the system of combinations, but also to introduce restrictive rules into the system itself. In the case of Llull, what we have is a proposal for a universal and limitless system of combinations, which as such will fascinate later thinkers, but which at its very inception is severely limited, for reasons both theological and logical.

Llull's *Ars* involves an alphabet of nine letters, from B to K (no distinction is made between I and J), and four combinatory figures. In a *Tabula Generalis,* Llull establishes a list of six sets of nine entities each (the six are: Absolute Principles or Divine Dignities, Relative Principles, Questions, Subjects, Virtues, Vices). Each entity may be assigned to one of the nine letters (our Figure 10.1).

Taking Aristotle's list of categories as a model, the nine Divine Dignities or attributes of God's being (*Bonitas, Magnitudo, Aeternitas* or *Duratio,*

---

six triplets (ABC, ACB, BAC, BCA, CAB, CBA), distinguished only by the order of their elements.

5. The formula is $n! / (n - t)!$. For example, given four elements ABCD, they can be arranged into twelve possible duplets.

6. The formula is $n! / t! (n - t)!$. Given the four elements ABCD, they can be combined into six possible duplets.

	Principia absoluta	Principia relativa	Quaestiones	Subjecta	Virtutes	Vita
B	Bonitas	Differentia	Utrum?	Deus	Iustitia	Avaritia
C	Magnitudo	Concordantia	Quid?	Angelus	Prudentia	Avaritia
D	Aetaernitas	Contrarietas	De quo?	Coelum	Fortitudo	Luxuria
E	Potestas	Principium	Quare?	Homo	Temperantia	Superbia
F	Sapientia	Medium	Quantum?	Imaginatio	Fides	Acidia
G	Voluntas	Finis	Quale?	Sensitiva	Spes	Invidia
H	Virus	Maioritas	Quando?	Vegetativa	Charitas	Ira
I	Veritas	Aequalitas	Ubi?	Elementativa	Patientia	Mendacium
K	Gloria	Minoritas	Quomodo? Cum quo?	Instrumentativa	Inconstantia	

Figure 10.1

Potestas, Sapientia, Voluntas, Virtus, Veritas, and *Gloria*) are subjects of predication while the other five columns contain predicates.

The *Ars* includes four figures or illustrations, which in the various manuscripts are highlighted in different colors.[7]

PRIMA FIGURA. Llull's first figure represents a case of *disposition.* The nine Absolute Principles are assigned to the letters. Llull explores all the possible combinations among these principles so as to produce propositions such as *Bonitas est magna* ("Goodness is great"), *Duratio est gloriosa* ("Duration is glorious"), and so on. The principles appear in nominal form when they are the subject and in adjectival form when they are the predicate, so that the sides of the polygon inscribed in the circle are to be read in two directions (we may read *Bonitas est magna,* as well as *Magnitudo est bona*). The possible dispositions of nine elements two by two, when inversions of order are also allowed, permit Llull to formulate seventy-two propositions (see Figure 10.2).

The figure permits regular syllogisms "ut ad faciendam conclusionem possit medium invenire" ("if the middle term be suitable for reaching a conclusion") (*Ars brevis* II).[8] To demonstrate that Goodness can be great, it is

---

7. The woodcuts that follow are taken from Bernardus de Lavinheta, *Practica compendiosa artis Raymundi Llulli* (Lyon, 1523).

8. It will be seen that, by "middle term," Llull means something different from what was understood by Scholastic syllogists. However that may be, excluded

·PRIMA·FIGVRA

Figure 10.2

argued that "omne id quod magnificetur a magnitudine est magnum—sed Bonitas est id quod magnificetur a magnitudine—ergo Bonitas est Magna" ("everything made great by greatness is great—but Goodness is what is made great by greatness—therefore Goodness is great").

SECUNDA FIGURA. Llull's circle (unlike the one in his first figure) does not involve any system of combinations. It is simply a visual-mnemonic device that allows us to remember the connections (already foreordained) among various types of relationships and various types of entities (see Figure 10.3).

For example, both difference and concordance, as well as contrariety, can be considered with reference to (i) two sensitive entities, such as stone and plant; (ii) one sensitive and one intellectual, such as body and soul; and (iii) two intellectual entities, such as soul and angel.

---

from this first table are self-predicatory combinations like BB or CC, because for Llull the premise "Goodness is good" does not permit us to come up with a middle term (cf. Johnston 1987: 234).

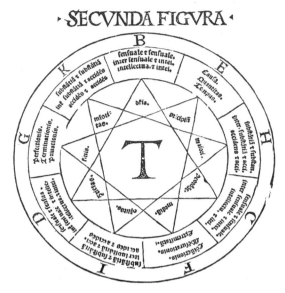

Figure 10.3

TERTIA FIGURA. This figure evidently represents a case of *combination,* considering that in it all possible pairings of the letters are considered, excluding inversions of order (the table includes BC, for example, but not CB), and the doublets generated are thirty-six, inserted into what Llull dubs thirty-six *chambers.* But the chambers are virtually seventy-two, because each letter may indifferently become subject or predicate, that is, a BC can also be read as a CB (*Bonitas est magna* also gives *Magnitudo est bona,* see *Ars magna* VI, 2, and Figure 10.4).[9]

Once the combinatory system has been set in motion, we proceed to what Llull calls the "evacuation of the chambers." For example, taking the BC chamber, and referring to the *Tabula Generalis,* we first read chamber BC according to the Absolute Principles and we obtain *Bonitas est magna,* then we read it according to the Relative Principles and we obtain *Differentia est*

---

9. Our references to Llull's texts are to the Zetzner edition (Strasburg, 1598), since it is on the basis of this edition that the Llullian tradition is transmitted to later centuries. Therefore, by *Ars magna* we mean the *Ars generalis ultima,* which in the 1598 edition is entitled *Ars magna et ultima.*

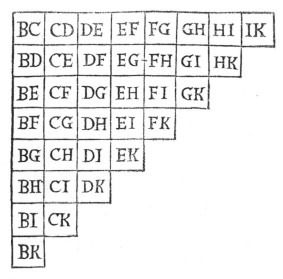

BC	CD	DE	EF	FG	GH	HI	IK
BD	CE	DF	EG	FH	GI	HK	
BE	CF	DG	EH	FI	GK		
BF	CG	DH	EI	FK			
BG	CH	DI	EK				
BH	CI	DK					
BI	CK						
BK							

Figure 10.4

concordans (*Ars magna* II, 3). In this way we obtain twelve propositions: *Bonitas est magna, Diffferentia est magna, Bonitas est differens, Differentia est bona, Bonitas est concordans, Differentia est concordans, Magnitudo est bona, Concordantia est bona, Magnitudo est differens, Concordantia est differens, Magnitudo est concordans, Concordantia est magna*. Returning to the *Tabula Generalis* and assigning to B and C the corresponding questions (*utrum* or "whether" and *quid* or "what") with their respective answers, we can derive, from the twelve propositions, twenty-four questions (of the type *Utrum Bonitas sit magna?* [Whether Goodness is great?] and *Quid est Bonitas magna?* [What is great Goodness?]) (see *Ars magna* VI, 1).

QUARTA FIGURA. In this case the mechanism is mobile, in the sense that we have three concentric circles decreasing in circumference, placed one on top of the other, and usually held together at the center with a knotted string. Revolving the smaller inner circles, we obtain triplets (see Figure 10.5).

These are produced from the combination of nine elements into groups of three, without the same element being repeated twice in the same triplet or *chamber*. Llull, however, adds to each triplet the letter *t*—an operator by which it is established that the letters that precede are to be read with reference to

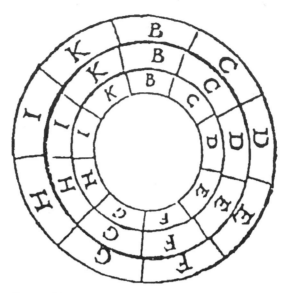

Figure 10.5

the first column of the *Tabula Generalis,* as Principles or Dignities, whereas those that follow are to be read as Relative Principles. Since the *t* changes the meaning of the letters, as Platzeck (1954: 140–143) explains, it is as if Llull were composing his triplets by combining, not three, but six elements (not merely BCD, for instance, but BCDbcd). The combinations of six elements into groups of three give (according to the rules of the combinatory system) twenty chambers.

Consider now the reproduction in Figure 10.6 of the first of the tables elaborated by Llull to exploit to the full the possibilities of his fourth figure (each table being composed of columns of twenty chambers each). In the first column we have BCDbcd, in the second BCEbce, in the third BCFbcf, and so on and so forth, until we have obtained eighty-four columns and hence 1,680 chambers.

If we take, for instance, the first column of the *Tabula Generalis,* the chamber bctc (or BCc) is to be read as *b=bonitas, c=magnitudo, c=concordantia.* Referring to the *Tabula Generalis,* the chambers that begin with *b* correspond to the first question *(utrum),* those that begin with *c* to the second question *(quid),* and so on. As a result, the same chamber *bctc* (or BCc) is to be read as *Utrum bonitas in tantum sit magna quod contineat in se res*

bcdt	bcet	bcft	bcgt	bcbt	bcit	bckt
bctb	bctb	bctb	bctb	bctb	bctb	bctb
bctc	bctc	bctc	bctc	bctc	bctc	bctc
bctd	bcte	bctf	bctg	bctb	bcti	bctk
bdtb	betb	bftb	bgtb	bbtb	betb	bktb
bdtc	betc	bftc	bgtc	bbtc	bitc	bktc
bdtd	bete	bftf	bgtg	bbtb	biti	bktk
btbc	btbc	btbc	btbc	btbc	btbc	btbc
btbd	btbe	btbf	btbg	btbb	btbi	btbk
btcd	btce	btcf	btcg	btcb	btci	btck
cdtb	cetb	cftb	cgtb	cbtb	citb	cktb
cdtc	cetc	cftc	cgtc	cbtc	citc	cktc
cdtd	cete	cftf	cgtg	cbtb	citi	cktk
ctbc	ctbc	ctbc	ctbc	ctbc	ctbc	ctbc
ctbd	ctbe	ctbf	ctbg	ctbb	ctbi	ctbk
ctcd	ctce	ctcf	ctcg	ctcb	ctci	ctck
dtbc	etbc	ftbc	gtbc	btbc	itbc	ktbc
dtbd	etbe	ftbf	gtbg	btbb	itbi	ktbk
dtcd	etce	ftcf	gtcg	btcb	itci	ktck
tbcd	tbce	tbcf	tbcg	tbcb	tbci	tbck

Figure 10.6

concordantes et sibi coessentiales ("Whether goodness is great insofar as it contains within it things in accord with it and coessential to it").

Quite apart from a certain arbitrariness in "evacuating the chambers," in other words, in articulating the reading of the letters of the various chambers into a discourse, not all the possible combinations (and this observation is valid for all the figures) are admissible. After describing his four figures in fact, Llull prescribes a series of Definitions of the various terms in play (of the type *Bonitas est ens, ratione cujus bonum agit bonum* ["Goodness is something as a result of which a being that is good does what is good"]) and Necessary Rules (which consist of ten questions to which, it should be borne in mind, the answers are provided), so that such chambers generated by the combinatory system as contradict these rules *must not be taken into consideration.*

This is where the first limitation of the *Ars* surfaces: it is capable of generating combinations that right reason must reject. In his *Ars magna sciendi*, Athanasius Kircher will say that one proceeds with the *Ars* as one does when working out combinations that are anagrams of a word: once one has obtained the list, one excludes all those permutations that do not make up an existing word (in other words, twenty-four permutations can be made of the letters of the Italian word ROMA, but, while AMOR, MORA, ARMO, and RAMO make sense in Italian and can be retained, meaningless permutations like AROM, AOMR, OAMR, or MRAO can, so to speak, be cast aside). In fact Kircher, working with the fourth figure, produces nine syllogisms for each letter, even though the combinatory system would allow him more, because he excludes all the combinations with an undistributed middle, which precludes the formation of a correct syllogism.[10]

This is the same criterion followed by Llull, when he points out, for example, in *Ars magna, Secunda pars principalis,* apropos of the various ways in which the first figure can be used, that the subject can certainly be changed into the predicate and vice versa (for instance, *Bonitas est magna* and *Magnitudo est bona*), but it is not permitted to interchange Goodness and Angel. We interpret this to mean that all angels are good, but that an argument that asserts the "since all angels are good and Socrates is good, then Socrates is an angel" is unacceptable. In fact we would have a syllogism with an unquantified middle.

But the combinatory system is not only limited by the laws of the syllogism. The fact is that even formally correct conversions are only acceptable if they predicate according to the truth criteria established by the rules—which rules, it will be recalled, are not logical in nature but philosophical and theological (cf. Johnston 1987: 229). Bäumker (1923: 417–418) realized that the aim of the *ars inveniendi* (or art of invention) was to set up the greatest possible number of combinations among concepts already provided, and to draw from them as a consequence all possible questions, but only if the resulting questions could stand up to "an ontological and logical examination," permitting us to discriminate between correct combinations and false propositions. The artist, says Llull, must know what is convertible and what is not.

Furthermore, among the quadruplets tabulated by Llull there are—by virtue of the combinatory laws—a number of repetitions. See, for example, in the columns reproduced in Figure 10.6, the chamber *btch,* which recurs in the second place in each of the first seven columns, and which in the *Ars magna* (V, 1) is translated as *utrum sit aliqua bonitas in tantum magna quod*

10. Athanasius Kircher, *Ars magna sciendi* (Amsterdam: Jannson, 1669).

sit differens ("whether a certain goodness is great insofar as it is different") and in XI, 1, by the rule of obversion, as *utrum bonitas possit esse magna sine distinctione* ("whether goodness can be great without being different")—permitting a positive answer in the first case and for a negative one in the second. The fact that the same demonstrative schema should appear several times does not seem to worry Llull, and the reason is simple. He assumes that the same question can be resolved both by each of the quadruplets in the single column that generates it and by all the other columns. This characteristic, which Llull sees as one of the virtues of the *Ars*, signals instead its second limitation: the 1,680 quadruplets do not generate original questions and do not provide proofs that are not the reformulation of previously tried and tested arguments. Indeed, in principle the *Ars* allows us to answer in 1,680 different ways a question to which we already know the answer—and it is not therefore a logical tool but a dialectical tool, a way of identifying and remembering all the useful ways to argue in favor of a preestablished thesis. To such a point that there is no chamber that, duly interpreted, cannot resolve the question to which it is adapted.

All of the above-mentioned limitations become evident if we consider the dramatic question *utrum mundus sit aeternus,* whether the world is eternal. This is a question to which Llull already knows the answer, which is negative, otherwise we would fall into the same error as Averroes. Seeing that the term *eternity* is, so to speak, "explicated" in the question, this allows us to place it under the letter D in the first column of the *Tabula Generalis* (see Figure 10.1). However, the D, as we saw in the second figure, refers to the contrariety between sensitive and sensitive, intellectual and sensitive, and intellectual and intellectual. If we observe the second figure, we see that the D is joined by the same triangle to B and C. Moreover, the question begins with *utrum,* and, on the basis of the *Tabula Generalis,* we know that the interrogative *utrum* refers to B. We have therefore found the column in which to look for the arguments: it is the one in which B, C, and D all appear.

At this point all that is needed to interpret the letters is a good rhetorical ability, and, working on the BCDT chamber, Llull draws the conclusion that, if the world were eternal, since we already know that Goodness is eternal, it should produce an Eternal Goodness, and therefore evil would not exist. But, Llull observes, "evil does exist in the world, as we know from experience. Therefore we conclude that the world is not eternal."

Hence, after having constructed a device (*quasi-electronic,* we might be tempted to say) like the *Ars,* which is supposed to be capable of resolving any question all by itself, Llull calls into question its output on the basis of a datum of experience (external to the *Ars*). The *Ars* is designed to convert Averroistic infidels on the basis of a healthy reason, shared by every human being (of whom it is the model); but it is clear that part of this healthy reason is the conviction that if the world were eternal it could not be good.

Llull's *Ars* seduced posterity who saw it as a mechanism for exploring the vast number of possible connections between one being and another, between beings and principles, beings and questions, vices and virtues. A combinatory system without controls, however, was capable of producing the principles of any theology whatsoever, whereas Llull intends the *Ars* to be used to convert infidels to Christianity. The principles of faith and a well-ordered cosmology (independently of the rules of the *Ars*) must temper the incontinence of the combinatorial system.

We must first bear in mind that Llull's logic comes across as a logic of first, not second, intentions, that is, a logic of our immediate apprehension of things and not of our concepts of things. Llull repeats in various of his works that, if metaphysics considers things outside the mind while logic considers their mental being, the *Ars* considers them from both points of view. In this sense, the *Ars* produces surer conclusions than those of logic: "Logicus facit conclusiones cum duabus praemissis, generalis autem artista huius artis cum mixtione principiorum et regularum. . . . Et ideo potest addiscere artista de hac arte uno mense, quam logicus de logica un anno" ("The logician arrives at a conclusion on the basis of two premises, whereas the artist of this general art does so by combining principles and rules. . . . And for this reason the artist can learn as much of this art in a month as a logician can learn of logic in a year") (*Ars magna, Decima pars,* ch. 101). And with this self-confident final assertion Llull reminds us that his is not the formal method that many have attributed to him. The combinatory system must reflect the very movement of reality, and works with a concept of truth that is not supplied by the *Ars* according to the forms of logical reasoning, but instead by the way things are in reality, both as they are attested by experience and as they are revealed by faith.

Llull believes in the extramental existence of universals, not only in the reality of genera and species, but also in the reality of accidental forms. On the one hand, this allows his combinatory system to manipulate, not only genera and species, but also virtues, vices, and all *differentiae* (cf. Johnston 1987: 20, 54, 59, etc.). Nevertheless, these accidents cannot rotate freely because they are determined by an ironclad hierarchy of beings: "Llull's *Ars* comes across as solidly linked to the knowledge of the objects that make up the world. Unlike so-called formal logic it deals with things and not just with words, it is interested in the structure of the world and not just in the structure of discourse. An exemplaristic metaphysics and a universal symbolism are at the root of a technique that presumes to speak both of logic and of metaphysics together and at the same time, and to enunciate the rules that form the basis of discourse and the rules according to which reality itself is structured" (Rossi 1960: 68).

10.2. Differences Between Llullism and Kabbalism

We can now grasp what the substantial differences were between the Llullian combinatory system and that of the Kabbalists.

True, in the *Sefer Yetzirah (The Book of Creation)*, the materials, the stones, and the thirty-two paths or ways of wisdom with which Yahweh created the world are the ten Sephirot and the twenty-two letters of the Hebrew alphabet.

> He hath formed, weighed, transmuted, composed, and created with these twenty-two letters every living being, and every soul yet uncreated. From two letters, or forms He composed two dwellings; from three, six; from four, twenty-four; from five, one hundred and twenty; from six, seven hundred and twenty; from seven, five thousand and forty; and from thence their numbers increase in a manner beyond counting; and are incomprehensible. (I, 1)[11]

The *Sefer Yetzirah* was assuredly speaking of factorial calculus, and suggested the idea of a finite alphabet capable of producing a vertiginous number of *permutations*. It is difficult, when considering Llull's fourth figure, to escape the comparison with Kabbalistic practices—at least from the visual point of view, given that the combinatory system of the *Sefer Yetzirah* letters was

---

11. *Sefer Yetzira*, University Press of America, 2010.

associated with their inscription on a wheel, something underscored by a number of authors who are nonetheless extremely cautious about speaking of Kabbalism in Llull's case (see, for example, Millás Vallicrosa 1958 and Zambelli 1965, to say nothing of the works of Frances Yates). Llull's fourth figure, however, does not generate *permutations* (i.e., anagrams), but *combinations*.

But this is not the only difference. The text of the Torah is approached by the Kabbalist as a symbolic apparatus that speaks of mystic and metaphysical realities and must therefore be read distinguishing its four senses (literal, allegorical-philosophical, hermeneutical, and mystical). This is reminiscent of the theory of the four senses of Scripture in Christian exegesis, but at this point the analogy gives way to a radical difference.

For medieval Christian exegesis the hidden meanings are to be detected through a work of interpretation (to identify a surplus of content), but *without altering the expression,* that is to say, the material arrangement of the text, but, on the contrary, making a supreme effort to establish the exact reading (at least according to the questionable philological principles of the day). For some Kabbalistic currents, however, reading anatomizes, so to speak, the very substance of the expression, by means of three fundamental techniques: Notarikon, Gematria, and Temurah.

Notarikon is the acrostic technique, Gematria is made possible by the fact that in Hebrew numbers are represented by letters of the alphabet, so that each word can be associated with a numerical value derived from the sum of the numbers represented by the individual letters—the idea is to find analogies among words with a different meaning that nevertheless have the same numerical value. But the possible similarities between Llull's procedures and those of the Kabbalists concern Temurah, the art of the permutation of letters, and therefore an anagrammatical technique.

In a language in which the vowels can be interpolated, the anagram has greater permutational possibilities than in other tongues. Moses Cordovero, for instance, wonders why in Deuteronomy we find the prohibition against wearing garments woven out of a mixture of linen and wool. His conclusion is that in the original version the same letters were combined to form another expression which warned Adam not to substitute his original garment of light with a garment of snakeskin, which represents the power of the demon.

In Abulafia we encounter pages in which the Tetragrammaton YHWH, thanks to the vocalization of its four letters and their arrangement in every conceivable order, produces four tables each consisting of fifty combinations. Eleazar of Worms vocalizes every letter of the Tetragrammaton with two vowels, using six vowels, and the number of combinations increases (cf. Idel 1988b: 22–23).

The Kabbalist can take advantage of the infinite resources of the Temurah because it is not only a reading technique, but the very process by which God created the world (as was already stated in the passage from the *Sefer Yetzirah* quoted above).

The Kabbalah suggests, then, that there may be a finite alphabet that produces a dizzying number of combinations, and the one who took the art of combination to its utmost limit is precisely Abulafia (thirteenth century) with his Kabbalah of names.

As we saw in Chapter 7, the Kabbalah of names, or ecstatic Kabbalah, is practiced by reciting the divine names hidden in the text of the Torah, playing upon the various combinations of the letters of the Hebrew alphabet, altering, separating, and recombining the surface of the text, down to the individual letters of the alphabet.

For the ecstatic Kabala, language is a universe unto itself, and the structure of language reflects the structure of reality. Therefore, conversely to what happens in the Western philosophical tradition and in Arab and Jewish philosophy, in the Kabbalah language does not represent the world in the sense that a significant expression represents an extralinguistic reality. If God created the world through the emission of sounds and letters of the alphabet, these semiotic elements are not representations of something pre-existent, but the forms on which the elements that compose the world are modeled.

A linguistic form that produces the world, and a series of symbols that can be infinitely combined, without the interference of any limiting rule: these are the two points on which the Kabbalistic tradition substantially differs from Llull's *Ars*. As Platzeck (1964: 1:328) remarks: "Llull's combinatory system, as a pure combination of concepts, is wholly inspired by the rigid spirit of Western logic, while the kabbalistic combinatory system is a philological game."

10.3. Llull's Trees and the Great Chain of Being

If Llull's ideas did not come from the Hebrew Kabbalah, where did he get them from?

An admiring reader of the Catalan mystic, Leibniz (in his 1666 *Dissertatio de arte combinatoria*) asked himself why Llull had stopped at such a limited number of elements. Given that the virtues are traditionally seven (four cardinal virtues and three theological), why did Llull, who increases them to nine, not go further? If, among the Absolute Principles, Truth and Wisdom are included, why not Beauty and Number?

In point of fact, in various of his works, Llull had proposed at one time ten, at another twelve, and at yet another twenty principles, finally settling on nine. Scholars have inferred—given that his Absolute Principles are nine, plus a tenth (labeled with an A) that is left out of the combinatory pool, because it represents divine Unity and Perfection—that he was influenced by the ten Sephirot of the Kabbalah (cf. Millás Vallicrosa 1958). But we have already seen that this analogy will not get us far. Platzeck (1953: 583) observes that a comparable list of Dignities could be found in the Koran, while, in his *Compendium artis demonstrativae* ("De fine hujus libri"), Llull claims to have borrowed the terms of the *Ars* from the Arabs.

Still, we are not obliged to recognize at all costs extra-Christian influences, because the list of divine Dignities could have been handed down to him from a long and venerable Classical, Patristic, and Scholastic tradition. From the *Divine Names* of Pseudo-Dionysius the Areopagite to the thought of mature Scholasticism, we find an idea, Aristotelian in origin, which runs through the entire reflective tradition of the Christian world, the idea of the transcendental properties of being: there are certain characteristics common to all being and found supereminently in the divine being, such as the One, the Good, the True (some include the Beautiful), and all of these properties are mutually converted into one another, in the sense that everything that is true is good and vice versa, and so on and so forth.

Furthermore, all the experts concur in identifying in Llull two basic sources of inspiration.

(i). One has its origin in Augustine Platonism, for which there exists a world of divine ideas which we know by internal enlightenment and innate disposition. In chapter 7 of his *De Trinitate,* Augustine affirms that God is called great, good, wise, blessed, and true, and His very greatness is His wisdom, while His goodness, which is greatness and wisdom, is truth, and to be blessed and wise means nothing more than to be true and good, and so on. These are pretty much Llull's Dignities, which, as was the case in Augustine, cannot but be known a priori, since they are imprinted by God himself on our souls. If Llull had not been convinced of this innatism he would not have thought it possible to dialogue with the infidels on the basis of the fundamental notions common to all mankind.

Platzeck (1953, 1954) has reconstructed a series of sources that Llull could have drawn upon in formulating his own list of divine Dignities, from Boethius to Richard of Saint Victor, from John of Salisbury to Arabic logicians like Algazel (on whom Llull wrote a commentary), not to mention Euclid, filtered through Boethius, who speaks of a number of principles that ought to be well known in and of themselves (*dignitas* would in that case be a translation of *axioma*): "The fact that the three religious communities present in the Mediterranean basin—Christian, Arab, and Hebrew—averred that these dignities or perfections were absolute in God authorized Llull to posit them, in imitation of Euclid's, as prior axioms or *dignitates* or *conceptiones animi communes*" (Platzeck 1953: 609).

(ii). The other source is the idea, Neo-Platonic in origin, of the Great Chain of Being (cf. Lovejoy 1936). Primitive Neo-Platonism, taken up in the Middle Ages in more or less tempered form, taught that the universe, entirely divine in nature, is the emanation of an unknowable and ineffable One, through a series of degrees of being, or hypostases, produced by necessity down to the lowest matter. Beings are thus arranged at progressively increasing distances from the divine One, and participate to an ever-decreasing extent in a divine nature that becomes degraded little by little to the point of disappearing altogether on the lower rungs of the ladder (or chain) of beings. From this state of affairs two principles follow, one cosmological, the other ethical-mystical. In the first place, if every step on the ladder of being is a phase of the same divine emanation, there exist relations of similarity, kinship, analogy between a lower state and the higher states— and from this root are derived all the theories of cosmic similarity and sympathy. In the second place, if the emanational ladder, on the one hand, represents a descent from the inconceivable perfection of the One to the lower degrees of matter, on the other, knowledge, salvation, and mystic union (strongly identified with each other in the Neo-Platonist view) imply an ascent, a return to the higher planes of the Great Chain of Being.

This tempered medieval Neo-Platonism will endeavor to reduce as much as possible the identity between the divine nature and the various states of creation, and, with Thomas Aquinas, will finally see the chain in terms of participation (which implies, not a necessary emanation of the divinity, but a free act by which God confers existence on his own creatures; and the stages of the chain are related to each other, not by an inevitable inner likeness, but by analogy. Nevertheless, this image of the Great Chain of Being is always in some way present in medieval thought, even when we cannot trace a direct relationship to Neo-Platonism. We have only to recall that every medieval thinker had meditated upon a text of the third or fourth century, the commentary to the Ciceronian *Somnium Scipionis* by Macrobius, whose Platonic and Neo-Platonic inspiration is obvious. Macrobius places at the top of the ladder of being the Good, the first cause of all things, then the Nous or Intelligence, born of God himself, which contains the Ideas as archetypes of all things. The Nous, contemplating itself and knowing itself, produces a World-Soul, which is diffused—preserving its unity—throughout the multiplicity of the created universe. Not a number, but the origin and matrix of all numbers, the Soul generates the numbered plurality of beings, from the celestial spheres down to the sublunar bodies: "Mind emanates from the Supreme God and Soul from Mind, and Mind, indeed, forms and suffuses all below with life, and since this is the one splendor lighting up everything and visible in all, like a countenance reflected in many mirrors arranged in a row, and since all follow on in continuous succession, degenerating step by step in their downward course, the close observer will find that it creates all the following things and fills them with life, and since this unique light illuminates everything and is reflected in everything, and just as a single countenance may be reflected in various consecutive mirrors, all things follow each other in a continuous succession, degenerating bit by bit down to the end of the series—so that the attentive observer may seize an interconnection of the parts, from God on High down to the last dregs of things, bound to each other without any interruption" (Macrobius 1952).

There is a passage in Llull's *Rhetorica* (ed. 1598: 199) that is practically a literal echo of Macrobius and confirms this basic principle of likeness among the various levels of being, as a result of which what was predicated in the definition of the original Dignities is realized in each being: "things receive from their likeness with the Divine Principle their conceptually defined places that at the same time correspond to their level of being" (Platzeck 1953: 601).

Through a thorough comparison not only of their texts but also of the illustrations that appear in various manuscripts of the two authors, Yates (1960) believed she could identify an unmediated source in the thought of John Scotus Eriugena. It is significant that for Eriugena the Divine Names or attributes are seen as primordial causes, eternal forms on the basis of which the world is configured, and from them there proceeds a primary matter, *hyle* or *chaos,* which we reencounter in the thought of Llull, author of a *Liber Chaos* or Book of Chaos). Along these lines, Yates (1960: 104 et seq.) identifies the first idea of the *Ars* in a passage from Eriugena's *De divisione naturae,* in which fifteen primordial causes are mentioned (Goodness, Essence, Life, Reason, Intelligence, Wisdom, Virtue, Beatitude, Truth, Eternity, Greatness, Love, Peace, Unity, Perfection), but Eriugena adds that the number of causes is infinite and that they can therefore be arranged, for purposes of contemplation, in a series of arbitrary successions (the term Eriugena uses is *convolvere,* to cause them to rotate, so to speak, and Yates moreover reminds us that Eriugena, like other authors of his time, used the method of concentric circles to define the divine attributes and their combinations— though for contemplative and not inventive purposes). Obviously, the analogy with Kabbalistic procedures does not escape Yates, though she does not attempt to explain it in terms of direct dependence: "We should ask, not so much whether Llull was influenced by the Kabbalah, but whether Kabbalism and Llullism, with its Scotist basis, are not phenomena of a similar type, the one arising in the Jewish, and the other in the Christian tradition, which both appear in Spain at about the same time, and which might, so to speak, have encouraged one another by engendering similar atmospheres, or perhaps by actively permeating one another" (1960: 112; Llull and Bruno. Collected Essays 1982, p. 112).

Maybe Yates allowed herself to be bedazzled by similarities that seem less surprising when we recall that many analogous themes are to be found in other medieval Neo-Platonic texts (of the School of Chartres, for example). But precisely because of this it is undeniable that there are present in Llull's texts ideas that Eriugena bequeathed to subsequent thinkers. Moreover, in the ninth century, Eriugena had contributed to the diffusion of the treatise by Pseudo-Dionysius *On the Divine Names,* one of the most important sources of medieval Neo-Platonic thought, at least in its tempered medieval form.

From the point of view of our investigation, ascertaining exactly where Llull got the idea of the Dignities is less relevant than recognizing that "Llull is a Platonist or a Neo-Platonist from top to bottom" (Platzeck 1953: 595). It is important to stress that the Dignities are not produced by the *Ars,* but constitute its premises, and they are the premises of the *Ars* because they are the roots of a chain of being.

To understand the metaphysical roots of the *Ars* we must turn to Llull's theory of the *Arbor scientiae* (1296). Between the first versions of the *Ars* and that of 1303, Llull has come a long way (his journey is described by Carreras y Artau and Carreras y Artau 1939: 1:394), making his device capable of resolving, not only theological and metaphysical problems, but also problems of cosmology, law, medicine, astronomy, geometry, and psychology. The *Ars* becomes more and more a tool to take on the entire encyclopedia of learning, picking up the suggestions found in the countless medieval encyclopedias and looking forward to the encyclopedic utopia of Renaissance and Baroque culture.

The *Ars* may appear at first sight to be free from hierarchical structures, because, for example, the divine Dignities are defined in a circular fashion one being used to define the other. The relationships are not arranged in a hierarchical system (though they in fact refer to an implicit hierarchy between things sensitive and things intellectual, or between substances and accidents). But a hierarchical principle insinuates itself into the list of questions (whether something exists, what it is, in what way does it exist, etc.) and the list of Subjects is certainly hierarchical (God, Angel, Heaven, Man, down to the elements and tools). The Dignities are defined in a circular fashion because they are determined by the First Cause: but, it is on the basis of the Dignities that the ladder of being begins. And the *Ars* is supposed to make it possible to argue about every element in this ladder, or about every element in the furniture of the universe, about every accident and every possible question.

The image of this ladder of being is the Tree of Science, which has as its roots the nine Dignities and the nine Relations, and is then subdivided into sixteen branches, to each of which corresponds a separate tree. Each of these sixteen trees, to which an individual representation is dedicated, is divided into seven parts (roots, trunk, limbs, branches, leaves, flowers and fruit). Eight trees clearly correspond to eight subjects in the *Tabula Generalis,* and constitute the *Arbor Elementalis* (which represents the *elementata,* that is, the objects of the sublunar world made up of the four elements, stones, trees, animals), the *Arbor Vegetalis,* the *Arbor Sensualis,* the *Arbor Imaginalis* (the mental images that are the likenesses of the things represented in the other trees), the *Arbor Humanalis* (which concerns memory, understanding, and will and includes the various sciences and arts invented by man), the *Arbor Coelestialis* (astronomy and astrology), the *Arbor Angelicalis* and the *Arbor Divinalis* (the divine Dignities). To this list should be added the *Arbor Moralis* (virtues and vices), the *Arbor Eviternalis* (the realms of the afterworld), the *Arbor Maternalis* (Mariology), the *Arbor Christianalis* (Christology), the *Arbor Imperialis* (government), the *Arbor Apostolicalis* (the Church), the *Arbor Exemplificalis* (the contents of knowledge), and the *Arbor Quaestionalis* (which includes 4,000 questions on the various arts). But it can be definitively said that this forest of trees corresponds to the columns of the *Tabula Generalis,* even if we cannot always identify what term corresponds to what other.

As Llinares writes (1963: 211–212):

the various trees are hierarchically arranged, the higher trees participate of the lower. The "vegetable" tree, for instance, participates of the tree of the elements, the "sensual" tree of both, while the tree "of imagination" is constructed on the preceding three, at the same time as it makes comprehensible the tree that follows, in other words, the "human" tree. In this way, in an ascending movement, Ramon Llull constructs a system of the universe and of human knowledge grouped around three central themes: the world, man, and God. . . . Logic has given way to metaphysics, which is concerned first of all to explain and interpret, since the philosopher considers the primitive and real elements, and through them descends to particular objects, which he studies thanks to them.[12]

---

12. That the emanative or participative process goes from the root to the leaves is simply a question of iconographic convention. Note how Kircher, in his *Ars magna sciendi,* constructs his tree of the sciences, on a model related to the Porphyrian tree, with the Dignities at the top. As for Llull, in works like the *Liber de*

Carreras y Artau and Carreras y Artau (1939: 1:400), followed by Llinares (1963: 208 et seq.), note that an almost biological dynamism is evident in the trees, in contrast with the logical-mathematical staticity of Llull's *Ars* in the preceding period. But we have already observed that the mastery of the *Ars* presupposes a preliminary knowledge that is precisely that conveyed by the trees. At least this is fully the case with the *Ars generalis ultima* and the *Ars brevis,* both subsequent in date to the formulation of the *Arbor scientiae.*

As we saw in Chapter 1, medieval thought has recourse to the figure of the tree (the Porphyrian tree) to represent the way in which genera formally include species and species are included in genera. If we observe just one of the illustrations in the *Logica nova* of 1303, we see a Porphyrian tree to which Llull affixes both the letters from B to K and the list of Questions. We might be tempted to conclude that the Dignities, and all the other entities of the *Ars,* are themselves the genera and species of the Porphyrian tree. But it is no accident that the illustration should be entitled *Arbor naturalis et logicalis.* Llull's tree is not only logical, but natural too.

A Porphyrian tree is a formal structure. It defines formally the relationship between genera and species. (It is only a didactic convention that in its canonical form it always represents substances like Body or Animal.) The Porphyrian tree is initially an empty tree that anyone and everyone can fill out according to the classification they wish to produce. The trees that Llull presents in his *Arbor scientiae* on the other hand are "full" trees, or, if you will, representations of the Great Chain of Being as it metaphysically is— and *must* be. Platzeck (1954: 145 et seq.) is right therefore when he affirms that the analogy between Llull's trees and the Porphyrian tree is only apparent: "its gradation is not the fruit of a logical framework but of the fact that the dignities manifest themselves, in created things, in different degrees."

Llull too (Platzeck reminds us) needs a *differentia specifica,* but it is not an accident (however essential) that can be abstracted from the species under consideration: instead, it represents the degree of its ontological participation. This is why Llull's criticism (see *De venatione medii inter subjectum et praedicatum* in *Opera parva* [Palma, 1744], I: 4) of the syllogism *Every ani-*

---

ascensu et descensu intellectus (1304), the hierarchy of beings is represented as a ladder on which the artist proceeds from the effects to the causes, from the sensitive to the intellectual, and vice versa.

mal is a substance, Every man is an animal, Therefore every man is a sub-stance is so interesting. The syllogism seems to be formally valid, but for Llull it is not "necessary" because the way in which man is a substance is marked by the distance between man and the first causes in the descent of the Great Chain of Being (therefore, man is indeed a substance, but only to a certain degree). Llull needs to come up with a "natural medium" that is non-logical, a sort of immediate kinship. He therefore reformulates the syllogism (and accepts it) as follows: *Every rational animal is a rational substance, Every man is a rational animal, Therefore every man is a rational substance.* This looks like mere terminological wordplay, but for Llull it is a question of find-ing a kind of soft affinity among things, with neither leap nor interruption. And here we recognize that rationality is a difference that already divides the substance, that reappears at each step of the ladder, and that is conferred upon man alone through a chain of descending steps.

"The Scholastic logician uses only definitions adapted to the logic of the classes; the Raimondist admits every kind of distinction, as long as they are based on a real relationship between things" (Platzeck 1954: 155).

Llull's presumed logic is not formal, it is a rhetoric that serves to express an ontology.[13]

In the light of these remarks it is understandable why on the one hand Llull organizes his *Ars* so as to find, in every possible argument, a middle term that allows him to form a demonstrative syllogism, but excludes some syllo-gisms, however correct, even if formally there is a middle term. *His middle term is not that of formal scholastic logic.* It is a middle that binds by likeness the elements of the Great Chain of Being, it is a substantial middle, not a formal one. This is why Llull is able to reject certain premises as unaccept-able, even though the combinatory system makes them imaginable. The middle does not unite things formally, *it is in things.* Llull's middle is not the middle term of an Aristotelian syllogism, it does not establish the cause identi-fied by the definition, or the genus under which a species is to be subsumed:

---

13. "We are . . . a thousand leagues away from modern formal logic. What we have here is a logic that is material in the highest degree, and therefore a kind of Topics or art of invention" (Platzeck 1953: 579). And again: "truth or logical correctness is never formally appreciated for its own sake, but always with reference to gnoseologi-cal truth" (Platzeck 1954: 151).

it is a "general label" that characterizes every form of participation, connection, kinship between two things, to such an extent that, in the elementary predications of his first and third figures, Llull does not even need to insert a copula. The greatness of goodness is not predicated, their consubstantial, incontrovertible, self-evident identity is simply recognized.[14]

Furthermore, in the rhymed Catalan version of his *Logica Algazelis,* Llull declares: "De la logica parlam tot breu—car a parlar avem de deu" ("Of logic we will speak briefly—because we have to speak of God"). The *Ars* is not a revelatory mechanism capable of designing cosmological structures as yet unknown: it discovers nothing; it supports probable arguments on the basis of ideas already known (or assumed to be known).

10.4. Pico's *Revolutio Alphabetaria*

We have one more knot to untie, a knot that lies at the junction between medieval Llullism and Renaissance and Baroque Llullism (and beyond)—it regards the supposed Llullism of Pico della Mirandola. Whether or not Pico was influenced by Kabbalistic texts is no longer an issue. At most, the discussion is still moot as to exactly what texts friends like Flavius Mithridates and others introduced him to. Idel (1988a: 205) reminds us that, for Yohanan Alemanno, friend and inspirer of Pico, "the symbolic cargo of language was becoming transformed into almost mathematical type of command. Thus, Kabbalistic symbolism was transformed (or retransformed) into a magical incantatory language." Hence, Pico could affirm that no word can have any virtue in magical operations if it is not Hebrew or coming from Hebrew: "nulla nomina ut significativa, et in quantum nomina sunt, singula et per se sumpta, in Magico opere virtutem habere possunt, nisi sint Hebraica, vel inde proxima derivata" ("No name, insofar as it is endowed with meaning and insofar as it is a name, taken singly in and of itself, can produce a magi-

---

14. See Johnston (1987), chapter 15, entitled "Natural Middle," in which these points are persuasively and searchingly discussed. "[The *Ars*] does not require systematic coherence of a deductive nature among its arguments; it is endlessly capable of offering yet another analogical explanation of the same idea or concept, or of restating the same truth in different terms. This explains both the volume and exhaustively repetitive character of nearly all of Llull's 240 extant writings" (Johnston 1987: 7).

cal effect, unless it is Hebrew or closely derived from Hebrew") (*Conclusiones cabalisticae* 22).[15]

What is the source, however, of the conviction, which we find in a number of authors, that Pico's Kabbalism owed a debt to Llull (whose *Ars brevis* and *Ars generalis ultima* Pico was certainly familiar with; see Garin 1937: 110)? To give but one example, the most curious document regarding this association is probably the book by Jean-Marie de Vernon (*Histoire véritable du bienheureux Raymond Lulle*, Paris, 1668: 347–348), which, attributing to Llull no fewer than 4,000 works declares that 2,225 of them were in the library of Pico!

The answer is simple, at least in the first instance. The responsibility must be ascribed to a few lines—anything but perspicuous—in Pico's *Apologia*, where, speaking of the Kabbalistic tradition, Pico draws a parallel that, to quote Wirszubski (1989: 259), is "the first of its kind in modern letters":

Duas scientias hoc etiam nomine honorificarunt. Unam quae dicitur חכמת הצרדך [*hokmat haseruf*], id est *ars combinandi*, et est modus quidam procedendi in scientijs et est simile quid sicut apud nostros dicitur *ars Raymundi, licet forte diverso modo procedant*. Aliam quae est de virtutibus rerum superiorum que sunt supra lunam et est pars magiae naturalis supremae. Utraque istarum apud Hebraeos etiam dicitur Cabalam propter rationem iam dictam, et de utraque istarum etiam aliquando fecimus mentionem in conclusionibus nostris. Illa enim est *ars combinandi* quam ego in conclusionibus meis voco *alphabetariam revolutionem*. Et ista quae est de virtutibus rerum superiorum

---

15. On the other hand, Agrippa's point of departure is the principle that "although all the demons or intelligences speak the language of the nation over which they preside, they make exclusive use of Hebrew when they interact with those who understand this mother tongue. . . . These names . . . though of unknown sound and meaning, must have, in the work of magic . . . greater power than significant names, when the spirit, dumbfounded by their enigma . . . fully convinced that it is acting under some divine influence, pronounces them in a reverent manner, even though it does not understand them, to the greater glory of the divinity" (*De occulta philosophia libri III* [Paris: Ex Officina Jacobi Dupuys, 1567], III:23–26). John Dee evokes angels of dubious celestiality with invocations such as *Zizop, Zchis, Esiasch, Od, Iaod* (cf. *A True and Faithful Relation* (London, printed by D. Maxwell for T. Garthwait, 1659).

quae uno modo potest capi ut pars magiae naturalis. (They also honored two sciences with this name. One is called חכמת הצרדך [*hokmat haseruf*], that is the combinatory art, and it is a certain way of proceeding in the sciences, similar to what we call the *ars Raymundi, even though on occasion they may proceed in a different manner.* The other which has to do with the powers of the higher things that are above the moon is part of the supreme natural magic. Both these two sciences are called Kabbalah among the Hebrews for the reason previously mentioned. And we have spoken of both some time ago in our *Conclusiones.* The first in fact is the *combinatory art* that I refer to in my *Conclusiones* as the *revolutio alphabetaria.* And the second is the one that has to do with the powers of higher things, which can be thought of as a part of natural magic) (*Apologia*, 5, 28, my emphasis).

Let us consider this fundamental moment in the *Apologia*. The trouble is that, in drawing this parallel between the *ars combinandi* and the *ars Raymundi*, Pico is more interested in the differences than in the similarities. In the passage cited, Pico makes a distinction between a Kabbalah of names and a theosophical Kabbalah. Now the first part of the Kabbalah, or the first way of understanding the Kabbalah, is the *ars combinandi*, which Pico has already (in the *Conclusiones cabalisticae*) dubbed the *revolutio alphabetaria*. Observe that, in the Abulafian tradition, the word *revolutio* stands for combination in general (Wirszubski 1989: 137), but the term certainly implies a rotatory connotation, which calls to mind the Kabbalistic or Llullian wheels (or, as we will see, steganographic wheels, à la Johannes Trithemius). In any case, the term could be also used metaphorically, as a more or less visual image of the combinatory swirling typical of the Kabbalistic technique of the anagram or Temurah. Frances Yates, while recognizing that Pico's *ars combinandi* is derived from the combinatory practices of Abulafia, decides to deal only with the second type of Kabbalah—something she has of course every right to do—dismissing the first by saying that Pico considers it to be somehow similar to the art of Raimon Llull (Yates 1964: 113).

However that may be, a combination of letters cannot help recalling the techniques of Llull, and this is why Pico says that the two practices are similar. Whereupon, however, he points out that the similarity is only apparent: "licet *forte* diverso modo procedant" ("even though *by chance/perhaps* they may proceed in a different manner"). The ambiguous adverbial expression *forte* ("perhaps" or "by chance") is a teaser. If Pico had wished to allude to a substantial difference, he would have had his good reasons: as we have seen, the letters in Llull's combinatory system refer to theological entities, to divine Dignities, and they therefore refer to a system of combinations which, though it appears to occur at the alphabetical level, in fact subsists in the realm of contents. The Abulafian Kabbalistic system, on the other hand, is exercised on the substance of the expression, on letters of the Torah, or on those elements of the form of the expression that are the letters of the alphabet.

Still, this explanation could easily be confuted on the basis of the Kabbalistic belief that every letter of the Hebrew alphabet has a meaning, at least a numerological meaning. So the Kabbalah too, though it may seem to be combining and permutating alphabetical elements, is really permutating and combining concepts. Apart, then, from their different theological backgrounds, *ars Raymundi* and *ars combinandi* are not *substantialiter* different from each other. They are so *forte,* "by chance," or with regard to their outcomes, or the way they are used.

It is our conviction that Pico had understood that what distinguished Kabbalistic thought from that of Llull was that the reality that the Kabbalistic mystic must discover is not yet known and can reveal itself only through the spelling out of the letters in their whirlwind permutations. Consequently, though it may be only in a mystical sense (in which the combinations serve only as a motor of the imagination), the Kabbalah pretends to be a true *ars inveniendi,* in which what is to be found is a truth as yet unknown. The combinatory system of Llull, on the other hand, is (as we saw) a rhetorical tool, through which the already known may be demonstrated—what the ironclad system of the forest of the various trees has already fixed once and for all, and that no combination can ever subvert.[16]

That Pico had understood perfectly, with his aside, this point, is also confirmed by his *Conclusiones cabalisticae:*

Nullae sunt litterae in tota lege, quae in formis, coniunctionibus, separationibus, tortuositate, directione, defectu, superabundantia, minoritate, maioritate, coronatione, clausura, apertura, & ordine, decem

---

16. Hillgarth (1971: 283) states that Pico, more interested in Kabbalism than in the *Ars* of Llull, cited Llull because he was better known than the Hebrew Kabbalah. For a subtle difference of opinion on this point, see Zambelli (1995[1965]: 59, n. 14).

numerationum secreta non manifestent. (There are no letters in the whole Law which in their forms, conjunctions, separations, crookedness, straightness, defect, excess, smallness, largeness, crowning, closure, openness and order, do not reveal the secrets of the ten numerations.) (Farmer 1998: 359)

Furthermore, if we bear in mind that these *numerationes* are the Sephirot, we can appreciate the revelatory power with which he endows his *ars combinandi*. What results this whirling dervish of an art leads him to, well beyond all philological common sense, but evincing without question a combinatorial energy that knows no limits, we may gather from the famous passage in the *Heptaplus* dedicated to the *Bereishit*.

Here for the first time we encounter what will turn out to be a distinguishing feature not only of Kabbalism but of the whole later hermetic tradition: given a discourse that already in and of itself dares to enunciate unfathomable mysteries, it is assumed to allude even further, to mysteries still higher and more occult. For Pico, in the Second Proem, the Mosaic account of the creation of the world alludes, in every one of its parts, and according to seven different levels of reading, to the creation of the world of the angels, of the celestial world and the sublunar world, as well as to man as microcosm: "Thus indeed this book of Moses, if any such, is a book marked with seven seals and full of all wisdom and all mysteries" (Pico della Mirandola 1965: 81). In the sixth chapter of the *Third Exposition* ("On the Angelic and Invisible World"), for instance, the creation of the fish, birds, and earthbound animals is seen as a revelation of the creation of the angelic cohorts. If there are unfathomable and unfathomed mysteries to discover, nothing must be taken as known. The combinations must be venturesome and, at least as far as intentions go, innocent and open-minded. Here is the famous passage, typically Kabbalistic in tone, in which Pico launches into the most uninhibited permutational and anagrammatical operations:

Applying the rules of the ancients to the first phrase of the work, which is read *Beresit* by the Hebrews and "In the beginning" by us, I wanted to see whether I too could bring to light something worth knowing. Beyond my hope and expectation I found what I myself did not believe as I found it, and what others will not believe easily: the whole plan of the creation of the world and of all things in it disclosed and explained in that one phrase. . . . Among the Hebrews, this phrase is written thus: בראשיח, *berescith*. From this, if we join the third letter to the first, comes the word אב, *ab*. If we add the second to the doubled first, we get בבד, *bebar*. If we read all except the first, we get ראשית, *resith*. If we connect the fourth to the first and last, we get שבת, *sciabat*. If we take the first three in the order in which they come, we get כרא, *bara*. If, leaving out the first, we take the next three, we get ראש, *rosc*. If, leaving out the first and second, we take the two following, we get אש, *es*. If, leaving out the first three, we join the fourth to the last, we get שת, *seth*. Again, if we join the second to the first, we get רב, *rab*. If after the third we set the fifth and fourth, we get איש, *hisc*. If we join the first two to the last two, we get ברית, *berith*. If we add the last to the first, we get the twelfth and last word, which is תב, *thob*, the *thau* being changed into the letter *thet*, which is very common in Hebrew.

Let us see first what these words mean in Latin, then what mysteries of all nature they reveal to those not ignorant of philosophy. *Ab* means "the father"; *bebar* "in the son" and "through the son" (for the prefix *beth* means both); resit, "the beginning"; *sabath*, "the rest and end"; *bara*, "created"; *rosc*, "head"; *es*, "fire"; *seth*, "foundation"; *rab*, "of the great"; *hisc*, "of the man"; *berit*, "with a pact"; *thob*, "with good." If we fit the whole passage together following this order, it will read like this: "The father, in the Son and through the Son, the beginning and end or rest, created the head, the fire, and the foundation of the great man with a good pact." This whole passage results from taking apart and putting together that first word. (Pico della Mirandola 1965: 171–172)

Pico's *ars combinandi* has nothing in common with the *ars Raymundi*. Ramon Llull used his art to demonstrate credible things; Pico uses his to discover things incredible and unheard-of. Nevertheless, the various misapprehensions that will later arise probably derive from the fact that it is precisely Pico's example that will free Llullism from its original fetters.

It is certainly not a question of seeing in Pico's uncoupling of the Kabbalistic *Ars combinandi* from the *Ars Raymundi,* and in the dizzying permutational exercises that Pico encourages, the detonator that liberated in the coming centuries Llull's *Ars* from its early limitations, taking it (as we will

see), beyond theology and beyond rhetoric, to nourish the formal speculations of modern logic and the random brainstorming that characterizes so
much of contemporary heuristics.

What is certain is that with Pico is affirmed, in harmony with his defense
of the dignity and rights of man, the invitation to dare, to *invenire* or discover, even if it was more in keeping with the tendentious suggestions of
Flavius Mithridates than with those of factorial calculus. What was needed
at this point was for someone to suggest that, if we are going to continue to
talk about being, the being chosen must be a being as yet unmade, rather
than a being that already exists. And it was Pico who (perhaps without intending to) steered modern thought in this direction. Which is, when you get
down to it, another way of saying that "man, for Pico, is divine insofar as he
creates; because he creates himself and his world; not because he is born
God, but because he makes himself God. Throughout the entire universe,
operatio sequitur esse. . . . For Pico, in man, and in man alone, *esse sequitur
operari*" (Garin 1937: 95).

This is the sense in which, to use Pico's own words, the *ars combinandi*
and the *ars Raymundi* "diverso modo procedunt." In this sense we may cancel
the ambiguous expression *forte* ("by chance, perhaps, accidentally"), possibly
inserted out of prudence, possibly because Pico's intuition was still in its
first vague glimmerings. Once the adverb has been eliminated, in that brief
aside, we pass from the idea of man as subject to the laws of the cosmos to
that of a man who constructs and reconstructs without fear of the vertigo of
the possible, fully accepting its risk.

10.5. Llullism after Pico

With the advent of the Renaissance the unlimited combinatory system will
tend to express a content that is equally unlimited, and hence ungraspable
and inexpressible.

In the 1598 edition of Llull's combinatorial writings, a work entitled *De
auditu kabbalistico* appears under his name. Thorndike (1929, V: 325) already pointed out that the *De auditu* first appeared in Venice in 1518 as a
little work by Ramon Llull, "opusculum Raimundicum," and that it was
consequently a work composed in the late fifteenth century. He hypothesized that the work might be attributed to Pietro Mainardi, an attribution

later confirmed by Zambelli (1965). It is remarkable, however, that this opuscule of Mainardi's should be dated "in the last years of the fifteenth century, in other words, immediately following the drafting of Pico's theses and his *Apologia*" (Zambelli 1995[1965]: 62–63), and that this minor forgery was produced under his influence, however indirect (see Scholem 1979: 40–41). The brief treatise gives two etymological Arabic roots for the word "Kabbalah": *Abba* stands for father while *ala* means God. It is difficult not to be reminded of similar exercises on Pico's part.

This confirms that by this time Llull had been officially enrolled among the Kabbalists, as Tommaso Garzoni di Bagnacavallo will confirm in his *Piazza universale di tutte le professioni* (Venice, Somasco, 1585):

> The science of Ramon, known to very few, could also be called, though with an inappropriate word, Kabbala. And from it is derived that common rumor among all the scholars, indeed among all persons, that the Kabbala teaches everything . . . and to this effect there is in print a little book attributed to him (although this is the way that lies are composed beyond the Alps) entitled *De Auditu Cabalistico*, which is nothing more when you get down to it than a very brief summary of the *Arte magna*, which was definitely abbreviated by him in that other work, which he calls *Arte breve*.[17]

Among the later examples from "beyond the Alps," we may cite Pierre Morestel, who published in France in 1621, with the title *Artis kabbalisticae, sive sapientiae divinae academia,* a modest anthology of the *De auditu*[18] (with an official imprimatur no less, since the author proposed to demonstrate exclusively, as Llull himself did, Christian truths), with nothing Kabbalistic about it, apart from the title, the initial identification of *Ars* and Kabbalah, and the repetition of the etymology found in the *De auditu*.

---

17. *La piazza universale di tutte le professioni del mondo, Nuovamente Ristampata & posta in luce, da Thomaso Garzoni di Bagnacavallo. Aggiuntovi in questa nuova Impressione alcune bellissime Annotazioni a discorso per discorso* (Venice: Appresso Roberto Maietti, 1599).

18. *Artis kabbalisticae, sive sapientiae divinae academia: in novem classes amicissima cum breuitate tum claritate digesta* (Paris: Apus Melchiorem Nondiere, 1621).

Figure 10.7

An additional stimulus to Neo-Llullism came from ongoing research into coded writings or steganographies. Steganography developed as a ciphering device for political and military purposes, and the greatest steganographer of modern times, Trithemius (1462–1516) uses ciphering wheels that work in a similar way to Llull's moving concentric circles. To what extent Trithemius was influenced by Llull is unimportant for our purposes, because the influence would in any case have been purely graphic. The wheels are not used by Trithemius to produce arguments, simply to encode and decode. The letters of the alphabet are inscribed on the circles and the rotation of the inner circles decided whether the A of the outer circle was to be encoded as B, C, or Z (the opposite was true for decoding; see Figure 10.7).

But, although Trithemius does not mention Llull, he is mentioned by later steganographers. Vigenère's *Traité des chiffres*[19] explicitly takes up Llullian ideas at various points and relates them to the factorial calculus of the *Sefer Yetzirah*.

There is a reason why steganographies act as propagators of a Llullism that goes beyond Llull. The steganographer is not interested in the content (and therefore in the truth) of the combinations he produces. The elemen-

---

19. *Traité des chiffres, Ou Secretes Manieres d'Escrire* (Paris: Chez Abel L'Angelier, 1587).

tary system requires only that elements of the steganographic expression (combinations of letters or other symbols) may be freely correlated (in ever different ways, so that their encoding is unpredictable) to elements of the expression to be encoded. They are merely symbols that take the place of other symbols. The steganographer, then, is encouraged to attempt more complex combinations, of a purely formal nature, in which all that matters is a syntax of the expression that is ever more vertiginous, and every combination is an unconstrained variable.

Thus, we have Gustavus Selenus,[20] in his 1624 *Cryptometrices et Cryptographiae,* going so far as to construct a wheel of twenty-five concentric circles combining twenty-five series of twenty-four doublets each. And, before you know it, he presents us with a series of tables that record circa 30,000 doublets. The possible combinations become astronomical (see Figure 10.8).

If we are going to have combinations, why stop at 1,680 propositions, as Llull did? Formally, we can say everything.

It is with Agrippa that the possibility is first glimpsed of borrowing from both the Kabbalah and from Llullism the simple technique of combining the letters, and of using that technique to construct an encyclopedia that was not an image of the finite medieval cosmos but of a cosmos that was open and expanding, or of different possible worlds.

His *In artem brevis R. Llulli* (which appears along with the other works of Llull in the Strasburg edition of 1598) appears at first sight to be a fairly faithful summary of the principles of the *Ars,* but we are immediately struck by the fact that, in the tables that are supposed to illustrate Llull's fourth figure, the number of combinations becomes far greater, since repetitions are not avoided.

As Vasoli (1958: 161) remarks,

Agrippa uses this alphabet and these illustrations only as the basis for a series of far more complex operations obtained through the systematic combination and progressive expansion of Llull's typical figures and, above all, through the practically infinite expansion of the *elementa.* In this way the subjects are multiplied, defining them within their species

---

20. *Cryptomenytices et cryptographiae libri ix* (Lüneburg: Excriptum typis Johannis Henrici Fratrum, 1624).

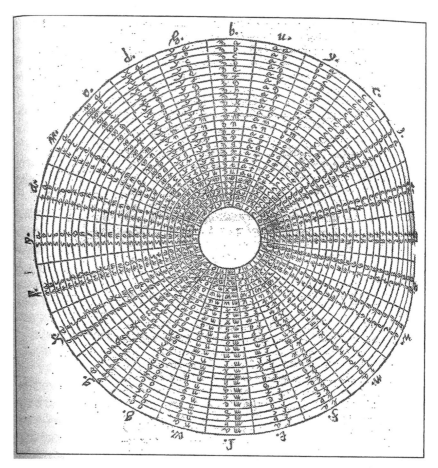

Figure 10.8

or tracing them back to their genera, placing them in relation with terms that are similar, different, contrary, anterior or posterior, or again, referring them to their causes, effects, actions, passions, relations, etc. All of which, naturally, makes feasible a practically infinite use of the *Ars*.

The Carreras y Artau brothers (1939: 220–221) observe that in this way Agrippa's art is inferior to Llull's because it is not based on a theology. But, at least from our point of view and from that of the future development of combinatory systems, this constitutes a strong point rather than a weakness. With Agrippa, Llullism is liberated from theology.

Rather, if we must speak of a limit, it is clear that, for Agrippa too, the point is not to lay the foundations for a logic of discovery, but instead for a wide-ranging rhetoric, at most to complicate the list of disciplines configured by his encyclopedia, but always in such a way as to provide—as is the case with a mnemonic technique—notions that can be manipulated by the proficient orator.

Llull was timid with respect to the form of the content. Agrippa broadens the possibilities of the form of the expression in an attempt to articulate vaster structures of content, but he does not go all the way. If he had applied the combinatory system to the description of the inexhaustible network of cosmic relations outlined in the *De occulta philosophia* he would have taken a decisive step forward. He did not.

Bruno, on the other hand, will try to make his version of Llull's *Ars* tell everything and more. Given an infinite universe whose circumference (as Nicholas of Cusa already asserted) was nowhere and its center everywhere, from whatever point the observer contemplates it in its infinity and substantial unity, the variety of forms to be discovered and spoken of is no longer limited. The ruling idea of the infinity of worlds is compounded with the idea that each entity in the world can serve at the same time as a Platonic shadow of other ideal aspects of the universe, as sign, reference, image, emblem, hieroglyphic, seal. By way of contrast too, naturally, because the image of something can also lead us back to unity through its opposite.

The images of his combinatory system, which Bruno finds in the repertory of the hermetic tradition, or even constructs for himself from his fevered phantasy, are not merely intended, as was the case with previous mnemonic techniques, for remembering, but also for envisaging and discovering the essence of things and their relationships.

They will connect with the same visionary energy with which Pico disassembled and reassembled the first word of the sacred text. A thing can represent another thing by phonetic similarity (the horse, in Latin *equus*, can represent the man who is *aequus* or just), by putting the concrete for the abstract (a Roman warrior for Rome), by the coincidence of their initial syllables (*asinus* for *asyllum*), by proceeding from the antecedent to the consequence, from the accident to the subject and vice versa, from the insignia to the one who wears it. Or, once again, by recurring to Kabbalistic techniques and using the evocative power of the anagram and of paronomasia (*palatio* for *Latio*, cf. Vasoli 1958: 285–286).

The combinatory technique becomes a language capable of expressing, not just the events and relationships of this world, but of all of the infinite worlds, in their mutual harmony with one another.

Where are the constraints imposed by a metaphysics of the Great Chain of Being now? The title of one of Bruno's mnemotechnical treatises, *De lampade combinatoria Lulliana* continues *ad infinitas propositiones et media invenienda*.[21] The reference to the infinity of propositions that can be generated is unequivocal.

The problem of combinatorial techniques will be taken up by other authors, though in an openly anti-Kabbalistic key, with the express purpose of displaying skepticism in the face of the proliferation of mystical tendencies, of demonstrating the weakness and the approximative nature of the Rabbinical calculus, and of bringing the technique back to a purely formal mathematical calculus (indifferent to meaning) but nevertheless capable of predicting how many new expressions and how many new languages could be produced using only the letters of the Latin alphabet.

In German Jesuit Christopher Clavius's *In Sphaerum Ioannis de Sacro Bosco*,[22] the author considers how many *dictiones*, or how many terms, could be produced with the twenty-three letters of the Latin alphabet (at the time there was no difference between *u* and *v* or *i* and *j*, and no *k* or *y*), combining them two by two, three by three, and so on, up to words made up of twenty-three letters. Clavius supplies the mathematical formulas for this calculus, but he stops short at a certain point before the immensity of the possible results, especially if repetitions were to be included.

In 1622, Pierre Guldin composed his *Problema arithmeticum de rerum combinationibus* (cf. Fichant 1991: 136–138), in which he calculates all the dictions that can be generated with twenty-three letters, regardless of whether they make sense or can be pronounced, but not including repetitions. He establishes that the number of words (of variable length from two to twenty-three letters) would be more than 70,000 billion billion (to write them out

---

21. *De lampade combinatoria Lulliana* (Wittenberg: Zacarius Cratius, 1587), inserted into the 1598 edition of Llull's works along with *De Lulliano Specierum Scrutinio, De Progressu Logicae Venationis* and *De Lampade Venatoria Logicorum*.

22. *In Sphaeram Ioannis de Sacro Bosco Commentarius* (Rome: Apud Victorium Helianum, 1570).

would require more than a million billion billion letters). To have an idea of the implications of this number, think of writing all of these words in registers of 1,000 pages, with 100 lines per page and sixty characters per line. They would fill 257 million billion such registers. And if we wished to house them in a library—Guldin studies point by point its arrangement, its extension, how one would navigate within it, if we had at our disposal cubic structures measuring 432 feet per side, each of them capable of holding 32 million volumes, 8,052,122,350 such bookcases would be required. But what realm could accommodate so many structures? Calculating the surface available throughout the entire planet, we could accommodate only 7,575,213,799 of them!

Marin Mersenne, in various of his writings (cf. Coumet 1975), wonders how many names it would take if we were to give a different name to each individual. And not only that: to every individual hair on the head of every human being. Maybe he was echoing the traditional medieval lament for the *penuria nominum* or penury of names, according to which there are more things in need of a name than there are names to go around. With the appropriate formula (and the calculations Mersenne engages in are dizzying), it would be possible to generate copious lexicons for all languages.

In addition to the alphabetical *dictiones*, Mersenne also takes into consideration the *canti* or musical sequences that can be produced without repetition over the space of three octaves (we may have here an initial allusion to the notion of the dodecaphonic series), and he observes that to record all these *canti* would require more reams of paper than, if they were piled on top of one another, would cover the distance from earth to the heavens, even if each sheet were to contain 720 *canti* each with 22 notes and every ream were compressed so as to measure less than an inch: because the *canti* that can be produced on the basis of 22 notes are 1,124,000,727,607,680,000, and dividing them by the 362,880 that will fit on a ream, the result would still be a number of 16 figures, while the distance from the center of the earth to the stars is only 28,826,640,000,000 inches (14 figures). And if we were to write down all these *canti,* at the rate of 1,000 a day, it would take 22,608,896,103 years and 12 days.

There is in all this giddy rapture a consciousness of the infinite perfectibility of knowledge, for which mankind, the new Adam, has the possibility in the course of the centuries to name everything that the first Adam did not find time to baptize. In this way, the combinations aspire to compete with that ability to know the individual that belongs solely to God (whose impossibility will be sanctioned by Leibniz). Mersenne had done battle against Kabbalah and occultism, but the vertiginous gyrations of the Kabbalah had evidently seduced him, and here he is spinning the Llullian wheels for all he's worth, no longer capable of distinguishing between divine omnipotence and the possible omnipotence of a perfect combinatorial language manipulated by man, to the point that in his *Quaestiones super Genesim* (cols. 49 and 52) he sees in the presence in man of the infinite a manifest proof of the existence of God.

But this ability to imagine the infinite possibilities of the combinatory technique manifests itself because Mersenne, like Clavius, Guldin, and others (the theme returns, for example, in Comenius, *Linguarum methodus novissima* III, 19),[23] is no longer calculating with concepts (as Llull did) but with alphabetical sequences, mere elements of expression, uncontrolled by any orthodoxy that is not that of the numbers. Without realizing it, these authors are already approaching that notion of "blind thought" that will be brought to fruition, with greater critical awareness, by Leibniz, the inaugurator of modern formal logic.

In his *Dissertatio de arte combinatoria,* the same Leibniz, after complaining (correctly) that Llull's whole method was concerned more with the art of improvising a discussion than with acquiring complete knowledge of a given subject, entertained himself by calculating how many possible combinations Llull's *Ars* really consented, if all of the mathematical possibilities permitted by nine elements were exploited; and he came up with the number (theoretical of course) 17,804,320,388,674,561.

But, to exploit these possibilities, one had to do the opposite from what Llull had done and to take seriously the combinatory incontinence of people like Guldin and Mersenne. If Llull had invented an extremely flexible syntax and then handicapped it with a very rigid semantics, what was needed was a syntax that was not hampered by any semantic limitations. The combinatory process ought to generate empty symbolic forms, not yet bound to any content. The *Ars* thus became a calculus with meaningless symbols.

This is a state of affairs that shows how much progress Llullism has made, providing tools for our contemporary theoreticians of artificial and comput-

---

23. The dates of composition are uncertain (ca. 1644–1648); the work was probably published at Leszno in 1648.

erized languages, while betraying the pious intentions of Ramon Llull. And that to reread Llull today as if he had had an inkling of computer science (apart from the obvious anachronism) would be to betray his intentions.

All Llull had in mind was speaking of God and convincing the infidel to accept the principles of the Christian faith, hypnotizing them with his whirling wheels. So the legend that claims he died a martyr's death in Muslim territory, though it may not be true, is nonetheless a good story.

11

The Language of the Austral Land

The subject of a perfect language has appeared in the cultural history of every people. Throughout the first period of this search, which continued until the seventeenth century, this utopia consisted in the search for the primigenial Hebrew in which God spoke to Adam or that Adam invented when giving names to the animals and in which he had had his first dialogue With Eve. But already in Dante's *De vulgari eloquentia* another possibility had been broached: that God had not given Adam primordial Hebrew but rather a general grammar, a transcendental form with which to construct all possible languages.

But this possibility was situated on the two horns of a dilemma. On the one hand, it was possible to conceive of a Chomskian God, who gave Adam some deep syntactical structures common to every language subsequently created by the human race, obeying a universal structure of the mind (without waiting for Chomsky, Rivarol, an eighteenth-century author, had defined French as the language of reason, because its direct order of discourse reproduces the logical order of reality). On the other hand, it could be supposed that God had given Adam some semantic universals (such as *high/low, to stand up, to think, thing, action,* and so on), a system of atomic notions by means of which every culture organizes its own view of the world.

Until the arrival of Humboldt, even if one accepted the so-called Epicurean hypothesis by which every people invents its own language to deal with its own experience, no one dared prefigure anything similar to the Sapir-Whorf hypothesis: that it is language that gives form to our experience of

---

This translation is a slightly revised version of the essay translated by William Weaver in Eco (1998b).

the world. Thinkers like Spinoza, Locke, Mersenne, and Leibniz admitted that our definitions (of *man, gold,* and so on) depend on our point of view about these things. Nobody, however, denied that it was possible to design a general system of ideas that somehow reflected the way the universe works.

Still, even before Dante, Ramon Llull had conceived the idea that there were universal notions, present in the language and in the thought of every people; he even believed that, by articulating and combining these concepts common to all men, it would be possible to convince the infidels—namely, the Muslims and the Jews—of the truth of the Christian religion.

This idea was revived at the dawn of the seventeenth century, after the discovery of Chinese ideograms, which were the same in Chinese, Japanese, and Korean (though pronounced differently), for these different peoples referred to the same concepts. The same thing, it was said, happens with numbers, where different words refer to the same mathematical entity. But numbers possessed another attractive aspect: independently of the variety of languages, all peoples (or very many of them) indicated them with the same cipher or character.

The idea that began to circulate, especially in Anglo-Saxon circles, inspired by the Baconian reform of knowledge, was this: postulate a priori a system of semantic universals, assign to each semantic atom a visual character or a sound, and you will have a universal language. As for the grammar, it would be a question, according to the project, of reducing the declensions or the conjugations themselves in order to derive the various elements of speech from a same root, indicating them with diacritical signs or some other criterion of economy.

The first idea of a universal character appeared in Francis Bacon and was to produce in England an abundant series of attempts, of which we would mention only those of George Dalgarno, Francis Lodwick, and John Wilkins. These inventors of languages, which will be called philosophic and a priori, because they were constructed on the basis of a given philosophical view of the world, no longer aimed merely at converting the infidel or recovering that mystic communion with God that distinguished the perfect language of Adam but rather at fostering commercial exchange, colonial expansion, and the diffusion of science. It is no accident that most of these attempts were linked to the work of the Royal Society in London, and many of the results—apparent failures—of these utopists contributed to the birth of the new scientific taxonomies.

But this project, even if abundantly stripped of the mystic-religious connotations of earlier centuries, had another feature in common with the yearned-for perfect language of Adam. It was said of Adam that he had given "proper" names to things, the names that the things should have as they expressed their nature. In earlier centuries and still in the heyday of the occult and the kabbalistic speculations of the seventeenth century (consider, above all, Athanasius Kircher), this kinship between names and things was understood in terms of onomatopoeia, on the basis of far-fetched etymologies. To give an idea of the flavor of these ways of thinking, it suffices to quote Estienne Guichard (*L'harmomie étymologique des langues,* Paris: Le Noir 1606), where, for example, the author shows how from the Hebrew word *batar* was derived the Latin synonym *dividere* (147). Shuffling the letters, the word becomes *tarab,* and from *tarab* derives the Latin *tribus,* which then leads to *distribuo* and finally to *dividere. Zacen* means "old"; transposing the radicals one gets *zanet,* whence the Latin *senex,* and with a subsequent shift of letters comes *zanec,* whence in Oscan *casnar,* from which the Latin *canus* would be derived (247).

In subsequent attempts, the criterion of correspondence, or isomorphism between word and thing, is, by contrast, "compositional": the semantic atoms are named arbitrarily, but their combination is motivated by the nature of the designated object. This criterion is similar to that followed by chemistry today: calling hydrogen H, oxygen O, and sulphur S is surely arbitrary, but calling water H_2O or sulfuric acid H_2SO_4 is motivated by the chemical nature of these compounds. If either the order or the nature of the symbols were altered, another possible compound would be designated. Naturally this language is universal because, while each people indicates water with a different linguistic term, all are able to understand and write chemical symbols in the same way.

The search for a priori philosophic languages and the impassioned debates and rejections they inspired are evidenced by those pages in *Gulliver's Travels* where Swift imagines an assembly of professors bent on improving the language of their country. The first project, you will recall, was to abbreviate speech, reducing all polysyllables to monosyllables and eliminating verbs and participles. The second tended to abolish all words completely, because it was quite possible to communicate by displaying things (a difficult project because the so-called speakers would be obliged to carry with them a sack containing all the objects they planned to mention).

But even earlier the subject of the philosophic language had rightfully entered the literary genre of seventeenth-century utopias. For that matter, already in the Basel edition (1518) of More's *Utopia,* published by Pieter Gilles, there was an illustration with writing in the language of that ideal island; Godwin spoke of the possible language of the Selenites in his *Man in the Moone* (1638); and Cyrano de Bergerac mentioned other-planetary languages on several occasions, both in *Les estats et les empires de la lune* (1657) and *Les estats et les empires du soleil* (1662).

Still, if we want two models of language that echo the a priori philosophical language of the Utopians, we must turn to two novels narrating journeys in the Austral Land, *La Terre australe connue* (1676), by Gabriel de Foigny, and *L'Histoire des Sevarambes* (1677–1679), by Denis Vairasse. Here, I will delve only into the first, which to me seems particularly instructive, because, as often happens with good caricatures, the parodistic deformation reveals some essential features of the caricatured object.

La Terre australe connue is naturally a work of the imagination. In distant, unknown lands an ideal community is supposedly discovered. In this ideal community the language, too, is ideal, and it is interesting to remark that Foigny writes in 1676, after the three significant a priori philosophic language projects have appeared: Lodwick's *Common Writing* (1647), Dalgarno's *Ars Signorum* (1661), and Wilkins's *Essay towards a Real Character* (1668).

Foigny's exposition, precisely because it is incomplete and a burlesque, takes up only a few pages of his ninth chapter, rather than the 500 (in folio!) of Wilkins's, the most voluminous and complete of all the projects of that century. Yet is worth taking Foigny's into consideration because, for all its terseness, it illustrates the advantages and limitations of a philosophic language. It reveals and magnifies—as only a parody can—the flaws of its models, but, as they are magnified, the better we are able to distinguish them.

In order to better understand Foigny it is useful to refer to Figure 11.1, where I try to extrapolate from his text a sort of Austral dictionary, along with some grammatical rules. Because the author is often reticent, I have inferred some rules from examples, while others remain unspecific (thus, for example, of thirty-six accidentals, I have been unable to reconstruct only eighteen).

Foigny's Austral inhabitants,

to express their thoughts, employ three modes, all used in Europe: signs, voice, and writing. Signs are very familiar to them, and I have noticed that they spend many hours together without speaking in any

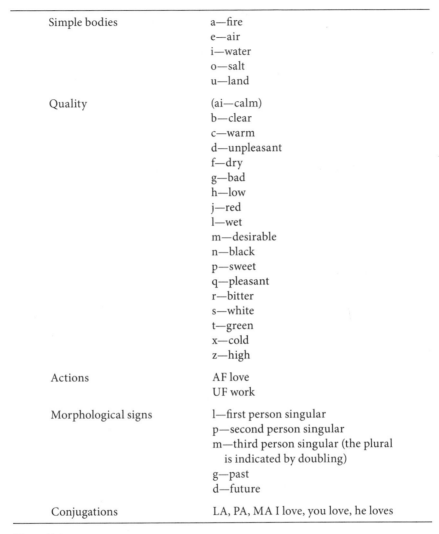

Simple bodies	a—fire
	e—air
	i—water
	o—salt
	u—land
Quality	(ai—calm)
	b—clear
	c—warm
	d—unpleasant
	f—dry
	g—bad
	h—low
	j—red
	l—wet
	m—desirable
	n—black
	p—sweet
	q—pleasant
	r—bitter
	s—white
	t—green
	x—cold
	z—high
Actions	AF love
	UF work
Morphological signs	l—first person singular
	p—second person singular
	m—third person singular (the plural is indicated by doubling)
	g—past
	d—future
Conjugations	LA, PA, MA I love, you love, he loves

Figure 11.1

other way, because they are ruled by this great principle: "that it is use-less to employ several ways of action, when one can act with few."

So they speak only when it is necessary to express a long series of propositions. All their words are monosyllabic, and their conjugations follow the same criterion. For example, *af* means "to love"; the present is *la, pa, ma*; I love, thou lovest, he loves; *lla, ppa, mma*; we love, you love, they love. They possess only one past tense, which we call the perfect: *lga, pga, mga,* I have loved, thou hast loved, etc.; *llga, ppga, mmga,* we have loved, etc. The future *lda, pda, mda,* I will love, etc., *llda, ppda, mmda,* we will love, etc. "To work," in the Austral language, is *uf: lu, pu, mu,* I work, thou workest, etc.; *lgu, pgu, ragu,* I have worked, etc.

They have no declensions, no article, and very few words. They express simple things with a single vowel and compound things through vowels that indicate the chief simple bodies that make up those compounds. They know only five simple bodies, of which the first and most noble is fire, which they express with *a;* then there is air, indicated with *e;* the third is salt, indicated with *o;* the fourth, water, which they call *i;* and the fifth, earth, which they define as *u.*

As differentiating principle they employ the consonants, which are far more numerous than those of the Europeans. Each consonant denotes a quality peculiar to the things expressed by the vowels, thus *b* means clear; *c,* hot; *d,* unpleasant; *f,* dry, etc. Following these rules, they form words so well that, listening to them, you understand immediately the nature and the content of what they signify. They call the stars *Aeb,* a word that indicates their compound of fire and air, united to clarity. They call the sun *Aab,* birds are *Oef,* sign of their solidity and their aeriform and dry matter. Man is called *Uel,* which indicates his substance, partly aerial, partly terrestrial, accompanied by wetness. And so it is with other things. The advantage of this way of speaking is that you become philosophers, learning the prime elements, and in this country, nothing can be named without explaining at the same time its nature, which would seem miraculous to those unaware of the secret that they use to this end.

If their way of speech is so admirable, even more so is their writing . . . and though to us it seems very difficult to decipher them, custom makes the practice very simple.[1]

---

1. The passage quoted here and subsequent quotations from the same author were presumably translated by Weaver from the Italian version cited by Eco, namely, Gabriel de Foigny. *La terra australe,* trans. Maria Teresa Bovetti Pichetto. Napoli: Guida, 1978. No page references are provided.

Instructions in the manner of writing follow; here vowels are indicated with dots marked in different positions, while the thirty-six consonants of the alphabet are little strokes that surround the dots and are recognized by their angles. Foigny mentions these graphic devices obviously making fun of similarly complicated systems, such as, for example, Joachim Becher's *Character pro notia linguarum universalis* (1661), which proposes a form of notation capable of completely muddling the reader's ideas. He then continues, citing composites that can be achieved:

> For example: *eb,* clear air; *ic,* hot water; *ix,* cold water; *ul,* damp earth; *af,* dry fire; *es,* white air. . . . There are another eighteen or nineteen, but in Europe we have no consonants corresponding to them.
>
> The more you consider this way of writing, the more you will discover secrets worthy of admiration: *b* means clear; *c* hot; *x* cold; *l* wet; *f* dry; *n* black; *t* green; *d* nasty; *p* sweet; *q* pleasant; *r* bitter; *m* desirable; *g* bad; *z* high; *h* low; *j* red; *a* joined with *i,* calm. The moment a word is spoken, they know the nature of what it denotes: to indicate a sweet and desirable apple, they write *ipm;* nasty and unpleasant fruit is *ind.* I cannot explain all the other secrets that they understand and reveal in their letters.
>
> The verbs are even more mysterious than the nouns. For example, they write and pronounce *af,* to say "to love"; *a* means fire, *f* means the scorching caused by love. They say *la* to mean "I Love," which means the secretion that love produces in us; *pa,* "thou lovest," sign of the lover's sweetness; *lla,* "we love," the double *ll* indicating the number of persons; *oz* means "to speak," the letter *o* standing for salt, which seasons out speech, while *z* indicates the inhaling and exhaling necessary to speech.
>
> When a child is being taught, the meaning of all the elements is explained to him, and when he unites them, he learns both the essence and the nature of all things he is saying. This is a wonderful advantage both for the individual and for society, because, when they have learned to read, as they always do by the age of three, they understand at the same time all the characteristics of all beings.

In this language the single letters are chosen arbitrarily, and each refers to a simple notion or to a thing. When compound entities are denoted, however, the syntax of expression appears isomorphic with reference to the content.

Assuming that stars are a compound of fire and clear-colored air, the syntagm *aeb* expresses "naturally" the nature of the thing. The expression is isomorphic to the content, to such a degree that changing one element of the expression denotes a different content. In fact, *aab* does not mean stars; it means *sun* because (in the astronomy of the Austral Land) the sun is obviously a double, clear fire. In this sense the language of real characters is distinguished from the natural languages where, if *month* means a length of time, the relationship between noun and notion (or thing) in both cases is entirely arbitrary. In other terms, if, by mistake, we write *catt,* this does not indicate, say, a cat with an extra leg, whereas, if in the Austral language you write, or say, *icc* instead of *ic,* probably you want to indicate water not hot but boiling hot.

As I said earlier, the system recalls the language of chemical formulas: if you write H_2Au instead of H_2O in theory you indicate a different chemical compound. But here the first drawback of the system crops up. In chemistry, the system remains, so to speak, open (accommodating neologisms) in case an absolutely new compound has to be named, but the acceptance of the neologism is conditioned by the system of the content. Because in nature the number of known or admitted compounds is limited, one may confidently read H_2Au as a mistake, a misspelling, as it were. But in the Austral language, what happens if one rungs into the syntagm *al?* Must one admit the possibility that there exists a "wet fire"?

A problem of this sort emerged in connection with the semantic universals that Ramon Llull subjected to combinations and permutations, where the free combination of letters could theoretically produce an utterance repellent to the philosophical bases of the system into which it was introduced (or, in other words, a heretical utterance, such as "truth is false" or "God is lascivious"). But in these cases Llull considered null the theologically unacceptable combination. This also occurred because the letters denoted metaphysical entities that, in the realm of the theology of reference, were precisely defined. *Bonitas est magna* means that Goodness is great, but as Goodness was already defined in this way, it was impossible to conceive of its opposite, *Bonitas est mala* (Goodness is evil). Likewise, the *Ars* did not contemplate the possibility of metaphorical expression or even of periphrases. The primitive terms employed defined the entire universe of what was theologically sayable. Llull, with his perfect theological language, was not interested in talking about stars or hot water.

On the contrary, the Austral language uses a very limited battery of primitives but must serve to express every possible experience, that is, to replace through compositions of primitives the entire vocabulary. Thus, as can be seen from the quotation above, it must employ periphrases that, in Foigny's satirical version, are highly questionable metaphors: apple becomes sweet and desirable water, and the act of loving is expressed as *af* (dry fire), or burning derived from the fire of passion. If *dry fire* means love, then why should *wet fire* not be able to mean metaphorically some other thing? The problem that arises, analyzing this caricature of language, is a serious problem: if a few primitives must denominate many things, it is indispensable to recur to periphrasis, and this is precisely what happens with the "serious" projects of Wilkins and Dalgarno. And the confines between periphrasis and metaphorical expression can become very hazy. In fact, in Dalgarno's serious project compounds were introduced on the order of "animal + full-hoofs + spirited" to signify horse and "animal + full-hoofs + huge" to signify elephant.

The equally serious project of Wilkins was based on the fact that all ambiguities of language had to be reduced so that every sign would refer to a single, rigorously defined concept. But some metaphorical operators were introduced to allow the language to express entities for which no terms existed in the philosophical dictionary, whose format had inevitably to be reduced. Wilkins asserts that it is not necessary to have a character for *calf* because the concept can be reached by combining *cow* and *young*; nor does one need a primitive *lioness*, since this animal can be denoted by combining the sign for *female* with that for *lion*. Thus Wilkins develops in his grammar (and then transforms into a system of special signs in the part devoted to the writing and pronunciation of the characters) a system of "Transcendental Particles" intended to amplify or alter the character to which they are applied. The list contemplates eight classes amounting to a total of forty-eight particles, but the criterion that assembles them is not at all systematic. Wilkins harks back to Latin grammar, which makes use of endings/suffixes (that allow the creation of terms like *lucesco, aquosus, homunculus*); of "segregates" such as *tim* and *genus* (allowing the creation, from a root, of *gradatim* or *multigenus*); and determination of place (hence *vestiarium*) and agent (cf. *arator*). Some of his particles are without doubt of a grammatical nature (for example, those that transform masculine into feminine or adult into young). But Wilkins himself recurs also to the criteria of rhetoric, citing metaphor, synecdoche, and metonymy, and, in fact, the particles in the metaphorical-like category are simply signs of rhetorical interpretation. Thus, adding one of these particles to *root* one gains *original,* while adding it to *light* yields *evident.* Finally, other particles seem to refer to the cause–effect relation, or container–thing contained, or function–activity, as in the following examples:

like + foot = pedestal
like + blood = crimson
place + metal = mine
officer + navy = admiral
artist + star = astronomer
voice + lion = roar

From the point of view of linguistic precision, this is the weakest part of the project. In fact, Wilkins, who supplies a long list of examples of the correct application of such particles, warns that they are, in fact, examples. Therefore the list is open, and its enrichment depends on the inventiveness of the speaker. It seems almost that Wilkins, concerned about the mechanical quality of his language, is anxious to leave room for its users' creativity. But once the user is free to apply these particles to any term, it is obvious that ambiguity will be hard to avoid.

And so the artificial language loses its one virtue: that of denoting always and only the same thing with the same character.

The Austral language (like the models it parodies) deliberately rejects the fundamental mechanism of every natural language, namely, double articulation. It is obvious how much double articulation (in which the units of second articulation are without meaning) can contribute to the free formation of neologisms. If, with three meaningless characters *(p, c, f),* I can compose six syntagma *(pot, top, opt, pto, otp, tpo),* and only three of these are admitted by the dictionary, the other three remain available for constructing neologisms or indicating the most subtle differences between otherwise similar entities. As long as they remain available, however, if they happen to appear in a context, they may be understood as errors in pronunciation or spelling.

Foigny's system, on the one hand, allows the creation of neologisms only through metaphor and, on the other, obliges us to seek out a meaning for every syntagm admitted by the ars *combinatoria,* because even the slightest phonetic or orthographic change immediately reflects on the content and denotes a different (and possible) entity.

Finally, the last limitation of the Austral language is—as occurred with many a priori philosophical languages—the absolute casualness with which the primitives are chosen. We will not speak of the so-called Anonymous Spaniard (Pedro Bermudo), who in his 1654 *Arithmeticus nomenclator* classified the primitives, subdividing them into:

(1) Elements (fire, wind, smoke, ash, hell, purgatory, and center of the earth). (2) Celestial entities (stars, lightning, rainbow). (3) Intellectual entities (God, Jesus, discourse, opinion, suspicion, soul, stratagem or specter). (4) Secular states (emperor, barons, plebs). (5) Ecclesiastical states. (6) Artificers (painter or sailor). (7) Instruments. (8) Affects (love, justice, lust). (9) Religion. (10) Sacramental confession. (11) Tribunal. (12) Army. (13) Medicine (doctor, hunger, enema). (14) Brute animals. (15) Birds. (16) Reptiles and fish. (17) Parts of animals. (18) Furnishings. (19) Foods. (20) Beverages and liquids (wine, beer, water, butter, wax, resin). (21) Clothing. (22) Silken stuffs. (23) Woolens. (24) Canvas and other textiles. (25) Navigation and spices (ship, cinnamon, anchor, chocolate). (26) Metals and coins. (27) Various artifacts. (28) Stones. (29) Jewels. (30) Trees and fruits. (31) Public places. (32) Weights and measures. (33) Numerals. (34–42) Various grammatical categories. (43) Persons (pronouns, forms of address such as His Eminence). (44) Travel (hay, road, robber) . . .

But Wilkins himself, though he discussed his list with students of botany, mineralogy, and zoology, put under the heading of Economic Relations not only cases of kinship, in which distinctions appear distorted by criteria such as Progenitor/Descendant, Brother/Half-brother, or *Coelebs*/Virgin (*Coelebs*, however, comprises both the bachelor and the spinster, whereas Virgin seems to refer only to a female condition), but also acts that refer to intersubjective relationships, such as Direct/Seduce or Defense/Desertion. Among the Private Relations appear also Provisions, where we find Butter/ Cheese but also Butchering/Cooking and Box/Basket.

Note the sly way that Foigny breaks the homogeneity of the list of the four classic elements by adding salt, which, if anything, would belong to another chemical-alchemistic taxonomy, including also mercury and sulfur. But the slyness is not gratuitous precisely because Wilkins added to the four elements a fifth, evident one: the Meteor.

As for the thirty-six accidentals, even if we know only eighteen of them, their heterogeneity is enough for us to infer that the list has prominent omissions. Here Foigny touches palpably the crucial question of the list of the primitives, and he resolves it more in the manner of the Anonymous Spaniard than in that of Wilkins, but only to insinuate (it seems) that, when it comes to incongruity, there is only a difference of degree between the two systems.

The final comic element in the Austral language is that it does not clarify when a letter has a lexical function or when it is morphemathic. It seems that *l, m,* and *p*—placed in the first position—function as pronouns. But, in analyzing *pa* (thou lovest), Foigny speaks of the sweetness of the lover. Thus he assigns two letters with morphemathic functions the meaning they have when they define accidentals. The solution is comic because it allows us to think that *lu* (I work) must be interpreted with reference to the sweat produced by the earth, but in that case why would there be sweetness in *pu* (thou workest)?

We cannot tell how consciously Foigny was being ironic about the fact that in the philosophical languages the entire grammar is semanticized, but this mischievousness is not to be overlooked.

Criticism of a priori philosophical languages for the most part appears, as I have shown, in French satirical works. Perhaps this is not an accident: it was in France that the first radical criticism of the project took shape in the serious works of Dalgarno, Wilkins, and Lodwick.

In 1629 the Minim friar Marin Mersenne sends his friend Descartes the project of a *nouvelle langue* by a certain des Vallées. In a letter to Mersenne on November 20, 1629, Descartes sends his impressions of that proposal. For every language, he says, it is necessary to learn a grammar and the meaning of the words. For the meaning of the words it would suffice to have a good dictionary, but the grammar is difficult. Nevertheless, if a grammar could be constructed free of the irregularities of the natural languages, which have been corrupted by use, the problem would be solvable. Thus simplified, this language would appear primitive compared to the others, which would appear as its dialects. And once the primitive terms were set (of which the terms of the other languages would be synonyms, such as *aimer* and *to love*), it would suffice to add the suffixes to obtain, for example, the corresponding substantive. Consequently, a system of universal writing could be developed in which every primitive term would be recorded with a number that would refer back to the synonyms in the different languages.

All the same, there would still remain the problem of the sounds to choose for these terms, inasmuch as certain sounds are pleasant and easy for one people and unpleasant for another. The sounds would thus be difficult to learn: if a speaker used synonyms in his own language for the primitive terms, then he would not be understood by speakers of other nations, except in writing. Yet learning the entire lexicon would require great effort, and if that were necessary, there would seem to be no reason not to use an international language already known to many, such as Latin.

Saying this, Descartes only repeated some ideas that were in the air in those decades. But at this point he saw that the central problem is something else altogether: to be able not only to learn but also remember the primitive nouns, these would have to correspond to an order of ideas, or of thoughts, that would have the same logic as the order of the numbers (where it is not necessary to learn them all but simply to generate them by succession). This problem coincides with another: that of a true philosophy able to define a system and distinct ideas. If a person were able to number all the simple ideas from which are then generated all the ideas that we are capable of thinking and to assign to each of these a character, we could then articulate, as we do with numbers, this sort of mathematics of thought. The words of our languages, on the other hand, refer to confused ideas.

In conclusion, Descartes affirmed: "Now I believe that this language is possible and that the learning on which it depends could be found, by which peasants will be able to judge the truth better than philosophers do now. But I have no faith in ever seeing it used; it presupposes great changes in the order of things, and the whole world would have to be nothing more than an earthly paradise, which can be proposed only in the land of novels."

The criticism of Descartes was correct. Every attempt to establish an architectonically perfect system of ideas composed of mutual dependences and strict classification from the general to the particular would prove to be a failure. At the end of the eighteenth century Joseph-Marie de Gérando, in *Des signes,* would isolate the secret termite that was gnawing at all the previous systems: either you create a logical dictionary confined to a very limited notional field or an encyclopedia of all our knowledge, that is, either a necessary but insufficient order of concepts or the flexible, infinitely amplifiable and variable order of a library.

On the other hand, Leibniz would acknowledge (in his *Nouveaux essais sur l'entendement humain*) that, having to depict the entire system of our learning, we would have a library where the doctrine of spirits could come under logic but also under morality, and all could come under the practical philosophy to the extent that it contributes to our happiness. A memorable story can be placed in the annals of universal history or in the specific history of a country or even in the biography of an individual. Anyone who is organizing a library often encounters the problem of deciding in which section a book should be cataloged.

So the only thing to do would be to essay a polydimensional encyclopedia (a hypertext, as we would say today). We can almost hear, in advance, the project that would be theorized by D'Alembert at the beginning of the *Encyclopédie*, where he speaks of the *Système Général des Sciences et des Arts* as a labyrinth. The philosopher is he who can discover the secret routes of this labyrinth, its temporary branches, the reciprocal dependences that compose this enclosure like a globe. Consequently, "one can create as many different systems of human knowledge as there are world maps having different projections. . . . But often such an object, which because of one or several of its properties has been placed in one class, belongs to another class by virtue of other properties and might have been placed accordingly."[2]

The criticism of the *Encyclopédie* puts an end to the dream of the grammar of ideas, even though further attempts would follow, down to our own day, when scholars are still studying the possibility of a so-called mentalese, a language written in the very convolutions of our brain, capable of supplying the deep structure of every expression in any natural language.

But as Descartes had announced, it is not impossible to write of ideal languages in the land of novels. Foigny did it, and two and a half centuries later, Borges was to do it, too.

In *Other Inquisitions*, Borges (1964), studying "the language of John Wilkins" (which, by his explicit admission, he knew only through an encyclopedia entry), recognizes at once the incongruity of the classification of the Wilkinsian semantic primitives (he discusses specifically the subdivisions

---

2. English translation: D'Alembert (1963: 46–49).

of stones), and it is in this same brief text that he invents the Chinese classification that Foucault quotes at the opening of *Les mots et les choses*. In this Chinese encyclopedia, entitled *Celestial Emporium of Benevolent Recognitions*, "it is written that the animals are divided into (a) those that belong to the Emperor, (b) embalmed ones, (c) those that are trained, (d) suckling pigs, (e) mermaids, (f) fabulous ones, (g) stray dogs, (h) those that are included in this classification, (i) those that tremble as if they were mad, (j) innumerable ones, (k) those drawn with a very fine camel's hair brush, (l) others, (m) those that have just broken a flower vase, (n) those that resemble flies from a distance."[3] Borges comes to the conclusion that no classification in the universe is not arbitrary and conjectural. But if it has to be arbitrary and conjectural, why not leave room not for the satire of utopian projects but for the utopia of linguistic fancy?

Borges, on at least two other occasions, returns to the question of ideal languages. In "Dr. Brodie's Report" Borges (1976) he examines the monosyllabic language of the Yahoos.

> Each monosyllabic word corresponds to a general idea whose specific meaning depends on the context or upon accompanying grimaces. The word "nrz," for example, suggests dispersion of spots and may stand for the starry sky, a leopard, a flock of birds, smallpox, something bespattered, the act of scattering, or the flight that follows defeat in warfare. "Hrl," on the other hand, means something compact or dense. It stands for the tribe, a tree trunk, a stone, a heap of stones, the act of heaping stones, the gathering of the four witch-doctors, carnal conjunction or a forest. Pronounced in another manner or accompanied by other grimaces, each word may hold an opposite meaning.[4]

This language of the Yahoos is not at all impracticable, as it seems at first glance. Note that the apparent polysemy of the term is, so to speak, held together by certain primitive special signs common to all its meanings. The grimaces that accompany the emission of sound function like the metaphorical operators of Wilkins. For the rest, the language simply carries to

---

3. See "The Analytical Language of John Wilkins" in Borges (1964: 103).
4. See "Doctor Brodie's Report" in Borges (1972: 117).

extremes the tendency of actual natural languages to contain expressions that mean different things in different contexts, and Borges hastens to remind his readers that this should not be surprising; after all, in English, to cleave means both "to split" and "to cling to."

Finally, in "Tlön, Uqbar, Orbis Tertius" Borges (1998) speaks of a language structured spatially and not temporally, which proceeds not through agglutinations as in the languages so far examined but only by expressing temporal flow. In this language, nouns do not exist, but only impersonal verbs qualified by monosyllabic suffixes and prefixes with adverbial value. In brief, "there is no word corresponding to the word "moon," but there is a verb which in English would be "to moon" or "to moonate." "The moon rose above the river" would thus be written *hlör u fang axaxaxas mlö*, or literally: "upward behind the onstreaming it mooned" (which sounds like a quote from Joyce's *Finnegans Wake*).[5]

The failure of the utopias of the a priori philosophical language has thus produced some interesting experiments in the Land of Novels that, instead of constructing perfect linguistic systems, have demonstrated how our imperfect languages can produce texts endowed with some poetic virtue or some visionary force. I consider this no small achievement.

---

5. See "Tlön, Ucbar, Orbis Tertius" in Borges (1962: 8).

12

The Linguistics of Joseph de Maistre

In the story of the centuries-old search for a perfect language, a central chapter must be devoted to the rediscovery of a series of *matrix languages* or of a primordial mother tongue. For many centuries, the leading claimant for the position of mother tongue was Hebrew. Subsequently, other candidates would appear upon the scene (even Chinese, for example), but finally the search would lose its utopian fervor and its mystical tension as the science of linguistics was born and, with it, the Indo-European hypothesis (see Eco 1993: ch. 5).

For a long time, though, the idea of a primigenial language not only had a historical significance (rediscovering the speech of all mankind before the confusion of Babel) but also a semantic one. In fact, this primigenial language was supposed to incorporate a natural relationship between words and things. The primigenial language also had revelatory value for, in speaking it, the speaker would recognize the nature of the named reality. This tendency, which Genette (1976) has called "mimologism," has an ancient and distinguished ancestry in Western tradition, its prime example being the *Cratylus* of Plato. The idea—already contested in the two previous centuries through the hypotheses known as Epicurean and polygenetic—underwent a crisis in what Rosiello (1976) would have called "the linguistic of enlightenment." But this crisis occurred at the level of the official (which is another way of saying victorious) philosophical and linguistic culture,

This translation is a minimally revised version of the translation by William Weaver that appeared in Eco (1998b). The quotations are here given in the version contained in "The Saint Petersburg Dialogues" in Lebrun (1993).

and the notion survived in many mystical and philosophical trends and has resurfaced even today in the work of those whom the nineteenth-century French tradition had begun calling *les fous du langage.*

I am indebted to Andrew White (1917: 2:189–208) for some suggestions on the way the mystical version of the monogenetic hypothesis was prolonged in the theosophical ambience of the late eighteenth century (in Louis-Claude de Saint Martin, *De l'esprit des choses,* for example) and among the French Catholic legitimists such as De Bonald (*Recherches philosophiques,* III, 2) and Lamennais (*Essai sur l'indifférence en matière de religion).* White also quotes Joseph de Maistre, an alluring clue, because Maistre represents a fusion of the themes of classic legitimism (of which he can be considered the initiator) and those of the theosophism hovering in the circles of Scottish and Templar masonry to which Maistre had at first belonged, though he broke with them for reasons of religious orthodoxy (reaffirming the authority of the Church and the pope against that of any clique of Illuminati).

In a debate on the subject, Raffaele Simone suggested that much of the search for a perfect language derived from a sort of neurotic uneasiness, because people would like to find in words an expression of the way the world works, and they are regularly disappointed. This is certainly true. In the legitimist tradition, the assertion of the sacrality of language aims not so much at reconstructing a primigenial language as at rediscovering the traces of our natural languages. The intent is first of all to question the materialistic claims of all the Epicurean, polygenetic hypotheses and then to reject every conventionalist theory as a way of separating language from the very source of Truth.

Since it is linguistically difficult to demonstrate that a relationship exists between words and the essence of things (not least because of the plurality of languages), the way followed by the monogeneticists does not differ much from that of the most fanciful etymologists of the past, Isidore of Seville at their head. The fact that many of these etymologies also reappear in some contemporary thought (in Heidegger, for example) only indicates the toughness of the dream, or perhaps an irrepressible need to have some contact with Being.

If we take a look at the text in which Maistre discussed at greatest length the nature of languages, his *Soirées de Saint-Pétersbourg,* we see that the first declarations simply repropose what is found even today among authors who hark back to tradition as the source of all knowledge, opposing the degenerate learning of a secularized culture, "modern," "enlightened," or "scientistic."

> Listen to what wise antiquity has to say about the first men; it will tell you that they were marvelous men, and that beings of a superior order deigned to favor them with the most precious communications. On this point there is no discord: initiates, philosophers, poets, history, fable, Asia and Europe, speak with one voice. Such agreement of reason, revelation, and every human tradition forms a demonstration that cannot be contradicted. So not only did men begin with science, but with a science different from our own, and superior to our own because it had a higher origin, which is what made it more dangerous. And this explains why science was always considered mysterious in principle, and why it was always confined to the temples, where the flame finally burned out when it could serve no purpose but to burn. (Second Dialogue 41)

But just when readers might expect proof of this theory, they always find themselves confronted by inconsistent, circular arguments. Maistre recalls that Julian the Apostate in one of his discourses called the sun "the seven-rayed god," and he wonders where the emperor found such a singular attribute. His answer is that the idea could have come to him only from the ancient Asiatic tradition to which he recurred in his theurgic renovation. Maistre cites, for example, "the sacred books of India," which speak of seven virgins gathered to celebrate the advent of Krishna when the god suddenly appears to them, inviting them to dance. When the virgins object that they have no dancing partners, the god divides into seven, giving each virgin her own Krishna.

There is really nothing so strange about Julian's choice of imagery, inasmuch as the hebdomad, the mystique of the number seven, is found in many ancient cultures, and Julian could have absorbed it either from Indian sources or from others. But what indicates a strange disjuncture of thought is the series of examples that follows hard upon Maistre's evocation of Julian. First of all, he notes, the "true" system of the universe was known from most remote antiquity, as is shown by the pyramids of Egypt, which are rigorously oriented according to astronomical criteria. Then, whether as proof or consequence of this fact, we observe that a people like the Egyptians, who could create colors that have lasted thirty centuries, raise boulders against every law of mechanics to a height of six hundred feet, carve in granite birds of all known species, could hardly fail to excel in every other art, and therefore they must have known things of which we are ignorant. Finally, in Asia, consider the ancient astronomical observations carved on the walls of Nimrud, which rose on land still damp from the Flood. All this drives one—notice the conclusion—to ask oneself, "So where will we place the so-called times of barbarism and ignorance?" (42).

We cannot see a direct rapport between the metaphor of the seven rays and the pyramids, unless it is to be found in the fact that different myths and archetypes tried to explain astronomical phenomena and furnished a pre-Galilean version of a world written in mathematical characters. But to confirm the existence of these trends Plato would again suffice, with his *Timaeus*. If anything, it is the knowledge that even more ancient images circulated in African and Asian culture that explains why Julian followed this tradition. Whether he followed it or revitalized it, however, this does not show that he was its direct and authorized heir or that the tradition spoke any truth.

But this reasoning had been typical of the same Masonic tradition that influenced Maistre: the fact that an association decided to hark back to the Templar tradition became a sign of direct descent.

It is obvious that in this reasoning there is no linguistic-etymological discovery, but only biased polemic against sick modern civilization: "Under skimpy northern dress, his head lost in the curls of deceptive locks, his arms loaded with books and instruments of all kinds, pale from long nights and work, the modern scientist drags himself along the road to truth, soiled with ink and panting, always bending his algebra-furrowed brow towards the earth" (43). Compared to that of our modern civilization, the knowledge of the origins reveals its obvious superiority:

> In so far as it is possible to perceive the science of early times at such a
> distance, one always see it free and isolated, soaring rather than walking,

and presenting in its whole being something airy and supernatural. Exposing to the winds the hair that escapes from an oriental *mitre,* an *efod* covering a breast uplifted with inspiration, it looked only to the heavens, and its disdainful foot seemed to touch the earth only to leave it. However, although it demanded nothing of anyone and seemed to know no human support, it is no less proven that it possessed the rarest knowledge. (43)

The proof of this primacy would lie in the fact that traditional science was exempted from the task imposed on modern science, while all the calculations that we base on experimentation are the most false that can be imagined. Whence we see that the thesis (modern civilization is inferior to ancient civilization) is reasserted as proof.

At this point the Greek myth of the golden age is proposed as proof that the state of perfect and luminous knowledge existed only in the civilizations of the origins (44). Thus the man who had written pages, truly beautiful from a literary point of view, on the revolution's crime, rediscovers the root of every Jacobin degradation in the act (so remote that it can no longer be collocated in history) with which language fell away from the original tree (44).

Seekers after original Hebrew, even they could retrace its origin only into a past Eden (of which they had to make an effort, moreover, to offer, however fancifully, a chronology) did not therefore refrain from reconstructing its grammar. Compared with the efforts of a man such as Athanasius Kircher to decipher Egyptian hieroglyphics and study the generating of alphabets, the efforts of Maistre seem fairly puerile: "Here is the mystery, gentlemen: one generation said *ba,* the other said *be;* the Assyrians invented the nominative, and the Medes, the genitive" (116)—which, if anything, would be proof not of a divine origin of languages but precisely of their slow evolution. Maistre asks himself why, in the languages of the ancient peoples, we find reflections of knowledge that those people could not have possessed. The correct question naturally would not be "why" but "whether." In fact, Maistre goes on to illustrate not inconceivable knowledge but proofs of the fact, common among ancients as among moderns, that poets are capable of finding ingenious metaphors to name phenomena fundamental to human experience.

For example, from where did the Greeks, at least three thousand years ago, take the epithet *Physizoos* (giving or possessing life), which Homer sometimes gives to the earth? Or that of *Pheresbios,* very nearly synonymous, which he attributes to Hesiod? From where did they take the still more singular epithet *of Philemate* (*amorous or thirsty for blood*), given to the earth in a tragedy? Who would have taught them to call sulphur, which is the cipher of fire, *the divine*? I am no less struck by the name *Cosmos* given to the world. The Greeks named it *beauty* because *all order is beauty,* as the good Eustathius said somewhere, and supreme order is in the world. The Latins encountered the same idea and expressed it by their word *Mundus,* which we have adopted by merely giving it a French ending, except however that one of these words excludes disorder and the other excludes defilement. Nevertheless it is the same idea, and the two words are equally correct and equally false. But again tell me, I ask you, how these ancient Latins, when they still knew only war and ploughing, thought to express by the same word ideas of prayer and torture? And who taught them to call fever *the purifier* or *the expiator*? We would not say that there is here a real knowledge of cause by which a people affirmed the correctness of a name. But do you believe that these sorts of judgment could have belonged to a time when they scarcely knew how to write, when the dictator spaded his own garden, when they wrote verses that Varro and Cicero no longer understood? These words and still others that could be cited, and that belong completely to oriental metaphysics, are the evident debris of more ancient languages destroyed or forgotten. (48–49)

Here we are simply demonstrating that every epoch had its poets, capable of naming things in an unusual and perspicacious fashion. Or, at most, we are repeating, in a simplified form, a thesis inspired by Vico on the metaphoric origin of language that is, if anything, a reflection of the perceptive freshness of ancient peoples, not of their presumed occult knowledge. It hardly seems that any profound learning was necessary for agrarian peoples to call the earth "life-giving" as they lived, in fact, on the earth's fruits.

Maistre was a vigorous thinker, capable of historically based critical judgments (it suffices to look at his contestations of the Templar myth of the

Scottish masonry). And he was not ignorant of the attempts made to construct an a priori philosophical language, from Bacon to Wilkins and beyond. He perceives the contrivances of the artificial languages proposed in the course of the previous two centuries, to which common sense would reply that natural languages seem more flexible in handling our experience. But then this position (which, thus enunciated, would prove disastrously "enlightened") in Maistre's discourse is radically transformed. To demonstrate the agility of natural languages Maistre cannot avoid recurring to another notion, born in the eighteenth century: that of the "genius" of languages. But the notion of genius recalls that of polygenesis, or at least of autonomous development, unreconcilable with any monogenetic hypothesis. Maistre thus finds himself entangled in a line of reasoning that leads to wild paralogisms:

> I do not want to take up the question of the origins of language (the same, it must be noted in passing, as that of innate ideas), in the most refined of centuries, drew attention to this talent in nascent peoples, but what I can assure you of, for nothing is clearer, is the prodigious talent of infant peoples in forming words and of the absolute incapacity of philosophers to do the same thing. I recall that Plato, in the most refined of centuries, drew attention to this talent in nascent peoples. What is remarkable about this is that it has been said they proceeded by way of deliberation, in virtue of a determined system of agreement, although such a thing would have been rigorously impossible in every respect. Each language has its genius, and this genius is ONE, in a way that excludes all idea of composition, or arbitrary formation, or anterior convention. (49)

The notion of genius does not exclude convention, unless the former is understood as a kind of mystical insufflation that comes from outside the linguistic formative process. Maistre decides to isolate the "genius" specific to Greek and to Latin in some morphological characteristics of the two languages, an admissible method, without making any decision as to the precision of the analysis. Thus he observes that in Greek compound words can be formed in which the two parts generate a second meaning, without therewith becoming unrecognizable, whereas Latin tends to shatter the words in

such a way that from their fragments, chosen and joined through some unknown and quite singular agglutinations, are born new words of surprising
beauty, whose elements are no longer recognizable except to a trained eye
(49). But here is the proof:

> From these three words, for example, CA*ro* DA*ta* VER*mibus* they
> made CADAVER, *flesh abandoned to the worms.* From the words
> M*Agis and vo*LO, NO*n* and *vo*LO, they made *MALO* and *NOLO,* two
> excellent verbs that every language, even Greek, might envy Latin. . . .
> The French are not absolutely unacquainted this system. Those who
> were our ancestors, for example, knew very well how to name theirs by
> a partial union of the word ANCI*ien* with ÊTRE, just as they made *bef-*
> *froi* from B*el* EFFROI. See how they worked with the two Latin words
> DU*o* and IRE, from which they made DUIRE, *going two together,* and
> by a very natural extension, *mener, conduire.* From the personal pro-
> noun SE, from the relative adverb of place HORS, and the verbal end-
> ing TIR, they made S-OR-TIR, that is to say SEHORSTIR, or *to put*
> *one's person outside the place where it was,* which appears marvelous to
> me. (49–50)

This passage displays two contradictions. In the first part, the fact that two
languages evolved through different morphological rules is, if anything (as
we have said), an argument against monogenetism. In the second part, with
a specific quotation from Isidore, Maistre tries to play the etymological
card. But at least the etymology of the seventeenth-century monogeneticists
consisted of showing how the words of each language had developed from a
single Hebrew root (the only one, for that matter, to have a presumed
"iconic" or motivated relationship with the thing signified). Here, on the
contrary, the game consists of demonstrating that within each language,
and with quite different mechanisms, compound words can be created
whose meanings are born from the sum of the meanings of their simple
components, which is what happens in the natural languages when they
compose terms like *screwdriver, corkscrew, parasol,* or when spontaneous
agglutinations are born, as in the transformation of Mediolanum into
Milan—though, alas, this never happened with the Latin word *cadaver.*
Even if Isidore's etymology of *cadaver* were plausible, and even if had

the etymology attributed to it by Maistre, this would in no way prove any iconic and motivated relation between simple words and signified reality but rather, if anything, that new coinages are often born from the word-play typical of the rhetors of decadence and not from an instinctive folk wisdom.

The fact that this aspect could escape Maistre is explained only by the religious—and not linguistic—exigency that he convince his readers (almost pedagogically) that language says originally the Truth. And we sense this from some expressions of outright joy with which he glimpses the action, within every human language, of this impulse to tell always the truth, no matter what: "It is a pleasure to be present, so to speak, at the work of this hidden principle that forms languages. Sometimes you see it struggling against some difficulty that impedes its development: it searches a form that it lacks; its materials resist it; then it will extricate itself from its embarrassment with a happy solecism, and it will say very effectively, 'Rue passante,' 'couleur voyante' 'place marchande' 'métal cassant,' etc." (51).

No objection would be made as to the efficacy of these compounds, were it not for the fact that Maistre is not always fond of compounds (or of the hidden action a language forms in order to mint them), as if a language, in some of its vicissitudes, remained faithful to its own obligation to truth and in other instances degenerated. As examples of degeneration, he cites the fact that already in his own day (and in the St. Petersburg familiar to him) on visiting cards one could find titles such as *Minister, Général, Kammerherr, Fräulein, Général-Anchef, Général-Dejournei, Joustizii-Minister,* and that on commercial posters words like *magazei, fabrica, meubel,* or that in the course of military drills commands were heard such as *directii na prava, na leva, deployade en échiquier, en echelon, contre-marche,* or that in the army functions should be named *haupt-wacht, exercise hause, ordonnance-hause, commisariat, cazarma, canzellari.*

Immediately afterward, he mentions terms considered "beautiful, elegant, and expressive" that presumably existed in "your primitive language": *souproug* (bridegroom), which precisely means "he who is attached with another to a single yoke," and he comments that "nothing more correct or more inspired" could have been found, just as "we must admit that the savages or the barbarians who once deliberated to form such nouns surely did not lack refinement" (52).

It is obvious that there is no reason (except the imponderable one of taste) to decide that *place marchande* is legitimate and *contremarche* is not. It is unclear why to describe the bridegroom as someone attached to the same yoke (which could be simply a carnival taunt) seems beautiful, whereas it is horrible to give an order for an army to deploy itself like a chessboard (an effective spatial metaphor). Perhaps here Maistre laments only the introduction of barbarisms and therefore the pollution of one language with terms borrowed from another. In any case, he seems to react according to his personal stylistic preferences, "by ear."

The point is that, if language must be considered the only way to enter into a rapport with the Sacred, every etymology must be "good"; in every metaphor, even the most banal, there should shine a truth, even in *screwdriver*. Since *rue passante* is not ancient to belong to the golden age, in recognizing it as an undegenerate expression Maistre is simply privileging the freshness of popular language over that of bureaucratic language. If he were to trace these and other discriminants, he would shift from mystical linguistics to sociolinguistics, an intention that is very far from his mind.

In fact, he returns constantly to the idea that the perfect language is that of the origins:

> The formation of the most perfect, the most meaningful, the most philosophic words, in the full force of the term, invariably belongs to the time of ignorance and simplicity. One must add, to complete this great theory, that similarly the name-making talent invariably disappears in the measure that one descends to the epochs of civilization and science. In all the writings of our time on this interesting question, there has been a continuously expressed wish for a *philosophic language*, but without anyone knowing or even suspecting that the most philosophic language is that in which philosophy is least involved. Two little things are lacking to philosophy to create words: the intelligence to invent them and the power to get them adopted. If it sees a new object, it pages through its dictionaries to find an antique or foreign word, and almost always it turns out badly. The word *montgolfière*, for example, which is national, is correct, at least in one sense, and I prefer it to *aréostat*, which is the scientific term and which says nothing. One might as well call a ship a *hydrostat*. See this crowd of new words borrowed from

the Greek this past twenty years, as crime or folly has found the need:
almost all have been taken or formed in a way that is contrary to their
literal meaning. The word *théophilanthrope,* for example, is more foolish than the thing, which is to say a lot: an English or German school-
boy would have known how to say, on the contrary, *théanthrophile.* You
tell me that this word was invented by wretches in a wretched period;
but chemical nomenclature, which was certainly the work of very enlightened men, begins with a solecism of the worst sort, *oxygène* instead of *oxygone.* Moreover, although I am not a chemist, I have excellent reasons to think that this whole dictionary will be effaced; but
merely looking at the matter from the philological and grammatical
point of view, it would be perhaps the most unfortunate thing imaginable if the recently disputed metric nomenclature did not win the all-
time award for barbarism. (56–57)

Why should *oxygen* be more unhappy than the very unhappy *oxygon?*
This is what Maistre does not explain. If language is seen as what the world
was for the Middle Ages, as a natural revelation of Truth, nothing in language should be wrong. As medieval thinkers said, even monsters should
show the power of God. Furthermore, as Maistre is the first to assert, in
language there is a glottogonic force that overcomes all human resistance
(and hence language is always right).

It must, however, be said that, at least in one case, Maistre's reasoning
finds a logically plausible formulation. He seeks, in effect, to distinguish
three concepts: (1) the historical paternity through which every language
derives from another, all tracing their ancestry back to the same, primigenial source; (2) the autonomous force whereby every language develops its
own genius, and (3) the presence within each language of a "superlinguistic"
force, a sort of divinely bestowed *energheia* that causes, within each language, without necessarily any historical descendance or borrowing, the
same miracle of the primordial language to take place. Thus the following
passage becomes comprehensible, as it denies thesis 1 in the first paragraph
and affirms thesis 2 in the second:

And what can we say of the surprising analogies that can be noticed
between languages separated by time and space to the point of never
having been able to influence each other?

1. Please notice that I am not to be understood to be speaking of simple conformities of words acquired simply by way of contact or communication;

2. I speak only of conformities of ideas, proved by synonyms of sense, totally different in form, *which excludes all idea of borrowing*. I will only have you notice one very singular thing, which is that when it is a question of rendering some of those ideas whose natural expression would in some way offend delicacy, the French often chanced upon the same turns of phrase formerly employed by the Greeks in their day to save these shocking naïvetés, that must appear quite extraordinary since in this regard we acted on our own without asking anything of our intermediaries, the Latins. (52, my emphasis)

But after the assertion that every language resolves its own problems by itself, thesis 3 emerges, which sets out to prove that it is no longer a language's autonomy but rather the existence of an original and divine force, the word, that becomes the source of every language.

If, on this point of the origin of language, as on so many others, our century has missed the truth, it is because it has a mortal fear of meeting it. Languages began, but *the word* never, and not even with man. The one has necessarily preceded the other, since *the word* is possible only through the VERB [i.e., the Word of God]. Every particular language comes into being like an animal, by birth and development, so that man never passed from a state of *voicelessness* to the use of the word. He has always spoken, and it is with sublime reason that the Hebrews called him a TALKING SOUL. (54)

But then, immediately afterward, and without a break, thesis 1, rejected in the first paragraph, is reproposed:

When a new language takes form, it is born in the midst of a society that is in the full possession of language; and the action or the principle that presides at this formation cannot arbitrarily invent one word. It uses those it finds around it or *that it calls from farther away;* it nourishes itself on them, it chews them, it digests them, and it never adopts them without modifying them to some degree. (54, my emphasis)

Finally, to underline the (always good) naturalness with which each single language, grinding or digesting previous elements, forms always suitable words, there is a gloss: "In a century passionate for every gross expression excluding order and intelligence, they have talked a lot about arbitrary symbols; but there are no arbitrary symbols, every word having its reason" (54). This negates what was previously asserted, namely, that having invented *oxygen* was a sign of degeneration. In fact, Maistre is biased: he thinks (from the beginning) that the modern inventors of *oxygen* were degenerate (inasmuch as they were modern), while the ancient inventors of *cadaver* were right (inasmuch as they were ancient). He is not seized by the suspicion that not even the ancient inventors of *cadaver* were the original Name Giver.

However, we also accept the proposition according to which languages live on borrowings; they transform and adapt, and yet their every word is natural and motivated. If Maistre returned to his example of *rue passante,* he would find that there is a motivation for the compound, but he would not be able to explain the motivation of *rue* and of *passer,* unless he repeated all the contortions of the classic etymologists. Thus, arriving at the crucial point, he gives up. Or, rather, he probably believes that he is not giving up, if the following passage is the expected demonstration. But the total mutual contradiction of the provided examples forces us—in the interest of the reader—to mark within the passage the various theses (all in disagreement among themselves) that it demonstrates. In our view, the theses are the following:

1. *Thesis of obscure borrowing.* Sometimes in a language there existed a word that then somehow passed into another language, which abandoned it but passed it on to a local dialect; for this reason, we may find in an Alpine locality a word used today in the Slavic area. This thesis, however, does not explain why words must reflect the nature of things, nor does it say that they do reflect it.

2. *Thesis of autonomous invention.* Sometimes a word is invented by analogy with a foreign term, sometimes by metaphor. Then each language invents its own terms and does so following quite different criteria.

3. *Thesis of original iconism.* A language does not invent words; it finds them already made, in accord with nature. (No proofs follow.)

    4. *Thesis of evident and multiple borrowing.* One language borrows words from different languages, for the widest variety of reasons.

This is how, without a break, four mutually incompatible theses are affirmed.

    [*Thesis of obscure borrowing*] Perhaps you will remember that in that country French *son* (in Latin *furfur*) is called *Bren*. On the other side of the Alps an owl is called *Sava*. If someone were to ask you why the two peoples have chosen these two arrangements of sound to express these two ideas, you would have been tempted to reply: *Because they judged it appropriate; things of this sort are arbitrary.* However you would have been in error; for the first of those two words is English and the second is Slavic; and from Ragusa to Kamchatka the word is used to signify in the beautiful Russian language what it signifies eight hundred leagues from here in a purely local dialect. You will not be tempted, I hope, to tell me that men deliberating on the Thames, on the Rhine, on the Obi, or on the Po, would by chance come across the same sounds to express the same ideas. Therefore the two words already pre-existed in the two languages that presented them to the two dialects. Would you like to think that the four peoples received them from some previous people? I know nothing of it, but I admit, it: in the first place it is the consequence of the fact that these two immense families, the Teutonic and the Slavic, did not arbitrarily invent these two words, but that they received them. Then the question begins again with respect to earlier nations. Where did they get them? One must answer in the same way, they received them; *and so one goes back to the origin of things.* (54–55)

    [*Thesis of autonomous invention*] The candles that are being carried in at the moment remind me of their name: at one time the French carried on a great commerce with the city of *Botzia* in the Kingdom of Fez; they brought from there a great quantity of wax candles that they took to naming *botzies*. Soon the national genius shaped this word and made *bougies* of it. The English retained the old expression *wax-candle*, and the Germans prefer to say *wachslicht* (light of wax); but everywhere you see the cause that determined the word. Even if I had not run across the etymology of *bougie* in the preface of Thomassin's Hebrew dictionary, where I certainly would never have looked for it, would I have been less sure of some such etymology? To be in doubt on such a matter, one would have to extinguish the flame of analogy, which is to say one would have to renounce reasoning. (55)

[*Thesis of original iconism*] Notice, if you will, that the very word *etymology* is already a great proof of the prodigious talent of antiquity to run across or adopt the most perfect words, for it presupposes that each word is *true*, which is to say that it is not imagined arbitrarily—which is enough to lead a good mind a long way. Because of induction, what one knows in this genre demonstrates a great deal about other cases. What one does not know, on the contrary, proves nothing except the ignorance of the one who is looking. An arbitrary sound never expresses and can never express an idea. As thought necessarily exists prior to words, which are only the physical symbols of thought, words, in their turn, exist prior to the formation of every new language, which receives them ready-made and then modifies them to its own taste. Like an animal, the genius of each language hunts every source to find what suits it. (55–56)

[*Thesis of evident and multiple borrowing*] In our language, for example, *maison* is Celtic, *palais* is Latin, *basilique* is Greek, *honnir* is Teutonic, *rabot* is Slavic, *almanach* is Arab, and *sopha* is Hebrew. Where does all this take us? It matters little to me, at least at the moment: it suffices for me to prove to you that languages are only formed from other languages, which they usually kill to nourish themselves, in the manner of carnivorous animals. (56)

The passage concludes: "So let us never speak of *chance* or of arbitrary symbols" (56). Yet, on the contrary, all the arguments that have gone before seem to militate in favor of a supreme arbitrariness of decisions on the part of the languages. And we are puzzled by the question "Where does all this take us?" which insinuates the idea of a deep source of words. We have just been told where they come from: Celtic, Greek, Latin, Arabic, Turkish, Hebrew.

We have said that the four theses contemporaneously enunciated are not compatible. We will be more specific: all together, they are not compatible with a strong idea of the birth and development of languages, but they would be compatible if we admitted that languages are a historical-cultural phenomenon, that they grow without an order decided by a supernatural will, and that they gradually arrive at their stability through borrowings (deliberate or unconscious), poetic inventions, conventional whims, and "iconic" attempts. But in this case languages would achieve their organic condition just as, from an evolutionist perspective devoid of any idea of providence, only giraffes would survive in certain conditions because they have the longest necks.

This is what Maistre cannot accept. And this is how he then concludes his linguistic excursus: with a series of thoughts, each of them perhaps acceptable, though when taken all together they seem a fireworks display of non sequiturs.

> Or, if you would like me to employ another turn of phrase, the word is eternal, and every language is as old as the people who speak it. Some, without reflection, might object that there is no nation that can understand its ancient language—but what, I ask you, does it matter? Do alterations that do not touch principle exclude identity? Would someone who had seen me in my cradle recognize me today? However I think I have the right to say that I am *the same*. It is no different with language: it is the same as long as the people is the same. The poverty of languages in their beginnings is another assumption made with *the full power and authority* of philosophy. New words prove nothing, since in the measure that they are acquired others are lost, in who knows what proportions. What is sure is that people have always spoken and they have spoken precisely as they have thought and as well as they have thought, for it is equal foolishness to believe that there is a symbol for a thought that does not exist as to imagine that a thought exists without a symbol to express it. (57–58)

It is true that the *Soirées* record conversations, but surely in this philosophical dialogue Maistre did not wish to give the impression of inconclusive chatter. The lack of conclusion, the iron chain of non sequiturs, reveals a method, not an interlocutory lapse.

For that matter, Maistre himself said as much. Look again at the passage entitled *Thesis of autonomous invention,* and you will see that, in order to believe in etymologies, the "flame of analogy" (56) must not be extinguished, reasoning must not be renounced. This is Maistre's idea of Reason: to reason means to entrust oneself to any analogy that establishes an unbroken network of contacts between every thing and every other thing. This can be said, and it must be done, because it has been assumed that this network has existed since the Origin; indeed it is itself the basis of all knowledge.

It is typical of reactionary thought to establish a double equation, between Truth and Origin and between Origin and Language. The Thought of Tradition serves only to confirm a mystical belief that arrests any further reasoning.

13

On the Silence of Kant

Paragraph II.4 of linguist Tullio De Mauro's *Introduzione alla semantica* ("*Introduction to Semantics*") is entitled "Il silenzio di Kant" ("The Silence of Kant") and clearly alludes (given the context) to Kant's silence regarding the problem of language. Since then, much has been written on the subject of Kantian semiotics (we have only to think, in Italian, of the contributions of Emilio Garroni). But did De Mauro's title really exclude Kant from a history of linguistics, if not semiotics? If Kant was (putatively) silent on the issue, not so De Mauro, who immediately went on to point out two crucial passages in which Kant had posed the problem of meaning, perhaps without being fully aware of what he was doing. One was the section in the *Critique of Pure Reason*, entitled *Analytic of Principles,* where the German philosopher speaks of the schema, and the other was paragraph 59 of the *Critique of Judgment.*[1] We will have occasion to come back to both of them, but let us first consider De Mauro's comments on the passage concerning the schema:

A revised version of "Il silenzio di Kant sull'ornitorinco" (Eco 1998a). The subject is treated at greater length in Eco (1997b: ch. 2).

1. For the works of Kant we will use the following abbreviations: *Critique of Pure Reason* (CPR/A and CPR/B, according to whether the reference is to the first or second edition), *Critique of Judgment* (CJ), *Prolegomena* (P), *Logic* (L), and *Opus Postumum* (OP). [*Translator's note:* The present translation has greatly benefited from the example of Alastair McEwen's excellent English version of Eco's *Kant and the Platypus*, which, in ch. 2 "Kant, Peirce and the Platypus," covers much of the same ground.]

What can this mysterious technique be if not the ability to connect signs of generic value with single images and concepts? We may ask ourselves whether it is possible for Kant not to have been aware that this is precisely the essential function performed by language in Locke and Berkeley's system, especially when the expressions and examples he uses coincide with those adopted by Locke and Berkeley with reference to the meaning of words. (De Mauro 1965: 65)

We can only confirm our agreement and attempt to develop a few suggestions of our own.

13.1. Empirical Concepts

In Kant the semiotic problem has the right of citizenship, for him as much as it did for Aristotle, if we consider the purely verbal origins of his categorial apparatus (based, in the last analysis, on the structures of their respective languages). In the work he devoted to Kant, Heidegger (1997: 19) remarked: "Finite, intuiting creatures must be able to share in the specific intuition of beings. First of all, however, finite intuition as intuition always remains bound to the specifically intuited particulars. The intuited is only a known being if everyone can make it understandable to oneself and to others and can thereby communicate it."

To speak of what *is* signifies making communicable what we know about it. But to know it, and communicate it, implies appealing to the generic, which is already an effect of semiosis, and depends on a segmentation of the content of which Kant's system of categories, anchored to a venerable philosophical tradition, is itself a cultural product already established, culturally rooted, and linguistically fixed. When the manifold of the intuition is referred to the unity of the concept, the *percipienda* are by now already perceived just as culture has taught us to speak of them.[2]

---

2. Semiotic interests are evident in some pre-*Critique* writings such as paragraph 10 Kant's inaugural dissertation, *De mundi sensibilis atque intelligibilis forma et principiis* ("On the Forms and Principles of the Sensible and Intelligible World"), while, in his *Anthropology from a Pragmatic Point of View* (http://link .springer.com/content/pdf/bfm%3A978-94-010-2018-3%2F1.pdf), we see how, in

Yet if a semiosic foundation is implied by the general framework of Kantian doctrine, that is one thing; it is entirely another question whether Kant ever developed a theory of how we assign names to the things we perceive, whether they be trees, dogs, stones, or horses. Given the question "How do we assign names to things?," as Kant had inherited the problem of a theory of knowledge, the responses were essentially two. One came from the tradition that we may call "Scholastic" (but which begins with Plato and Aristotle): things present themselves to the world already ontologically defined in their essence, matter organized by a form. It is not important to decide whether this (universal) form is *ante rem* or *in re*: it is offered to us, it shines in the individual substance, it is grasped by the intellect, it is thought and defined (and therefore *named*) as a quiddity. Our mind has no work to do, or only insofar as the agent intellect does, which (wherever it may work) does so in a flash.

The second response was that of British empiricism. We know nothing of substances, and even if they existed, they would reveal nothing to us. For Locke, what we have are sensations, which propose simple ideas to us, either primary or secondary, but still unconnected: a rhapsody of weights, measures, sizes, and then colors, sounds, flavors, reflections changing with the hours of the day and the conditions of the subject. Here the intellect acts, in the sense that it *works:* it combines, correlates, and abstracts, in a way that is certainly spontaneous and natural to it, but only thus does it coordinate simple ideas to form those complex ideas to which we give the name of man, horse, tree, and then again, triangle, beauty, cause and effect. To know is to give names to these compositions of simple ideas. For Hume, the work of the intellect, as regards the recognition of things, is even simpler (we work directly on impressions of which ideas are faded images): the problem arises, if anything, in positing relations between ideas of things, as occurs in affirmations of causality. Here we would say that there is work, but performed without effort, by dint of habit and a natural disposition toward belief, even if we

---

the courses taught in his later years, Kant outlined (at least as a didactic tool) a summary theory of the sign—not original, but indebted to traditional doctrines, from Sextus Empiricus to Locke and perhaps Lambert, but nevertheless showing a respectful interest in the theme of semiotics. For Kant and semiotics, see Garroni (1972, 1977).

are required to consider the contiguity, priority, or constancy in the succession of our impressions.

Kant certainly does not believe that the Scholastic solution can be proposed again. Indeed, if there is truly a Copernican aspect to his revolution, it lies in the fact that he suspends all judgment on form *in re* and assigns a productive-synthetic, and not merely abstractive, function to the traditional agent intellect. As for the English empiricists, Kant seeks a transcendental foundation for the process they accepted as a reasonable way of moving in the world, whose legality was confirmed by the very fact that, when all was said and done, it worked.

At the same time, however, Kant noticeably shifts the focus of interest for a theory of knowledge. It is rash to say, as Heidegger (1997) did, that the *Critique of Pure Reason* has nothing to do with a theory of knowledge but is rather a questioning by ontology of its intrinsic possibility. Yet, it is also true, to quote Heidegger again, that it has little to do with a theory of ontic knowledge, in other words, of experience.

Nevertheless, Kant believed in the evidence of phenomena, he believed that our sensible intuitions came from somewhere, and he was concerned to articulate a rebuttal of idealism. But it appears to have been Hume who roused Kant from his dogmatic sleep, problematizing the causal relationship between things, and not Locke, though it was Locke who brought to the table the problem of an activity of the intellect in the naming of things.

A fundamental problem for the empiricists was saying why we decide, upon receiving sensible impressions from something, whether they refer to a tree or a stone. Yet it seems to have become a secondary problem for Kant, who was too preoccupied with guaranteeing our knowledge of heavenly mechanics.

In fact, the first *Critique* does not construct a gnoseology so much as an epistemology. As Rorty (1979) sums it up, Kant wasn't interested in *knowledge of* but in *knowledge that*: not, then, in the conditions of knowledge (and therefore the naming) of objects. Kant asked himself how pure mathematics and physics are possible, or how it is possible to make mathematics and physics two theoretical fields of knowledge that must determine their objects a priori. The nucleus of the first *Critique* concerns the search to provide philosophical warrant for a legislation of the intellect regarding those *propositions* that have their model in Newton's laws—and that, out of the need for exemplification, are sometimes illustrated by more comprehensible and venerable propositions such as *All bodies are heavy*. Kant is concerned to guarantee the knowledge of those laws fundamental to nature, understood as *the totality of objects of experience*. But he appears uninterested (at least until his *Critique of Judgment*) in clarifying how we know the objects of daily experience, what nowadays we call *natural kinds*, for example, camel, beech tree, beetle—with which the empiricists, on the other hand, were concerned.

Husserl, a philosopher interested in *knowledge of*, realized this, with evident disappointment (*Investigation* VI, ch. 8, para. 66):

> In Kant's thought categorial (logical) functions play a great role, but he fails to achieve our fundamental extension of the concepts of perception and intuition over the categorial realm. . . . He therefore also fails to distinguish between concepts, as the universal meanings of words, and concepts as species of *authentic* universal presentation, and between both, and concepts as universal objects, as the intentional correlates of universal presentations. Kant drops from the outset into the channel of a metaphysical epistemology in that he attempts a critical 'saving' of mathematics, natural science and metaphysics, before he has subjected knowledge as such, the whole sphere of acts in which pre-logical objectivation and logical thought are performed, to a clarifying critique and analysis of essence, and before he has traced back the primitive logical concepts and laws to their phenomenological sources.[3]

Husserl's disappointment is converted into satisfaction for someone who maintains instead that the problem of knowledge can be resolved only in terms internal to language, namely in terms of coherence among propositions. And here Rorty (1979: sect. 3.3) takes issue with the idea that knowledge must be "the Mirror of Nature," and he even asks how it was possible for Kant to assert that intuition offers us the manifold, when this manifold is known only after it has been unified in the synthesis of the intellect. In this sense, Kant would have taken a step forward with regard to the gnoseological tradition going from Aristotle to Locke, a tradition in which

---

3. Husserl (1970a: 2, 833).

philosophers attempted to model knowledge on perception. Kant would have liquidated the problem of perception, insisting that knowledge concerns propositions and not objects.

Rorty's satisfaction has evident reasons: although he proposes to challenge the very paradigm of analytical philosophy, it is this paradigm that is his point of departure, and therefore Kant seems to him to have been the first to suggest to the analytical tradition that we should not be asking what a dog is but rather what follows if the proposition *dogs are animals* is true.

What Rorty seems not to consider is that, if the opposition is between *knowing what X is like* and *knowing what type of thing X is* (as he himself quotes Sellars), we would still have to ask how one could respond to this second question without having responded to the first one.[4] And it is worthwhile asking ourselves to what extent the opposition cited reproposes the old question (treated in Chapter 1 of the present volume) between encyclopedia and dictionary knowledge.

Kant's position is still more embarrassing. He not only appears uninterested in explaining how we understand *what X is like,* but also incapable of explaining how we decide *what type of thing X is.* In other words not only is the problem of how one understands that a dog is a dog and not a cat absent from the first *Critique,* but even the problem of how we are able to say that a dog is a mammal.

More than of a lack of interest on Kant's part, we should perhaps speak of a cultural difficulty.[5] Kant, as an example of rigorous knowledge constructible a priori, had mathematical and physical sciences at his disposal, as established and laid down from Newton onward, and knew very well how to define weight, extension, force, mass, a triangle, and a circle. On the other hand, he did not have at his disposal a science of dogs, beech or linden trees, or beetles. When Kant writes his first *Critique,* hardly more than twenty years had passed since the definitive edition of Linnaeus's *Systema naturae,* the first attempt to establish a classification of natural species. The older editions of the classic Italian dictionary first published in 1612 by the Accademia della Crusca still defined a dog as a "well-known animal," the attempts

---

4. Cf. the objections by Marconi and Vattimo (1986: xix) in their introduction to the Italian translation of Rorty (1979).

5. I owe this reflection to Ugo Volli (personal communication).

at universal classification like those of Dalgarno or Wilkins (seventeenth century) used taxonomies that we would today call approximate (as we have seen, in this volume, in both Chapters 1 and 11. This is why Kant spoke of *empirical* concepts, and often repeated that we couldn't know all of the marks of these concepts. To take up our main point again, he was concerned by the fact that encyclopedic knowledge was potentially infinite. Thus the first *Critique* opens (Introduction, VII) with the declaration that concepts containing empirical elements must not appear in transcendental philosophy. The object of an a prior synthesis cannot be the nature of things, which in itself is "unlimited."

But even if Kant had been conscious of reducing knowledge to knowledge of propositions (and hence to linguistic knowledge), he still would not have been able to formulate the problem, which Peirce on the other hand will formulate, of the nonexclusively linguistic but *semiosic* nature of knowledge. To be more precise, if he fails to do so in the first *Critique*, he will move in this direction in the third. But to be able to set out along this road, he needed to bring the notion of *schema* into the picture.

According to one of Kant's examples, you can go from an unrelated succession of phenomena (there is a stone, it is struck by the sun, the stone is hot—and, as we will see, this is an example of perceptual judgment) to the proposition *the sun heats up the stone* (P, 23). Let us suppose that the sun is A, the stone B, being hot C, and we can say that A is the cause by which B is C.

The tables of categories, transcendental schemata, and principles of the pure intellect instruct us on how to proceed. The axioms of intuition tell us that all intuitions are extensive quantities and, through the schema of number, we apply the category of singularity to A and B. Through the anticipations of perception, applying the schema of Degree, the reality of the phenomenon (in the existential sense of *Realität*) supplied by our intuition is affirmed. Through the analogies of experience, A and B are seen as substances, permanent in time, to which accidents inhere. We therefore establish that accident C (heat) of B (stone) is caused by A (sun). And thus we finally decide that what is connected to the material conditions of experience is real (reality in the modal sense, *Wirklichkeit*) and applying the schema of existence in a determined time, we assert that the phenomenon is truly the case. Likewise, if the proposition was *by the law of nature, it happens that always and necessarily the light of the sun heats up (all) stones,* the category of unity should first be applied, and finally that of necessity. Accepting the transcendental foundation of synthetic judgments a priori (but this isn't the matter in contention), Kant's theoretical apparatus has explained to us why one can say with certainty that A necessarily causes the fact that B is C.

But why is A perceived as sun and B as stone? How do the concepts of the pure intellect intervene to make it possible to understand a stone as such, as distinct from the other stones in the heap of stones, from the solar light heating it up, from the rest of the universe? The concepts of the pure intellect that constitute the categories are too vast and too general to allow us to consent to recognize the stone, the sun, and the heat. Kant promises (CPR/B: 94) that once a list of pure primitive concepts has been designated, we will "easily" be able to add those derived from and subordinate to them; however, since at the present time he is concerned not with the completeness of the system but with its principles, he will reserve this supplement for another work. Furthermore, he informs us that in any case all we have to do is to consult the manuals of ontology, thus deftly subordinating the predicates of force, action, or passion to the category of causality, or the predicates of being born, perishing, or changing to the category of modality. But this is not enough, because we are still at such a level of abstraction that we are not able to say *this B is a stone.*

The table of categories does not allow us to say how we perceive a stone as such. The concepts of the pure intellect are only logical functions, not concepts of objects (P, 39). But, if we are not able to say not only that this A is the sun and this B is a stone, but also that this B is at least a body, all the universal and necessary laws that these concepts guarantee are worth nothing, because they could refer to any datum of experience. One could perhaps say that there is an A that heats up everything, whatever constraints there might be on variable B, but we still wouldn't know what this entity is that heats things up, because variable A would remain unconstrained. The concepts of the pure intellect not only need sensible intuition, but also the concepts of the objects to which they must be applied.

The empirical concepts of sun, stone, water, and air are not very different from what the empiricists called "ideas" (of genera and species). Sometimes Kant speaks of generic concepts, which are concepts, but not in the sense in which he often calls concepts "categories," which are indeed concepts, but of the pure intellect. Categories are extremely abstract concepts, such as unity, reality, causality, possibility, and necessity. We cannot determine the concept of horse through the application of pure concepts of the intellect. Horse is instead an empirical concept deriving from sensation, through comparison of the objects of experience.

Empirical concepts are not studied by general logic, which is not supposed to investigate "the *source* of concepts, or the way in which concepts have an *origin*, insofar as they are representations" (L I, 55, my emphasis). Nor are empirical concepts studied by critical philosophy, which deals not with "the genesis of experience, but about that which lies in experience"; of the two objects of study, "the former belongs to empirical psychology" (P, 21). We ought to say then that we arrive at the formulation of empirical concepts in ways that have nothing to do with the legislative activity of the intellect, which rescues the matter of the intuition from its own blindness. In which case we should know horses and houses either through their manifest quiddities (as occurred in the Aristotelian-Scholastic line of thought) or through a simple task of combination, correlation, and abstraction, as was the case for Locke.

There is a passage from the *Logic* that could confirm our interpretation:

> In order to make our presentations into concepts, one must thus be able to *compare, reflect,* and *abstract,* for these three logical operations of the understanding are the essential and general conditions of generating any concept whatever. For example, I see a fir, a willow and a linden. In firstly comparing these objects, I notice that they are different from one another in respect of trunk, branches, leaves and the like; further, however, I reflect only on what they have in common, the trunk, the branches, the leaves themselves, and abstract from their size, shape, and so forth; thus I gain a concept of tree. (L, 100)

But the passage would be Lockean if a term like "understanding" were to retain what is, after all, its weak meaning of "Human Understanding." Instead, this could not happen in the case of the mature Kant, who had already published the three *Critiques*. Whatever process the intellect goes through in order to understand that a willow and a linden are trees, it does not find this "treeness" in the sensible intuition. And in any case Kant has not told us why having a given intuition allows us to understand that it is an intuition of a linden tree.

Even "to abstract" in Kant doesn't mean *take from* or make *spring from* (which would still be the Scholastic prospective), and not even *construct by means of* (which would be the empirical position): it is purely *considering separately*, it is a negative condition, a supreme maneuver of the intellect that knows that the opposite of abstraction would be the *conceptus omnimode determinatus*, the concept of an individual, which in the Kantian system is impossible. Sensible intuition must be worked upon by the intellect and illuminated by general or generic determinations.

The cited passage perhaps responded to necessities of didactic simplification (in a text that gathers and certainly reelaborates notes taken by others in the course of his lectures, and is approved by an already mentally weakened Kant), because it is in clear contrast with what is said two pages before: "the empirical concept derives from the senses by the comparison of objects of experience and only receives the form of universality thanks to the intellect" (L 1, 3). "Only" here appears to be a euphemism.

13.2. Judgments of Perception

When Kant dealt with empirical psychology, in the decade preceding the first *Critique* (and here, too, we have to rely on lectures given somewhat under constraint and transcribed by others[6]), he already knew that knowledge provided by the senses is not sufficient, because it is necessary for the intellect to reflect on what the senses have offered it. The fact that we believe we know things on the basis of the sole testimony of the senses depends on a *vitium subreptionis:* from infancy we are so used to grasping things as if they already appeared given in our intuition that we have never made an issue out of the role performed by the intellect in this process. Not being aware that the intellect is in action does not mean that it is not working. Thus, in his *Logic* Kant alludes to many automatisms of this kind, such as when we speak, demonstrating that we know the rules of language; and yet, if asked, we wouldn't be able to say what they were, and maybe we wouldn't be even able to say they exist (L, Intro. I, 13).

Today we would say that to obtain an empirical concept we must be able to produce a judgment of perception or perceptual judgment. But we under-

---

6. See Kant (1968: 221–301).

stand perception as a complex act, an interpretation of sensible data that involves memory and culture and that results in our grasping the nature of the object. Kant, on the other hand, speaks of *perceptio* or *Wahrnehmung* only as a "representation with consciousness." Such perceptions can be distinguished into sensations, which simply modify the state of the subject, and forms of objective knowledge. As such, they can be empirical intuitions, which through sensations refer to the singular object, and are still only appearances, devoid of concept and therefore blind. Or else they are imbued with concept, through a distinctive sign common to many things, a *note* (CRP/B: 249).

What would a perceptual judgment *(Wahrnehmungsurteil)* be, then, for Kant and how is it to be distinguished from a judgment based on experience *(Erfahrungsurteil)*? Perceptual judgments are an inferior logical activity (L, I, 57) that creates the subjective world of personal consciousness; they are judgments such as, *When the sun shines on a stone it gets warm.* They can also be erroneous and are in any case contingent (P, 20, 22 and footnotes). Judgments of experience, on the other hand, establish a necessary connection (for example, they assert in fact that *The sun warms up the stone).*[7] It would seem, then, that the categorial apparatus is only involved in judgments of experience.

Why, then, are perceptual judgments "judgments"? Judgment is nonimmediate but mediated knowledge of an object: in every judgment there is a concept valid for a plurality of representations (CPR/B: 85). It cannot be denied that having the representation of the stone and its warming already represents a unification effectuated in the manifold of the sensible. To unite representations in a consciousness is already "to think" and "to judge" (P, 22), and judgments are a priori rules (P, 23), "all synthesis, without which even perception would be impossible, is subject to the categories" (CPR/B: 125). It cannot be that (as Kant says in P, 21) "the a priori principles of the

---

7. In P, para. 18 he also speaks of a kind of superordinate genus of empirical judgments *(Empirischen Urteile),* based on the perception of the senses, to which judgments of experience add the concepts originating in the pure intellect. It is not clear how these empirical judgments differ from perceptual judgments, but here perhaps (without getting into Kantian philology) we can limit the comparison to perceptual judgments and judgments of experience.

possibility of all experience . . . are nothing other than propositions *(Sätze)* that subsume all perception . . . under those pure concepts of the understanding *(Verstandesbegriffe)*". A *Warnehmungsurteil* is already woven, penetrated with *Verstandesbegriffe*. There can be no argument: recognizing a stone as such is already a perceptual judgment, a perceptual judgment is a judgment, and therefore it too depends on the legislation of the intellect. The manifold is given in the sensible intuition, but the conjunction of a manifold in general can enter into us only through an act of synthesis on the part of the intellect.[8]

In short, Kant postulates a notion of empirical concepts and perceptual judgment (a crucial problem for the empiricists), but he does not succeed in rescuing both from a quagmire, from the muddy terrain between sensible intuition and the legislatory intervention of the intellect. But for his critical theory this no-man's-land *cannot* exist.

The various stages of knowledge, for Kant, could be represented by a series of verbalizations in the following sequence:

1. This stone.
2. This is a stone (or: Here there is a stone).
3a. This stone is white.
3b. This stone is hard.
4. This stone is a mineral and a body.
5. If I throw this stone it will fall back to earth.
6. All stones (being minerals and therefore bodies) are heavy.

---

8. CPR/B: 107. Therefore, "the question is not at all resolved" (Martinetti 1946: 65) concerning the difference between judgments of perception and judgments of experience. Cassirer (1918) realized this too, although he only alludes to it in note 20 of chapter II, 2: "it must be noted that a similar exposition of empirical knowledge . . . is not so much the description of a real objective fact, as much as the construction of a borderline case. . . . For Kant, no 'singular judgment' is given that does not already claim some form of 'universality.' No 'empirical' proposition exists that does not include in itself something asserted 'a priori': since the very form of the judgment already contains this claim to 'universal objective validity.'" Why such an important statement only in a footnote? Because Cassirer knows that he is extrapolating according to good sense and systematic coherence what Kant should have said plainly, in order to exclude any other ambiguous formulation.

The first *Critique* certainly deals with propositions like (5) and (6). It is doubtful whether it really deals with propositions like (4), and it leaves vague the legitimacy of propositions from (1) through (3b). We are entitled to wonder if (1) and (2) express different locutionary acts. Except in infantile holophrastic language, it is impossible to conceive of someone uttering (1) when confronted with a stone—if anything, this syntagm could only occur in (3a) or (3b). But no one has ever said that there must be a verbalization, or even an act of self-consciousness, that corresponds to every phase of knowledge. Someone can walk along a road, without paying attention to the heaps of stones piled up on either side; but if someone asks the walker what there was by the side of the road, the walker could very well reply that there were only stones.[9] Therefore, if the fullness of perception is actually already a perceptual judgment—and if we insist on verbalizing it at all costs, we would have (1) which is not a proposition and therefore does not imply a judgment—by the time we get to verbalizing it we are immediately at (2).

Therefore, if someone who has seen a stone is questioned about what they have seen or are seeing, they would either answer (2) or there would be no guarantee that they had perceived anything. As for (3a) and (3b), the subject can have all possible sensations of whiteness or hardness, but when he predicates whiteness or hardness he has already entered into the categorial, and the quality he predicates is applied to a substance, precisely to determine it at least from a certain point of view. They may start with something expressible, such as *this white thing*, or *this hard thing*, but even so he would already have begun the work of hypothesis.

It remains to be decided what happens when our subject says that this stone is a mineral and a body. Peirce would have said that we had already entered into the moment of interpretation, whereas for Kant we have constructed a generic concept (but, as we have seen, he is very vague about this). Kant's real problem, however, concerns (1–3).

There is a difference between (3a) and (3b). For Locke, while the first expresses a simple secondary idea (color), the second expresses a simple primary idea. Primary and secondary are qualifications of objectivity, not of the

---

9. Here we will leave undecided whether he has perceived the stones, but has repressed this perception, so to speak, or whether he perceives only when he responds, interpreting memories of still unconnected visual sensations.

certainty of perception. A by no means irrelevant problem is whether someone seeing a red apple or a white stone is also able to understand that the
apple is white and juicy inside, and that the stone is hard inside and heavy.
We would say that the difference depends on whether the perceived object is
already the effect of our segmentation of the continuum or whether it is an
unknown object. If we see a stone, "we know" in the very act of recognizing
that it is a stone what it is like inside. The person seeing a fossil of coral origin for the first time (a stone in form, but red in color) did not yet know what
it was like inside.

But even in the case of a known object, what does it mean that "we know"
that the stone, white on the outside, is hard on the inside? If someone were
to ask us such an irritating question, we would reply: "I imagined so: that's
how stones usually are."

It seems curious to put an image at the base of a generic concept. What does
"imagine" mean? There is a difference between "to imagine₁," in the sense of
evoking an image (here we are in the realm of daydreams, of the delineation
of possible worlds, as when we picture to ourselves in our minds a stone we
would like to find to split open a nut—and this process does not require the
experience of the senses) and "to imagine₂," in the sense that, upon seeing a
stone as it is, precisely because of and in concomitance with the sensible
impressions that have stimulated our visual organs, *we know* (but we do not
see) that it is hard.

What interests us is "to imagine" in this second meaning. As Kant would
say, we can leave the first meaning to empirical psychology; but the second
meaning is crucial for a theory of understanding, of the perception of things,
or—in Kantian terms—in the construction of empirical concepts. And,
in any case, even the first meaning of "imagine" is possible—the desire
for a stone to use as a nutcracker—because, when we imagine₁ a stone, we
imagine₂ it to be hard.

Sellars (1978) proposes reserving the term *imagining* for "imagine₁," and
using *imaging* for "imagine₂." I propose to translate *imaging* with "to figure"
(both in the sense of constructing a figure, of delineating a structural framework, and in the sense in which we say, on seeing the stone, "I figure" it is hard
inside).

In this act of *"figuring"* some of the stone's properties, a choice is made,
we "figure" it from a certain point of view. If, when seeing or imagining the

stone, we did not intend to crack a nut but rather to chase away a bothersome animal, we would also see the stone in its dynamic possibilities, as an object that can be thrown and, due to its heaviness, has the property of falling toward the target rather than rising up in the air.

This "figuring" in order to understand and understanding through "figuring" is crucial to the Kantian system, both for the transcendental grounding of empirical concepts and for permitting perceptual judgments (implicit and nonverbalized) such as (1).

13.3. The Schema

In Kant's theory, we must explain why categories so astrally abstract can be applied to the concreteness of the sensible intuition. We see the sun and the stone and we must be able to think *that* star (in a singular judgment) or *all* stones (in a still more complex, universal judgment, because we have actually seen just one stone, or a few stones, warmed by the sun). Now, "Special laws, therefore, as they refer to phenomena that are empirically determined, cannot be completely derived from the categories. . . . Experience must be superadded" (CPR/B: 127). But, since the pure concepts of the intellect are heterogeneous with respect to sensible intuitions, "in every subsumption of an object under a concept" (CPR/B: 133; though in fact we should say "in every subsumption of the subject of the intuition under a concept, so that an object may arise"), a third, mediating element is called for that makes it possible, so to speak, for he concept to wrap itself around the intuition and renders the concept applicable to the intuition. This is how the need for a *transcendental schema* arises.

The transcendental schema is a product of the imagination. Let us set aside for now the discrepancy that exists between the first and the second editions of the *Critique of Pure Reason*, as a consequence of which in the first edition the Imagination is one of the three faculties of the soul, together with Sense (which empirically represents appearances in perception) and Apperception, while in the second edition, Imagination becomes simply a capacity of the Intellect, an effect that the intellect produces on the sensibility. For many of Kant's interpreters, like Heidegger, this transformation is immensely relevant, so much so in fact as to oblige us to return to the first edition, overlooking the changes in the second. From our point of view, however, the issue is of minor importance. Let us admit, then, that the Imagination, whatever type of faculty or activity it may be, provides a schema to the intellect, so that it can apply it to the intuition. Imagination is the capacity to represent an object even without its being present in the intuition (but in this sense it is "reproductive," in the sense we have called "imagining₁"), or it is a *synthesis speciosa,* "productive" imagination, the capacity for "*figuring.*"

This *synthesis speciosa* is what allows us to think the empirical concept of a plate, through the pure geometrical concept of a circle, "because rotundity, which is thought in the first, can be intuited in the second" (CPR/B: 134). In spite of this example, the schema is still not an image; and it therefore becomes apparent why we preferred "figure" to "imagine." For instance, the schema of number is not a quantitative image, as if we were to imagine the number 5 in the form of five dots placed one after the other as in the following example: • • • • •. It is evident that in such a way we could never imagine the number 1,000, to say nothing of even greater numbers. The schema of number is "rather the representation of a method of representing in one image a certain quantity . . . according to a certain concept" (CRP/2: 135), so that Peano's five axioms could be understood as the elements of a schema for representing numbers. Zero is a number; the successor to every number is a number; there are no numbers with the same successor; zero is not the successor of any number; every property belonging to zero, and the successor to every number sharing this property, belongs to all numbers. Thus any series x0, x1, x2, x3 . . . xn is a series of numbers, under the following assumptions: it is infinite, does not contain repetitions, has a beginning; and, in a finite number of passages, does not contain terms that are unreachable starting from the first.

In the preface to CPR/B Kant cites Thales who, from the figure of one isosceles triangle, in order to discover the properties of all isosceles triangles, does not follow step by step what he sees, but has to produce, to *construct* the isosceles triangle in general.

The schema is not an image, because the image is a product of the reproductive imagination, while the schema of sensible concepts (and also of figures in space) is a product of the pure a priori capacity to imagine, "a monogram, so to say" (CPR/B: 136). If anything it could be said that the Kantian schema, more than what we usually refer to with the term "mental image" (which evokes the idea of a photograph) is similar to Wittgenstein's *Bild,* a proposition that has the same form as the fact that it represents, in the same sense in which we speak of an *iconic* relation for an algebraic formula, or a *model* in a technical-scientific sense.

Perhaps, to better grasp the concept of a schema, we could appeal to the idea of the *flowchart,* used in computer programming. The machine is capable of "thinking" in terms of *if . . . then go to,* but a logical system like this is too abstract, since it can be used either to make a calculation or to design a geometrical figure. The flowchart clarifies the steps that the machine must perform and that we must order it to perform: given an operation, a possible alternative is produced at a certain juncture; and, depending on the answer that appears, a choice must be made; depending on the new response, we must go back to a higher node of the flowchart, or proceed further; and so on. The flowchart has something that can be intuited in spatial terms, but at the same time it is substantially based on a temporal progression (the flow), in the same sense in which Kant reminds us that the schemata are fundamentally based on time.

The idea of the flowchart seems to provide a good explanation what Kant means by the schematic rule that presides over the conceptual construction of geometrical figures. No image of a triangle that we find in experience— the face of a pyramid, for example—can ever be adequate to the concept of the triangle in general, which must be valid for every triangle, whether it be right-angled, isosceles, and scalene (CPR/B: 136). The schema is proposed as a rule for constructing in any situation a figure having the general properties triangles have (without resorting to strict mathematical terminology if we have, say, three toothpicks on the table, one of the steps that the schema would prescribe would be not to go looking for a fourth toothpick, but simply to close up the triangular figure with the three available).

Kant reminds us that we cannot think of a line without tracing it in our mind; we cannot think of a circle without describing it (in order to describe a circle, we must have a rule that tells us that all points of the line describing the circle must be equidistant from the center). We cannot represent the three dimensions of space without placing three lines perpendicular to each other. We cannot even represent time without drawing a straight line (CPR/B: 120, 21 ff.). At this point, what we had initially defined as Kant's implicit semiotics has been radically modified, because thinking is not just applying pure concepts derived from a preceding verbalization, it is also entertaining diagrammatical representations, for example, flowcharts.

In the construction of these diagrammatical representations, not only is time relevant, but memory too. In the first edition of the first *Critique* (CPR/A: 78–79), Kant says that if, while counting, we forget that the units we presently have in mind have been added gradually, we cannot know the production of plurality through successive addition, and therefore we cannot even know the number. If we were to trace a line with our thought, or if we wished to think of the time between one noon and the next, but in the process of addition we always lost the preceding representations (the first parts of the line, the preceding parts in time) we would never have a complete representation.

Look how schematism works, for example, in the anticipations of perception, a truly fundamental principle because it implies that observable reality is a segmentable continuum. How can we anticipate what we have not yet intuited with our senses? We must work as though degrees could be introduced into experience (as if one could *digitize* the continuous), though without our digitization excluding infinite other intermediate degrees. As Cassirer (1918: 215) points out, "Were we to admit that at instant a a body presents itself in state x and at instant b it presents itself in state x' without having travelled through the intermediate values between these two, then we would conclude that it is no longer the 'same' body. Rather, we would assert that the body at state x disappeared at instant a, and that at instant b another body in state x' appeared. It results that the assumption of the continuity of physical changes is not a single result from observation but a presupposition of the knowledge of nature in general," and therefore this is one of those principles presiding over the construction of the schemata.

13.4. Does the Dog Schema Exist in Kant?

So much for the schemata of the pure concepts of the intellect. But it so happens that it is in the very same chapter on schematism that Kant introduces examples that concern empirical concepts. It is not simply a question of understanding how the schema allows us to homogenize the concepts of unity, reality, inherence, subsistence, possibility, and so on, with the manifold of the intuition. There also exists the *schema of the dog*: "the concept of a dog indicates a rule, according to which my for imaginative capacity can universally trace the figure of a four-legged animal, without being restricted to either a unique particular figure supplied by experience, or to any possible image that I am able to portray *in concrete*" (CPR/B:136).

Right after this example, a few lines further on, Kant writes the famous sentence stating that this schematism of our intellect, which also concerns the simple *form* of appearances, is an art hidden in the depths of the human soul. Schematism is an art, a procedure, a task, a *construction,* but we know very little about how it works. Because it is clear that our analogy of the flowchart, which was useful in understanding how the schematic construction of the triangle takes place, doesn't work as well for the dog.

What is certain is that a computer is able to construct the image of a dog, if it is provided with the appropriate algorithms. But if someone who had never seen a dog were to study the flowchart to see how it was constructed, they would have trouble forming a mental image of it (whatever a mental image may be). We would find ourselves once more faced with a lack of homogeneity between categories and intuition, and the fact that the schema of the dog can be verbalized as a *four-legged animal* only brings us back to the extreme abstractness of every predication by genus and specific *differentia,* without helping us distinguish a dog from a horse.

Deleuze (1963:73) reminds us that "the schema does not consist in an image, but *in spatiotemporal relations that incarnate or realize some purely conceptual relations*" (my emphasis), and this seems right as far as the schemata of the concepts of the pure intellect go. But it doesn't seem sufficient when it comes to empirical concepts, since Kant was the first to tell us that to think of a plate we must resort to the image of the circle. While the schema of the circle is not an image but a rule to follow in constructing the image, nevertheless in the empirical concept of plate the constructability of its *form* should find a place somehow, and precisely in a visual sense.

We can only conclude that when Kant thinks of the schema of the dog he is thinking of something very close to what Marr and Nishishara (1978), in the field of modern cognitive sciences, called a "3D Model," which is nothing but a three-dimensional schematization (through the composition and articulation of more elementary forms) of various objects that we are able to recognize. To put it plainly, the 3D model of a human being—thinking of it only in the form of cylindrical elements—is composed of a smaller cylinder attached to a longer cylinder, from which cylindrical joints branch off, corresponding to the upper and lower limbs, including the elbows and knees.

In the perceptual judgment the 3D model is applied to the manifold of experience, and an x is distinguished as a man and not as a dog. This should demonstrate how a perceptual judgment is not necessarily resolved into a verbal statement. In point of fact, it is based on the application of a structural diagram to the manifold of sensation. The fact that further judgments are required to determine the concept of man with all his possible characteristics is something else entirely (and, as is the case for all empirical concepts, the task appears to be infinite, and never fully realized). With a 3D model, we could even mistake a man for a primate and vice versa—which is exactly what sometimes happens, although it is unlikely that a man would be confused with a snake. The fact is that we somehow start out with this type of schema, even before knowing or asserting that man has a soul, speaks, or even has an opposable thumb.

We might go so far as to say, then, that the schema of the empirical concept turns out to coincide with the concept of the object and that therefore *schema, concept,* and *meaning* are being identified with one another. Producing the schema of the dog implies having at least an initial essential concept of it. A 3D model of a man does not correspond to the concept of man in the classic categorial definition ("mortal rational animal"). But it works as far as recognizing a human being goes, and subsequently adding the characteristics that derive from this first identification. Which explains why Kant (L II, 103) pointed out that a synthesis of empirical concepts can never be complete, because over the course of experience it will always be possible to identify further notes of the object *dog* or *man.* Except that, with an overstatement, Kant declared that empirical concepts therefore "cannot even be defined." We would say instead that they cannot be defined once and for all, like mathematical concepts, but that they do allow a first nucleus to be formed, around which successive categorial definitions will gel (or arrange themselves harmoniously).

Can we say that this first conceptual nucleus is also the meaning that corresponds to the term with which we express it? Kant doesn't often use the word *meaning (Bedeutung),* but he does use it precisely when he is speaking of the schema.[10] Concepts are completely impossible, nor can they have

---

10. See, on this issue, Garroni (1968: 123; 1986, III, 2, 2) and also De Mauro (1965: 2, 4).

any meaning, unless an object is given either to the concepts themselves or at least to the elements of which they consist (CPR/B: 135). Kant is suggesting in a less explicit way that coincidence of *linguistic meaning* and *perceptual meaning*, which will later be energetically asserted by Husserl: it is in a "unity of act" that the red object becomes recognized as red and named as *red*. "To 'call something red'—in the fully actual sense of 'calling' which presupposes an underlying intuition of the so called—and to 'recognize something as red,' are in reality synonymous expressions" (Husserl 1970a: II, 691).

But, that being the case, not only the notion of empirical concept, but also that of the meaning of terms referring back to perceivable objects (for example, the names of natural genera) opens up a new problem. This first nucleus of meaning, the one identified with the conceptual schema, cannot be reduced to mere categorial information: the dog is not understood and identified (and recognized) because it is a mammiferous animal, but because it has a certain *physical form*. The form of circularity must of necessity correspond to the concept of plate, and Kant has told us that the fact that the dog has paws (four of them altogether) is part of the schema of the dog. A man (in the sense of a member of the human race) is nonetheless something that moves fin accordance with the articulations provided for by the 3D model.

Now, while a reflection on the pure intuition of space was sufficient in the case of the schemata of geometrical figures, and therefore the schema could be drawn from the very constitution of our intellect, this is certainly not the case for the schema (and therefore the concept) of dog. Otherwise we would have a repertoire, if not of innate ideas, of innate schemata, including the schema of doghood, horsehood, and so on, until the whole furniture of the universe had been exhausted.

If that were the case, we would also have innate schemata of things we didn't yet know, and Kant would certainly not subscribe to this type of Platonism—and it is debatable whether Plato himself subscribed to it.

The empiricists would have said that the schema is drawn from experience, and the schema of the dog would be nothing but the Lockean *idea* of the dog. But this is unacceptable to Kant, seeing that we have experience precisely by applying the schemata. We cannot abstract the schema of the dog from the data of intuition, because that data becomes *thinkable* precisely as a result of applying the schema. And therefore we are in a vicious circle of reasoning from which, it would seem, the first *Critique* does nothing to help us escape.

There is one other solution left: that by reflecting on the data from the sensible intuition, by comparing it and evaluating it, by activating an arcane and inborn art hidden in the depths of the human soul (and therefore existing within our own transcendental apparatus), we do not abstract but rather we *construct* the schemata. The schema of the dog comes to us from our education, and we don't even realize that we are applying it since, by a *vitium subreptionis*, we are led to believe that we are seeing a dog because we are receiving sensations.

That Kantian schematism implies—in the sense that it cannot help leading us to think of it—a kind of constructivism is not an original idea, especially given the sort of return to Kant discernible in many contemporary cognitive sciences. But to what degree the schema can and must be a construction ought not to emerge from the fact that preconstructed schemata (such as that of the dog) are applied; the real problem is *What happens when we have to construct the schema of an object we do not yet know?*

13.5. How to Construct the Schema of an Unknown Object

In Eco 1997, we discussed at length the history of the platypus, which was discovered in Australia at the end of the eighteenth century. When a stuffed platypus was brought to England, the naturalists believed that it was a taxidermist's joke. Not surprisingly, the debate became even more heated when this animal with a bill and webbed feet, but at the same time covered in fur and with a beaver's tail, was found to nurse its young and lay eggs. The platypus appears in the Western world when Kant had already written his works—and indeed had already fallen into a period of mental obnubilation—and when it was finally decided that the platypus is a mammal that lays eggs, Kant had already been dead for some eighty years. To ask ourselves how Kant would have reacted when confronted with a platypus is no more than a mental experiment, but the experiment is useful precisely because it provides an occasion for reflection on how the theory of schematism might explain the experience of an unknown object.

Kant would have had to figure out the platypus schema, starting from sense impressions, but these sensible impressions would not have fit into any previous schema (how could Kant have *conceived* of a quadruped bird, or a quadruped with a beak?). Kant, the confuter of idealism, would have been well aware that if the platypus was offered to him by sensible intuition, it *existed,* and therefore must be thinkable. And, wherever the form he would give it might come from, it had to be possible to construct it. So what problem would he have found himself faced with?

By introducing schematism into the first version of his system, as Peirce suggested, Kant finds himself holding an explosive concept that compels him to go further: in the direction of the *Critique of Judgment.* Judgment is the faculty of thinking of the particular as contained in the general, and if the general (the rule, the law) is already given, the judgment is *determinant.* But if *only the particular is given and the general must be sought,* the judgment is then *reflecting* or *reflective.* Once one arrives at reflective judgment from the schema, the very nature of determinant or determining judgments becomes problematic. Because the capacity of determinant judgment (as we learn in the chapter in the *Critique of Judgment* on the dialectic of the capacity of teleological judgment) "does not have in itself principles that found *concepts of objects.*" Determinant judgment limits itself to subsuming objects under given laws or concepts such as principles. "Thus the capacity of transcendental judgment, which contained the conditions for subsumption under categories, was not in itself nomothetic, but simply indicated the conditions of the sensible intuition under which a given concept may be given reality." Therefore, for any concept of an object to be well-founded, it must be fixed by the reflective judgment, which "is supposed to subsume under a law that is yet to be given" (CJ, para. 69, 257).

His fundamental realistic assumption prevents Kant from thinking that natural objects somehow do *not* exist independently from us. They are there in front of us, they function in a certain manner, and they develop by themselves. One tree produces another tree—of the same species—and at the same time it grows and therefore also produces itself as an individual. The bud of one tree leaf grafted onto the branch of another tree produces one more plant of the same species. The tree lives as a whole on which the parts converge, since the leaves are produced by the tree, but defoliation would affect the growth of the trunk. The tree therefore lives and grows by following its own internal organic law (CJ, para. 64).

But one cannot learn from the tree what this law is, since phenomena do not tell us anything about the noumenal. Nor do the a priori forms of the pure intellect have anything to tell us about it, because natural beings respond to multiple and particular laws. And yet, they should be considered necessary according to the principle of the unity of the manifold, which in any case is beyond our ken.

These natural objects (over and above the extremely general laws that render the phenomena of physics thinkable) are dogs, stones, horses—and platypuses. We must be able to say how these objects are organized into genera and species, but (and this is important), genera and species do not depend on a classificatory judgment of ours: "There is in nature a subordination of genera and species that we can grasp; that the latter in turn converge in accordance with a common principle, so that a transition from one to the other, thereby to a higher genus is possible" (CJ, Intro., v).

And so we try to construct the concept of the tree (we assume it) *as if* trees were the way we can think of them. Something is thought of as possible according to the concept (we try to harmonize the form with the possibility of the thing itself, even if we do not have any concept of it) and we think of it as an organism that obeys certain ends.

To interpret something *as if* it was in a certain way means to advance an hypothesis, because the reflective judgment must subsume under a law that is not yet given "and which is in fact it only a principle for reflection on objects for which we are objectively entirely lacking a law or a concept of the object that would be adequate for the cases that come before us" (CJ, para. 69). Moreover, it must be a very risky type of hypothesis, because we must infer an as yet unknown Rule from the particular (from a Result); and to come up with the Rule we must hypothesize that that Result is a Case of the Rule to be constructed. Kant certainly never put it that way, though the Kantian Peirce did. It is clear however that reflective judgment is nothing more or less than an *abduction*.

In this abductive process, as we said, genera and species are not merely arbitrary classifications—and if they were, they could only become established once the abduction had taken place, at an advanced stage of conceptual elaboration. In the light of the third *Critique* it must be admitted that the reflective judgment, insofar as it is teleological, already assigns a character of "animality" (or of "living being") in the construction of schemata. Let us reflect for a moment on what would have happened if Kant had ever seen a platypus. He would have had the intuition of a multiplicity of traits, compelling him to construct the schema of an autonomous being, not moved by external forces, which exhibited coordination in its own movements, an organic and functional relationship between bill (which allows it to take nourishment), paws (that allow it to swim), head, trunk, and tail. The animality of the object would have seemed to him a fundamental element of the schema of perception, not as a successive abstract attribution (which would have merely served to ratify conceptually what the schema already contained).[11]

It appears that one must therefore speak of a form of *pre-categorial perception* that precedes conceptual categorization, whereby the animality that one perceives on seeing a dog or a cat has nothing to do with the genus ANIMAL on which semantics has insisted at least since the time of the Porphyrian tree. If Kant had been able to observe the platypus (morphology, customs, and behavior), as has been done in the two centuries since Kant, he would have probably have come to the same conclusion as Gould (1991: 277): that this animal is not just a clumsy experiment of nature but a masterpiece of design, a perfect example of environmental adaptation. Indeed, its fur protects it from cold water, it can regulate its own body temperature, its morphology makes it adapted for diving into water and finding food with its eyes and ears closed, its anterior limbs allow it to swim, its posterior limbs and tail act as a rudder, its ankle spurs enable it to compete with other males in mating season. But Gould would probably not have been able to give this "teleological" reading of the platypus if Kant hadn't suggested to us that "an

---

11. On the other hand, let us put ourselves in the shoes of a hypothetical Adam who sees a cat for the first time, without ever having seen any other animals. For this Adam, a cat will be schematized as "something that moves," and for the moment this quality will make the cat similar to water and to clouds. But one imagines that it will not take Adam long to place the cat together with dogs and hens, among moving bodies that react unforeseeably to his solicitation and quite foreseeably to his call. Thus he will distinguish the cat from water and clouds, which appear to move, but are indifferent to his presence.

organized product of nature is that in which everything is an end and reciprocally a means as well" (CJ, para. 66), as well as suggesting that the products of nature appear (unlike machines, which are moved by mere driving
force, a *bewegende Kraft*) as organisms moved from within by a *bildende
Kraft*, a capacity, a formative force.

And yet Gould, in attempting to define this *bildende Kraft*, couldn't come
up with anything better than the outdated metaphor of design, which is a
way of forming nonnatural beings. I don't think Kant could have said he was
wrong, even if in so doing he would have gotten himself into a happy contradiction. The fact is that the Capacity of Judgment, once it comes on the
scene as reflective and teleological, overwhelms and dominates the entire
universe of the knowable, and invests every thinkable object, even a chair. It
is true that a chair, as an object of art, could be judged only as beautiful, as a
pure example of finality without a goal and universality without a concept, a
source of disinterested pleasure, the result of the free play of the imagination
and the intellect. But at this point you do not need much to add a rule and an
purpose where we have already tried to abstract them, and the chair will be
seen, as was the intention of whomever conceived it, as a functional object
oriented toward its own goal, organically structured so that each of its parts
supports the whole.

It is Kant who moves quite nonchalantly on from teleological judgments
concerning natural entities to teleological judgments concerning products
of artifice:

> If someone were to perceive a geometrical figure, for instance a regular
> hexagon, drawn in the sand in an apparently uninhabited land, his re-
> flection, working with a concept of it, would become aware of the unity
> of the principle of its generation by means of reason, even if only ob-
> scurely, and thus, in accordance with this, would not be able to judge as
> a ground of the possibility of such a shape the sand, the nearby sea, the
> wind, the footprints of any known animals, or any other nonrational
> cause, because the contingency of coinciding with such a concept,
> which is possible only in reason, would seem to him so infinitely great
> that it would be just as good as if there were no natural law of nature,
> consequently no cause in nature acting merely mechanically, and as if
> the concept of such an object could be regarded as a concept that can be

given only by reason and only by reason compared with the object, thus as if only reason can contain the causality for such an effect, consequently that this object must be thoroughly regarded as an end, but not a natural end, i.e., as a product of **art** *(vestigium hominis video).* (CJ, para. 64, emphasis in text)

Kant has just told us how one develops an abduction worthy of Robinson Crusoe. And if someone were to observe that in this case art has nonetheless imitated a regular figure, not invented by art, but produced by pure mathematical intuition, we have only to cite an example that occurs shortly before the one just quoted. In that case, as an illustration of empirical finality (as opposed to the pure finality of the circle, which seems to have been invented for the purpose of highlighting all of the demonstrations that can be deduced from it), Kant pictures a beautiful garden, in the French style with its well-ordered flowerbeds and avenues, where art prevails over nature; and he speaks of empirical, certainly, and of real finality, for we are well aware that the garden has been planned with an aim and a function in mind. We may say that seeing the garden or the chair as a organism oriented toward an end calls for a less risky hypothesis, because I already know that artificial objects respond to the intentions of the artificer, while judgment postulates purpose (and indirectly a creative formativity, a sort of *natura naturans*) as the only way to understand it. But in any case even the artificial object cannot help being invested with reflective judgment.

This teleological version of the schema is not developed with absolute clarity even in the third *Critique.* See, for instance, the famous paragraph 59 which has always seduced anyone who attempted to find in Kant the elements of a philosophy of language. In the first place, a distinction is made between *schemata*, specific to the pure concepts of the intellect, and *examples (Beispiele)*, valid for empirical concepts. The idea in itself is not without its appeal: in the schema of the dog or the tree *prototypical* ideas come into play, as if all dogs could be represented by the *ostension* of a dog (or by the image of a single dog). It remains to be seen how this image, which is supposed to mediate between the manifold of the intuition and the concept, can avoid being interwoven with concepts—being the image of a dog *in general* and not of *that* dog. And, once again, what "example" of a dog could mediate between intuition and concept, since it certainly appears that for empirical concepts the schema ends up coinciding with the possibility of "figuring" a generic concept?

Immediately afterward, Kant says that making something perceptible to the senses ("hypotyposis") may be *schematic* when a concept grasped by the intellect is given the corresponding intuition is given (and this is valid for the schema of the circle, indispensable for understanding the concept of "plate"). On the other hand, Kant continues, it is *symbolic* when, to a concept that only Reason can think of, to which there exists no corresponding intuition, one is provided by analogy, as would be the case, for example, if I chose to represent the monarchical state as a human body. Here certainly Kant is speaking not only of symbols in the logical-formal sense (which for him are mere "characterisms") but also of phenomena such as metaphor or allegory. But a gap still remains between schemata and symbols (we have only to think of the platypus): there is intuition, but not yet the concept, and I cannot recognize it or define it through a metaphor.

13.6. *Opus Postumum*

Kant bridges this gap in his *Opus Postumum*, in which he again tries even harder to determine the various particular laws of physics that cannot be deduced from the categories alone. In order to ground physics, he must postulate the ether as matter that, distributed throughout cosmic space, is found in and penetrates all bodies.

External perceptions, as material for a possible experience, which lack only the form of their connection, are the effect of the moving (or driving) forces of matter. Now, to mediate the application of these motor forces to the relations that occur in experience calls for identifying empirical laws. These latter are not given a priori, they need concepts *constructed* by us *(selbstgemachte)*. These are not concepts given by reason or experience but *factitious* concepts. They are *problematic* (and we recall that a problematic judgment depends on the Postulate of Empirical Thought in General, so that what is in harmony with the formal conditions of experience is possible).

Concepts of this kind must be thought as the foundation of natural inquiry. We must therefore postulate (in the case of the factitious concept of ether) an absolute whole that subsists in matter. Kant repeats on various occasions that this concept is not a hypothesis but a postulate of reason, but his suspicion of the term *hypothesis* has Newtonian roots. In fact, a concept (built on nothing, so to speak) that renders possible the totality of experience is an abduction, which, in order to explain certain Results, appeals to a Rule constructed *ex novo*.[12]

As Mathieu (1984) observes, apropos of Kant's last writings, "The intellect makes experience by designing the structure according to which the driving forces of the object can act." The reflective judgment, more than observing (and subsequently producing schemata), produces schemata so as to observe and test. And "such doctrine goes beyond that of the first *Critique* for the freedom that it assigns to the intellectual designing of the object" (Mathieu 1984: 231, n. 1). It is Mathieu (1984: 21) who again observes that "even keeping unchanged the necessary structure of the categories, one can equally take a further spontaneous activity into consideration, which the intellect performs *starting with* categories, but without remaining stalled at them . . . constructing not simply what *derives* from them, but all that we are able to think, and without falling into contradiction." Perhaps to arrive at such boldness Kant had needed to pass through the aesthetic reflection of the third *Critique*; only then "is a new schematism born—the free schematism *of the imagination*, without concepts—as the primary capacity to organize perceptions" (cf. Garroni 1986: 226).

With this late schematism the intellect does not construct the simple definition of a possible object, but *makes* the object, *constructs* it, and in this activity (problematic in itself) it proceeds by trial and error.

At this point the notion of trial and error becomes crucial. If the schema of empirical concepts is a construct that attempts to make the objects of nature thinkable, and if a complete synthesis of empirical concepts can never be given, because new notes of the concept can always be discovered through experience (LI, 103), then the schemata themselves can only be revisable, fallible, destined to evolve over time. If the pure concepts of the

---

12. In "Horns, Hooves, Shoes" (in Eco 1990b) I defined the phenomenon we are dealing with as *creative abduction*, Cf. also Bonfantini and Proni (1983). Even though the postulate of ether was subsequently shown to be erroneous, it worked pretty well for a considerable time. Abductions (one thinks of the theory of epicycles and deferents) are shown to be helpful when they hold up for a long time, until a more suitable, economical, and potent abduction comes onto the scene.

intellect were to constitute a sort of intemporal repertoire, empirical concepts can only become "historic," or cultural, however you choose to say it.[13]

Kant did not, in fact, say this, but it seems hard not to say it if one takes the doctrine of schematism to its logical conclusions. Peirce, for one, saw it this way, firmly putting the entire cognitive process down to hypothetical inference. Sensations appear as interpretations of stimuli; perceptions as interpretations of sensations; judgments of perception as the interpretation of perceptions; particular and general propositions as interpretations of perceptual judgments; and scientific theories as interpretations of a series of propositions (cf. Bonfantini and Grazia 1976: 13).

Given the infinite segmentability of experience, both perceptual schemata and propositions concerning the laws of nature themselves carve out entities or relations that—to a greater or lesser degree—always remain hypothetical and subject to the possibility of fallibilism.

Naturally at this point transcendentalism too will undergo its Copernican revolution. The guarantee that our hypotheses are "right" (or at least acceptable as such until proved otherwise) will no longer be sought in the a priori of the pure intellect (though its most abstract logical forms will be retained) but rather in the consensus, historic, progressive, and temporal of the Community.[14] In the face of the risk of fallibilism, the transcendental too becomes historicized, an accumulation of received interpretations, accepted after a process of discussion, selection, and repudiation.[15] An unsta-

---

13. Or, as Paci (1957: 185) has it, they are founded not on necessity but on *possibility:* "a synthesis is impossible without time and therefore without the schema, without an image which is always something more than the simple projection, something new, or as we would say, something projecting, open to the future, open to the possible."

14. Cf. Apel (1995). The transcendental subject of knowledge becomes the community that almost "evolutionistically" approaches what could become knowable "in the long run," through processes of trial and error. See also Apel (1975). This induces us to reread the anti-Cartesian polemic and the refusal to admit unknowable data, which could be defined as a cautious and preemptive distancing from the Kantian idea of the thing in itself. The Dynamic Object starts as something in itself but in the process of interpretation becomes ever more—even if only potentially—appropriate.

15. The rehabilitation of Kant by Popper (1969, I, I, v) should be read in this sense. "When Kant said, 'Our intellect does not draw its laws from nature but

ble foundation, if you will, based on the pseudo-transcendental of the Community (an optative idea more than a sociological category); and yet it is the Consensus of the Community that today makes us incline toward the Keplerian abduction rather than that of Tycho Brahe. Naturally the Community has come up with what we call called proofs, but it is not the authority of the proofs in themselves that convinces us, or keeps us from falsifying them. Rather, it is the difficulty of calling into question one proof without overturning the entire system and the paradigm on which it is based.

This detranscendentalization of knowledge comes up again, thanks to the explicit influence of Peirce, in Dewey's notion of the "warranted assertion" (or, as we prefer to call it today, "warranted assertibility") and remains present in the various holistic conceptions of knowledge.

—Translated by Jacob D. Blakesley and Anthony Oldcorn

---

imposes its laws upon nature,' he was right. But in thinking that these laws are necessarily true, or that we necessarily succeed in imposing them upon nature, he was wrong. Nature very often resists quite successfully, forcing us to discard our laws as refuted; but if we live we may try again." Therefore Popper reformulates Kant's dictum: "The intellect does not draw its laws from nature but tries (with a variable possibility of success) to impose on it the laws it freely invents" (I, 8).

14

Natural Semiosis and the Word in Alessandro Manzoni's *The Betrothed* (*I promessi sposi*)

Writing the history of semiotic ideas does not only mean examining the philosophical or linguistic theories that deal explicitly with the sign or with communication. Often ideas that are not altogether irrelevant concerning these phenomena are expressed, however indirectly, in the declarations writers and artists have made about their poetics, or, alternatively, they can be extrapolated from the way in which processes of signification and communication are staged at the level of the narrative.

From this point of view it is legitimate, though by no means common practice, to ask oneself whether there exists a Manzonian semiotics, deducible not so much from Manzoni's theoretical and critical writings, in which he discusses the genre of the historical novel and other problems we would define today as problems of literary theory, as from his narrative performance itself.

14.1. Action and Word

"By their actions, my dear fellow: all men are known by their actions" (p. 139), says the village innkeeper in chapter 7 of *I promessi sposi*, no less adept than the host of the Full Moon tavern in distinguishing a law-abiding citizen from an informer by the cut of his clothes, his tone of voice, and his overall bearing. Not so Renzo; a page earlier, when he entered the inn and saw one bravo, who did not stand aside to let him in, standing there on

This essay originally appeared in Manetti (1989) and was republished in Eco (1998c).

sentry duty, armed with a cudgel, with a red velvet cap over his quiff, his pigtails pinned with a comb at the back of his neck, while his comrades went on playing the game of *morra,* all of them exchanging eloquent nods among themselves. In this bildungsroman, Renzo is the last one to grow up, to become familiar, that is, with the signs and the way other people interpret them (only at the very end of the story will he have learned not to hold door knockers in his hand for too long and not to tie bells on his ankles). At this stage of the game, Renzo "looked at his two guests [Tonio and Gervaso], uncertain, as if hoping to find an explanation of those signals in their faces" (p. 137), clues he still has trouble deciphering. But he has not lived long enough yet, and, as we will learn later, only "a man's life is the touchstone of his words" (pp. 403–404).

Suspicious of the notion that the course of human history unfolds in a rational manner, wary of every good intention which does not allow for the heterogenesis of ends, fearful of the evil that lurks in the things of this world, diffident toward the powerful and the arts by which they take advantage of the meek, Alessandro Manzoni appears to have synthesized his Enlightenment common sense and his Jansenistic rigor into a semiotic formula that can be extrapolated from many pages of his novel: (i) there is a natural semiosis, employed almost instinctively by those among the meek who have accumulated experience, according to which the various aspects of reality, when interpreted with prudence and a knowledge of the ways of the world, present themselves as symptoms, clues, *signa* or *semeia* in the classic sense of the term; and (ii) there is the artificial semiosis of verbal language which, either turns out be inadequate to give an account of reality or is used explicitly and maliciously to mask it, almost always for the purposes of exercising power. Verbal language, then, is deceptive by its very nature, whereas natural semiosis leads to errors and blunders only when it is polluted by language, which restates it and interprets it, or when its interpretation is clouded by the passions.

Behind this semiotics there lies a metaphysics: reality exists, and can be investigated, so long as people follow "a method which has been recommended to them for long enough—the method of observing, listening, comparing and thinking before they begin to talk" (p. 583). This rule is not as simplistic as it might appear at first sight. It repeats in a popular form a precept of Galileo's, which the positive and prudent characters in the novel, however, when confronted with everyday reality, put into practice in the light of common sense and not according to the dictates of the Accademia del Cimento. But when it comes to applying it to historical reconstruction, Manzoni shows us nonetheless how it works. Given that words are misleading, and what we know about things that happened in the past we know only through verbal accounts, Manzoni instinctively appeals to a precept already formulated by Saint Augustine in his *De Doctrina Christiana*. When confronted with the various versions of the sacred books, all of them translations of translations, while the mystery of the original Hebrew text, by now hopelessly adulterated, remains unknown, all we can do is compare the versions among themselves, set them one against the other, and obtain from the one clarification of what is lacking in the other.

This is what Manzoni does, in dealing with the manuscript of the anonymous author, which has unreliability, so to speak, written all over it, given the verbal excesses with which, with typical baroque emphasis, it is embellished. Since he feels that behind this discourse (which is verbal) there lies "such a good story" (and a story is a *fabula*, a sequence of events or, as Aristotle would have said, the imitation of an action, something nonverbal), Manzoni decides "to search among the memoirs of the period, to satisfy ourselves whether that was really the way things happened in those days" (p. 21). And his investigation, in the form of a collation of texts, dissipates all doubt: though camouflaged by so much literary artifice, something must indeed have occurred.

The same procedure is followed with regard to the plague. Consider the opening of chapter 31: "The plague . . . really had arrived,"[1] where that word "really," a verificative intrusion of the narrative voice, liquidates once and for all any doubts to which the conflicting verbal texts might give rise. The thing in itself, the Dynamical Object, is there somewhere or other, or was there; our problem is to interpret the signs and make it reappear. But even here, as long as what we are dealing with are verbal accounts, "Every one of them leaves out essential facts which others record . . . every one of them

---

1. [*Translator's note:* This is a literal translation of Manzoni's Italian. Bruce Penman's English translation (Manzoni 1972), which we have otherwise followed and to which subsequent page numbers in the text refer, does not follow Manzoni's precise wording at this point and omits the adverb "really" *(davvero).*]

contains material errors, which can be recognized and corrected with the help of one of the others, or of the few official documents that have come down to us in published or unpublished form. Often one writer gives us the cause of effects which we have already seen floating unconnectedly in the pages of another" (p. 564). And therefore, "examining and collating" the various sources we may hope, not only to identify the most salient facts, but also "to arrange them in the order in which they happened" (p. 565).

We are dealing here, not with Manzoni's idea of historical truth or with his theory of knowledge, which is what it is. What we want to underscore is that, unless philological scrupulousness is exercised to the full, verbal accounts are deceptive by their very nature. The author Manzoni may well reconstruct the order of events through language, but the characters in the novel are either poor devils or persecutors of poor devils (only the positive characters are gifted with a kind of paraphilological, so to speak, intuition), and as a rule, in the novel, language is a bearer of wind, if not of lies.

Let us take a look at the passage which Manzoni (not Quine) devotes in chapter 27 to the impossibility, not so much of translation between one language and another, but of that daily process of interpretation by which an illiterate person tells the scrivener what he wants to say, the scrivener writes down what he understands to have happened or what he thinks should have happened, the reader recruited by the addressee interprets it for himself, and the illiterate addressee, seeking criteria for interpretation in the facts that he knows, distorts the message in his turn. This is an extremely effective representation of how, through successive interpretations, the message becomes completely garbled and is made to express, not only what the original sender did not mean to say, but also what the same message, as the linear manifestation of a text, set against a code, ought not to say, if a community of interpreters inspired by common sense and respect for the rules were to get together and agree on a publicly acceptable reading. Which is not what happens; and Manzoni's description comes across as a portrait of a process of interpretive drift. With, in the end, "the two sides . . . at the same stage of mutual understanding as two medieval scholars might once have been after four hours of argument about the entelechy" (p. 497).

The peasant who cannot write, and needs something written, turns to someone who has learned to use a pen. He chooses him, as far as he can, among those of his own class; for he is either shy of approaching others, or does not trust them sufficiently. He tells the man what has gone before, with such clarity and logical order as he can muster, and then tells him, in the same style, what he wants to say. The literate friend understands part of what he says, and misunderstands another part; he advises him, suggests a couple of changes, and then says 'Leave it to me!' He takes up his pen, and puts the first man's thoughts in literary form, as best he can; corrects them or improves on them, adds emphasis or takes it away, even leaves bits out, as seems best to him. For there is no getting away from it—a man who knows more than his neighbors does not care to be a passive tool in their hands, and once he has become involved in their affairs, wants to give them a little guidance. Moreover, the literate friend may not always succeed in saying what he means. Sometimes he says something quite different. (We professional writers of books have been known to do the same.) When such a letter reaches the other correspondent, who is equally ignorant of his ABC, he takes it to another learned man of the same caliber, who reads it and explains it to him. Then doubts arise over what the letter really means. The interested party, with his knowledge of what has gone before, maintains that certain words must mean one thing; but the man who is doing the reading, from his knowledge of the written language, claims that they must mean something else. In the end the man who cannot write must put himself in the hands of the of the man who can, and must charge him with the task of replying. The answer will be composed in the same fashion as the first letter, and will be submitted to the same sort of interpretation. (p. 497)

And if that wasn't enough to make us distrustful of language, we have only to see what Don Ferrante, with his extensive library, does with it when it comes to discussing the plague (chapter 37). After two chapters of nonverbal evidence, thanks to which the reader is by now fully informed, the Aristotelian librarian, with a few well-chosen syllogisms (the contagion cannot be a substance) and an equal number of paralogisms (the contagion cannot be an accident), succeeds in covering up reality to such a point that he can recognize it only when he will no longer be conscious of it. And, as just punishment for the arrogance of the word, his famous library "may well be still lying around on the secondhand bookstalls" (p. 700).

That discourses lie, or can never be sufficiently explicit, seems clear enough. If proof were required, we need only recall the fact that many readers, of Manzoni's novel, with understandable indolence, skip all the examples of those inconclusive, ambiguous, and confused discourses, living parasitically off one other, that are the seventeenth-century edicts against the bravoes.

What is it then that, read correctly, does not lie? I would say, primarily, what is not oral, but visual, and, if it is oral, what belongs to the sphere of the paralinguistic, the suprasegmental, or the tonemic—the inflections, volume, and rhythms of the voice.

14.2. Popular Semiosis

We referred at the beginning to a natural semiosis as opposed to the semiosis of the word. It would be inexact to say that in Manzoni the classical distinction between motivated, unintentional, natural semiosis and conventional and arbitrary semiosis is clearly discernible. The best I can do, to define the first term of the opposition, is to call it "popular" semiosis. On the one hand we have verbal language, artificial (deceptive), at the beck and call of the powerful, on the other we have various systems of signs, which of course include the so-called natural signs, medical and atmospheric symptoms, physiognomic traits, but also those "languages" that are not natural, and are instead the effect of rules and habits, like dress, bodily posture, pictorial representations, the productions of folklore, liturgy—that somehow appeal to an ancestral and instinctive competence that belongs, not only to the learned, but also to the meek. Because of the *natural* nature of this competence, of the instinctive popularity of the encyclopedia to which it refers, we could call this type of semiosis, though it may be founded on rules and custom, the natural effect of a long-term deposit in the collective memory, not subject to the same rapid and reserved variations as the exercise of the verbal arts.

It is not that popular semiosis is more "true" that the verbal kind: we will see how and to what extent it too can give rise to misunderstanding and mendacity. But to the meek it seems more comprehensible than verbal language, and they therefore consider it more reliable. So much so that when they make a mistake or are deceived about these forms of signification, they appear more vulnerable, because they do not employ the same systematic diffidence toward them that they employ toward verbal language. Take what happens (and we will have more to say about this later) during Renzo's visit to Azzeccagarbugli (Dr. Quibbler) or in the entire case of the plague and the anointers *(untori)*.

The meek are suspicious of verbal language because it imposes a logical syntax abolished by natural semiosis, since the latter does not proceed by linear sequences but by "pictures," or lightning "iconologemes." Whereas the threads of the linguistic sequences may multiply ad infinitum, while the simple-minded become lost in this dark wood, natural semiosis on the other hand permits, or seems to permit, an easier access to the truth of things, of which it is a spontaneous vehicle: an authentic, instinctive gesture can reveal the intentional falsity of a previous gesture. The notary who arrests Renzo speaks to him encouragingly, Renzo distrusts the words but he could be taken in by the tone; the notary, however, has him handcuffed, and, seeing this sign, Renzo realizes without the shadow of a doubt that he is in trouble.

The object of the narration is this popular semiosis in all its forms, because from it and through it the reader, no less than the characters, learns what is really happening, in other words the *story,* beneath the veil of the *discourse.*

We constantly find, throughout the novel, this opposition between "natural" sign and verbal sign, between visual sign and linguistic sign. Manzoni is always so embarrassed by the verbal sign, so anxious to demonstrate his diffidence, that in all the instances of enunciation with which the novel is studded, he makes excuses for the way he is telling the story, whereas, when he assumes a veridictive tone, it is to point out the credit that must be given to a proof, a piece of evidence, a trace, a symptom, a clue, a finding.

His characters act in the same way: either they speak with the deliberate intention of using language to lie, confuse, or conceal the proper relationships between things, or they apologize and complain that they are incapable of saying what they know. Though Renzo wants his children to learn how to read and write, he cannot help calling these verbal and grammatological artifices *birberie,* "a scoundrelly business" (p. 719). Renzo is suspicious of the language par excellence, Latin, and the only time that he quotes it he makes up a Babelic version (*siés baraòs trapolorum*, p. 279). Only once, in the final chapter, when by that time he has made his peace with Don Abbondio, does he say that he accepts the Latin of the wedding ceremony and the mass, but that is because it is "an honest, holy sort of Latin . . . and besides, you clerical gentlemen have to read what's written in the book" (p. 709). The *good* Latin of the liturgy is not a spoken language; it is chant, formula, psalmody, plainsong, gesture, but it does not say anything and therefore cannot be false. It is like an article of clothing, a wave of the hand, a facial expression: all signs (and "signs" [*segni*] is what Manzoni calls them over and over again) that are part of a natural semiosis.

At this point we would be advised to go through the entire novel to see if our hypothesis holds, whether it is true that at every stage there is this clear opposition between natural semiosis and language. It will be sufficient for now, however, to verify it in a few essential episodes.

14.3. The Meeting with the Bravoes

Don Abbondio has lived, and he is able to interpret many signs. He comes on the scene exhibiting the sign par excellence, the index finger, which he places in his breviary (*per segno*, as a sign, Manzoni naturally remarks). He passes an example of visual communication, a clumsily painted tabernacle, in which there can be no doubt that certain "long, snaky shapes with pointed ends . . . were meant by the artist and understood by the local inhabitants to be flames" (p. 27), and he sees "something he did not expect or want to see at all" (p. 28). Don Abbondio's entire life, lived under the sign of tranquility, rests upon his faith in tried and true patterns of action, habitual frames and scenarios; and his tragicomedy begins the moment these expectations are frustrated—from then on he starts to see a number of things that he could never have expected, including a scoundrel who becomes a saint. Don Abbondio immediately recognizes the bravoes by "certain unmistakable signs"—their dress, their attitudes, their appearance—"which left no doubt about what they were" (p. 28). There follows the famous description of the bravoes, on the strength of which the reader will be able to recognize them every time they appear in the novel—except when they are described in words by the edicts, because from that confused set of injunctions, threats, and prescriptions the descriptions that emerge are vague and poorly defined.

Don Abbondio recognizes the bravoes for what they are because he is in possession of a behavioral, vestimentary, and kinesic code. Otherwise, it would be hard to understand why he is able to identify them at first sight as "individuals of the species known as bravoes" (p. 28). (It is curious how scholastically rigorous Manzoni is at this point, how, using Aristotelian terms, he is able to suggest the semiotic relationship between *type* and *token*.)

We may note in passing that Don Abbondio is fully aware that the habit and not the name make the monk. In the last chapter he will jestingly discuss with Renzo the inanity of the decree that grants to cardinals the title of "eminence" (p. 707). It has come about because at this point everybody was called "monsignor" or "your grace," but before long everybody will want to be called "eminence," and the linguistic innovation will have done nothing to bring order to the universe of ecclesiastical dignity and human vanity.

The meeting with the bravoes takes place under the sign of the opposition between word and visual evidence. The bravoes speak, but what Don Abbondio understands always anticipates their words. The priest realizes "by certain unmistakable signs" (p. 32) that he is the one they are waiting for; he puts on a casual attitude, in the vain hope of deceiving the threatening characters who are lying in wait for him, running the first two fingers of his left hand under his collar; he decides that to run for it would have lent itself to an inauspicious interpretation ("it would have been the same as saying, follow me, or worse"); once more he pretends to be relaxed, reciting a verse or two out loud; he composes his face into as calm and carefree an expression as he can muster (because he knows that, since gestures and facial expressions speak, they can be manipulated in order to lie); he prepares a smile; and, to indicate his submission, he comes to a halt.

As for the bravoes, when they speak (and so far they speak saying nonthreatening things), they speak with a menacing attitude, they speak in his ear "in a tone of impressive command" (p. 33), and they know full well that their attitude speaks louder than their words, because "if these things had to be settled by talk, [Don Abbondio with his book learning] would make rings round [them]" (p. 33).

There's just one thing, at the end of the episode, that seems to challenge our hypothesis, and to this we must now turn our full attention.

14.4. Proper Names

The bravoes mention the name of Don Rodrigo and "The effect of that name on Don Abbondio's mind was like a flash of lightning in the middle of the storm at night, which illuminates one's surroundings confusedly for a moment, and makes them more terrifying than before" (p. 34). Confronted with this power of the name, it has to be said that, of all the *flatus vocis* that we cannot trust, proper names, because of their indexical nature, take on a particular status which makes them cognate with symptoms or visual signs.

The novelist must certainly have faith in proper names, to identify his characters without ambiguity. Now it appears that when he needs these indispensable labels, for Renzo, Lucia, Agnese, Tonio, or Donna Prassede, Manzoni makes the most neutral choices possible, dipping into the liturgical calendar or into the Scriptures,

For the historical characters in the background, he uses the names that history obliges him to use (Federigo, Ambrogio Spinola, Ferrer), but for the most part he could not be more careful about using as few surnames and place names as he can, resulting in the great abundance of asterisks that we are all familiar with, and the unrevealing antonomasias like "the Signora," arriving finally at that masterpiece of reticence that is the name of the Unnamed, written with a lower case initial in the original no less.

In other words, Manzoni has the same reluctance to divulge names that Renzo demonstrates at the inn in the presence of the pseudo-Ambrogio Fusella. And he does not appear to do so merely in obedience to the rules of the genre. He seems to lack faith in names because he realizes that, even regarding names, the chronicles, which speak of facts, are ambiguous, so much so that we do not even know what the correct name is of the man who was the first bearer of the contagion, and we have to choose between two, both of which are probably false. And when havoc has been wreaked upon real names (as in the case of the name of Giangiacomo Mora), an image that does not correspond to reality has attached itself to the label, connoting in infamous fashion a name that ought by rights to evoke feelings of pity.

Proper names, then, embarrassing signs, are not reliable as words, and are in danger of being even less so as "rigid designators." The fewer of them mentioned the better. But, as labels, they serve their purpose: little by little the reader *hangs* on the name Lucia everything that the actions of the young woman have done to define her, and the characters in the novel do likewise. Obviously, the name is all the more effective the more it provides a label for a series of characteristics already defined from the outset, as is the case with Don Rodrigo, and for characters already fully defined by a hagiography that is never called into question, as is the case with Cardinal Federigo Borromeo. Don Rodrigo and Federigo are both clichés—the first damned from the opening chapters (so much so that we will never learn whether or not he was touched by grace at the point of death), the second wearing a halo of holiness before he even comes onstage. This is why their names have an almost magical power, hearing them one either shudders or is reassured.

But, both in the case of already defined characters like Federigo, and those in the process of being defined like the Unnamed, Manzoni can name names—sidestepping his distrust of the verbal—because as a good storyteller he knows that proper names are merely hooks on which to hang precise descriptions, and the descriptions come from a playbook of behaviors and actions that manifest themselves in terms of natural semiotics.

In any case, we cannot say that Manzoni exploits names to suggest connotations of character. The case of the defamatory nicknames of the bravoes does not count, because the bravoes appear onstage already characterized for what they are and what they have no option but to be. Let us consider instead a borderline case, that of the aforementioned pettifogging lawyer Azzeccagarbugli (Dr Quibbler).

He seems to be defined from the start by his nickname, but this is not altogether true. The theater of visual appearances that he deploys around himself seduces Renzo in the beginning: the actions of the pettifogger are marked by humanity, his rooms are a guarantee of his learning and respect for the law (the portraits of the twelve Caesars, the bookshelf full of dusty old volumes, the table littered with statements, pleas, applications, and edicts). Nor should we forget that the dressing gown he is draped in is a legal robe, however threadbare. Renzo is taken in by a seductive mise-en-scène, and he concludes that a quibbler can quibble for a just cause as well as an evil one. The name has not yet condemned the character, indeed the mise-en-scène exalts him, at least in the eyes of someone without experience of the world. All the doctor's gestures are reassuring to Renzo, showing him the edicts, letting him see with his own eyes that the laws exist, and so on. Azzeccagabugli only becomes odious when Renzo realizes that all this talk about the rule of law hides his desire to get around it, and the good doctor reveals his true self when he talks like Don Abbondio, using language, that is, to duck the request that is being made. At that point his gestures are unequivocal, shooing Renzo out and especially (the exercise of the symbolic has a material cost) giving him back his brace of capons.

14.5. The Pardon of Father Cristoforo

The solemn scene of the pardon in Chapter 4 is symbolic and liturgical in its staging. Given the solemn comportment of the actors, the time and place of the meeting, and the elaborately theatrical orchestration of the action, as well as the costumes and poses of the figures who are to decide upon the life or death of the penitent, words become irrelevant.

The duel itself had already occurred because there were rules of behavior and precedence to be observed, in which left and right, frowns and tones of voice counted. Ludovico/Cristoforo's repentance and his conversion were a consequence of his revulsion from the offense he had committed. "Though murder was so common in those days that everyone was used to the news of violent death and the sight of blood, the impression made on him by the spectacle of the man who had died for him, and the man who had died at his hands, was something novel and indescribable—a revelation of feelings he had never known before. To see his enemy fall to the ground, to see the change in his face, as it passed in a moment from fury and menace to the vanquished, solemn peace of death, was an experience which transformed the soul of the killer" (p. 83). But let us come to the scene of the pardon.

Blood will have blood: the fact that Cristoforo has repented, that he is seeking forgiveness, that he has gone so far as to renounce the world and take the habit of a Franciscan friar, cannot wash away the offense. It is washed away by a magnificently mounted scenario that articulates, in terms of a strict code of etiquette, what words cannot say—a seventeenth-century idea if ever there was one, which Manzoni captures with a fine pictorial sense. Hence the gathering of all the deceased's relatives in the great reception hall, with capes, plumes, ceremonial swords, starched and pleated ruffs, flowing simars—a secular aristocratic liturgy.

The two friars process ritually between the two wings of the crowd, and already at that point "Brother Cristoforo's face and manner proclaimed unmistakably to the assembled company" (p. 88) that he had truly repented. Whether Cristoforo is sincere or not is unimportant: he behaves in a sincere way, with the tone of a sincere man, which he somehow instinctively theatricalizes, true son of his century that he is, and cannot help theatricalizing, since he must stay within the parameters that have been carefully preordained. After which Cristoforo sticks to his script. He kneels, crosses his hands over his chest, bows his shaved head. At that point he speaks and pronounces words of forgiveness, but it is clear from the narrative that it is not those words that convince the dead man's brother and the crowd of nobles. Their conviction has already taken place. The dead man's brother's "stance was meant to suggest strained condescension and suppressed wrath" (he strikes a pose, like a character in an opera), but the gestures of the penitent (his ritual posturings) make it clear that the bearing of the offended party may now be modified. This is the context, liturgical and clearly ecclesiastical in nature, for the embrace and the kiss of peace, the petition for and the bestowing of the bread of forgiveness.

Cristoforo is fully aware that this bread is something more than part of the paraphernalia of the ceremony, that, rather than being mere evidence of his forgiveness, it has performatively created that forgiveness and will continue to keep it alive as long as the bread itself lasts. He will carry a morsel of that bread with him for the rest of his life. In the plague hospital, after reminding Renzo that in thirty years he has still not found peace for what he did, he entrusts the bread to the two betrothed as inheritance, warning, pledge, and viaticum. Cristoforo does not feel blasphemous using that bread as a relic, because he knows that it has been consecrated in the course of a ritual.

14.6. Further Examples

We could continue, and heaven help us if we couldn't. In the meeting between Don Rodrigo and Father Cristoforo, the courteous words Don Rodrigo pronounces at the start of their conversation are belied by "his way of uttering them" (p. 108). Don Rodrigo asks in what way can he be of service, but his tone plainly says: remember whom you are speaking to. And Cristoforo indulges in a little stage business himself when, in order to strike terror into the heart of the villain, given the patent inadequacy of verbal threats of divine retribution, he has recourse (or Manzoni has recourse for him, which amounts to the same thing) to striking another theatrical pose, this time more nineteenth-century than baroque: "stepping back a couple of paces, poised boldly on his right foot, with his right hand on his hip, he raised the other hand with his forefinger outstretched towards Don Rodrigo and looked him straight in the eye with a furious glare" (pp. 110–111).

Before the reader has learned about her terrible life, the Signora of Monza is introduced, in a passage that owes much to the Gothic novel, behind the convent grille, condemned by her physiognomic ambiguities, by her gaze, by the not unworldly way her waist is laced and a curl of black hair allowed to emerge from the band on her forehead, against every rule of the cloister (p. 171). As yet we know nothing about Gertrude, and already we can guess a great deal. The only ones who cannot guess are Lucia, she too as yet a novice when it comes to the codes of natural semiosis, and the Father Superior, who has given up trying to read behavior for political reasons.

Moreover, Gertrude's entire education consists of visual signs more than words, from the religious dolls given to her as a child down to her segregation as a consequence of her rebellion, a segregation that takes the form of a play of absences, evasive glances, silences, reticence: "The days went by, without her father or anyone else talking to her about her application, or her change of mind, and without any course of action whatever being urged upon her, either with caresses or with threats. Her parents' behavior to her was unsmiling, gloomy and harsh, but they never told her why" (p. 182). The opportunity to speak, and at some length, is restored to her only after she has surrendered, because by now what she was expected to understand she has understood without words.

On the other hand Gertrude, in the end, sentences herself to burial in the cloister precisely because words are extorted from her that she would have preferred not to utter, that do not express what she feels, but, since they are ritual gestures with a performative value, no sooner have they been said than they can no longer be taken back.

In the course of his visit to the Unnamed in chapter 20, the way Don Rodrigo offers his respects is through a complex liturgy of greetings and gifts to the bravoes of his host, while the latter—whose profession is announced by room after room whose walls are covered with muskets, sabers, and halberds—at once, even before speaking, scrutinizes Don Rodrigo's hands and his face.

In chapter 33, when Don Rodrigo experiences the first signs of the plague, he becomes aware of unequivocal internal symptoms, about which he cannot be deceived, and Griso immediately grasps his master's state by observing his face. In a universe in which, as Manzoni has told us in the foregoing pages, the whole of society has vied with one another in ignoring or not comprehending the symptoms of the sickness—and was able to do so by translating the visual evidence into verbal reports—Don Rodrigo's symptoms can only be interpreted in the correct way, because they cannot be verbally mediated. We are faced with the natural evidence of "a filthy bubonic swelling, of a livid purplish color" (p. 608). Language, however, immediately steps in to cover up the reality. Don Rodrigo lies, saying he feels well. Griso lies, encouraging him, with words, and professing his obedience, and all the while he is preparing to hand him over to the scavenging *monatti*. Don Rodrigo and Griso understand each other with looks and deceive each other with words.

14.7. Public Madness and Public Folly

But if so far we have tried to extrapolate from various episodes an implicit semiotics, Manzoni is far more explicit in the chapters on the plague (31 and 32).

When he recounts how the contagion spread, while the whole of society repressed the idea, and how, when the reality of the disease became undeniable, a human agent was invented and the figure of the "anointer" *(untore)* was constructed (in the sense in which the press constructs a monster or a conspiracy), Manzoni speaks of "public madness" (p. 581) and "a confused and terrifying accumulation of public folly" (p. 601). A delirium of reason, to be sure, but the way in which the author explains it is a description of a process of semiosic teratology, a chronicle of falsification of signifiers and of substitution of signifieds.

The first signs that appear (a number of corpses) are without a code—"symptoms [*segni*] quite unfamiliar to most of the survivors" (p. 566). It is Ludovico Settala, a doctor who has lived through the previous plague, who provides the code to interpret them. But when similar symptoms occur in Lecco, the commissioners send representatives who gather evidence—verbal evidence—from an ignorant barber, who provides a different, mendacious code: autumnal vapors from the marshes, the privations and torments caused by German troops.

Fresh proofs arrive: the "marks" (p. 567) of the pestilence are found in various localities. The usual reports are sent, in writing, to the Governor, who takes them for what they are worth and protests that he is too busy with the weightier affairs of war. For its part the population, passionately concerned to suppress its fears, compete among themselves in giving credit to the most bizarre codes, attributing the symptoms to the most unheard-of causes.

Finally somebody sees a bubo for the first time. In this case the signifier ought to be referred, according to a tried and true symptomatological tradition, to its proper signified. But the majority have only heard *talk* about the bubo, seen only by a few. On the other hand the edicts, which proliferate in an inane manner in the hope of forestalling contagion, add to the verbal confusion, and are as usual ignored. Furthermore, it seems that the news that arrives is insufficient, and "the rarity of the cases itself diverted most minds from the truth" (p. 572). Here begins a process that an epistemologist would attribute to the intrinsic weakness of any inductive method (how many cases are needed to justify the formulation of a law?) but which in fact brings into play a rhetorical insecurity, a perplexity over how consistent a part must be before it can represent the whole by synecdoche, or how evident an effect must be to be a good metonymy for the cause. However that may be, confronted with the uncertainty with regard to the symptoms, the doctors have an effective verbal stratagem to fall back on. They attribute to the imprecise symptoms "various names of ordinary diseases [which they had] ready to describe all the instances of plague that they were called on to treat, whatever signs or symptoms they might exhibit" (p. 572).

The opposition between symptoms and signs and names is clear. The natural visual signifier is hidden by a verbal signifier that prevents it from being recognized.

Still, there are persons who, in spite of everything, are able to "see" the approaching catastrophe. And they are branded with the "name" of enemies of their country. The case of Ludovico Settala, who risks lynching for insisting on saying what he had seen, is typical. Against him there arise the negligent doctors, who, faced with "those sinister livid patches and bubonic swellings," take refuge in "a mere fraudulent play on words" and speak of "pestilent fever" (p. 574).

At this point a kind of new rhetorical figure comes into play, which articulates the universe of natural semiosis. The deaths of personages who are well-known (by antonomasia) become more convincing than the deaths already known. Somehow or other what had so far been *said* now becomes of necessity *seen,* in the form, if nothing else, of a conspicuous absence.

In this tangle of visual signs confused by verbal definitions, it finally occurs to someone that only public visual proof can combat the manipulations of the word. "At the time of day when the crowd was at its thickest, in the midst of the throng of carriages, riders and people on foot, the corpses of that family were carried, by order of the commission of health, to the same cemetery. They were borne naked on a cart, so that the crowd could see the manifest signs of the plague on their bodies. . . . There was more belief in the existence of the plague after that" (p. 582).

At this point it would seem that the plague should become self-evident and its symptoms begin to be interpreted correctly. But the manipulations of a false conscience are reproduced on another level. No longer able to deny the existence of the evil, the deniers try to hide the causes of the contagion (so successfully that the Cardinal will be obliged to hold a solemn public propitiatory procession, thereby increasing, of course, the opportunities for infection). The promotion of the myth of the anointers has begun.

At the end of chapter 31, Manzoni himself sums up what has taken place in this process of semiosic pestilence as an action performed by the spoken language (which defines and names) upon the natural expressivity of natural signs, already abundantly misunderstood on account of the preceding encrustations of passion that had obfuscated right reason.

(i) "In the beginning, then, there had been no plague, no pestilence, none at all, not on any account. The very words had been forbidden."

(ii) "Next came the talk of 'pestilent fever'—the idea being admitted indirectly, in adjectival form": the signifier is modified to avoid evoking its proper signified.

(iii) "Then it was 'not a *real* pestilence'—that is to say, it was a pestilence, but only in a certain sense." And now the content has begun to be modified.

(iv) "Last of all, it became a pestilence without any doubt or argument—but now a new idea was attached to it, the idea of poisoning and witchcraft, and this corrupted and confused the sense conveyed by the dreaded word" (pp. 582–583). And here, as can be seen, a radical transformation has taken place, whereby the word, which has as its content a symptom that refers to a cause *p,* is made to correspond to a symptom which ought to have as its content a cause *q.* A total alteration of the meaning, using the possibility language offers of modifying the natural expressivity of visual signs and natural symptoms.

Here it appears that, instead of arranging words to mask the visual evidence, the bad conscience of society begins to operate through the staging of visual evidence. Some people "thought they saw" someone anointing a partition in the cathedral; the partition was brought, along with several pews, outside the church, where it was decided to give them a wash. But "the sight of that mass of woodwork had a very frightening effect on the crowd" and "it was generally said and believed that all the benches in the cathedral had been anointed" (p. 579). A curious process of amplification: if previously many deaths had not provided a sufficient synecdoche for the disease, now a few planks of wood provide a more than sufficient synecdoche for the entire temple, and for the general pollution. The following morning "another sight, stranger still and more significant" appeared. If the pews outside the church door had been an accidental mise-en-scène, now this "strange sort of yellowish or whitish filth," daubed over doors and walls, whether a practical joke or an act of terrorism, is quite clearly an intentional mise-en-scène.

This is where the folly or madness really gets going. Manzoni knows, or suspects, that the history of this delirium is not just a psychiatric history, but the history of a machination, or at least the history of a metastasis of demented semiosis, since he declares that "the most interesting and instructive aspect that we can study, when considering human errors—especially those of the crowd—is their mode of progression, the shapes they take on and the methods they adopt to obtain entry into the minds of men and dominate them" (p. 580). It seems to me that there is no better way to indicate a process of formation of public opinion through a distorted interpretation of signs, whether it occur for casual and instinctive reasons, or as the result of a project or "wicked plot" (p. 579).

Prepared for by the protracted deceit of the experts, who under various pretexts had denied the contagion, and by the simple fear of the uninformed, who out of natural passion had attempted to suppress the evidence, the popular semiosic ability, which throughout the course of the novel has combated the word of the schemers, has become definitively corrupted. The story of the anointers is a story of collective dementia, in which a distorted meaning is attributed to every symptom, or in which every fact, every gesture, forcibly isolated from its everyday context, from the customary scenarios, is transformed into a symptom of a single obsessive signified. People recognized as strangers by their dress are seen as anointers, an elderly man is lynched because he has dusted a pew, Renzo is practically lynched because he knocks on a door. Someone asks directions, removing his hat, and people immediately suspect that he has the powder he plans to throw at his victim in the brim of his hat; someone else touches the facade of the cathedral to see what the stone feels like, and the crowd charges at him like a wild beast . . .

The system of normal expectations collapses. Don Abbondio, seeing the bravoes, had seen something unexpected, because he knew what he was supposed to see and what, if he saw it, would be a harbinger of bad news. Now no one can see anything anymore, no one expects anything; or rather, they see and they expect, they expect and therefore they see, always the same sign. A single signifier for a single signified. That is what obsession is like; that is public madness.

14.8. In Conclusion

Verbal language versus popular semiosis? To invalidate this conjecture all we have to do is to observe how Manzoni, in his novel, celebrates the defeat of the word and the triumph of popular semiosis, precisely by means of the narrative word. But this objection strikes at the implicit semiotics of Manzoni, who is not celebrating the limits of language, but demonstrating how an author can set forth (in words, of course) his pessimistic conception of the power of the word. A happy contradiction, that becomes somewhat less contradictory when we realize that every novel presents itself as a machine (necessarily linguistic) which strives to bring to life, linguistically, signs that are not themselves linguistic, signs which accompany, precede, or follow language, with their own instinctive and violent autonomy.

This ability that verbal language has to evoke that which is not verbal has a name in rhetorical terminology: hypotyposis.

Since we cannot avoid using words ("talking—just talking, by itself—is so much more easy than any of the other activities mentioned, or all of them put together, that we human beings in general deserve a little indulgence in this matter" [p. 583]), we will say that Manzoni's *I promessi sposi* succeeds in elaborating and exemplifying its own implicit semiotics, and presenting itself as a verbal celebration of popular semiosis, only thanks to an uninterrupted chain of examples of hypotyposis.

A linguistic machine that celebrates itself by negating itself, the novel tells us something about other ways of signifying, and it suggests that, as a verbal object, it is at the service of these other ways, because it is a narration not of words but of actions, and even when it narrates words it narrates them to the extent to which they have assumed the function of actions.

15

The Threshold and the Infinite

Peirce and Primary Iconism

This essay was written in response to a number of objections raised by the section in my *Kant and the Platypus* (hereinafter *K & P*) in which I proposed the notion of "primary iconism" to explain the perceptual processes. I hypothesized a starting point or *primum,* which was at the origin of all subsequent inferential processes. The fact that I insisted on this point reflected a concern first evidenced in 1990 with my *Limits of Interpretation* and which became clearer in philosophical terms in the opening chapter of *K & P,* where I postulated a "hard core of Being." The nucleus of my thesis was that, if and precisely because we are arguing for a theory of interpretation, we cannot avoid admitting that we have been *given* something to interpret.

Let me make it clear from the outset, if it were not already obvious, that the *primum* that forms the starting point for any interpretation may also be a previous interpretation (as when, let's say, a judge interprets the statements of a witness who gives his own interpretation of what took place). In such cases too, however, the previous interpretation (to be interpreted) is taken as a *given,* and that, and nothing else, is what is to be interpreted. If anything, the interesting problem is why the judge decides to start from that particular piece of evidence and not another. But this is precisely the theme of what follows.

Originally written for the miscellany *Studi di semiotica interpretativa* (Paolucci 2007), which collected the contributions presented at the Scuola Superiore di Studi Umanistici of the University of Bologna during the academic years 2004–2005 and 2005–2006. [*Translator's note:* Quotations from *Kant and the Platypus* are from the translation by Alastair McEwen (Eco 2000).]

15.1. Peirce Reinterpreted

Having made that clear, let me recap briefly what I said in *K & P*. First of all, I put this whole discussion into a section (2.8) entitled "Peirce reinterpreted." This title was ambiguous since it could be understood in two different ways: as just one more interpretation of Peirce's theory (but such, naturally, as to present itself as the only faithful and trustworthy reading) or as a free reformulation of some of Peirce's suggestions.

The fact that what I was proposing was meant in fact to be a reformulation ought to have been clear from the section's beginning, where I reminded the reader that Peirce, in endeavoring to steer a course between Ground, perceptual judgment, and Immediate Object, was attempting to solve, from the standpoint of an inferential view of knowledge, the problem of Kantian schematism. Since, however, Peirce himself had given not one but several different answers, I felt authorized to come up with one of my own, without claiming it was his. In fact, I wrote: "And so I don't think it is enough to trust in philology, at least I have no intention of doing so here. What I shall do is try to say how I think Peirce should be read (or reconstructed, if you will); in other words, I shall try to make him say what I wish he had said, because only that way will I be able to understand what he meant to say" (*K & P*, p. 99).

Suffice it to say therefore that my proposals regarding primary iconism were all my own work and that, not being Peirce, I have the right to think differently from him, so I can't be accused of saying something that cannot be justified from the standpoint of Peircean semiotics.

As the Italian proverb says, it's not fair to throw a stone and then hide your hand in your pocket (*tirare il sasso e nascondere la mano*). Not only were my proposals constantly based on Peirce's texts, but the problem at issue touched closely on one of the fundamental principles of his semiotics, his anti-intuitionism, a principle with which I am still inclined to agree. Finally, the object of my discourse was precisely that stage of the semiosic process that Peirce called Firstness, and it is undeniable that Peirce identified Firstnesss with the Icon (as he identified Secondness with the Index and Thirdness with the Symbol), and this explains my use of a term like "primary iconism," despite the fact that for some time now I have been attempting to demonstrate that "iconism" is an umbrella term that covers a range of phenomena differing considerably among themselves.

Reflecting today on what I wrote ten years ago, I believe we must make a clear distinction between "-ists" and "-ologists." Thinkers who have not created a militant posterity are the objects of straight historiography and philology (of the kind "what did Plato really say?" or "what was Aristotle getting at?") and the people who write about them are the "-ologists," if we are at liberty to coin terms such as "Plato-oloists" or "Platologists," in other words, specialists on Plato. There also exist, however, thinkers of whom many people still declare themselves to be militant followers: hence, there have been and continue to be Neo-Aristotelians, Neo-Thomists, Neo-Hegelians, and Neo-Kantians, and these are the ones I call, for convenience, "-ists."

What distinguishes an "-ist" from an "-ologist"? The "-ologist," often engaging in honest-to-goodness textual criticism, is supposed to tell us if such and such a thinker really did say such and such a thing. For example, a Thomologist has to admit that Thomas Aquinas really did say that original sin is transmitted by the semen like a natural infection (*Summa Theologica,* I–II, 81, 1), whereas the soul is individually created, because it cannot be dependent on corporal matter. (Thomas was a creationist not a traducianist). For Thomas vegetables have a vegetative soul, which in animals is absorbed by the sensitive soul, while in human beings these two functions are absorbed by the rational soul. But God introduces the rational soul only when the fetus has gradually acquired, first the vegetative, then the sensitive soul. Only at that point, when the body has already been formed, is the rational soul created (*Summa Theologica* I, 90 and *Summa contra gentiles* II, 89). Embryos have only a sensitive soul (*Summa Theologica* I, 76, 2 and I, 118, 2) and therefore cannot participate in the resurrection of the flesh (*Supplementum* 80, 4).

This is what makes a Thomologist. A Thomist on the other hand is someone intent on thinking *ad mentem divi Thomae,* as if Thomas were speaking today. Thus, a present-day Thomist might develop Saint Thomas's premises to define lines of ethical conduct with regard to the current debates on abortion, the use of stem cells, and so on.

I still maintain that there exists a third position, between "-ists" and "-ologists," and the best term I can come up with is that of "reconstructionists." I take this position because, in my first work of philosophical history, devoted to the aesthetics of Thomas Aquinas, I found myself faced with the following problem: Thomas never devoted a specific text to aesthetics but simply scattered his works with statements regarding the nature of art and the beautiful. If he had had to write a specific text (the hypothesis is not too far-fetched, since for some time a *De pulchro et bono,* which turned out to be the work of his teacher Albertus Magnus, was attributed to him) or if he had been quizzed about it (then, in his own times), what would he have said, in the light (and only in the light) of the system that was in fact his (as even the "-ologists" describe it)? When one conducts experiments like this, one runs the risk of discovering that any system, subjected to an inspection of this kind, may reveal a few cracks. This is precisely what happened to me in the case of Thomas, in which, while recognizing that he had an implicit theory of beauty which could readily be reconstructed, I finally pointed out an aporia to be found in his system (precisely when that system was faithfully interpreted, as an "-ologist" ought to interpret it).

I am still pleased with the vaguely Gödelian flavor of that conclusion, but the purpose of this whole preamble is to say that in *K & P* I had made the "-ist" choice, while the objections subsequently brought against me (see section 15.2) were aimed at reconstructing the problem from an "-ologist" point of view.

My starting point was in fact a suggestion made by Armando Fumagalli (1995: ch. 3), who saw in the post-1885 Peirce an almost Kantian return to the immediacy of intuition, antecedent to any inferential activity (the Ground is no longer a predicate but a sensation, and indexicality becomes the kind of experience which takes the form of a *shock;* it is an impact with an individual, which "strikes" the subject without yet being a representation). In this connection, I attempted to say why precisely Peirce's Firstness was exactly that, a "firstness" *(primità),* a sort of auroral moment that gives rise to the perceptual process. Speaking of the Ground, Peirce informs us that it is a Firstness, and if on occasion it has been interpreted as "background" or "basis," or "foundation," it is certainly not so in an ontological sense but in a gnoseological one. It is not *something* that presents itself as a candidate to be a *subjectum,* it is a possible predicate itself, more like the immediate recognition expressible as "red!" (comparable to the response "ouch!" to a blow that causes pain) than like the judgment expressible as "*this* is red." In that phase there is not even something that resists us (this would be the moment of Secondness), and at a certain point Peirce tells us that it is "pure *species,*" in the sense of appearance, aspect (cf. Fabbrichesi 1981: 471), and he calls it icon, semblance, *likeness.*[1]

---

1. See Peirce, *Collected Papers* (1931–1958)(hereinafter "CP") 1:307: "any feeling must be identical with any exact duplicate of it," and therefore the icon is a likeness, not in the sense that is like something else, but because it is the phenomenon

Peirce says that the idea of the First is "so tender that you cannot touch it without spoiling it" (CP 1.358). The Firstness is a presence "such as it is," a positive characteristic (CP 5.44), a "quality of feeling," like a purple color noticed without any sense of the beginning or the end of the experience, it is not an object nor is it initially inherent to any recognizable object, it has no generality (CP 7.530). Only when both Secondness and Thirdness come into play can the interpretive process begin. But Firstness is still "mere maybe" (CP 1.304), "potentiality without existence" (CP 1.328), "mere possibility" (CP 8.329), and in any case the possibility of a perceptual process (CP 5.119), something that cannot be thought in an articulate way or asserted (CP 1.357). Elsewhere, by *feeling* Peirce means "that kind of consciousness which involves no analysis, comparison or any process whatsoever, nor consists in whole or in part of any act by which one stretch of consciousness is distinguished from another, which has its own positive quality which consists of nothing else, and which is of itself all that it is" (CP 1.306).

I thought I had recognized that, though this Firstness had the character of a nonmediated apprehension, it still could not be assimilated to Kantian intuition: it is not at all an intuition of the manifold offered by experience, but instead something absolutely simple, that I tried to assimilate to the phenomenon of *qualia* (cf. Dennett 1991).

Apropos of a *quale* Peirce is still not talking about perceptual judgment but about a mere "tone" of consciousness, which he defines as being resistant to all possible criticism. Peirce is telling us not that the sensation of red is "infallible," but simply that once it has been, even if it was an illusion of the senses, it is indisputable that it has been. In this connection I gave the example (and it wasn't meant to be flippant) of the housewife in the commercial, who declares: "I thought my sheet was white, but now that I've seen yours . . ." Seeing the detergent commercial, Peirce would have told us that the housewife initially perceived the whiteness of the first sheet (pure "tone" of awareness); then, once she had moved on to the recognition of the object (Secondness) and set in motion a comparison packed with inferences (Thirdness), she was able to declare that the second sheet was whiter than

---

that founds any possible judgment of similarity, without being able to be founded by it. This also explains my choice of the perhaps misleading term, "primary iconism."

the first. But she could not cancel out the preceding impression, which as a pure quality *has been,* and therefore she says: "I was sure [*before*] I had seen something white, but *now* I recognize that there are different degrees of whiteness." Only at this point, reacting to the *album* (white) of at least two different sheets, has the housewife moved on to the predicate of the *albedo* (whiteness), that is, to a *general* which can be named and for which there is an Immediate Object. It is one thing to perceive an object as white, without having become aware as yet that we are dealing with something external to our awareness, and it is another to perform the prescission whereby one predicates of that object the quality of being white.

But how are we to justify the fact that the starting point of all knowledge is not inferential in nature, because it is immediately manifest, without being open to discussion or denial, when Peirce's entire anti-Cartesian polemic is based on the assumption that all knowledge is always inferential in nature?

15.2. Peirce and the Coffeepot

In his doctoral thesis Claudio Paolucci (2005) maintains with a wealth of arguments that there is no "realistic" turning-point in Peirce that leads him to consider the possibility of intuitions of a Kantian type, and in so doing he is very polemical in his criticism of both Fumagalli (1995) and Murphey (1961), to whom Fumagalli is referring. Let me say at once that I have no intention of contesting this contestation of Paolucci's. I simply want to point out that in *K & P* I wrote: "Fumagalli observes that we have a Kantian return here to the immediacy of intuition, prior to all inferential activity. Nevertheless, since this intuition, as we shall see, remains the pure sentiment that I am confronted with something, the intuition would still be devoid of all intellectual content, and therefore (it seems to me) it could withstand the young Peirce's anti-Cartesian polemic" (p. 99).

Paolucci still finds this "I am confronted with something" embarrassing, and he writes: "There is no question that Peirce, to describe the formal moment that gives body to the second phenomenological category, describes on several occasions a type of nonmediated relationship between a subject and an individual external object (a *haecceitas* or thisness). Should this type of relationship turn out to be a *cognition* (but, as we shall see, it isn't), it would certainly be correct to speak of a return on the part of Peirce to the immediacy of intuition, since we would be dealing with a cognition not determined by previous cognitions." *Quod est impossibile,* if we assume that Peirce always remained anti-Cartesian.

But, in *K & P,* was I really talking about *cognitions?*

The position Paolucci has always defended, including in his thesis, is that Peirce's notion of synechism has to do, not with an amorphous *continuum* to be segmented (à la Hjelmslev), but with the series of cognitive inferences that, proceeding *en abyme,* always lead us to make a supposed *primum* that offers itself to our experience, the point of departure for a subsequent inference (and it is no accident that Paolucci has always appealed in this regard to the principles of infinitesimal analysis). Therefore, every cognitive phenomenon, even the most aurorally primal, must call upon all three categories. Assuredly, there are moments in which Firstness or Secondness seem preeminent, but they are never the exclusive components of the process because any kind of experience always needs to be made up of all three phenomenological categories. How then can we speak of a primary experience?

This is not all, but for Peirce the three categories are not cognitions but formal structures that found the possibility of all cognition (in this sense Peirce was a Kantian), or they are not kinds of experience but pure forms that make up experience. Therefore, if a sensation of redness is an example of Firstness or, in one of the examples I provided at the time, the burning I feel when I touch a hot coffeepot, this Firstness in itself is still nothing from the point of view of my cognitions (a "mere maybe"), and I recognize it as a burn from the coffeepot only if it is immediately placed in relation to Secondness and Thirdness.[2]

---

2. Claudio Paolucci recently suggested (in a private communication) that "obviously the burning sensation produced by the coffeepot is a Firstness for Peirce too, i.e., 'the emergence of something new.' Except that in Peirce Firstnesses 'do not spring up isolated; for if they did, nothing could unite them. They spring up in reaction upon one another, and thus in a kind of existence'" (CP 6.199). The emergence of the Firstnesses through their being opposed to one another (Secondness) starting from the regularity of the habit (Thirdness) for Peirce is an *event* (CP 6.200), i.e., a singularity, a point at which something occurs. . . . In this way the spontaneity of Firstness, whose irregular and singular nature Peirce underlines (CP 6.54), turns out to be nothing other than an infinitesimal deviation from the law and from the regularity on whose basis it is produced

Naturally I agree that, indeed let me remind you that in *K & P* I made it clear that, even in the face of the immediacy of a *quale* (a sensation of redness, a burning feeling, the whiteness of a sheet), I can always become aware later, precisely when that Firstness becomes defined as such in the interplay of all three categories, that my first reaction was the result of an error (that I had experienced as red or scorching something that wasn't), and that I might have received the stimulus in conditions (external or internal) that were such as to "deceive" my nerve terminals. Except that, as Peirce himself made clear, even after recognizing that my senses have been deceived, I cannot say that I *have not* experienced (let alone "that I have not *known*"!) a sensation of redness or excessive heat. Going back to the housewife with her sheet, she might say: "A short time ago, after having made my first over-hasty perceptual inference, *I entertained the belief* [(a cognitive fact)] that *I had experienced* a sensation of whiteness, upon further reflection however . . ."

Paolucci's objection is that, given that Peirce denies all power to intuition and asserts that all cognition arises from a previous cognition, not even a

---

(CP 6.59). Peirce calls habit, or Thirdness, this very regularity starting from which it is possible to generate the singular spontaneity of the Firstnesses in their opposition to one another (Secondness). . . . In other words, somehow, the very spontaneity of the event, of the emergence of something new (Firstness) is nothing but the habit of a regular series (Thirdness) which differentiates itself at certain given points: the singular emerges from the regular from which it detaches itself as a consequence of an instability effect. . . . In this way, since, as Peirce says, Firstnesses do not occur in isolation, the feeling of pain that emerges in the example of my morning coffee (Firstness) is a quality that emerges from a background of experiential habits (getting up in the morning, picking up the coffeepot, putting it on the burner, not turning the gas up too high, placing the coffeepot in just the right place: a whole syntax of habits and regularities of everyday experience). So the sensation of pain (Firstness) arises against a background of habits (Thirdness) that did not imply it (it is not regular to encounter pain in the breakfast scenario) and pain can only arise in opposition (Secondness) to this background of habits. So, even on the cognitive level, we find the pattern of the Logic of Relatives: on the basis of a series of regularities and habits that define the laws of my morning breakfast (Thirdness), a tendency to be distinguished from it may be created, out of which something new emerges, something for which the regularity of the local system does not make allowance. Firstness is an event of this kind, which arises in opposition (Secondness) to a regular background of Thirdness."

unrelated sensation, be it thermal, tactile, or visual, can be recognized (and therefore known) except by bringing into play an inferential process that, however instantaneous and unconscious it may be, guarantees its reliability.

Nevertheless, the problem that ought to interest a reconstructionist (more "-ologist" than "-ist") is the following: Is it possible that a sensible person like Peirce should deny that in some fashion the inferential process that leads me to say "I burned myself by touching the coffeepot" arises from a sensation of scorching that compels me (like any other animal) to withdraw the limb from the point of stimulus, even before recognizing it as something other than myself that opposes resistance? Furthermore, Peirce could not deny it because his realism, whether Scotist or otherwise, was based on the fact that all knowledge refers to a Dynamical Object that *lies outside of myself* and my cognitive acts, and precedes every possible inference—even if by chance this Dynamical Object were to remain forever unattainable, multiplying itself into an infinite series of Immediate Objects. Peirce could not deny that the perceptual process seems to begin in a vague and marshy zone between Firstness, Secondness, and Thirdness, and the knot of inferences that leads it to perfect itself in perceptual judgment appears to situate itself after the apparition of *something,* not before—which is tantamount to saying that in order to interpret there must be something there to interpret, otherwise we would not be Peirceans but Deconstructionists or Nietzscheans (see *K & P*, sect. 1.9).

How can we, then, from an anti-intuitionist standpoint, according to which all experience is always of an inferential nature, how can we speak of a point where inference begins? Is this *primum* a *primum* in absolute terms or it is a *primum* for me, at that moment, and (to use a Peircean expression) is it such only *in some respect or capacity?*

The problem, quintessentially Peircean, of the respect or capacity that makes something a sign, licenses me to introduce a distinction between *molecular* pertinentization and *molar* pertinentization.

15.3. Peirce vs. The Phantom Blot

In January 2006 I engaged in a debate in Rome with Achille Varzi, inspired by his 2005 essay "Teoria e pratica dei confini," ("The Theory and Practice of

Boundaries").[3] Taking the notion of "boundary" as his starting point, Varzi proceeded to discuss the evident difference between purely *de dicto* demarcations (like the boundaries between two states) and demarcations we might be tempted to consider *de re* (like the boundary that separates the inside of an apple from its outside, a human body from what surrounds it, or even life from nonlife or life from death, as is the case in discussions about abortion, stem cells, or euthanasia). Varzi recognized that:

> it is not clear what the relationship is between a boundary and the entity *of which* it is the boundary. . . . We never encounter points, lines and surfaces in complete isolation. We cannot eat all the three-dimensional parts of an apple and keep only its surface, if by surface we mean, not the peel (which is a solid part), but the perfectly two-dimensional entity that circumscribes the peel on the outside, just as we cannot display in a museum the boundary of our town or the point of intersection between the equator and the Greenwich meridian. Still, this relationship of dependency is reciprocal: neither can we think of an apple without a surface, or a town without boundaries. . . . Certain entities commence their existence only when a boundary is drawn.[4]

And, after referring to the uncertain boundary between the water of the sea and the air of the sky remarked on by Leonardo, Varzi got to Peirce *(The Logic of Quantity)* and to the edge of a black spot on a white surface—a problem that seemed similar to him to the Aristotelian question whether at the precise moment when a body begins to move we should say that the body is at rest or in motion (*Physics* VI, 234a et seq.).

Varzi remarked, citing Jackendoff (1987), that we might be dealing with asymmetrical configurations in which one of the two entities is a *figure* in

---

3. Varzi (2005) returns to themes previously discussed in Smith and Varzi (2000: 401–420). [*Translator's note:* The Phantom Blot is a Walt Disney character (Macchia Nera in Italian). He is an archenemy of Mickey Mouse and first appeared in the comic strip *Mickey Mouse Outwits the Phantom Blot* by Floyd Gottfredson in 1939.]

4. [*Translator's note:* The quotation from Varzi's article appears in the original Italian in Eco's text.]

relation to the other which is the *background:* thus the spot is imposed on the sheet of paper that acts as the background, and so the line of demarcation that Peirce was looking for belongs to the spot not to the paper. The water wins out over the air that acts as the background, and hence the line of demarcation Leonardo was concerned with belongs to the sea. We never have two solid bodies in contact with each other, but always a body inserted into a certain background context, and it is therefore to the body itself that the boundary is to be assigned. Nevertheless, Varzi did not find the idea very convincing:

> But what happens when two figures collide? We throw a stone into the sea. The stone is "closed," and so is the water. How does the stone manage to enter, if two closed bodies cannot even touch each other? And granted that it manages to enter, which of them does the boundary line between stone and water belong to? Are we to say that upon entering the stone opened? That the sea is closed on the outside (toward the air) but open on the inside (toward the stone)? Or let us think of the white cliffs of Dover: it is hard to think of them as a topologically open background against which the waters of the English Channel stand out. This is also because the cliffs stand out in their turn against the sky. Are we to say then that that the cliffs are open along the zone that separates them from the water, but closed for that part of their surface that separates them from the air? And what are we to say of the line along which water, air and rock meet? If we grant that the water continues to win out, how do the air and the rock manage to touch if they are both open? Obviously something is wrong. The topology of the continuous excludes the possibility of two closed bodies touching, but it also that of two open bodies touching. . . . The gradual process of dematerialization of matter that has marked the development of modern and contemporary physical theories presents us with a world in which even objects that to us appear perfectly rigid and compact are, if we look closely, swarms of microscopic particles frenetically in motion in the wide open spaces that surround them (the volume of an apple, if by this we mean the material part of the fruit, is less than a thousandth of what we are accustomed to calculate), and the surfaces of these systems of particles are no more smooth and continuous than a fakir's bed of

nails. If this is how things are, it makes no sense to speak of contiguous objects separated by a common boundary line. It makes no sense to ask ourselves *to which of them* the boundary between two objects belongs. There are only dancing particles, and if we really insist on insisting, we will say that each of them must have its own boundary that separates it from the void: there is *nothing else* that can claim its possession. Put in another way, if we look closely, the spatial boundaries of common physical objects are imaginary entities whose form and localization involve the same degree of arbitrariness as the lines of a graph based on a limited amount of data, the same degree of idealization as a drawing obtained by "following the dots" on the page of a puzzle book, the same degree of abstraction as the outlines of the figures in an Impressionist painting. To ask ourselves who or what *these* lines belong to makes no sense, or it makes sense only if we conceive of them as abstract boundaries drawn by our unifying action, *de dicto* boundaries which, as such, may well be undetermined, as we have seen.

Varzi seemed to me to be tending toward an overconventional vision of the notion of boundary, going so far indeed as to extend the *de dictu* modalities to cover all those that were presumably *de re*.[5] Still, in the course of the discussion that ensued, I accepted the idea that "even what are for us the most salient events and actions, that seem to be defined by *de re* boundaries,

---

5. Nevertheless, with reference to the *Phaedrus,* in which Plato recommends that we divide being into species "according to the natural formation, where the joint is, not breaking any part as a bad carver might" (Benjamin Jowett trans.), Varzi reminded us that, if all boundaries were the product of a conventional decision, then our knowledge of the world would be reduced to a knowledge of the maps we have drawn of it (an example of the total substitution of facts by interpretations). But, without postulating a totally realistic solution (according to which the world presents itself to our experience already prepackaged into objects, events, and natural properties), he cited my proposal (from *K & P*) as a compromise solution: though in different cultures veal may be carved in different ways (so that the names of certain dishes are not always translatable from one language to another), it would be very hard to think of a cut that offered at the same time the end of the snout and the end of the tail. Even if there were no one-way streets in the world, there would still be no-entries, in other words objective limits to our ability to organize the content of experience.

emerge upon further consideration from an intricate system of underlying processes that we select and unify according to laws that reflect our cognitive biases." The problem of cognitive biases seems to bring us back to the difference between molecular and molar.

It is certainly difficult to define the boundaries of a black spot on a white sheet of paper, just as it is difficult to define the boundaries of a hole. Granted, it is usually the body that is topographically closed while the background remains open. But who decides which is the body and which the background? As a collector of rare books, I know that, when I come across a wormhole in the page of an incunabulum, I am concerned, not with the boundaries of the hole, but with the boundaries of the page, because it is on the page that a letter may be eaten away or even cancelled by the hole. And when I write in my catalogue "with the partial loss of a letter on leaf A6 recto," it is with the margins of the page and not of the hole that I am concerned.

This might mean that the definition of the limits (and of the relationship of figure to background) is merely a question of *negotiation*: it is a question of negotiation if I think like a collector and not like an informal artist who wishes to pantograph the hole (or the spot) and would be interested in that case in defining its edges with microscopic exactness. For a theorist of fractals, the edges of the hole could be analyzed *en abyme* so as to identify their curves and folds beyond any limit conceivable in terms of our normal perceptual habits. But, from my standpoint as collector and bibliophile, I respect the limits of my perceptual abilities, and I consider as undivided something that is, cosmologically speaking, susceptible *in posse* to further division.

This is also true of the boundary that separates an apple from its outside. Clearly, in terms of subatomic physics, what we have along that borderline, and before it and after it, is a host of dancing particles and not a line. But I was once guilty of an error in this connection. In *La struttura assente*, arguing against ingenuous conceptions of iconism, I said that a line drawing of a horse in profile, which ought to imitate the properties of a horse, exhibits the one property that a horse does not have, namely, a solid black line that separates the inside of the horse from the outside. I was forced to recant, following the lead of Gombrich (1982), who, correcting a conventionalist position he had taken earlier, observed that if it had once been affirmed that there are no lines in nature and that outlines are a human artifice, psychologists today tend to see them as a perceptual "surrogate" and as "indicators of discontinuity." In fact "the outlines may serve as an anticipation of the motion parallax effect, because objects within our reach always stand out from their background, but will retain an intrinsic coherence however slightly we move our heads" (Gombrich 1985: 233).

This does not mean that the outline *belongs* to the horse, because, depending on whether I look up at the horse from a lying position or down from a balcony, I will see different aspects of the horse, and therefore the outline will shift with my point of view; and yet, even though it does depend on my point of view, at the moment when I look, the outline is an *objective* datum that I cannot ignore. The horse may display an infinite number of outlines, but *in that particular respect or capacity* it has only one.

Once I have decided to consider the leaf of the book from the collector's point of view, if I write that there is a hole with the loss of one or two letters or half a letter, it is objectively true that one or two letters or half a letter is missing, and the difference between one or two letters is not a question of negotiation or of infinitely subdivisible borders. Either the letter is missing or it isn't.

Once the level of pertinence has been decided—or the level of interest with which I focus on things (and in my case I have chosen a molar rather than a molecular level)—not only do nonnegotiable objective impossibilities become evident, but also *starting points* from which my inferential activity begins.

Let us talk, not about the borderline case of the holes, but about the normal case of the absence of holes. There can be no doubt that if I take a fresh sheet of standard 8.5 x 11 typing paper there are no holes in it. Similarly, if I were to attempt to walk from one room to another without using the door but by going through the wall (or going through the looking glass like Alice), I would come up against the fact that there are no holes (or ways through of any kind) in the paper or the wall or the looking glass. And yet—as one would have to admit from a molecular, if not a molar, point of view—using an extremely powerful microscope I would see in both the paper and the wall an infinite number of holes or empty spaces, just as I am aware that the crystal atoms of the mirror are miniature solar systems with empty interstellar spaces.

The point is that *from my own point of view,* or in some respect or capacity, those empty spaces are of no interest, and therefore as far as I am concerned *do not exist.*

15.4. Peirce and the Brain

Whether we call it primary iconism or use some other name, there is something we cannot get around as soon as we introduce an interpreting subject into the process of semiosis. In other words, if primary iconism does not exist cosmologically, it exists for the subject.

Let us take another look at the Peircean concepts. In CP 5.213 it is specified that "the term *intuition* will be taken as signifying a cognition not determined by a previous cognition of the same object, and therefore so determined by something out of the consciousness."[6] If denying all intuition, however, meant denying that everything that happens in our minds is not determined by something outside of our consciousness, we might be tempted to believe that Peirce was opting for a magical idealism à la Novalis. But Peirce does not say "everything that happens outside of our minds"; instead he speaks of cognitions. If someone kicks me and I cry out (and feel pain) can we speak of cognition? I would speak simply of stimulus-response, which is nonetheless something that involves our neuronal processes. Now, Peirce never said that stimulus-response processes are cognitions, or that the stimulus that I feel when kicked does not come from something outside of our minds (or our brain). Can we reasonably speak, without being accused of not thinking *ad mentem divi Caroli,* of the sensation of pain I would feel if (for example and *per absurdum*) Paolucci were to kick me in the shins?

Faced with this stimulus, my brain would probably perform processes of whose complexity I have no inkling, as it does when it inverts (as if there were nothing to it!) the retinal image. We can say therefore that processes occur in my neuronal circuit that we may define as inferential or in any case interpretive. But about these processes *I know nothing* and, just as it seems natural to see Paolucci walking with his feet on the ground and his head in the air, it seems natural to react with a cry of pain to his kick in the shins, even if to invite me to emit it my brain has performed who knows what labor. And that the brain labors to interpret, often making mistakes in interpretation, is proven by the fact that the brains of amputees cause them to suffer painful sensations that appear to come from the limb they have lost.

---

6. Originally published as "Questions concerning Certain Faculties Claimed for Man," *Journal of Speculative Philosophy* (1868) 2, 103–114].

This does not exclude the possibility that the sensation of pain itself (once involved in the triadic process that transforms it into cognition) may take on a semiosic character: it becomes a sign, to be specific a sign of the fact that someone (who through subsequent inferences I will discover was Paolucci) has given me a kick. But as soon as I become aware of pain and cry out, I assume that pain as *a point of departure in an upward direction,* to find out what it is and what caused it, and not *in a downward direction,* to understand how my brain *processed* the external stimulus. I consider that *quale* beneath a *molar* respect and capacity.

It is true (see Proni 1990: sect. 1.5.2.3.1, n. 6) that Peirce remains very ambiguous on the definition of sensation, and at times what I am calling the sensation of a *quale* is for him an impression (in the sense of a nonorganized aggregate of sensorial data), but there is no call (with a thinker who changed his terminology so often) to split hairs over lexical issues. In CP 1.374 it is said that the three categories, though they are imposed by logic and have a metaphysical valency, nevertheless have their origin in the nature of the mind and are "constant ingredients of our knowledge." Of course, this could be simply meant to confirm that they are transcendental forms in the Kantian sense, and in fact Peirce makes it clear that *they are not sensations.* But in CP 1.381 he says that "*feelings,* in the sense in which alone they can be admitted as a great branch of mental phenomena, form the warp and woof of cognition" (emphasis mine), while in CP 1.386 he speaks of feeling as "immediate consciousness," and something that "arises *in a active state of nerve-cells*" (emphasis mine). Nor can we forget that from CP 1.374 to 1.394 he speaks of the triads in psychology and physiology.

In short, if Peirce does not speak of sensations, and if he is vague when he speaks of impressions, he nonetheless alludes to states of *immediate consciousness* (see also CP 1.306). In CP 1.317 he says that "the whole content of consciousness is made up of qualities of feeling, as truly as the whole of space is made up of points or the whole of time of instants," and in CP 1.318 he writes that these qualities of feeling are "a pure *priman.*"

I believe (when I read CP 5.291 carefully) that a sensation, insofar as it is recognized as such in an interpretive process, is already a semiosic phenomenon and functions as a hypothesis; but, as pure *feeling,* "a mere feeling of a particular sort, it is determined only by an *inexplicable, occult power;* and so far, it is not a representation, but only the material quality of a representation" (emphasis mine). "A feeling, therefore, as a feeling, is merely the *material qual-ity* of a mental sign" (emphasis in original). What does the material quality of a mental sign mean? It means, I believe, that if I do not consider the word *dog* as a sign (and therefore, we would argue today, as a composite of expression and content, or signifier and signified), but consider only the phonation *dog* as it can be physically recorded and played back by someone who does not know English, I find myself faced with the material quality of the sign (the substance of the expression, so to speak), but not yet with the semiotic phenomenon developed and concluded in a representation and an act of cognition. The *feeling,* then, is not yet a hypothesis but the material occasion offered me or offered to my brain as a stimulus *provided* to allow it to proceed to the infer-ence. "The hypothetic inference of the sensation is two-thirds written (the premises) by the nature of our sensorial system: it is a hypothesis, but our conscious intervention is limited simply to drawing the conclusion, which is obtained in an automatic manner. . . . The laws of logic construct the form of the sensation, but its content, that which arrives from without, is not part of it: the *feeling* is the *material quality* of the perceptual sign" (Proni 1990: 106).

I believe it is possible to reconcile this idea of the sensation as *priman* with a nonintuitionist theory of all knowledge as inference. Provided that what I assume to be the initial sensation or stimulus is recognized as such, at the molar level, in the respect and capacity of something that *interests me at that moment,* independently of all cosmological considerations.

15.5. Peirce and the Tortoise

When reading Peirce, we must not confuse cosmology and gnoseology. As I already remarked in *K & P,* two different but mutually interdependent per-spectives are interwoven in Peirce's thought: the metaphysical-cosmological and the cognitive. Unless we read them in a semiotic key, Peirce's metaphys-ics and cosmology remain incomprehensible. But we would have to say the same thing of his semiotics with respect to his cosmology. Categories such as Firstness, Secondness, Thirdness, and the concept of interpretation itself not only define *modi significandi,* that is, the ways in which the world can be known: they are also *modi essendi,* ways in which the world *behaves,* proce-dures through which the world, in the course of evolution, interprets itself.

In *K & P*, I cited Mameli (1997: 4): "Given that Peirce thinks and demonstrates that intelligibility is not an accidental characteristic of the universe, that it is not, that is, a mere epiphenomenon of how things are, but a characteristic that 'shapes' the universe, it follows that a theory of intelligibility is also a metaphysical theory of the structure of the universe" (*K & P*, p. 399, n. 28). The theory of intelligibility and metaphysical theory, however, must sometimes be kept separate.

Kant said that the fact that we believe we know things on the basis of the mere evidence of our senses depends on a *vitium subreptionis* or subreption: we are so accustomed from childhood to grasp things as if they appeared to us already given in intuition that we have never thematized the role played by the intellect in this process. Therefore even what were for him empirical intuitions were already the result of a work of inference.

We can construct a semiotics without a subject or (what amounts to the same thing) in which the subject is everywhere. In this semiotics there will never be a *priman* because interpretation will proceed by *mise en abyme*. But, if from the cosmological point of view the inferential process is infinite, because there are no intuitions, we cannot ignore the cognitive instance, that is, that edge of the semiosis that is formed when a subject (any instance capable of saying *I* that somehow enters into the semiosis from the material and corporal outside—what I am speaking about is a brain) installs itself and touches off a chain of inferences under the stimulus of something that, from its own point of view and only in this precise spatiotemporal segment, *attracts its attention.*[7] The I in this case stands on that edge where on the one hand there stands, let's say, the dog—the thing that interests him at that moment—and on the other hand, everything else—which does not interest him.

In this phase Firstness, as we saw, is a presence "such as it is," nothing but a positive characteristic, like a purple color perceived without any sense of the beginning or the end of the experience, without any self-awareness separate from the sensation of the color; it is a potentiality without existence, the simple possibility of a perceptual process. In order to contest these *qualia*

---

7. At this point we might be tempted to open up another can of worms: Why does one thing attract my attention at the expense of another? But reconstructing a theory of attention in Peirce lies beyond my capabilities, and beyond the scope of this chapter.

that precede any inference, we must take as our point of departure the principle that they constitute an intuitive moment, without our being able to conceive of further inferential processes behind it, in a sort of infinite fractalization. But I would like to remind the reader that the infinite fractalization of a sea coast does not prevent a human subject, who has a molar view compared with the molecular view of an ant, from covering in a single step what would be for the ant an extremely long and tortuous trajectory.

We are back, if you will, to the paradox of Achilles and the tortoise, in which we must take into account the distinction between *potential infinity* and *infinity in act,* already present in Aristotle.

In the paradox Achilles must first cover half the distance, but before that he must cover a quarter, and before that an eighth, and so on ad infinitum, so that he will never succeed in catching up with the tortoise. It has been observed, however, that, although this process of fractalization can continue infinitely, its result will never be greater than one—as occurs in any case with irrational numbers, so that 3.14, however successful we may be in analyzing it, will never be 4.

If we apply this argument to the fractal length of a coast, where the *potential* process of division could be infinite, at least insofar as we can always postulate smaller and smaller microbes, this does not prevent Achilles in practice covering this space with a single stride. Achilles will cover a unit of distance appropriate to him in a unit of time appropriate to him.

Already Aristotle (*Physics* III, 8, 206) objected to Zeno that, among magnitudes, there exists infinity by addition (I can always find an even number greater than the preceding one) but not by division, insofar as the infinity of the subintervals into which a unit of length is divisible is always contained in a limited totality (never greater than one) which may constitute the object of an empirical intuition.

In other words, if, cosmologically speaking, there is never perhaps a Firstness that is not the result of a previous Thirdness, cognitively speaking there is a limit to our perceptive abilities, which experience as undivided something that, cosmologically speaking, is *in posse* capable of being further divided. What is *in posse* belongs to cosmology. What is *in actu* belongs to the agent subject.

What happens when we put ourselves in the place of a perceiving subject? Zellini (2003: 26–27) reminds us that:

Adolf Grünbaum [(1969)] recently demonstrated that the measured structure of physical time justifies applying the arithmetical theory of limits to the solution of the paradox. Human awareness of time has a base limit of perceptibility, that is, a minimal threshold beyond which temporal intervals vanish into inconceivable smallness. If we consciously tried to contemplate 'all' the intervals of the series (a), it would be realized concretely as a countable infinity of mental acts, and the duration of each of these would be larger than the minimal threshold that time allows. But this insuperable 'minimum' is an Archimedean quantity: when added to itself infinite times, it yields an infinite result. Consequently, the mental contemplation of the entire series would result in an impossibly unlimited period of time. This would happen, for example, if one 'counted' the intervals of (a) one by one, assigning to each of them an ordinal number. This would take more time than the necessary minimum just to conceive or pronounce them. (But it is absurd, Aristotle objected [*Physics* 8, 8, 263a–263b], to maintain that whatever moves, moves while counting.) In reality, by raising doubts about the possibility of traversing the interval (0–1), Zeno exploits the unacceptable delay that is implied by reducing the series (a) to the corresponding mental acts of the counting process, but he fails to make clear that this process does not reproduce exactly the measurement of the physical time involved in the actual traversal.

Thus, Grünbaum finds Zeno's argument illegitimate because it uses what is basically an inevitable confusion between two incompatible forms of thought. He explains that we do not experience the intervals into which we subdivide the traversal in any measure that corresponds to their actual nature. Rather, we derive our impression of their duration from the time needed for our acts of mental contemplation, which for each fraction of the distance must perforce exceed our minimal threshold or limit.

In other words, our perception is not mathematical but ingenuous, just as our perception of the supposed movement of the sun is ingenuous and not astronomical. Zellini (1980: 44) reminds us that the existence of a *threshold of observability* is a postulate both of physics and of the psychology of perception.

Zellini also appeals to Hume: our imagination must be capable of reaching a minimum beyond which we cannot conceive of further subdivisions. We can speak of the thousandth or ten-thousandth part of a grain of sand, but (apart from the fact that we cannot see it—which from the point of view of perception is no small matter) we can't even imagine it except with the same dimensions as the grain of sand itself: "The idea of a grain of sand is not distinguishable, nor separable into twenty, much less into a thousand, ten thousand, or an infinite number of different ideas."

"Put," said Hume, "a spot of ink upon paper, fix your eyes upon that spot, and retire to such a distance, that at last you lose sight of it; 'tis plain, that the moment before it vanish'd the image or impression was perfectly indivisible" (*Treatise of Human Nature,* I, 2, 27) At a certain point, the spot will become invisible, because it is too far away, but when it is on the point of disappearing, it will still be visible as a punctual and indivisible *minimum.* As is the case for the ideas of the imagination, an ultimate conceivable term is given for our sense impressions, whereby we go directly from nothing to a minimal perceivable reality not resolvable into smaller parts.

Hume might have added that—while it may be true that under the microscope the same ink blot would reveal a universe of bacteria that made it look like a painting by Kandinsky—from the point of view of our perceptual abilities, it is a black spot, nothing more or less.

If it can be granted that for Peirce the Ground is what I referred to as primary iconism, let us bear in mind that the Ground is an element, a marker, a quality that is (for whatever reason) being isolated and considered in itself. *By whom* is it isolated? Potentially isolable, it becomes isolated when a subject isolates it, from a certain point of view, and at that point it becomes the terminus a quo of an inferential process, *in an upward* and not a downward direction—toward the series of relationships, in other words, that bind that spot to me and to my perceptual interests, not toward the series of the infinite possible decompositions of the spot itself.

This, it seems to me, is exactly what happens when Peirce tells us that we feel the blackness of the ink as Firstness. It is possible that—to be able to recognize that what strikes our senses is a quality of blackness—the brain deep down performs an immense number of successive operations. I also agree with Paolucci (2005) that, for the empirical concept of *dog* as well, the Kantian intellect may make use, not of images, but of a flowchart. But, aside from the fact that the brain too, as a computational machine, must come to a stop at a certain point in order to be able to transmit "blackness," at the level of conscious perception we are not aware of that additional fractalization. There is a threshold on this side of which we perceive or sense "black" as Firstness, primary iconism (or whatever you choose to call it), and that is the starting point for our all subsequent inferences.

Commenting on Hume, William James (1987: 1061) declared: "Either your experience is of no content, of no change, or it is of a perceptible amount of content or change. Your acquaintance with reality grows literally by buds or drops of perception. Intellectually and on reflection you can divide these into components, but as immediately given they come totally or not at all."

Zellini also cites Wittgenstein (*Notebooks*, 18, 6, 15):

> If the complexity of an object is definitive of the sense of the proposition, then it must be portrayed in the proposition to the extent that it does determine the sense. And to the extent that its composition is *not* definitive of *this* sense, to this extent the objects of this proposition are *simple*. THEY *cannot* be further divided. . . .
>
> What I mean is: if, e.g. I say that this watch is not in the drawer, there is absolutely no need for it to FOLLOW LOGICALLY that a wheel that is in the watch is not in the drawer, for perhaps *I had not the least knowledge* that the wheel was in the watch, and hence could not have meant by "this watch" the complex in which the wheel occurs. And it is certain— moreover—that I do not see all the parts of my *theoretical* visual field. Who knows *whether* I see infinitely many points?
>
> Let us suppose that we were to see a circular patch: is the circular form its *property*? Certainly not. It seems to be a "structural" property. And if I notice that a spot is round, am I not noticing an infinitely complicated structural property? . . .
>
> A proposition can, however, quite well treat of infinitely many points without being infinitely complex in a particular sense.[8]

Let us attempt a paraphrasis in terms of perception. The complexity of a *quale,* if it is definitive of the meaning of a perception or a perceptual

---

8. English translation: Wittgenstein (1961: 63e–65e).

judgment, must be present and recognized as pertinent to the perception insofar as it determines the meaning of the perception. And to the extent to which the further segmentability of the *quale* is not definitive for *this* perception, to the same extent that *quale* is simple or primary. It is valid as Firstness and there are no *pertinent* inferential processes below its threshold.

To conclude (seeing that I began with Saint Thomas), I would like to quote Nicholas of Cusa: "Only in a finite fashion is the infinite form received," *Of Learned Ignorance*, II, 11).

16

The Definitions in Croce's *Aesthetic*

It may seem odd to include a critique of Benedetto Croce's *Aesthetic* in a collection of essays devoted to the history of semiotics and the philosophy of language. But, apart from the fact that the full title of Croce's work *(The Aesthetic as the Science of Expression and of the Linguistic in General)*[1] entitles us to speculate on what "linguistics in general" might mean for Croce, the present chapter will deal for the most part with the lack of precision of the definitions on which the *Aesthetic* is founded. In a volume that opened

---

A reworking of a book review, written for *La rivista dei libri* in October 1991, of the new edition of Croce's *Estetica* published in 1990 by Adelphi. The essay was republished in Eco (1997) with the title "Croce e l'intuizione" (but it was not included in the English translation of that work, *Kant and the Platypus* [Eco 2000]). [*Translator's note:* Page references to Croce's *Estetica* in this chapter are to the English translation by Colin Lyas (Croce 1992).]

1. The work was first published by Sandron in 1902 (when Croce was thirty-five years old) and represented the point of arrival of a study begun in 1898. After an initial reprint by Sandron in 1904, subsequent editions were published by Laterza, with the ninth edition—the last in the author's lifetime—appearing in 1950. For three of these reprintings, Croce wrote new prefaces (dated November 1907, September 1921, and January 1941) pointing out corrections that he had made in the text (see Maggi 1989) to bring it into line with the subsequent development of his thought (his *Logica, Filosofia della pratica, Teoria e storia della storiografia,* and, naturally, his *Breviario d'estetica, Aesthetica in nuce, Problemi di estetica, Nuovi saggi di estetica,* and *La poesia*). Since the author did not make any changes after the 1941 edition, we must presume that he still considered it current at mid-century. The 1941 *ne varietur* is the text reprinted by Adelphi and discussed in what follows.

with a critique of the most venerable model of definition (the Porphyrian tree)—whose inability to define we attempted to demonstrate, but to which we must at least grant an almost heroic effort of logical rigor—we feel duty bound to examine a theoretical work which undermines its own project through the dramatically approximate nature of the definitions it pretends to provide.

Rereading the *Aesthetic* today, we encounter a number of ideas that have become part of received wisdom, as well as the record of a series of battles lost from the outset. Among the latter, this is not the place to tackle the indefensible equation between aesthetics and "linguistics in general," a paradox of such proportions as to call for a separate treatment of its own.[2] What seems to me more urgent is an examination of Croce's theory of intuition, not just because this is the first topic the work addresses, but because with it Croce intends to lay the cornerstone of his entire system.

1. The book's incipit asserts that knowledge takes two forms: it is either intuitive or logical, and, consequently, knowing means producing either representations or concepts. But, after passing in review several traditional woolly notions regarding the nature of *intuition,* Croce confronts the problem himself, not by definition but by example: "the net result in the case of a work of art is an intuition" (p. 2). The procedure would be incorrect if it was Croce's intention to demonstrate what art is, taking the notion of intuition as his starting point; but in fact his intention is to demonstrate what intuition is, taking as his starting point the experience we have of art. Even in this latter case, we would simply have gone from example to antonomasia, if it were not for the fact that the antonomasia in fact conceals an absolute identity.

For Croce, intuition is not pure sensation (which in any case is not pure, but matter without form, passivity), even when the latter is seen, in Kantian fashion, as formed and organized in space and time (we have intuitions outside of space and time, such as when we react with a spontaneous cry to a sensation of pain or a sentimental impulse). It would appear at first blush, however, that the result of perception is intuition. True, Croce's intuition has wider implications, since we have intuitions of what today we would call "counterfactual" states of affairs, while successful perception requires repre-

---

2. The reader is referred to De Mauro (1965: ch. IV).

sentation and reality to be congruent. Our author suggests, however, that what we call a representation or an image could be intuition, especially when we reflect that the phenomenon of intuition also applies to the nonverbal or to what cannot necessarily be put into words, as is the case, for instance, when we intuit the form of a triangle.

Nevertheless, the intuitive nature of perception becomes problematic once Croce introduces (p. 8) the twin category that dominates his aesthetics, affirming that every true intuition and representation is also, inseparably, *expression,* because "the spirit only intuits by making, forming, expressing" (pp. 8–9). Intuiting a geometrical figure, then, means having its image so clear in one's mind as to be able to trace it immediately on paper or on a blackboard.

At this point Croce has not yet excluded perceptions from the category of intuitions, but he leads us to suspect that, if indeed they are intuitions, they are extremely imperfect ones. The uneducated fisherman, who may not even know how to use a sextant, can find his way back to port even at the height of a storm, because he "recognizes" every feature of the coast, every indentation. This is because he is working with a stored system of perceptions, present and past. But if he were asked to make a drawing of the coastline, he would be incapable of doing so. The anthropologists have given us many examples of natives who know every bend of the river they sail on every day, but when confronted with a map are completely at a loss. Or again, it is a common experience for lovers who are apart not to be able to picture the features of the beloved, however fully and adoringly they "perceive" those features when the beloved is present. They are frustrated by this form of expressive impotence, though the sentiment that accompanies this imperfect reevocation remains extremely vivid (and recognition of the beloved when he or she appears is of course immediate, even at a great distance, as if we knew their most imperceptible movements by heart).

If perceiving and representing to oneself were the same thing as intuition, which coincides with the most complete kind of expression, what happens when, having known someone at the age of twenty, young, clean-shaven with a shock of curly hair, I run into him again at forty, bald or white-haired, with a grey beard? The completeness of today's intuition not being commensurate with the completeness of yesterday's intuition, I ought not to recognize anything at all. Instead I say: "How you've changed, it doesn't look like you!" This implies that knowing a person means selecting as pertinent certain features, in a kind of mnemonic schema (not necessarily exclusively morphological, because I may have selected a twinkle in the eye or a crease at the corner of the mouth), and preserving in our memories a "type" with which we compare every "token" of the person, each time I see him or her. The type of the beloved breaks down precisely because I try to pack in an infinite number of pertinent traits, the voracity of my passion makes me want to memorize too much. Croce is the first to recognize that "even of our closest friend, the person to whom we are close every hour of every day, we possess intuitively only a very few physiognomic traits" (p. 10).

In the face of these problems, Croce decides (pp. 13–14) that

> the world that we normally intuit is a petty thing and translates itself into petty expressions that are gradually enlarged and made more adequate only by an increasing spiritual concentration at certain given moments. They are the internal words that we say to ourselves, the judgments we express tacitly: 'there's a man, there's a horse, this is heavy, this is bitter, I like this, etc., etc.': it is a dazzle of light and colour that, pictorially, could only find a true and proper expression in a hotchpotch [the word Croce uses is *guazzabuglio*] of colour, and from which one could hardly extract a few distinct details. These, and nothing else, are what we possess in our everyday lives and are what serves as the basis of our everyday actions. (p. 10)

Guazzabuglio or "hotchpotch" seems to me an extremely effective term to describe what we are faced with in everyday life, and I shall use it. What is it that rises above this quotidian hotchpotch? The intuition-expression of Raphael, who sees, knows, and reproduces on canvas *La Fornarina*. Intuition-expression belongs only to art, and "good" art at that, given that Croce is prepared to assign to the hotchpotch the imperfect expressions of Manzoni, Proust, Mallarmé, and many others.

Hence, the first form of the spirit, the form onto which the lucidity of the concept *and* ethical action *and* economic action must be grafted, is that of great art. The rest—our perceptions of the world, our encounters with other people and nature—belongs to the territory of the *guazzabuglio*.

2. At this point we might expect Croce to define art, or the moment when intuition-expression occurs in the pure state. And in fact, in his "Conclusion," he writes: "having defined the nature of intuitive or expressive knowledge, the aesthetic or artistic act (I and II), and noted the other forms of knowledge, and the further combinations of this form" (p. 154). Unfortunately, this affirmation is false: nowhere in the *Aesthetic* do we find a definition of art that is not a definition of intuition, and nowhere do we find a definition of intuition that does not refer to the definition of art. The reason would seem to be that "the boundaries between the expression-intuitions that are called 'art' and those that are commonly called 'non-art' are purely empirical: they cannot be defined" (p. 14). Thus, Croce takes, so to speak, the experience of art (the confident immediate recognition of what art is) as a primitive that acts as a starting point for conferring on intuition all the (undefined) characteristics of art. Nor do things change when we proceed to formulas such as "lyrical intuition" (*Breviario d'estetica*, 1), since we discover that "lyrical" is not a specific *difference*, but a synonym of "intuition." For a devotee of the Circle, the demonstrative circularity is perfect: the only intuition is artistic intuition, and art is intuition. This definitional circularity may have relieved Croce's earliest readers of critical responsibility, reassuring them that art was nothing more or less than what they felt art was, and all the rest was professorial hair-splitting, to which the second part of the book, devoted to the history of aesthetics, does summary justice.

If this seems like a harsh judgment, we have only to consider such glaring tautologies as "it seems appropriate for us to define the beautiful as successful expression, or better, as expression *simpliciter,* since expression, when it is not successful, is not expression" (p. 87); or examples of woolliness that would not be countenanced even in a beginner, such as when, on page 78, the author, distinguishing "successful expressions" from those that are "flawed," compares two pairs of paintings, of which we are told nothing except that one is "devoid of inspiration" and the other "inspired," one "strongly felt," the other "coldly allegorical," though no explanation is offered of exactly what a "strongly felt" painting might look like. You can't help thinking that many of Croce's readers must have been delighted to see the feeble interjections they used in the cultural circles of the provincial Italy of the late nineteenth century raised to the level of critical categories.

The elusive nature of aesthetic form deprives Croce of a flexible theory of judgment and interpretation. A promising idea is presented in the fourth chapter: namely, that forming an aesthetic opinion means putting oneself in the artist's place and following the process of creation "with the assistance of the physical sign he has produced." Genius and taste are, then, substantially identical. But the fact that they share the same nature does not necessarily mean that any judgment of taste must fit the work of art in the same way and from the same point of view. Croce is not unaware of the empirical phenomenon of the variety of judgments, due to the evolution of cultural conditions as well as to the physical nature of the work. But he considers it is always possible, with a proper philological effort, to recreate the original conditions and retrace the process in the only correct way possible. Either everything the artist intuited is fully reproduced, or the process is stymied. *Tertium non datur.* There is no third way. Since he did not develop a theory of the conditions that make a form what it is, the suspicion could not cross Croce's mind that a form might lend itself to several different interpretations, each of which captures it fully from a separate point of view (as will be the case in Pareyson's aesthetics). Even his 1917 reflections on the cosmic character of art presuppose that the successful work is like Borges's Aleph from which one may view the entire cosmos: it's all or nothing. Croce's theory of form ignores Nicholas of Cusa's *complicatio,* which is likewise ignored in his history of aesthetics.

3. We feel a similar sense of unease when Croce announces his explanation of what he means by *conceptual* knowledge, as opposed to the intuitive form. His model of pure knowledge is the lucid and complete logical concept. When it comes to knowledge directed toward practical ends, all we have are his notorious pseudo-concepts. But if we take a closer look at what pseudo-concepts mean for Croce, we realize that they are far more important for him than they would later become for so many of his followers. In the opinion of the latter, they were mere mechanical lucubrations that the philosopher would be well advised not to meddle with. Croce on the other hand meddles as a matter of principle, because the pseudo-concepts of the sciences are fundamental to the orientation of our practical actions. We realize, with some satisfaction, that the pseudo-concepts too belong to the world of the inchoate hotchpotch in which our perceptions are formed, and like them proceed by standardizations, incomplete profiles of reality, and can

always be jettisoned, as we all do with our own perceptions of the day before ("I must admit that that wardrobe seemed bigger than it really is"). The world of the hotchpotch is the everyday territory we live in, in which we proceed by trial and error, assays, conjecture, and, seeing a shadow pass by in the dark, we hazard a guess that it must have been a dog, and discovering that Mars passes through two points that cannot belong to a circle, we hazard a guess, as Kepler did, that the orbits of the planets may be elliptical.

Croce grasps this world very concretely, with a keen sense of life's flux, and he describes it vividly: but after having recognized it, he loses interest, as if philosophy were not supposed to get involved with the human condition as it really is, but only with the way things ought to be, with forms so pure that they defy any attempt at definition. And yet Croce expects philosophy to prompt his readers to exclaim "I felt that too!," and he remarks: "There is no greater satisfaction for a philosopher than to discover his philosophical ideas in the opinions of common sense" (Croce 1995: 211). It is as if Croce were tempted to flatter false common sense when he is explaining what pure intuition is by talking about a "strongly felt" painting, and that he turns away out of boredom when common sense is recognized in the everyday hotchpotch.

The quest after pure conceptual knowledge gives rise to a fair number of embarrassments. In chapter 3 of the *Aesthetic* an attempt is made to define it as "knowledge of the relationships between things, and the things are intuitions" (p. 24). "Intuitions are: this river, this lake, this brook, this rain, this glass of water; concept is: "water." But we have been told that "this lake" is a true intuition only when painted by a great painter, whereas the lake I intuit is a schema, a sketch, or a label. If conceptual knowledge consists in establishing relationships among drafts and sketches, what we are really talking about are pseudo-concepts. And if it consists in establishing relationships between fully realized intuitions, the pure concept of water can only emerge from the relationship among the various intuitions of water had, say, by Dante, Leonardo, and Canaletto. We could get to this point, if, treating spiritual phases and historical phases as identical, we were to take in a chronological sense Vico's proposal that the original idiom of mankind was a poetical language: "were it not for the fact that a wholly poetical period in the history of humanity, without abstractions and without reasoning, never existed, indeed could not even be imagined" (p. 293). But Vico never believed that, except in a metaphorical sense, seeing that, while he posits a hieroglyphic language more fantastic than the symbolic and *pistolare* or "epistolary" languages, still "as gods, heroes and men began at the same time (for they were after all men who imagined the gods and believed their own heroic nature to be a mixture of the divine and human natures), so these three languages began at the same time" (*Scienza Nuova Seconda,* 2, 2, 4, p. 189, my translation).

With a much greater sense of concreteness, and less exclusive obsession with distinctions, the Croce of the 1909 *Logica* will posit, as strictly complementary to definitional judgment (which in the *Aesthetic* still figures as the only manifestation of logical thought [p. 48]), individual "or perceptive" judgment. Each of the two presupposes the other, and hence perception is shot through with concept: "to perceive means to apprehend a given fact as having such and such a nature, and is therefore the same as thinking and judging it. Not even the most fleeting impression, the most inconsequential fact is perceived by us except insofar as it is thought" (*Logica,* p. 109). Conversely, every universal definition will appear as the answer to a specific question, historically situated, starting from "a darkness that is in search of light," to the point where "the nature of the question will lend its color to the answer." How, then, are we to remove the logical form itself from the generous and vital territory of the hotchpotch and from the gamble of conjecture?

Once more, Croce succumbs to the fascination of the hotchpotch, but he does not ask himself, for instance, what are the probabilities that a perception or a definition may be, if not true, at least acceptable—and this despite the fact that, starting with the *Aesthetic,* he reserved this very concern for history, which, as knowledge of individual facts, neither unreal nor fantastic, must nevertheless resort to conjectures, suppositions, probabilities (p. 32).

4. Prepared to compromise on the hotchpotch as far as conceptual knowledge goes, the Croce of the *Aesthetic* seems determined not to give ground as far as intuition is concerned. Intuition is always without a conceptual component; at most it may employ concepts as the subject of artistic expression—but in that case "They were, indeed, once concepts, but have now become simply components of intuitions" (p. 2).

This explains why the Croce of the *Aesthetic* declares war on prescriptive rules: no doubt out of the need to distance himself from the preceding tradition, but in the end throwing out the baby with the bath water. In combating the rules, whether they are rhetorical rules, the classification of literature into genres, or the phenomenology of "styles," Croce forgets that, in the hotchpotch of conjecture, we make ample use of formulas such as "military bearing" or "sickly complexion," without these formulas exhausting or reducing the perception we may have of an individual in his or her irreducible peculiarity. If I say: "Yesterday I met the minister's new assistant, I was expecting some kind of seminarist, but he looks more like a tennis player," it does not imply pigeonholing a new experience in terms of a stereotype; on the contrary, it means using clichés to underline its novelty. In the same way, classifying something as a historical novel or a metaphor defines in the first case the expectations we bring to the work (expectations that may in fact be unexpectedly thwarted), and in the second the umpteenth but completely original variation on a rhetorical schema that has assumed a wide variety of forms over the centuries. While it is undeniable that "every true work of art has violated an established genre" (p. 41), the very fact that Croce realizes it merely highlights the role played by his awareness of the genre and his expectations and suspicions of it in generating his surprise and his positive judgment of taste. Much of Ariosto's irony and his humor would be lost if, in his *Orlando Furioso,* he had not been playing fast and loose with the genre of the chivalric epic.

"The amount of damage wreaked by these [rhetorical] distinctions" (p. 77) is something that we all know, and maybe in 1902 there was some point in combating the facile rhetoric taught in Episcopal seminaries. But how much harm Croce did by broadcasting his scorn for rhetoric (with a rhetorical ability and a gift for polemical oversimplification that entranced his readers) has not perhaps been sufficiently realized. See, for instance, the argument against the definition of metaphor as "a word used in place of the literally correct one" (p. 77). The definition is certainly inadequate, but Croce is not in the least concerned with the problem—which still exercises not ignoble minds—of defining what really happens, not merely to language but to our cognitive structures themselves, when we use a trope. He simply comments: "And why give oneself the trouble of substituting a different word in place of the literally correct one and of taking the longer and worse way when the shorter and better is known to us? Perhaps because, as it is commonly said, the literal word, in certain cases, is not as expressive as the supposed nonliteral or metaphorical word? But if this is the case, the metaphor just is in this event the 'literal' word; and that which is usually called 'literal,' if it were used in this case, would be less expressive and therefore wholly improper" (p. 77). "Similar observations of elementary common sense," however, are precisely that, elementary, and, instead of addressing the question, repeat it back as the answer. We are all aware that, when Dante says "conobbi il tremolar della marina" ("I recognized the trembling of the sea"), he is using a most felicitous expression, but the problem is to explain what made *both* Dante's text *and* the entire patrimony of the language take a quantum leap, when the new expression is adjudged "perfectly proper" and takes the place of another whose meaning, however, is not cancelled. To address problems like these is the least we can expect of an aesthetics that claims at the same time to be a general linguistics.

It should be said in Croce's defense that all his polemical exaggerations are always tempered with a great deal of common sense. Thus, having condemned the notion of literary genres, he is prepared to admit their practical utility. While such "groupings" retain their usefulness as criteria for classifying books in a library, they are also useful for selecting certain books and reading them with a certain attitude of mind—the attitude that will allow Croce to define as "tragic" in Torquato Tasso "the vital impulse and *joie de vivre* that at times find their issue in suffering and death and are thereby redeemed." What's more, the genres thrown out the door come back in again through the window when Croce finds himself having to explain how an architectural work, whose practical intentions no one can deny, can produce an aesthetic effect: all the artist has to do is to make "the destination of the object that is to serve a practical end enter as material for his aesthetic intuition and external expression. He has no need to add anything to the object in order to make it an instrument for aesthetics impressions: it will be such if perfectly adapted to its purposes" (p. 113). Excellently put: but why not apply the principle to someone proposing to produce a chivalric epic, a seascape, or a madrigal?

As for rhetoric, Croce is the first to see in its classifications a way of identifying a "family likeness" (a fine pre-Wittgensteinian expression)—resemblances, in other words, which reveal spiritual relationships between artists. It is by considering these procedural similarities that we can confer a minimum of legitimacy on translations, "not insofar as they are reproductions (which it would be useless to attempt) of the original expressions, but insofar as they are productions of expressions which resemble their originals more or less closely" (p. 81).

5. More embarrassing is the discourse Croce broaches in chapter 6 of the *Aesthetic,* devoted to the difference between theoretical activity and practical activity, in which the incredible proposition is announced whereby the intuition-expression of art is entirely contained in its inner elaboration, while its technical and material exteriorization, in marble, on canvas, in emitted vocal sounds, is totally accessory and inessential, having as its only end the "conservation and reproduction" of the original inner illumination (p. 108). Just a minute! Isn't this the same author who a hundred pages earlier had declared "One often hears people claim to have in their heads many important thoughts but not to be able to express them. But the truth is that if they *truly* had them, they would have coined them in so many ringing words" (p. 9)? Of course, Croce can tell us that putting those thoughts into concrete words is no more than an empirical necessity, a stenographic device, so to speak, for the record, to let him or another judge know that the thoughts really were there. But what are we to say of the famous tenor who one night, after having a perfect internal intuition of a magnificent high C, is hooted off the stage by the gallery merely because he had tried to externalize it, just for the record, only to have his vocal cords fail him? Who knows his craft but has a trembling hand, as Dante put it (*Paradiso,* XIII, 78). The fact is that what Croce says does not correspond to what we know from the practice of other artists, who have made sketch after sketch trying to come up with the definitive image, or who have struggled with a set square and a pair of compasses to produce a perfect vanishing point.

On this point, however, Croce's convictions are unfortunately adamant and seem to spring from an extremely limited familiarity with the arts, not only in the sense of his never having practiced one, but also in the sense that he never had much interest in what artists actually did. Croce condemns as superficial the observation that "the artist creates his expressions in the act of painting and sketching, writing and composing," because artists "in fact, do not make strokes of the brush without first having seen [the work] by means of the imagination" (p. 114). But if the word "reality" has any meaning in Croce's system, actual artists in fact never tire of recounting how the consistency of the material stimulated their imaginations, and it is only when reciting their rough drafts aloud that some poets find the clue that leads them to change the rhythm and come up with the right word. Croce, however, states, in *La poesia,* that poets abhor the empirical externalization of their inner intuitions to the point that are reluctant to recite their poems out loud. Which is statistically inaccurate as far as the poets I know are concerned.

In his *Breviario d'estetica* Croce demonstrates the inessential nature of the technical aspects of art, citing the cases of very great painters who have used colors that faded over time; but in so doing he confuses artistic technique with the science of materials. In the *Aesthetic* there is an interesting page describing the efforts of a poet who tries out different words and phrases in search of "an expression for an impression he feels, or of which he has a presentiment" (p. 132); but only a few pages earlier he had said that artists whose expression is still unformed apply an experimental brushstroke "not to externalize their expressions (which do not then exist), but as if to try out and to have a simple point of support" or as a "heuristic device" (p. 114). What Croce calls a "point of support" is like the hotchpotch of our everyday perception: it's all we have. But what common sense recognizes as everything, for philosophy becomes nothing, with the minor inconvenience that everything that's left becomes impalpable.

I believe it can be pacifically agreed that in these pages Croce affirms the exact contrary of the truth, if the truth is what common sense concedes in the light of a thousand recorded experiences. I am not sufficiently familiar with the entirety of his works to know whether Croce ever commented on the sonnet in which Michelangelo reminds us that: "Non ha l'ottimo artista alcun concetto / c'un marmo solo in sé non conconscriva / col suo soverchio, e solo a quello arriva / la man che ubbidisce all'intelletto" ["The best of artists does not have any concept / that a single [block of] marble does not encompass / with its excess, and only to that [concept] arrives / the hand that obeys the intellect"]. If he read it, he forgot it, on purpose. Because what Michelangelo is telling us here is that the artist finds his intuition-expression in a dialogue with his materials, with their vein, their bias, the possibilities they offer. Indeed Michelangelo goes still further, for the sake of hyperbole: the statue is already present in the marble, and all the artist has to do is to remove the excess that conceals it.

And here we have Croce, as it were, contradicting Michelangelo, speaking of the "piece of marble *that embodies* the statue of Moses and of the piece of coloured wood *embodying* the Transfiguration" (p. 112, my emphasis). The citation leaves no room for doubt: what we consider works of art (over whose deterioration, restoration, counterfeiting ,or theft we agonize) are merely the *containers* of the only, unique, true (and at this point unattainable) works that existed in the completely inward intuitions of their authors. Elsewhere, speaking of how the judgment of taste retraces the genesis of the original intuition, Croce will refer to these physical embodiments as mere "signs," instruments practically didactic in nature that facilitate the process of reconstruction. Not realizing that, for a philosopher reluctant to acknowledge the social existence of systems of signs, with their own laws and definable unities, who sees instead every expressive act as a *unicum* in which the language is, as it were, reborn as though for the first time, a sign ought not be something negligible, and the relationship between sign and intuition should be understood to be less accidental and external.

Croce tells us that that block of marble and that wooden panel are said to be beautiful only as a metaphor. Then it occurs to him that we really are using a metaphor when we say the score that contains Mozart's *Don Giovanni* is beautiful, and he recognizes that the first metaphor is more immediate than the second. But, for an author who has refused to define metaphor, the solution leaves something to be desired. What does this difference in immediateness between metaphors conceal? And what is the status of the *Don Giovanni* contained in the score? Is it something that exists in the realm of sound (and therefore physically externalized and externalizable) or is it the original intuition that Mozart could even have refused to perform? And why does it continue to be performed today, rather than simply evoked by reading the score, as Croce believes dramatic works should be read, instead of seeing them externalized on the stage?

It seems clear that what Croce is articulating (encouraged by his lack of interest in everything that goes by the name of "nature," and dominated by his humanistic education with its verbo-centric model, whereby beauty is inevitably defined with reference to verbal poetry) is a complex paralogism whose phases it will be useful to follow.

(i) First of all he is aware that there exist *volatile* expressions (in the sense in which *verba volant* ["words fly away"] and do not congeal in mid-air as Rabelais put it) and *permanent* expressions, such as statues or drawings. The difference is so evident that humankind has developed means by which to make the first permanent, from writing to magnetic tapes—authentic physical vehicles for the recording of previous expressions in the realm of sound.

(ii) From this correct empirical observation he draws the erroneous conclusion that volatile expressions are not material facts, as if writing and recordings did not record sounds. His verbal experience must have made him think of poets who mouth their poems to themselves, thinking of the sound they could give them. But they do so because they have already had experience of what sounds they could produce, so that an experimental psychologist (a category Croce didn't have much time for) might argue that, when we think of Pavarotti hitting a high C, our organs of phonation, however imperceptibly, imitate the externalization we are thinking of. When we intuit, what we intuit are externalizations; when we think, we do not think outside the body but with the body. Croce is sufficiently well aware of this to have devoted a rather memorable passage to the phenomenon of synesthesia, in which he says that words on the page evoke not just thoughts but auditory, tactile, and thermal sensations. If Michelangelo had been born blind, he could never have "intuited" his Moses.

(iii) Beguiled by his (empirical) experience of discourses that take place in the mind (of which, however, we become fully aware only when they have been "minted in the currency of words"—and the physical metaphor of coining is worth noting), Croce makes this possibility into an absolute and extends it to the arts of permanence. Of course, we can all imagine a sculptor who, away from his workshop, imagines down to the tiniest details the statue he could produce with his chisel. But he can do so only because he has sweated over marble before, because he has hammered away in his shop; he can do so in the same way anyone can intuit that if they swallow a cube of ice they will feel a pain in the middle of their forehead, because they recall having already felt it under similar circumstances. Without the memory of our previous natural experiences we can intuit nothing, and someone who has never smelled a verbena can never intuit the scent of a verbena, just as someone born blind can never intuit what a *dolce color d'oriental zaffiro* ("sweet color of an oriental sapphire" [Dante, *Purgatory,* I, 13]) might be.

When we consider these paradoxes we understand why the generations that came after Croce were fascinated by alternative theories: by Pareyson's appeal to the fundamental importance of the materials in the genesis of a work of art, by Anceschi's concern for the artist's poetics, by Dorfles and

Formaggio's emphasis on artistic techniques, by Morpurgo Tagliabue's return to the hoary concepts of style and rhetorical apparatus, by Della Volpe's insistence on the "rational" moment in the artistic process, not to mention the liberation that came with reading Dewey's *Art as Experience,* in which the fullness of naturalistic empiricism is revalued. The question was what was the place of "the philosophy of the four words" (the polemical characterization is Gentile's) within that vital flux to which Croce was after all so attentive.[3] How to do justice to Croce himself, in whom there was constantly "a hiatus, as it were, a hidden conflict between his extremely detailed analysis of vast sectors of human experience and culture, and his 'system.' . . . On the one hand, part and parcel of the precise discussion of cultural data and experience, we find 'concepts,' extremely 'impure' if you will, but precious if we are to understand, in other words, connect and clarify, the multiple forms taken by human action and history. On the other, a few extremely abstract ideas, whose development is affirmed rather than demonstrated" (Garin 1966: 2:1315).

6. Perhaps, however, it is the unresolved persistence of this gap that accounts for the influence Croce's works have enjoyed: readers grasped the abstractness of the few ideas, but they were attracted to them because they saw them as the logical conclusion of the concrete analysis, admirable for its common sense, clarity, and penetration. In the hotchpotch the readers recognized both the embarrassments of their own personal experience and their longing for an uncontaminated idea of beauty, truth, goodness, and the useful itself—values that all the metaphysical systems so abhorred by Croce had defined in their hyperuranic spiritual nature, without descending to compromise with that corporality that is mere envelope, mortal coil, the prison of the soul. In Croce they saw both the confirmation of the inevitable and the promise of the desirable, interpreting as systematic mediation what was instead an unresolved contradiction.

These readers were delighted to be told that art was fundamentally what they were hoping it was, and non-art what they—perturbed and disturbed— could witness all around them. What exactly pure forms were they did not know, but they were quick to embrace a judgment of taste such as that on

---

3. [*Translator's note:* This characterization of Croce's philosophy is that of fellow Italian Idealist and sometime collaborator Giovanni Gentile (1875–1944). The four words in question were aesthetics, logic, economics, and ethics.]

Proust: "one feels that what is dominant in the author's soul is a rather perverse sensual eroticism, an eroticism that already permeates his eagerness to relive the sensations of a distant past. But this state of mind does not achieve clarity in a lyric motif or a poetic form, as occurs instead in the better works of the less complicated but more inspired Maupassant" ("Postille" to *La poesia*). Of Manzoni's *I promessi sposi*, Croce asserts "the critics stubbornly continue to analyze and discuss it as an inspired and poetically successful novel," whereas all it is "from one end to the other, is a novel of moral exhortation, measured and conducted with a firm eye" (*La poesia*, VII). And, if I may be forgiven the invidious comparison (the two texts after all display certain similarities), when in 1937, one year after the appearance of *La poesia*, a much lesser writer attempted to justify his Philistine parody of Manzoni, after praising the author's workmanship in *I promessi sposi* ("ah! what a genius he was!"), he adduced the following alibi for the sacrilege he was about to commit: "The truth is this: that in Manzoni the only thing missing is the poet. . . . Is there a single episode, a character, a personage that remains impressed on my mind with the same ever purer and more glittering clarity that characterizes the immortal creations of art? Well, if I must be sincere, I have to reply in the negative" (Da Verona 1937: viii–xiii).

The thought occurs to us that, instead of Croce creating a readership of Croceans, a readership that already existed, with its own myths and its own unshakable uncertainties regarding the good and the beautiful, adopted him as their spokesperson.

For this readership (and for our good fortune) Croce was then obliged (in *La poesia*) to open up a no man's land (no man's and everyman's), where hotchpotch and purity could live together in peace and reconciliation, a space he called *literature*. To this space Croce could allocate the entertainments composed by the likes of Dumas and Poe, whom he basically enjoyed, as well as the works of authors he did not relish, like Horace and Manzoni. "Literature" is not a spiritual form, it is a part of civility and good manners, it is the realm of prose and civil conversation.

And this is the region from Croce writes. Why are Croce's readers not aware of the unresolved contradiction, why do they see a well-knit system where things were falling apart? Because Croce is a masterly writer. The rhythm, the subtle dosage of sarcasm and pacific reflection, the perfection of his periodic sentences, make everything he thinks or says persuasive. When he says something, he says it so well, that, being said so well, it is unthinkable that it shouldn't also be true. Croce, the great master of oratory and style, succeeds in convincing us of the existence of Poetry (incorporeal and angelified as he understands it) through a corporeal, courtly, harmonious example of Literature.[4]

---

4. [*Translator's note:* In his criticism Croce opposes *poesia* (=poetry), the term he applies to inspired art, and *non-poesia* (=non-poetry), which he also he calls *allotria* (=extraneous matter, padding), *struttura*, or simply, with negative implications, *letteratura* (=literature or intellectual confectionery). Croce's dichotomy is famously hard on the structural elements in that most structured of works, Dante's *Divine Comedy*. Croce and his disciples dominated Italian literary criticism in the first half of the twentieth century and beyond.]

17

Five Senses of the Word "Semantics," from Bréal to the Present Day

The term "semantics" has a number of different meanings, several of which seem to be completely at odds with one another. This state of affairs is often a source of considerable embarrassment in dealing with our students, to whom we find ourselves having to explain that our discipline is a bit like the country where some people call "red" what others call "white" and vice versa. With the result that, every time we use the word "red," we would have to assign it a superscript or subscript number, specifying that we mean "red$_1$ in such and such a sense."

Still, although the term "semantics" may have a number of meanings, those meanings are less irreconcilable than might at first appear.

In 1883 Michel Bréal *(Les lois intellectuelles du langage: Fragment de sémantique)* defined semantics as the science of meaning, but when he came to publish his *Essai de sémantique* in 1897 he gave it the more general subtitle *Science des significations,* and only in chapter IX, in which he proposed to examine "by what causes words, once created and endowed with a certain meaning, are induced to restrict, to extend, to transfer this meaning from one order of ideas to another, to raise or to lower its dignity, in short to

Paper presented at the symposium "La semantica *fin de siècle*: Dalla fondazione di Michel Bréal all'attualità della ricerca" ("*Fin de siècle* semantics: From Michel Bréal's foundation to contemporary research"), held at the Center for Semiotic and Cognitive Studies of the University of San Marino in November 1997. It was later published with the title "Cinque sensi di 'semantica'" ["Five Meanings of 'Semantics'"] (Eco 2001).

change it," does he say "it is this second part which, properly speaking con-stitutes Semantics or the Science of Significations."[1]

Semantics, then, is the science of meanings, but, for Bréal, only insofar as they are subject to historical development. And this is not all. Each time Bréal has to deal with the meaning of a word he proves incapable of isolating it from the set of enunciates, or more extensive fragments of text, in which the word appears. To give but a single example, in the chapter on the laws of specialization, Bréal is less interested in defining the meaning of the French word *plus* than in the fact that it takes on different meanings in dif-ferent expressions.

The notion of semantics, then, is born, historically speaking, in reference to that imponderable entity we label meaning, but only to a lesser extent is it concerned with the meaning of words, or, to put it differently, of terms in iso-lation. For this, what was needed was not a science but an empirical praxis, lexicography in its most hands-on sense, that is, the actual compilation of dictionaries. Still, we must not forget that the whole of lexicography is simply the description of a *langue,* and therefore of an abstract entity, and not of the practical use of *parole* by means of which the speaker "means" something.

17.1. Various Meanings of Semantics

I would argue that the more or less explicit semiotics of former centuries did not question the fact that terms expressed something, but they did not pre-sume that a special science was needed to clarify what that something was. Knowing the signs implied knowing either the things they referred to or the ideas they brought to mind, or the definitions given them by common con-sent, according to which the Latin *homo,* for instance, signified "a mortal rational animal." In any case, for Aristotle, providing correct definitions was a task either for logic (see the *Analytics*) or for the various natural sci-ences, as is seen in his definitions of animals.

If we examine Abelard's use of terminology, we remark that a verbal ex-pression (i) *significat* a mental concept, (ii) *designat* or *denotat* its definition or "meaning," and (iii) *nominat* the thing.

---

1. English translation: Bréal (1964: 99).

What we have here are three notions of semantics: (i) as the study of cognitive processes, (ii) as the study of dictionary or encyclopedia definitions, and (iii) as the study of the truth conditions of sentences. Many of our current problems stem from these medieval perplexities (and they are indeed perplexities: what exactly does a *vox significativa* do—signify, denote, or name?). Furthermore, Abelard's threefold division is missing a fourth dimension, not unknown to previous semiotics, that of the disambiguation of complex texts (see Augustine's *De doctrina christiana*, which is concerned with the "meaning" of a text like that of Scripture). And, lastly, there is also a fifth dimension missing, whose absence in Abelard does not imply its absence in medieval thought. What is missing is what we would call today a *structural semantics* as a theory of content, already present in the binary system of the division of predicables as represented in the *Arbor Porphyriana* (see Chapter 1).

Let us go back then, or let us look forward, beyond Abelard and beyond Bréal, and observe that, in the course of the debates on meaning, five areas of investigation have been identified, sometimes proceeding independently of each other, sometimes contradicting each other, and sometimes one of them presupposing—however acritically—the other:

1. *Semantics as the study of the meaning of terms removed from any context* (for instance, Carnap's theory of meaning postulates, much of componential semantics, and the various forms of semic analysis, not to mention lexicography of every kind and tendency).

2. *Semantics as the study of content systems or structural semantics* (Hjelmslev and structural approaches to semantic fields in general *et similia*).

3. *Semantics as the study of the relation between term (or sentence) and referent, or as the study of reference* (for instance, Morris, Ogden, and Richards, much of analytic philosophy, and *in primis* Kripke). Let me remind the reader, however, of the distinction I posited in *Kant and the Platypus* between (i) providing instructions to identify the possible referent of a term and (ii) the act of reference itself.

4. *Semantics as the study of the truth conditions of propositions expressed by sentences.*

5. *Semantics as the study of the particular meaning that terms or sentences assume in context or in the text as a whole* (this is a vast and variegated field that is concerned with the meaning of the same sentences in different con-

texts and circumstances, for which we may cite in first and foremost the later Wittgenstein, as well as the theory of different discursive isotopies, etc.).

Any student of semiotics is familiar with all these meanings of semantics, and yet it would be optimistic to claim that this awareness is shared by all students of language—not to mention the fact that the semioticians themselves, though well aware of the definition of semantics cited in 3 and 4 above, are often prone to reject it as nonpertinent, or to consider it as a single problem, whereas in fact it involves two quite different problems.

17.2. Encyclopedia Entries

Let us consider a few examples of how the different conceptions of semantics may fail to recognize one another. In the *Dictionnaire raisonné des sciences du langage* of Greimas and Courtés, "truth" is defined.[2] The concept of truth might be foreign to a semanticist in senses 1 and 2, but it is certainly central for anyone concerned with senses 3 and 4 and, as Greimas demonstrates, it cannot be sidestepped by someone concerned with sense 5:

> Truth designates the complex term which subsumes the terms *being* and *seeming* situated on the axis of contraries within the semiotic square of veridictory modalities. It might be helpful to point out that the true is situated within the discourse, because it is the fruit of veridiction operations; this thus excludes any relation (or any homologation) with an external referent.

I suspect that an analytic philosopher would find this definition confused and troublesome. But it would also be troublesome for someone concerned with semantics in sense 3, while it would have to be viewed with some indulgence by someone concerned with sense 4. In fact a truth-conditional approach is not concerned with establishing whether a given proposition is true but rather with what inferences one might legitimately draw *if the proposition were true*. What is certain is that, for someone who subscribes to sense 4, these truth conditions are posited within a "corporate body," or coherent set of assumptions. When, however, doubt is cast upon the existence of this *holistic*

---

2. English translation: Greimas and Courtés (1982: 432).

system, as it is in Davidson, we may say that the principle of charity leads us to assume that a proposition makes sense and is therefore true within a discursive exchange (even if the sentence that conveys it does not present itself as especially perspicuous). Are we then to say that Greimas's definition is so foreign to the analytical *koine?* I am not so sure. Granted, if someone says to me on the freeway "Look out, there's a train ahead," and I am aware that what is in front of me is a trailer truck, given that I have certain convictions concerning the real world, and appealing to the principle of charity, I assume that the speaker meant to say that there was a big rig ahead, and I let the communicative interaction go forward without a hitch. But do I only exercise the principle of charity in cases where I am able to counter an ambiguous sentence with certain convictions based on experience (that is, on what I consider to be true in the outside world), or do I not also behave in the same way when I attribute to someone else convictions that coincide with those I hold on the basis of a shared system of assumptions?

Let us suppose that a student of astronomy were to say to me: "Assuming that, after Galileo, the sun revolves around the earth and not vice versa," I understand perfectly well, based on a shared system of assumptions, that he is asserting something false, but, applying the principle of charity, I assume that what he meant to say was what I consider to be true, in other words, the exact opposite of what he actually said (and that what he said was a common or garden *lapsus*), and I go on listening to his argument. In such a case I would be considering as true not what is confirmed by my experience of the outside world but what is guaranteed to be true by the holistic system of our received assumptions. We have only to stretch a little the notion of "situated within the discourse" for the conversation between a Greimasian and a Davidsonian, provided each of them exercises a reasonable principle of charity, to lose its dramatic edge.

But let us proceed with our examples. In the Einaudi *Enciclopedia,* under the entry "Semantica," Diego Marconi—after defining semantics as the study of meaning—assumes that standard semantics is concerned only with natural languages. He devotes the bulk of his article to model semantics (sense 4), the semantics of possible worlds (senses 3 and 4), the dictionary vs. encyclopedia discussion (sense 1), but only in his introduction does he mention the existence of another tendency known as componential analysis (which is certainly concerned with meaning 1 and, for the purpose of establishing theoretically the number of components, presupposes sense 2).

The fact is that Marconi, at the time of writing, was an orthodox analyst and shared the conviction, common to many of his persuasion, that these problems were part and parcel of lexicography (senses 1 and 2); and for the analysts lexicography had nothing to do with semantics.

In the *Encyclopedic Dictionary of Semiotics* edited by T. A. Sebeok (1986), the entry "Semantics," written by Bierwisch, at first tries to elude the often mortal embrace between semantics and the study of natural languages. After defining semantics as the study of meaning, Bierwisch excogitates the formula "A interprets B as representing C," in which B is an object or an event, which permits it to be understood as something different from a phonation or a verbal enunciate. The author lists all the problems and takes into account the various positions, but in the body of the article he gives his own personal solution to these problems. Thanks to a happy decision by the editorial board, an entry on "Seme" (by Schogt) follows, in which we find a broad investigation into other linguistic positions, for the most part structural in their orientation (Lyons, Lamb, Pottier, Apresjan, Coseriu, Buyssens, Prieto, Greimas, etc.). Unfortunately, there is no mention of truth-conditional semantics—for some scholars the only semantics worthy of the name.

On the other hand, the Greimas-Courtés *Dictionnaire,* through a number of different entries, provides a review of the various lexicographical theories in the semantic and notional fields. They examine the componential theory, taken to the Hjelmslevian extreme of its own ambitions (how from "a score of binary semic categories, considered as the taxonomical basis of possible combinations" one can succeed "in producing several million sememic combinations"). They assume as prerequisites of any semantics that it be at once *generative* (recognizing too the work of the post-Chomskyan generativists), *syntagmatic* (attempting to overcome the limits of linguistic taxonomism and come to grips with a semantics of the sentence and finally of the text, sense 5), and *general;* semantics is not limited to the investigation of linguistic meanings but must address the semantics of the natural world insofar as it is made manifest by the various semiotics. I would say that senses 1, 2, and 5 are covered, and at this point we cannot expect Greimas to give his attention to model semantics or to the semantics of possible worlds (given that his treatment takes no account whatsoever of modal logic) or to truth-conditional semantics, considering the position he has staked out with regard to truth. The dictionary proceeds, then, with entries dedicated to Discursive semantics, Fundamental semantics, Generative semantics, Narrative semantics, Seme and Sememe, all, however, in a strictly Greimasian key.

The most balanced treatment is the one appearing in John Lyons's two-volume *Semantics,* which represents a tolerant approach to all of the relevant traditions. Being on the one hand a linguist, exposed to the sirens of European theory, and on the other an insular Briton, did not prove a disadvantage for Lyons. But he does not formulate a theory, he expounds what has previously been said on the subject, and he can therefore afford to be ecumenical. Ecumenical, but hardly systematic.

Is ecumenism a *pis aller,* a necessity for the popularizer, or may it also be a theoretical choice? I would choose the second option. The problem of meaning is so complex that it is preferable to be syncretistic rather than a dogmatist and fundamentalist on the subject.

17.3. Does the Notion of Meaning Still Have a Meaning?

I remarked earlier that it is still a moot point whether or not semantics is concerned with the meaning of words (sense 1). It would appear that all we need do is pass from sense 1 to the subsequent meanings to accept that semantics is still concerned with meaning. It is arguable, however, whether the notion of meaning still enjoys citizenship rights in sense 3 (for some—for instance Quine—meaning can be shelved as long as one has a good theory of reference). Most interestingly, it is also debatable whether the notion of meaning (at least in the sense of a meaning conventionally agreed—sense 1) still has citizenship rights in sense 5. So long as, apropos of sense 5, we have in mind Greimas, in whom a generative semantics of texts is preceded by a structural semantics, there is no reason for this suspicion. But deconstructionists and Davidsonians, or those like Sperber and Wilson who subscribe to the theory of inference, can also be subsumed under sense 5.

Here meaning itself is called into question. In the case of Derrida, the denial of so-called transcendental meaning seems to be directed rather at the single meaning of a text (which he certainly calls into question) while sense 1 is not in question. In his *De la grammatologie (Of Grammatology)* he declares that, without the tools of criticism and traditional philology (including, I presume, dictionaries), interpretation could take off in any direction and consider itself authorized to say whatever it liked. Only he adds that this indispensable guardrail protects but does not initiate a reading, and he is evidently convinced that existing grammars and dictionaries are sufficient to protect a reading.

In the case of Davidson and the various theories of inference, he chooses to ignore the fact that terms have meanings fixed by the community (the ones provided by dictionaries) because what counts is that I take for granted that anyone speaking to me sees the world as I see it and intends to say what I would say in the same circumstances. It would therefore seem irrelevant that a boat be designated as a "boat," because if someone were to say to me "Let's get on that wagon," pointing to a boat, I would understand, through the principle of charity, that he meant to refer to the boat and I don't go splitting hairs about the "conventional" meaning of the terms.

The example, however, presupposes that all there is in front of us a boat, and not a boat and a wagon, and that the direction in which I am pointing is unambiguous. In the latter case, and in the absence of any further circumstantial indicators, if the speaker says "Let's get on that wagon," I understand that he wants to get on the wagon and not on the boat. This is a consequence of the fact that social and linguistic conventions assign two different meanings to the words "boat" and "wagon" independently of any context or act of charity. Of course, out of a principle of charity that, under the circumstances, would be tantamount to a "principle of malevolence," I could always assume that the person speaking had a selection disturbance and said "wagon" whenever he meant "boat," but we do not usually push the malevolence principle that far. We assume that there is a semantics in sense 1 involved, in which words have a certain meaning independently of any specific context.

Note that not even Davidson denies this evidence—see "Communication and Convention" (Davidson 1984b)—in which he asks himself if we need a convention to tie every word to a fixed meaning for all speakers, and assumes, as a condition of the existence of a convention, the position of Lewis, which is clearly more valid for poker than for languages. At this point Davidson realizes that we can even understand terms we are not familiar with and decides that all conventions are useful but not necessary. The argument is that we simply tend to speak like everyone else—and this would shift the problem of the existence of a code to that of consistency of usage.

To be quite frank, this strikes me as merely playing with words. Saying that we regularly associate the word "boat" with a floating vessel and saying that the code establishes that a boat is a floating vessel doesn't change much. In fact when linguists speak of a code they are speaking of a statistical extrapolation from common usage: the *code de la langue* that De Saussure talked about is a fiction based on consistency of usage.

Otherwise, it would be like saying that it is not true that the penal code establishes that whoever kills someone else must serve x number of years in prison, but that "usually" (that is, as a rule) whoever kills someone else gets x number of years in prison. If this were the only difference between Roman Law and Common Law, what we would have is identical conventions. The difference is that, in order to decide what is customary, Common Law, has recourse, not to a rule fixed once and for all, but to the precedent set by a previous case.

Now, Davidson does not deny that there are conventions according to which a "boat" always signifies a floating vessel; he simply decides that this is a marginal or obvious case (obvious because it is marginal and marginal because it is obvious), and he prefers to give his attention to the more dramatic cases. The dramatic cases are when we use the word "boat" to indicate something other than a floating vessel. The most convincing example, of course, is that of metaphor (think of the example of "sauce boat"). But we cannot build a theory of a language on its use of metaphor, unless it be to say that the meaning of all linguistic terms is originally metaphorical—and I do not believe this was Davidson's intent.

The confusion lies in demonstrating that what is dramatic is normal and what is normal marginal, whereas in science the dramatic cases are always used as marginal examples to demonstrate that the normal cases are not as simple as we think. True, the principle that the exception confirms the rule is scientifically infantile (something proved by Popper's falsificationist theory, according to which an exception calls the rule into question), but to state, as humorist Achille Campanile does, that "rules made up entirely of exceptions are rules fully confirmed," is to state a paradox, and it is equally paradoxical to claim that the exception constitutes the rule. The rule for defining a rule, in the human sciences, is that it must allow for a number of exceptions, but that they must be controllable, that is to say, predictable. In the physical sciences, either all bodies fall according to the laws of gravity or, if only one body does not, the laws of gravity must be called into question. In the human sciences, on the other hand, the statistical rule is that the majority of human beings come together in heterosexual congress in order to procreate (otherwise our number would not have increased from two to six billion in a matter of fifty years), but this does not exclude the fact that some human beings choose not to procreate, which allows us to include Catholic priests and homosexuals among human beings.

Were it true that there is no such thing as meaning in the sense of sense 1, we would have no end of trouble understanding each other, and in fact, Davidson, though through gritted teeth, has never defended this thesis. What we may be sure of is that, in terms of sense 5, the principle of charity theory must be taken very seriously. It is then that we discover that Davidson, by suggesting that he is contesting sense 1 (which he nevertheless presupposes) and seeming to place in discussion, for purely academic reasons, senses 3 and 4, was in fact proposing the principles of the semantics in sense 5—in other words, a semantics not of terms, or of sentences, but of texts. From the lexicographic point of view, Davidson seems to be denying the evidence, but from the point of view of a theory of textual interpretation he is a fairly sane person, or—though he is not aware of it—someone with something serious to say about the interpretation of the meaning of texts (texts that, on top of everything else, produced as they are in complex situations, are always multimedia; made up, in other words, of words, demonstrative and deictic gestures, paralinguistic elements, and maybe even hypoiconic supports).

Allow me to remind you of a well-known example of Ducrot's. The expression *je suis le rognon* ("I am the kidney"), uttered by a human being, is false (from the point of view of senses 3 and 4), but, when said in the context of a restaurant, accompanied by a gesture first pointing to the dish in the waiter's hand and then to the speaker himself, it signifies unequivocally that the speaker is affirming that he is the one who ordered the kidney and not the one who ordered the sirloin steak.

17.4. The Identification of Meaning and Synonymy

In order to deny that semantics makes sense in sense 1, to affirm, that is, that words do not have meanings agreed upon by convention, it is customary to employ a quite fallacious argument. Meaning is identified with synonymy. Philosophers of language are more responsible for this fallacy than lexicographers. No sensible person versed in languages can believe that there are two synonyms that really do mean the same thing (and even the authors of dictionaries of synonyms offer their alternatives as possibilities *faute de mieux,* as stylistic variants to be evaluated on a case-by-case basis, not as absolute equivalents). Once meaning and synonymy have been identified, however, the tendency is to demonstrate that, since there is no such thing as absolute synonymy (so much is obvious), there can be no meaning (which is not so obvious). This is the argument of those who hold that translation is an impossibility.

Let us consider a fairly curious text of Quine's, "The Problem of Meaning in Linguistics," which appears in his *From the Logical Point of View.* In it Quine speaks of lexicography and lexicographers, saying that lexicographers seem to be interested in the problem of meaning, and he is certainly correct. After which he opines that a lexicographer "differs from the so-called formal linguists only in that he is concerned to correlate linguistic forms with one another in his own special way, namely, synonyms with synonyms" (Bréal 1900). If by "lexicographer" we understand the author of a dictionary of synonyms, this is certainly what he does, though with all due caution, as we said before. But Quine seems to think that the only thing the lexicographer is interested in is deciding what linguistic forms are synonymous, that is, "alike in meaning." This is not true. The lexicographer's first task is precisely to establish why the same expression may have different meanings in different contexts. Rather than cultivate the myth of synonymy, a good lexicographer contests it.

If by "lexicographer" we understand someone who is writing a dictionary for tourists, and if he tells us "steak" is a synonym of *bistecca,* he may be taking advantage of the work of other lexicographers, but he is deliberately impoverishing it, though he may make it possible for an English-speaking tourist to order a *bistecca* if he happens to be in Italy. The good lexicographer is the one who explains that *cagna* is not a synonym of "bitch," except in a few rare cases, so that in Italian I may define a lousy singer as a *cagna,* however impeccable her morals, but I could not call her a "bitch" in English without suggesting that she is of easy virtue (though her singing may be divine).

So lexicographers, real lexicographers, are indeed semanticists in sense 1, in that they endeavor to establish on what common bases we may legitimately use a word, but they are above all semanticists in sense 2 when they try to decide the nature of our lexicographic conventions, not in the caricatural terms of synonymy and homonymy, but on the basis of an inspection of the systems of content and basing their findings on a broad survey of previous texts and their meaning (sense 5).

When Quine says that lexicographers do not hold the monopoly on the problem of meaning, he appears to have in mind the authors of pocket dictionaries for tourists, rather than lexicographers who are scholars of structural semantics.

Just how debatable Quine's ideas about lexicography are can be seen from the paragraphs which follow, in which he equiparates the work of the lexicographers to that of the phonologists who decide whether two phonemes are different according to whether or not the meaning of the word changes if we substitute one for the other within the same language. It is true that the phonologist decides that a given phoneme is different from another because, if we substitute one for the other within the same syntagm, we obtain two words with two different meanings (*ship* and *sheep,* for instance), but, when he does so, the phonologist is not concerned with the notion of meaning. He simply assumes that the native speaker (of whom he himself is a reliable sample) perceives a variation in meaning in the passage from one phoneme to another. He merely registers a fact, he does not remotely presume to define what a ship or a sheep is. The lexicographer on the other hand takes as a given the proof of substitution provided by the phonologist and is concerned with defining the difference between a ship and a sheep.

17.5. Truth-Conditional Semantics

Let us go on to the fourth sense of semantics. It goes without saying that if we have such an impoverished notion of lexicography and meaning as that of synonymy, we are free to experiment with phenomena such as the substitution of apparently synonymous terms in opaque contexts (and clearly, someone who believes that Aristotle wrote the *Metaphysics* does not automatically believe that Alexander's teacher wrote the *Metaphysics*). These are exercises of considerable importance for the study of logic, but not very important for understanding the way we speak. No speaker in his right mind, once it had been affirmed that "Giorgione" has three syllables, would affirm that "Barbarelli" too had three syllables.[3] I am one of the first to admit how

---

3. [*Translator's note:* The Venetian painter Giorgione was born Giorgio Barbarelli. The two names are used as a paradoxical example in Quine 2004.]

many things we would have failed to understand if we had not performed exercises of this kind, but they have nothing at all to do with at least four of the five senses of semantics that I am talking about.

Let us come now to the differences between sense 3 and sense 4. It is my conviction that a truth-conditional semantics has nothing to do with the problem of reference. The problem of reference has to do with our ability to designate objects and states of the world, to reach an understanding on this act of designation (and hence it has something to do with sense 1), and—eventually (but this is not a semantic but an epistemological and gnoseological problem)—to say whether the object or the state of the world we referred to exists or is taking place to the extent that we referred to it. In simple terms, if I say that it is raining today, we have to be agreed on the meaning of "rain," we have to grant that the speaker is saying that water is falling from the sky, and that (another problem) water is actually falling from the sky.

Let us take a look at Tarsky's truth criterion. Its concern is with how to define the truth conditions of a proposition, but not with how to establish if the proposition is true when used for acts of reference. And saying that understanding the meaning of a sentence means knowing its truth conditions (that is, on what conditions the proposition expressed would be true) it is not the same thing as proving the sentence to be true or untrue.[4]

Agreed, the paradigm is nowhere near as homogeneous as is usually maintained, and there are those who tend to interpret Tarsky's criterion according to a correspondentist epistemology. But, whatever Tarsky may have thought,[5] it is hard to read in a correspondentist sense his famous definition:

The sentence [i] "snow is white" is true if, and only if, [ii] snow is white.

---

4. "To understand a proposition means to know what is the case if it is true" (Wittgenstein 1922: 4.024). Nevertheless, we know the truth conditions of the proposition: "At twelve noon on August 2, 1810, all living cats made up an odd number," but it is unlikely that either today or in the future anyone will ever be able to say whether it is true or false.

5. In any case, here is what Tarsky thought in 1944: "We may accept the semantic conception of truth without giving up any epistemological attitude we may have had; we may remain naive realists, critical realists or idealists, empiricists or metaphysicians—whatever we were before. The semantic conception is completely neutral toward all these issues."

We are in a position to say what kind of logical and linguistic entity [i] is—it is a sentence in an object language L that conveys a proposition—but we have no idea what [ii] is. If it were a state of affairs (or a perceptive experience) we would be extremely embarrassed: a state of affairs is a state of affairs and a perceptive experience is a perceptive experience, not a sentence. If anything, a sentence is produced to express a state of affairs or a perceptive experience. But if what appears in [ii] is a sentence about a state of affairs or a perceptive experience, it cannot be a sentence expressed in L, since it must guarantee the truth of the proposition expressed in [i]. It must be, then, a sentence expressed in a metalanguage L_2. But in that case Tarsky's formula ought to be translated as follows:

[i] The proposition "snow is white," conveyed by the sentence (in L) *snow is white*
    is true if, and only if,
[ii] the proposition "snow is white" conveyed by the sentence (in L_2) *snow is white* is true.

It is clear that this solution is destined to produce a sorites of infinite sentences, each one expressed in a new metalanguage. If we assume Tarsky's example in a naïve fashion, we find ourselves in the same boat (or wagon) as the editors of De Saussure who represented the relationship between signifier and signified with an oval split into two superimposed halves, in which the word *arbre* is contained in the bottom half while the top half contains a drawing of a tree. Now, the signifier *arbre* is certainly a word, but the drawing of the tree is not intended to be and cannot be the signified or a mental image (because what it is, if anything, is another nonverbal signifier that interprets the word below it). Seeing that the design excogitated by De Saussure's editors had no formal ambition, only a mnemonic function, we can forget about it. But the problem with Tarsky is different.

We could of course interpret the definition in a strictly behaviorist sense: snow is white if, when confronted by the stimulus snow, every speaker reacts by saying it is white. But, apart from the fact that we would find ourselves up to our necks in the difficulties of radical interpretation, I do not believe this was what Tarsky had in mind, and, even if this was his intention, this would not be a way to decide whether a proposition is true, because it would simply tell us that all speakers are guilty of the same error of perception, just as the fact that for thousands of years all speakers declared that the sun sinks into the sea in the evening does not prove that the proposition was true.

It seems more convincing to admit that, in Tarsky's formulation, [ii] stands conventionally for *the assignment of a truth value to* [i]. The Tarskyan state of affairs is not something we can check in order to recognize the proposition that expresses it as true; on the contrary, it is what a true proposition, or indeed anything that is expressed by a true proposition, corresponds to (cf. McCawley 1981: 161), in other words its truth value. In this sense Tarsky's notion does not tell us whether it is more true to say that a cat is a cat than it is to say that a cat is a mammal.

17.6. Meaning, Referent, Reference

This node, between truth-conditional semantics, reference semantics, semantics of the sentence, and textual semantics compels us to revise a few concepts, something I attempted to do in my *Kant and the Platypus*.

1. Meaning of a term like *cat*. It may contain categorial elements like *mammal* and *feline,* but it also contains instructions to define the referent. But the referent of *cat* is not some individual cat, but cats in general. In this sense, terms that denote nonexistent objects may contain reference instructions (for instance, "unicorn"). It is possible to transmit and understand instructions for identifying the referent without having had and without ever having the occasion of referring to something.

2. References to cats *(My cat is in the kitchen)*. Reference as a linguistic act, to be negotiated. The reference, however, is completely unconnected either to the empirical truth of the proposition (if I am lying or mistaken, the cat is not there) or to any discussion of its truth value. To be sure, if there is a cat in the kitchen, there is a feline mammal in the kitchen (sense 4), I am certainly referring to a specific cat, mine (sense 3), but it might not be true that it is in the kitchen. Senses 1 and 2 are presupposed by semantics of the third type, and can be taken into consideration by semantics of the fourth, but the converse is not true. Let us not forget that Morris (1938) reminded us that semantics is concerned with the relationship between a sign and its *designata,* that a semantic rule establishes under what conditions a sign is applicable to an object, but that the notion of *designatum* has nothing to do with

the existence of the object; the *designatum* of a sign is something the sign may denote—but establishing whether there really are objects of this kind goes beyond the competence of semiotics.

Let us now suppose that I were to visit a culture (with a language adequate to express it) in which only two animals are known: the cat, hairy, smaller than a human being, domesticated, and harmless, and the crocodile, usually bigger than a human being, and scaly. For the members of that culture, based on such an elementary system of oppositions, which constitutes the full extent of their classification of the animal kingdom (a cat is everything a crocodile is not, and vice versa), if a dog were to show up, given that it was hairy, domesticated, and friendly, it would be defined as a cat (however unusual its appearance) and certainly not as an unusual crocodile. Let us suppose again that I realize that there is a boa constrictor behind my native interlocutor's back. I wouldn't be able to tell him that it was a boa because there is no adequate term in his language, and I couldn't describe the strange and unusual animal without wasting precious time. I would therefore have to tell him that there was a crocodile behind him, assuming that, since in that culture animals are divided into harmless and hostile, I would thus be informing him that he was in a dangerous situation. This example is not chosen at random because in some medieval encyclopedias, not knowing how to define a crocodile (since the author had probably never seen one), they were content to call it a *serpens acquaticus.*

If I succeed in causing my interlocutor to be concerned, as was my intention, and if I obtain his consent to my proposition (he turns around, gives a start and concedes that the animal, obviously not a cat, is indeed a crocodile), I will have behaved according to certain methodological principles of sense 2, to make a successful reference in the sense of sense 3, obtaining his consent in terms of sense 4.

But in fact all this is because I am basing myself on the principles of sense 5, according to which it is the text and the context that have the last word in defining the meaning of terms.

This whole discourse will no doubt lead someone to opine that there is no semantics that does not need to be backed up by a pragmatics. I can only agree, as indeed I always have, from my *A Theory of Semiotics* (1976) to *Kant and the Platypus* (2000).

18

Weak Thought versus
the Limits of Interpretation

In 1983, a symposium entitled *Il pensiero debole (Weak Thought)*, edited by Gianni Vattimo and Pier Aldo Rovati, was published by Feltrinelli. The notion of "weak thought" had been proposed by Vattimo, and in that collection of essays thinkers of various stripes were invited to discuss its definition. To my knowledge, not all of those invited to join in the debate agreed to take part, and so my own contribution appeared in a context in which those who bought into the project of "weak thought" were more numerous than those with reservations. Furthermore, in their introduction, Vattimo and Rovatti, after pointing out that the essays in the volume were not to be lumped together under the label of a school, "given the heterogeneous provenance and theoretical orientations of their authors," nonetheless claimed that what they all had in common was the idea that the various discourses on the crisis of reason had still not thoroughly explored "the experience of the forgetfulness of being, or the 'death of God', of which Heidegger and especially Nietzsche had brought the tidings to our culture" (p. 9).

Anyone rereading my contribution to that symposium—entitled "L'anti-porfirio" ("The Anti-Porphyry": a good deal of which is recapitulated in the

A further revisited version of the paper delivered at the conference, attended by Gianni Vattimo, entitled "Autour d'Umberto Eco: Signes, réprésentations, interprétations," ("Apropos of Umberto Eco: Signs, Representations, Interpretations") held in Sofia in November 2004 (originally published as "La notion de limite" [Eco 2005]), and subsequently reelaborated as "Weak Thought and the Limits of Interpretation" (Eco 2007).

Chapter 1 of this book)[1]—will observe that I showed no interest in the theories of Heidegger or Nietzsche or in the death of God, so much so that Cesare Cases, in a review in the periodical *L'Espresso* dated February 5, 1984, could write: "with the exception of Umberto Eco, who sticks to the encyclopedists, the others see it [i.e., weak thought] embodied above all in Nietzsche."

What possible connection could I have pointed out between a hypothetical metaphor of "weak thought" and the encyclopedists? On that occasion I argued against the model of thought represented by dictionary semantics, to which I opposed an encyclopedic semantics. My presentation (though it took up and anticipated what is for me a central theme which received its definitive formulation the following year in the 1984 Italian edition of *Sémiotique: Dictionnaire raisonné de la théorie du langage* (see Greimas and Courtés 1982) was not totally alien to Vattimo and Rovatti's proposal, since I argued that, from the point of view of an encyclopedic semantics— dominated by the Peircean idea of interpretation and hence of unlimited semiosis—no thought expressed in language ever claims to reflect in a definitive fashion the *Dynamical Object* (or thing in itself) but is aware that what it is putting into play are *Immediate Objects* (pure content), interpretable in their turn by other expressions that refer back to other Immediate Objects in a self-sustaining semiotic process.

Naturally, I alluded to the question, developed at length elsewhere, that, from the Peircean perspective, the "flight" of the interpretants does not resolve our conception of the world into a mere sequence of interpretations, but generates *habits* and therefore modes of transformation of the natural world. In that communication, however, I was content to take for granted as obvious my conviction that semiosis is an activity that takes place in a world of facts, since the position of weak thought had not yet been summed up in the catchphrase according to which *there are no facts, only interpretations.* In other words, I had not yet realized that the return to Nietzsche on the part of many of my accidental fellow travelers implied this very catchphrase; and I became aware of it only when, as we shall see, the slogan was also attributed to me.

At the time, all I was arguing was that an encyclopedic semantics may be called "weak," not in the sense that it is insufficient to explain how we

---

1. See Eco (1985c).

use language to signify and define the world, but because it submits the laws of signification to the constant determination of context and circumstances. I wrote:

> An encyclopedic semantics has no problem providing rules for the generation and interpretation of the expressions of a language, but its rules are orientated toward contexts, and semantics incorporates pragmatics (the dictionary incorporates, albeit in a semioticized form, our knowledge of the world). What makes the encyclopedia weak, but fruitfully so, is the fact that the representation it provides is never closed and definitive, and that an encyclopedic representation is never global but always local; produced to deal with given contexts and circumstances, the perspective it provides on semiotic activity is a limited one.... The encyclopedia does not provide a complete model of rationality (it does not reflect an ordered universe in an unambiguous fashion), but instead it provides *rules of reasonableness,* rules, that is, for negotiating at each stage the conditions that permit us to use language to give an account—according to some provisional criterion of order—of a disorderly world (or a world whose criteria of order escape us)" (Eco 1983b: 75).

I was referring back implicitly to a review I had written of the collection of essays edited by Aldo Gargani (1979),[2] in which, against a number of "strong" definitions of Reason, either as the ability of knowing the Absolute through direct vision, or as a Platonic belief in a system of universal innate principles, or as the conviction that the order of language mirrors unproblematically the order of the world while truth is always and in every instance *adaequatio rei et intellectus* ("the correspondence of a thing to the intellect"). I defended the rights of critical reasonableness, of a series of conjectural procedures that called at a minimum for the pooling of certain instruments of verification. And I concluded with a eulogy of the *modus ponens,* while admitting that it had no place in poetry, dreams, or the language of the unconscious. I ended (parodying the slogans of the Maoism fashionable at the time): "Comrades, long live the *Modus Ponens!*"—and adding: "As the case may be!"

---

2. My review was published in *Alfabeta,* January 1, 1980, and later reprinted in Eco (1983c).

Can someone who sings the praises of the *modus ponens* become a charter member of the sect of weak thought?

Be that as it may, such is the mass-media power of the slogan that I have frequently since found myself automatically enrolled among the devotees of weak thought, simply because I once contributed (it obviously didn't matter what) to a volume with that title. This display of superficiality was joined by a number of professors of philosophy, whom one might have expected to be a little more attentive to what a colleague had written, and several respectable clerics, who had perhaps gotten their notions of philosophy from the conning of glossy magazines.

It is understandable why the question should be of concern to ingenuous realists or guarantors of absolute truths: if thinking in a "weak" way meant asserting that there are no facts only interpretations, the notion of a "fact" as something independent of our interpretations is thrown in doubt, and by the same token we deny the very concept of Truth, falling as a consequence into that murky recess which neoreactionary thought identifies confusedly with "relativism" (just as the ultraconservative Thomists of the nineteenth century saw "the Kantian poison" in every aspect of modern thought).

I do not believe that even the most extremist champion of weak thought insists that there are no facts, only that such notions of fact as we possess come to us through the series of our interpretations—so that we ought not to waste time investigating facts but attempt to understand the mutable history of their representation. What is sure is that the debate between the proponents of weak thought and its opponents turns on whether the preceding affirmation should stop there, or whether it ought not to imply as its natural corollary the issue (to which Peirce was sensitive) of whether or not, against the background of the sequence of interpretations, the ineluctable presence of a *Dynamic Object* inevitably rears its head. Since the idea of a sequence of interpretations is conceivable and makes sense only if we admit that there is *something to interpret,* wouldn't it make sense too to come to grips with that *something?*

This is the problem I came back to definitively in *Kant and the Platypus,* but, even prior to that, it was hard to credit me with the idea that there are no facts, only interpretations, considering I had written a book entitled—no less!—*The Limits of Interpretation.* And the problem had already come up previously in some of my earlier writings. In the face of the affirmation that there are no facts only interpretations, I have always maintained that every fact is the occasion for diverse and conflicting interpretations, but one curious thing about facts is that they resist interpretations they do not legitimate or support. In other words, though it may be difficult to decide whether one interpretation is better than another, we can always recognize untenable interpretations. And finally, though facts are always known and communicable by means of interpretations, they also somehow stand as parameters of our interpretations.

In 1986, I wrote an essay on Latin thought for a symposium edited by Georges Duby. In it I identified the notion of limit as the fundamental concept of Latinity. From Greek rationalism to its medieval progeny, knowing meant reconstructing causes. To explain the world we must postulate the idea of a unidirectional causal chain: if a movement goes from Alpha to Omega, no force can make it invert its direction and go from Omega to Alpha (in Aesop's fable the wolf is cheating because he claims to turn this principle on its head). The necessary foundations of this idea of a unidirectional chain are the principles of identity, noncontradiction, and the excluded middle or the excluded third *(principium tertii exclusi)*. The typical way of reasoning of Western rationalism is based on the *modus ponens:* if *p* then *q;* but *p:* therefore *q.*

Latin rationalism had basically accepted the principles of Greek rationalism, transforming and enriching them, however, in a juridical-contractual direction, so as to set up as a fundamental principle the notion of *limes* or frontier, and hence limit. The obsession with the spatial frontier is present in Latin culture right from its foundation myth: Romulus draws a line of demarcation and slays Remus because he has violated it. If the frontier is not recognized there can be no *civitas.* Bridges are sacrilegious because they cross the *sulcus,* the circular moat of water that defines the limits of the city, so much so that they can only be administered under the ritual control of the *pontifex.* The ideology of the *pax romana* is based on the precise nature of its boundaries. The strength of the empire lies in knowing on which *vallum,* within which *limen,* its system of defense must be organized. When this notion of boundaries was no longer clear, when the barbarians (nomads who had abandoned their territories of origin and crossed all other territories as if the territories belonged to them, only to abandon them the following day) imposed their nomadic vision, whereupon the capital of the empire could be moved anywhere and, little by little, losing its center and its periphery, the empire collapsed.

When he crosses the Rubicon, Caesar is aware of committing a sacrilege, and he knows, that, once he is on the other side of the river, he cannot turn back: *alea jacta est* (the die is cast). Not only space, but time too had its limits: we cannot fix it so that what has already happened did not happen. The direction and order of time, which establish a linear cosmological continuity, become the system of logical subordination in the *consecutio temporum*. The ablative absolute establishes that, once something has happened or been presupposed, it can no longer be placed in discussion.

In his *Quaestio quodlibetalis* V, 2, 3, Thomas Aquinas asks "utrum Deus possit virginem reparare" ("Can God repair the loss of a girl's virginity?"). His answer is that God certainly has the power to forgive or therefore repair the moral wound, just as he has the power to work miracles and give the girl back an intact hymen; but he cannot bring it about that the violation never occurred, because this negation of what has already happened would be contrary to God's very nature. For God too *alea jacta est*.

Still, in addition to Aristotelian logic, hermetic thought too is part and parcel of the Greco-Roman heritage. The Greek world was always attracted by the infinite, which has neither limits nor direction, as well as by the figure of Hermes, at once father of the arts and protector of thieves and merchants, *juvenis* and *senex* at one and the same time. In the myth of Hermes, the principles of identity, contradiction, and the excluded middle are contested, the causal chains are twisted into spirals in which what comes after may precede what comes before.

Now, if I go back and review the entire gist of my philosophical reflections, I realize that I always placed them under the sign of the limit—confining my fascination with the limitless to my occasional narrative divagations, where my intentions were to present it as grotesque.

It might be objected that, though I began my philosophical research with studies on the aesthetics of the Middle Ages, I later turned my reflection to the infinity of the interpretations of a work of art, and this is precisely why a work I wrote in 1962 was entitled *L'opera aperta (The Open Work)*. The closing pages of the book were devoted to the most limitless and open of works, Joyce's *Finnegans Wake*. Consequently, when, almost thirty years later, I came to write *The Limits of Interpretation,* some critics were led to wonder whether I had reneged on my eulogy of an open interpretation. But what they failed to take into account was that it should have been evident (starting with the very title of *The Open Work*) that what interpretation was supposed to "open" was nonetheless a *work*, and therefore a form, something that preceded the act of interpretation and in some sense conditioned it, even though it did not steer it toward a unique end. In fact I was following (though in a secularized version) the thought of Luigi Pareyson,[3] based upon a constant dialectic between the legality of a form and the initiatives of its interpreters, between faithfulness and freedom (see Pareyson 1954).

This was the course I had already embarked upon in 1979 with *Lector in fabula* (*The Role of the Reader*), which, from its very title, on the one hand announced the importance to the life of a text of the interpretive collaboration of its empirical reader, while defending on the other the rights of the *fabula* to design its own Model Reader.

If these were the premises, it was natural that eventually (in *The Limits of Interpretation*) I should find myself criticizing the various forms of deconstruction (especially the American varieties, for which Derrida was not wholly responsible)[4] which could be summed up in Valéry's affirmation, according to which "il n'y a pas de vrai sens d'un texte" ["there is no true meaning of a text"].

I was following a principle along the Popperian model, according to which, though we cannot recognize "good" interpretations, we can always point out which are the "bad" ones. In this way, the text became the parameter for judging its interpretations even though it was precisely and only the interpretations that could tell us what the text was. At this point it ought to be clear that, from the point of view of the dialectic between an object and its interpretations, all differences between *facts* and *texts* disappear. And not in the fashion that many American analysts ascribe to continental philosophy, by insisting that facts are texts too or may be analyzed as texts (a position assumed by some poststructuralist tendencies), but, on the contrary, by affirming that *texts are facts* (i.e., something that

---

3. [*Translator's note:* Both Eco and Vattimo were students of the philosopher Luigi Pareyson.]

4. For Derrida, deconstruction was not a method of artistic or literary criticism but a method of interrogating philosophical texts, and he always maintained that every reading should respect certain *garde-fous* or guardrails that would act as philosophical checks on the free drift of interpretation.

exists prior to its interpretations and whose rights of precedence cannot be called into question).

Elsewhere I have attempted to demonstrate how not even the most radical of deconstructionists, though they may maintain that every interpretation is a misunderstanding or a *misprision,* can deny the text a controlling role over its own interpretations. Given two texts Alpha and Beta and an interpretation Gamma, is it possible to decide whether Gamma is an interpretation of Alpha or of Beta? If it is not possible, if Gamma could be seen indifferently as an interpretation not only of Alpha and of Beta but also of any other text, then there would be no interpretations, only production of texts without any relationship between them, pure solipsistic babble. If on the other hand it is possible, then we have a parameter that permits us to discriminate between reliable interpretations and unreliable ones. In order to conclude, for instance, that Gamma is not an interpretation of Beta, we must still affirm that Beta is *not* the Thing it is talking about. Now, not even the most rabid advocate of deconstructionism would ever affirm that the 1825 *Iliade* by Vincenzo Monti (well known to be a free translation of previous translations of Homer) could be read as if it were a translation of the *Aeneid.* Homer's *Iliad,* then, is a text (an object, a fact) that determines the recognition of Monti's *Iliade* as one of its possible interpretations, at the same time as it excludes the sixteenth-century Italian translation of the *Aeneid* by Annibal Caro from the ranks of possible translations of the *Iliad.*

Is it possible, given an object that exists prior to its interpretations, that the interpretations of that object could be so different from one another, perhaps potentially infinite, or at least indefinite in number, without however our being able to ignore that they have to do with something that precedes them?

In *Kant and the Platypus* I proposed a mental experiment. Let an elementary model be constructed that contains a World along with a Mind that knows and names it. The World is a whole made up of elements (we could call them atoms, in the sense of the Greek *stoicheia*), structured according to reciprocal relations. As for the Mind, we do not have to think of it as a *res cogitans:* it is simply a device for organizing sequences of elements valid as descriptions of the real World or of possible worlds. These elements could be understood as neurons, bytes, or *stoicheia,* but for the sake of convenience let's call them *symbols.*

By World we mean the universe in its "maximal" version, inasmuch as it includes both what we consider to be the current universe and the infinity of possible universes. This universe can therefore also include God, or any other original principle.

Theoretically, there would be no need to assume that we have on the one hand a thinking substance and on the other the universe of things that may be thought. Both atoms and symbols may be conceived of as ontologically homologous entities, *stoicheia* made from the same basic material. The Mind should be thought of simply as a device that forms part of the World; or alternatively the World should be thought of as something capable of interpreting itself, which delegates part of itself to this purpose, so that among its infinite or indefinite number of atoms some serve as symbols that represent all the other atoms, exactly as when we human beings, speaking of phonology or phonetics, delegate a limited number of sounds to represent every possible phonation. The Mind ought, then, to be represented, not as standing in front of the World, but as contained in the World, and it should be structured in such a way as to be able to speak, not only of the World (which is opposed to it), but also of itself as part of the World, and of the very process by means of which it, as part of what is interpreted, can function as an interpretant. At this point, however, we would no longer have a model, but exactly what the model is attempting, however clumsily, to describe.[5]

Let us agree, then, for the sake of convenience and in the interests of simplification, to think of a World on the one side and on the other a Mind that interprets it, enriching it at the same time with fresh possible configurations.

FIRST HYPOTHESIS. Let us imagine that the World is made up of three atoms (1, 2, 3) and the Mind of three symbols (A, B, C). They could combine

---

5. I realize this hypothesis comes close to Schelling's notion of the Absolute, in which there is no longer any difference between the subject thinking of the thing in itself and what was previously considered the thing in itself. But perhaps Schelling was much less of an "idealist" (in the negative sense of the term) than has been thought—and was instead something of a Spinozan. I had no intention of saying that nothing exists outside of thought and that the world is the creation of the subject, but that subject and object are two aspects of the same universal substance—and that we (that is, culture) assuredly know the world in the form in which we think it, but we think it in that form precisely because we are part of it.

in six different ways, but if we limit ourselves to thinking of the World in its current state (including its history), we might suppose it to be endowed with a stable structure given by the sequence 123 (as in Figure 18.1). If knowledge were specular, and the truth Aquinas's *adaequatio rei et intellectus*, the Mind would assign *nonarbitrarily* symbol A to atom 1, symbol B to atom 2, symbol C to atom 3, and would represent the structure of the world with the ordered triplet of symbols ABC. In point of fact, the Mind would not be "interpreting" the world but *representing it in a specular fashion*.

But if the assignment of symbols to the atoms was arbitrary, then the Mind could also assign A, B, and C to any of the atoms it so desired, and by combinatory calculus it would have six possible ways of faithfully representing the same 123 structure. The six descriptions would furthermore be six specular representations *in six different languages,* but the metaphor of six different specular images of the same object suggests that either the object or the mirror moves each time, providing six different angles.

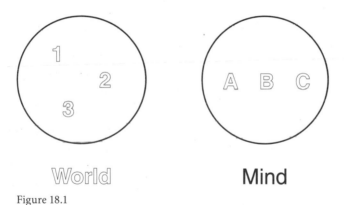

Figure 18.1

SECOND HYPOTHESIS. The symbols used by the Mind are fewer in number than the atoms of the World. The symbols used by the Mind are still three, but the atoms of the World are ten (1, 2, 3 . . . 10). If the World were still structured in triplets of atoms, by factorial calculus it could group its ten atoms in 720 different ternary structures. In that case the Mind would have six triplets of symbols as in the first hypothesis (ABC, BCA, CAB, ACB, BAC, CBA) to account for 720 triplets of atoms (as in Figure 18.2). Different worldly events, from different perspectives, could be interpreted by the same symbols. For example, we would always be obliged to use the triplet of symbols ABC to represent 123, or 345, or 547. This might constitute an embarrassing superabundance of homonyms, but it might also permit us to discover (creatively) that between, let's say, the worldly triplets 123 and 345 there exist analogies or elements in common, to the point that they can be represented by the same triplet of symbols. The poverty of the Mind therefore would not preclude it from making more and more fresh discoveries.

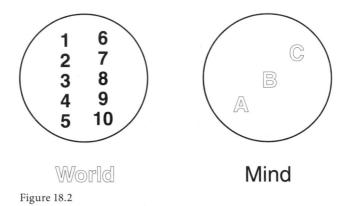

Figure 18.2

The problem would be no different—it would just become more complicated—if the World were not ordered in a stable way, but chaotic (and capable of evolving and restructuring itself over time). Constantly changing the structures of its triplets, the language of the Mind would have to keep constantly adapting itself to the changing situations.

And if, on the other hand, the World were hyperstructured in a stable way, that is, if it were organized according to a single structure given by a particular sequence of ten atoms, the Mind would still only have six triplets of symbols to describe this hyperstructure. It would be obliged, then, to attempt to describe it piecemeal, from local points of view, and would never be able to describe it in its entirety. But it would be precisely the choice of these partial solutions that made ever more innovative and original points of view possible.

THIRD HYPOTHESIS. The Mind has more elements than the World. The Mind has ten symbols at its disposal (A, B, C, D, E, F, G, H, I, J) and the World only three atoms (1, 2, 3), as in Figure 18.3. This is not all—the

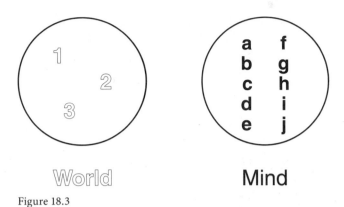

Figure 18.3

Mind can combine these ten symbols in duplets, triplets, quadruplets, and so on. Which is the same thing as saying that the cerebral structure would have more neurons and more combinatory possibilities among neurons than the number of atoms and their combinations identifiable in the World.

Clearly, this hypothesis would have to be abandoned immediately, because it conflicts with the original assumption that the Mind is part of the World. In order to consent this hypothesis, the Mind would have to step out of the World: it would be a kind of intensely thinking divinity compelled to account for an extremely impoverished world, a world that, on top of that, it does not know, because it was cobbled together by a Demiurge with no imagination. We could also think of a World that somehow secretes more *res cogitans* than *res extensa*, a World that has produced, that is, a fairly limited number of thinkable structures, using few atoms, and is holding others in reserve to use them as symbols of the Mind. It would follow that the Mind would have an astronomical number of combinations of symbols to represent a 123 structure of the world (or at most its six possible combinations), always from a different point of view. The Mind could, for example, represent 123 (by combinatory calculus) by means of 3,628,800 decuplets, each of which would not only be designed to account for 123 but also for the day and the hour when it is represented, for the internal state of the Mind itself at that moment, and for the intentions and purposes with which the Mind was representing it. There would be an excess of thought with respect to the simplicity of the World, and the supply of possible representations would exceed the number of possible existing structures. And maybe this is what really happens, seeing that we are able to lie and construct fantastic worlds, and imagine and anticipate alternative states of things (Figure 18.4).

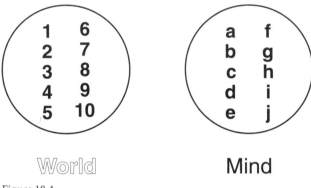

Figure 18.4

FOURTH HYPOTHESIS. The Mind has ten symbols, and the atoms of the World are ten. Both Mind and World can combine their elements, as in the third hypothesis, in duplets, triplets, quadruplets ... decuplets (see Figure 18.4). The Mind would then have an astronomical number of propositions at its disposal to describe an astronomical number of worldly structures. And this is not all—given the abundance of as yet unrealized worldly combinations, it could plan modifications of the World, as it could be continually taken by surprise by worldly combinations it had not foreseen; in addition to which, it would be kept very busy explaining in different ways how it itself worked.

What we would have would be, not so much an excess of thought with respect to the simplicity of the world—as was the case with the third hypothesis—but a kind of constant challenge among contenders fighting on potentially equal terms, though in fact changing weapons with each attack and putting the adversary at a disadvantage. The Mind would confront the World from an excess of perspectives, the World would elude the snares of the Mind by constantly changing the rules of the game (including the Mind's own rules).

Now, it is not a question of deciding which of the four hypotheses is the correct one. The mental experiment was designed to demonstrate that, *however things may go,* not only is it possible for a plurality of interpretations to coexist with the presumed legality of the interpreted object, but also that it would not even make sense to try out all the interpretations unless we were to presuppose that there was something there to interpret.

I believe that recognizing the legality of the object leads us to distinguish a philosophy of conjecture and interpretance from a philosophy of weak thought. There is a minimal and noningenuous definition of realism, according to which a realist is someone who believes that things *go a certain way*—even though we may not know which way and may never succeed in knowing. And even if they were convinced that they will never know how things go, this kind of realist continues to investigate how they go, hoping to reach a satisfactory approximation, and forever prepared to correct their interpretations should things oppose the slightest resistance to their "readings" of them. The point is that this realist of ours starts out from the premise that, even if things were to go a different way every day (if the world had no rules), this too would still be the way things went (the ironclad law that guarantees permanent irregularity). So that, though we may accept that the descriptions we give of the World (or of a text as World) are always prospective, this ought not to prevent our readings from attempting to keep pace with the world, at least from a certain point of view, without ever pretending that the said readings, even when they seem on the whole to be "good," are to be considered definitive. And, since in this series of interpretations we stick to the parameters offered by the facts to be interpreted (even if only locally and from a certain perspective), we must presume that the readings we give of the facts may be accurate or they may be completely off the wall.

But did anyone ever really believe that there are no facts, only interpretations? Vattimo and Rovatti were not wrong in appealing to Nietzsche, because that is where this very theory is explained, in an especially intense manner in "Ueber Wahrheit und Lüge im aussermoralischen Sinne" ("On Truth and Lies in a Nonmoral Sense") (1873), a text I already discussed in *Kant and the Platypus*. Since nature has thrown away the key, the intellect plays with fictions that it calls truth, or a system of concepts, based on the legislation of language. We think we are talking about (and knowing) trees, colors, snow, and flowers, but they are metaphors that do not correspond to the original essences. Every word immediately becomes a concept, draining away with its pallid universality the differences between fundamentally unequal things: so we believe that compared to the multiplicity of individual leaves there exists a "primal" leaf "from which all leaves were woven, drawn, delineated, dyed, curled, painted—but by a clumsy pair of hands, so that no single example turned out to be a faithful, correct and reliable copy of the primal form" (Nietzsche 1873: 145). It is difficult for us to admit that birds or insects perceive the world differently from us, and it makes no sense either to say which perception is the correct one, because this would call for that criterion of "exact perception" that does not exist because "nature knows neither forms nor concepts and hence no species, but only an 'X' which is inaccessible to us and indefinable by us" (ibid.: 145).

Truth, then, becomes "a mobile army of metaphors, metonymies, and anthropomorphisms," produced poetically, only to become fossilized into knowledge, "illusions of which we have forgotten that they are illusions" (ibid.: 146), coins whose images has been rubbed away and are now considered simply as pieces of metal and no longer as coins. We thus become accustomed to lying according to convention, having reduced the metaphors to *schemata* and *concepts*. Thence a pyramidal order of castes and ranks, laws and delimitations, entirely constructed by language, an immense "Roman *columbarium*" of concepts, the graveyard of intuition.

No question but that this is a fascinating account of how the edifice of language regiments the landscape of the world, but Nietzsche fails to consider two intuitively evident phenomena. One is that, if we adapt ourselves to the constrictions of the columbarium, we can still manage to give some kind of account of the World (if someone goes to see a doctor and tells him he has been bitten by a dog, the doctor knows what sort of injection to give him, even if he is not familiar with the particular dog that bit him). The other is that every now and then the World forces us to adapt the columbarium, or even to choose an alternative model to the columbarium (which is, at the end of the day, the problem of the revolution of cognitive paradigms).

Nietzsche is undeniably cognizant of the existence of natural constrictions and can see a way to change. The constrictions seem to him to be "terrible forces" that constantly press upon us, countering "scientific" truths with other truths of a different nature; but he evidently refuses to recognize them by conceptualizing them in their turn, given that it is in order to escape them that we have wrought, by way of a defense, our conceptual suit of armor. Change is possible, though not in the form of tinkering with the structure, but instead in the form of a permanent poetic revolution: "if each of us still had a different kind of sensuous perception, if we ourselves could only perceive now as, variously, a bird, a worm, or a plant does, or if one of us were to see a stimulus as red, a second person were to see the same stimulus as blue, while a third were even to hear it as a sound, nobody would ever speak of nature as something conforming to laws" (ibid.: 149).

Therefore, art (and with it myth) "constantly confuses the cells and the classifications of concepts by setting up new translations, metaphors, metonymies; it constantly manifests the desire to shape the given world of the waking human being in ways which are just as multiform, irregular, inconsequential, incoherent, charming and ever-new, as things are in the world of dream" (ibid.: 151).

If these are the premises, our first option would be to reject what surrounds us (and the way in which we vainly try to reduce it to order) and take refuge in dreams as a flight from reality. Nietzsche in fact cites Pascal, for whom, in order to be happy, all it would take would be to dream *every night* of being king, but he then admits that this dominion of art over life, however delightful, would be a deception. Otherwise, and this is what Nietzsche's heirs have taken as the real lesson, art can say what it says because it is Being itself, in its weakness and generosity, that accepts any definition, and takes pleasure from seeing itself seen as changeable, a dreamer, extenuatingly vigorous and victoriously weak, no longer as "fullness, presence or foundation, but rather as fracture, absence of foundation, work and pain" (Vattimo 1993: 73). Being can therefore only be spoken insofar as it is in decline; instead of imposing itself, it withdraws. Thus we have arrived at an "ontology organized into 'weak' categories" (ibid.: 5). Nietzsche's announcement of the death of God is nothing more than the proclamation of the end of the stable structure of Being (Vattimo 1984: 158). From now on, Being will present itself only "as suspension and withdrawal" (Vattimo 1997: 13).

It is not my intention to discuss whether, from the point of view of weak thought, Being should still be written with a capital B (and in fact Vattimo does not do so). I will stick to the mental experiment previously proposed, and I will speak not of Being but of the World (if "Die Welt ist alles, was der Fall ist" ["The world is everything that is the case"—Wittgenstein], and if we call World what happens to be the case). The problem is that what prevents us believing that all points of view are equally valid, that the World is merely the effect of language and, in addition to being malleable and weak, is a mere *flatus vocis,* and is therefore the work of Poets, characterized as daydreamers, liars, imitators of the nonexistent, capable of irresponsibly placing a horse's head on a human body and turning every entity into a chimera.

The trouble is, in the first place, that, once we had settled our accounts with the World, we would still find ourselves having to settle them with the subject that emits this *flatus vocis* (a problem which is in any case the limit of any magic idealism). And, in the second place, if it is a hermeneutic principle that there are no facts, only interpretations, this still does not exclude the possibility of "bad" interpretations. There is no winning hand at poker that has not been *put together* by a choice of the player (encouraged maybe by chance), but this does not mean that every hand assembled by the player is a winning hand. All it would take is for my opponent to respond to my three aces with a straight flush for my wager to turn out to have been a bad bet. There are times in our game with the World when the World responds to our three aces with a straight flush. Furthermore, there are players who make a bet and are eventually obliged to show a hand that, according to the laws of poker, contains no valid combination of cards: and the others, in unison, observe that the player must be crazy, or doesn't know how to play, or is bluffing. What is the status of bluffing in a universe in which one interpretation is as good as another? What are the intersubjective criteria that allow us to define that particular combination of cards as off the wall? What criterion allows us to distinguish between dreams, poetic inventions, and LSD trips (there are people who after taking LSD have thrown themselves out of windows convinced they could fly and finished up in a heap on the sidewalk—contrary, mind you, to all their hopes and intentions), and, on the other hand, acceptable statements concerning the things of the physical or historical world that surrounds us?

Let us posit, as Vattimo does (1994: 100), a difference between epistemology, as "the construction of a body of rigorous knowledge and the solution of problems in the light of paradigms that lay down the rules for the verification of propositions" (which seems to correspond to Nietzsche's picture of the conceptual universe of a given culture) and hermeneutics, as "the activity that takes place during the encounter with different paradigmatic horizons, which do not allow themselves to be assessed on the basis of some kind of conformity (to rules or, in the final analysis, to the thing) but exist as 'poetic' proposals of other worlds, of the establishment of new rules" (Vattimo 1997: 79). What new rule should the Community prefer, what rule should it condemn as folly? There are still people hell-bent on demonstrating that the earth is square, that we live not on but beneath its crust, that statues weep, that forks can be bent by television, that the apes are descended from man—and we have to come up with a public criterion by which to judge whether their ideas are in some way acceptable.

In a debate that took place in 1990 (published in Eco 1992), on whether or not criteria for textual interpretation exist, Richard Rorty—broadening the discourse to include criteria for interpreting things in the world—argued against the notion that the use of a screwdriver for screwing in screws is imposed by the object itself, while its use for opening a package is imposed by our own subjectivity (he was discussing my distinction between the *interpretation* and *use* of a text (cf. Eco 1979).

In the oral debate, Rorty had polemically asserted his right to go so far as to interpret a screwdriver as something useful for scratching your ears. This explains my reply, which still survives in the printed version of the debate because I was unaware that in the version of his contribution submitted by Rorty to the publisher that example had been left out. Rorty had evidently concluded that it was more of a boutade than a logical argument, but since another critic (less inclined to self-criticism than Rorty) might still conceivably use the wisecrack as an argument, my objection is still valid: a screwdriver can certainly be very useful for opening a package but it is not advisable to use it for poking about in your ear, because it is too sharp and too long for the hand to be able to exercise control over its movements; and therefore it would be better to use a light plastic stick with a wad of cotton at either end. Which is the same thing as appealing to the notion of *affordance* proposed by Gibson (1966) or to that of pertinence with respect to a practice proposed by Prieto (1975). There is something about the conformation of my body and that of the screwdriver that does not permit me to interpret and use the latter as the whim takes me.

This is why, in *Kant and the Platypus*, I argued that we have to recognize a *hard core of being*, such that some of the things that we say about it or for it cannot and must not be taken as "valid" (and if they are said by the Poets they should be taken as valid only insofar as they refer to a possible world and not to the world of real facts).

In speaking of a "hard core" I did not mean something like a "stable kernel" which we might identify sooner or later, not the Law of Laws, but, more prudently, *lines of resistance* that render some of our approaches fruitless. It is precisely our faith in these lines of resistance that ought also to guide the discourse on hermeneutics, because, if that discourse were to assume that one can say anything and everything one pleases about being and the World, the intellectual and moral tension that guides its continual interrogation would no longer make sense—and it would be content to amuse itself with the Futurists' *parole in libertà*. In any case, Heidegger himself recognized limits, otherwise he would not have concentrated so much on the problem of Death—the limit, the cosmic *tendency,* par excellence.

When we claim to have learned from experience that nature exhibits stable tendencies, there is no need to think of complex laws like the law of universal gravity, but of experiences that are simpler and more immediate, like the apparent rising and setting of the sun, the fact that things fall downward and not upward, the existence of species. Universals may well be a figment and an infirmity of thought, but once a dog and a cat have been identified as belonging to a species, we immediately learn that if we couple a dog with a dog what is born is a dog, and if we couple a dog with a cat nothing is born— and even if something were born it would be unable to reproduce itself.. This does not yet mean that what we have recognized is the reality (Darwinian or Platonic) of genera and species. All it is meant to suggest is that speaking *per generalia* may well be a result of our *penuria nominum,* but that *something* resistant has driven us to invent general terms (whose extension we can always revise and correct). The objection that biotechnology may one day render these tendencies obsolete and create a new species halfway between a cat and a dog is not relevant. The fact that a technology (which by definition alters the limits of nature) is required in order to violate them means that the limits of nature exist.

We use expressions to express a content, and this content is carved up and organized differently by different cultures (and languages). Out of what is it carved? Out of an amorphous magma, which *was there* before language performed its vivisections and which we may call the *continuum* of the content, all that can be experienced, all that can be said, all that can be thought—if you will, the infinite horizon of all that is, was, and will be, either of necessity or by contingency. It would seem that, before a culture has organized it linguistically in the form of content, this continuum is everything and nothing, and therefore eludes all definition. Nevertheless, when Hjelmslev

(1943: 13 and 46–48) speaks of this amorphous continuum that every language organizes in a different way, he says that linguistic chains such as *I do not know, je ne sais pas, en tiedä, naluvara, jeg véd det ikke,* despite their differences, express the same *mening,* that is, the same thought. The Danish term *mening* is a cognate of *meaning,* and for the English version of his work Hjelmslev accepted the term *purport.* How can an amorphous continuum have a meaning or a purport?

As a matter of fact Hjelmslev was not speaking of a linguistic phenomenon but rather of an extralinguistic one: he said that the purport could be described by various extralinguistic disciplines. Thus languages are obliged to recognize extrasemiotic constrictions that they cannot ignore. In other words different expressions such as *it is raining, il pleut,* and *piove* all refer to the same phenomenon. Which amounts to saying that in the magma of the continuum there are lines of resistance and possibilities for flow, like the grain in wood or marble that makes it easier to cut it one way rather than another. Every culture runs up against the extralinguistic problem of rain; it rains or doesn't rain in every culture, and *tertium datur* only when it drizzles or when hoarfrost forms.

If the continuum itself has lines of tendency, we are not entitled to say whatever we like. There are *directions,* maybe not compulsory directions, but certainly directions to which entry is *forbidden.* There are things we cannot say. It doesn't matter if these things were once said. We subsequently "banged our heads into" evidence that convinced us that we could no longer say what we formerly said.

Although we talk about encountering something that obliges us to recognize lines of tendency and resistance, we are not yet ready to start defining "laws." If, on the path I am taking through the woods, I find a boulder blocking my way, I have no choice but to turn left or right or decide to go back (though, unlike Chrysippus's dog, I could also stop and lean back against the rock and dedicate the remainder of my life to contemplating the Tao). But I have no reassurance that the decision I make will help me get to know the woods better. The occurrence merely interrupts my initial project and induces me to come up with another. Stating that there are lines of resistance does not amount to saying, as Peirce claims, that there are universal laws that operate in nature. The hypothesis of a law is only one of the ways in which we can react to the encounter with a resistance. Habermas, in seeking to identify the kernel of Peirce's criticism of Kant's thing-in-itself, stresses the fact that Peirce's problem is not saying that something (hidden behind the appearances that aspire to mirror it) has, like a mirror, a reverse side that eludes reflection, a side that we are almost certain to discover one day, so long as we can circumvent the figure that we see: the fact is that reality imposes restrictions on our knowledge only in the sense that it does not permit false interpretations (Habermas 1995: 251).

Stating that there are lines of resistance simply means that, even if it appears as an effect of language, the World always presents us with something that is *already given* and not *posited* by us. What is *already given* are precisely the lines of resistance.

In *Kant and the Platypus*, I expressed my opinion that the appearance of these resistances is the closest thing we can find, before any First Philosophy or Theology, to the idea of God or the Law. Certainly, this is a God who manifests Himself as pure Negativity, pure Limit, pure "No"—something quite different from the God of revealed religions, of whom he retains only the severest traits, as exclusive Lord of Interdiction, ever intent only upon repeating "Of this tree thou shalt not eat." Since, however, a tendentious reader has seen in these affirmations of mine a proposal for a new proof for the existence of God, I find myself obliged to make up for his lack of sensitivity to the stratagems of *elocutio* by pointing out (as in the most desperate cases we may be obliged to explain we were making a joke) that the lines of resistance are not a metaphor for God, but, on the contrary, the idea of a God who says "No" functions as a metaphor for the lines of resistance.

And, seeing that our need not to be misunderstood compels us to explain even our metaphors, labeling them as such, let me make it clear that it is also a metaphor to say that the lines of resistance confront us with a no. The World says no in the same way a mole would say no if we asked it to fly. It is not as if the mole is aware that he cannot fly. The mole proceeds on his terrestrial and subterranean way, and does not know what it means not to be a mole. He plays the mole to his own moliness.

To be sure, animals run into obstacles too, and struggle to overcome them: think of the dog that barks and scratches at the closed door and bites at the handle. But in a case like this the animal is already approaching a condition similar to our own; it evinces desires and intentions, and the limit is a limit with respect to its desires (or its instincts). A closed door in and of itself is not a no, indeed it could be a yes for someone seeking privacy and protection behind it. It becomes a no only for the dog who wants to come in.

It is we who, since the Mind can also provide imaginary representations of impossible worlds, ask things to be what they are not and, when they continue to be what they are, conclude they are answering no, opposing a limit. But the limit lies in our desire, in our aspiration toward absolute freedom. Death itself appears to us as a limit, when as living creatures we fear it. But at the moment of death it arrives just when things are going exactly the way they must go—the very idea that death arrives is no more than a metaphor: no one arrives, heart and brain simply stop, from the most natural causes.

In the face of the *already given,* we proceed by conjecture, and we do our best to get others to accept our conjectures. That is to say, we publicly compare our conjectures with what others know of the *already given.* It may be that this attitude does not define a "strong" thought, in the sense in which the various tribunals of Reason and Faith (more closely related than may appear at first blush) see themselves as strong. But it certainly defines a thought that continually runs up against the "forces" that oppose it. And since racing improves the breed, a conjectural thought, while it may not be strong, may not be weak either, but it will be *well-tempered.*

If Vattimo were to admit that his "weakness" is also a metaphor for a well-tempered thought, he would be welcome to become a member of my sect. But if a weak thinker should happen to agree with Nietzsche that everything is a metaphor, could we still recognize a metaphor for what it is?

References

Abelard, Peter. 1956. *Dialectica,* ed. L. M. de Rijk. Van Gorcum: Assen.

Albano Leoni, F., et al. eds. 1998. *Ai limiti del linguaggio.* Bari: Laterza.

Alighieri, Dante. 1909. *Convivio,* trans. William Walrond Jackson. Oxford: Clarendon Press.

Angelini, Cesare. 1969. "Introduzione and commento all'Apocalisse." In *Apocalisse Xilografica Estense,* trans. Cesare Angelini. Parma: Franco Maria Ricci.

Apel, Karl-Otto. 1975. *Der Denkweg von Charles S. Peirce.* Frankfurt: Suhramp.

——. 1995. "Transcendental Semiotics and Hypothetical Metaphysics of Evolution: A Peircean or Quasi-Peircean Answer to a Recurrent Problem of Post-Kantian Philosophy." In Ketner, ed. 1995.

Apresjian, Jurij. D. 1966. "Analyse distributionnelle des significations et des champs sémantiques structurés." *Langages* 1: 44–74.

Aquinus, St. Thomas. 1983. *On Being and Essence,* translated with an introduction and notes by Armand Maurer, C.S.B., 2nd revised edition. Toronto: Pontifical Institute of Medieval Studies (Second edition 1968, Reprinted).

Aristotle. 1926. *The "Art" of Rhetoric,* trans. John Henry Freese. Cambridge, MA: Harvard University Press.

Assunto, Rosario. 1961. *La critica d'arte nel pensiero medievale.* Milan: il Saggiatore.

Auerbach, Heinrich. 1944. "Figura." In *Neue Dantenstudien* 5.

Balme, David M. 1961. "Aristotle's Use of Differentiae in Zoology." In S. Mansion, ed., *Aristote and les problèmes de méthode.* Leuven: Publications Universitaires de Louvain.

Barney, Stephen A., W. J. Lewis, J. A. Beach, and Oliver Berghof, trans. with Introduction and Notes. 2006. *The Etymologies of Isidore of Seville.* Cambridge: Cambridge University Press.

Barsalou, Lawrence. 1992. "Frames, Concepts and Conceptual Fields." In A. Lehrer and E. Feder Kittay, eds., *Frames, Fields and Contrasts.* Hillsdale, NJ: Erlbaum.

Barthes, Roland. 1964. "Elements de sémiologie." *Communications* 4: 91–144.

Battistoni, Giorgio. 1995. "Tramiti ebraici e fonti medievali accessibili a Dante. 2. Manoello Giudeo." *Labyrinthos* 27–28: 35–69.

———. 1999. "Tramiti ebraici e fonti medievali accessibili a Dante: 3. Dante nel 'Paradiso' di Manoello Giudeo." *Labyrinthos* 35–36: 41–80.

Baudry, Léon. 1958. *Lexique philosophique de Guillaume d'Ockham: Etude des notions fondamentales*. Paris: Lethielleux.

Bäumker, Clemens. 1923. "Die europeische Philosophie des Mittelalters." In Wilhelm Wundt et al., *Allgemeine Geschichte der Philosophie*, 2nd ed. Berlin: Teubner.

Beato di Liébana. 1985. *Sancti Beati a Liébana Commentarius in Apocalypsin*, ed. E. Romero-Pose. Rome: Poligrafico dello Stato.

Beltran, Evencio. 1998. "Les questions sur la rhétorique d'Aristote de Jean de Jandun." In Dahan and Rosier-Catach, eds. 1998.

Beonio-Brocchieri Fumagalli, Mariateresa. 1969. *La Logica di Abelardo*. Florence: La Nuova Italia.

———. 1987. "L'intellettuale." In Jacques Le Goff, ed., *L'uomo medievale*. Bari: Laterza.

———, ed. 1981. *Le enciclopedie dell'occidente medievale*. Turin: Loescher.

Berg, Jan. 1983. "Aristotle's Theory of Definition." *In Atti del congresso internazionale di storia della logica. 4–8 dicembre 1982*. Bologna: Clueb.

Bertini, Ferruccio. 2003. "Da Cicerone alla Poetria Nova di Geoffroy de Vinsauf." In L. Calboli Montefusco, ed., *Papers on Rhetoric V*. Rome: Herder.

Biard, Joël. 1998. "Science et rhétorique dans les Questions sur la Rhétorique de Jean Buridan." In Dahan and Rosier-Catach, eds., 1998.

Bierwisch, Manfred. 1970. "Semantics." In J. Lyons, ed., *New Horizons in Linguistics*. Harmondsworth: Penguin Books.

———. 1971. "On Classifying Semantic Features." In D. Steinberg and L. A. Jakobovits, eds., *Semantics*. London: Cambridge University Press.

———. 1986. "Semantics." In T. A. Sebeok, ed., *Encyclopedic Dictionary of Semiotics*, vol. 2. Berlin: Mouton de Gruyter.

Binkley, Peter. 1997. "Preachers' Response to the Thirteenth Century Encyclopedism." In Binkley, ed., 1997.

———, ed. 1997. *Pre-Modern Encyclopedic Texts*. Leiden: Brill.

Black, Deborah. 1990. *Logic and Aristotle's Rhetoric and Poetics in Medieval Arabic Philosophy*. Leiden: Brill.

Black, Max. 1955. "Metaphor." In *Proceedings of Aristotelian Society* 55: 273–294.

———. 1979. "More about Metaphor." In Ortony, ed., 1979.

Boas, George. 1973–1974. "Teriophily." In Philip P. Wiener, ed. in chief, *Dictionary of the History of Ideas*. New York: Scribner's Sons.

Boehner, Philothetus. 1958. "Ockham's Theory of Signification." In E. Buytaert, ed., *Collected Articles on Ockham*. St. Bonaventure, New York: The Franciscan Institute (originally published in *Franciscan Studies* 6 [1946]).

Boethius, Anicius Manlius Torquatus Severinus. 1988. *Boethius's In Ciceronis Topica*, trans. with notes and an introduction by Eleonore Stump, Ithaca, NY: Cornell University Press.

———. 1998. *De divisione liber.* Critical edition, translation, prolegomena, and commentary by John Magee. Leiden: Brill.

Bogges, W. F. 1970. "Aristotle's Poetics in the Fourteenth Century." *Studies in Philology* 67: 278–294.

———. 1971. "Hermannus Alemannus's Rhetorical Translations." *Viator* 2: 227:250.

Bolzoni, Lina. 1995. *La stanza della memoria.* Turin: Einaudi.

Bonfantini, Massimo, and Giampaolo Proni. 1983. "To Guess or Not to Guess." In Eco and Sebeock, eds., 1983.

Bonfantini, Massimo, and Roberto Grazia. 1976. "Teoria della conoscenza and funzione dell'icona in Peirce." In *Versus* 15: 1–16.

Bonomi, Andrea, ed. 1973. *La struttura logica del linguaggio.* Milan: Bompiani.

Bord, Janet. 1976. *Mazes and Labyrinths of the World.* London: Latimer.

Borges, Jorge-Luis. 1962. *Labyrinths: Selected Stories and Other Writings.* Edited by Donald A. Yates & James E. Irby. New York: New Directions.

———. 1964. *Other Inquisitions, 1937–1952,* trans. Ruth L. C. Simms. Austin: University of Texas Press.

———. 1972. "Doctor Brodie's Report." In *Doctor Brodie's Report,* trans. Norman Thomas di Giovanni. New York: E. P. Dutton.

———. 1998. *Collected Fictions,* trans. Andrew Hurley. New York: Viking-Penguin.

Bori, Pier Cesare. 1987. *L'interpretazione infinita. L'ermeneutica cristiana antica and le sue trasformazioni.* Bologna: il Mulino.

Bosanquet, Bernard. 1904. *A History of Aesthetic.* London: Swan Sonnenscheit.

Bréal, Michel. 1883. "Les lois intellectuelle du langage. Fragment de sémantique." In *L'Annuaire de l'Association pour l'encouragement des ètudes grecques en France XVII.*

———. 1897. *Essai de Sémantique: Science des significations.* Paris-Genève: Slatkine (Reprint Paris: Hachette, 1924).

———. 1900. *Semantics: studies in the science of meaning,* trans. Nina Cust. New York: Henry Holt (Reprint with a new introduction by Joshua Whatmough. NY: Dover, 1964).

Brown, Mary Franklin. 2012. *Reading the World: Encyclopedic Writing in the Scholastic Age.* Chicago: University of Chicago Press.

Bruner, Jerome. 1990. *Acts of Meaning.* Cambridge, MA: Harvard University Press.

Busi, Giulio. 2004. "La Qabbalah secondo Dante." *Il Sole-24 Ore,* October 17.

Butterworth, Charles E. 1986. *Averroes' Middle Commentaries on Aristotle's Poetics.* Princeton: Princeton University Press.

Buyssens, Eric. 1943. *Le langage et le discours.* Brussels: Officine de Publicité.

Calboli, Gualtiero 2005. "La metafora tra Aristotele e Cicerone, e oltre." In Lorusso, ed., 2005.

Calboli Montefusco, Lucia. 2005. "La percezione del simile: metafora and comparazione in Aristotele." In Lorusso, ed., 2005.

Calimani, Riccardo. 1987. *Storia dell'ebreo errante.* Milan: Rusconi.

Camón Aznar, José. 1960. "La miniatura española en el siglo X." In *Gesammelte Aufsätze zur Kulturgeschichte Spaniens* 16.

Campanelli, Cosimo. 1996. *Arte and poesia nella filosofia di Jacques Maritain.* Salerno: Palladio.

Carnap, Rudolf. 1955. "Meaning and Synonymy in Natural Languages." *Philosophical Studies* 7: 33–47.

Carreras y Artau, Joaquim. 1957. "Raimundo Lulio y la Cabala." *Las ciencias* 22: 146–150.

Carreras y Artau, Tomás, and Joaquím Carreras y Artau. 1939. *Historia de la filosofia española: Filosofos cristianos de los siglos XII al XV.* 2 vols. Madrid: Real Academia de sciencias exactas, Fisicas y Naturales.

Carruthers, Mary. 1990. *The Book of Memory: A Study of Memory in Medieval Culture.* London: Cambridge University Press.

Casciato, Maristella et al., eds. 1986. *Enciclopedismo in Roma barocca.* Venice: Marsilio.

Cassirer, Ernst R. 1981. *Kant's Life and Thought*, trans. James Haden. New Haven and London: Yale University Press. (German original: 1918).

Cavazza, Marc, and Pierre Zweigenbaum. 1995. "Lexical Semantics. Dictionary or Encyclopedia?" In P. Saint-Di-zier and E. Viegas, eds., *Computational Lexical Semantics: Studies in Natural Language Processing.* Cambridge: Cambridge University Press.

Cavini, Walter. 1977. "Appunti sulla prima diffusione in Occidente delle opere di Sesto Empirico." *Medioevo* 3: 1–20.

Ceñal, Ramón. 1946. "Un anonimo español citado por Leibniz." *Pensamiento* 6: 201–203.

Cevolini, Alberto. 2006. *De arte excerpendi: Imparare a dimenticare nella modernità.* Florence: Olschki.

Chenu, M.-D. 1950. *Introduction à l'étude de Saint Thomas d'Aquin.* Paris: Vrin.

Cherchi, P. 1990. *Encyclopedism: From Pliny to Borges.* Chicago: University of Chicago Press.

Cicero. 1954. *Rhetorica ad Herennium.* Trans. Harry Caplan, Cambridge, MA: Harvard University Press.

Coleridge, Samuel Taylor. 1983. *Biographia Literaria*, edited by James Engell and W. Jackson Bate. *Collected Works* 7. Bollingen Series LXXV. Princeton: Princeton University Press.

Collison, R. 1966. *Encyclopaedias: Their History throughout the Ages: A Bibliographical Guide with Extensive Historical Notes to the General Encyclopaedias Issued throughout the World from 350 B.C. to the Present Day.* New York: Hafner.

Compagnon, Antoine. 1979. *La seconde main.* Paris: Seuil.

Comparetti, Domenico. 1937. *Virgilio nel Medioevo.* 3rd rist. Florence: La Nuova Italia 1967.

Corcoran, John, ed. 1974. *Ancient Logic and Its Modern Interpretations.* Dordrecht: Reidel.

Corti, Maria. 1981. *Dante a un nuovo crocevia.* Società Dantesca Italiana, Quaderno I. Florence: Libreria Commissionaria Sansoni.

Corvino, Francesco. 1955. "Sette questioni inedite di Ockham sul concetto." *Rivista critica di storia della filosofia* 10: 265–288.

Corvino, Francesco, et al. 1983. *Linguistica medievale.* Bari: Adriatica.

Coseriu, Eugenio. 1962. *Teoria del languaje y linguistica general.* Madrid: Gredos.

Coumet, Ernest. 1975. "Mersennes: dictions nouvelles à l'infini." *XVIIᵉ siècle* 109: 3–32.

Croce, Benedetto. 1902. *Estetica come scienza dell'espressione and linguistica generale.* Milan: Sandron (9th ed., Bari: Laterza, 1950).

———. 1955. *Cultura e vita morale,* 3rd ed. Bari: Laterza.

———. 1992. *The Aesthetic as the Science of Expression and of the Linguistic in General,* trans. Colin Lyas. Cambridge: Cambridge University Press.

Curley, Michael J., trans. 1979.*Physiologus: A Medieval Book of Nature Lore.* Austin: University of Texas Press.

Curtius, Ernst Robert. 1948. *Europäische Literatur und lateinisches Mittelater.* Bern: Francke.

Dahan, G., and I. Rosier-Catach, eds. 1998. La Rhétorique d'Aristote. Traditions et commentaires de l'antiquité au XVII siècle. Paris: Vrin.

Dahan, Gilbert. 1980. "Notes et textes sur la Poétique au Moyen Age." *Archives d'histoire doctrinale et littéraire du Moyen Age* 47: 171–239.

———. 1992. "Saint Thomas d'Aquin et la métaphore: Rhétorique et herméneutique." *Medioevo* 18: 85–117.

———. 1998. "L'entrée de la Rhétorique d'Aristote dans le monde latin entre 1240 et 1270." In Dahan and Rosier-Catach, eds., 1998.

D'Alembert, Jean Le Rond. 1963. *Preliminary Discourse to the Encyclopedia of Diderot,* trans. Richard N. Schwab. The Library of Liberal Arts. Indianapolis: Bobbs-Merrill.

Dante. 1961. *Divine Comedy 3: Paradiso,* trans. John D. Sinclair. Oxford: Oxford University Press.

———. 1982. *The Divine Comedy: Paradiso,* trans. Allen Mandelbaum. Berkeley: University of California Press.

———. 1996. *De vulgari eloquentia,* ed. and trans. Steven Botterill. Cambridge: Cambridge University Press.

Davidson, Donald. 1984a. "On the Very Idea of Conceptual Scheme." In *Inquiries into Truth and Interpretation.* Oxford: Oxford University Press.

———. 1984b. "Communication and Convention." In *Inquiries into Truth and Interpretation.* Oxford: Clarendon: 265–280.

———. 1986. "A Nice Derangement of Epitaphs." In E. Lepore and B. McLaughlin, eds., *Actions and Events: Perspectives on the Philosophy of Donald Davidson*. Oxford: Blackwell.

De Bruyne, Edgar. 1928. *S. Thomas d'Aquin: le milieu, l'homme, la vision du monde*. Paris: Beauchesne.

———. 1930a. "Du rôle de l'intelligence dans l'activité esthétique." In Rintelen, ed., 1930.

———. 1930b. *Esquisse d'une philosophie de l'art*. Brussels: Dewit.

———. 1946. *Etudes d'esthétique médiévale*. Bruges: De Tempel (Reprint Paris: Albin Michel, 1998).

———. 1947. *L'esthétique du moyen Âge*. Leuven: Edition de l'Institut supérieur de philosophie (included in the 1998 Albin Michel edition of De Bruyne 1946).

———. 1952–1955. *Geschiedenis van de aesthetica*. Antwerp-Amsterdam: Standaard-Boekhandel.

De Ghellinck, Joseph. 1939. "Originale et originalia." *Archivum Latinitatis Medii Aevi* 14: 95–105.

De Leo, Pietro. 1974. *Ricerche sui falsi medievali*. Reggio Calabria: Editori Meridionali Riuniti.

De Lubac, Henri. 1959–1964. *Exégèse médiévale: Les quatre sens de l'Ecriture*. Paris: Aubier.

De Mauro, Tullio. 1965. *Introduzione alla semantica*. Rome-Bari: Laterza.

De Munnynk, Maurice. 1923. "L'esthétique de Saint Thomas." In *San Tommaso d'Aquino*. Milan: Vita and Pensiero.

De Rijk, Lambert. 1962–1967. *Logica Modernorum: A Contribution to the History of Early Terminist Logic*. Assen: Van Gorcum.

———. 1975. "La signification de la proposition *(dictum propositionis)* chez Abelard." In *Studia Mediewistyczne* 16: 155–161.

———. 1982. "The Origins of the Theory of the Property of Terms." In Kretzmann et al., eds., 1982.

Debenedetti Stow, Sandra. 2004. *Dante and la mistica ebraica*. Florence: Giuntina.

Deely, John N. 1985. *Tractatus de signis: The Semiotic of John Poinsot*. Berkeley: University of California Press.

———. 1988. "The Semiotic of John Poinsot." *Semiotica* 69, nos. 1–2.

Deely, John, Brooke Williams, and Felicia E. Kruse, eds. 1986. *Frontiers in Semiotics*. Bloomington: Indiana University Press.

Deleuze, Gilles. 1963. *La philosophie critique de Kant*. Paris: PUF.

Deleuze, Gilles and Guattari, François. 1976. *Rhizome*. Paris: Minuit.

Demaria, Cristina. 2006. *Semiotica and memoria*. Rome: Carocci.

Dennett, Daniel. 1991. *Consciousness Explained*. New York: Little Brown.

———. 1978. *Brainstorms*. Montgomery: Bradford Books.

Derrida, Jacques. 1967. *De la grammatologie*. Paris: Minuit.

Desmond, Henry P. 1964. *The* De Grammatico *of St. Anselm: The Theory of Paro-nymy.* Notre Dame: University of Notre Dame Press (Publications in *Medieval Studies* 18).

Dragonetti, Robert. 1961. "La conception du langage poétique dans le De vulgari eloquentia de Dante." In *Aux frontières du langage poétique. Romanica Gandensia* IX.

Dronke, Peter. 1974. *Fabula: Explorations into the Use of Myth in Medieval Platonism.* Leiden: Brill.

———. 1986. *Dante and Medieval Latin Tradition.* Cambridge: Cambridge University Press.

Ducrot, Oswald. 1972. *Dire et ne pas dire.* Paris: Hermann.

Dummett, Michael. 1973. *Frege: Philosophy of Language.* London: Duckworth.

———. 1986. "A Nice Derangement of Epitaphs: Some Comments on Davidson and Hacking." In E. Lepore, ed., *Truth and Interpretation: On the Philosophy of Donald Davidson.* Oxford: Blackwell.

Ebbesen, Sten, ed. 1995. *Sprachtheorien in Spätantike und Mittelalter.* Tübingen: Gunter Narr.

Eco, Umberto. 1956. *Il problema estetico in San Tommaso.* Turin: Edizioni di "Filosofia" (2nd enlarged ed., Milan: Bompiani, 1970).

———. 1959. "Sviluppo dell'estetica medievale." In *Momenti and problemi di storia dell'estetica,* vol. 1. Milan: Marzorati (new enlarged edition Eco 1987a).

———. 1961. "Storiografia medievale ed estetica teorica." *Filosofia* 12: 505–524.

———. 1962a. *La struttura assente.* Milan: Bompiani.

———. 1962b. *L'opera aperta.* Milan: Bompiani.

———. 1971. "Semantica della metafora." In *Le forme del contenuto.* Milan: Bompiani.

———. 1973. "Palinsesto su Beato." In *Beato di Liébana.* Milan: Franco Maria Ricci.

———. 1975. *Trattato di semiotica generale.* Milan: Bompiani.

———. 1979a. *Lector in fabula.* Milan: Bompiani.

———. 1979b. *A Theory of Semiotics.* Bloomington, IN: Indiana University Press.

———. 1981. "Dall'albero al labirinto." In A. Bonito Oliva, ed., *Luoghi del silenzio imparziale.* Milan: Feltrinelli.

———. 1983a. "Corna, zoccoli, scarpe." In U. Eco and T. A. Sebeok, eds., *Il segno dei tre.* Milan: Bompiani (also in Eco 1990).

———. 1983b. "L'antiporfirio." In G. Vattimo and A. Rovatti, eds., *Il pensiero debole.* Milan: Feltrinelli, 1983 (also in Eco 1985c).

———. 1983c. *Sette anni di desiderio: Cronache 1977-1983.* Milan: Bompiani.

———. 1984a. *Semiotica and filosofia del linguaggio.* Turin: Einaudi.

———. 1984b. *Semiotics and the Philosophy of Language.* Bloomington, IN: Indiana University Press.

—————. 1984c. *The Role of the Reader. Explorations in the Semiotics of Texts.* Bloomington, IN: Indiana University Press.

—————. 1985a. "L'antiporfirio." In Eco 1985c.

—————. 1985b. "L'Epistola XIII and l'allegorismo medievale." In Eco 1985c.

—————. 1985c. *Sugli specchi.* Milan: Bompiani.

—————. 1986a. *Art and Beauty in the Middle Ages,* trans. Hugh Bredin. New Haven: Yale University Press.

—————. 1986b. "La ligne et le labyrinthe: les structures de la pensée latine." In G. Duby, ed., *Civilisation latine.* Paris: Orban.

—————. 1987a. "Ars oblivionalis." *Kos* 3: 40–53.

—————. 1987b. *Arte and bellezza nell'estetica medievale.* Milan: Bompiani.

—————. 1988. *The Aesthetics of Thomas Aquinas,* trans. Hugh Bredin. Cambridge, MA: Harvard University Press.

—————. 1989. "La semiosi ermetica and il paradigma del velame." In Pozzato, ed., 1989.

—————. 1990a. *I limiti dell'interpretazione.* Milan: Bompiani.

—————. 1990b. *The Limits of Interpretation.* Bloomington, IN: Indiana University Press.

—————. 1991. "La lingua universale di Ramón Llull." *Cahiers Ferdinand de Saussure* 45: 121–149.

—————. 1992a. "Forma locutionis." In Gianni Vattimo, ed., *Filosofia 91.* Bari: Laterza.

—————. 1992b. *Interpretation and Overinterpretation.* Cambridge: Cambridge University Press.

—————. 1992c. "Pourquoi Llulle n'était pas un kabbaliste." *Magie du Livre, Livres de Magie=Aries* 15: 85–93.

—————. 1993. *La ricerca della lingua perfetta.* Rome-Bari: Laterza.

—————. 1995. *The Search for the Perfect Language,* trans. James Fentress. Oxford: Blackwell.

—————. 1996a. *The Island of the Day Before,* trans. William Weaver. New York: Penguin Books.

—————. 1996b. "Jerusalem and the Temple as Signs in Medieval Culture." In Manetti, ed., 1996.

—————. 1996c. "Ostrigotta, ora capesco." Introduction to James Joyce, *Anna Livia Plurabelle,* ed. Rosa Maria Bosinelli. Turin: Einaudi.

—————. 1997a. "I rapporti tra *Revolutio Alphabetaria* e Lullismo." In G. C. Garfagnini, ed., *Giovanni Pico della Mirandola: Convegno Internazionale di Studi nel Cinquecentesimo Anniversario della morte (1494–1994), Mirandola, 4–8 ottobre 1994.* Florence: Olschki.

—————. 1997b. *Kant and l'ornitorinco.* Milan: Bompiani.

—————. 1998a. "Il silenzio di Kant sull'ornitorinco." In F. Albano Leoni et al., eds., *Ai limiti del linguaggio.* Bari: Laterza.

————. 1998b. *Serendipities: Language and Lunacy.* New York: Columbia University Press.

————. 1998c. *Tra menzogna e ironia.* Milano: Bompiani.

————. 2000. *Kant and the Platypus*, trans. Alastair McEwen. New York: Harcourt Brace.

————. 2001. "Cinque sensi di 'semantica.'" *Versus* 88–89: 21–35.

————. 2002. *Sulla letteratura.* Milan: Bompiani.

————. 2003. *Dire quasi la stessa cosa.* Milan: Bompiani.

————. 2004a. "L'esthétique médiévale d'Edgar de Bruyne." In M. Storme et al., eds., *Ethiek, Esthetieck en Cultuurfilosofie biy Edgar de Bruyne.* Brussels: Koninlijke Vlaamse Academie van Belgie poor Wetenschappen en Kunsten.

————. 2004b. *On Literature*, trans. Martin McLaughlin. New York: Harcourt.

————. 2004c. "Fakes in Arts and Crafts." In Roland Posner, Klaus Robering, and Thomas A. Sebeok, eds., *Semiotik/Semiotics: Ein Handbuch zu den zeichentheoretischen Grundlagen von Natur und Kultur/A Handbook in the Sign-Theoretic Foundations of Nature and Culture*, 4 vols. Berlin: Walter de Gruyter.

————. 2005. "La notion de limite." *Divinatio* 21: 11–30.

————. 2007. "Weak Thought and the Limits of Interpretation," trans. Antonio Calcagno. In Santiago Zabala, ed., *Weakening Philosophy: Essays in Honour of Gianni Vattimo.* Montréal: McGill University Press.

Eco, Umberto, and Costantino Marmo. 2005. "La teoria aristotelica della metafora nel Medioevo." In Lorusso, ed., 2005.

————, eds. 1989. *On the Medieval Theory of Signs.* Amsterdam: Benjamins.

Eco, Umberto, and Thomas A. Sebeok, eds. 1983. *The Sign of Three.* Bloomington, IN: Indiana University Press.

Eco, Umberto, Roberto Lambertini, Costantino Marmo, and Andrea Tabarroni. 1986. "'Latratus canis' or: the Dog's Barking." In John Deely, Brooke Williams, and Felicia E. Kruse, eds., *Frontiers in Semiotics.* Bloomington, IN: Indiana University Press.

Eco, Umberto, and Patrizia Violi. 1987. "Instructional Semantics for Presuppositions." In *Semiotica* 64, nos. 1–2.

Eco, Umberto, and Marilyn Migiel. 1988. "An *Ars Oblivionalis*? Forget It." *PMLA*, 103, 254–261.

Eliot, Charles W., ed. 1909. *Prefaces and Prologues to Famous Books.* New York: P. F. Collier & Son, The Harvard Classics.

Esposito, Elena 2001. *La memoria sociale: Mezzi per comunicare and modi di dimenticare.* Rome-Bari: Laterza.

Evans, Robert J. W. 1973. *Rudolf II and His World: A Study in Intellectual History, 1576–1612.* Oxford: Clarendon.

————. 1985. *The Making of Habsburg Monarchy, 1500–1700.* Oxford: Oxford University Press.

Fabbrichesi Leo, Rossella, 1981. "L'iconismo and l'interpretazione fenomeno-
    logica del concetto di somiglianza in C. S. Peirce." In *ACME, Annali della
    Facoltà di Lettere and Filosofia dell'Università degli Studi di Milano*,
    XXXIV, iii. Enlarged ed. published as *Sulle tracce del segno*. Florence: Nu-
    ova Italia, 1986.

Faral, Edmond. 1924. *Les arts poétiques du XIIᵉ et du XIIIᵉ siècle*: Recherches et
    documents sur la technique littéraire du Moyen Age. Paris: Champion.

Farmer, Steve A. 1998. Syncretism in the West: Pico's 900 Theses (1486). Tempe,
    AZ: MRTS.

Federici Vescovini, Graziella. 1965. *Studi sulla prospettiva medievale*. Turin:
    Giappichelli.

Fernandez, Ramona. 2001. "Imagining Literacy: Rhythms of Knowledge." In
    American Culture and Literature. Austin: University of Texas Press.

Ferreiro Alemparte, J. 1983. "Hermann el Alemán, traductor del siglo XIII en
    Toledo." In *Hispania sacra: Revista de historia ecclesiástica de España* 35.

Feyerabend, Paul K. 1975. *Against Method*. London: NLB.

Fichant, Michel. 1991. Postfazione a Gottfried W. Leibniz, *De l'horizon de la doc-
    trine humaine*. Paris: Vrin.

Fillmore, Charles J. 1968. "The case for case." In E. Bach and Robert T. Harms,
    eds., *Universals in Linguistic Theory*. New York: Holt Rinehart and
    Winston.

———. 1969. "Types of Lexical Information." In F. Kiefer, ed., *Studies in Syntax
    and Semantics*. Dordrecht: Reidel.

———. 1977. "The Case for Case Reopened." In P. Cole et al., eds., *Syntax and Se-
    mantics: Grammatical Relations*. New York: Academic Press.

Focillon, Henri. 1938. *Art d'Occident*. Paris: Colin.

———. 1952. *L'an mil*. Paris: Colin.

Formigari, Lia. 1970. *Linguistica ed empirismo nei seicento inglese*. Rome-Bari:
    Laterza.

Foucault, Michel. 1966. *Les mots et les choses*. Paris: Gallimard.

———. 1970. *The Order of Things: An Archeology of the Human Sciences*. Pantheon
    Books.

Fowler, Robert. 1977. "Encyclopedias: Definitions and Theoretical Problems." In
    Binkley, ed., 1997.

Frank, Thomas. 1979. *Segno and significato: John Wilkins and la lingua filosofica*.
    Naples: Guida.

Frawley, William. 1981. "In Defense of the Dictionary: A Response to Haiman."
    Lingua 55: 53–61.

Fredborg, K. M., L. Nielsen, and J. Pinborg, eds. 1978. "An Unedited Part of Roger
    Bacon's Opus Maius: 'De signis.'" *Traditio* 34: 75–136.

Frege, Gottlob. 1892. "Uber Sinn und Bedeutung." In *Zeitschrift für Philosophie
    und Kritik* 100: 25–50.

French, Peter J. 1972. *John Dee: The World of an Elizabethan Magus*. London: Routledge.

Fumagalli, Armando. 1995. *Il reale nel linguaggio: Indicalità and realismo nella semiotica di Peirce*. Milan: Vita and Pensiero.

Gallavotti, Carlo. 1974. "Introduzione." In *Aristotele, Dell'arte poetica*. Rome: Fondazione Valla.

Gargani, Aldo G. 1971. *Hobbes and la scienza*. Turin: Einaudi.

———, ed. 1979. *Crisi della ragione*. Turin: Einaudi.

Garin, Eugenio. 1937. *Giovanni Pico della Mirandola: Vita and dottrina*. Florence: Le Monnier.

———. 1966. *Storia della filosofia italiana*. Turin: Einaudi.

Garroni, Emilio. 1968. *Semiotica ed estetica*. Rome-Bari: Laterza.

———. 1972. *Progetto di semiotica*. Rome-Bari: Laterza.

———. 1977. *Ricognizione della semiotica*. Rome: Officina.

———. 1986. *Senso and paradosso*. Rome-Bari: Laterza.

Geach, Peter. 1962. *Reference and Generality*. Ithaca: Cornell University Press.

Genette, Gérard. 1976. *Mimologiques: Voyage en Cratylie*. Paris: Seuil.

Genot-Bismuth, Jacqueline. 1988. *"Pommes d'or masquées d'argent": Les sonnettes italiennes de Manoel Giudeo (Immanuel de Rome)*. Paris: Mimeo.

Gensini, Stefano, ed. 1990. *G. W. Leibniz: Dal segno alle lingue*. Casale M.: Marietti Scuola.

Geyer, B. ed. 1927. *Peter Abaelards philosophische Schriften, Münster: Aschendorff* (Beiträge zur Geschichte der Philosophie des Mittelalters 21).

Ghisalberti, Alessandro. 1981. "La semiotica medievale: I terministi." In Lendinara and Ruta, eds. 1981.

Gibson, James J. 1966. *The Senses Considered as Perceptual Systems*. Boston: Houghton Mifflin.

Gil, Ferdinando. 1981. "Sistematica and classificazione." In *Enciclopedia Einaudi XII*. Turin: Einaudi.

Gilbert, Katharine, and Helmut Kuhn. 1939. *A History of Esthetics*. London: Macmillan (rev. ed. Bloomington, IN: Indiana University Press, 1954).

Gilby, Thomas, trans. 2006. *Summa Theologiae, Volume 1, Christian Theology*. Cambridge: Cambridge University Press.

Gilson, Etienne. 1919. *Le thomisme, introduction au système de saint Thomas*. Paris: Vrin.

———. 1952. *La philosophie au Moyen Age*. Paris: Payot.

Glunz, Hans. H. 1937. *Die Literarästhetik des europäischen Mittelalters*. Bochum: Pöppinghaus.

Gombrich, Ernst. 1982. *The Image and the Eye: Further Studies in the Psychology of Pictorial Representation*. Oxford: Phaidon.

———. 1985. *L'immagine e l'occhio: Altri studi sulla psicologia della rappresentazione pittorica*, trans. A. Cane. Turin: Einaudi.

Goodman, Nelson. 1968. *Languages of Art*. Indianapolis: Bobbs-Merrill.

Gorni, Guglielmo. 1990. *Lettera nome numero: L'ordine delle cose in Dante*. Bologna: Il Mulino.

Gouguenheim, Sylvain. 2000. *Les fausses terreurs de l'an mil*. Paris: Picard.

Gould, Stephen Jay. 1991. *Bully for Brontosaurus*. London: Hutchinson Radius.

Grabmann Martin. 1906–1911. *Die Geschichte der scholastischen Methode*. Freiburg: Herder.

Gregory, Tullio. 1961. *Scetticismo and empirismo: Studio su Gassendi*. Bari: Laterza.

———. 1985. "Discorso di chiusura." In *L'uomo di fronte al mondo animale nell'alto Medioevo*. Spoleto: Centro Italiano di Studi sull'alto Medioevo 2.

Greimas, Algirdas J., and Joseph Courtés. 1966. *Sémantique structurale*. Paris: Larousse.

———. 1979. *Sémiotique: Dictionnaire raisonné de la théorie du langage*. Paris: Hachette.

———. 1982. *Semiotics and Language: An Analytical Dictionary*, trans. Larry Christ, Daniel Patte, James Lee, Edward McMahon II, Gary Phillips, and Michael Rengstorf. Bloomington, IN: Indiana University Press.

Groupe m. 1970. *Rhétorique générale*. Paris: Larousse.

Gruber, Tom R. 1993. "A Translation Approach to Portable Ontology Specifications." *Knowledge Acquisition* 5: 199–220.

Grünbaum, Adolf. 1969. "Can an Infinitude of Operations Be Performed in a Finite Time?" *The British Journal for the Philosophy of Science* 20: 203–218.

Habermas, Jürgen. 1995. *Peirce and Communication*. In Ketner, ed., 1995.

Hackett, Jeremiah, ed. 1997. *Roger Bacon and the Sciences*. Leiden: Brill.

———. 1997. "Roger Bacon on Rhetoric and Poetics." In Hackett, ed., 1997.

Haiman, John. 1980. "Dictionaries and Encyclopedias." *Lingua* 50: 329–357.

———. 1982. "Dictionaries and Encyclopedias again." *Lingua* 56: 353–355.

Halm, Carolus. 1863. *Rhetores latini minores*. Lipsia: Teubner.

Havet, Julien. 1889. *Lettres de Gerbert*. Paris: Picard.

Haywood, Ian. 1987. *Faking It: Art and the Policy of Forgery*. New York: St. Martin's Press.

Heidegger, Martin. 1915. "Die Kategorien und deutungslehre des Duns Scotus." In *Frühe Schriften*. Frankfurt/M: Klostermann, 1972.

———. 1973. *Kant und das Problem der Metaphysik*, 4th ed. Frankfurt/M.: Klostermann.

———. 1997. *Kant and the Problem of Metaphysics*, 5th enlarged ed., trans. Richard Taft. Bloomington, IN: Indiana University Press.

Henri, Desmond P. 1964. *The De Grammatico of St. Anselm: The Theory of Paronymy*. Notre Dame, IN: University of Notre Dame Press.

Herren, Michael W. 1974. *The Hisperica Famina*. Toronto: Pontifical Institute of Medieval Studies.

Hillgarth, Jocelyn N. 1971. *Ramon Lull and Lullism in Fourteenth-Century France.* Oxford: Clarendon.

Hjelmslev, Louis. 1961. *Prolegomena to a Theory of Language,* trans. Francis J. Whitfield. Madison, WI: Wisconsin University Press. Originally published in 1943, in Danish.

Hogrebe, Wolfram. 1974. *Kant und das Probleme einer traszendentalen Semantik.* Freiburg: Alber.

Höltgen, Carl Josef. 1998. "Clever Dogs and Nimble Spaniels." *Explorations in Renaissance Culture* 24: 1–36.

Holtz, L. 1981. *Donat et la tradition de l'enseignement grammatical: Etude sur l'Ars Donati et sa diffusion (IVe–IXe siècle) et édition critique.* Paris: Editions du CNRS.

Hookway, Christopher. 1988. "Pragmaticism and 'Kantian Realism?'" *Versus* 49: 103–112.

Huizinga, Johan. 1919. *Herfsttij der Middeleeuwen.* Haarlem: Tjeenk Willink & Zoon.

Hungerland, Isabel C., and George R. Vick. 1981. "Hobbes' Theory of Language, Speech and Reasoning." In Thomas Hobbes, *Computatio sive logica.* New York: Abaris Books.

Husserl Edmund. 1922. *Logische Untersuchungen,* 3rd ed. Halle: Niemayer.

———. 1970a. *Logical Investigations,* trans. J. N. Findlay. London: Routledge and Kegan Paul.

———. 1970b. "Zur Logik der Zeichen (Semiotik)," in H. L. van Breda, ed., *Husserliana,* vol. XII. Den Haag: Nijhoff.

Huysmans, Joris-Karl. 2003. *Against Nature,* trans. by Robert Baldick with an introduction and notes by Patrick McGuinness. London & New York: Penguin Books.

Idel, Moshe. 1988a. *Kabbalah: New Perspectives.* New Haven: Yale University Press.

———. 1988b. *The Mystical Experience of Abraham Abulafia.* Albany: State University of New York Press.

———. 1988c. *Studies in Ecstatic Kabbalah.* Albany: State University of New York Press.

———. 1989. *Language, Torah and Hermeneutics in Abraham Abulafia.* Albany: State University of New York Press.

Isidore of Seville, *Etymologies,* trans. with introduction and notes by Stephen A. Barney, W. J. Lewis, J. A. Beach, and Oliver Berghof. Cambridge: Cambridge University Press, 2006.

Jackendoff, Ray. 1987. *Consciousness and the Computational Mind.* Cambridge, MA: MIT Press.

Jakobson, Roman. 1979. "Coup d'oeil sur le développement de la sémiotique." In S. Chatman et al., eds., *A Semiotic Landscape. Panorama Sémiotique: Proceedings of the First Congress of the International Association for Semiotic Studies.* The Hague: Mouton.

Jakobson, Roman, and Morris Halle. 1956. *Fundamentals of Language*. The Hague: Mouton.

James, Williams. 1987. *Writings, 1902–1910*. New York: Library of America.

Jeauneau, Edouard. 1967. "Nani gigantium humeris insidentes: Essai d'interprétation de Bernard de Chartres." *Vivarium* 5: 79–99.

John of St. Thomas. 1930. *Cursus Philosophicus Thomisticus, Ars Logica seu de forma et material ratiocinandi*, ed. B. Reiser. Turin: Marietti. Originally published in Spain, 1631–1635. (Reprint Hildesheim: Georg Olms, 2008, in 3 volumes, with introductory remarks by John Deely ["On the Value of Poinsot's Work to Philosophy Today"]).

Johnston, Mark D. 1987. *The Spiritual Logic of Ramon Llull*. Oxford: Clarendon.

Kant, Immanuel. 1968. *Kant gesammelte Schriften*, XXVIII "Vierte Abteilung, Vorlesungen, Fünfter Band, Herste hälfte." Berlin: De Gruyter.

———. 1974. *Logic*, trans. with an introduction by Robert S. Hartman and Wolfgang Schwartz. Indianapolis, IN: Bobbs-Merrill.

———. 1993. *Opus Postumum*, trans. by Eckart Förster and Michael Rosen. Cambridge: Cambridge University Press.

———. 1998. *Critique of Pure Reason*, trans. and ed. by Paul Guyer and Allen W. Wood. Cambridge: Cambridge University Press.

———. 2000. *Critique of the Power of Judgment*, trans. Paul Guyer and Eric Matthews. Cambridge: Cambridge University Press.

———. 2004. *Prolegomena to Any Future Metaphysics*. Revised edition, trans. and ed. by Gary Hatfield. Cambridge: Cambridge University Press.

Katz, Jerry, and Jerrold Fodor. 1963. "The Structure of a Semantic Theory." In *Language* 39: 170–210.

Katz, Jerrold J. 1972. *Semantic Theory*. New York: Harper and Row.

Kelemen, Jànos. 1991. "La comunicazione estetica nella *Critica del Giudizio*: Appunti per la ricostruzione della semiotica di Kant." *Il cannocchiale* 3: 33–50.

Kern, Hermann. 1981. *Labyrinthe*. Munich: Prestel Verlag.

Ketner, Kenneth L. ed. 1995. *Peirce and Contemporary Thought*. New York: Fordham University Press.

Klinkenberg, Jean-Marie. 1983. "Problèmes de la synecdoque: Du sémantique à l'encyclopédique." *Le français moderne* 51: 289–299.

———. 1984. "Le rôle du composant encyclopédique en linguistique." In Tasso Borbé, ed., *Semiotics Unfolding: Proceedings of the Second Congress of the International Association for Semiotic Studies*, vol. 3. Berlin: Mouton: 1169–1174.

Kovach, Francis. 1961. *Die Ästhetik des Thomas von Aquin*. Berlin: De Gruyter.

Kretzmann, Norman. 1974. "Aristotle on Spoken Sound Significant by Convention." In Corcoran, ed. 1974.

Kretzmann, Norman et al., eds., 1982. *The Cambridge History of Later Medieval Philosophy: From the Rediscovery of Aristotle to the Disintegration of Scholasticism, 1100–1600*. Cambridge: Cambridge University Press.

Kripke, Saul. 1972. "Naming and Necessity." In D. Davidson and G. Harman, eds., *Semantics of Natural Languages*. Dordrecht: Reidel.

Labarrière, Jean-Louis. 1997. "Logos endiathetos et logos prophorikos dans la polémique entre le Portique et la Nouvelle-Académie." In Barbara Cassin and Jean-Louis Labarrière, eds., *L'animal dans l'antiquité*. Paris: Vrin.

———. 2000. "Les animaux pensent-ils?." *Terrain* 34: 37–54.

Lakoff, George, and Mark Johnson. 1980. *Metaphors We Live By*. Chicago: University of Chicago Press.

Lamb, Sidney M. 1964. "The Sememic Approach to General Semantics." In A. K. Romney and R. G. D'Andrade, eds., *Transcultural Studies in Cognition* (*American Anthropologist* 66, no. 3, pt. 2).

Lambertini, Roberto. 1984. "L'origine è la meta: Percorsi dell'interpretazione contemporanea dei modisti." In *Versus* 38–39: 91–113.

Landes, Richard. 1988. "Lest the Millennium Be Fulfilled: Apocalyptic Expectations and the Pattern of Western Chronology 100–800 CE." In W. D. F. Werbeke et al., eds. *The Use and Abuse of Eschatology in the Middle Ages*. Mediaevalia Lovaniensia I/15. Leuven: Louvain University Press.

LeBrun, Richard A., trans. 1993. *The Collected Works of Joseph De Maistre*. Montreal: McGill-Queen's University Press.

Leclerc, Henri and Fernand Cabrol, eds. 1913–1953. *Dictionnaire de l'archéologie chrétienne et de liturgie*, 30 vols. Paris: Letousey & Ané.

Le Goff, Jacques. 1964. *La civilisation de l'occident médiéval*. Paris: Arthaud.

Leech, Geoffrey. 1974. *Semantics: A Study of Meaning*. Harmondsworth: Penguin Books.

Lemay, Richard. 1997. "Roger Bacon's Attitude toward the Latin Translations and Translators of the Twelfth and Thirteenth Century." In Hackett, ed., 1997.

Lemoine, Michel. 1998. "Postface" to the 1998 edition of De Bruyne 1946.

Lendinara, Patrizia, and Ruta, Maria Caterina, eds. 1981. *Per una storia della semiotica: teorie and metodi*. Palermo: Quaderni del Circolo Semiologico Siciliano.

Lewis, David K. 1969. *Convention: A Philosophical Study*. Cambridge, MA: Harvard University Press.

Llinares, Armand. 1963. *Raymond Lulle, Philosophe de l'action*. Paris: PUF.

Lo Piparo, Franco. 2000. "Le théorème de Pythagore dans la linguistique grecque." *Histoire Epistémologie Langage* 22: 51–67.

Lorusso, Anna Maria. 2005. "Tra cannocchiali, lenti, riflessi and specchi: la lezione aristotelica nel Cannocchiale del Tesauro." In Lorusso, ed., 2005.

Lorusso, Anna Maria, ed. 2005. *Metafora and conoscenza*. Milan: Bompiani.

Lotman, Jurij. 1984. "O semiosfere." *Trudy po znakovym sistemam* 17: 5–23.

———. 2005. "On the Semiosphere," trans. Wilma Clark. *Sign Systems Studies* 33: 205–229.

Lotman, Jurij M., and Boris A. Uspenskij. 1975. *Tipologia della cultura*. Milan: Bompiani.

Lovejoy, Arthur. 1936. *The Great Chain of Being.* Cambridge, MA: Harvard University Press.

Luisetti, Federico 2001. *Plus Ultra: Enciclopedismo barocco and modernità.* Turin: Trauben.

Lupieri, Edmondo. 1999. *L'Apocalisse di Giovanni.* Milan: Valla-Mondadori.

Lyons, John. 1968. *Introduction to Theoretical Linguistics.* Cambridge: Cambridge University Press.

——. 1977. *Semantics I–II.* Cambridge: Cambridge University Press.

Lyttkens, Hampus. 1952. *The Analogy between God and the World.* Uppsala: Almqvist & Wiksell.

Macrobius. 1952. *Commentary on the Dream of Scipio by Macrobius,* trans. with an introduction and notes by William Harris Stahl. New York: Columbia University Press.

Maggi, Michele. 1989. *La filosofia di Benedetto Croce.* Florence: Ponte alle Grazie.

Mahoney, Edward P. 1982. "Sense, Intellect, and Imagination in Albert, Thomas and Siger." In Kretzmann et al., eds., 1982.

Maierú, Alfonso. 1972. *Terminologia logica della tarda scolastica.* Rome: Edizioni dell'Ateneo.

——. 1981. "Signum dans la culture mediévale." *Miscellanea mediaevalia* 13: 51–72.

——. 1983 "Dante al crocevia?" *Studi Medioevali* 3: 735–748.

Mâle, Emile. 1922. *L'art religieux du XIIe siècle en France.* Paris: Colin.

Maloney, Thomas S. 1983. "The Semiotics of Roger Bacon." In *Medieval Studies* 45: 120–154.

Mameli, Matteo. 1997. *Synechism: Aspetti del pensiero di C. S. Peirce.* Tesi di Laurea, Università di Bologna.

Manetti, Giovanni. 1987. *Le teorie del segno nell'antichità classica.* Milan: Bompiani.

——. 2005. "Aristotele and la metafora: Conoscenza, similarità, azione, enunciazione." In Lorusso, ed., 2005.

——, ed. 1989. *Leggere* I promessi sposi. Milano: Bompiani.

——, ed. 1996. *Knowledge through Signs: Ancient Semiotic Theories and Practices.* Turnhout, Belgium: Brepols.

Manzoni, Alessandro. 1972. *The Betrothed,* trans. Bruce Penman. Harmondsworth: Penguin Books.

Marconi, Diego. 1981. "Semantica." In *Enciclopedia Einaudi XII.* Turin: Einaudi.

——. 1982. *Dizionari and enciclopedie.* Turin: Giappichelli.

——. 1999. *La competenza lessicale.* Rome-Bari: Laterza.

Marconi, Diego, and Gianni Vattimo. 1986. "Nota introduttiva." Introduction to the Italian translation of Rorty 1979. [*La filosofia e lo specchio della natura.* Milan: Bompiani, 1986.]

Marigo, Aristide. 1938. *De Vulgari Eloquentia ridotto a miglior lezione and commentato da A. Marigo.* Florence: Le Monnier.

Maritain, Jacques. 1920. *Art et scolastique.* Paris: Art Catholique.

——. 1932. *Les degrés du savoir.* Paris: Desclée.

——. 1935. *Les frontières de la poésie.* Paris: Rouart.

——. 1938a. "De la connaissance poétique." *Revue thomiste* 44: 87–98.

——. 1938b. "Signe et symbole." *Revue thomiste* 44: 229–330.

——. 1944. *De Bergson à Thomas d'Aquin—Essai de métaphysique et de morale.* New York: Editions de la Maison française (2nd ed. Paris: Hartmann, 1947)

——. 1947. *Court traite de l'existence et de l'existant.* Paris: Hartmann.

——. 1953. *Creative Intuition in Art and Poetry.* New York: Pantheon Books.

——. 1961. *La responsabilité de l'artiste.* Paris: Fayard.

——. 1962. *Art and Scholasticism and The Frontiers of Poetry,* trans. Joseph W. Evans. New York: Charles Scribner's Sons.

Marmo, Costantino. 1984. "Guglielmo di Ockham and il significato delle proposizioni." *Versus* 38–39: 115–148.

——. 1990. "*Suspicio:* A Key Word to the Significance of Aristotle's Rhetoric in Thirteenth-Century Scholasticism." *Cahiers de l'Institut du Moyen-Age Grec et latin* 60: 145–198.

——. 1992. "Retorica and motti di spirito. Una quaestio inedita di Giovannni di Jandun." In P. Magli et al., eds., *Semiotica, storia, interpretazione.* Milan: Bompiani.

——. 1994. *Semiotica and linguaggio nella scolastica.* Rome: Istituto Storico Italiano per il M.E.

——. 1998. "L'utilizzazione delle traduzioni latine della Retorica nel commento di Egidio Romano (1272–1273)." In Dahan and Rosier-Catach, eds., 1998.

Marr, David, and H. Keith Nishishara. 1978. "Visual Information Processing: Artificial Intelligence and the Sensorium of Sight." *Technology Review* 81: 2–23.

Marrone, Caterina. 1986. "Lingua universale and scrittura segreta nell'opera di Kircher." In Casciato et al. eds. 1986.

Marrou, Henri Irenée. 1958. *Saint Augustin et la fin de la culture antique,* 4th ed. Paris: Boccard.

Martinetti, Piero. 1946. *Kant.* Milan: Bocca.

Mathieu, Vittorio. 1984. "Introduzione" to I. Kant, *Opus Postumum.* Rome-Bari: Laterza.

Mayoux, Jean-Jacques. 1960. *Vivants piliers.* Paris: Maurice Nadeau.

McCawley, James D. 1981. *Everything That Linguists Have Always Wanted to Know about Logic.* Chicago: University of Chicago Press.

McGarry, Daniel, trans. 1955. *The Metalogicon, a twelfth-century defense of the verbal and logical arts of the trivium.* Berkeley: University of California Press.

McKeon, Richard. 1952. "Rhetoric in the Middle Ages." In R. S. Crane et al., eds., *Critics and Criticism.* Chicago: The University of Chicago Press.

Meier, Christel. 1997. "Organization of Knowledge and Encyclopedic Ordo." In Binkley, ed. 1997.

Menendez y Pelayo, Marcelino. 1883. *Historia de las idea estéticas en España*. Madrid: Perez Dubrull (3rd ed. Madrid: Consejo Superior de Investigaciones Cientificas, 1962).

Mengaldo, Pier Vincenzo. 1979. Introduzione e note al *De vulgari Eloquentia*. In Dante Alighieri, *Opere Minori*, vol. 2. Naples: Ricciardi.

Merton, Robert. 1965. *On the Shoulders of Giants*. New York: Free Press.

Mill, John Stuart. 1898. *A System of Logic*. London: Routledge. Originally published 1843.

Millás Vallicrosa, José M. 1958. "Las relaciones entre la doctrina luliana y la Cábala." In *L'homme et son destin: Actes du premier congrès international de philosophie médiévale*. Leuven-Paris, 1960.

Minio-Paluello, L. ed. 1968. *De arte poetica*. Aristoteles Latinus 33. Leiden: Brill.

Mondolfo, Rodolfo. 1934. L'infinito nel pensiero dei greci. Florence: Le Monnier.

Montano, Rocco. 1954. "L'estetica nel pensiero cristiano." In *Grande Antologia Filosofica* V. Milan: Marzorati.

Moody, Ernest A. 1935. *The Logic of William of Ockham*. New York: Sheed & Ward.

Morris, Charles. 1938. *Foundations of a Theory of Signs*. Chicago: University of Chicago Press.

———. 1946. *Signs, Language, and Behavior*. New York: Prentice Hall.

Murphey, Murray G. 1961. *The Development of Peirce's Philosophy*. Cambridge, MA: Harvard University Press.

Murphy, James B. 1974. *Rhetoric in the Middle Ages*. Berkeley: University of California Press.

———. 1991. "Nature, Custom, and Stipulation in the Semiotic of John Poinsot." *Semiotica* 83 1/2: 33–68.

Nardi, Bruno. 1985. *Dante and la cultura medievale*. Rome-Bari: Laterza.

Neubauer, Fritz, and János S. Petöfi. 1981. "Word Semantics, Lexicon Systems, and Text Interpretation." In Hans-Jürgen Eikmeyer and Hannes Rieser, eds., *Words, Worlds, and Contexts: New Approaches in Word Semantics*. Berlin: Walter de Gruyter.

Nietzsche, Friedrich. 1873. "On Truth and Lying in a Non-Moral Sense." *In The Birth of Tragedy and Other Writings*, trans. by Ronald Speirs, edited by Raymond Geuss and Ronald Speirs. Cambridge: Cambridge University Press.

———. 1874. "On the Uses and Disadvantages of History for Life." In *Untimely Meditations*, trans. R. J. Hollingdale with an Introduction by J. P. Stern. Cambridge : Cambridge University Press.

Nuchelmans, Gabriël. 1973. *Theories of the Proposition: Ancient and Medieval Conceptions of the Bearers of Truth and Falsity*. Amsterdam: North Holland.

Ogden, C. K., and I. A. Richards. 1923. *The Meaning of Meaning*. London: Routledge.

Ortega y Gasset, José. 1947. "Entorno a Galileo" in *Obras completas* V, Madrid: Revista de Occidente.

Ortony, Andrew, ed. 1979. *Metaphor and Thought.* Cambridge: Cambridge University Press.

Ottaviano, Carmelo. 1930. *L'Ars Compendiosa de R. Lulle.* Paris: Vrin (2nd ed. 1981).

Owens, Joseph. 1951. *The Doctrine of Being in the Aristotelian "Metaphysics."* Toronto: Pontifical Institute.

Paci, Enzo. 1957. "Relazionismo and schematismo trascendentale." In *Dall'esistenzialismo al relazionismo.* Messina: D'Anna.

Pagani, Ileana. 1982. *La teoria linguistica di Dante.* Rome: Liguori.

Panofsky, Erwin, ed. 1946. *Abbot Suger in the Abbey Church of St. Denis and Its Art Treasures.* Princeton: Princeton University Press.

———. 1957. *Gothic Architecture and Scholasticism.* London: Thames.

Paolucci, Claudio. 2005. "Appendice peirciana." In *Antilogos, Logica delle relazioni and semiotica interpretativa. Tesi di dottorato,* Università di Bologna.

———. ed. 2007. *Studi di semiotica interpretative.* Milan: Bompiani.

Paulmier-Foucart, Monique, and Serge Lusignan. 1990. "Vincent de Beauvais et l'histoire du 'Speculum Maius.'" *Journal des Savants:* 97–124.

Pareyson, Luigi. 1954. *Estetica.* Turin: Edizioni di 'Filosofia' (Reprint Milan: Bompiani, 1988).

Pavel, Tomas. 1986. *Fictional Worlds.* Cambridge, MA: Harvard University Press.

Peeters, Bert. 2000. "Setting the Scene: Recent Milestones in the Lexicon-Encyclopedia Debate." In B. Peeters, ed., *The Lexicon-Encyclopedia Interface.* Current Research in the Semantics/Pragmatics Interface 5. Oxford: Elsevier Science.

Peirce, Charles S. 1931–1958. *Collected Papers.* Cambridge, MA: Harvard University Press.

Pellerey Roberto. 1984. "Tommaso d'Aquino: semiotica naturale and processo gnoseologico." *Versus* 38–39: 39–61.

Pépin, Jean. 1958. *Mythe et allégorie.* Paris: Montaigne.

———. 1970. *Dante et la tradition de l'allégorie.* Paris: Vrin.

Perani, Mauro, and Enrica Sgradini. 2004. *Talmudic and Midrashic Fragments from the "Italian Genizah."* Florence: Giuntina.

Petitot Jean. 1979. "Locale/globale." In *Enciclopedia Einaudi VIII.* Turin: Einaudi.

Pico della Mirandola, Giovanni. 1965. *Heptaplus, On the Sevenfold Narration of the Six Days of Genesis,* trans. by Douglas Carmichael, in *On the Dignity of Man, and Other Works.* New York: Bobbs-Merrill.

Pike, Joseph B. 1938. *Frivolities of Courtiers and Footprints of Philosophers.* Being a Translation of the First, Second, and Third Books and a Selection from the

Seventh and Eighth Books of the *Policraticus* of John of Salisbury. Minneapolis: University of Minnesota.

Pinborg, Jan. 1961. "Interjektionen und Naturlaute." *Classica et Mediaevalia* 22: 117–138.

———. 1962. "Sprachdenken der Stoa und Augustins Dialektik." In *Classica et Mediaevalia* 23: 148–177.

———. 1972. *Logik und Semantik im Mittelalter: Ein Überblick.* Stuttgart-Bad Cannstatt: Fromann-Holzboog.

Pini, Giorgio. 1999. "Species, Concept and Thing: Theories of Signification in the Second Half of the Thirteenth Century." *Medieval Philosophy and Theology* 8: 21–52.

Platzeck, Erhard-Woffram. 1953. "La combinatoria lulliana." *Revista de filosofia* 12: 575–609.

———. 1954. "La combinatoria lulliana. Conclusiones." *Revista de filosofia* 13: 125–165.

———. 1964. *Ramon Lull: Sein Leben, Seine Werke, Die Grundlagen seines Denkens,* 2 vols. Düsseldorf: Schwann.

Pohlenz, Max. 1948–1955. *Die Stoa. Die Geschichte einer geistigen Bewegung,* 2 vols. Göttingen: Vandenhoeck und Ruprecht.

Polara, G., ed. 1979. *Virgilio Marone grammatico: Epitomi ed epistole.* Rome: Liguori.

Pombo Olga et al., eds. 2006. *Enciclopédia e Hipertexto.* Lisbon: Editora Duarte Reis.

Pombo, Olga. n.d. *O projecto enciclopedista.* www.educ.fc.ul.pt/hyper/enciclopedia.

Pons, Alain. 1966. "L'avventura dell'Enciclopedia." In *Enciclopedia.* Milan: Feltrinelli, vol. 1.

Ponzio, Augusto. 1983. "La semantica di Pietro Ispano." In F. Corvino et al., *Linguistica Medievale.* Bari: Adriatica.

Popper, Karl R. 1959. *The Logic of Scientific Discovery.* London: Hutchinson [original German ed. Vienna: 1935).

———. 1969. *Conjectures and Refutations.* London: Routledge.

Pottier, Bernard. 1965. "La définition sémantique dans les dictionnaires." *Travaux de Linguistique et de Littérature* 3: 33–39.

Pouillon, Henry. 1939. "Le premier traité des propriétés transcendentales." *Revue Néoscolastique de Philosophie* 42: 40–77.

———. 1946. "La beauté, propriété transcendentale chez les Néoscolastiques (1220–1270)." *Archives d'Histoire Doctrinale du Moyen Âge* 15: 263–329.

Pozzato, Maria Pia, ed. 1989. *L'idea deforme.* Milan: Bompiani.

Prieto, Luis. 1964. *Principes de noologie.* The Hague: Mouton.

———. 1975. *Pertinence et pratique.* Paris: Minuit.

Proni, Giampaolo. 1990. *Introduzione a Peirce.* Milan: Bompiani.

Pseudo-Dionysius. 1987. The Complete Works, trans. by Colm Luidheid and Paul Rorem. New York: Paulist Press.

Putnam, Hilary. 1975. "The Meaning of Meaning." In K. Gunderson, ed., *Language, Mind, and Knowledge*. Minneapolis: University of Minnesota Press. Included in H. Putnam, *Mind, Language and Reality*. London: Cambridge University Press.

Quillian, Ross. 1968. "Semantic Memory." In Marvin Minsky, ed., *Semantic Information Processing*. Cambridge, MA: MIT Press.

Quine, Willard V. O. 1951. "Two Dogmas of Empiricism." In *Quine* 1953a.

———. 1953a. *From a Logical Point of View*. Cambridge, MA: Harvard University Press.

———. 1953b. "The Problem of Meaning in Linguistics." In Quine 1953a.

———. 2004. *Quintessence: basic readings from the philosophy of W. V. Quine*. Edited by Roger F. Gibson Jr. Cambridge, MA: Harvard University Press.

Rabelais, François. 2006. *Gargantua and Pantagruel,* trans. and ed. with an introduction and notes by M. A. Screech. London: Penguin Books.

Renucci, Paul. 1958. *Dante*. Paris: Hatier.

Ricoeur, Paul. 1975. *La métaphore vive*. Paris: Seuil.

Rintelen, F. H. von, ed. 1930. *Philosophia perennis: Abhandlungen zu ihren Vergangenheit und Gegenwart*. Regensburg: Habbel.

Rivers, Kimberly. 1997. "Memory, Division and the Organization of Knowledge in the Middle Ages." In Binkley, ed. 1997.

Roland-Gosselin, M.-D. 1930. "Peut on parler d'intuition intellectuelle dans la philosophie thomiste?" In Rintelen, ed. 1930.

Romano, Immanuello. 2000. *L'Inferno e il Paradiso,* ed. Giorgio Battistoni. Florence: Giunta.

Rorem, Paul. 1993. *Pseudo-Dionysius. A Commentary on the Texts and an Introduction to their Influence*. New York, Oxford: Oxford University Press.

Rorty, Richard. 1979. *Philosophy and the Mirror of Nature*. Princeton: Princeton University Press.

Rosenau, Helen. 1979. *Vision of the Temple*. London: Oresko Books.

Rosenstiehl, Pierre. 1979. "Labirinto." In *Enciclopedia Einaudi VIII*. Turin: Einaudi.

Rosiello, Luigi. 1976. *Linguistica illuminista*. Bologna: il Mulino.

Rosier-Catach, Irène. 1997. "Prata rident." In A. De Libera et al., eds., *Langages et philosophie*. Paris: Vrin.

———. 1998. "Roger Bacon, al-Farabi et Augustin. Rhétorique, logique et philosophie morale." In Dahan and Rosier-Catach, eds. 1998.

———. 2006. " 'Solo all'uomo fu dato di parlare.' Dante, gli angeli and gli animali." *Rivista di filosofia Neoscolastica* 3: 435–465.

Rossano, Pietro, ed. 1963. *Nuovo testamento*. Turin: Utet.

Rosselli, Cosma. 1579. *Thesaurus Artificiosae Memoriae*. Venice: Paduanius.

Rossi, Paolo. 1957. *Francesco Bacone: Dalla magia alla scienza*. Bari: Laterza (2nd ed. Turin: Einaudi 1974).

————. 1960. *Clavis Universalis: Arti della memoria and logica combinatoria da Lullo a Leibniz.* Milan: Ricciardi (2nd ed. Bologna: il Mulino, 1983).

————. 1988. "La memoria, le immagini, l'enciclopedia." In P. Rossi, ed. 1988.

————. 1998. "La storia della scienza: la dimenticanza and la memoria." In L. Bolzoni et al., eds., *Memoria and memorie.* Florence: Olschki.

Rossi, Pietro, ed. 1988. *La memoria del sapere.* Rome-Bari: Laterza.

Russell, Bertrand. 1905. "On Denoting." *Mind* 14: 479–493.

Saintsbury, George. 1900–1904. *A History of Criticism and Literary Taste in Europe: The Earliest Texts to the Present Day.* Edinburgh: Blackwood.

Salsano, Alfredo. 1977. "Enciclopedia." In *Enciclopedia Einaudi I.* Turin: Einaudi.

Sanders, Henry. 1930. *Beati in Apocalipsin libri duodecim.* Rome: American Academy.

Santarcangeli, Paolo. 1967. *Il libro dei labirinti.* Florence: Vallecchi (Reprint Milan: Frassinelli, 2005, with a preface by Umberto Eco).

Schaer, R., ed., 1996. *Tous les savoirs du monde.* Paris: Flammarion.

Schank, Roger C., and Robert P. Abelson. 1977. *Scripts, Plans, Goals and Understanding: An Inquiry into Human Knowledge Structures.* Hillsdale, NJ: Lawrence Erlbaum.

Schank, Roger C., and Peter G. Childers. 1984. *The Cognitive Computer.* Reading, MA: Addison-Wesley.

Schlosser-Magnino, Julius. 1924. *Die Kunstliteratur.* Wien: Schroll.

Schneider, Bernhard, ed. 1978. *Rhetorica, Translatio anonyma sive Vetus et Translatio Guillielmi de Moerbeka.* Aristoteles Latinus 30. Leiden: Brill.

Schogt, H. G. 1986. "Seme." In T. A. Sebeok, ed., *Encyclopedic Dictionary of Semiotics,* vol. 2. Berlin: Mouton de Gruyter.

Scholem, G. et al. 1979. "Kabbalistes chrétiens." In *Cahiers de l'Hermetisme.* Paris: Albin Michel.

Sebeok, T. A., ed. 1986. *Encyclopedic Dictionary of Semiotics,* 3 vols. Berlin: Mouton De Gruyter.

Secret, François. 1964. *Les Kabbalistes chrétiens de la renaissance.* Paris: Dunod (Reprint Milan: Sebastiani, 1985).

Sellars, Wilfrid. 1978. "The Role of Imagination in Kant's Theory of Experience." In Henry W. Johnstone Jr., ed., *Categories: A Colloquium.* Pennsylvania: Pennsylvania State University Press.

Setz, Wolfram. ed. 1988. *Fälschungen im Mittelalter,* 5 vols. Schriften der Monumenta Germaniae Historica 33. Hannover: Hahn, 1988.

Simson, Otto von. 1956. *The Gothic Cathedral.* New: York: Pantheon Books.

Sirridge, M. 1997. "The Wailing of Orphans, the Cooing of Doves, and the Groans of the Sick: The Influence of Augustine's Theory of Language on Some Theories of Interjection." In C. Marmo, ed., *Vestigia, imagines, verba: Semiotics and Logic in Medieval Theological Texts (XIIth–XIVth Century).* Turnhout, Belgium: Brepols.

Slaughter, Mary. 1982. *Universal Languages and Scientific Taxonomy in the Seventeenth Century.* London: Cambridge University Press.

Smith, Barry. 2003. "Ontology." In L. Floridi, ed., *The Blackwell Guide to Philosophy of Computing Information.* Malden: Blackwell.

Smith, Barry, and Achille C. Varzi, 2000. "Fiat and Bona Fide Boundaries." *Philosophy and Phenomenological Research* 60: 401–420.

Sorabji, Richard. 1996. "Animal Minds, Human Morals." *The Philosophical Review* 105.

Sowa, John, ed., 1991. *Principles of Semantic Networks: Explorations in the Representation of Knowledge.* San Mateo: Morgan Kaufmann Publishers.

———. 2000. "Ontology, Metadata, and Semiotics." In B. Ganter and G. W. Mineau, eds., *Conceptual Structures: Logical, Linguistic, and Computational Issues.* Berlin: Springer.

Spade, Paul V. 1980. "Notes on Richard Lavenham's So Called 'Summulae Logicales', with a Partial Edition of the Text." *Franciscan Studies* 40: 370–407.

———. 1982. "The Semantics of Terms." In Kretzmann et al., eds., 1982.

Sperber, Dan, and Deirdre Wilson. 1986. *Relevance.* Cambridge, MA: Harvard University Press.

Svoboda, Karl. 1927. *L'esthétique de Saint Augustin et ses sources.* Paris-Brno: Belles Lettres.

Tabarroni, Andrea. 1984. "Segno mentale and teoria della rappresentazione in Ockham." *Versus* 38–39: 63–90.

Tarsky, Alfred. 1944. "The Semantic Conception of Truth and the Foundations of Semantics." *Philosophy and Phenomenological Research,* 4: 241–275.

Tatarkiewicz, Wladislaw. 1962. *Historia estetyki.* Warsaw: Pafstwowe Wydawnictwo Naukowe.

Tega, Walter. 1983. *L'Unità del sapere and l'ideale enciclopedico nel pensiero moderno.* Bologna: il Mulino.

———. 1984. Arbor scientiarum: *Enciclopedie and sistemi in Francia da Diderot a Comte.* Bologna: il Mulino.

———. 1995. "La follia dell'ordine alfabetico and la concatenazione delle scienze: L'enciclopedia come sistema tra XVIII and XX secolo." In *Storia della filosofia and storia della scienza: Studi in onore di Paolo Rossi.* Florence: La Nuova Italia.

———. 1999. "Il prisma di Alsted." In W. Tega, ed., *Le origini della modernità.* Florence: Olschki. Also published as "Le prisme d'Alsted: l'encyclopédie comme système de systèmes." In B. Saint Girons, ed., *Art et science a l'age classique.* Paris: Vrin 2000.

———. 2004. "Enciclopedie and sistemi tra XVIII and XIX secolo." In *Studi in onore di Cesare Vasoli.* Florence: Olschki.

Tesauro, Emanuele. 1968. *Il cannocchiale aristotelico,* herausgegeben und eingeleitet von August Buck. Bad Homburg: Verlag Gehlen. (A facsimile of the Zavatta edition published in Turin in 1670).

Thorndike, Lynn. 1929. *A History of Magic and Experimental Science.* New York: Columbia University Press.

Thurot, Charles. 1869. *Extraits de divers manuscrits latins pour servir à l'histoire des doctrines grammaticales du Moyen Age.* Paris: Bibliothèque Impériale (Reprint Frankfurt: Minerva, 1964).

Todorov, Tzetan. 1982. *Theories of the Symbol,* trans. Catherine Porter. Ithaca: Cornell University Press (Originally published in French, 1977).

Trier, Jost. 1931. *Der deutsche Wortschatz im Sinnberzirk des Verstandes.* Heidelberg: Winter.

Valente, Luisa. 1995. "Une sémantique particulière: La pluralité du sens dans les Saintes Ecritures (XIIe siècle)." In Ebbesen, ed. 1995.

Varzi, Achille C. 2005. "Teoria e pratica dei confine." *Sistemi Intelligenti* 17: 399–418.

Vasoli, Cesare. 1958. "Umanesimo and simbologia nei primi scritti lulliani and mnemotecnici del Bruno." In E. Castelli, ed., *Umanesimo and simbolismo.* Padova: Cedam.

———. 1978. *L'enciclopedismo del seicento.* Naples: Bibliopolis.

Vattimo, Gianni. 1980. *Le avventure della differenza.* Milan: Garzanti.

———. 1983. "Dialettica, differenza, pensiero debole." In G. Vattimo and P. A. Rovatti, eds., *Il pensiero debole.* Milan: Feltrinelli.

———. 1984. "Dialectics, Difference and Weak Thought," trans. Thomas Harrison. *Graduate Faculty Philosophy Journal* 10: 151–164.

———. 1993. *The Adventures of Difference: Philosophy after Nietzsche and Heidegger,* trans. Cyprian Blamires with the assistance of Thomas Harrison. Baltimore: Johns Hopkins University Press.

———. 1994. *Oltre l'interpretazione.* Rome-Bari: Laterza.

———, ed. 1992. *Filosofia 91.* Bari: Laterza.

Vecchio, Sebastiano. 1994. *Le parole come segni: Introduzione alla linguistica agostiniana.* Palermo: Novecento.

———. 1997. *Beyond Interpretation,* trans. David Webb. Cambridge: Polity Press.

Verbeke, Gerard. 1961. *Commentaire sur le* Peri hermeneias *d'Aristote, traduction de Guillaume de Moerbeke, ed. critique et étude sur l'utilisation du Commentaire dans l'oeuvre de saint Thomas par G. Verbeke.* Leuven: Publications Universitaires.

Verona, Guido da. 1937. *I promessi sposi di Alessandro Manzoni e Guido Da Verona.* Milan: Unitas.

Viano, Carlo Augusto. 1988. "La biblioteca and l'oblio." In P. Rossi, ed. 1988.

Vico, Giambattista. 1984. *The New Science of Giambattista Vico,* trans. Thomas Goddard Bergin and Max Frisch. Cornell: Cornell University Press.

———. 1942. *La scienza nuova seconda giusta l'edizione del 1744,* a cura di Fausto Nicolini. Bari: Laterza.

Virgil. 1999. *Eclogues, Georgics, Aeneid I–VI,* trans. H. Rushton Fairclough, rev. G. P. Goold. Cambridge, MA: Harvard University Press.

Violi, Patrizia. 1997. *Significato and esperienza*. Milan: Bompiani.

———. 2001. *Meaning and Experience*. Bloomington, IN: Indiana University Press, 2001.

Weinrich, Harald. 2004. *Lethe: The Art and Critique of Forgetting*, trans. Steven Rendall. Ithaca, NY: Cornell University Press.

Wencelius, Léon. 1932. *La philosophie de l'art chez les néo-scolastiques de langue français*. Paris: Alcan.

West, William N. 1997. "Public Knowledge at Private Parties: Vives, Jonson, and the Circulation of the Circle of Knowledge." In Binkley, ed. 1997.

White, Andrew D. 1917. *A History of the Warfare of Science with Theology in Christendom*. New York: Appleton.

Wierzbicka, Anna. 1972. *Semantic Primitives*. Frankfurt: Athenäum.

———. 1995. "Dictionaries and Encyclopedias: How to Draw the Line." In Philip W. Davis, ed., *Alternative Linguistics. Descriptive and Theoretical Modes*. Amsterdam: Benjamins.

———. 1996. *Semantics: Primes and Universals*. Oxford: Oxford University Press.

Wilks, Yorick. 1977. "Good and Bad Arguments about Semantic Primitives." *Communication and Cognition* 10: 181–221.

Williams, John. 1994–2003. *The Illustrated Beatus: a corpus of the illustrations of the Commentary on the Apocalypse*. 5 vols. London: Harvey Miller.

Wilson, N. L. 1967. "Linguistical Butter and Philosophical Parsnips." *Journal of Philosophy* 64: 55–67.

Wirszubski, Chaim. 1989. *Pico della Mirandola's Encounter with Jewish Mysticism*. Cambridge, MA: Harvard University Press.

Wittgenstein, Ludwig. 1922. *Tractatus Logico-Philosophicus*. London: Routledge.

———. 1953. *Philosophische Untersuchungen*. Oxford: Blackwell.

———. 1961. *Notebooks 1914–1916*, ed. C. H. von Wright and G. E. M. Anscombe with an English translation by G. E. M. Anscombe. Oxford: Basil Blackwell.

Worch, J. Hershy. 2010. *Sefer Yetzira. Chronicles of Desire*. A new Hebrew/English translation and commentary by J. Hershy Worch. Lanham, MD: University Press of America.

Worth, Sol. 1975. "Pictures Can't Say Ain't." *Versus* 12: 85–108.

Yates, Frances. 1954. "The Art of Ramon Lull." *Journal of the Warburg and Courtauld Institutes* 17: 115–173 (included in F. Yates, *Lull and Bruno: Collected Essays I*. London: Routledge, 1982).

———. 1960. "Ramon Lull and John Scotus Eriugena." *Journal of the Warburg and Courtauld Institutes* 23: 1–44 (included in F. Yates, *Lull and Bruno, Collected Essays I*. London: Routledge, 1982).

———. 1964. *Giordano Bruno and the Hermetic Tradition*. London: Routledge.

———. 1966. *The Art of Memory*. London: Routledge.

———. 1982. *Lull and Bruno. Collected Essays*. London: Routledge.

Zambelli, Paola. 1965. "Il De auditu Kabbalistico and la tradizione lulliana nel Rinascimento." In *Atti dell'accademia toscana di scienze and lettere 'La Colombaria' XXX* (included in P. Zambelli, *L'apprendista stregone: Astrologia, cabala and arte lulliana in Pico della Mirandola and seguaci.* Venice: Marsilio, 1995).

Zellini, Paolo. 1980. *Breve storia dell'infinito.* Milan: Adelphi.

———. 2003. *A Brief History of Infinity,* trans. David Marsh. London: Penguin Books.

Index